# Lecture Notes in Computer Science 3936

Commenced Publication in 1973
Founding and Former Series Editors:
Gerhard Goos, Juris Hartmanis, and Jan van Leeuwen

## Editorial Board

David Hutchison
   *Lancaster University, UK*
Takeo Kanade
   *Carnegie Mellon University, Pittsburgh, PA, USA*
Josef Kittler
   *University of Surrey, Guildford, UK*
Jon M. Kleinberg
   *Cornell University, Ithaca, NY, USA*
Friedemann Mattern
   *ETH Zurich, Switzerland*
John C. Mitchell
   *Stanford University, CA, USA*
Moni Naor
   *Weizmann Institute of Science, Rehovot, Israel*
Oscar Nierstrasz
   *University of Bern, Switzerland*
C. Pandu Rangan
   *Indian Institute of Technology, Madras, India*
Bernhard Steffen
   *University of Dortmund, Germany*
Madhu Sudan
   *Massachusetts Institute of Technology, MA, USA*
Demetri Terzopoulos
   *University of California, Los Angeles, CA, USA*
Doug Tygar
   *University of California, Berkeley, CA, USA*
Moshe Y. Vardi
   *Rice University, Houston, TX, USA*
Gerhard Weikum
   *Max-Planck Institute of Computer Science, Saarbruecken, Germany*

Mounia Lalmas   Andy MacFarlane
Stefan Rüger   Anastasios Tombros
Theodora Tsikrika   Alexei Yavlinsky (Eds.)

# Advances in Information Retrieval

28th European Conference on IR Research, ECIR 2006
London, UK, April 10-12, 2006
Proceedings

Volume Editors

Mounia Lalmas
Anastasios Tombros
Theodora Tsikrika
Queen Mary, University of London
Department of Computer Science
London E1 4NS, UK
E-mail:{mounia,theodora,tassos}@dcs.qmul.ac.uk

Andy MacFarlane
City University
Department of Information Science
Northampton Square, London EC1V OHB, UK
E-mail: andym@soi.city.ac.uk

Stefan Rüger
Alexei Yavlinsky
Imperial College London
Department of Computing
South Kensington Campus, London SW7 2AZ
E-mail:{s.rueger,alexei.yavlinsky}@imperial.ac.uk

Library of Congress Control Number: 2006923244

CR Subject Classification (1998): H.3, H.2, I.2.3, I.2.6-7, H.4, H.5.4, I.7

LNCS Sublibrary: SL 3 – Information Systems and Application, incl. Internet/Web
and HCI

ISSN        0302-9743
ISBN-10     3-540-33347-9 Springer Berlin Heidelberg New York
ISBN-13     978-3-540-33347-0 Springer Berlin Heidelberg New York

This work is subject to copyright. All rights are reserved, whether the whole or part of the material is
concerned, specifically the rights of translation, reprinting, re-use of illustrations, recitation, broadcasting,
reproduction on microfilms or in any other way, and storage in data banks. Duplication of this publication
or parts thereof is permitted only under the provisions of the German Copyright Law of September 9, 1965,
in its current version, and permission for use must always be obtained from Springer. Violations are liable
to prosecution under the German Copyright Law.

Springer is a part of Springer Science+Business Media

springer.com

© Springer-Verlag Berlin Heidelberg 2006
Printed in Germany

Typesetting: Camera-ready by author, data conversion by Scientific Publishing Services, Chennai, India
Printed on acid-free paper      SPIN: 11735106      06/3142      5 4 3 2 1 0

# Preface

These proceedings contain the refereed papers and posters presented at the $28^{th}$ Annual European Conference on Information Retrieval (ECIR 2006), which was held at Imperial College London in South Kensington between April 10 and 12, 2006. ECIR is the annual conference of the British Computer Society's Information Retrieval Specialist Group. The event started its life as a colloquium in 1978 and was held in the UK each year until 1998, when the event took place in Grenoble, France. Since then the venue has alternated between the UK and Continental Europe. In the last decade ECIR has grown to become the major European forum for the discussion of research in the field of information retrieval.

ECIR 2006 received 177 paper and 73 poster submissions, largely from the UK (18%) and Continental Europe (50%), but we had many sub- missions from further afield including America (7%), Asia (21%), Middle East and Africa (2%), and Australasia (2%). In total 37 papers and 28 posters were accepted, and two papers were converted to posters. All contributions were reviewed by at least three reviewers in a double anonymous process and then ranked during a Programme Committee meeting with respect to scientific quality and originality. It is a good and healthy sign for information retrieval in general, and ECIR in particular, that the submission rate has more than doubled over the past three years. The downside, of course, is that many high-quality submissions had to be rejected owing to a limited capacity of the conference.

ECIR has always been popular with research students and established researchers alike, and this year 73% of the accepted papers and 66% of the accepted posters turned out to have a research student as their main author. The 67 accepted publications span a wide range of cutting-edge themes ranging from formal models (5) over document & query representation and text understanding (5), design and evaluation (8), topic identification and news retrieval (3), user interests and workspaces (5), clustering and classification (8), refinement and feedback (4), performance and peer-to-peer networks (4), Web search (3), structure/XML (6), multimedia (8), cross-language retrieval (6) to genomic information retrieval (2).

We are greatly indebted to the reviewers who spent a great deal of their time giving useful feedback, ensuring the high quality and standard of the selected publications and adhering to rather tight deadlines. We thank the Prize Committee for identifying the very best publications. Thanks go to our platinum sponsors EPSRC, European Information Retrieval Specialist Group of CEPIS, Google, and GCHQ; our golden sponsors Microsoft Research Cambridge, Yahoo Research Barcelona, Sharp Laboratories of Europe, Apriorie, and Lemur Consulting; and our silver sponsors the Multimedia Knowledge Management Network, Imperial College London, Queen Mary, University of London, and Elsevier. Together, the sponsors provided a significant amount of money that, amongst other things, helped more than 40 students to attend the conference. We are immensely grateful to David Hawking, who agreed to come all the way from Canberra, Australia, to give the keynote talk on Enterprise Search. Last, not least, we thank our universities Imperial College London, City University and Queen Mary, University of London, and the countless local helpers at each place who ensured the smooth organization of ECIR 2006.

February 2006

Mounia Lalmas
Andrew MacFarlane
Stefan Rüger
Anastasios Tombros

# Organization

ECIR 2006 was jointly organized by Imperial College London; Queen Mary, University of London; and City University under the patronage of the Information Retrieval Specialist Group of the British Computer Society.

## Organizing Committee

| | |
|---|---|
| General Chair | Stefan Rüger, Imperial College London |
| Programme Chair | Mounia Lalmas, Queen Mary, University of London |
| Poster Chair | Anastasios Tombros, Queen Mary, University of London |
| PC Management System | Theodora Tsikrika, Queen Mary, University of London |
| Web, Sponsorship and Finances Chair | Andrew MacFarlane, City University London |
| Registration Chair | Alexei Yavlinsky, Imperial College London |
| Local Organization | Paul Browne, Imperial College London |
| | Peter Howarth, Imperial College London |
| | Gabriella Kazai, Queen Mary, University of London |
| | João Magalhães, Imperial College London |
| | Simon Overell, Imperial College London |
| | Zoltán Szlávik, Queen Mary, University of London |

## Programme Committee

Mounia Lalmas, Queen Mary, University of London (Programme Chair)
Anastasios Tombros, Queen Mary, University of London (Poster Chair)
Trond Aalberg, NTNU Norwegian University of Technology and Science, Norway
Giambattista Amati, Fondazione Ugo Bordoni, Italy
Massih-Reza Amini, LIP6, Paris, France
Leif Azzopardi, University of Strathclyde, UK
Ricardo Baeza-Yates, Universitat Pompeu Fabra, Spain and Universidad de Chile, Chile
Mark Baillie, University of Strathclyde, UK

Micheline Beaulieu, University of Sheffield, UK
Catherine Berrut, Université Joseph Fourier - Grenoble I, France
Gloria Bordogna, IDPA CNR, Italy
Theo Bothma, University of Pretoria, South Africa
Mohand Boughanem, Université Paul Sabatier, France
Luis de Campos, University of Granada, Spain
David Carmel, IBM Haifa, Israel
Joe Carthy, University College Dublin, Ireland
You-Jin Chang, Queen Mary, University of London, UK
Stavros Christodoulakis, Technical University of Crete, Greece
Paul Clough, University of Sheffield, UK
Nick Craswell, Microsoft Research Cambridge, UK
Fabio Crestani, University of Strathclyde, UK
Gaël Dias, University of Beira Interior, Portugal
Sándor Dominich, University of Veszprém, Hungary
Antoine Doucet, University of Helsinki, Finland
Juan M. Fernández-Luna, University of Granada, Spain
Ingo Frommholz, University of Duisburg-Essen, Germany
Pablo de la Fuente, University of Valladolid, Spain
Norbert Fuhr, University of Duisburg-Essen, Germany
Patrick Gallinari, LIP6, Paris, France
Eric Gaussier, XEROX Europe, France
Mark Girolami, University of Glasgow, UK
Ayse Göker, Robert Gordon University, UK
Julio Gonzalo, UNED, Spain
Cathal Gurrin, Dublin City University, Ireland
Daniel Heesch, Imperial College London, UK
Andreas Henrich, Bamberg University, Germany
Monika Henzinger, EPFL, Lausanne, Switzerland
Djoerd Hiemstra, University of Twente, The Netherlands
Eduard Hoenkamp, University of Nijmegen, The Netherlands
Gilles Hubert, Université Paul Sabatier, France
Peter Ingwersen, Royal School of Library and Information Science,
    Denmark
Gareth Jones, Dublin City University, Ireland
Joemon Jose, University of Glasgow, UK
Jaap Kamps, University of Amsterdam, The Netherlands
Jussi Karlgren, Swedish Institute of Computer Science, Sweden
Gabriella Kazai, Queen Mary, University of London, UK
Jaana Kekäläinen, University of Tampere, Finland
Wessel Kraaij, TNO, The Netherlands
Udo Kruschwitz, University of Essex, UK
Monica Landoni, University of Strathclyde, UK
Birger Larsen, Royal School of Library and Information Science, Denmark
Hyowon Lee, Dublin City University, Ireland

Xuelong Li, Birkbeck College, UK
David Losada, University of Santiago de Compostela, Spain
Andrew MacFarlane, City University London, UK
Massimo Melucci, University of Padova, Italy
Stefano Mizzaro, University of Udine, Italy
Dunja Mladenić, Jožef Stefan Institute, Slovenia
Marie-Francine Moens, Katholieke Universiteit Leuven, Belgium
Christof Monz, Queen Mary, University of London, UK
Josiane Mothe, Université Paul Sabatier, France
Philippe Mulhem, CLIPS-IMAG, Grenoble, France
Michael Oakes, University of Sunderland, UK
Farhad Oroumchian, University of Wollongong Dubai Campus,
    United Arab Emirates
Iadh Ounis, University of Glasgow, UK
Gabriella Pasi, ICT CNR, Italy
Daniela Petrelli, University of Sheffield, UK
Nils Pharo, Oslo University College, Norway
Victor Poznanski, Sharp, UK
Andreas Rauber, Vienna University of Technology, Austria
Jane Reid, Queen Mary, University of London, UK
Maarten de Rijke, University of Amsterdam, The Netherlands
Keith van Rijsbergen, University of Glasgow, UK
Ian Ruthven, University of Strathclyde, UK
Michail Salampasis, Technology Education Institute of Thessaloniki,
    Greece
Eero Sormunen, University of Tampere, Finland
Jacques Savoy, Université de Neuchâtel, Switzerland
Ralf Schenkel, MPI Informatik, Saarbrücken, Germany
Tomás Skopal, Charles University in Prague, Czech Republic
Barry Smyth, University College Dublin, Ireland
Dawei Song, The Open University, UK
Umberto Straccia, ISTI CNR, Italy
John Tait, University of Sunderland, UK
Ulrich Thiel, Fraunhofer IPSI, Germany
Pertti Vakkari, University of Tampere, Finland
Robert Villa, ITIM CNR, Italy
Jesus Vegas, University of Valladolid, Spain
Anne-Marie Vercoustre, INRIA, France
Arjen de Vries, CWI, Netherlands, The Netherlands
Theo van der Weide, Radboud University Nijmegen, The Netherlands
Thijs Westerveld, CWI, The Netherlands
Hugo Zaragoza, Microsoft Research, UK
Roelof van Zwol, Utrecht University, The Netherlands

# Best Student Paper Award Committee

Gareth Jones, Dublin City University, Ireland
David Losada, University of Santiago de Compostela, Spain
Michael Oakes, University of Sunderland, UK

# Best Student Poster Award Committee

Mohand Boughanem, Université Paul Sabatier, France
Birger Larsen, Royal School of Library and Information Science, Denmark
Christof Monz, Queen Mary, University of London, UK

# Additional Reviewers

Eija Airio
Matjaz Bevk
Janez Brank
Gudrun Fischer
Blaz Fortuna
Leo Galamboš
Franc Grootjen
Juan Huete
Aleks Jakulin
Valentin Jijkoun
Hideo Joho
Heikki Keskustalo
Gary Marchioni
Rudolf Mayer

Vojkan Mihajlović
Gilad Mishne
Ragnar Nordlie
Henrik Nottelmann
Blaz Novak
Georg Pölzlbauer
Andreas Pesenhofer
Georgina Ramírez
Erik Tjong Kim Sang
Dacheng Tao
Miha Vuk
Murat Yakici
Yuan Yuan

# Previous Venues of ECIR

2005 Santiago de Compostela, Spain
2004 Sunderland, UK
2003 Pisa, Italy
2002 Glasgow, UK
2001 Darmstadt, Germany
2000 Cambridge, UK
1999 Glasgow, UK
1998 Grenoble, France
1997 Aberdeen, UK
1996 Manchester, UK
1995 Crewe, UK
1994 Drymen, UK
1993 Glasgow, UK
1992 Lancaster, UK

1991 Lancaster, UK
1990 Huddersfield, UK
1989 Huddersfield, UK
1988 Huddersfield, UK
1987 Glasgow, UK
1986 Glasgow, UK
1985 Bradford, UK
1984 Bradford, UK
1983 Sheffield, UK
1982 Sheffield, UK
1981 Birmingham, UK
1980 Leeds, UK
1979 Leeds, UK

# Sponsors

## Platinum

EPSRC

Engineering and Physical Sciences
Research Council

★ CEPIS ★

Google™

GCHQ

## Golden

Microsoft® **Research** YAHOO! RESEARCH

SHARP
Laboratories of
Europe Limited

Apr**i**orie
Information    Management

lemur consulting
the information experts

## Silver

MM KM
http://www.mmkm.org

**Imperial College**
London

Queen Mary
University of London

ELSEVIER

# Table of Contents

## Topic Identification and News Retrieval

## Clustering and Classification

## Refinement and Feedback

# Performance and Peer-to-Peer Networks

# Web Search

# Structure/XML

# Multimedia

# Cross-Language Retrieval

# Genomic IR

# Posters

# Progress in Information Retrieval

Mounia Lalmas[1], Stefan Rüger[2], Theodora Tsikrika[1], and Alexei Yavlinsky[2]

[1] Department of Computer Science, Queen Mary, University of London, UK
{mounia, theodora}@dcs.qmul.ac.uk
http://qmir.dcs.qmul.ac.uk
[2] Department of Computing, Imperial College London, UK
{s.rueger, alexei.yavlinsky}@imperial.ac.uk
http://mmis.doc.ic.ac.uk

**Abstract.** This paper summarises the scientific work presented at the 28th European Conference on Information Retrieval and demonstrates that the field has not only significantly progressed over the last year but has also continued to make inroads into areas such as Genomics, Multimedia, Peer-to-Peer and XML retrieval.

**Introduction.** Information Retrieval is certainly one of those thriving research fields that — despite being relatively old and established — still generates an enormous amount of new interest: the last decade has not only seen eminently successful commercial applications that survived the dot-com bubble but also new challenges such as the hidden and visible Web, enterprise repositories, digital libraries, multimedia, semi-structured documents and new theoretical approaches. It appears that, now more than ever, new and diversified approaches are necessary to stem the tide of information that engulfs us in all shapes and forms. Document collections that increase in size, vary in type and prompt different user needs have driven the information retrieval community to revisit established formal models and create new ones; to look at appropriate document & query representation and increase automated text understanding; to rethink experimental design and evaluation; to improve topic identification and news retrieval; to research user interests and workspaces; to develop specific clustering and classification approaches; to work on query refinement and feedback; to increase performance and design peer-to-peer networks; to contribute to Web search approaches; to create novel XML query approaches; to shift paradigms for multimedia retrieval; to refine methods in cross-language retrieval; and to establish more methods for the new field of genomic Information Retrieval. All this proves that Information Retrieval as a research field continues to push the boundaries of the scientific state of the art and proceeds to positively change the way we all browse, search, select, assess and evaluate, ie, ultimately access and use information.

**Formal Models.** Amati [1] introduces three hypergeometric models, namely KL, DLH and DLLH, using the Divergence from Randomnesss approach, and compares these models to other relevant models of Information Retrieval. Experiments show that these models have an excellent performance with small and

M. Lalmas et al. (Eds.): ECIR 2006, LNCS 3936, pp. 1–11, 2006.
© Springer-Verlag Berlin Heidelberg 2006

very large collections. Azzopardi and Losada [2] present an efficient implementation of the multiple-Bernoulli language model, which makes it comparable in speed to traditional term matching algorithms. Fernández *et al.* [3] argue that the performance of score-based aggregation is affected by artificial deviations consistently occurring in the input score distributions. They propose to rectify this by normalising the scores to a common distribution before combination. Wan and Yang [4] propose a novel document similarity measure based on the Proportional Transportation Distance. They show, using the TDT-3 data, that this measure improves on the previously proposed similarity measure based on optimal matching by allowing many-to-many matching between subtopics of documents. Wang *et al.* [5] propose a probabilistic user-item relevance model to re-formulate the problem of implicit acquisition of user preferences for log-based collaborative filtering to perform recommendations. They show that the approach provides a better recommendation performance on a music play-list data set.

**Document & Query Representation and Text Understanding.** Chang and Poon [6] propose a common phrase index as an efficient index structure to support phrase queries in a very large text database. The structure is an extension of previous index structures for phrases and achieves better query efficiency with negligible extra storage cost. Ernst-Gerlach and Fuhr [7] describe a new approach for retrieval in texts with non-standard spelling, which is important for historic texts in English or German. The approach is based on a new algorithm for generating search term variants in ancient orthography and is shown to outperform competing methods. Karbasi and Boughanem [8] develop a method to assess the potential role of the term frequency-inverse document frequency measures commonly used in text retrieval systems. They identify a novel factor, which is shown to be significant for retrieving relevant documents, especially in large collections.

Kane *et al.* [9] use a machine learning approach for classifying document readability based on a simple set of features that attempt to measure the syntactic complexity of text. Meyer zu Eissen and Stein [10] propose a novel plagiarism detection method that identifies potentially plagiarised passages by analysing a single document with respect to variations in writing style; they also identify new features for the quantification of style aspects for this purpose.

**Design and Evaluation.** Clough *et al.* [11] argue that, within the framework of geographic information retrieval, spatial relevance should be considered independently from thematic relevance. They suggest that spatial relevance requires greater assessor effort and more localised geographic knowledge than judging thematic relevance. Demartini and Mizzaro [12] classify 44 different information retrieval evaluation metrics according to the notions of document relevance and of retrieval. Kirsch *et al.* [13] research whether the inclusion of information about a user's social environment and his or her position in the social network of his or her peers leads to an improvement in search effectiveness. Liang *et al.* [14] present a new metric for measuring summary quality based on representativeness and judgeability. They argue that the elements that make up an evaluation methodology are interdependent, and the way in which they are combined is critical to its effectiveness. Della Mea *et al.* [15] carry out a number of text retrieval experiments using the Average Distance Measure and show that it is highly correlated with traditional effectiveness metrics. Mooney *et al.* [16] carry out a physiological user study that shows that users exhibit galvanic skin response when watching movies engaging in interactive tasks. They examine how these data might be exploited for indexing of data for search and within the search process itself. Vinay *et al.* [17] investigate the problem of some text collections being more difficult to search or more complex to organise into topics than others. Using the Cox-Lewis statistic to measure this complexity, they demonstrate that this analysis is useful in text retrieval. Wen *et al.* [18] investigate the effect of topic familiarity on users' relevance judgements and find that users employ different relevance criteria when searching on less familiar topics.

**Topic Identification and News Retrieval.** Parapar and Barreiro [19] present two sentence retrieval methods, Latent Semantic Indexing retrieval and a topic identification method based on Singular Value Decomposition. Experiments on the TREC novelty track data show these techniques as valid alternative approaches to other more ad-hoc methods devised for this task. Smith and Rodríguez [20] present an algorithm for topic detection that considers the temporal evolution of news and the structure of Web documents, the result of which is used for searching and navigating in an online news source. Yao *et al.* [21] present a novel method to identify important news in the Web environment that consists of diversified online news sites. Their method uses a tripartite graph to capture the facts that a piece of important news generally occupies a visually significant place in some homepage of a news site and that important news events will be reported by many news sites.

**User Interests and Workspaces.** Bogers and van den Bosch [22] present a novel method of re-ranking search results within closed-community search environments; it utilises information related to topical expertise of workgroup members. Boydell and Smyth [23] describe how snippet-text and title similarities can be used to promote documents without selection history in collaborative retrieval environments. Freschi *et al.* [24] propose a technique for filtering obfuscated spam e-mail using approximate pattern matching performed on the original message and on its phonetic transcription. Tamine-Lechani and Boughanem [25] present a retrieval model based on influence diagrams to incorporate long-term interests of the users into the retrieval process. Vildjiounaite and Kyllönen [26] deploy a Support Vector Machine classifier to learn how to associate user information needs with the contents of their electronic calendar to facilitate proactive information collection and presentation.

**Clustering and Classification.** Bouma and de Rijke [27] investigate the impact on classification accuracy of broadness and narrowness of categories in terms of their distance to the root of a hierarchically organised thesaurus. Carpineto *et al.* [28] present Credino, a clustering engine for PDAs based on the theory of concept lattices that can help overcome some specific challenges posed by small-screen, narrow-band devices. Chakraborti *et al.* [29] adapt Latent Semantic Indexing for document classification by treating class labels as additional terms. Ke *et al.* [30] present an improved procedure for automatically categorising e-mails into user-defined folders that have few example messages. Naughton *et al.* [31] cluster text spans in a news article that refer to the same event and exploit the order in which events are described for better clustering. Osinski [32] shows how approximate matrix factorisations can be used to organise document summaries returned by a search engine into meaningful thematic categories. San-Juan and Ibekwe-SanJuan [33] present a new method for clustering multi-word terms based on general lexico-syntactic relations that does not require prior domain knowledge or the existence of a training set. Yin and Power [34] present a machine-learning approach for ranking Web documents according to the proportion of procedural text they contain, where "procedural text" refers to ordered lists of steps, which are very common in some instructional genres such as online manuals.

**Refinement and Feedback.** Clinchant *et al.* [35] investigate various lexical entailment models in information retrieval, using the language modelling framework. They show that lexical entailment potentially provides a significant boost in performance, similar to pseudo-relevance feedback, but at a lower computational cost. Keskustalo *et al.* [36] define a user model, which helps to quantify some interaction decisions involved in simulated relevance feedback. They use the model to construct several simulated relevance feedback scenarios in a laboratory setting. Rode and Hiemstra [37] propose a new kind of relevance feedback that shows how so-called query profiles can be employed for disambiguation and clarification. Yamout *et al.* [38] demonstrate a new relevance feedback technique which propagates relevance information of individual documents to unlabelled documents within a given neighbourhood.

**Performance and Peer-to-Peer Networks.** Büttcher and Clarke [39] present a hybrid approach in which long posting lists are updated in-place, while short lists are updated using a merge strategy. Experimental results show that better indexing performance is obtained with this hybrid approach than either method (in-place, merge-based) alone. Kohlschütter *et al.* [40] introduce a two-dimensional Web model and adapt the PageRank algorithm to efficiently compute an exact rank vector of Web pages, which even for large-scale Web graphs, requires only a few minutes and iteration steps. Nottelmann and Fuhr [41] investigate different building blocks of peer-to-peer architectures, among them the decision-theoretic framework, CORI, hierarchical networks, distributed hash tables and HyperCubes. Siersdorfer and Sizov [42] describe an efficient method to construct reliable machine learning applications in peer-to-peer networks by building ensemble-based meta methods.

**Web Search.** Joho and Jose [43] carry out a comparative evaluation of textual and visual forms of document summaries as an additional document surrogate in the search result presentation. Mishne and de Rijke [44] present an analysis of a large blog search engine query log, exploring a number of angles such as query intent, query topics, and user sessions, and show that blog searches have different intents than general Web searches. Song *et al.* [45] suggest the use of the location of query terms occurring in a URL for measuring how well a Web page is matched with a user's information need in Web search. This is done through an estimate of URL hit types, i.e. the prior probability of being a good answer given the type of query term hits in the URL.

**Structure/XML.** Caracciolo and de Rijke [46] examine multiple query-independent ways of segmenting texts into coherent chunks that can be returned in response to a query. They show this approach to be a viable solution for providing a "go-read-here" functionality. Cornacchia and de Vries [47] use array comprehensions as a novel way to bridge the gap between databases and information retrieval. Schenkel and Theobald [48] present a framework that expands a keyword query into a full-fledged content-and-structure query for relevance feedback in XML retrieval. Extensive experiments on INEX benchmark show the feasibility of the approach. Van Zwol *et al.* [49] present a visual query formulation technique for structured document retrieval that aims at reducing the complexity of the query formulation process and required knowledge of the underlying document structure for the user, while maintaining full expression power, as offered by the NEXI query language for XML retrieval. Vittaut and Gallinari [50] use a model trained to optimise a ranking loss criterion to improve the performance of a baseline structured document retrieval system. The model uses a learning ranking algorithm that operates on scores computed from document elements and from their local structural context. Wang and Rölleke [51] investigate a new, parameter free, ranking method for structured documents based on context-specific inverse document frequency.

**Multimedia.** Chen *et al.* [52] consider episodic memory, based on time and location, for system design in image retrieval. Their user studies show that the browser that clusters images based on time and location data combined was significantly better than four other more standard browsers. Demuth *et al.* [53] propose an efficient motion retrieval system based on the query-by-example paradigm. This system employs qualitative, geometric similarity measures, which allows for intuitive and interactive browsing in a purely content-based fashion without relying on textual annotations. Gurrin *et al.* [54] investigate the use of relevance feedback in a text-based video retrieval setting and identify an optimal number of terms for composing new queries based on feedback data. Schedl *et al.* [55] investigate approaches for album cover retrieval that use image search functions of popular search engines and complement them with content analysis. Smeaton *et al.* [56] investigate a novel, object-based modality for video retrieval, where objects appearing in the video are segmented from their background and are used for retrieval based on their low-level visual features. Urban and Jose [57] propose a novel image retrieval system that incorporates a workspace where users can organise their search results. A task-oriented and user-centred experiment shows that the proposed approach leads to a more effective and enjoyable search experience. Wilkins *et al.* [58] automatically determine visual feature weights for content-based image retrieval using a subset of top query results. Zhang *et al.* [59] propose decision fusion and hierarchical classifier approaches to combine short and long term audio features for detecting game highlights in TV tennis videos.

**Cross-Language Retrieval.** Alberair and Sanderson [60] study how morphological variants of Arabic queries affect retrieval accuracy. Awadallah and Rauber [61] introduce novel techniques for generating answer choices in a multiple choice question answering setting and evaluate it on English and Arabic question answering data. Hoenkamp and van Dijk [62] use the analogy of fingerprinting as employed in forensics to investigate whether Latent Semantic Analysis, and the hyperspace analog to language are directed towards meaning, and this across languages. Koolen *et al.* [63] propose a cross-language approach to historic document retrieval. In particular, they investigate the automatic construction of translation resources for historic languages and the retrieval of historic documents using cross-language information retrieval techniques. Whittaker *et al.* [64] describe how their statistical pattern classification approach can be used for the rapid development of a Question Answering system in a new language. Zhang *et al.* [65] present a system that automatically collects high quality parallel bilingual corpora from the Web. The proposed system use multiple features to identify parallel texts via a $k$-nearest-neighbour classifier.

**Genomic Information Retrieval.** Bernstein and Cameron [66] present an approach based on document fingerprinting for identifying highly similar sequences in large genomic collections. Their approach is shown to use a modest amount of memory and to execute in a time roughly proportional to the size of the collection. Zhou *et al.* [67] focused on addressing the synonym and polysemy issue within the language model framework. A comparative experiment on the TREC 2004 Genomics Track data shows that significant improvements are obtained by incorporating concept-based indexing into a basic language model for this task.

# References

1. Giambattista Amati. Frequentist and Bayesian approach to Information Retrieval. In *Proceedings of the 28th European Conference on Information Retrieval*, volume 3936 of *Lecture Notes in Computer Science*, pages 13–24. Springer-Verlag, 2006.
2. Leif Azzopardi and David E. Losada. An efficient computation of the multiple-Bernoulli language model. In *Proceedings of the 28th European Conference on Information Retrieval*, volume 3936 of *Lecture Notes in Computer Science*, pages 480–483. Springer-Verlag, 2006.
3. Miriam Fernández, David Vallet, and Pablo Castells. Probabilistic score normalization for rank aggregation. In *Proceedings of the 28th European Conference on Information Retrieval*, volume 3936 of *Lecture Notes in Computer Science*, pages 553–556. Springer-Verlag, 2006.

4. Xiaojun Wan and Jianwu Yang. Using proportional transportation distances for measuring document similarity. In *Proceedings of the 28th European Conference on Information Retrieval*, volume 3936 of *Lecture Notes in Computer Science*, pages 25–36. Springer-Verlag, 2006.
5. Jun Wang, Arjen P. de Vries, and Marcel J.T. Reinders. A user-item relevance model for log-based collaborative filtering. In *Proceedings of the 28th European Conference on Information Retrieval*, volume 3936 of *Lecture Notes in Computer Science*, pages 37–48. Springer-Verlag, 2006.
6. Matthew Chang and Chung Keung Poon. Efficient phrase querying with common phrase index. In *Proceedings of the 28th European Conference on Information Retrieval*, volume 3936 of *Lecture Notes in Computer Science*, pages 61–71. Springer-Verlag, 2006.
7. Andrea Ernst-Gerlach and Norbert Fuhr. Generating search term variants for text collections with historic spellings. In *Proceedings of the 28th European Conference on Information Retrieval*, volume 3936 of *Lecture Notes in Computer Science*, pages 49–60. Springer-Verlag, 2006.
8. Soheila Karbasi and Mohand Boughanem. Document length normalization using effective level of term frequency in large collections. In *Proceedings of the 28th European Conference on Information Retrieval*, volume 3936 of *Lecture Notes in Computer Science*, pages 72–83. Springer-Verlag, 2006.
9. Lorna Kane, Joe Carthy, and John Dunnion. Readability applied to Information Retrieval. In *Proceedings of the 28th European Conference on Information Retrieval*, volume 3936 of *Lecture Notes in Computer Science*, pages 523–526. Springer-Verlag, 2006.
10. Sven Meyer zu Eissen and Benno Stein. Intrinsic plagiarism detection. In *Proceedings of the 28th European Conference on Information Retrieval*, volume 3936 of *Lecture Notes in Computer Science*, pages 565–569. Springer-Verlag, 2006.
11. Paul D. Clough, Hideo Joho, and Ross Purves. Judging the spatial relevance of documents for GIR. In *Proceedings of the 28th European Conference on Information Retrieval*, volume 3936 of *Lecture Notes in Computer Science*, pages 548–552. Springer-Verlag, 2006.
12. Gianluca Demartini and Stefano Mizzaro. A classification of IR effectiveness metrics. In *Proceedings of the 28th European Conference on Information Retrieval*, volume 3936 of *Lecture Notes in Computer Science*, pages 488–491. Springer-Verlag, 2006.
13. Sebastian Marius Kirsch, Melanie Gnasa, and Armin B. Cremers. Beyond the Web: Retrieval in social information spaces. In *Proceedings of the 28th European Conference on Information Retrieval*, volume 3936 of *Lecture Notes in Computer Science*, pages 84–95. Springer-Verlag, 2006.
14. Shao Fen Liang, Siobhan Devlin, and John Tait. Evaluating Web search result summaries. In *Proceedings of the 28th European Conference on Information Retrieval*, volume 3936 of *Lecture Notes in Computer Science*, pages 96–106. Springer-Verlag, 2006.
15. Vincenzo Della Mea, Gianluca Demartini, Luca Di Gaspero, and Stefano Mizzaro. Experiments on average distance measure. In *Proceedings of the 28th European Conference on Information Retrieval*, volume 3936 of *Lecture Notes in Computer Science*, pages 492–495. Springer-Verlag, 2006.
16. Colum Mooney, Micheál Scully, Gareth J. F. Jones, and Alan F. Smeaton. Investigating biometric response for Information Retrieval applications. In *Proceedings of the 28th European Conference on Information Retrieval*, volume 3936 of *Lecture Notes in Computer Science*, pages 570–574. Springer-Verlag, 2006.

17. Vishwa Vinay, Ingemar J. Cox, Natasa Milic-Frayling, and Ken Wood. Measuring the complexity of a collection of documents. In *Proceedings of the 28th European Conference on Information Retrieval*, volume 3936 of *Lecture Notes in Computer Science*, pages 107–118. Springer-Verlag, 2006.
18. Lei Wen, Ian Ruthven, and Pia Borlund. The effects on topic familiarity on online search behaviour and use of relevance criteria. In *Proceedings of the 28th European Conference on Information Retrieval*, volume 3936 of *Lecture Notes in Computer Science*, pages 456–459. Springer-Verlag, 2006.
19. David Parapar and Álvaro Barreiro. Sentence retrieval with LSI and topic identification. In *Proceedings of the 28th European Conference on Information Retrieval*, volume 3936 of *Lecture Notes in Computer Science*, pages 119–130. Springer-Verlag, 2006.
20. Simón C. Smith and M. Andrea Rodríguez. Clustering-based searching and navigation in an online news source. In *Proceedings of the 28th European Conference on Information Retrieval*, volume 3936 of *Lecture Notes in Computer Science*, pages 143–154. Springer-Verlag, 2006.
21. Jinyi Yao, Jue Wang, Zhiwei Li, Mingjing Li, and Wei-Ying Ma. Ranking Web news via homepage visual layout and cross-site voting. In *Proceedings of the 28th European Conference on Information Retrieval*, volume 3936 of *Lecture Notes in Computer Science*, pages 131–142. Springer-Verlag, 2006.
22. Toine Bogers and Antal van den Bosch. Authoritative re-ranking of search results. In *Proceedings of the 28th European Conference on Information Retrieval*, volume 3936 of *Lecture Notes in Computer Science*, pages 519–522. Springer-Verlag, 2006.
23. Oisín Boydell and Barry Smyth. Title and snippet based result re-ranking in collaborative Web search. In *Proceedings of the 28th European Conference on Information Retrieval*, volume 3936 of *Lecture Notes in Computer Science*, pages 484–487. Springer-Verlag, 2006.
24. Valerio Freschi, Andrea Seraghiti, and Alessandro Bogliolo. Filtering obfuscated email spam by means of phonetic string matching. In *Proceedings of the 28th European Conference on Information Retrieval*, volume 3936 of *Lecture Notes in Computer Science*, pages 505–509. Springer-Verlag, 2006.
25. Lynda Tamine-Lechani and Mohand Boughanem. Influence diagrams for contextual Information Retrieval. In *Proceedings of the 28th European Conference on Information Retrieval*, volume 3936 of *Lecture Notes in Computer Science*, pages 464–467. Springer-Verlag, 2006.
26. Elena Vildjiounaite and Vesa Kyllönen. Learning links between a user's calendar and information needs. In *Proceedings of the 28th European Conference on Information Retrieval*, volume 3936 of *Lecture Notes in Computer Science*, pages 557–560. Springer-Verlag, 2006.
27. Lucas Bouma and Maarten de Rijke. Specificity helps text classification. In *Proceedings of the 28th European Conference on Information Retrieval*, volume 3936 of *Lecture Notes in Computer Science*, pages 539–542. Springer-Verlag, 2006.
28. Claudio Carpineto, Andrea Della Pietra, Stefano Mizzaro, and Giovanni Romano. Mobile clustering engine. In *Proceedings of the 28th European Conference on Information Retrieval*, volume 3936 of *Lecture Notes in Computer Science*, pages 155–166. Springer-Verlag, 2006.
29. Sutanu Chakraborti, Robert Lothian, Nirmalie Wiratunga, and Stuart Watt. Sprinkling: Supervised Latent Semantic Indexing. In *Proceedings of the 28th European Conference on Information Retrieval*, volume 3936 of *Lecture Notes in Computer Science*, pages 510–514. Springer-Verlag, 2006.

30. Shih-Wen Ke, Chris Bowerman, and Michael Oakes. PERC: A personal email classifier. In *Proceedings of the 28th European Conference on Information Retrieval*, volume 3936 of *Lecture Notes in Computer Science*, pages 460–463. Springer-Verlag, 2006.

31. Martina Naughton, Nicholas Kushmerick, and Joe Carthy. Clustering sentences for discovering events in news articles. In *Proceedings of the 28th European Conference on Information Retrieval*, volume 3936 of *Lecture Notes in Computer Science*, pages 535–538. Springer-Verlag, 2006.

32. Stanislaw Osinski. Improving quality of search results clustering with approximate matrix factorisations. In *Proceedings of the 28th European Conference on Information Retrieval*, volume 3936 of *Lecture Notes in Computer Science*, pages 167–178. Springer-Verlag, 2006.

33. Eric SanJuan and Fidelia Ibekwe-SanJuan. Phrase clustering without document context. In *Proceedings of the 28th European Conference on Information Retrieval*, volume 3936 of *Lecture Notes in Computer Science*, pages 496–500. Springer-Verlag, 2006.

34. Ling Yin and Richard Power. Adapting the naive Bayes classifier to rank procedural texts. In *Proceedings of the 28th European Conference on Information Retrieval*, volume 3936 of *Lecture Notes in Computer Science*, pages 179–190. Springer-Verlag, 2006.

35. Stéphane Clinchant, Cyril Goutte, and Eric Gaussier. Lexical entailment for Information Retrieval. In *Proceedings of the 28th European Conference on Information Retrieval*, volume 3936 of *Lecture Notes in Computer Science*, pages 217–228. Springer-Verlag, 2006.

36. Heikki Keskustalo, Kalervo Järvelin, and Ari Pirkola. The effects of relevance feedback quality and quantity in interactive relevance feedback: A simulation based on user modeling. In *Proceedings of the 28th European Conference on Information Retrieval*, volume 3936 of *Lecture Notes in Computer Science*, pages 191–204. Springer-Verlag, 2006.

37. Henning Rode and Djoerd Hiemstra. Using query profiles for clarification. In *Proceedings of the 28th European Conference on Information Retrieval*, volume 3936 of *Lecture Notes in Computer Science*, pages 205–216. Springer-Verlag, 2006.

38. Fadi Yamout, Michael Oakes, and John Tait. Relevance feedback using weight propagation. In *Proceedings of the 28th European Conference on Information Retrieval*, volume 3936 of *Lecture Notes in Computer Science*, pages 575–578. Springer-Verlag, 2006.

39. Stefan Büttcher and Charles L.A. Clarke. A hybrid approach to index maintenance in dynamic text retrieval systems. In *Proceedings of the 28th European Conference on Information Retrieval*, volume 3936 of *Lecture Notes in Computer Science*, pages 229–240. Springer-Verlag, 2006.

40. Christian Kohlschütter, Paul-Alexandru Chirita, and Wolfgang Nejdl. Efficient parallel computation of PageRank. In *Proceedings of the 28th European Conference on Information Retrieval*, volume 3936 of *Lecture Notes in Computer Science*, pages 241–252. Springer-Verlag, 2006.

41. Henrik Nottelmann and Norbert Fuhr. Comparing different architectures for query routing in peer-to-peer networks. In *Proceedings of the 28th European Conference on Information Retrieval*, volume 3936 of *Lecture Notes in Computer Science*, pages 253–264. Springer-Verlag, 2006.

42. Stefan Siersdorfer and Sergej Sizov. Automatic document organization in a P2P environment. In *Proceedings of the 28th European Conference on Information Retrieval*, volume 3936 of *Lecture Notes in Computer Science*, pages 265–276. Springer-Verlag, 2006.
43. Hideo Joho and Joemon M. Jose. A comparative study of the effectiveness of search result presentation on the Web. In *Proceedings of the 28th European Conference on Information Retrieval*, volume 3936 of *Lecture Notes in Computer Science*, pages 302–313. Springer-Verlag, 2006.
44. Gilad Mishne and Maarten de Rijke. A study of blog search. In *Proceedings of the 28th European Conference on Information Retrieval*, volume 3936 of *Lecture Notes in Computer Science*, pages 289–301. Springer-Verlag, 2006.
45. Ruihua Song, Guomao Xin, Shuming Shi, Ji-Rong Wen, and Wei-Ying Ma. Exploring URL hit priors for Web search. In *Proceedings of the 28th European Conference on Information Retrieval*, volume 3936 of *Lecture Notes in Computer Science*, pages 277–288. Springer-Verlag, 2006.
46. Caterina Caracciolo and Maarten de Rijke. Generating and retrieving text segments for focused access to scientific documents. In *Proceedings of the 28th European Conference on Information Retrieval*, volume 3936 of *Lecture Notes in Computer Science*, pages 350–361. Springer-Verlag, 2006.
47. Roberto Cornacchia and Arjen P. de Vries. A declarative DB-powered approach to IR. In *Proceedings of the 28th European Conference on Information Retrieval*, volume 3936 of *Lecture Notes in Computer Science*, pages 543–547. Springer-Verlag, 2006.
48. Ralf Schenkel and Martin Theobald. Structural feedback for keyword-based XML retrieval. In *Proceedings of the 28th European Conference on Information Retrieval*, volume 3936 of *Lecture Notes in Computer Science*, pages 326–337. Springer-Verlag, 2006.
49. Roelof van Zwol, Jeroen Baas, Herre van Oostendorp, and Frans Wiering. Bricks: the building blocks to tackle query formulation in structured document retrieval. In *Proceedings of the 28th European Conference on Information Retrieval*, volume 3936 of *Lecture Notes in Computer Science*, pages 314–325. Springer-Verlag, 2006.
50. Jean-Nöel Vittaut and Patrick Gallinari. Machine learning ranking for structured Information Retrieval. In *Proceedings of the 28th European Conference on Information Retrieval*, volume 3936 of *Lecture Notes in Computer Science*, pages 338–349. Springer-Verlag, 2006.
51. Jun Wang and Thomas Rölleke. Context-specific frequencies and discriminativeness for the retrieval of structured documents. In *Proceedings of the 28th European Conference on Information Retrieval*, volume 3936 of *Lecture Notes in Computer Science*, pages 579–582. Springer-Verlag, 2006.
52. Chufeng Chen, Michael Oakes, and John Tait. Browsing personal images using episodic memory (time + location). In *Proceedings of the 28th European Conference on Information Retrieval*, volume 3936 of *Lecture Notes in Computer Science*, pages 362–372. Springer-Verlag, 2006.
53. Bastian Demuth, Tido Röder, Meinard Müller, and Bernhard Eberhardt. An Information Retrieval system for motion capture data. In *Proceedings of the 28th European Conference on Information Retrieval*, volume 3936 of *Lecture Notes in Computer Science*, pages 373–384. Springer-Verlag, 2006.
54. Cathal Gurrin, Dag Johansen, and Alan F. Smeaton. Supporting relevance feedback in video search. In *Proceedings of the 28th European Conference on Information Retrieval*, volume 3936 of *Lecture Notes in Computer Science*, pages 561–564. Springer-Verlag, 2006.

55. Markus Schedl, Peter Knees, Tim Pohle, and Gerhard Widmer. Towards automatic retrieval of album covers. In *Proceedings of the 28th European Conference on Information Retrieval*, volume 3936 of *Lecture Notes in Computer Science*, pages 531–534. Springer-Verlag, 2006.

56. Alan F. Smeaton, Gareth J. F. Jones, Hyowon Lee, Noel E. O'Connor, and Sorin Sav. Object-based access to TV rushes video. In *Proceedings of the 28th European Conference on Information Retrieval*, volume 3936 of *Lecture Notes in Computer Science*, pages 476–479. Springer-Verlag, 2006.

57. Jana Urban and Joemon M. Jose. Can a workspace help to overcome the query formulation problem in image retrieval? In *Proceedings of the 28th European Conference on Information Retrieval*, volume 3936 of *Lecture Notes in Computer Science*, pages 385–396. Springer-Verlag, 2006.

58. Peter Wilkins, Paul Ferguson, Cathal Gurrin, and Alan F. Smeaton. Automatic determination of feature weights for multi-feature CBIR. In *Proceedings of the 28th European Conference on Information Retrieval*, volume 3936 of *Lecture Notes in Computer Science*, pages 527–530. Springer-Verlag, 2006.

59. Bin Zhang, Weibei Dou, and Liming Chen. Combining short and long term audio features for TV sports highlight detection. In *Proceedings of the 28th European Conference on Information Retrieval*, volume 3936 of *Lecture Notes in Computer Science*, pages 472–475. Springer-Verlag, 2006.

60. Asaad Alberair and Mark Sanderson. Morphological variation of Arabic queries. In *Proceedings of the 28th European Conference on Information Retrieval*, volume 3936 of *Lecture Notes in Computer Science*, pages 468–471. Springer-Verlag, 2006.

61. Rawia Awadallah and Andreas Rauber. Web-based multiple choice question answering for English and Arabic questions. In *Proceedings of the 28th European Conference on Information Retrieval*, volume 3936 of *Lecture Notes in Computer Science*, pages 515–518. Springer-Verlag, 2006.

62. Eduard Hoenkamp and Sander van Dijk. A fingerprinting technique for evaluating semantics based indexing. In *Proceedings of the 28th European Conference on Information Retrieval*, volume 3936 of *Lecture Notes in Computer Science*, pages 397–406. Springer-Verlag, 2006.

63. Marijn Koolen, Frans Adriaans, Jaap Kamps, and Maarten de Rijke. A cross-language approach to historic document retrieval. In *Proceedings of the 28th European Conference on Information Retrieval*, volume 3936 of *Lecture Notes in Computer Science*, pages 407–419. Springer-Verlag, 2006.

64. Edward W.D. Whittaker, Julien Hamonic, Dong Yang, Tor Klingberg, and Sadaoki Furui. Rapid development of Web-based monolingual question answering systems. In *Proceedings of the 28th European Conference on Information Retrieval*, volume 3936 of *Lecture Notes in Computer Science*, pages 501–504. Springer-Verlag, 2006.

65. Ying Zhang, Ke Wu, Jianfeng Gao, and Phil Vines. Automatic acquisition of Chinese-English parallel corpus from the Web. In *Proceedings of the 28th European Conference on Information Retrieval*, volume 3936 of *Lecture Notes in Computer Science*, pages 420–431. Springer-Verlag, 2006.

66. Yaniv Bernstein and Michael Cameron. Fast discovery of similar sequences in large genomic collections. In *Proceedings of the 28th European Conference on Information Retrieval*, volume 3936 of *Lecture Notes in Computer Science*, pages 432–443. Springer-Verlag, 2006.

67. Xiaohua Zhou, Xiaodan Zhang, and Xiaohua Hu. Using concept-based indexing to improve language modeling approach to genomic IR. In *Proceedings of the 28th European Conference on Information Retrieval*, volume 3936 of *Lecture Notes in Computer Science*, pages 444–455. Springer-Verlag, 2006.

# Enterprise Search — The New Frontier?

David Hawking

CSIRO ICT Centre, Canberra, Australia
David.Hawking@csiro.au
http://es.cmis.csiro.au/people/Dave/

The advent of the current generation of Web search engines around 1998 challenged the relevance of academic information retrieval research – established evaluation methodologies didn't scale and nor did they reflect the diverse purposes to which search engines are now put. Academic ranking algorithms of the time almost completely ignored the features which underpin modern web search: query-independent evidence and evidence external to the document. Unlike their commercial counterparts, academic researchers have for years been unable to access Web scale collections and their corresponding link graphs and search logs.

For all the impressive achievements of the Web search companies, great search challenges remain. Nowhere is this more so than behind the organisational firewall, where employees cry out for effective search tools to permit them to find what they need among huge accumulations of text data, heterogeneous both in type and in format, and subject to security and privacy restrictions. Worldwide, there are almost certainly hundreds of thousands of organisations whose electronic text holdings are larger than (but very different from!) the TREC ad hoc corpus. Do we as an academic community know anything about the character of these collections? Do we know how employees search? What they search for? How they judge the value of what is retrieved? Do we have effective algorithms which can deliver results tailored to the context of their search? Enterprise search is at a more manageable scale than the Web, but nonetheless presents formidable problems for academic researchers. Can academic researchers overcome them, or will the field be left to commercial companies?

The talk will outline the nature of the enterprise search domain, review the current state of research in the area, present some research results, highlight some non-standard applications of search, discuss evaluation methodologies and pose challenges.

**Biography.** David Hawking is the founder and chief scientist of CSIRO's enterprise search engine project (Funnelback: http://funnelback.com). Funnelback is a commercial product permitting effective metadata and/or content search of heterogeneous enterprise information sources including websites, email, fileshares and databases. David was a coordinator of the Web track at the international Text Retrieval Conference from 1997-2004 and has been responsible for the creation and distribution of text retrieval benchmark collections now in use at over 120 research organisations worldwide. In 2003 he was awarded an honorary doctorate from the University of Neuchatel in Switzerland for his contributions to the objective evaluation of search quality. He won the Chris Wallace award for contribution to computer science research in Australasia, for the years 2001-2003.

M. Lalmas et al. (Eds.): ECIR 2006, LNCS 3936, p. 12, 2006.
© Springer-Verlag Berlin Heidelberg 2006

# Frequentist and Bayesian Approach
# to Information Retrieval

Giambattista Amati

Fondazione Ugo Bordoni, Rome, Italy

**Abstract.** We introduce the hypergeometric models KL, DLH and DLLH using the DFR approach, and we compare these models to other relevant models of IR. The hypergeometric models are based on the probability of observing two probabilities: the relative within-document term frequency and the entire collection term frequency. Hypergeometric models are parameter-free models of IR. Experiments show that these models have an excellent performance with small and very large collections. We provide their foundations from the same IR probability space of language modelling (LM). We finally discuss the difference between DFR and LM. Briefly, DFR is a frequentist (Type I), or combinatorial approach, whilst language models use a Bayesian (Type II) approach for mixing the two probabilities, being thus inherently parametric in its nature.

## 1 Introduction

In a problem of statistical inference, the distribution generating the empirical data have a mathematical form and contains certain parameters, such as mean, variance or other characteristics with unknown values. In Information Retrieval (IR), statistical inference is a very complex type of inference since it involves stratified textual data and different populations, different types of information tasks and information needs, and more importantly a relevance relation is defined over the set of documents. Models for IR may therefore contain parameters whose estimation is based on relevance data.

Language Modelling (LM) [5, 7, 14] is an example of application of statistical inference to IR. According to the language modelling approach to IR [19, 6, 15] a document is a sample of the population, and language model computes the probability that a query is generated by a document. In LM we may use either the mixing or the compounding of two probability distributions, the first distribution models the document, the second one models the collection. The combination of these two probability distributions has the effect of *smoothing* the raw likelihood of occurrence of a term in a document. The statistical combination, whether it is of mixing or compounding type, contains a parameter. In general the value of this parameter is determined by a set of training data made up of a set of topics together with the complete set of relevance values made by some assessors. It is a matter of fact that the optimal value of this parameter varies according to the size, the content of the collection, as well as to the length of the queries, and thus performance may significantly change from collection to collection, and for different query-lengths.

Although DFR baseline models were originally motivated by providing parameter-free models for IR [4], recent developments of the DFR approach have shown that a refinement of the term frequency normalization component (also known as the *document*

M. Lalmas et al. (Eds.): ECIR 2006, LNCS 3936, pp. 13–24, 2006.
© Springer-Verlag Berlin Heidelberg 2006

*length normalization* problem) may improve the performance of DFR models [2, 12]. A parameter $c$ was introduced to define how "large" is the standard document length in the collection. Term-frequencies are then resized according to the standard length. In general the standard length is the average document length in the collection, and in such a case $c$ is set to 1.

Since LM and the most general form of the DFR models use a parameter, the existence of a highly performing model of IR, easy to implement and completely free from parameters, is still an open problem. The introduction of new parameter-free models must however perform consistently well on small and very large collections, and with different query lengths.

The present investigation on parameter free models for IR thus is important from both theoretical and pragmatical perspectives. The main result of this paper is the definition of very simple but highly performing models of IR that make only use of the textual data and not of the relevance data.

There are other two well known parameter-free models of IR: the vector space model [23, 25, 24, 20] and Ponte and Croft's model [19]. Except Ponte and Croft's model, we here show that language modelling is inherently Bayesian, and it is thus based on parameter smoothing techniques.

Our analysis will start with two foundational views: frequentist and Bayesian. We revisit the information retrieval inference problem assuming these alternative positions. With the aim of producing a parameter free model for IR in mind, we finally provide a document-query matching function based on the information theoretic definition of divergence given by the hypergeometric distribution. Also, we experimentally compare the frequentist approach to language modelling, BM25 and to other DFR models.

## 2    The Metaphor of the Urn Models for IR Models

We assume that IR is modeled by a set of urns or recipients. Sampling consists in the experiment of drawing balls of different colours $\mathbf{V}$ (the vocabulary or the index) from these urns. In the urn paradigm the population of balls represent all tokens of the collection, and the colours are simply the terms listed in the index. Each urn (document) has a prior probability to be selected P(d), and the balls (tokens) of the same colour (term) have a prior probability P(t) to be drawn. A document is thus regarded as a sample of the population. In the DFR approach the matching function between a query-term and a document is the probability of extracting a number tf (term frequency) balls of the same colour out of l(d) trials (document length).

An alternative approach is used by Language Modelling. It computes the probability of the query-term in the document by smoothing the maximum likelihood estimate (MLE) of the term-frequency in the document, $\hat{p} = \dfrac{tf}{l(d)}$, with the relative term-frequency in the collection, $P(t) = \dfrac{TF}{TFC}$, where tf is the within-document frequency, l(d) the document length, TF is the number of tokens of that term in the collection and TFC is the overall number of tokens in the collection. Smoothing can be obtained by either mixing these two probabilities, or extracting the MLE from the compounding of the multinomial distribution with a prior distribution, for example Dirichlet's Priors.

Let us see in details similarities and differences of these two approaches.

## 2.1  Types of Urns

We may classify IR models according to the way we interpret the stratification of the population [10]. We can imagine an ordinary sampling experiment as the selection of balls from a single urn, in general with replacement and shuffling. This is called a Type I model. We may select before a urn at a random, and then make an experiment as described by a Type I model. The urn selection generates a Type II model. Type III model is similarly defined. Translating this hierarchy to IR, we may say

- IR model of Type I. One single urn, where the urn can be either a document or a collection.
- IR model of Type II. We have several urns, which represent either a set of documents or a set of collections.
- IR model of Type III. Different urns containg other urns (set of sets of documents/collections).

Before we construct the frequentist (non-Bayesian) model, we would like to quote Good's argument on the choice of Type I or Type II model for probability estimation [10, page 5-11]:

[...] The Bayesian will wish to ascribe different weights to different initial (or Type II) distributions. [...] Just as the non-Bayesian finds it expedient to construct mathematical models of Type I probability distributions in which he tries to minimize the number of parameters, the Bayesian will do the same, but with both the Type I and Type II probability distributions. This leads to Type II problems of estimation and significance.

If the Type II probability distribution is unknown, like with the Dirichlet priors in LM, then the Bayesian methodology necessarily leads to the parameter estimation problem.

## 2.2  IR Model of Type I: The Document as a Sample of the Collection

The natural choice for generating a language model of a document is the binomial process. The document is a finite binary sequence of Bernoulli trials whose outcome can be either *a success*, that is an occurrence of the term, or *a failure*, that is an occurrence of a different term. To be more precise, we also assume that the finite binary sequence is *random*, that is any trial is statistically independent from its preceding trials. In a Bernoulli process the probability of a given sequence is

$$P(\text{tf}|d, p) = p^{\text{tf}} \cdot (1\text{-}p)^{l(d)-\text{tf}}$$

where p is the probability of occurrence of the term.

There are $\binom{l(d)}{\text{tf}}$ of *exchangeable sequences* (in IR they are also called *a bag of words*), therefore the probability is given by the binomial

$$P(tf|d, p) = \binom{l(d)}{tf} p^{tf} \cdot (1-p)^{l(d)-tf} \tag{1}$$

The best value for the parameter p in the binomial is unknown. We note that the likelihood $P(tf|d, p)$ is maximised when $\dfrac{dP(tf|d, p)}{dp} = 0$ which is equivalent to set p to the *maximum likelihood estimate MLE* of the term in the document:

$$\hat{p} = \frac{tf}{l(d)} \text{ (MLE)} \tag{2}$$

When the prior p is unknown, then the MLE is a good estimate for p. However we know that the prior probability of occurrence of the term t is the relative term-frequency in the collection:

$$P(t) = \frac{TF}{TFC} \tag{3}$$

But, what does happen if we substitute the prior $P(t)$ for p in Equation 1?

Let us then substitute $P(t)$ for p in Equation 1. For each document d the prior, $P(t)$ of Equation 3, will be fixed, whilst $\hat{p}$ of Equation 2 will vary. We have seen that the probability in Equation 1 is maximised with documents d for which $\hat{p}$ goes towards the value $P(t) = \dfrac{TF}{TFC}$. That is, the maximum likelihood estimator coincides with the prior $P(t)$ when the sample is selected randomly, or better, when the tokens of the term in the document occur randomly. In summary, when the document is little informative, the MLE $\hat{p}$ of a term in the document approaches the prior $P(t)$. For non informative terms, we may say that they occur *randomly*. There are words which always fit to this random behaviour. These are the functional words, and they are also called *non-specialty words* [11]. Usually these words are kept in a list of non-informative words, that constitute the so called *stop list*.

But, documents are not built randomly, and thus documents cannot be regarded as they were random samples of the population of the collection. Frequencies of words are biased by some content or semantics. The more a document model diverges from a random behaviour, the more informative it is. In such a case, if the MLE $\hat{p}$ of a term and its prior $P(t)$ diverge, the binomial probability diminishes, and the term conveys information. We may assume that the divergence given by the binomial can be used as a measure of the significance of the term (the smaller the binomial, the more significant the term). The mechanism of the DFR models, but also of the 2-Poisson and BM25 models (see a formal derivation of the BM25 from a DFR model [4]), encompasses explicitly such a divergence measure. Then, following our intuition on the divergence from randomness, it would be very natural to use the probability

$$P(tf|d) = \binom{l(d)}{tf} P(t)^{tf} (1 - P(t))^{l(d)-tf} \tag{4}$$

to define a measure of divergence of the probabilities $\hat{p}$ and $P(t)$[1].

---

[1] The same formula is used for query expansion by merging top-ranked documents into a single sample.

*Document ranking is thus obtained by ordering the documents which minimize Equation 4.* As we already observed Equation 4 is maximised when the MLE is equal to $P(t)$, and in such a case the term distributes randomly (non informative terms), but Equation 4 is minimised when the two probabilities $\hat{p}$ and $P(t)$ diverge (informative terms). In other words the probability of Equation 4 is *inversely* related to a measure of informativeness of the term. We may soon regard Equation 4 as primitive. However, we want to derive Equation 4 by using aType I model. Doing this we see that the DFR approach is thus frequentist, since it comes from a Type I model, and in contraposition we see that LM employs a Bayesian Type II model. Never the less, both LM and DFR share the same basic probabilistic space. Let us explore these aspects in details.

## 3  Type I Model: The Hypergeometric Model

We said that a DFR model assumes *a high divergence between MLEs and prior probabilities* as a measure of a high informativeness of the term. In other words $P(tf|d, p = P(t))$ of Equation 4 and information content are inversely related. We need a function which is additive on independent events (terms), and the logarithmic function is the only function which satisfies such a condition:

$$\text{Inf}(tf\|d) = -\log_2 P(tf|d, p = P(t))$$

We now want to show Equation 4 with a direct derivation from a frequentist approach. The frequentist approach to IR yields the system of probabilities using the paradigm of the occupancy numbers, or with a less sophisticated terminology, transforming the IR inference problem into a combinatorial form. A well known combinatorial problem is the following: in a population of TFC balls there are TF red balls. What is the probability that in a sample of cardinality $l(d)$ there is exactly a number tf of red balls? There are $\binom{TF}{tf}$ ways to choose a red ball, and there are $\binom{TFC - TF}{l(d) - tf}$ to choose a ball of different colour. All possible configurations are $\binom{TFC}{l(d)}$. Therefore the probability is

$$P(tf|d) = \frac{\binom{TF}{tf} \cdot \binom{TFC - TF}{l(d) - tf}}{\binom{TFC}{l(d)}} \tag{5}$$

The probability distribution of Equation 5 is called the *hypergeometric distribution.* An equivalent formula can be obtained by swapping $l(d)$ with TF:

$$P(tf|d) = \frac{\binom{l(d)}{tf} \cdot \binom{TFC - l(d)}{TF - tf}}{\binom{TFC}{TF}}$$

A limit theorem for the hypergeometric distribution is (see [9, page 59]):

$$\binom{l(d)}{tf} \left(P(t) - \frac{tf}{TFC}\right)^{tf} \left(1 - P(t) - \frac{l(d) - tf}{TFC}\right)^{l(d) - tf}$$
$$< P(tf|d) <$$
$$\binom{l(d)}{tf} P(t)^{tf} (1 - P(t))^{l(d) - tf} \left(1 - \frac{l(d)}{TFC}\right)^{-l(d)}$$

where $P(t)$ is the frequency $\dfrac{TF}{TFC}$ of the term in the collection. Therefore, the binomial distribution of Equation 4

$$\mathcal{B}(l(d), tf, P(t)) = \binom{l(d)}{tf} P(t)^{tf} (1 - P(t))^{l(d) - tf}$$

is obtained as a limiting form of the hypergeometric distribution when the population TFC is very large and the size of the sample is very small, that is when both $\dfrac{l(d)}{TFC} \sim 0$ and $\dfrac{tf}{TFC} \sim 0$. *Thus, we have formally derived the Equation 4*:

$$Inf(tf\|d) = - \log_2 P(tf|d, p = P(t)) = - \log_2 \mathcal{B}(l(d), tf, P(t))$$
$$= - \log_2 \left[\binom{l(d)}{tf} P(t)^{tf} (1 - P(t))^{l(d) - tf}\right]$$

We need to simplify relation 4 to have a workable model of IR. To obtain this, we start with a very useful relation that relates the binomial distribution to the information theoretic *divergence* $\mathcal{D}$ of $\phi$ from $\psi$ (also called the symmetric Kullback-Leibler divergence):

$$\mathcal{D}(\phi, \psi) = \phi \cdot \log_2 \frac{\phi}{\psi} + (1 - \phi) \cdot \log_2 \frac{(1 - \phi)}{(1 - \psi)} \tag{6}$$

Renyi [21] indeed proves the following relation:

$$\mathcal{B}(l(d), tf, P(t)) \sim \frac{2^{-l(d) \cdot \mathcal{D}(\hat{p}, P(t))}}{(2\pi \cdot tf(1 - \hat{p}))^{\frac{1}{2}}} \tag{7}$$

where $\hat{p}$ is the MLE of the probability of the term in the document d of Equation 2. We may delete the contribution of $(1 - \hat{p}) \cdot \log_2 \dfrac{(1 - \hat{p})}{(1 - P(t))}$ in Equation 7 because it is very small. Using the asymmetric Kullback-Leibler divergence

$$\mathbf{KL}(\hat{p}\|P(t)) = \hat{p} \cdot \log_2 \left(\frac{\hat{p}}{P(t)}\right)$$

we can further simplify the information content:

$$Inf(tf\|d) \sim l(d) \cdot \mathcal{D}(\hat{p}, P(t)) + 0.5 \log_2 (2\pi \cdot tf \cdot (1 - \hat{p}))$$
$$\sim l(d) \cdot \mathbf{KL}(\hat{p}\|P(t)) + 0.5 \log_2 (2\pi \cdot tf \cdot (1 - \hat{p}))$$
$$\sim tf \cdot \log_2 \left(\frac{\hat{p}}{P(t)}\right) + 0.5 \log_2 (2\pi \cdot tf \cdot (1 - \hat{p}))$$

## 3.1 DLH and DLLH: Parameter-Free Models of IR

To obtain the matching function we use the *average amount of information* of the term. Instead of using the raw average information carried by a term, that is $\frac{\mathrm{Inf}(tf||d)}{tf}$, we use the *cross-entropy function*. With cross-entropy the average information is a *smoothed* with the Laplace normalization $L$ [4]. The Laplace smoothing is similar to Robertson and Walker's normalization used for the family of BM models [22]. Briefly, we derive the model DLH (DFR model based on the Hypergeometric distribution and the Laplace normalization) as:

$$
\mathrm{weight} = \frac{\mathrm{Inf}(tf||d)}{tf+1} = \frac{-\log_2 \mathcal{B}(l(d), tf, P(t))}{tf+1} =
$$
$$
= \frac{tf \cdot \log_2\left(\frac{\hat{p}}{P(t)}\right) + 0.5 \cdot \log_2\left(2\pi \cdot tf \cdot (1-\hat{p})\right)}{tf+1} \quad \text{(DLH)} \tag{8}
$$

Instead of the average information we may also use the product of two information contents:[2]

$$
\mathrm{weight} = \log_2\left(1+\frac{1}{tf}\right) \cdot \left(tf \cdot \log_2\left(\frac{\hat{p}}{P(t)}\right) + 0.5 \cdot \log_2\left(2\pi \cdot tf \cdot (1-\hat{p})\right)\right) \text{(DLLH)} \tag{9}
$$

Since the first addendum of Equation 8 is related to the asymmetric Kullback-Leibler divergence as follows:

$$
l(d) \cdot \mathbf{KL}(\hat{p}||P(t)) = tf \cdot \log_2\left(\frac{\hat{p}}{P(t)}\right)
$$

This suggest to use a further simplified parameter-free model of IR, called KL:

$$
\mathrm{weight} = \frac{l(d) \cdot \mathbf{KL}(\hat{p}||P(t))}{tf+1} = \frac{tf}{tf+1} \cdot \log_2\left(\frac{\hat{p}}{P(t)}\right) \text{(KL)} \tag{10}
$$

where $\hat{p}$ is the MLE as defined in Equation 2 and $P(t)$ is the prior given by Equation 3. The use of KL divergence is also used in LM [26, 15]. The query expansion weighting function as used in language modeling approach is obtained by *minimizing* the KL-divergence between the document language model and the feedback set of returned documents.

---

[2] Now, $\hat{p} = \frac{tf}{l(d)}$ and $P(t) = \frac{TF}{TFC}$, and also $TFC = N \cdot \mathbf{avg\_length}$, where $N$ is the number of documents in the collection and $\mathbf{avg\_length}$ is the average length. Thus the ratio $\frac{\hat{p}}{P(t)} = \left(\frac{tf}{l(d)}\right) \setminus \left(\frac{TF}{N \cdot \mathbf{avg\_length}}\right)$ contains very small probability factors. In the implementation these small factors might lead to errors. We suggest to associate the statistics contained in the formula differently, to avoid the appearance of very small numbers, as follows:

$$
\log_2\left(\frac{\hat{p}}{P(t)}\right) = \log_2\left(\left(tf \cdot \frac{\mathbf{avg\_length}}{l(d)}\right) \cdot \left(\frac{N}{TF}\right)\right)
$$

## 4  Type II Model: Language Models

Let us take again the binomial distribution of Equation 1 as the *likelihood* probability with parameter p unknown. Bayes' Theorem compounds the likelihood distribution with Type II priors P(p|d) over the document collection. The Dirichlet distribution can be used to assign the priors. In such a case, the compound generates the *generalised hypergeometric distribution*:

$$P(d|tf) = \frac{\binom{l(d)}{tf} p^{tf} \cdot (1-p)^{l(d)-tf} \cdot P(p|d)}{\int_0^1 \binom{l(d)}{tf} P(tf|d,p) \cdot P(p|d)dp} \tag{11}$$

Dirichlet priors has a set of parameters $A_1, \ldots, A_V > 0$, one parameter for each term $t_i$ of the vocabulary of size $V$. The term-frequencies obviously satisfy the condition $tf_1 + \ldots + tf_V = l(d)$. The Dirichlet priors are:

$$P(p_1, \ldots, p_V | d, A_1, \ldots, A_V) = \frac{\Gamma(A)}{\Gamma(A_1) \cdots \Gamma(A_V)} p_1^{A_1-1} \cdots p_V^{A_V-1}$$

$$A = \sum_{i=1}^V A_i \text{ and } \sum_{i=1}^V p_i = 1$$

The *a posteriori* probability distribution after conditionalizing on the Type II distribution $P(p_1, \ldots, p_V | d, A_1, \ldots, A_V)$ takes the same form of Equation 4, that is:

$$P(d|tf_1, \ldots, tf_V, A_1, \ldots, A_V) =$$
$$= \frac{\Gamma(A + l(d))}{\Gamma(A_1 + tf_1) \cdots \Gamma(A_V + tf_V)} p_1^{tf_1+A_1-1} \cdots p_V^{tf_V+A_V-1}$$

Setting $A_t = \mu \cdot P(t)$ with $\mu$ an unknown parameter, the MLE of the compound of the likelihood with probability P as defined by Equation 11 or 4 is:

$$\hat{p}_{LM} = \frac{tf + \mu \cdot P(t)}{l(d) + \mu}$$

Using additivity on independent events of the logarithmic function, we have:

$$p(Q|\mu, d) \propto \frac{1}{|Q|} \sum_{i=1}^{|Q|} \log_2 \left( \frac{tf_i}{\mu P(t_i)} + 1 \right) - \log_2(l(d) + \mu) \ (\text{ LM }).$$

## 5  Comparison of the Frequentist with the Bayesian Approach

We have seen that the frequentist approach defines a parameter-free model of IR, while the Bayesian approach leads to the construction of a parameter based model of IR. The main difference between the two approaches are

**Table 1.** Short queries (Title) of the Robust Track of TREC 2004 (250 queries)

| Model | MAP | R Prec. | Prec. at 5 | Prec. at 10 |
|---|---|---|---|---|
| DLLH | 0.2483 | 0.2887 | 0.4651 | 0.4281 |
| DLH | 0.2438 | 0.2858 | 0.4843 | 0.4373 |
| KL | 0.2343 | 0.2765 | 0.4763 | 0.4289 |
| Ponte & Croft | 0.2383 | 0.2847 | 0.4297 | 0.3972 |
| LM ($\mu = 600$) | 0.2519 | 0.2939 | 0.4803 | 0.4313 |
| BM25 (b=0.75, k=1.2) | 0.2418 | 0.2858 | 0.4731 | 0.4273 |
| PL2 (c=6) | **0.2563** | **0.2979** | **0.4876** | **0.4430** |

1. DFR approach computes the probability of observing two probabilities, while LM smoothes the MLE of a term in the document.
2. DFR approach weights terms according to the *im*probability of observing the MLE of a term in the document given the prior, and it is based on information theoretic notions, such as amount of information and uncertainty. LM instead weights the probability of observing the term in a document given a prior distribution.
3. In DFR approach there are no *non-zero probabilities*, that is when a term does not occur in a document it does not contribute at all to the document score. On the contrary, a term that does not appear in a document plays an important role in LM approach. This requires extra computational costs either in terms of additional index or retrieval structures.
4. The basic DFR models (such as Formulas 10, 8 and 9) can be used as they are for query expansion. A parameter free model of query expansion can be also defined [3]. Also Kullback-Leibler divergence based techniques for query expansion [8, 26], as it was here shown, are approximations of the hypergeometric model and the binomial model.
5. With DFR approach we can combine LM with DFR models or BM25 into a single model, with the advantage of not having non-zero probabilities [1, 13].
6. On the other hand, Bayesian approach is flexible and easy to be applied with a stratified population and in presence of other parameters, while frequentist approach requires a major attention to model complex combinatorial problems.

**Table 2.** Short queries (Title) with DFR Query Expansion of Robust Track 2004 (250 queries) with 40 most informative terms from 8 topmost-retrieved documents

| Model | MAP | R Prec. | Prec. at 5 | Prec. at 10 |
|---|---|---|---|---|
| DLLH | **0.3052** | **0.3303** | 0.5012 | 0.4538 |
| DLH | 0.2912 | 0.3181 | 0.4980 | 0.4514 |
| KL | 0.2821 | 0.3096 | 0.4948 | 0.4462 |
| LM ($\mu$=400) | 0.2968 | 0.3245 | 0.4867 | 0.4562 |
| BM25 (b= 0.75, k=1.2) | 0.2950 | 0.3182 | 0.4956 | 0.4482 |
| PL2 (c=6) | 0.2984 | 0.3253 | **0.5052** | **0.4622** |

**Table 3.** Title and DFR Query Expansion (QE) - Terabyte Track 2004 (GOV2). In order to make a comparison with DLH, we here display the best baseline run. It is relative to the same system that obtained the best TREC run, but using query expansion and single keyword approach only.

| Model | MAP |
|---|---|
| DLH | 0.277 |
| best TREC | 0.284 |
| baseline (with QE) of the best TREC | 0.253 |

## 6    Experiments

We used two test collections of TREC (Text REtrieval Conference). The first collection is from disks 4 and 5 of TREC minus the CR collection and consists of about 2 Gbytes of data, with 528,107 documents and 91,088,037 pointers. The second collection is the terabyte collection GOV2 and consists of about 426 GB Gbytes of data, with about 25 million documents. We used 250 queries (queries 300-450 and 600-700) of the Robust (ad hoc) track of TREC 2004 with the 2GB collection. These queries are ad hoc topics used i since TREC 7. We used also 50 topics of the Terabyte track of TREC 2004. The optimal performance value of $c$ of the DFR models depends on either the query-length (short or long, with or without query expansion) or the collection. The length of the query with query expansion can be regarded short in the case of the Terabyte collection because only 10 additional terms were added to the topics, while it must be considered long in the case of the 2GB collection, because 40 additional terms were added to the topics. We have compared the new models KL, DLH and DLLH with BM25, LM, Ponte and Croft's parameter free model of LM , and the Poisson model PL2, that was shown to have an excellent performance in both .GOV and the terabyte collection GOV2 at the TREC conference [17, 18]. We have used a default value $c = 6$ for PL2. On the other hand, we have used different optimal values of $\mu$ for the model LM. The same query expansion techniques as described in [3] has been applied to all models.

## 7    Discussion of the Results and Conclusions

We have derived from the frequentist approach of IR some very simple document-ranking models which we have shown to perform very well with two different collection sizes (a collection of 2 GB and a collection of 426 GB). These models are free from parameters and can be used with any collection without tuning parameters. The problem of parameter tuning is instead important in the language modelling approach. Zhai and Lafferty report [27] that an inadequate smoothing may hurt the performance more heavily in the case of long and verbose queries. Also, the optimal value of the LM parameter $\mu$ tends to be larger for long queries than for short queries. They observe that smoothing plays a more important role for long queries than for short queries. They also observe that Dirichlet prior performs worse on long queries than title queries on the web collection. In particular, for each subcollection contained in the 2GB collection the optimal value of $\mu$ varies from 500 to 4000 for the short queries and from 2000 to 5000 for the long queries. They conclude that the optimal value of $\mu$ depends both on the collection and the verbosity of the query.

The hypergeometric models have very good performance. In particular, they have the best MAP for short queries with query expansion on the 2GB collection. As for the Terabyte collection, they have better performance than the best TREC run that uses query expansion and single keyword approach, and a close performance to the best run, which however uses additional document and term structures.

## Acknowledgments

This paper was given as oral contribution at the "IR & Theory workshop", held in Glasgow the 25th July 2005. We thank Keith van Rijsbergen, Iadh Ounis for infinitely long discussions on DFR approach, and University of Glasgow for support. Special gratitude goes to Ben He who ran the experiments with the GOV2 collection. All experiments of this paper have been conducted using the Terrier version 1.0.2 [16]. The second addendum of Equation 6, implemented in DLH version of Terrier, was not here used.

## References

1. AMATI, G. *Probability Models for Information Retrieval based on Divergence from Randomness*. PhD thesis, University of Glasgow, June 2003.
2. AMATI, G., CARPINETO, C., AND ROMANO, G. FUB at TREC 10 web track: a probabilistic framework for topic relevance term weighting. In *In Proceedings of the 10th Text Retrieval Conference TREC 2001* (Gaithersburg, MD, 2002), E. Voorhees and D. Harman, Eds., NIST Special Pubblication 500-250, pp. 182–191.
3. AMATI, G., CARPINETO, C., AND ROMANO, G. Fondazione Ugo Bordoni at TREC 2004. In *In Proceedings of the 13th Text Retrieval Conference TREC 2001* (Gaithersburg, MD, 2004), E. Voorhees and D. Harman, Eds., NIST Special Pubblication 500-261.
4. AMATI, G., AND VAN RIJSBERGEN, C. J. Probabilistic models of information retrieval based on measuring the divergence from randomness. *ACM Transactions on Information Systems (TOIS) 20*, 4 (2002), 357–389.
5. BAHL, L. R., JELINEK, F., AND MERCER, R. L. A maximum likelihood approach to continuous speech recognition. *IEEE Transactions on Pattern Analysis and Machine Intelligence PAMI-5*, 2 (Mar. 1983), 179–190.
6. BERGER, A., AND LAFFERTY, J. Information retrieval as statistical translation. In *SIGIR '99: Proceedings of the 22nd annual international ACM SIGIR conference on Research and development in information retrieval* (New York, NY, USA, 1999), ACM Press, pp. 222–229.
7. BROWN, P. F., COCKE, J., DELLA PIETRA, S. A., DELLA PIETRA, V. J., JELINEK, F., LAFFERTY, J. D., MERCER, R. L., AND ROOSSIN, P. S. A statistical approach to machine translation. *Computational Linguistics 16*, 2 (June 1990), 79–85.
8. CARPINETO, C., DE MORI, R., ROMANO, G., AND BIGI, B. An information theoretic approach to automatic query expansion. *ACM Transactions on Information Systems 19*, 1 (2001), 1–27.
9. FELLER, W. *An introduction to probability theory and its applications. Vol. I*, third ed. John Wiley & Sons Inc., New York, 1968.
10. GOOD, I. J. *The Estimation of Probabilities: an Essay on Modern Bayesian Methods*, vol. 30. The M.I.T. Press, Cambridge, Massachusetts, 1968.
11. HARTER, S. P. *A probabilistic approach to automatic keyword indexing*. PhD thesis, Graduate Library, The University of Chicago, Thesis No. T25146, 1974.

12. HE, B., AND OUNIS, I. A study of parameter tuning for term frequency normalization. In *Proceedings of the twelfth International Conference on Information and Knowledge Management* (2005), Springer.

13. HE, B., AND OUNIS, I. A study of the Dirichlet priors for term frequency normalisation. In *SIGIR '05: Proceedings of the 28th annual international ACM SIGIR conference on Research and development in information retrieval* (New York, NY, USA, 2005), ACM Press, pp. 465–471.

14. JELINEK, F., AND MERCER, R. Interpolated estimation of markov source parameters from sparse data. In *Pattern Recognition in Practice* (Amsterdam, Netherlands, 1980), North-Holland, pp. 381–397.

15. LAFFERTY, J., AND ZHAI, C. Document Language Models, Query Models, and Risk Minimization for Information Retrieval. In *Proceedings of ACM SIGIR* (New Orleans, Louisiana, USA, September 9-12 2001), ACM Press, New York, NY, USA, pp. 111–119.

16. OUNIS, I., AMATI, G., V., P., HE, B., MACDONALD, C., AND JOHNSON, D. Terrier Information Retrieval Platform. In *Proceedings of the 27th European Conference on IR Research (ECIR 2005)* (2005), vol. 3408 of *Lecture Notes in Computer Science*, Springer, pp. 517 – 519.

17. PLACHOURAS, V., HE, B., AND OUNIS, I. University of Glasgow at TREC2004: Experiments in Web, Robust and Terabyte tracks with Terrier. In *Proceedings of the 13th Text REtrieval Conference (TREC 2004)* (Gaithersburg, MD, 2004), NIST Special Pubblication 500-261.

18. PLACHOURAS, V., AND OUNIS, I. Usefulness of hyperlink structure for query-biased topic distillation. In *Proceedings of the 27th annual international conference on Research and development in information retrieval* (2004), ACM Press, pp. 448–455.

19. PONTE, J., AND CROFT, B. A Language Modeling Approach in Information Retrieval. In *The 21st ACM SIGIR Conference on Research and Development in Information Retrieval* (Melbourne, Australia, 1998), B. Croft, A. Moffat, and C. Van Rijsbergen, Eds., ACM Press, pp. 275–281.

20. RAGHAVAN, V. V., AND WONG, S. K. A critical analysis of the vector space model for information retrieval. *Journal of the American Society for Information Science 37*, 5 (1986), 279–287.

21. RENYI, A. *Foundations of probability*. Holden-Day Press, San Francisco, USA, 1969.

22. ROBERTSON, S., AND WALKER, S. Some simple approximations to the 2-Poisson Model for Probabilistic Weighted Retrieval. In *Proceedings of the Seventeenth Annual International ACM-SIGIR Conference on Research and Development in Information Retrieval* (Dublin, Ireland, June 1994), Springer-Verlag, pp. 232–241.

23. SALTON, G. *The SMART Retrieval System*. Prentice Hall, New Jersey, 1971.

24. SALTON, G., AND MCGILL, M. *Introduction to modern Information Retrieval*. McGraw-Hill, New York, 1983.

25. SALTON, G., WONG, A., AND YANG, C. S. A vector space model for automatic indexing. *Commun. ACM 18*, 11 (1975), 613–620.

26. ZHAI, C., AND LAFFERTY, J. Model-based Feedback in the Language Modeling Approach to Information Retrieval. In *ClKM 2001* (Atlanta, Georgia, USA, November 5-10 2001), ACM Press, New York, NY, USA, pp. 334–342.

27. ZHAI, C., AND LAFFERTY, J. A Study of Smoothing Methods for Language Models Applied to Information Retrieval. *ACM Transactions on Information Systems 22*, 2 (April 2004), 179214.

# Using Proportional Transportation Distances for Measuring Document Similarity

Xiaojun Wan and Jianwu Yang

Institute of Computer Science and Technology, Peking University, Beijing 100871, China
{wanxiaojun, yangjianwu}@icst.pku.edu.cn

**Abstract.** A novel document similarity measure based on the Proportional Transportation Distance (PTD) is proposed in this paper. The proposed measure improves on the previously proposed similarity measure based on optimal matching by allowing many-to-many matching between subtopics of documents. After documents are decomposed into sets of subtopics, the Proportional Transportation Distance is employed to evaluate the similarity between sets of subtopics for two documents by solving a transportation problem. Experiments on TDT-3 data demonstrate its good ability for measuring document similarity and also its high robustness, i.e. it does not rely on the underlying document decomposition algorithm largely as the optimal matching based measure.

## 1 Introduction

Measuring pairwise document similarity is critical to various text applications, such as document clustering, document filtering, and nearest neighbor search. Most text applications aim to measure document similarity by how much information (content) the documents share. Lin [11] clarifies the intuitions about similarity as follows: The similarity between documents A and B is positively related to their commonality and negatively related to the differences between them. The commonality and difference between documents are measured based on the co-occurrences of words or phrases in the documents. If two documents share more words/phrases while keep less different words/phrases, the documents are more similar. Most popular similarity measures, such as the Cosine measure, the Dice measure, the Jaccard measure, the Overlap measure [3, 18] and the information-theoretic measure [2], all observe the above intuitions.

However, the above similarity measures do not take into account the document structure, e.g. the subtopic[1] structure, thus losing the information of word distribution over the document structure. Wan and Peng [19] propose an optimal matching based similarity measure to take into account the subtopic structures of documents, with the TextTiling algorithm to decompose the documents and the optimal matching technique to match the subtopics and get the overall similarity value. However, the optimal matching based measure is limited by allowing only one-to-one matching between subtopics. In reality, the one-to-one matching between subtopics is not the same as human's cognition. From human's perspective, any two subtopics are more or less similar, thus can be matched more or less. In other words, one subtopic in a

---

[1] In this paper, a subtopic is represented by a coherent block of text, either contiguous or incontiguous.

M. Lalmas et al. (Eds.): ECIR 2006, LNCS 3936, pp. 25–36, 2006.
© Springer-Verlag Berlin Heidelberg 2006

document should be allowed to be matched to more than one subtopic in the other document with different weights, and thus the many-to-many matching is allowed between the subtopics of two documents.

In this study we propose a novel measure based on the Proportional Transportation Distance (PTD) to evaluate document similarity by allowing many-to-many matching between subtopics. First, documents are decomposed into sets of subtopics, each subtopic being represented by a contiguous or incontiguous block of text, and then the Proportional Transportation Distance is employed to evaluate the similarity between two sets of subtopics for two documents by solving a transportation problem. Experiments evaluate the performance of a number of popular similarity measures and results show the PTD-based measure outperforms all other similarity measures, including the optimal matching based measure. We also explore the sentence clustering algorithm for document decomposition in addition to the TextTiling algorithm, and the experimental results show that the PTD-based measure has a stably high performance with either the sentence clustering algorithm or the TextTiling algorithm for document decomposition, while the optimal matching based measure performs poorly with the sentence clustering algorithm. In other words, the proposed PTD-based measure does not rely largely on the document decomposition algorithm, while the optimal matching based method relies largely on the TextTiling composition algorithm.

The rest of this paper is organized as follows: Section 2 reviews the popular similarity measures, including the Cosine measure, the information theoretic measure, the optimal matching based measure and the measures derived from popular retrieval functions. In Section 3, we propose the new similarity measure based on the Proportional Transportation Distance. Experiments and results are described in Section 4. Section 5 gives our conclusions and future work.

## 2  Popular Similarity Measures

### 2.1  The Cosine Measure

The Cosine measure is the most popular measure for document similarity based on vector space model (VSM). The vector space model creates a space in which documents are represented by vectors. For a fixed collection of documents, an $m$-dimensional vector is generated for each document from sets of terms with associated weights, where $m$ is the number of unique terms in the document collection. Then, a vector similarity function is used to compute the similarity between vectors.

In VSM, weights associated with the terms are calculated based on term frequency $tf_{d,t}$ and inverse document frequency $idf_t$. The similarity $sim(a,b)$, between two documents $a$ and $b$, can be defined as the normalized inner product of the two vectors $\vec{a}$ and $\vec{b}$ :

$$sim_{\cos ine}(\mathrm{a},\mathrm{b}) = \frac{\vec{a} \bullet \vec{b}}{|\vec{a}||\vec{b}|} = \frac{\sum_{t \in a \cap b}(w_{a,t} \cdot w_{b,t})}{\sqrt{\sum_{t \in a} w_{a,t}^2 \times \sum_{t \in b} w_{b,t}^2}} \tag{1}$$

where $t$ represents a term. $a \cap b$ gets the common words between $a$ and $b$. Document weight $w_{d,t}$ is computed by $tf_{d,t} * idf_t$.

## 2.2 The Information Theoretic Measure

Aslam and Frost [2] extend the concept that the assessment of pairwise object similarity can be approached in an axiomatic manner using information theory and delevop an information-theoretic measure for pairwise document similarity as follows:

$$\text{Sim}_{\text{IT-sim}}(a, b) = \frac{2 \cdot \sum_t \min\{p_{a,t}, p_{b,t}\} \log \pi(t)}{\sum_t p_{a,t} \log \pi(t) + \sum_t p_{b,t} \log \pi(t)}. \qquad (2)$$

In the above equation, the probability $\pi(t)$ is simply the fraction of corpus documents containing term $t$. For each document d and term t, let $p_{d,t}$ be the fractional occurrence of term $t$ in document $d$; thus, $\sum_t p_{d,t} = 1$ for all d. Two (normalized) documents $a$ and $b$ share $\min\{p_{a,t}, p_{b,t}\}$ amount of term t in "common," while they contain $p_{a,t}$ and $p_{b,t}$ amount of term $t$ individually.

## 2.3 The Optimal Matching Based Measure

A similarity measure taking into account the subtopic structure is proposed by Wan and Peng [19]. Given two documents $X$ and $Y$, the TextTiling algorithm [7] is adopted to get their subtopic structures. The subtopic structures are represented by the sequences of TextTiles $X=\{x_1, x_2, ..., x_n\}$ and $Y=\{y_1, y_2, ... y_m\}$, respectively, where $x_i$ represents a subtopic (TextTile) in document $X$ and $y_j$ represents a subtopic (TextTile) in document $Y$. Then a bipartite graph $G=\{X, Y, E\}$ is built for the documents $X$ and $Y$. A weight $w_{ij}$ is assigned to every edge $e_{ij}$, measuring the similarity between $x_i$ and $y_j$ with the Cosine measure. Lastly the Kuhn-Munkres algorithm [20] is applied to acquire the total value of the optimal matching in the graph. In order to balance the effect of the lengths of different documents, the total value is normalized as follows:

$$sim_{\text{OM}}(a, b) = \frac{optmatch(a, b)}{\min(length(a), length(b))} \qquad (3)$$

where $optmatch(d_1, d_2)$ represents the total value of the optimal matching for $d_1$ and $d_2$. $length(d)$ represents the count of text segments in document $d$ and $min(a,b)$ returns the minimal value of $a$ and $b$. The normalized value is taken as the final similarity between the two documents.

The TextTiling algorithm will be described in detail later. The optimal matching (OM) is a classical problem in graph theory. A matching $M$ of the bipartite graph $G$ is a subset of the edges with the property that no two edges of $M$ share the same node. OM is basically an extension of maximum matching (MM) and aims to find the matching $M$ that has the largest total weight. According to its definition, the optimal matching allows only one-to-one matching between subtopics in the documents.

## 2.4 Measures Derived from Retrieval Models

### 2.4.1 The BM25 Measure

The BM25 measure [13, 14] is one of the most popular retrieval models in a probabilistic framework and is widely used in the Okapi system. In this study, we use the

BM25 model to compute the similarity value between documents by using one document as the query. Given the query document $q$, the similarity score for the document $d$ is defined as follows:

$$\text{score}_{\text{BM25}}(q,d) = \sum_{t \in q} f_{q,t} \times \log(\frac{N - n_t + 0.5}{n_t + 0.5}) \times \frac{(K+1) \times f_{d,t}}{K \times \left\{ (1-b) + b\frac{dlf_d}{avedlf} \right\} + f_{d,t}} \quad (4)$$

where $t$ represents a unique term; $N$ is the number of documents in the collection; $n_t$ is the number of documents in which term t exists; $f_{q,t}$ is the frequency of term $t$ in $q$; $f_{d,t}$ is the frequency of term $t$ in $d$; $dlf_d$ is the sum of term frequencies in $d$; $avedlf$ is the average of $dlf_d$ in the collection; $K$=2.0, $b$=0.8 are constants.

Note that given two documents $a$ and $b$, the similarity value computed with this measure when $a$ is taken as the query would be different from the similarity value when $b$ is taken as the query. In the experiments, the query documents are selected beforehand, and so we can apply this measure directly, so do the following PivoitedVSM measure and language model measure.

### 2.4.2  The Vector Space Model with Pivoted Document Length Normalization

The vector space model with pivoted document length normalization [17] is also a popular retrieval model and is used in the Smart system [16]. In this study, we use this retrieval model to compute the similarity value between documents by using one document as the query. Given the query document $q$, the similarity score for the document $d$ is defined as follows:

$$\text{score}_{\text{PivotedVSM}}(q,d) =$$

$$\sum_{t \in q} (1 + \log(f_{q,t})) \times idf_t \times \frac{1 + \log(f_{d,t})}{1 + \log(avef_d)} \times \frac{1}{avedlb + S \times (dlb_d - avedlb)} \quad (5)$$

where $t$ represents a unique term; $f_{q,t}$ is the frequency of term $t$ in $q$; $f_{d,t}$ is the frequency of term $t$ in $d$; $idf_t$ is the inverse document frequency of term $t$; $dlf_d$ is the sum of term frequencies in $d$ (or the document length of $d$); $dlb_d$ is the number of unique terms in $d$; $avef_d$ is the average of term frequencies in $d$ (i.e., "$dlf_d/dlb_d$"); $avedlb$ is the average of $dlb_d$ in the collection; $S$=0.2 is a constant.

### 2.4.3  The Language Model Measure

The language model measure [5, 22] adopts a probabilistic framework and it interprets the relevance between a document and a query as the probability of generating the query from the document. We use the frequently used the Dirichlet prior smoothing method for the unigram document model $\theta_d$. Given the query document $q$, the similarity score for the document d is defined as follows:

$$\text{score}_{\text{LM}}(q,d) = \prod_{t \in q} p(t \mid \theta_d) = \sum_{t \in q} \log(\lambda \times \frac{f_{d,t}}{dlf_d} + (1-\lambda) \times P_{\text{MLE}}(t \mid C)) \quad (6)$$

where $f_{d,t}$ is the frequency of term $t$ in $d$; $dlf_d$ is the sum of term frequencies in $d$ (or the document length of $d$); $\lambda = dlf_d/(dlf_d + \mu)$, and $P_{\text{MLE}}(t \mid C)$ is the maximum likelihood estimate of the probability of term $t$ in collection $C$. $\mu$ is a parameter and is usually set to be multiples of the average document length.

## 3   The Proposed PTD-Based Measure

The proposed measure circumvents the problem of the optimal matching based measure by employing the Proportional Transportation Distance to allow many-to-many matching between subtopics, thus benefiting the evaluation of document similarity based on subtopic structure.

Similarly, the framework of the proposed PTD-based measure is composed of the following two steps: 1) Decompose documents into sets of subtopics; 2) Evaluate document similarity based on the subtopic sets.

In the first step, different algorithms can be adopted to decompose documents, such as the TextTiling algorithm and the sentence clustering algorithm. In the second step, the proposed measure formalizes the problem as a transportation problem and adopts the Proportional Transportation Distance to solve this problem, while the previous optimal matching based measure formalizes the problem as an optimal matching problem and adopts the Kuhn-Munkres algorithm to solve this problem.

### 3.1   Document Decomposition

#### 3.1.1   TextTiling

A document usually has a discourse structure and the structure can be characterized as a sequence of subtopical discussions that occur in the context of a few main topic discussions. For example, a news text about China-US relationship, whose main topic is the good bilateral relationship between China and the United States, can be described as consisting of the following subdiscussions (numbers indicate paragraph numbers):

*1 Intro-the establishment of China-US relationships*
*2-3 The officers exchange visits*
*4-5 The culture exchange between the two countries*
*6-7 The booming trade between the two countries*
*8 Outlook and summary*

Texttiling is a technique for automatically subdividing text into multi-paragraph units that represent subtopics.

The algorithm of TextTiling detects subtopic boundaries by analyzing patterns of lexical connectivity and word distribution. The main idea is that terms that describe a subtopic will co-occur locally, and a switch to a new subtopic will be signaled by the ending of co-occurrence of one set of terms and the beginning of the co-occurrence of a different set of terms. The algorithm has the following three steps:

1) Tokenization: The input text is divided into individual lexical units, i.e. pseudosentences of a predefined size;

2) Lexical score determination: All pairs of adjacent lexical units are compared and assigned a similarity value;

3) Boudary identification:  The resulting sequence of similarity values is graphed and smoothed, and then is examined for peaks and valleys. The subtopic boundaries are assumed to occur at the largest valleys in the graph.

For TextTiling, subtopic discussions are assumed to occur within the scope of one or more overarching main topics, which span the length of the text. Since the segments are adjacent and non-overlapping, they are called TextTiles.

The computational complexity is approximately linear with the document length, and more efficient implementations are available, such as Kaufmann's work [10] and JTextTile [4].

### 3.1.2  Sentence Clustering

The clustering algorithm is often used to automatically discover the subtopics in a set of documents and group the documents by those subtopics. Similarly, the clustering technique can be taken to automatically discover the subtopics in a set of sentences of a document and group the sentences by those subtopics, such as Zha's work [21]. In this study, we employ the hierarchical agglomerative clustering algorithm to group sentences in a document and get the subtopic structure. Note that the sentences within one of the resultant subtopics might not be consecutive, while the sentences within one of those subtopics produced by the TextTiling algorithm are consecutive.

The algorithm is as follows: initially, each sentence is an individual cluster; then we iteratively merge two sentences with the largest similarity value to form a new cluster until this similarity value is below a pre-set merging threshold. The merging threshold can be determined through cross-validation. We employ the widely used average-link method to compute the similarity between two clusters as follows:

$$sim\ (c_1, c_2) = \frac{\sum_{i=1}^{m} \sum_{j=1}^{n} sim\ (s_i, s_j)}{m \times n} \tag{7}$$

where $s_i$, $s_j$ are sentences in cluster $c_1$ and cluster $c_2$ respectively, and $m$ is the number of sentences in cluster $c_1$ and $n$ is the number of sentences in cluster $c_2$.

Finally, the sentences in a cluster represent a subtopic.

The computational complexity of the clustering algorithm is $O(n^3)$, where $n$ is the number of sentences in a document.

### 3.1.3  The PTD-Based Measure

Giannopoulos and Veltkamp [6] propose the Proportional Transportation Distance (PTD) in order to get a similarity measure based on weight transportation such that the surplus of weight between two point sets in taken into account and the triangle inequality still holds. The PTD evaluates dissimilarity between two weighted point sets where a distance measure between single points, which we call the ground distance is given. The PTD "lifts" this distance from individual points to full sets.

In our context, the point sets are the subtopic sets for documents, and a weighted graph is constructed to model the similarity between two documents, and then PTD is employed to compute the minimum cost of the weighted graph as the similarity value between two documents. The problem is formalized as follows:

Given two document $A$ and $B$, a weighted graph $G$ is constructed as follows:

Let $A = \{(t_{a1}, w_{a1}), (t_{a2}, w_{a2}), ..., (t_{am}, w_{am})\}$ as the weighted point set of document $A$, $t_{ai}$ represents a subtopic in document $A$ and its weight $w_{ai}$ is the total number of the words in the sentences within the subtopic $t_{ai}$.

Let $B = \{(t_{b1}, w_{b1}), (t_{b2}, w_{b2}), ..., (t_{bn}, w_{bn})\}$ as the weighted point set of document B, $t_{bj}$ represents a subtopic in document B and its weight $w_{bj}$ is the total number of the words in the sentences within the subtopic $t_{bj}$.

Let $D = \{d_{ij}\}$ as the distance matrix where $d_{ij}$ is the distance between subtopics $t_{ai}$ and $t_{bj}$. In our case, $d_{ij}$ is computed by 1-$s_{ij}$, where $s_{ij}$ is the Cosine similarity between the two blocks of texts for subtopics $t_{ai}$ and $t_{bj}$.

Let $G = \{A, B, D\}$ as a weighted graph constructed by A, B and D. $V = A \cup B$ is the vertex set while $D = \{d_{ij}\}$ is the edge set. $W_A$, $W_B$ are the total weights of A, B respectively.

In the weighted graph G, the set of all feasible flows $\xi = [f_{ij}]$ from A to B is defined by the following constraints:

$$f_{ij} \geq 0 \quad 1 \leq i \leq m \quad 1 \leq j \leq n \tag{8}$$

$$\sum_{j=1}^{n} f_{ij} = w_{ai} \quad 1 \leq i \leq m \tag{9}$$

$$\sum_{i=1}^{m} f_{ij} = \frac{w_{bj} W_A}{W_B} \quad 1 \leq j \leq n \tag{10}$$

$$\sum_{i=1}^{m} \sum_{j=1}^{n} f_{ij} = W_A \tag{11}$$

Constraint (8) allows moving words from A to B and not vice versa. Constraint (9) and (11) force all of A's weight to move to the positions of points in B. Constraint (10) ensures that this is done in a way that preserves the old percentages of weight in B.

The PTD(A,B) is given by:

$$\text{PTD}(A, B) = \frac{\min_{F \in \xi} \sum_{i=1}^{m} \sum_{j=1}^{n} f_{ij} d_{ij}}{W_A}. \tag{12}$$

Finally, the similarity between documents A and B is defined as:

$$Sim_{\text{PTD}}(A, B) = 1 - \text{PTD}(A, B). \tag{13}$$

$Sim_{PTD}(A,B)$ is normalized in the range of [0,1]. The higher the value of $Sim_{PTD}(A,B)$, the more similar the documents A and B.

The PTD is in fact a modification of the Earth Mover's Distance (EMD) [15] and has all properties of the EMD for equal total weight sets. For example, it naturally extends the notion of a similarity distance between subtopics to that of a similarity distance between subtopic sets, or documents by allowing for many-to-many matches among subtopics according to their similarity.

The PTD is calculated by first dividing, for both point sets, every point's weight by its point set's total weight, and then calculating the EMD for the resulting point sets. Efficient algorithms for the transportation problem are available, which are important to compute EMD efficiently. We used the transportation simplex method [8], a streamlined simplex algorithm that exploits the special structure of the transportation problem. A theoretical analysis of the computational complexity of the transportation simplex is hard, since it is based on the simplex algorithm which can have, in general, an exponential worst case. However, in our context, the performance is improved by the fact that the size of the vertex set in the graph is small. Other efficient methods to solve the transportation problem have been developed, such as interior-point algorithms [9] which have polynomial time complexity.

## 4 Experiments

### 4.1 Experimental Setup

In order to evaluate the performance for the similarity measures, we use a number of documents as queries and retrieve similar documents from a document corpus based on different similarity measures. Then the returned list of 200 documents is compared with the ground truth list. The higher the document is in the ranked list, the more similar it is with the query document.

As a Java implementation of the TextTiling algorithm, the JTextTile with the recommended parameter settings is used to segment texts into contiguous topic segments. For the sentence clustering algorithm, we explore different merging thresholds.

To perform the experiments, a ground truth data set is required. As in previous work [19], we build the ground truth data set from the TDT-3 corpus, which has been used for evaluation of the task of topic detection and tracking [1] in 1999 and 2000. TDT-3 corpus is annotated by Linguistic Data Consortium (LDC) from 8 English sources and 3 Mandarin sources for the period of October through December 1998. 120 topics are defined and about 9000 stories are annotated over these topics with an "on-topic" table presenting all stories explicitly marked as relevant to a given topic.

According to the specification of TDT, the on-topic stories within the same topic are similar and relevant. After removing the stories written in Chinese, we use 40 topics and more than 2500 stories as a test set, while the others are used as a training set. Sentence tokenization is firstly applied to all documents. The stop word list in Smart is employed in order to remove stop words. Then we use Porter's stemmer [12] to remove common morphological and inflectional endings from English words. The TextTiling algorithm and the sentence clustering algorithm are adopted to decompose documents respectively. The total stories are considered as the document collection for search, and for each topic we simulate a search as follows: The first document within the topic is considered as the query document and all the other documents within the same topic are the relevant (similar) documents, while all the documents within other topics are considered irrelevant (dissimilar) to the query document. Then the system compares the query document with all documents in the document collection with one of the similarity measures, returning a ranked list of 200 documents.

The higher the document is in the ranked list, the more similar it is with the query document.

As in TREC[2] experiments, we use the average precisions ($P$) at top $N$ results, i.e. *P@5* and *P@10*, and the non-interpolated mean average precision (MAP) to measure the performance. Note that the number of documents within each topic is different and some topics contain even less than 5 documents, so its corresponding precisions may be low. But these circumstances do not affect the comparison of the performance for different measures.

## 4.2 Experimental Results

### 4.2.1 Similarity Measure Comparison

The results of MAP, *P@10* and *P@20* for different similarity measures are shown and compared in Figure 1. For the PTD-based measure and the OM-based measure, the performance is dependent on the document decomposition algorithm, so we plot the highest precisions they achieve based on the TextTling algorithm. We mainly concern about the MAP value. The upper bounds are the ideal values under the assumption that all the relevant (similar) documents are retrieved and ranked higher than those irrelevant (dissimilar) documents in the ranked list. If the number of relevant documents for a query document is smaller than 5 or 10, the *P@5* or *P@10* for this query will never reach 100%. There are a few such queries in the TDT3 corpus, so the average *p@5* or *P@10* (i.e. the upper bounds of *P@5* or *P@10*) will not reach 100%.

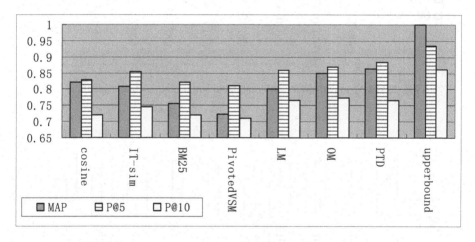

**Fig. 1.** Performance comparison for different similarity measures

Seen from Figure 1, the PTD-based measure outperforms all other similarity measures on MAP and *P@5*, including the optimal matching based measure. Other observations are similar to those in previous work [5], e.g. the measures derived from the popular retrieval functions perform poorly because the full document query differ

---

[2] http://trec.nist.gov

from the short query in that the full document contains more redundant and ambiguous information and even greater noise effects; the Cosine measure has a high performance for evaluating document similarity.

### 4.2.2 Performance Comparison for Document Decomposition Algorithms

Both the proposed PTD-based measure and the OM-based measure rely on the subtopic sets, which can be produced by either the TexTiling algorithm or the sentence clustering algorithm described earlier. Figures 2, 3 and 4 show the MAP, *P@5*, *P@10* results for the PTD-based measure and the OM-based measure with different document decomposition algorithms, respectively. The TextTiling algorithm and the sentence clustering algorithm with different merging similarity thresholds are compared in the figures. For example, "cluster(0.01)" refers to the sentence clustering algorithm with the merging similarity threshold set to 0.01.

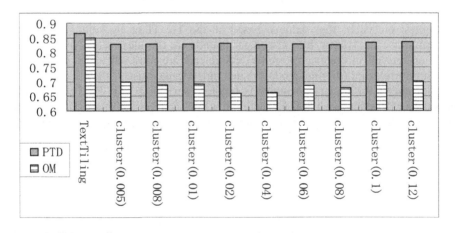

**Fig. 2.** MAP comparison for different document decomposition algorithms

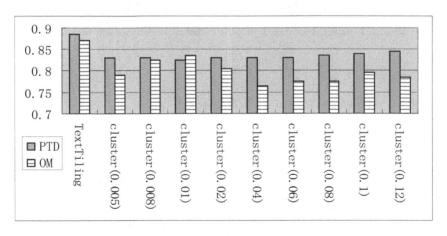

**Fig. 3.** P@5 comparison for different document decomposition algorithms

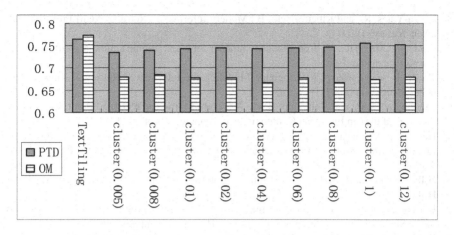

**Fig. 4.** P@10 comparison for different document decomposition algorithms

We can see from Figures 2, 3 and 4 that with the sentence clustering algorithm for document decomposition, the PTD-based measure performs much better than the OM-based measure, though both measures have better performance with the TextTiling algorithm than that with the sentence clustering algorithm. Moreover, the PTD-based measure has a stably high performance for different document decomposition algorithms, while the OM-based measure relies largely on the TextTiling algorithm for document decomposition. In other words, the PTD-based measure is much more robust than the OM-based measure.

## 5 Conclusions

In this paper, a novel measure based on the Proportional Transportation Distance (PTD) is proposed to evaluate document similarity by allowing many-to-many matching between subtopics. The proposed measure overcomes the problem in the existing optimal matching based measure that only one-to-one matching is allowed between subtopics. We also explore different algorithms to decompose documents. Experimental results show the high performance and robustness of the PTD-based measure.

In future work, we will apply the proposed measure to evaluate the semi-structured document similarity. Other tasks, such as document clustering will also be explored based on the proposed measure.

## References

1. Allan, J., Carbonell, J., Doddington, G., Yamron, J. P., Yang, Y.: Topic detection and tracking pilot study: final report. In *Proceedings of DARPA Broadcast News Transcription and Understanding Workshop* (1998) 194-218
2. Aslam, J. A., and Frost, M.: An information-theoretic measure for document similarity. In Proceedings of the 26th International ACM/SIGIR Conference on Research and Development in Information Retrieval (2003)

3.  Baeza-Yates, R., and Ribeiro-Neto, B.: Modern Information Retrival. ACM Press and Addison Wesley (1999)
4.  Choi, F.: JTextTile: A free platform independent text segmentation algorithm. http://www.cs.man.ac.uk/~choif
5.  Croft, B., and Lafferty, J.: Language Modeling for Information Retrieval. Kluwer Academic Publishers (2003)
6.  Giannopoulos, P., and Veltkamp, R. C.: A Pseudo-Metric for Weighted Point Sets. In Proceedings of the 7th European Conference on Computer Vision (ECCV) (2002) 715–730
7.  Hearst, M. A.: Multi-paragraph segmentation of expository text. In Proceedings of the 32$^{nd}$ Meeting of the Association for Computational Linguistics (ACL), Los Cruces, NM (1994) 9-16
8.  Hillier, F. S., and Liberman, G. J.: Introduction to Mathematical Programming. McGraw-Hill (1990)
9.  Karmarkar, N.: A new polynomial-time algorithm for linear programming. In Proceedings of the Sixteenth Annual ACM Symposium on Theory of Computing (1984) 302-311
10. Kaufmann, S.: Cohesion and collocation: using context vectors in text segmentation, Proceedings of the 37th conference on Association for Computational Linguistics (1999) 591-595
11. Lin, D.: An information-theoretic definition of similarity. In Proc. 15th International Conf. on Machine Learning (1998)
12. Porter, M. F.: An algorithm for suffix stripping. *Program* **14-3** (1980) 130-137
13. Robertson, S., Walker, S.: Some simple effective approximations to the 2-poisson model for probabilistic weighted retrieval. In Proeedings. of the 17th International ACM/SIGIR Conference on Research and Development in Information Retrieval (1994) 232-241
14. Robertson, S., Walker, S., and Beaulieu, M.: Okapi at TREC–7: automatic ad hoc, filtering, VLC and filtering tracks. In Proceedings of TREC'99 (1999)
15. Rubner, Y., Tomasi, C., and Guibas, L.: The Earth Mover's Distance as a metric for image retrieval. Int. Journal of Computer Vision **40-2** (2000) 99-121
16. Salton, G.: The SMART retrieval system: experiments in automatic document processing. Prentice-Hall (1991)
17. Singhal, A., Buckley, C., and Mitra, M.: Pivoted document length normalization. In Proceedings of SIGIR'96 (1996)
18. van Rijsbergen, C. J.: Information Retrieval. Butterworths, London (1979)
19. Wan, X. J., and Peng, Y. X.: A new retrieval model based on TextTiling for document similarity search. Journal of Computer Science & Technology **20-4** (2005) 552-558.
20. Xiao, W. S.: Graph Theory and Its Algorithms. Beijing: Aviation Industry Press (1993)
21. Zha, H.: Generic summarization and keyphrase extraction using mutual reinforcement principle and sentence clustering. In Proc. of 25$^{th}$ SIGIR conference (2002) 113-120
22. Zhai, C., and Lafferty, J.: A study of smoothing methods for language models applied to ad hoc information retrieval. In Proceedings of SIGIR'01 (2001)

# A User-Item Relevance Model for Log-Based Collaborative Filtering

Jun Wang[1], Arjen P. de Vries[1,2], and Marcel J.T. Reinders[1]

[1] Information and Communication Theory Group,
Faculty of Electrical Engineering, Mathematics and Computer Science,
Delft University of Technology,
Mekelweg 4, 2628 CD Delft, The Netherlands
j.wang@ewi.tudelft.nl
[2] CWI, Amsterdam, The Netherlands

**Abstract.** Implicit acquisition of user preferences makes *log-based* collaborative filtering favorable in practice to accomplish recommendations. In this paper, we follow a formal approach in text retrieval to re-formulate the problem. Based on the classic probability ranking principle, we propose a probabilistic user-item relevance model. Under this formal model, we show that user-based and item-based approaches are only two different factorizations with different independence assumptions. Moreover, we show that smoothing is an important aspect to estimate the parameters of the models due to data sparsity. By adding linear interpolation smoothing, the proposed model gives a probabilistic justification of using TF×IDF-like item ranking in collaborative filtering. Besides giving the insight understanding of the problem of collaborative filtering, we also show experiments in which the proposed method provides a better recommendation performance on a music play-list data set.

## 1   Introduction

Generally, a collaborative filtering algorithm uses a collection of user profiles to identify interesting "information" for these users. A particular user gets a recommendation based on the user profiles of other, similar users. User profiles are commonly obtained by explicitly asking users to rate the items. Collaborative filtering has often been formulated as a self-contained problem, apart from the classic information retrieval problem (i.e. ad hoc text retrieval). Research started with heuristic implementations of "Word of Mouth" (e.g. user-based approaches [1]), and moved to item-based approaches [17], and, more recently, various model-based approaches have been introduced ([8, 13]).

Previous research ([3]) has shown that users are very unlikely to provide an explicit rating. Asking the user to rate items is annoying and should be avoided when possible. Alternatively, user profiles can also be obtained by implicitly observing user interactions with the system. For instance, music play-list indicates the music taste of a user, and web query logs could indicate the interest of a user for certain web sites. The implicit acquisition of user preferences makes

M. Lalmas et al. (Eds.): ECIR 2006, LNCS 3936, pp. 37–48, 2006.
© Springer-Verlag Berlin Heidelberg 2006

the so-called "log-based" collaborative filtering more favorable in practice (see Section 2).

Therefore, this paper focuses on log-based collaborative filtering. We identify a close relationship between log-based collaborative filtering and text information retrieval. We build a user-item relevance model to re-formulate collaborative filtering under the classic probability ranking principle. Given our user-item relevance models, we also introduce a linear interpolation *smoothing* into collaborative filtering. We show that the smoothing is important to estimate the model parameters correctly due to the data sparsity. Similar to the situation in text retrieval, the user-item relevance model provides a probabilistic justification of using TF×IDF like item weighting in collaborative filtering.

## 2   Background

### 2.1   Rating-Based Collaborative Filtering

The preference information about items can either be based on ratings (explicit interest functions) or log-archives (implicit interest functions). Their differences lead, to our view, to two different ways to approach collaborative filtering: *rating-based* and *log-based*. Rating-based collaborative filtering is based on user profiles that contain rated items. The majority of the literature addresses rating-based collaborative filtering, which has been studied in depth ([13]). Different rating-based approaches are often classified as memory-based or model-based. In the memory-based approach, all rating examples are stored *as-is* into memory (in contrast to learning an abstraction). In the prediction phase, similar users or items are sorted based on the memorized ratings. Based on the ratings of these similar users or items, a recommendation for the query user can be generated. Examples of memory-based collaborative filtering include item correlation-based methods ([17]), user clustering ([20]) and locally weighted regression ([1]). The advantage of the memory-based methods over their model-based alternatives is that they have less parameters to be tuned, while the disadvantage is that the approach cannot deal with data sparsity in a principled manner.

In the model-based approach, training examples are used to generate a model that is able to predict the ratings for items that a query user has not rated before. Examples include decision trees ([1]), latent class models ([8]), and factor models ([2]). The 'compact' models in these methods could solve the data sparsity problem to a certain extent. However, the requirement of tuning an often significant number of parameters or hidden variables has prevented these methods from practical usage.

Recently, to overcome the drawbacks of these approaches to collaborative filtering, researchers have started to combine both memory-based and model-based approaches ([14, 19]).

### 2.2   Log-Based Collaborative Filtering

Implicit interest functions usually generate binary-valued preferences. That is a one indicates as a "file is downloaded", or a "web-site is visited". Few log-based collaborative filtering approaches that deal with such data have been developed thus far. Two examples are the item-based Top-N collaborative filtering approach ([4, 10]) and Amazon's item-based collaborative filtering ([12]).

The following characteristics make log-based collaborative filtering more similar to the problem of text retrieval than the rating-based approaches:

- Log-based user profiles, e.g., play-lists, are usually binary-valued. Usually, one means 'relevance' or 'likeness', and zero indicates 'non-relevance' or 'non-likeness'. Moreover, in most of the situations, non-relevance and non-likeness are hardly observed. This is similar to the concept of 'relevance' in text retrieval.
- The goal for rating-based collaborative filtering is to predict the rating of users, while the goal for the log-based algorithms is to rank the items to the user in order of decreasing relevance. As a result, evaluation is different. In rating-based collaborative filtering, the mean square error (MSE) of the predicted rating is used, while in log-based collaborative filtering, recall and precision are employed.

Therefore, this paper proposes to apply the probabilistic framework developed for text retrieval to log-based collaborative filtering. We consider the following formal setting. The information that has to be filtered, e.g., images, movies or audio files, is represented as a set of *items*. We introduce discrete random variables $U \in \{u_1, ..., u_K\}$ and $I \in \{i_1, ..., i_M\}$ to represent a user and an item in the collection, respectively. $K$ is the number of users while $M$ is the number of items in the collection. Let $L_{u_k}$ denote a user profile list for user $u_k \in U$. $L_{u_k}$ is a set of items that user $u_k$ has previously shown interest in. $L_{u_k}(i_m) = 1$ (or $i_m \in L_{u_k}$) indicates that item $i_m \in I$, is in the list while $L_{u_k}(i_m) = 0$ (or $I_m \notin L_{u_k}$) otherwise. The number of items in the list is denoted as $|L_{u_k}|$.

The purpose of log-based collaborative filtering is to rank the relevance of a target item to a user. This could be represented by the retrieval status value (RSV) of a target item towards a user, denoted as: $RSV_{u_k}(i_m)$. Heuristic implementations of 'Word of Mouth' introduced in [4, 6] give the following basic item-based and user-based approaches to calculate the RSV when we consider the binary case:

$$\text{User-based} : RSV_{u_k}(i_m) = \sum_{\text{Top-N similar } u_b} s_U(u_k, u_b)L_{u_b}(i_m)$$

$$\text{Item-based} : RSV_{u_k}(i_m) = \sum_{\forall i_b : i_b \in L_{u_k}} s_I(i_b, i_m) \tag{1}$$

where $s_I$ and $s_U$ are the two similarity measures between two items and two users, respectively. The two commonly used similarity measures are the Pearson Correlation and the Cosine similarity ([1]). Alternatively, frequency counting has been used as a basis for similarity measures in ([4, 10]). To suppress the influence of items that are being purchased frequently, they have introduced a TF×IDF-like weighting (similarity) function:

$$s_I(i_b, i_m) = \frac{c(i_b, i_m)/c(i_m)}{c(i_b)^\alpha} \qquad (2)$$

where $c(i_b, i_m) = \sum_{k=1}^{K} L_{u_k}(i_m) \cap L_{u_k}(I_b))$ is the number of user profiles in which both items $i_b$ and $i_m$ exist (i.e., items they *co-occur*); and $c(i)$ is the number of user profiles containing item $i$. $\alpha$ is a tuning parameter.

# 3   A User-Item Relevance Model

In log-based collaborative filtering, users want to know which items fit their interests best. This section adopts the probabilistic relevance model proposed in text retrieval domain ([11, 15]) to measure the relevance between user interests and items. We intend to answer the following basic question:

– What is the probability that *this* item is relevant to *this* user, given his or her profile.

To answer this question, we first define the sample space of relevance: $\Phi_R$. It has two values: 'relevant' $r$ and 'non-relevant' $\bar{r}$. Let $R$ be a random variable over the sample space $\Phi_R$. Likewise, let $U$ be a discrete random variable over the sample space of *user id*'s: $\Phi_U = \{u_1, ..., u_K\}$ and let $I$ be a random variable over the sample space of *item id*'s: $\Phi_I = \{i_1, ..., i_M\}$, where $K$ is the number of users and $M$ the number of items in the collection. In other words, $U$ refers to the user identifiers and $I$ refers to the item identifiers.

We then denote $P$ as a probability function on the joint sample space $\Phi_U \times \Phi_I \times \Phi_R$. In a probability framework, we can answer the above basic question by estimating the probability of relevance $P(R = r|U, I)$. The relevance rank of items in the collection $\Phi_I$ for a given user $U = u_k$ (i.e. retrieval status value (RSV) of a given target item toward a user) can be formulated as the odds of the relevance:

$$RSV_{u_k}(i_m) = \frac{\log P(r|u_k, i_m)}{\log P(\bar{r}|u_k, i_m)} \qquad (3)$$

For simplicity, $R = r$, $R = \bar{r}$, $U = u_k$, and $I = i_m$ are denoted as $r$, $\bar{r}$, $u_k$, and $i_m$, respectively.

Hence, the evidence for the relevance of an item towards a user is based on both the positive evidence (indicating the relevance) as well as the negative evidence (indicating the non-relevance). Once we know, for a given user, the RSV of each item $I$ in the collection (excluding the items that the user has already expressed interest in), we sort these items in decreasing order. The highest ranked items are recommended to the user.

In order to estimate the conditional probabilities in Eq. 3, i.e. the relevance and non-relevance between the user and the item, we need to factorize the equation along the item or the user dimension. We propose to consider both *item-based generation* (i.e., using items as features to represent the user) and *user-based generation* (i.e., treating users as features to represent an item). Since the two generative models are very similar to each other, for readability, the remainder of the paper presents our results using the item-based generation model; the analogous model based on user-based generation is given in Appendix A.

## 3.1 Item-Based Generation

By factorizing $P(\bullet|u_k, i_m)$ with $\frac{P(u_k|i_m, \bullet)P(\bullet|i_m)}{P(u_k|i_m)}$, the following log-odds ratio can be obtained from Eq. (3):

$$RSV_{u_k}(i_m) = \log \frac{P(r|i_m, u_k)}{P(\bar{r}|i_m, u_k)} = \log \frac{P(u_k|i_m, r)}{P(u_k|i_m, \bar{r})} + \log \frac{P(i_m|r)P(r)}{P(i_m|\bar{r})P(\bar{r})} \quad (4)$$

Without explicit evidence for non-relevance, and following the language modelling approach to information retrieval ([11]), we now assume that: 1) independence between $u_k$ and $i_k$ in the non-relevance case ($\bar{r}$), i.e., $P(u_k, |i_m, \bar{r}) = P(u_k|\bar{r})$; and, 2) equal priors for both $u_k$ and $i_m$, given that the item is non-relevant. Then the two non-relevance terms can be removed and the RSV becomes:

$$RSV_{u_k}(i_m) = \log P(u_k|i_m, r) + \log P(i_m|r) \quad (5)$$

Note that the two negative terms in Eq. (4) can always be added to the model, when the negative evidences are captured.

To estimate the conditional probability $P(u_k|i_m, r)$ in Eq. (5), consider the following: Instead of placing users in the sample space of user id's, we can also use the set of items that the user likes ($L_{u_k}$) to represent the user ($u_k$). This step is similar to using a 'bag-of-words' representation of queries or documents in the text retrieval domain ([16]). This implies: $P(u_k|i_m, r) = P(L_{u_k}|i_m, r)$. We call these representing items as *query items*. Note that, different with the target item $i_m$, the query items do not need to be ranked since the user has already expressed interest in them.

Further, we assume that the items in the user profile list $L_{u_k}$ (query items) are conditionally independent from each other. Although this naive Bayes assumption does not hold in many real situations, it has been empirically shown to be a competitive approach (e.g., in text classification ([5, 18]). Under this assumption, Eq. (5) becomes:

$$\begin{aligned} RSV_{u_k}(i_m) &= \log P(L_{u_k}|i_m, r) + \log P(i_m|r) \\ &= \sum_{\forall i_b: i_b \in L_{u_k}} \log P(i_b|i_m, r) + \log P(i_m|r) \end{aligned} \quad (6)$$

The conditional probability $P(i_b|i_m, r)$ corresponds to the relevance of an item $i_b$, given that another item $i_m$ is relevant. This probability can be estimated by counting the number of user profiles that contain both items $i_b$ and $i_m$, divided by the total number of user profiles in which $i_m$ exists (see also, [10]):

$$P_{ml}(i_b|i_m, r) = \frac{P(i_b, i_m|r)}{P(i_m|r)} = \frac{c(i_b, i_m)}{c(i_m)} \quad (7)$$

## 3.2  Probability Estimation and Smoothing

Using the frequency count in Eq. (7) to estimate the above probability corresponds to using its maximum likelihood estimator. However, many item-to-item co-occurrence counts will be zero, due to the sparseness of the user-item matrix. Therefore, we apply a smoothing technique to adjust the maximum likelihood estimation ([18]).

In information retrieval ([21]), most smoothing methods apply two different distributions: one for the words that occur in the document, and one for the words that do not. Here, we also adopt this formulation. To estimate $P(i_b|i_m, r)$, we use $P_s(i_b|i_m, r)$, when $c(i_b, i_m) > 0$, while when $c(i_b, i_m) = 0$ (i.e., $i_b$ and $i_m$ do not co-occur in any of the user profiles), we assume the probability is proportional to the general frequency of $i_b$ for the whole user profile set. That is $P(i_b|i_m, r) = \alpha_{i_m} P(i_b|r)$, where $\alpha_{i_m}$ depends on item $i_m$. Then, the conditional probability between a user and an item can be formulated as follows:

$$
\begin{aligned}
\log P(u_k|i_m, r) &= \log P(L_{u_k}|i_m, r) \\
&= \sum_{\forall i_b : i_b \in L_{u_k} \cap c(i_b, i_m) > 0} \log P_s(i_b|i_m, r) + \sum_{\forall i_b : i_b \in L_{u_k} \cap c(i_b, i_m) = 0} \log \alpha_{i_m} P(i_b|r) \\
&= \sum_{\forall i_b : i_b \in L_{u_k} \cap c(i_b, i_m) > 0} \log \frac{P_s(i_b|i_m, r)}{\alpha_{i_m} P(i_b|r)} + \sum_{\forall i_b : i_b \in L_{u_k}} \log \alpha_{i_m} P(i_b|r) \qquad (8) \\
&= \sum_{\forall i_b : i_b \in L_{u_k} \cap c(i_b, i_m) > 0} \log \frac{P_s(i_b|i_m, r)}{\alpha_{i_m} P(i_b|r)} + |L_{u_k}| \log \alpha_{i_m} + \sum_{\forall i_b : i_b \in L_{u_k}} \log P(i_b|r)
\end{aligned}
$$

Since the last term is independent from the target item $i_m$, it can be dropped when we calculate the RSV of item $i_m$. Combining Eq. (6) and Eq. (8), we obtain the following:

$$
\begin{aligned}
&RSV_{u_k}(i_m) \\
&= \sum_{\forall i_b : i_b \in L_{u_k} \cap c(i_b, i_m) > 0} \log \frac{P_s(i_b|i_m, r)}{\alpha_{i_m} P(i_b|r)} + |L_{u_k}| \log \alpha_{i_m} + \log P(i_m|r) \qquad (9)
\end{aligned}
$$

Eq. (9) gives a generative ranking formula. Next, we consider a special case: a linear interpolation smoothing.

**The Linear Interpolation Smoothing.** A linear interpolation smoothing can be defined as a linear interpolation between the maximum likelihood estimation and background model. To use it, if we define:

$$
\begin{aligned}
P_s(i_b|i_m, r) &= (1 - \lambda) P_{ml}(i_b|i_m, r) + \lambda P(i_b|r) \\
\alpha_{i_m} &= \lambda
\end{aligned}
\qquad (10)
$$

where $P_{ml}(i_b|i_m, r)$ is the maximum likelihood estimation as given in Eq. (7). The item prior probability $P(i_b|r)$ is used as background model. Furthermore, the parameter $\lambda \in [0,1]$ is a parameter that balances the maximum likelihood estimation and background model (a larger $\lambda$ means more smoothing). Usually, the best value for $\lambda$ is found from a training data. The linear interpolation smoothing leads to the following RSV:

$$RSV_{u_k}(i_m)$$
$$= \sum_{\forall i_b : i_b \in L_{u_k} \cap c(i_b, i_m) > 0} \log(1 + \frac{(1-\lambda)P_{ml}(i_b|i_m, r)}{\lambda P(i_b|r)}) + \log P(i_m|r). \quad (11)$$

## 3.3 Discussion

**IDF.** The usage of TF×IDF-like ranking shown in Eq. 2 was studied in [4] and has been shown to have the best performance. However, [4] does not provide the justification about the usage of the *inverse item frequency* $(1/P(i_b|r))$ by probability theory. By considering the log-based collaborative filtering probabilistically and proposing the linear interpolation smoothing, our user-item relevance model in Eq. 11 provides a probabilistic justification. Our ranking formula can directly be interpreted as TF×IDF-like ranking, since:

$$P_{ml}(i_b|i_m, r) \propto c(i_b, i_m)/c(i_m) \text{ and } P(i_b|r) \propto c(i_b) \quad (12)$$

Also, Eq. 11 allows a very intuitive understanding of the statistical ranking mechanisms that play a role in log-based collaborative filtering:

- The relevance rank of a target item $i_m$ is the sum of both its popularity (prior probability $P(i_m|r)$) and its co-occurrence (first term in Eq. 11) with the items $(i_b)$ in the profile list of the target user. The co-occurrence is higher if more user expresses interest in target item $(i_m)$ as well as item $i_b$. However, the co-occurrence should be suppressed more when the popularity of the item in the profile of the target user $(P(i_b|r))$ is higher.
- When $\lambda$ approaches 0, smoothing from the background model is minimal. It emphasizes the co-occurrence count, and the model reduces to the traditional item-based approach ([12]). When the $\lambda$ approaches 1, the model is more smooth, emphasizing the background model. When the parameter equals 1, the ranking becomes equivalent to *coordination level matching* ([7]), which is simply counting the number of times for which $c(i_b, i_m) > 0$.

**Two Representations.** Traditionally, collaborative filtering makes a distinction between user-based and item-based approaches. Our probabilistic user-item relevance model, derived with an information retrieval view on collaborative filtering, demonstrates that the user-based (Eq. 16) and item-based (Eq. 11) models are equivalent from the probabilistic point of view, since they have actually been derived from the same generative relevance model (Eq. 3). The only difference in derivation corresponds to the choice of independence assumptions, leading to the two different factorizations.

Consequently, this formula gives a much better understanding of the underlying statistical assumptions that are made in these two approaches. In the user-based approach, a target item is assumed to be judged or rated independently (see the Appendix A) while in the item-based approach, a target user is assumed to independently judge or rate each query item. Besides the differences in the number of users ($K$) and the number of items ($M$), we believe that these underlying assumptions are the major factors to influence the performances of these two approaches in practice.

## 4   Experiments

The standard data set used in the evaluation of collaborative filtering algorithms (MovieLens) is rating-based, which is not suitable for testing our method using log-based user profiles. The user logs we used were collected from the *Audioscrobbler*[1] community. The audioscrobbler data set is collected from the play-lists of the users in the community by using a plug-in in the users' media players (for instance, Winamp, iTunes, XMMS etc). Plug-ins send the title (song name and artist name) of every song users play to the Audioscrobbler server, which updates the user's musical profile with the new song. That is, when a user plays a song in a certain time, this transaction is recorded as a form of {userID, itemID, $t$} tuple in the database.

For computational reasons, we randomly sampled the data set to limit the number of users to 428 users and the number of items to 516. The sparsity (percentage of zero values in the user-item matrix) is 96.86% .

For cross-validation, we randomly divided this data set into a training set (80% of the users) and a test set (20% of the users). Results are obtains by averaging 5 different runs (sampling of training/test set). The training set was used to estimate the model. The test set was used for evaluating the accuracy of the recommendations on the new users, whose user profiles are not in the training set. For each test user, 50% of the items of a test user were put into the user profile list. The other 50% of the items were used to test the recommendations. By doing so, the number of items in the user profiles reflects the distribution in the overall data set.

The effectiveness of the log-based collaborative filtering experiments can be measured using the *precision* and *recall* of the recommendations. Precision measures the proportion of recommended items that are ground truth items (only partially known, by the half of the user profiles). The recall measures the proportion of the ground truth items that are recommended. Note that the items in the profiles of the test user represent only a fraction of the items that the user *truly* liked. Therefore, the measured precision *underestimates* the true precision ([9]). In the case of making recommendations, precision seems more important than recall. However, to analyze the behavior of our method, we report both metrics on our experimental results.

We first studied the behavior of the linear interpolation smoothing. For this, we plotted the average precision and recall rate for the different values of the smoothing parameter $\lambda$. This is shown in Fig. 1.

---

[1] Audioscrobbler is found at http://www.audioscrobbler.com/

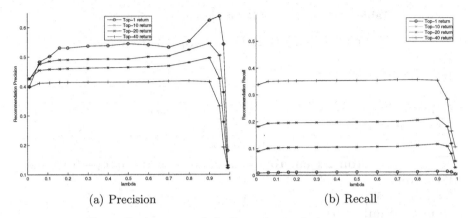

(a) Precision                                      (b) Recall

**Fig. 1.** Performance of the linear interpolation smoothing

Fig. 1 (a) and (b) show that both precision and recall drop when $\lambda$ reaches its extreme values zero and one. The precision is sensitive to $\lambda$, especially the early precision (when only a small number of items are recommended). Recall is less sensitive to the actual value of this parameter, having its optimum at a wide range of values. Effectiveness tends to be higher on both metrics when $\lambda$ is large; when $\lambda$ is approximately 0.9, the precision seems optimal. An optimal range of $\lambda$ near one can be explained by the sparsity of user profiles, causing the prior probability $P(i_b|r)$ to be much smaller than the conditional probability $P_{ml}(i_b|i_m, r)$. The background model is therefore only emphasized for values of $\lambda$ closer to one. In combination with the experimental results that we obtained, this suggests that smoothing the co-occurrence probabilities with the background model (prior probability $P(i_b|r)$) improves recommendation performance.

Next, we compared our user-item relevance model to other log-based collaborative filtering approaches. Our goal here is to see, using our user-item relevance model, whether the smoothing and inverse item frequency should improve recommendation performance with respect to the other methods. For this, we focused on the item-based generation (denoted as UIR-Item). We set $\lambda$ to the optimal value 0.9. We compared our results to those obtained with the *Top-N-suggest* recommendation engine, a well-known log-based collaborative filtering implementation ([10]).[2] This engine implements a variety of log-based recommendation algorithms. We compared our own results to both the item-based TF×IDF-like version (denoted as ITEM-TFIDF) as well the user-based cosine similarity method (denoted as User-CosSim), setting the parameters to the optimal ones according to the user manual. Additionally, for item-based approaches, we also used other similarity measures: the commonly used cosine similarity (denoted as Item-CosSim) and Pearson correlation (denoted as Item-CorSim). Results are shown in Table 1. For the precision, our user-item relevance model with the item-based generation (UIR-Item) outperforms other log-based collaborative filtering approaches for all four different number of returned items. Overall,

---

[2] http://www-users.cs.umn.edu/~karypis/suggest/

**Table 1.** Comparison of Recommendation Performance

|  | Top-1 Item | Top-10 Item | Top-20 Item | Top-40 Item |
|---|---|---|---|---|
| **UIR-Item** | 0.62 | 0.52 | 0.44 | 0.35 |
| **Item-TFIDF** | 0.55 | 0.47 | 0.40 | 0.31 |
| **Item-CosSim** | 0.56 | 0.46 | 0.38 | 0.31 |
| **Item-CorSim** | 0.50 | 0.38 | 0.33 | 0.27 |
| **User-CosSim** | 0.55 | 0.42 | 0.34 | 0.27 |

(a) Precision

|  | Top-1 Item | Top-10 Item | Top-20 Item | Top-40 Item |
|---|---|---|---|---|
| **UIR-Item** | 0.02 | 0.15 | 0.25 | 0.40 |
| **Item-TFIDF** | 0.02 | 0.15 | 0.26 | 0.41 |
| **Item-CosSim** | 0.02 | 0.13 | 0.22 | 0.35 |
| **Item-CorSim** | 0.01 | 0.11 | 0.19 | 0.31 |
| **User-CosSim** | 0.02 | 0.15 | 0.25 | 0.39 |

(b) Recall

TF×IDF-like ranking ranks second. The obtained experimental results demonstrate that smoothing contributes to a better recommendation precision in the two ways also found by [21]. On the one hand, smoothing compensates for missing data in the user-item matrix, and on the other hand, it plays the role of inverse item frequency to emphasize the weight of the items with the best discriminative power. With respect to recall, all four algorithms perform almost identically. This is consistent to our first experiment that recommendation precision is sensitive to the smoothing parameters while the recommendation recall is not.

## 5   Conclusions

This paper identified a close relationship between log-based collaborative filtering and the methods developed for text information retrieval. We have built a user-item relevance model to re-formulate the collaborative filtering problem under the classic probability ranking principle. Using this probabilistic framework of user-item relevance models, we introduced a linear interpolation *smoothing* in collaborative filtering. We showed that smoothing is an important aspect to estimate models due to the data sparsity. Similar to the situation in text retrieval, the user-item relevance model provides a probabilistic justification of using TF×IDF-like item weighting in collaborative filtering.

Our further research aims to introduce relevance feedback into collaborative filtering. One of the powerful characteristics of linear interpolation smoothing is that we can vary smoothing parameter: $\lambda \to \lambda(i_b)$ for the different items $i_b$ in the user profile. It can then be treated as the importance of the query item. In the beginning, all the items in the user profile are treated equally. From relevance feedback, the importance value for different query items can be updated by using EM algorithm ([7]).

# References

1. J. S. Breese, D. Heckerman, and C. Kadie. Empirical analysis of predictive algorithms for collaborative filtering. In *Proc. of UAI*, 1998.
2. J. Canny. Collaborative filtering with privacy via factor analysis. In *Proc. of SIGIR*, 1999.
3. M. Claypool, M. W. P. Le, and D. C. Brown. Implicit interest indicators. In *Proc. of IUI*, 2001.
4. M. Deshpande and G. Karypis. Item-based top-n recommendation algorithms. *ACM Trans. Inf. Syst.*, 22(1):143–177, 2004.
5. S. Eyheramendy, D. Lewis, and D. Madigan. On the naive bayes model for text categorization. In *Proc. of Artificial Intelligence and Statistics*, 2003.
6. J. L. Herlocker, J. A. Konstan, A. Borchers, and J. Riedl. An algorithmic framework for performing collaborative filtering. In *Proc. of SIGIR*, 1999.
7. D. Hiemstra. Term-specific smoothing for the language modeling approach to information retrieval: the importance of a query term. In *Proc. of SIGIR*, 2002.
8. T. Hofmann and J. Puzicha. Latent class models for collaborative filtering. In *Proc. of IJCAI*, 1999.
9. D. Hull. Using statistical testing in the evaluation of retrieval experiments. In *Proc. of SIGIR*, 1993.
10. G. Karypis. Evaluation of item-based top-n recommendation algorithms. In *Proc. of CIKM*, 2001.
11. J. Lafferty and C. Zhai. Probabilistic relevance models based on document and query generation. *Language Modeling and Information Retrieval, Kluwer International Series on Information Retrieval*, V.13, 2003.
12. G. Linden, B. Smith, and J. York. Amazon.com recommendations: Item-to-item collaborative filtering. *IEEE Internet Computing*, Jan/Feb.:76–80, 2003.
13. B. Marlin. Collaborative filtering: a machine learning perspective. Master's thesis, Department of Computer Science, University of Toronto, 2004.
14. D. M. Pennock, E. Horvitz, S. Lawrence, and C. Giles. Collaborative filtering by personality diagnosis: a hybrid memory and model based approach. In *Proc. of UAI*, 2000.
15. J. M. Ponte and W. B. Croft. A language modeling approach to information retrieval. In *Proc. of SIGIR*, 1998.
16. G. Salton and M. J. McGill. *Introduction to modern information retrieval.* New York : McGraw-Hill, 1983.
17. B. Sarwar, G. Karypis, J. Konstan, and J. Riedl. Item-based collaborative filtering recommendation algorithms. In *Proc. of the WWW Conference*, 2001.
18. C. J. van Rijsbergen. *Information Retrieval.* Butterworths, London, 1979.
19. J. Wang, J. Pouwelse, R. Lagendijk, and M. R. J. Reinders. Distributed collaborative filtering for peer-to-peer file sharing systems. In *Proc. of the 21st Annual ACM Symposium on Applied Computing*, 2006.
20. G.-R. Xue, C. Lin, Q. Yang, W. Xi, H.-J. Zeng, Y. Yu, and Z. Chen. Scalable collaborative filtering using cluster-based smoothing. In *Proc. of SIGIR*, 2005.
21. C. Zhai and J. D. Lafferty. A study of smoothing methods for language models applied to ad hoc information retrieval. In *Proc. of SIGIR*, 2001.

## A    User-Based Generation

By factorizing $P(\bullet|u_k, i_m)$ with $P(i_m|u_k, \bullet)P(\bullet|u_k)/P(i_m|u_k)$, the following log-odds ratio can be obtained from Eq. 3 :

$$
\begin{aligned}
RSV_{u_k}(i_m) &= \log \frac{P(r|i_m, u_k)}{P(\bar{r}|i_m, u_k)} \\
&= \log \frac{P(i_m|u_k, r)}{P(i_m|u_k, \bar{r})} + \log \frac{P(u_k|r)P(r)}{P(u_k|\bar{r})P(\bar{r})} \\
&\propto \log \frac{P(i_m|u_k, r)}{P(i_m|u_k, \bar{r})}
\end{aligned}
\tag{13}
$$

When the non-relevance evidence is absent, and following the language model ([11]), we now assume equal priors for $i_m$ in the non-relevant case. Then, the non-relevance term can be removed and the RSV becomes:

$$
RSV_{u_k}(i_m) = \log P(i_m|u_k, r)
\tag{14}
$$

Instead of using the item list to represent the user, we use each user's judgment as a feature to represent an item. For this, we introduce a list $L_{i_m}$ for each item $i_m$, where $m = \{1, ..., M\}$. This list enumerates the users who have expressed interest in the item $i_m$. $L_{i_m}(u_k) = 1$ (or $u_k \in L_{i_m}$) denotes that user $u_k$ is in the list, while $L_{i_m}(u_k) = 0$ (or $u_k \notin L_{i_m}$) otherwise. The number of users in the list corresponds to $|L_{i_m}|$.

Replacing $i_m$ with $L_{i_m}$, after we assume each user's judgment to a particular item is independent, we have:

$$
RSV_{u_k}(i_m) = \log P(i_m|u_k, r) = \sum_{\forall u_b : u_b \in L_{i_m}} \log P(u_b|u_k, r)
\tag{15}
$$

Similar to the item-based generation, when we use linear interpolation smoothing to estimate $P(u_b|u_k, r)$, we obtain the final ranking formula:

$$
\begin{aligned}
RSV_{u_k}(i_m) &= \sum_{\forall u_b : u_b \in L_{i_m}} \log P(u_b|u_k, r) \\
&\propto \sum_{\forall u_b : u_b \in L_{i_m} \cap c(u_b, u_k) > 0} \log(1 + \frac{(1 - \lambda)P_{ml}(u_b|u_k, r)}{\lambda P(u_b|r)}) + |L_{i_m}| \log \lambda
\end{aligned}
\tag{16}
$$

where $\lambda \in [0, 1]$ is the smoothing parameter.

# Generating Search Term Variants for Text Collections with Historic Spellings

Andrea Ernst-Gerlach and Norbert Fuhr

University of Duisburg-Essen
ernst@is.informatik.uni-duisburg.de, fuhr@uni-duisburg.de

**Abstract.** In this paper, we describe a new approach for retrieval in texts with non-standard spelling, which is important for historic texts in English or German. For this purpose, we present a new algorithm for generating search term variants in ancient orthography. By applying a spell checker on a corpus of historic texts, we generate a list of candidate terms for which the contemporary spellings have to be assigned manually. Then our algorithm produces a set of probabilistic rules. These probabilities can be considered for ranking in the retrieval stage. An experimental comparison shows that our approach outperforms competing methods.

## 1 Introduction

In 2005, we have seen a number of initiatives addressing the problem of digitising books and making them available on the Internet, following earlier less ambitious projects like e. g. project Gutenberg[1]. The US search engine Google proclaimed an effort to digitise 15 million books. Some months later, the Open Content Alliance[2] was formed by several companies, research institutes and universities from the US. Since these initiatives are focusing on books in English only — and mainly as a reaction to the Google digitisation initiative — the European Union plans to create a European digital library in order to preserve the culture of the European countries. This library should include texts from the traditional European libraries and make them available on the Internet. So far, 19 European libraries have signed the corresponding manifest [6]. There have been already several digitisation projects in the past, but only a small fraction of the library content is digitised so far. With a European digital library project, the collections that are available in the Internet could be growing exponentially.

In contrast to countries with institutions defining spelling standards (e.g. Spain, France), English[3] and German [11] spelling was not stable over several centuries. English spelling was more or less fixed around 1800. In contrast, German spelling was not standardised until 1901/1902. Before that date, there was the rule 'write as you speak' (phonological principle of spelling) [8]. Because of the various dialects and the variations over time, German spelling before 1900 was highly time- and region-dependent. But even for languages like French where the orthography has been standardised, early spelling variants are occurring [2]. Furthermore, the predominant part of the 6,000

---

[1] http://www.gutenberg.org/

[2] http://www.opencontentalliance.org/

[3] http://en.wikipedia.org/wiki/English_spelling, access 20 January 2005 11:05.

M. Lalmas et al. (Eds.): ECIR 2006, LNCS 3936, pp. 49–60, 2006.
© Springer-Verlag Berlin Heidelberg 2006

contemporary spoken languages never became official languages and thus, they have never been standardised at all [15].

The non-standard spelling produces problems when searching in the historic parts of digital libraries. Most users will enter search terms in their contemporary language which differs from the historic language used in the documents. In order to solve this problem, our project deals with the research and development of a search engine where the user can formulate queries in contemporary language for searching in documents with an old spelling that is possibly unknown to the user. For this purpose, we are developing transformation rules for generating historic spellings from a given word.

More specifically, our project aims at the following goals:

- The development of time- and location-specific rule sets. The revision of rules from the text basis and from statistical analyses should be possible.
- The development of new distance measures for spelling variants on the basis of a modified Levenshtein similarity measure.
- Application of the search engine in other German digitisation projects (e.g. the Nietzsche project [1]).

The search engine under development is based on the probabilistic information retrieval engine PIRE [9] and will create a platform that supports the interactive, iterative development of new rules.

The paper has the following structure. In Section 2, we give a brief survey over related work. Section 3 discusses approaches for the search in text collections with non-standard spelling, and outlines our work. The core of our approach is presented in Section 4, where we specify the generation of rules for transforming words into their ancient spellings. Our approach is evaluated in Section 5, and the last section concludes the paper and gives an outlook on future work.

## 2   Related Work

Rayson et.al. [14] describe a project for dealing with historic spellings of English. They developed a variant detector for English texts from the 16th-19th century. A major difference to our work consists in the fact that German is a highly inflected language, in contrast to English. Thus approaches developed for English can hardly be applied for German.

Previous digitisation projects for the German language (e.g the Bayrische Staatsbibliothek[4]) employed standard search engines. Some of them are thesaurus-based (in combination with manual indexing), but they do not offer specific support for searching in historic texts. Other approaches use dictionaries for this purpose. However, this approach covers only the words contained in the dictionary. Furthermore, the time and effort for the manual construction of the word entries is rather high.

We want to overcome this disadvantage with a rule-based approach, in order to be able to cover the complete vocabulary (and thus increase recall). On the other hand, the rules to be developed should be sufficiently precise, for distinguishing between spelling variants of the search term and other words.

---

[4] http://www.bsb-muenchen.de/mdz/

The topic addressed in this paper is related to problem of approximate name matching [10]. There names with an incorrect spelling have to be found in a list of names. However, the major difference between the two problems consists in the fact that names usually differ only in their spelling, but not in their pronunciation. In contrast, words from historic texts may also differ in their pronunciation, mainly due to regional dialects [15]. These differences can also have effects on the spelling (see section 1).

The problem studied here is also somewhat related to cross-language information retrieval [12], since in both cases mappings between words are considered. However, our problem can be solved by means of mappings at the grapheme level, while only dictionary-based approaches are suitable for cross-language information retrieval.

## 3    Searching in Text Collections with Non-standard Spelling

There are two possible approaches for searching in texts with spelling variants:

1. Stemming at indexing time: This standard information retrieval method requires the set of stemming rules to be known at indexing time. In the case of spelling variants, also rules for the standardisation of the different spellings are necessary. However, the German language is a highly inflected language. Rule-based stemming for contemporary German requires rather complex rule sets, so it would be very difficult to find the inflection rules which map the ancient spelling onto the associated contemporary radical. In our case, no rule set for spelling standardisation exists (and, due to the time- and region-dependence, will probably never become available).

2. Generation of search term variants at retrieval time: For this query expansion again rules for inflections and derivations of words as well as for handling spelling variants are required, but this time in the opposite direction, i.e. we need a mapping

   search term → contemporary inflections (or derivations) → spelling variants

   This approach is more flexible, as new rule sets can easily be adopted.

Indeed, the first approach would be a lot faster than the second one, because the time-sensitive processing of the transformation happens once when a new collection gets indexed. However, we assume that rule sets for spelling variations will not be fixed for quite a long time and so only the second approach gives us the necessary flexibility.

In the latter approach, we first have to deal with morphological variations, before we can start constructing the rules for spelling variants. For this purpose, we are using a contemporary dictionary[5] containing the full word forms [13]. Thus, when the user enters a search term (in its basic word form), the dictionary yields all inflected forms. This way, we can focus on the second mapping, i.e. the generation of spelling variants of the inflected forms.

By comparing the inflected forms of the dictionary with the word list of our corpus (or using a spell checker), we are getting a list of candidate words in non-standard spelling (some words also may not be contained in the dictionary, though). On the other hand, this method will not be able to detect homographs (ancient spelling that matches

---

[5] http://wortschatz.uni-leipzig.de/

a different contemporary word); this issue will be addressed at a later stage of our project. This way, we get a list of candidate words from our corpus. Then, we have to check manually if the words are really in a non-standard spelling, and have to assign the equivalent words in the contemporary standard spelling. After that, we can focus on the second step — the building of new rules.

Even though the studied language is German we also found examples for English [14] where our approach could be employed. E. g. always — alwaies (y $\longrightarrow$ ie), sudden — suddain (e $\longrightarrow$ ai), and publicly — publikely (c $\longrightarrow$ ke).

In the following we list some example rules developed manually for the 19th century German (Table 1).

**Table 1.** Example rules for German

| Contemp. spelling | 19th century | rules | |
|---|---|---|---|
| wiedergaben | widergaben | wieder $\longrightarrow$ wider | (1) |
| | | ie $\longrightarrow$ i | |
| akzeptieren | acceptieren | kz $\longrightarrow$ cc | (2) |
| | | k $\longrightarrow$ c $\wedge$ z $\longrightarrow$ c | |
| überall | ueberall | ü $\longrightarrow$ ue | (3) |
| seht | sehet | t $\longrightarrow$ et | (4) |

The first example shows two rules at different levels of specialisation. The first rule transforms a prefix whereas the second one only transforms an allograph (see section 5.2). The next example also offers two possibilities. In this case the transformation can consist of one rule or the concatenation of two rules. However it becomes apparent that the precision of the first rule would be much higher than that of the second rule. The third case shows a very common rule for umlauts. The last example contains a very general rule, but it could reach a higher precision if the rule is connected with context information (in this case the end of the word). So not only the transformation itself is important, but also the associated position.

Even though our approach requires a substantial manual effort at the beginning, we expect that only little additional work is required later when the collection is growing continually — due to the fact that we are working at the grapheme level.

## 4    Generation of Transformation Rules

As described above, our rule generation method starts with a training sample of historic texts, on which we run a spell checker for contemporary German[6]. For all words marked as incorrect spelling, the contemporary word form has to be assigned manually; furthermore, we determine $cf$ the number of occurrences of each historic word form. Thus, we have a set $H$ of triplets $(\mathbf{a}, \mathbf{h}, cf)$ (contemporary word form $a$, full word form $h$, collection frequency $cf$).

---

[6] We are not using the contemporary dictionary for this purpose, since it contains a large number of spelling errors, due to the fact that it was built automatically from large volumes of Web pages.

In the following, we denote a character string **a** also as a sequence $a_0 \ldots a_n$. Furthermore, if $n = 0$, then $a_0 \ldots a_n$ denotes the empty string $\varepsilon$, and $a|b$ denotes the concatenation of strings (for convenience, we don't distinguish between characters and strings of length 1 here). The definitions apply accordingly for a character string **h**. Furthermore, we assume that each word form has a leading and a trailing blank. For lists we use the Prolog-like notation $[l_1, \ldots, l_k]$, and we also use the notation $[h|t]$ for splitting a list into head $h$ and tail $t$.

For generating transformation rules, we use the set $H$ containing the contemporary words and their historic spellings. First, we compare the two words and determine so-called 'rule cores', i.e. the necessary transformations. In a second step, we generate rule candidates that also consider context information from the word **a**. Finally, in the third step, we select the useful rules by pruning the candidate set. For describing the different steps, we are specifying the functions involved — the corresponding algorithms offer various possibilities for optimisations, which are still under development (a straightforward implementation could be achieved by using Prolog or a function-oriented programming language).

## 4.1 Generate Rule Cores

For the rule cores, we determine the necessary transformations and also identify the corresponding contexts. First, we define a function $rcg1()$, which creates a mixed list of transformations and contexts when being called with two words and an empty string as initial value. For example, for **a**=' unnütz ' and **b**=' unnuts ', $rcg(\mathbf{a}, \mathbf{b}, \text{' '})$ would yield p= [' unn',('ü','u'),'t',('z','s'),' '].

$$rcg1(a_0 \ldots a_n, h_1 \ldots h_m, p) =$$
$$\begin{cases} [p] & \text{, if } n = m = 0 \\ rcg1(a_2 \ldots a_n, h_2 \ldots h_m, p|a_1) & \text{, if } a_1 = h_1 \\ [p, (a_1 \ldots a_j, h_1 \ldots h_l)|rcg1(a_j \ldots a_n, h_l \ldots h_m, \varepsilon)] & \\ \quad \text{so that } a_{j+1} = h_{l+1} \text{ and } j + m \text{ is minimum} & \text{, if } a_1 \neq h_1 \end{cases}$$

Given such a list $L$, we now generate the rule cores, i.e. the transformations with the left and right contexts, by means of the following recursive function:

$$rcg(L) =$$
$$\begin{cases} \emptyset & \text{, if } |L| = 1 \\ rcg(L') \cup \{(l,t,r)\} \text{ with } L = [l,t,r|R] \text{ and } L' = [r|R] & \text{, otherwise} \end{cases}$$

For our example from above, we would get the following 2-element set of rule cores:
{(' unn',('ü','u'),'t'), ('t',('z','s'),' ').

## 4.2 Generate Rule Candidates

For each rule core, we want to generate a set of rule candidates, by successively adding left and right context to the left-hand side of a transformation rule. Besides considering the exact characters occurring in the context, we also regard abstractions to the two character classes vowels and consonants denoted by V and C, respectively. In addition,

B denotes a blank. Thus, the left context of a transformation has the general syntax B?[C/V]\*['a'..'z']\* [7], and the right context follows the grammar ['a'..'z']\*[C/V]\*B?.

For each element $(l,(s,d),r)$ from our list of rule cores, we call the function $rg(l,r,(\varepsilon,s,\varepsilon,d))$ which is defined as follows:

$$rg(l,r,t) = rgcl(l,r,t) \cup rgcr(l,r,t) \cup rge(l,r,t)$$
$$rge(l,r,t) = rgl(l,r,t) \cup rgr(l,r,t) \cup \{r\}$$

$$rgcl(l_1 \ldots l_n, r_1 \ldots r_m, (f,s,b,d)) =$$
$$\begin{cases} rg(l_1 \ldots l_{n-1}, r_1 \ldots r_m, (l_n|f,s,b,d)) & \text{, if } n > 0 \\ \emptyset & \text{, otherwise} \end{cases}$$

$$rgcr(l_1 \ldots l_n, r_1 \ldots r_m, (f,s,b,d)) =$$
$$\begin{cases} rg(l_1 \ldots l_n, r_2 \ldots r_m, (f,s,b|r_1,d)) & \text{, if } m > 0 \\ \emptyset & \text{, otherwise} \end{cases}$$

$$rgl(l_1 \ldots l_n, r_1 \ldots r_m, (f,s,b,d)) =$$
$$\begin{cases} rge(l_1 \ldots l_{n-1}, r_1 \ldots r_m, (cc(l_n)|f,s,b,d)) & \text{, if } n > 0 \\ \emptyset & \text{, otherwise} \end{cases}$$

$$rgr(l_1 \ldots l_n, r_1 \ldots r_m, (f,s,b,d)) =$$
$$\begin{cases} rge(l_1 \ldots l_n, r_2 \ldots r_m, (|f,s,b|cc(r_1),d)) & \text{, if } m > 0 \\ \emptyset & \text{, otherwise} \end{cases}$$

Here rgcl() and rgcr() generate rules containing literal characters, whereas rge() produces rules with the generalisations mentioned above. rgl() generalises the next character of the left context, and rgr() the next character on the right. In practical applications, we further restrict the number of candidate rules generated by these functions by defining a maximum length for the left and right context to be considered.

For our example from above, the following candidate rules are generated (among others: $(\varepsilon,\ddot{u},\varepsilon,u)$, $(n,\ddot{u},\varepsilon,u)$, $(\varepsilon,\ddot{u},t,u)$, $(n,\ddot{u},t,u)$ (C,$\ddot{u}$,$\varepsilon$,u), $(\varepsilon,\ddot{u},C,u)$, (C,$\ddot{u}$,C,u).

Given these candidate rules for a contemporary word **a** and its historic form **h**, we generate a tuple $(\mathbf{a},\mathbf{h},cf,(f,s,b,d))$ for each candidate rule; in addition, $cf$ denotes the collection frequency of **h**. The set of these tuples for all our triplets from $H$ forms the set of training instances $E$.

### 4.3   Rule Set Pruning

The generation of the final transformation rules can be regarded as a classification task, where we have to distinguish between 'correct' and 'incorrect' rules. The set $E$ of instances $e_i = (\mathbf{a}_i, \mathbf{h}_i, cf_i, (f_i, s_i, b_i, d_i)) \in E$ with the rule candidates contains the positive examples. The negative examples consists of the words **a** in $E$ where a rule can be applied, but has not been generated [8].

---

[7] According to the notation of regular expressions, ? denotes an occurrence once or not at all and \* denotes an occurrence zero or more times.

[8] This is only an approximation, but a proper set of negative examples would require a huge manual effort.

For deriving a good set of transformation rules, we have developed an extension of the PRISM algorithm developed in data mining [4]. PRISM assumes that we have a set of instances to be classified into a set of classes (in our case: correct/incorrect rules). Instances are described by a fixed set of attributes with values from a nominal scale. For each class $C$, the algorithm tries to find a set of high-precision rules for identifying the instances belonging to $C$.

```
For each class C
  Initialise E to the instance set
  While E contains instances in C
    Create a rule R with an empty left-hand side that predicts C
    Until R is perfect (or there are no more attributes to use) do
      For each attribute A not mentioned in R, and each value v,
        Consider adding the condition A=v to the left-hand side of R
        Select A and v to maximise the accuracy p/t
          (break ties by choosing the condition with the largest p)
      Add A=v to R
    Remove the instances covered by R from E
```

Unfortunately, we cannot apply PRISM directly, for two major reasons:

1. We are not aiming at perfect rules, since this would result in rules which are specific for each contemporary word form — and thus, hardly any words not seen before would be covered by these rules (i.e. we would get a high precision, but very low recall).
2. Instead of a set of attributes with fixed sets of nominal values, we have a possibly infinite set of left-hand sides of rules. For this reason, we are generating rule candidates from examples, whereas PRISM generates rules independent from examples and then tests their quality. In PRISM, adding a condition to a rule results in a more specific rule. In our case, we also have generalisation/specialisation relationships between rule antecedents, which we can exploit for directing the search.

Based on these considerations, we have developed the rule pruning algorithm that takes the candidate set $E$ and outputs a final set $F$ of rules. (Similar algorithms have been proposed for text categorisation, see e. g. [5], but they do not consider the specialisation hierarchy on rule conditions.) As additional parameters, two cutoff values have to be specified for this algorithm: $q_{min}$ denotes the minimum number (of tokens) of correct applications of a rule, and $p_{min}$ is the minimum precision of rules to be considered.

Let us assume that we have a Boolean function $match(r, \mathbf{a})$ which tests if the word $\mathbf{a}$ satisfies the right-hand side of rule $r$. Based on this function, the most expensive step in our algorithm is the search for all word forms where $match()$ yields true. In order to speed up this process, we first sort the instances by the rule itself; thus, we have to perform the search only once for each rule (and not once per instance). Due to the regular structure of our rules, we can use an access structure like a PAT array [7] for determining all matching word forms.

In the following $q_i$ denotes the number of positive occurrences of rule r and $p_i$ denotes the precision of rule r.

For each training instance $e_i$, let

$$E_i = \{r | r \in E \wedge r = (\mathbf{a}, \mathbf{h}, cf, (f_i, s_i, b_i, d_i))\}$$

$$m_i = \sum_{e_j \in E \wedge match(e_i, \mathbf{a}_j)} cf_j$$

$$q_i = \sum_{e_j \in E_i} cf_j$$

$$p_i = \frac{q_i}{m_i}$$

Remove all instances $e_i$ from $E$ where $p_i < p_{\min} \vee q_i < q_{\min}$.
Let $F = \emptyset$.

while $E \neq \emptyset$ do

1. from the instances with the highest $p$ values, select those with the highest $q$ values and among those, choose one for which there is no instance in $E$ with a more general rule. Let $e_i$ denote this instance.
2. $F = F \cup (e_i, p_i)$.
3. remove all instances from $E$ where $e_i$ applies: let

$$D = \{e_j | e_j \in E \wedge e_j = (\mathbf{a}_j, \mathbf{h}_j, cf_j, (f_j, s_j, b_j, d_j)) \wedge$$
$$\exists e_k \in E \wedge e_k = (\mathbf{a}_j, \mathbf{h}_j, cf_k, (f_i, s_i, b_i, d_k))\}$$

Then set $E := E - D$.

od.

### 4.4  Rule Application

Given the set of probabilistic rules as described above, they can be applied in our search engine. For a contemporary word $\mathbf{a}$, we want to generate all historic spellings. Thus, for any element $(r_i, p_i) \in F$, if $match(r_i, \mathbf{a})$, $r_i$ is applied to $\mathbf{a}$, thus yielding the word $\mathbf{a}_i$. This way we are generating a set of historic spellings for a single word $\mathbf{a}$, by application of single rules. Obviously, these word forms are not all equally precise. Therefore, these words should be assigned weights which reflect the precision of the rules they resulted from [17].

Our retrieval engine considers the precision of rules in the following way:

For a spelling variant $w$ generated from a search term $t$, we interpret $p$ as the probability $p = P(t \rightarrow w)$ that $t$ implies $w$. Since our search engine is based on retrieval as uncertain inference, these probabilities can be easily incorporated into the retrieval process (e.g. in the simple case of binary indexing and single-term queries, $p$ would be the weight of a document containing $w$).

## 5  Evaluation

For evaluation, we compared our new approach with two other methods developed before. Here we first describe the alternative methods, and then we present the experimental results.

### 5.1 Manually-Built Rules

In [11], the manual construction of two rule sets for 19th century German texts is described. For the first rule set, each rule can only be applied at most once at a specific position in a word (e. g. ä ⟶ e). In contrast, the rules from the second rule set (e. g. aa ⟶ a) can be applied an arbitrary number of times. Due to the fact that spelling variants often occur because of differences in pronunciation, a part of the rules have been developed by comparing pronunciations. Other rules have been developed by literature research. For each word in question, these rules are applied onto the contemporary and the historic word form. If the results of the transformations are equal, this means that a historic spelling variant has been found.

### 5.2 Variant Graph

The approach presented in [2] is similar to phonetic name matching. For each graphem, the appropriate allographs are generated. For example, the grapheme $f$ has the allographs $\{u, v, f, ff, pf\}$. Given the set of allographs for each graphem, a variant graph can be build for each input word in contemporary spelling. For each grapheme in the input word this graph contains the corresponding allographs; each path in the graph produces one variant spelling. As an example, Figure 1 shows the variant graph for the word 'Himmel' (sky).

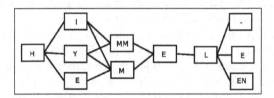

**Fig. 1.** The variant graph for 'himmel'

### 5.3 Experiments

For a comparative evaluation of the different approaches, we used documents from the Nietzsche collection and other smaller collections containing texts from the 19th century. The manually build rule set had been developed only based on the Nietzsche collection while the rule set for the other two approaches had been developed for the whole test collection. Our small collection contains 64290 word tokens, with 11326 different words (types). After feeding the types into the spell checker, followed by manual checking of the marked words, we were left with 717 different words in historic spellings.

Since our new approach requires a training sample, we split the available data such that two thirds of the instances were used as training sample, and the remaining third as test sample.

The recall and precision values are based on collection frequency of the retrieved full word forms. The results of applying the three approaches to the test sample are shown in Table 2.

**Table 2.** Recall and precision figures of the three approaches

| Approach | Precision | Recall |
|---|---|---|
| Manual rules | 0.53 | 0.09 |
| Variant graph | 0.48 | 0.69 |
| Automatic rules | 0.45 | 0.88 |

The manually developed rules from [11] perform poorly, as they achieve a precision of 0.53, but only a recall of 0.09. In addition to the low quality, a major disadvantage of the manual rules is the intellectual effort for their development. Thus, this approach does not seem to be suitable for supporting retrieval of texts in historic spelling, because we did not even get an expected high precision for the available rules.

With the variant graph, we reach a similar precision, but a recall level of 0.69. Roughly speaking, this approach misses one out of three words in historic spelling; this is not a satisfying result - even though only a fraction of all words occur in non-standard spelling. Another drawback of the variant graph method is the large number of spelling variants generated (e. g. 18 in Figure 1), which increases retrieval times substantially.

The automatic generated rules reach a precision of 0.45 and a recall of 0.88. In comparison to the other two approaches, precision is slightly inferior. On the other hand, the recall is 28 % better as that of the variant graph method.

With the automatically generated rules, it is also simple to look at the precision values for single rules. These precision values are based on the collection frequency of full word forms and the false positives the rules are used for. Table 3 shows some frequently used rules with their corresponding precision values.

We generated a first rule set with the parameters $p_{min} = 0.0$ and $q_{min} = 1$. By applying higher thresholds values $p_{min}$ in our rule pruning algorithm, we can increase the precision on the test sample. Table 4 shows the corresponding results. A reasonable threshold seems to be 0.4, because recall decreases only slightly from 0.88 to 0.86, while precision decreases from 0.45 to 0.77 and is consequently superior to the precision values of the other two approaches.

**Table 3.** Frequently used rules

| Rules | Context | Frequency | Precision | Examples |
|---|---|---|---|---|
| t $\longrightarrow$ th | | 116 | 0.67 | Einteilung - Eintheilung |
| ä $\longrightarrow$ ae | post: $C$ | 42 | 0.98 | Ämter - Aemter |
| s $\longrightarrow$ ß | | 35 | 0.62 | aus - auß |
| k $\longrightarrow$ c | | 32 | 0.8 | Kollegien - Collegien |
| ü $\longrightarrow$ ue | | 20 | 0.69 | Übertragung - Uebertragung |
| ä $\longrightarrow$ ai | | 18 | 1.0 | souverän - souverain |

**Table 4.** Recall and Precision for different threshold values $p_{min}$

| $p_{min}$ | 0.0 | 0.1 | 0.2 | 0.3 | 0.4 | 0.5 | 0.6 | 0.7 | 0.8 | 0.9 | 1.0 |
|---|---|---|---|---|---|---|---|---|---|---|---|
| Recall | 0.88 | 0.87 | 0.87 | 0.87 | 0.86 | 0.73 | 0.73 | 0.69 | 0.65 | 0.63 | 0.29 |
| Precision | 0.45 | 0.65 | 0.65 | 0.75 | 0.77 | 0.93 | 0.94 | 0.96 | 0.98 | 0.99 | 1.00 |

Overall, these results the implementation of our new approach show that automatically generated rules outperform previous methods, and that we are on the right track to achieve a high quality in the generation of historic spellings.

## 6   Conclusion and Future Work

In this paper, we have discussed the problem of retrieval in historic texts with non-standard spelling. We have shown that due to the large variations in historic spellings, the standard stemming approach cannot be applied. Instead, historic variants of the search terms have to be generated. By using a contemporary dictionary containing the inflected word forms, we first map the search term onto its inflected forms, and then generate the corresponding historic variants. For this purpose, we have described a machine learning method for generating appropriate transformation rules. Since the rules have probabilistic weights, these weights can be considered in retrieval for weighting the documents matched by search terms generated through weighted rules.

So far, we have only a first version of our algorithm. As an obvious extension of the basic algorithm, we should consider better parameter estimation methods for estimating the precision of rules with a small number of positive examples. The manual analysis of the errors on the test set has shown that a large number of errors is caused by a few words. Thus, these words should be considered as exceptions in the rules — so the rule generation algorithm should be modified accordingly.

For an application of our approach to large corpora, we are also working on the development of an interactive tool for rule generation. Instead of assessing a large number of 'misspelled' words before starting rule generation, the interactive tool would start with a few assessed examples only, generate rule candidates and then ask the user for judging about (a representative sample of) other words where these rules apply.

So far, our method has been applied to German texts only. However, by exchanging the linguistic resources (i.e. the dictionary containing the full word forms) it can be easily applied to other languages.

The module for generating historic variants of search terms will be integrated in a probabilistic engine for the retrieval of historic texts. Only through retrieval experiments with historic collections, we can assess the ultimate quality of the new method presented here.

## Acknowledgements

This work is supported by the DFG (project RSNSR).

## References

[1] Biella, D., Dyllong, E., Kaiser, H., Luther, W., and Mittmann, T.: Edition électronique de la réception de Nietzsche des années 1865 à 1945." In: Proc. ICHIM03, Paris, 2003.
[2] Biella, D., Dyllong, E., H., Luther, W., and Pilz, T.: An On-line Literature Research System with Rule-Based Search, In: Proc. of the 4th European Conference on e-Learning (ECEL2005). Amsterdam, 2005.

[3] Camps, R., Daudé, J.: Improving the efficacy of approximate personal name matching. In: Proc. 8th International Conference on Applications of Natural Language to Information Systems (NLDB 03). 2003. http://www.lsi.upc.es/dept/techreps/ps/R03-9.ps.gz.

[4] Cendrowska, J.: PRISM: An algorithm for inducing modular rules. International Journal of Man-Machine Studies, 27(4), pp. 349-370. 1987.

[5] Cohen, W., W., Singer, Y.: Context-sensitive learning methods for text categorization. In ACM Trans. Inf. Syst. Vol. 17, No. 2, pp 141-173. ACM Press, New York, NY, USA. 1999.

[6] De Roux, E.: 19 bibliothèques en Europe signent un manifeste pour contrer le projet de Google. Le Monde, Paris, 28.04.2005.

[7] Frakes, W., B., Baeza-Yates, R., A.: Information Retrieval: Data Structures & Algorithms Context-sensitive learning methods for text categorization. Prentice-Hall, 1992. DBLP, http://dblp.uni-trier.de.

[8] Keller, R.: Die Deutsche Sprache und ihre historische Entwicklung. Hamburg: Helmut Buske Verlage, 1986.

[9] Nottelmann, H.: PIRE: An extensible IR engine based on probabilistic Datalog. ECIR 2005.

[10] Pfeifer, U., Poersch, T., and Fuhr, N.: Retrieval Effectiveness of Proper Name Search Methods. Information Processing and Management Vol. 32, No. 6, pp. 667-669. 1996.

[11] Pilz, Th.: Unscharfe Suche in Textdatenbanken mit nichtstandardisierter Rechtschreibung am Beispiel von Frakturtexten zur Nietzsche-Rezeption. Staatsexamensarbeit. Universität Duisburg-Essen, 2003.

[12] Peters, C. (Hrsg.): Cross-Language Information Retrieval and Evaluation, Vol. 2069 von Lecture Notes in Computer Science, Heidelberg et al. Springer. 2001.

[13] Quasthoff, U.: Projekt Der Deutsche Wortschatz. In Heyer, G., Wolff, Ch. (eds.) (1998). Linguistig und neue Medien. In: Proc. from the GLDV-Tagung, 17.-19. März 1997 at Leipzig, Deutscher Universitätsverlag, pp. 93-99, 1998.

[14] Rayson, P., Archer, D., Smith, N.: VARD versus Word. A comparison of the UCREL variant detector and modern spell checkers on English historical corpora. In proceedings of the Corpus Linguistics 2005 conference. Birmingham, UK. In: Proc. from the Corpus Linguistics Conference Series on-line e-journal, Vol. 1, No. 1., 2005.

[15] Strunk, J.: Information Retrieval for Languages that lack a fixed orthography. 2003. http://www.linguistics.ruhr-uni-bochum.de/~strunk/LSreport.pdf.

[16] Witten, I., Frank, E.: Data Mining: Practical Machine Learning Tools and Techniques with Java Implementations. Morgan Kaufmann Publishers, San Francisco, CA, 2000.

[17] Zobel, J. and Dart, P.: Phonetic String Matching: Lessons from Information Retrieval. 1996. In Frei, H.-P.; Harman, D.; Schäuble, P.; Wilkinson, R. (eds.): Proc. 19th Inter. Conf. on Research and Development in Information Retrieval (SIGIR), New York, 1996, pp. 166-172.

# Efficient Phrase Querying with Common Phrase Index*

Matthew Chang and Chung Keung Poon

Dept. of Computer Science, City U. of Hong Kong, China
{kcmchang, ckpoon}@cs.cityu.edu.hk

**Abstract.** In this paper, we propose a *common phrase index* as an efficient index structure to support phrase queries in a very large text database. Our structure is an extension of previous index structures for phrases and achieves better query efficiency with negligible extra storage cost. In our experimental evaluation, a common phrase index has 5% and 20% improvement in query time for the overall and large queries (queries of long phrases) respectively over an *auxiliary nextword index*. Moreover, it uses only 1% extra storage cost. Compared with an *inverted index*, our improvement is 40% and 72% for the overall and large queries respectively.

## 1 Introduction

In this information age, search engine acts as an efficient tool for seeking information from a vast heap of online texts. By providing an ad hoc query, we can immediately get a set of texts from gigabytes text database. As the Internet is growing at an extremely fast pace, the number of hosts available increased more than 130 folds (from 1.3 to 171 millions[1]) in the last decade. Hence, search engines should be able to evaluate queries efficiently and effectively. In other words, the systems should resolve queries quickly and also provide accurately what the users want [13]. In order to improve the effectiveness of searching, considering phrases in searching and indexing seems to be an interesting idea for the following reasons:

- Phrases come closer than individual words or their stems to express structured concepts.
- Phrases have a smaller degree of ambiguity than their constituent words. That is, while two words are both ambiguous, the combination is not, since each of its two constituent words creates a context for the unambiguous interpretation of the other.
- By using phrases as index terms, a document that contains a phrase would be ranked higher than a document that just contains its constituent words in unrelated contexts.

---

* The work described in this paper was fully supported by a grant from the Research Grants Council of the Hong Kong Special Administrative Region, China [Project No. CityU 1198/03E].

[1] Source: Internet Software Consortium (http://www.isc.org/).

M. Lalmas et al. (Eds.): ECIR 2006, LNCS 3936, pp. 61–71, 2006.
© Springer-Verlag Berlin Heidelberg 2006

Previous research works on phrase recognition and automatic phrase formation [6, 7, 8] resulted in improved retrieval effectiveness. Also, an amalgamated hierarchical browsing and hierarchical thesaurus browsing can be used to display the result set of documents in a more effective way than simply listing the results [11].

To efficiently resolve a query with gigabytes of online texts, an efficient way of indexing is essential. A conventional and practical way of indexing is the *inverted index* [17]. For each term in the index, there are a list of postings with document identification numbers, within-document frequencies and offsets at which the term appears. To resolve a query, we can simply combine the lists attached to each of the query terms to get the results. It is straightforward to intersect the lists with the consideration of the offsets of the terms to produce the result set for a phrase query. However, for evaluating common words, the process of merging is slow due to the long list of postings retrieved. Even if we use pruning techniques like *frequency-sorted indexing* and *impact-sorted indexing* so that we need not retrieve the whole postings list of a term [1, 2, 5, 12], the number of retrieved highest-scored postings of a common word can still reach several megabytes. Also, these early termination heruistics do not retain the complete set of result documents.

*Nextword index* provides a fast alternative for resolving phrase queries, phrase browsing, and phrase completion [15]. Unlike an inverted index, it has a list of nextwords and positions following each distinct word. The set of first words is known as the *vocabulary* or *firstword*. The words following the firstwords are called *nextwords*. The major drawback of using *nextword index* is its large space consumption which is around 60% of the size of the indexed data. With careful optimization techniques [3], the size of a nextword index file can be reduced to 49% of the indexed data. An *auxiliary nextword index* proposed by Bahle et. al [4] further reduces the space overhead to only 10% of the size of the inverted index file.

In this paper, we propose a new indexing structure which we call *common phrase index*. Building on the ideas of the inverted index and auxiliary nextword index, it divides the vocabulary into two sets: *rare words* and *common words*. We attach a list of postings to each of the rare words as in an inverted index. For the common words, it differs from the nextword index structure in that it has a collection of trees such that each root-to-leaf path represents a phrase starting from a common word and ending in a terminal word. Moreover, postings lists are only attached to the leaf nodes of the tree. This combination of structures breaks down the original inverted lists of terms and provides useful additional information for evaluating phrases efficiently from a large text database. Similar to our index, Moffat and Zobel [10] proposed that inverted lists can be broken into groups by introducing *synchronization points*. However, our index applied the concept of phrase and hence has the following advantages over it. First, it supports fast phrase query evluation. Also, it breaks only some inverted lists but provides significant improvement in efficiency. Last, it is not required to determine the number of document pointers in a group.

In our experiments, we implemented a prototype system to compare an inverted index, auxiliary nextword index, and common phrase index against a set of benchmark documents and query logs. Our results show that common phrase index speeds up the overall efficiency and large-sized query evaluation by 5% and 20% respectively. Both the inverted index and nextword index have a significant increase in the query time as the size of query increases. In contrast, common phrase index shows only a slight increase in query time as the query size increases. Also, the storage usage is just increased by about 1% of the auxiliary nextword index.

The rest of this paper is organized as follows. Section 2 and 3 describe the inverted index, nextword index, and auxiliary nextword index. Section 4 introduces our common phrase index and its interesting characteristics. Section 5 explains our experiment setup and presents our results. Section 6 is our conclusion and future work.

## 2   Inverted Indexes

*Inverted index*, or inverted file structure, is the most commonly used index structure for database management and information retrieval systems [9]. An inverted index is a two-level structure. The upper level is all the index terms for the collection. For text database, the index terms are usually the words occurring in the text, and all words are included. The lower level is a set of postings lists, one per index term. Following the notation of Zobel and Moffat [16], each posting is a triple of the form:

$$< d, f_{d,t}, [o_1, ..., o_{f_{d,t}}] >$$

where $d$ is the identifier of a document containing term $t$, the frequency of $t$ in $d$ is $f_{d,t}$, and the $o$ values are the positions in $d$ at which $t$ is observed. To evaluate a query, each query term is used to fetch a postings list via the vocabulary search. For instance, suppose we have the following four documents associated with their contents:

```
Document 1 {Computer Science}
Document 2 {Computer Engineering}
Document 3 {Search Engine}
Document 4 {Computer Science: Search Engine}.
```

Then, the postings lists of "computer" and "science" are:

```
<computer,    3, <1, 1, [1]>, <2, 1, [1]>, <4, 1, [1]>>
<science,     2, <1, 1, [2]>, <4, 1, [2]>>.
```

It indicates that document 1, 2, and 4 have one occurrence of "computer" each at the position 1 of the documents. The term "science" exists at position 2 of both document 1 and 4. To resolve a phrase query "Computer Science", we first retrieve the corresponding postings list of each query term and then we sort the lists according to the value $f_t$ in ascending order. Finally we intersect the lists one by one from the rarest to the most common term with a temporary structure. When intersecting the sorted lists, we have to consider the proximity. The query terms "Computer" and "Science" have a position difference of one. Hence, for each intersect operation, we first see if there is any document identifier present in both structures. For each matched document, we check if the offsets of them are having a position difference of one. So, the results of the phrase query "Computer Science" are document 1 and 4.

## 3   Nextword Indexes and Auxiliary Nextword Indexes

Inverted index is not efficient for evaluating query with common terms since the three most common words account for about 4% of the size of the whole index file [4] and retrieving such long postings list can suffer a long operation time. Hence, nextword index [15] is proposed to construct an index by recording additional index for supporting fast evaluation of phrase queries.

A nextword index is a three-level structure. The highest level is of the distinct index terms in the collection, which we call *firstwords*. At the middle level, for each firstword there is a collection of *nextwords*, which are the words observed to follow that firstword in the indexed text. At the lowest level, for each nextword there is a postings list of the positions at which that firstword-nextword pair occur. Using the same example we employed in Section 2, the postings lists of all firstword-nextword pairs of the nextword index are shown below:

```
<computer_science,     2, <1, 1, [1]>, <4, 1, [1]>>
<computer_engineering, 1, <2, 1, [1]>>
<science_search,       1, <4, 1, [2]>>
<search_engine,        2, <3, 1, [1]>, <4, 1, [3]>>.
```

To pose a phrase query "Computer Science", nextword index just needs to fetch a single list of postings instead of retrieving two long lists of postings and performing intersection. This speeds up the evaluation of a phrase query. The applications of nextword index can be found in [15]. However, the size of index is large. Bahle et. al [4] observe the weakness of resolving phrase query by using an inverted index and the enormous size overhead of a nextword index and hence proposed auxiliary nextword index. The main idea of the auxiliary nextword index is that only the *top-frequency* words are to be indexed with nextwords. For example, using the same sample documents as Section 2 and assuming that "computer" is the only high-frequency or common word, all firstword-nextword pairs of the auxiliary nextword index are as:

```
<computer_science,     2, <1, 1, [1]>, <4, 1, [1]>>
<computer_engineering, 1, <2, 1, [1]>>.
```

To resolve a query, the steps are similar to an inverted index. However, the auxiliary nextword index first contends with the common words of query terms, and then the rest. Experimental result in [4] shows that having the three most common terms as firstwords consumes just 10% of space of the inverted index. Therefore, a huge amount of space is saved compared with nextword index. The ideal size of phrase query for an auxiliary nextword index is two because only one fetching is required. However, in the query log of Excite dating 1997 and 1999, queries of size two occupied only 35.28%. For queries of size one, which accounts for 25.36%, no index can be more efficient than an inverted index. For the remaining 39.36% of queries, a nextword index has to perform at least two fetchings and one intersection. We will show that a common phrase index can further improve the efficiency for query size larger than two.

## 4    Common Phrase Indexes

The main difference between a common phrase index and an auxiliary nextword index is that the additional index terms are not fix-sized *firstword-nextword* pairs but variable-sized *common phrases*. For each common phrase, there is a postings list of the positions at which that common phrase occur.

### 4.1    Common Phrases

We define *common phrase* as a sequence of two or more contiguous words that starts with a *common word* and ends in a *terminal word*.

We define common words as those words having the highest frequencies in a set of queries. Thus our notion of common word is sensitive to the query workload. For concreteness, we take the Excite query log dating 1997 and 1999 as reference. We first count the frequency of each distinct word of the query logs. The highest-frequency words are known as *common words* and the others are called *rare words*.

Terminal words are words which are likely to be the end of a phrase. We observe that in an auxiliary nextword index, some of the indexed pairs (e.g. "in_all", "in_new", "in_the") can actually be expanded in order to achieve further efficiency improvement. These *firstword-nextword* pairs do not end in a significant or *terminal* word (to be defined). We have investigated the 2.1 million queries in the query logs of the Excite dating 1997 and 1999. In the logs, we count the frequency of each function (or part-of-speech) of the last word of all queries by submitting the words to *Merriam-Webster OnLine* and retrieving the corresponding functions, see Table 1. If a word has more than one function, we take the most popular function of the word. Note that, the function *Others* includes misspellings and proper nouns. In the table, we observe that prepositions, adverbs, conjunctions, definite articles, indefinite articles, and pronouns occupy only 0.408% of all last words of the queries. That is, a query often contains a phrase with last word having other kinds of function. Thus, we define the *terminal word* of our common phrase as *any word whose function*

**Table 1.** Function Frequency of Query Last Word

| Function | Frequency | Percentage |
|---|---|---|
| adjective | 62482 | 2.938% |
| preposition | 1556 | 0.073% |
| adverb | 5116 | 0.241% |
| conjunction | 209 | 0.010% |
| definite article | 79 | 0.004% |
| indefinite article | 15 | 0.001% |
| verb | 126252 | 5.936% |
| noun | 1050804 | 49.410% |
| pronoun | 1686 | 0.079% |
| others | 878512 | 41.308% |

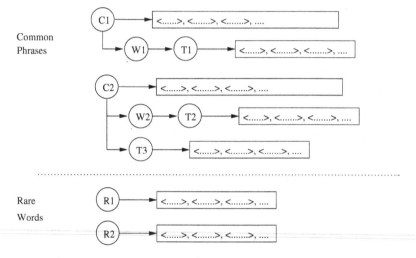

**Fig. 1.** Common Phrase Index Structure

*is not a preposition, adverb, conjunction, definite article, indefinite article, or pronoun.*

The structure of common phrase index is illustrated in Figure 1, where the $C$'s are common words, $R$'s are rare words, $T$'s are terminal words, and $W$'s are the others. The concept of common phrase index can be easily illustrated by using a simple example to compare the structure of auxiliary nextword index and common phrase index. For instance, suppose we have the following documents:

```
Document 1 {Students of the same year}
Document 2 {Computer and applications}
Document 3 {Usage of the Search Engine}.
```

For the sake of brevity, we omit all the postings lists of the rare words. Then, the auxiliary nextword index for the documents contains:

```
<and_applications,          1, <2, 1, [2]>>
<computer_and,              1, <2, 1, [1]>>
<of_the,                    2, <1, 1, [2]>, <3, 1, [2]>>
<the_same,                  1, <1, 1, [3]>>
<the_search,                1, <3, 1, [3]>>
```

while the common phrase index for the documents contains:

```
<and_applications,          1, <2, 1, [2]>>
<computer_and_applications, 1, <2, 1, [1]>>
<of_the_same_year,          1, <1, 1, [2]>>
<of_the_search,             1, <3, 1, [2]>>
<the_same_year,             1, <1, 1, [3]>>
<the_search,                1, <3, 1, [3]>>.
```

The number of contiguous words in an auxiliary nextword index is capped at two while that in a common phrase index is not limited. The size of a common phrase stops growing when it encounters a terminal word. In the above example, the postings list of the *firstword-nextword* pair "of_the" in the nextword index is broken down into "of_the_same_year" and "of_the_search" in the common phrase index. By issuing a query "computer and applications", auxiliary nextword index has to perform two fetchings and one intersection while the common phrase index has to perform just a single fetching.

Note that by using common phrase index, high efficiency in phrase evaluation can be sustained even if the query size is large. Our experiments in Section 5 show that improvement of common phrase index enlarges when the query size increases. The further breakdown of the postings lists in common phrase index supports high efficiency with low additional storage overhead comparing with auxiliary nextword index.

## 4.2   Query Evaluation

To evaluate a query with common phrase index, we perform the following steps:

1. Identify the first common word of the query.
2. Expand the common word to a common phrase by adding the succeeding words of it until a terminal word or end of query is reached. If the common phrase is found, fetch the postings list to a temporary structure. Then mark all the words of the common phrase as *covered*.
3. Find the next common word from the query terms that are not yet *covered*.
4. Repeat *Step 2* and intersect the fetched postings list with the temporary structure until all common words are *covered*.
5. For all the words not yet *covered*, which must be rare words, fetch the associated postings list and intersect with the postings list in the temporary structure.

## 4.3   Dynamic Nature of Common and Rare Words

Our experiments use a set of common words that is "ideal" for a certain set of queries. In reality, the set of highest-frequency words in query log keeps changing.

We have studied a report that analysed an Excite query log of 16 September 1997 [14] which listed the top 75 terms that are occurring more than 1110 times in the 531,416 unique queries. The top 8 terms with more than 5000 times each in unique queries are the words likely to have high-frequency at anytime, they are "and", "of", "sex", "free", "the", "nude", "pictures", and "in". These terms have 80778 or 15.2% of the total occurrences of the top 75 terms. However, some terms ranked in the top 75 are not that stable especially for those having less than 2000 times each in unique queries. They are popular for querying at a certain period of time because of some incidences. For example, the terms "princess" and "diana" which are having 1461 and 1885 times respectively in 1997 because many people are in memory of Diana, Princess of Wales. The high-frequency word "diana" is ranked at $31^{st}$ in 1997 but it falls to $315^{th}$ when we take both 1997 and 1999 Excite query log into consideration. The term "princess" is ranked from $45^{th}$ in 1997 and dropped to $362^{nd}$ in both 1997 and 1999.

Our observation suggests that common phrase index should be dynamically changing according to the high-frequency terms at that time. Basically, common phrase index is a combination of an inverted index and additional indexes of common phrases. By using this combination, it is easy for updating the index file. The system has to keep the frequency of each query term. For each word newly falling into the set of common words, we break down the corresponding postings list into several lists indexed by common phrases. In contrast, for each word that is newly excluded from the set of common words, we can union the lists of common phrases into one list.

## 5   Experiments

In our experiment, we implemented a prototype system to evaluate phrase queries for comparing the efficiency and total size of inverted index, auxiliary nextword index, and common phrase index. We used a database system, *MySQL*, to store all the postings lists, vocabularies, and dictionary. All experiments were run on an Intel 3 GHz Pentium 4-based server with 2 Gb of memory, running *Linux* operating system under light load.

We used a set of benchmark documents and query logs in our experiments. For test documents, we used the *.Gov* web research collection from TREC. This collection is especially for Information Retrieval systems in a Web context and large-scale information retrieval systems design and evaluation. It was collected in early 2002 and contains about 1.25 million .gov web pages with a total size of about 18.1 Gbytes. For test queries, we used the query logs provided by Excite dating to 1997 and 1999. These are the same query logs used by Bahle et. al [4]. There are 2.1 million queries in the query logs (including duplicates).

We did the following preprocessing to each document. First of all, any formatting information such as HTML or XML tags are removed from the document. Special characters are replaced by blanks and all upper-case letters are changed to lower-case. After these, a document becomes a sequence of words separated by blanks. We then constructed the postings lists for each kind of indexing and stored them in database.

In our experiments, we first focus on comparison in efficiency between auxiliary nextword index and common phrase index. We tried designating different number of words as common words in the vocabulary for both indexes, see Table 2. For each size of the set of common words, we show the overall efficiency and also break down the results according to the query size in order to pinpoint where improvements are made. For all the different sizes of the set of common words we have tested, we have about 4% improvement in the overall efficiency. For queries of size one and two, the common phrase index does not have any

**Table 2.** Efficiency in average milliseconds of Auxiliary Nextword Index (ANI) and Common Phrase Index (CPI) with 10, 20, and 255 common words. ($\Delta = ANI - CPI$)

| Query Size | ANI(10) | CPI(10) | $\frac{\Delta}{ANI(10)}$ | ANI(20) | CPI(20) | $\frac{\Delta}{ANI(20)}$ | ANI(255) | CPI(255) | $\frac{\Delta}{ANI(255)}$ |
|---|---|---|---|---|---|---|---|---|---|
| Overall | 367.47 | 352.30 | 4.13% | 359.34 | 341.72 | 4.90% | 247.77 | 237.55 | 4.12% |
| 1 | 79.99 | 79.98 | 0.01% | 80.05 | 79.66 | 0.49% | 77.36 | 76.88 | 0.62% |
| 2 | 302.49 | 302.42 | 0.02% | 300.69 | 299.60 | 0.36% | 243.04 | 241.44 | 0.66% |
| 3 | 452.96 | 448.21 | 1.04% | 445.90 | 438.91 | 1.57% | 322.16 | 311.65 | 3.26% |
| 4 | 643.85 | 619.25 | 3.82% | 625.79 | 596.87 | 4.62% | 383.80 | 362.47 | 5.56% |
| 5 | 708.75 | 642.19 | 9.39% | 680.87 | 608.02 | 10.70% | 375.01 | 335.58 | 10.52% |
| ≥ 6 | 980.00 | 804.69 | 17.89% | 921.68 | 729.56 | 20.85% | 397.77 | 331.88 | 16.56% |

**Table 3.** Efficiency in average milliseconds of Inverted Index (II), Auxilary Nextword Index (ANI) and Common Phrase Index (CPI) with 255 common words

| Query Size | II | ANI(255) | CPI(255) | $\frac{II-ANI(255)}{II}$ | $\frac{II-CPI(255)}{II}$ |
|---|---|---|---|---|---|
| Overall | 401.80 | 247.77 | 237.55 | 38.33% | 40.88% |
| 1 | 79.97 | 77.36 | 76.88 | 3.26% | 3.86% |
| 2 | 307.57 | 243.04 | 241.44 | 20.98% | 21.50% |
| 3 | 488.34 | 322.16 | 311.65 | 34.03% | 36.18% |
| 4 | 701.48 | 383.80 | 362.47 | 45.28% | 48.33% |
| 5 | 857.19 | 375.01 | 335.58 | 56.25% | 60.85% |
| ≥ 6 | 1223.12 | 397.77 | 331.88 | 67.48% | 72.87% |

**Table 4.** Size of Inverted Index (II), Auxilary Nextword Index (ANI) and Common Phrase Index (CPI) with 10, 20, and 255 common words

| Index(Common words) | Index Size (Gb) | $\frac{CPI(x)-ANI(x)}{ANI(x)}$ | $\frac{index(x)-II}{II}$ |
|---|---|---|---|
| II | 23.08 | - | - |
| ANI(10) | 25.67 | - | 11.24% |
| ANI(20) | 26.56 | - | 15.08% |
| ANI(255) | 26.86 | - | 16.38% |
| CPI(10) | 25.96 | 1.13% | 12.50% |
| CPI(20) | 26.94 | 1.44% | 16.73% |
| CPI(255) | 27.28 | 1.59% | 18.22% |

improvement as we have expected because it can at most extract phrases of the same length as in auxiliary nextword index. Note that, the improvement rate increases when the size of query increases. Common phrase index can even achieve more than 16% improvement when the query size is larger than or equal to six. We also compare the efficiency between the inverted index, auxiliary nextword index, and common phrase index, see Table 3. Again, we observe that common phrase index has a better improvement rate (the rightmost two columns) than auxiliary nextword index.

The total index sizes of different indexings are shown in Table 4. As can be seen, total index size of the common phrase index is just larger than that of the auxiliary nextword index by about 1.5%. It is a negligible trade-off for higher efficiency in query evaluation.

## 6    Conclusion

We have proposed a novel extension of auxiliary nextword index. Phrase queries on large text databases can be supported by using *common phrase index*. In this approach, all words in the text document are indexed the same as inverted index; in addition, the most common words are indexed via common phrase. Unlike the inverted index and auxiliary nextword index where the size of an index term is fixed (one word for an inverted index and two words for an auxiliary nextword index), common phrase index has variable-sized index term. These variable-sized index terms further break down the postings lists and support the fastest phrase query evaluation among inverted index and auxiliary nextword index. Having efficiency improvement especially for query size larger than or equal to three, the total size of it is just larger than that of an auxiliary nextword index by about 1.5%.

Our experimental results show that we can implement common phrase index for evaluating phrase queries with no significant storage overhead. The only additional requirement is having a dictionary for checking of terminal words. However, the dictionary is rather static. Therefore, it can be used for a long period of time after we built it once.

In our future work, we will also implement and experiment a version of our index that can adjust its structure according to the dynamic nature of common words. Since the performance of a common phrase index is highly related to the chosen common words, it requires the index to be updated after a certain period of time. We expect that our system will further improve the efficiency with the dynamic update nature implemented.

## References

1. V. Anh and A. Moffat. Compressed inverted files with reduced decoding overheads. In *Proc. of the 21th Annual SIGIR Conf. on Research and Development in information retrieval*, pages 290–297, 1998.
2. V. Anh and A. Moffat. Vector-space ranking with effective early termination. In *Proc. of the 24th Annual SIGIR Conf. on Research and Development in information retrieval*, pages 35–42, 2001.

3. D. Bahle, H. E. Williams, and J. Zobel. Compaction techniques for nextword indexes. In *Proc. 8th International Symposium on String Processing and Information Retrieval (SPIRE2001)*, pages 33–45, 2001.
4. D. Bahle, H. E. Williams, and J. Zobel. Efficient phrase querying with an auxiliary index. In *Proceedings of the 25th annual international ACM SIGIR conference on Research and development in information retrieval*, 2002.
5. S. Chaudhuri and L. Gravano. Optimizing queries over multimedia repositories. pages 91–102, 1996.
6. W. B. Croft, H. R. Turtle, and D. D. Lewis. The use of phrases and structured queries in information retrieval. In *Proceedings of the 14th Annual International ACM SIGIR Conference on Research and Development in Information Retrieval. Chicago, Illinois, USA, October 13-16, 1991 (Special Issue of the SIGIR Forum)*, pages 32–45, 1991.
7. E. F. de Lima and J. O. Pedersen. Phrase recognition and expansion for short, precision-biased queries based on a query log. In *Proceedings of the 22nd annual international ACM SIGIR conference on Research and development in information retrieval*, pages 145–152, 1999.
8. J. L. Fagan. *Experiments in automatic phrase indexing for document retrieval: a comparison of syntactic and non-syntactic methods*. PhD thesis, Cornell University, 1987.
9. G. Kowalski. *Information Retrieval Systems: Theory and Implementation*. Kluwer Academic Publishers, 1997.
10. A. Moffat and J. Zobel. Self-indexing inverted files for fast text retrieval. *ACM Transactions on Information Systems*, 14(4):349–379, 1996.
11. G. W. Paynter, I. H. Witten, S. J. Cunningham, and G. Buchanan. Scalable browsing for large collections: A case study. In *Proceedings of the Fifth ACM International Conference on Digital Libraries*, 2000.
12. M. Persin, J. Zobel, and R. Sacks-Davis. Filtered document retrieval with frequency-sorted indexes. *Journal of the American Society of Information Science*, 47(10):749–764, 1996.
13. G. Salton. *Automatic Text Processing: The Transformation, Analysis, and Retrieval of Information by Computer*. Addison-Wesley, 1998.
14. A. Spink, D. Wolfram, B. Jansen, and T. Saracevic. Searching the web: The public and their queries. *Journal of the American Society for Information Science*, 52(3):226–234, 2001.
15. H. E. Williams, J. Zobel, and P. Anderson. What's next? - index structures for efficient phrase querying. In *Proc. Australasian Database Conference*, pages 141–152, 1999.
16. J. Zobel and A. Moffat. Exploring the similarity space. In *ACM SIGIR Forum*, pages 18–34, 1998.
17. J. Zobel, A. Moffat, and K. Ramamohanarao. Inverted files versus signature files for text indexing. *ACM Transactions on Database Systems*, 23(4):453–490, 1998.

# Document Length Normalization Using Effective Level of Term Frequency in Large Collections

Soheila Karbasi and Mohand Boughanem

IRIT-SIG, Campus Univ. Toulouse III, 31062 Toulouse, Cedex 09, France
{karbasi, bougha}@irit.fr

**Abstract.** The effectiveness of the information retrieval systems is largely dependent on term-weighting. Most current term-weighting approaches involve the use of term frequency normalization. We develop here a method to assess the potential role of the term frequency-inverse document frequency measures that are commonly used in text retrieval systems. Since automatic information retrieval systems have to deal with documents of varying sizes and terms of varying frequencies, we carried out preliminary tests to evaluate the effect of term-weighing items on the retrieval performance. With regard to the preliminary tests, we identify a novel factor (effective level of term frequency) that represents the document content based on its length and maximum term-frequency. This factor is used to find the maximum main terms within the documents and an appropriate subset of documents containing the query terms. We show that, all document terms need not be considered for ranking a document with respect to a query. Regarding the result of the experiments, the effective level of term frequency (EL) is a significant factor in retrieving relevant documents, especially in large collections. Experiments were undertaken on TREC collections to evaluate the effectiveness of our proposal.

## 1 Introduction

As the volume of information increases, automatic and effective information retrieval methods become essential to deal with the growth of information. By far, many studies show that most information is text based and high retrieval performance is closely related to the use of appropriate term-weighting scheme [1]. Term weighting has been introduced to fit exhaustivity and specificity of the search, where the exhaustivity is related to recall and specificity to precision [2].

One of the most commonly used term weighting schemes is *tf-idf* model that is based on two basic principles:

- For a given term in a document, the more a term is frequent, the more likely the term is relevant to the document

- For a given term, the more the term occurs throughout all documents, the less likely the term discriminates between documents [3].

There are numerous variants of *tf-idf* weighting and selecting an appropriate scheme requires considering some constraints for study a new collection, especially large collections. The previous works show in spite of the fact that the number of index terms does not increase proportionally with collection size, the terms discrimination

M. Lalmas et al. (Eds.): ECIR 2006, LNCS 3936, pp. 72–83, 2006.
© Springer-Verlag Berlin Heidelberg 2006

problem is amplified in the large collections. Therefore the effectiveness of *tf-idf* measures needs to be revised with the increasing the collection size due to term heterogeneity.

In this paper, we investigate a basic existing weighting scheme to propose a new term-weighting approach supporting the *tf-idf* model. First, we present the factorial analysis of the weighting scheme. Next, we evaluate the impact of the document length on the different factor of this scheme. Based on our observations, we present a novel factor for document length normalization (effective level of term frequency) which is used to find the maximum main terms within the documents. We verify the impact of this factor on the large TREC collections.

The remainder of the paper is organized as follows. We present a simple overview of term significance and term weight normalization in Section 2. In Section 3, we describe our method for document length normalization in details. The retrieval model and test collections are described in Section 4. In Section 5, the evaluation of the new method and experimental results are presented. Finally, we discuss our findings and results in Section 6.

## 2  Models for Term Weight Normalization

The definition of term (the indexing unit), is very critical in the information retrieval field. Index terms can be used as meta-information that describes documents, and as key that helps for seeking information. Automatic document indexing removes the non significant terms (function terms) from the documents, so the documents will only be represented by content bearing terms [1]. This indexing can be based on term frequency, where terms that have both high and low frequency within a document are considered to be function terms [2].

Using the term frequency for indexing is one of the main issues in text retrieval domain which is stated by Luhn [4]. It is well known that term frequency is largely dependent on the document length (i.e. the number of tokens in a document) and needs to be normalized using a technique called *term frequency normalization* [5]. There are various normalized formulas such as "Okapi BM25" [6], "Lnu" [7], "dtu" [8], "Pivoted normalization" [9] that are used for the various IR models. Two important reasons for term frequency normalization are:

– The same term usually occurs repeatedly in long documents
– A long document has usually a large size of vocabulary [3].

## 3  Effective Level of Term Frequency

The main idea of the novel factor for document length normalization (effective level of term frequency) comes from observation of techniques embedded in any normalization method. Most of the common normalization methods, such as maximum term frequency, pivoted normalization, byte length normalization use the document length factor. In addition these methods involve the use of tuned parameters which have an important impact on the effectiveness of the IR systems [10]. Document length normalization is considered one of the more often studies in the text retrieval researches. Fang et al. present a set of basic constraints that correspond to the major well-known

IR heuristics, especially *tf-idf* weighting and document length normalization techniques [11]. Singhal et al. show the retrieval effectiveness is improved when a normalization scheme retrieves documents of all lengths with similar chances as their likelihood of relevance [9].

In our approach, we characterize a traditional retrieval function based on *tf-idf* measures by introducing an efficient constraint. The goal is to determine the importance degree of a query term within each document and collection by ranking terms based on term frequency.

We define an effective level factor, noted EL(d) , as a percentage (X%) of ranked terms based on term frequency in document d and $d^\circ(d,t)$ the importance degree (the rank) of term t within document d according to its frequency.

**Example:** Let us consider a document $d_1 = \{t_1, t_2, t_3, t_4, t_5, t_6\}$, with terms having the following frequency, noted f (d,t):

$$f(d_1, t_1) = 6, \ f(d_1, t_2) = 1, \ f(d_1, t_3) = 8, f(d_1, t_4) = 5, \ f(d_1, t_5) = 1, \ f(d_1, t_6) = 3.$$

The terms are ranked in decreasing order of their frequency in the document.

$$d^\circ(d_1, t_3) = 1, \ d^\circ(d_1, t_1) = 2, \ d^\circ(d_1, t_4) = 3, \ d^\circ(d_1, t_6) = 4, \ d^\circ(d_1, t_2) = 5, \ d^\circ(d_1, t_5) = 5.$$

If the terms $t_3$, $t_1$ and $t_4$ are considered as important in $d_1$ the $EL(d_1)$ will be 50%.

Note: the lower $d^\circ(d,t)$ is, the higher the importance of term t within document d is.

The value of EL factor regulates the interaction between frequency and importance degree of a term in the documents. This means that, a document is more relevant for a query term if this term is one of the important terms within the document. Based on this constraint, we must find the optimum value of EL which improves the retrieval efficiency. In Section 5, we apply this constraint to our retrieval function in two phases. In the first phase, we obtain the retrieval results for a set of 50 queries with the original retrieval function (see equation 2). Next, we repeat this experiment ten times by applying the EL factor to this function. Each time, we select X% of the documents' terms as important terms and we will not consider other terms for retrieval. In first time: we will consider just 5% of the document's terms by ranking terms based on term frequency, in second time: we will select 10% of the terms within documents as important terms and etc. In the second phase, we consider that X% of the document's terms are more important than the others and they will get too over-weighted. Based on this hypothesis, we will compare the results of experiments with the initial results.

# 4   Experimental Framework

## 4.1   Utilized Retrieval Model

We used Mercure model (an information retrieval system based on spreading activation process) [12]. Mercure is implemented a vector space model. The document terms are weighted using a kind of *tf-idf* measure inspired by OKAPI [13] and SMART term weighting. The weights of term-document are expressed by:

$$w_{ij} = \frac{tf_{ij} * \left( h_1 + h_2 * \log\left(\frac{N}{n_i}\right) \right)}{h_3 + h_4 * \frac{dl_j}{\Delta l} + h_5 * tf_{ij}} \tag{2}$$

where:

$w_{ij}$ : term-document weight of term $t_i$ and document $d_j$
- $tf_{ij}$: term frequency of $t_i$ in the document $d_j$
- N: total number of documents and $n_i$: number of documents containing term $t_i$
- $dl_j$: length of document $d_j$
- $\Delta l$ : average document length
- h1, h2, h3, h4 and h5: constant parameters.
In our experiments the constant parameters were set to 0.1, 0.8, 0.2, 0.7 and 1 respectively and the query terms are weighted according to their frequency within the query.

## 4.2  Test Collections

These experiments were undertaken on GOV1 (A crawl of .gov Web sites from early 2002) [14] and WT10G (A subset of the Web from TREC 2001) [15] of the TREC test collections. The details of these collections are shown in Table 1.

**Table 1.** Details of the test collections

| Collection | GOV1 | WT10G |
|---|---|---|
| # Documents[1] | 1,034,442 | 1,691,808 |
| # Terms | 1,679,541 | 3,024,452 |
| # Queries | 50 | 50 |
| Avg. Words per Document | 250 | 267 |
| Avg. Single Words per Document | 143.5 | 156.1 |
| Collection Size [2] | 18.1 GB | 10 GB |

**Table 2.** Summary statistics for used query setsCollection

| Collection | Topic set | Topic field | Min | Max length | Avg |
|---|---|---|---|---|---|
| GOV1 | 551 - 600 | Title & Description | 2 | 11 | 6 |
| WT10G | 501 - 550 | Title & Description | 1 | 9 | 4 |

The GOV1 collection has less documents than WT10G but has a much larger average document size (15k vs 7k). TREC topic sets (551- 600 for GOV1 and 501-550 for

---

[1] Number of indexed documents by Mercure.
[2] The collections have been compressed.

WT10G) and their corresponding relevance judgments are used in our experiments. Test queries are created using the Title and Description fields of these topic sets. The statistical information of the query sets is presented in Table 2. For each query, the first 20 documents retrieved by the system are returned. These experiments have been performed with no relevance feedback and no query expansion.

## 5   Experiments, Results and Discussion

### 5.1   Effect of Term-Weighting Items

We carried out preliminary tests to know the effect of term-weighing items in our retrieval model. We chose three factors: A (term frequency), B (inverse document frequency), C (normalized document length) and analysed the performance of the retrieval model with various factor combinations. Table 3 shows the precisions obtained with only *tf*, factor and its effectiveness. Table 4 illustrates the retrieval precisions obtained by combination of *tf* and the other factors for two collections. The following functions with various factor combinations have been used in this section.

*Factor*                                        *Retrieval function*

- *tf*
  $$w_{ij} = tf_{ij}$$

- *tf & idf*
  $$w_{ij} = tf_{ij} * \left( h_1 + h_2 * \log\left(\frac{N}{n_i}\right) \right)$$

- *tf &length*
  $$w_{ij} = \frac{tf_{ij}}{h_3 + h_4 * \frac{dl_j}{\Delta l} + h_5 * tf_{ij}}$$

In Table 4, the notation "*tf & idf & length*" indicates the use of original function (2).

Based on this analysis and its results, we notice that normalized document length is the most important factor and *idf* is the least important factor for two collections. In addition, Fig. 2 clearly depict that the effect of length factor will be more important in combination with *idf* factor for two test collections.

In reality, the importance of document length normalization is a recurring theme in IR and full-text retrieval necessitates a revision of document length normalization [16], especially in large collections. Following the above experiments, we tried to study more profoundly the effect of length factor. In Section 5.2, we will argue the impact of document length on term frequency and importance degree of term for two test collections.

**Table 3.** Retrieval precisions obtained with only *tf* factor

| GOV1 | | WT10G | |
|---|---|---|---|
| Factor | tf | Factor | tf |
| P@5 | 0.0286 | P@5 | 0.0440 |
| P@10 | 0.0245 | P@10 | 0.0500 |
| P@15 | 0.0224 | P@15 | 0.0487 |
| P@20 | 0.0173 | P@20 | 0.0490 |
| **Avg Precision** | **0.0227** | **Avg Precision** | **0.0474** |

**Table 4.** Retrieval precisions obtained with various factor combinations

| GOV1 | | | | WT10G | | | |
|---|---|---|---|---|---|---|---|
| Factor | tf & Idf | tf & length | tf & idf & length | Factor | tf & idf | tf & length | tf & idf & length |
| P@5 | 0.0449 | 0.1878 | 0.2286 | P@5 | 0.0640 | 0.2000 | 0.2960 |
| P@10 | 0.0388 | 0.1612 | 0.1755 | P@10 | 0.0700 | 0.1900 | 0.3000 |
| P@15 | 0.0360 | 0.1497 | 0.1581 | P@15 | 0.0653 | 0.1793 | 0.2683 |
| P@20 | 0.0327 | 0.1367 | 0.1490 | P@20 | 0.0560 | 0.1750 | 0.2590 |
| **Avg Precision** | **0.0376** | **0.1588** | **0.1770** | **Avg Precision** | **0.0628** | **0.1855** | **0.2800** |
| Δ (change) | 0.0149 | 0.1361 | 0.1543 | Δ (change) | 0.0154 | 0.1381 | 0.2326 |

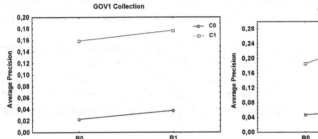
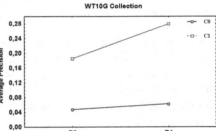

**Fig. 2.** Interaction between factor B (Idf) and factor C (Length) for two collections  (level **0**: leaving out the factor, level **1**: using the factor)

## 5.2   Document Length Analysis

The overall aim of the present section is to investigate the relationships between document length and the other factors of our retrieval function in the test collections. Since the collections contain the documents of varying lengths, we analysed the document length normalization technique which is used by retrieval function 2. In this function, all of the documents are retrieved with similar conditions as their likelihood of relevance. On the other hand, normalized document length decreases the retrieval chances of long documents in preference over shorter documents [16].

We analysed the impact of the length factor on the retrieval effectiveness and its impact on the other factors with calculating their correlation coefficients. Therefore, we chose a set of ten terms at random from each collection. We computed the correlation coefficients between different factors (term frequency, document length and importance degree) in the documents that contain these terms. Table 5 shows some characteristics of ten chosen terms and the computed correlation coefficients for two collections. The following notations are used in Table 5.

- N-Doc: number of documents containing the chosen term
- R1: correlation coefficient between term frequency $tf$ and document length $|d|$
- R2: correlation coefficient between term frequency $tf$ and importance degree $d°(d,t)$
- R3: correlation coefficient between document length $|d|$ and importance degree $d°(d,t)$

Looking at Table 5, we notice that there is not high correlation between $tf$ and document length factors. The maximum correlation coefficient between $tf$ and document length factors is 0.24 for GOV1collection and 0.17 for WT10G collection. This means that the relationship between two factors is weak. Afterwards, we verified the correlation coefficient between $tf$ and $d°(d,t)$ which is presented by R2. The small values of R2 (between -0.11 and -0.27 for GOV1 collection; between -0.03 and -0.13 for WT10G collection) show a low correlation between $tf$ and $d°(d,t)$. Consequently, the high frequency of a term is not a good reason to estimate that this term is located in a long document. Also, the high value of $tf$ cannot present a high importance degree of term. Indeed, using document length factor for term frequency normalization penalizes the term weights of a long document in according with its length. But, the retrieval chances of small documents containing the low frequency terms will be increased.

Next, we verified the correlation between document length and importance degree of term in the documents containing ten chosen terms. The R3 values present this correlation. These values show that the correlation between document length and importance degree of term is higher than the correlation between document length and term frequency. Therefore, the influence of $d°(d,t)$ can be verified for discrimination the documents' terms.

**Table 5.** Correlation coefficients between various factors in the documents containing the chosen terms

| GOV1 | | | | | WT10G | | | | |
|------|------|------|------|---|-------|-------|------|------|------|
| Term | N-Doc | R1 | R2 | R3 | Term | N-Doc | R1 | R2 | R3 |
| Bilingu | 2418 | 0.1876 | -0.1766 | 0.6933 | Biograph | 4762 | 0.1746 | -0.0859 | 0.7817 |
| Boll | 740 | 0.0451 | -0.2746 | 0.7177 | Booker | 1143 | 0.1659 | -0.1261 | 0.6191 |
| Diabet | 8759 | 0.0948 | -0.1996 | 0.6204 | Camel | 2348 | 0.0123 | -0.1058 | 0.8940 |
| Eradic | 3081 | 0.1176 | -0.2406 | 0.7372 | Humid | 4573 | 0.1080 | -0.1119 | 0.6726 |
| Farmer | 13802 | 0.1841 | -0.2093 | 0.6223 | Invent | 9069 | 0.1456 | -0.0990 | 0.7407 |
| Golf | 4587 | 0.1220 | -0.1106 | 0.7454 | Pheromone | 239 | 0.0941 | -0.1220 | 0.5744 |
| Mother | 10801 | 0.1596 | -0.2376 | 0.6650 | Referenc | 8036 | 0.1437 | -0.0262 | 0.7647 |
| Resort | 5677 | 0.0699 | -0.2209 | 0.7909 | Scar | 8163 | 0.0651 | -0.0581 | 0.7732 |
| Tornado | 6460 | 0.2404 | -0.1689 | 0.5855 | Solar | 9440 | 0.1023 | -0.0955 | 0.5970 |
| Visa | 7345 | 0.1123 | -0.2014 | 0.6985 | Steroid | 2140 | 0.0314 | -0.0670 | 0.7452 |

In conclusion, we can say as the length of a document grows, the importance degrees of the terms within this document decrease (as noted in Section 3, the lower $d°(d,t)$ is, the higher the importance of term $t$ in document $d$ is and inversely).

In the other word, all of the terms within a long document are not good indicators for document content and we should consider more significant terms for retrieval. We suggest that it will be useful to determine how many of document terms are significant and they should be relied upon more than the other terms in the retrieval process. In the next section, we continue to verify this analysis using the EL factor.

## 5.3   Analysis of the Effective Level of Term Frequency (EL)

In this study, our experiments focused on verifying the effectiveness of our hypothesis described in Section 3, and specifying the characteristics of test collections. Based on the previous analyses, we used the importance degree of term as a novel factor for document length normalization. We applied the EL factor to the retrieval function 2 in two phases.

### 5.3.1   Phase One

We obtained the retrieval results for a set of 50 queries (the queries sets are presented in Section 4.2), with considering X% of the documents' terms as important terms and we didn't consider the other terms of documents for retrieval. We repeated this experiment ten times with various values of X (i.e. on each time the number of considered terms for retrieving is changed). The new term-document weighting function using EL factor is as follows:

$$w_{ij} = \frac{tf_{ij} * R(t_{ij}) * \left( h_1 + h_2 * \log\left(\frac{N}{n_i}\right) \right)}{h_3 + h_4 * \frac{dl_j}{\Delta l} + h_5 * tf_{ij}} \tag{3}$$

with:

- $d^\circ(d_j, t_i)$ : the importance degree of term $t_i$ within document $d_j$

- EL($d_j$) : X% of ranked terms based on term frequency in document $d_j$  (X: 5, 10, 20,…, 90)

- R ($t_{ij}$) :   if   $d^\circ(d_j, t_i)$ <= EL($d_j$)   then   R($t_{ij}$) = 1 $\tag{4}$

else    R($t_{ij}$) = 0.

The obtained results in this phase and that obtained with original function are listed in Table 6.

For GOV1 collection, the values of P@5, exact precision and average precision are higher than those obtained by function 2 when EL has been set to 10%. In addition, the average precisions obtained in all of the ten experiments (10 cases) are higher than initial average precision.

For WT10G collection the 10%, 20% and 30% of ranked terms achieve the higher values for P@5 compared to function 2 but the average precisions are decreased. Following these observations, we reviewed the characteristic of WT10G collection.

We noticed that there are more than 3,000,000 indexed terms in WT10G collection but the number of indexed terms in GOV1 collection is smaller. Moreover, in WT10G collection, the number of terms with $tf=1$ is more than that is in GOV1 collection.

To verify the general applicability of effective level of term frequency (EL factor), we tested it again using a different scheme of the constraint 4.

**Table 6.** Precisions obtained with function 2 and function 3 (phase one)

| Retrieval Function | EL(%) | GOV1 | | | WT10G | | |
|---|---|---|---|---|---|---|---|
| | | P@5 | Exact Precision | Average Precision | P@5 | Exact Precision | Average Precision |
| Initial Function (2) | ----- | 0.2286 | 0.1227 | 0.1770 | 0.2960 | 0.1006 | 0.2800 |
| Function 3 | 5 (%) | 0.2245 | 0.1282 | 0.1892 | 0.2840 | 0.0847 | 0.2476 |
| | 10 (%) | **0.2367** | **0.1358** | **0.1919** | **0.3040** | 0.0804 | 0.2550 |
| | 20 (%) | 0.2327 | 0.1353 | 0.1903 | **0.3120** | 0.0808 | 0.2695 |
| | 30 (%) | 0.2204 | 0.1295 | 0.1835 | **0.3120** | 0.0915 | 0.2793 |
| | 40 (%) | 0.2204 | 0.1228 | 0.1846 | 0.2800 | 0.0901 | 0.2727 |
| | 50 (%) | 0.2286 | 0.1191 | 0.1827 | 0.2840 | 0.0901 | 0.2758 |
| | 60 (%) | 0.2245 | 0.1187 | 0.1806 | 0.2840 | 0.0901 | 0.2764 |
| | 70 (%) | 0.2245 | 0.1187 | 0.1806 | 0.2840 | 0.0901 | 0.2761 |
| | 80 (%) | 0.2245 | 0.1187 | 0.1806 | 0.2840 | 0.0901 | 0.2758 |
| | 90 (%) | 0.2245 | 0.1187 | 0.1806 | 0.2840 | 0.0901 | 0.2758 |

### 5.3.2  Phase Two

The obtained results from phase one show that the EL factor with preceding constraint does not achieve important improvements on WT10G. After verifying the indexed terms in WT10G collection, we observed that the document terms are very heterogeneous and the majority of terms are low frequency. In consequence, most of the low frequency terms are important and they should be considered for retrieving. Hence, we changed the constraint 4 to the following constraint:

$$-R\ (t_{ij}):\quad if\ \ d^{\circ}\!\left(d_j, t_i\right) <= EL(d_j)\quad then\quad R(t_{ij}) = 2 \tag{5}$$
$$else\quad R(t_{ij}) = 1.$$

This constraint means that we consider all of the documents' terms for retrieving but certain terms (identified by EL) are weighted twice as much as other terms. Like as previous phase, we applied this constraint to the initial function ten times (In first time EL=5%, in second time EL=10% and etc.). After comparing the obtained precisions, we noticed that in the second case (i.e. when the weights of 10% of ranked terms are doubled), the values of P@5, exact precision and average precision are higher than the others. Moreover the obtained precisions are higher than the results of function 2. For instance, the improvement of the average precision is +17.63% for GOV1 collection.

The obtained results from second case and those obtained by function 2 are listed in Table 7 and their Recall-Precision curves are presented in Fig. 3. As a result, the EL factor with constraint 5 improves the retrieval results in a large and heterogeneous collection such as WT10G. Finally, higher precisions explain that our proposed

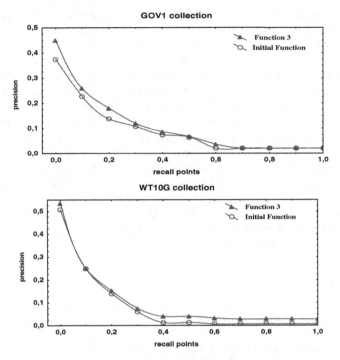

**Fig. 3.** Recall / Precision curves on GOV1 and WT10G (phase two, EL=10%)

**Table 7.** Precisions obtained with function 2 and function 3 (phase two, EL=10%)

| Retrieval Function | GOV1 | | | WT10G | | |
|---|---|---|---|---|---|---|
| | P@5 | Exact Precision | MAP | P@5 | Exact Precision | MAP |
| Initial Function (2) | 0.2286 | 0.1227 | 0.1770 | 0.2960 | 0.1006 | 0.2800 |
| Function 3 | 0.2653 | 0.1373 | 0.2082 | 0.3160 | 0.1126 | 0.2905 |
| **Improvement** | **+ 16.05 %** | **+ 11.90 %** | **+17.63 %** | **+ 6.76 %** | **+ 11.93 %** | **+3.75 %** |

technique performs well in two collections and we can say the EL factor is an effective factor for document lengths normalization.

## 6 Conclusion

The web information and data collections grow continuously and user's requests in information retrieval systems will be more special. Therefore, the new techniques and researches are necessary to deal with the explosive growth of information. It is well known that *tf-idf* weighting scheme is still one of the most plausible approaches to the text retrieval model. However, the heterogeneity becomes more important in large text collections and term discrimination problem is amplified in these collections.

In present paper we have described a new approach to document length normalization scheme called effective level of term frequency with identifying a novel factor (EL). By investigating a basic scheme of *tf-idf* weighting and measuring the effect of its items we proposed our new method, which can be used in large collections. We tested the new scheme using two large web collections and evaluated its retrieval performance. According to experimental results, we found that document length has a strong effect on the retrieval effectiveness. Furthermore, we applied our novel factor (EL) to Mercure IR system. In our approach, all document terms need not be used for ranking a document with respect to a query and it is not necessary to consider all of the documents containing the query terms. This method has shown its successful applicability and EL is a significant factor to retrieve relevant documents. In general this method increases the performance of the information retrieval systems and improves the query run-time, by considering just the important terms and identifying an appropriate data subset. In the future, we will verify the performance of EL factor by extended experiments and we will specify the optimal conditions for utilizing this factor in terabyte data collections.

# References

1. G.Salton and M.J.McGill. Introduction to Modern Information Retrieval. McGraw-Hill, New York 1983.
2. van Rijsbergen, C. J. *Information retrieval.* Butterworths, 1979.
3. G. Salton and C. Buckley, *Term-Weighting Approaches in Automatic Text Retrieval,* Information Processing & Management, 24(5), pp. 513-523, 1988.
4. Luhn, H. P. *The Automatic Creation of Literature Abstracts.* IBM Journal of Research and Development 2 (2), p. 159-165 and 317, April 1958.
5. Ben He and Iadh Ounis. Term Frequency Normalisation Tuniong for BM25 and DFR Models. In Proceedings of the 27 th European Conference on Information Retrieval (ECIR 05).
6. S. Robertson, S. Walker, M. M. Beaulieu, M. Gatford and A. Payne. Okapi at trec-4. In NIST Special Publication 500-236: The Fourth Text Retrieval Conference (TREC-4), pages 73 - 96, 1995.
7. C. Buckley, A. Singhal, M. Mitra and G. Salton (1996). New retrieval approaches using SMART. In *Proceedings of TREC-4,* (pp. 25-48). Gaithersburg, MD: NIST Publication #500-236.
8. A. Singhal, J. Choi, D. Hindle, D.D. Lewis and F. Pereira (1999). AT&T at TREC-7. In *Proceedings of TREC-7,* (pp. 239-251). Gaithersburg, MD: NIST Publication #500-242.
9. A. Singhal, C. Buckley, and M. Mitra. Pivoted document length normalization. In *Proceedings of the 19th Annual International ACM SIGIR Conference on Researchand Development in Information Retrieval,* pages 21–29, 1996.
10. B. He and I. Ounis. A study of parameter tuning for  term  frequency normalization, in Proceedings of the twelfth international conference on Information and knowledge management, New Orleans, LA, USA, 2003.
11. Hui Fang, Tao Tao, ChengXiang Zhai. A formal study of information retrieval heuristics. SIGIR 2004: 49-56.
12. M. Boughanem, C. Chrisment, C. Soulé-Dupuy. *Query Modification based on relevance back-propagation in adhoc environnement.* In : *Information Processing & Management,* Elsevier Science, V. 35, p. 121-139, avril 1999.

13. S. E. Robertson and S. Walker. Okapi/Keenbow at TREC- 8. In E M Voorhees and D K Harman, editors, The Eighth Text Retrieval Conference (TREC-8), pages 151- 162. Gaithersburg, MD: NIST, 2000. NIST Special Publication 500-246.

14. N. Craswell and D. Hawking, 2002. Overview of the TREC-2002 Web Track. *NIST Special Publication SP 500-251: The 11 th Text Retrieval Conference (TREC'2002)*. Gaithersburg, Maryland, USA.

15. Bailey, P., Craswell, N., Hawking, D.: Engineering a multipurpose test collection for web retrieval experiments draft. In: Proceedings of the 24th annual international ACM SIGIR conference (2001).

16. A. Singhal, G. Salton, M. Mitra, and C. Buckley: 1996, 'Document length normalization'. Information Processing & Management 32, 619–633.

# Beyond the Web: Retrieval in Social Information Spaces

Sebastian Marius Kirsch, Melanie Gnasa, and Armin B. Cremers

Institute of Computer Science III, University of Bonn, Römerstrasse 164,
53117 Bonn, Germany
{kirschs, gnasa, abc}@cs.uni-bonn.de

**Abstract.** We research whether the inclusion of information about an information user's social environment and his position in the social network of his peers leads to an improval in search effectiveness.

Traditional information retrieval methods fail to address the fact that information production and consumption are social activities. We ameliorate this problem by extending the domain model of information retrieval to include social networks.

We describe a technique for information retrieval in such an enviroment and evaluate it in comparison to vector space retrieval.

## 1 Introduction

In the late 1990s, the field of information retrieval rose to meet new challenges posed by the ubiquitous nature of the world wide web: Information retrieval in an environment where individual documents are not characterized only by their content, but also by their relationship to other documents. By the means of hyperlinks, a web author can express associations with other authors' documents that may reside anywhere on the web. Successful techniques for this task are primarily characterized by their reliance on the spectral properties of the web graph. Prime examples are the PageRank algorithm [1] and the HITS [2] algorithm, both of which represent first-order approximations of matrices derived from the web graph: The adjacency matrix in the case of PageRank, and the bibliographic and co-citation coupling matrices in the case of HITS. At the core of both algorithms is an acknowledgement of the democratic and social nature of the web: A human author's act of including a hyperlink to another page is an act of social interaction. A hyperlink expresses an endorsement of the page that is linked to. The sum of all hyperlinks is used to determine the relative importance of all pages – as a sum of judgements made by humans. This idea revolutionized the the field of web retrieval and shaped the nature of web retrieval systems for years to come.

However, the nature of the web has changed since the inception of spectral retrieval techniques. Whereas previously, web pages were crafted as individual documents, nowadays many web pages amount to nothing more than user interfaces: interfaces to an underlying database, an underlying information space that is made accessible via the web. Many of these information spaces model social relationships between their participants in a much more direct manner than

M. Lalmas et al. (Eds.): ECIR 2006, LNCS 3936, pp. 84–95, 2006.
© Springer-Verlag Berlin Heidelberg 2006

one could glean from analyzing the surface hyperlink structure of the interface. A logical next step is directly analyzing the social structure of the information space. This social structure may then be used for the purpose of information retrieval. This paper presents an attempt to leverage social networks for information retrieval, in environments that do not follow the usual presumptions made in web retrieval.

The rest of this paper is structured as follows: Sect. 2 lists related work. Sect. 3 describes social software on the web. Sect. 4 gives an extended information retrieval models which includes social relations, and explains a retrieval technique based on this model. Sect. 5 presents the evaluation of this technique. Sect. 6 concludes the paper.

## 2   Related Work

*Google* was one of the first web search engines to incorporate analysis of the web graph into its ranking algorithms. The PageRank algorithm [1] was a novelty among search engines at the time and was quickly singled out among independent observers as the main factor for its success. The impact of PageRank on the quality of Google's search results is not known; as is common for a web search engine, the innards of its scoring algorithm are kept secret. Evidence for the importance of PageRank in web retrieval is still scarce: According to [3], only 11 of 74 submitted runs at the TREC-2004 'Web' track used PageRank, and only one of the top systems used it.

*ReferralWeb* [4, 5] is a system for mining social relations from the web and exploring social networks. The authors describe it as 'combining of social networks and collaborative filtering'; its focus is extracting a social network from web pages, finding experts for a topic and linking the searcher to the expert by a path in the social network. ReferralWeb differs from other social networking applications because it extracts social links from publicly available information on the web; it does not require the user to sign up with a service and explicitly name his colleagues and collaborators. A formal evaluation of ReferralWeb's effectiveness, as compared to other information retrieval systems, was not conducted to our knowledge.

I-SPY [6] is an experimental meta search engine developed at University College, Dublin, Ireland. I-SPY implements collaborative ranking, borrowing ideas from collaborative filtering: It aggregates relevance judgements from a community of people and uses them in later searches for the same keywords to boost pages which are known to be good. Users are required to join a specific community before executing a query; one user can only be part of one community at a time, requiring the user to change the community as the subject matter of his search changes. I-SPY does not facilitate the formation of a community. It does not use information about the social relations between its users, and does not facilitate the formation of such relations.

ISKODOR is a prototype system developed at University of Bonn aiming to combine three aspects of user-centred information retrieval: personalization, collaboration and socialization. These principles form three pillars of a new web search paradigm called 'congenial web search' [7]. The framework supports a common representation of documents, queries, and relationships, which form individual context information of a user's search interest. The prototype employs a peer-to-peer architecture in order to share explicit feedback with other users. The user's faith in the service is strengthened, as he himself controls which information is stored and disseminated about him. Whereas personalized and collaborative aspects are already implemented in the prototype, research presented in this paper forms the basis of the social aspect of the system.

## 3   Social Software and the Web

One of the earliest applications of computer networks were electronic mailing lists and discussion groups. Precursors of the internet, for example BITNET and Usenet, already supported interaction and discussion among groups of users. Interaction between a large number of users is supported on these system at a negligible cost. Recently, the focus of social software has shifted from dedicated platforms to the web; popular examples include the following:

*Wikis* are a form of collaborative authoring environment that is characterized by the fact that every user can add, edit, and delete content at will. The first wiki was WikiWikiWeb, launched by Ward Cunningham in 1995 as a supplement to the Portland Pattern Repository, a web site about software design patterns. A number of software packages and similar projects followed; the largest wiki is purported to be Wikipedia, an online encyclopedia that employs the wiki principles. The quality of published content varies wildly; some wikis contain nothing more than a few quickly written ideas, others, like Wikipedia, aim for publication-quality content.

*Blogs* are an internet phenomenon originating in the late 1990s: Websites that continually publish new articles on their front page, written by one individual or a group of people. Blog entries can be tied to their author; linking between entries is supported in the form of comments or so-called 'trackback links', in which the author of another blog refers in his entry to the original entry. Blogs can take many forms, for example personal blogs, topical blogs or corporate blogs. Another typical feature is the so-called 'blogroll': A list of other blogs the author reads regularly. This may be used to determine social links between authors, but it is not universally adopted.

*Social networking platforms* like Friendster, orkut or openBC are dedicated web applications for the formation of social networks. Users have the ability to name their friends among the users explicitly and advertise them on a special page. Finding paths between two users in the social network is often supported, as are group discussions.

We call these systems 'social information spaces' [8] or 'social software'. The social interactions between users of these systems are hidden beneath the web front-end in databases, and thus are not directly accessible to web search engines. The resulting social network can be seen as the 'deep structure of the web'. Efforts of the Semantic Web initiative [9] aim to provide this information in machine-readable form, for example with the Dublin Core standard [10] for document metadata or the 'Friend of a Friend' standard [11] for expressing the relations between individuals.

With the increasing use of social software, social ties and the structure of the social network become tractable. In such a setting, incorporation of social networks into information retrieval processes is a desirable feature.

# 4    Models and Techniques for Social Retrieval

Social information retrieval systems are distinguished from other types of IR systems by the incorporation of information about social networks and relationships into the information retrieval process. This feature necessitates an extended model for information retrieval, as well as new techniques that make use of social information.

## 4.1    Domain Model for Social IR

The traditional models for information retrieval concern themselves with documents, queries, and their relations to each other: A document is relevant to a query, a document references other documents, a query is similar to other queries. Likewise, social network analysis models individuals and their relations with each other. Information retrieval systems traditionally do not model individuals, neither in their role as users of the system, nor as authors of the retrieved documents, and social networks do not incorporate retrievable content.

Social IR combines the models of information retrieval and social networks with each other. By incorporating individuals into the model, we gain a greater insight into their role in the information retrieval and production process (Fig. 1). New associations between the entities become apparent: Individuals appear in their role as information producers or information consumers, queries relate to an individual's information needs, or describe a topic about which an individual possesses knowledge.

A social IR system is characterized by the presence of all three types of entities: documents, queries, and individuals. Most systems will only use a subset of the possible associations between the entities, depending on the domain of the system. Modeling the relations between individuals is mandatory for a social IR system; all other types of associations are optional, as long as all three entities have an association with at least one other.

This characterization of a social IR system raises the question of suitable domains for such a system. The world wide web in its current state is evidently not a suitable domain: It lacks reliable authorship information, as well as information about social relations between authors. The increasing use of machine-readable

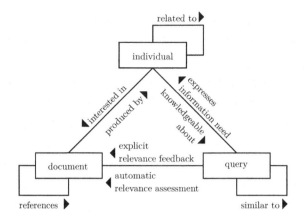

**Fig. 1.** A domain model for social information retrieval

metadata – for example in the aforementioned Dublin Core and 'Friend of a Friend' standards – gives hope that this will change in the long run. An attempt at mining social relations from the web is described in [4, 5].

Subsets of the web provide more suitable domains. The entirety of blog sites on the web (often called 'blogosphere') is one such domain: Blog entries can usually be associated with an author, and via comments or so-called trackback links, communication between blog authors can be ascertained, leading to a social network. Such information is usually not available in machine-readable format and has to be extracted using information extraction techniques. Some blogging services, for example LiveJournal [12], already provide it in machine-readable form. Wikis are also an environment that allows to ascertain authorship of a document, usually via the revision history. Interaction between users can be determined by co-authorship, or by discussions on dedicated talk pages; however, this information is often not portable between different wikis. Direct access to the underlying database often makes extraction of this information much easier.

For application of social IR to other domains, availability of the required information needs to be determined beforehand. Specialized techniques may have to be employed in order to extract it. We do however surmise that similar characteristics govern the structure of all social information spaces, and that similar techniques are applicable.

Traditional information retrieval techniques which are based solely on analysing document content, while very successful in many contexts, fail badly when the information need is underspecified, and when a large number of relevant documents exist. In this sense, social IR can be understood as a formalization of search techniques we commonly use to assess the quality of information – by looking at the author's standing in his community.

We use an associative network as the underlying representation. An associative network is a graph of information items, with unlabeled, weighted, directed or undirected edges ('associations') between nodes. In agreement with the domain model, we use three kinds of nodes: for individuals, documents, and queries.

**Definition 1.** *For a set of individuals $I$, a set of documents $D$, and a set of queries $Q$ the domain is represented by a weighted, directed graph $G = (V, E)$, where $V = I \uplus D \uplus Q$ and $E \subseteq V \times V$. A weight matrix $C \in \mathbb{R}_{\geq 0}^{|V| \times |V|}$ contains the weight of the edges. For edges between individuals $e \in I \times I$, the weight function expresses the strength of a social relationship between two individuals.*

We use this domain for retrieval of documents from keyword queries. This task is the most common task in information retrieval, which ensures comparability with other systems. Systems that store associations between users and queries, or between queries and documents, are mostly found in the experimental field of personalized and collaborative retrieval; they have not found their way into the mainstream of IR yet.

## 4.2 Techniques for Social IR

The domain model presented in the last section is able to accomodate many aspects of social information retrieval. We concentrate on retrieval of documents from keyword queries in an environment where authorship information is available.

A central idea is that the authority of an author can be inferred from his position in the social network, and that this authority measure can be applied to the documents he authored. Whether a document is relevant to a query can be determined using conventional IR techniques. A social IR system for this task is therefore composed of two parts: An authority measure for individuals in the social network, and a relevance measure for documents as regards queries. Both measures are combined to provide an improved ranking of documents.

In our experiments, we evaluate the use of PageRank as an authority measure for graphs. PageRank [1] is one of the most well-known algorithms for link analysis. In web retrieval, the PageRank algorithm is usually formulated based on a random surfer model: A user starts on a random web page and follows one outlink of this page at random and repeats this process on every page he reaches. Assuming that the link graph consists of a single strongly connected component (ie. there is a path from every page to every other page), the random surfer will eventually visit every page in the web graph. One may consider this sequence of pages as a Markov chain and compute the stationary probability of the random surfer being on a given page at any time. The stationary probability may be computed using linear algebra methods: Let $A$ be the adjacency matrix of the web graph $G$. Let $M$ be a row-normalized version of $A$, that is $(M)_{ij} = \frac{(A)_{ij}}{\sum_k (A)_{ik}}$. Then the PageRank vector $r$ is the maximal eigenvector of

$$\left( \frac{\epsilon}{|V|} \mathbf{1} + (1 - \epsilon)M \right)^{\top} ,$$

provided that $G$ is ergodic [13]. $\epsilon$ is the 'bias': The probability that the random surfer will teleport to a random page instead of following an outlink.

In order to get an idea of the application of PageRank to a social network, it is instructive to compute the PageRank scores for a well-known social network.

**Table 1.** PageRank scores for the coauthorship network of the SIGIR corpus. Scores are normalized and are computed with a teleportation probability of $\epsilon = 0.3$.

| rank name | PageRank |
|---|---|
| 1. Bruce W. Croft | 7.929 |
| 2. Clement T. Yu | 4.716 |
| 3. James P. Callan | 4.092 |
| 4. Norbert Fuhr | 3.731 |
| 5. Susan T. Dumais | 3.731 |
| 6. Mark Sanderson | 3.601 |
| 7. Nicholas J. Belkin | 3.518 |
| 8. Vijay V. Raghavan | 3.303 |
| 9. James Allan | 3.200 |
| 10. Jan O. Pedersen | 3.135 |

We computed PageRank scores for a coauthorship network extracted from 25 years of SIGIR proceedings (from 1978–2003); the ten highest-ranking authors are listed in Tab. 1.

In social IR, we apply the PageRank algorithm to the social network, ie. the graph $G[I]$. We compute a PageRank score $r_i$ for every node $i$ in the social network. We ignore the fact that several disconnected components may exist in the social network: Since they are small compared to the giant component, they can be expected to contribute little to the document set, which means that documents produced by individuals not in the giant component will only be relevant for very few of the expected queries. We use a bias of $\epsilon = 0.3$, further ameliorating the problem.

The score $r_i$ is then assigned to the documents:

$$\forall d \in D \forall i \in I : (i, d) \in E \Rightarrow r_d = r_i$$

If a document has more than one author, one has the option of either accumulating the PageRank scores ($r_d = \sum_{(i,d) \in E} r_i$), or of chosing either the maximum, minimum, or average of the PageRank scores of the authors. If the edges between nodes for individuals and document nodes are non-uniform in weight, one can also incorporate this weight information when transferring PageRank scores from authors to documents.

As a relevance measure for documents as regards a query, we employ a modified vector-space model. For a query $q$, the text retrieval component produces a set of relevant document $D_q \subset D$ as well as a score $\text{rel}(q, d)$ for every document. The inclusion of $r_d$ does not affect the result set $D_q$; it only influences the ranking of the documents, enabling the user to find relevant documents more quickly.

There are several models for combining PageRank with a text retrieval system. The simplest method is to sort the documents $d \in D_q$ by their PageRank score, and present those with the highest $r_d$ to the user first. However, this method only works when a high precision of the result set is ensured [1].

A very simple method of combining PageRank and relevance scores is

$$r_d \cdot \text{rel}(q, d) \ .$$

For our purposes, this method has the advantage of not having tunable parameters, and being invariant to normalization. We choose this method for our experiments.

## 5  Evaluation

We evaluate the techniques in a known-item retrieval setting and compare them to the baseline technique using the metrics average rank and inverse average inverse rank (IAIR). A known-item retrieval setting reduces the amount of manual labour required and allows a semi-automatic selection of items. By comparing with a baseline technique on the same index, we eliminate external factors that may account for differences in performance; this allows us to gauge the impact of social retrieval techniques on retrieval performance. We use a modified vector-space model as the baseline.

### 5.1  Setting

For evaluation, we use a mailing list archive from the years 2000–2005; the archive contains 44108 messages written from 1834 different email addresses. For evaluation, two different subsets of the corpus are used, one containing messages from 2000–2005, and one from 2004. We construct a full-text index from the message body, after removing quoted parts.

In addition to the full-text index, an associative network is constructed from the messages:

- An author node is constructed for each email address. No effort is made to reconcile different email addresses of one person.
- Every message is linked to its author, and every author is linked to his messages.
- Authors are linked to each other based on how often they respond to one another's messages.

The extracted social network displays characteristics typical for social networks: It exhibits a high degree of clustering and short average shortest path lengths, making it a 'small-world network' [14]. 70% of all authors are part of a giant weak component, and the degree distribution follows a power law.

### 5.2  Choosing Query Terms

For choosing appropriate query terms for known-item retrieval, the following strategy is used: From the subject lines of email messages, frequent bi- and trigrams are extracted. Subject lines are a good indicator of user information needs, as many threads on a mailing list start with a question, and the question is usually summarized in the subject. Bi- and trigrams are especially apt candidates, because 'real-world' queries have been found to average between two and three words [15].

Selecting $n$-grams by frequency alone is suboptimal, as some frequent $n$-grams correlate highly with the author of the containing messages. In order to remove these $n$-grams, the mutual information of the occurence of a specific $n$-gram in the subject line and the author of the messages is determined. A desirable $n$-gram for use as a query phrase therefore has a low mutual information with the author, and a high document frequency at the same time. We sort $n$-grams by mutual information divided by the frequency and use the $n$-grams with the lowest score for evaluation:

$$\text{score}(n-\text{gram}) = \frac{I(n-\text{gram}, \text{author})}{\text{df}(n-\text{gram})}$$

For each of the ten queries, one message is chosen as the 'known item', the objective of this search: Only messages from 2004 are considered as relevant, and only those messages are assessed that actually contain the sequence of query terms in the subject line. The criteria for relevance are selected to mimic a searcher looking for an item he has seen before.

The items to be retrieved are chosen by an expert in the subject matter, and by a complete novice. Using two different relevance assessments allows us to evaluate whether a social IR system caters more to novice users who desire more general results of high quality, but know next to nothing about the authors, or expert users who may have more specific interests, and can judge a person's authority within the community without assistance of the social IR system.

## 5.3   Results

Results of the evaluation are summarized in Tab. 2. For items chosen by an expert searcher, the combination of PageRank and the vector-space model performs better than the vector-space model alone for four of ten queries on the 2004 corpus; in one case, the result is a draw. While the average rank of the found documents increases for PageRank search, the inverse average inverse rank decreases: The average rank increases by $21.7\% \pm 2.4$, but the inverse average inverse rank decreases by $6.2\% \pm 0.5$. This means that some documents are found considerably later than with vector-space search, but for those documents in the earlier parts of the result list, PageRank combined with vector space performs better. This effect is even more pronounced on the 2000–2005 corpus, where the average rank increases by $69.9\% \pm 2.3$, but the inverse average inverse rank decreases by $24.6\% \pm 0.5$. On the 2000–2005 corpus, the combination performs better for six out of ten queries.

For the novice searcher, results are less pronounced. On the smaller corpus from 2004, both the average rank and inverse average inverse rank decrease (average rank by $13.1\% \pm 1.5$, IAIR by $1.5\% \pm 0.3$), whereas on the larger corpus, the average rank is unchanged, but the IAIR increases sharply (by $58.4\% \pm 0.4$.) On the smaller corpus, PageRank times vector space performs better for five out of ten queries, with one draw; for the larger corpus, it performs better for four out of ten queries, also with one draw.

**Table 2.** Known-item retrieval on mailing list data. Columns labelled 'VS' contain ranks from vector-space search, columns labelled 'PR×VS' contain ranks scored by pagerank times vector space score. Rows 'rank change' and 'IAIR change' contain the change compared to the baseline method 'VS' in percent.

| | VS | PR×VS | VS | PR×VS |
|---|---|---|---|---|
| method:<br>searcher: | expert | expert | novice | novice |
| *on messages from 2004:* | | | | |
| rank: | $14.75 \pm 0.25$ | $17.95 \pm 0.05$ | $17.5 \pm 0.3$ | $15.2 \pm 0$ |
| rank change [%]: | | $+21.7 \pm 2.4$ | | $-13.1 \pm 1.5$ |
| IAIR: | $7.548 \pm 0.032$ | $7.082 \pm 0.010$ | $4.670 \pm 0.013$ | $4.599 \pm 0$ |
| IAIR change [%]: | | $-6.2 \pm 0.5$ | | $-1.5 \pm 0.3$ |
| *on messages from 2000–2005:* | | | | |
| rank: | $24.4 \pm 0.3$ | $41.45 \pm 0.05$ | $39.35 \pm 0.35$ | $39.6 \pm 0$ |
| rank change [%]: | | $+69.9 \pm 2.3$ | | $+0.6 \pm 0.9$ |
| IAIR: | $8.787 \pm 0.040$ | $6.697 \pm 0.012$ | $4.962 \pm 0.013$ | $7.86 \pm 0$ |
| IAIR change [%]: | | $-24.6 \pm 0.5$ | | $+58.4 \pm 0.4$ |

This mirrors the results from [1], who report that 'the benefits of PageRank are the greatest for underspecified queries' and that 'for more specific searches where recall is more important, the traditional information retrieval scores and the PageRank should be combined.' The very nature of the known-item retrieval task places an emphasis on recall, since the objective is finding one *specific* document instead of just one of several that satisfy the information need.

## 6 Conclusion

We research how to integrate social networks in the information retrieval process and whether this integration leads to a performance improvement. Several applications of the internet are identified as social media, for example wikis, blogs, or mailing lists.

We propose a model for social information retrieval, which integrates the domains of social network analysis and information retrieval. Meaningful associations become apparent which are not part of the traditional models. We define social information retrieval as a retrieval process which includes a well-defined subset of the constituents of the social IR model.

We apply graph-based techniques to social networks, using them outside their traditional domains within information retrieval, namely web retrieval. We thereby extend the state of the art in graph-based retrieval techniques.

The commonly cited benefits of social software, for example improved communication among group members or emergence of communities, is important but intangible. We aim to derive tangible benefits from the application of social networks, namely improved retrieval performance – by providing retrieval techniques which are tailored to the emerging field of social software. We believe that these tangible benefits will accelerate the adoption of social software.

The main limitation of social IR follows from its domain model: it is only applicable where a social network is present in the domain, or can be derived. Furthermore, the quality of the social network is crucial. Limitations of other graph-based retrieval methods also apply to social information retrieval. Commonly cited limitations of PageRank are that its benefits are greatest for under-specified queries with many relevant results.

Evaluation of the prototype system was performed using non-standardized corpora and evaluation scenarios. For comparing the prototype system with current and future information retrieval systems, standardized corpora and evaluation scenarios must be constructed. Standardized scenarios also permit to tune the system for a particular retrieval task.

We chose not to base our evaluation on a web-based social information space, because of the associated problems of scale, and the difficulties in extracting suitable information. Instead, we use a mailing-list archive as an example of a social information space which lends itself readily to evaluation. The expected transferability of our results to other information spaces needs to be ascertained in further experiments.

An important next step is the integration of social IR in the ISKODOR prototype developed at University of Bonn, in order to implement the third pillar of the congenial web search paradigm [7].

We conclude that social network analysis is an important tool for information retrieval.

## Acknowledgements

We would like to thank Alan F. Smeaton for graciously providing a dataset containing 25 years of publications from the SIGIR conference proceedings, on which preliminary experiments were performed.

## References

1. Page, L., Brin, S., Motwani, R., Winograd, T.: The PageRank citation ranking: Bringing order to the Web. Technical report, Stanford University (1999)
2. Kleinberg, J.M.: Authoritative sources in a hyperlinked environment. Journal of the ACM **46** (1999) 604–632
3. Craswell, N., Hawking, D.: Overview of the TREC-2004 Web track. In Voorhees, E.M., Buckland, L.P., eds.: Proceedings of the Thirteenths Text REtrieval Conference (TREC 2004). Number 500-261 in NIST Special Publications, Gaithersburg, MD, U. S. National Institute of Standards and Technology (2004)
4. Kautz, H., Selman, B., Shah, M.: The hidden web. AI Magazine **18** (1997) 27–36
5. Kautz, H., Selman, B., Shah, M.: Referral web: combining social networks and collaborative filtering. Commununications of the ACM **40** (1997) 63–65
6. Freyne, J., Smyth, B.: An experiment in social search. In Nejdl, W., De Bra, P., eds.: Adaptive Hypermedia and Adaptive Web-Based Systems, Third International Conference, AH 2004, Eindhoven, The Netherlands, August 23-26, 2004, Proceedings. Volume 3137 of Lecture Notes in Computer Science. Springer (2004) 95–103

7. Gnasa, M., Won, M., Cremers, A.B.: Three pillars for congenial web search. Continuous evaluation for enhancing web search effectiveness. Journal of Web Engineering **3** (2004) 252–280
8. Lueg, C., Fisher, D., eds.: From Usenet to CoWebs. Interacting with social information spaces. Springer (2003)
9. Berners-Lee, T., Hendler, J., Lassila, O.: The semantic web. Scientific American **284** (2001) 34–43
10. Dublin Core Metadata Initiative: DCMI Metadata Terms. `http://dublincore.org/documents/dcmi-terms/` (2005)
11. Brickley, D., Miller, L.: FOAF vocabulary specification. `http://xmlns.com/foaf/0.1/` (2005)
12. Six Apart Ltd.: LiveJournal bot policy. `http://www.livejournal.com/bots/` (2006)
13. Flake, G.W., Tsioutsiouliklis, K., Zhukov, L.: Methods for mining web communities: Bibliometric, spectral, and flow. In Poulovassilis, A., Levene, M., eds.: Web Dynamics. Springer Verlag (2004) 45–68
14. Watts, D.J., Strogatz, S.H.: Collective dynamics of 'small-world' networks. Nature **393** (1998) 440–442
15. Silverstein, C., Marais, H., Henzinger, M., Moricz, M.: Analysis of a very large web search engine query log. SIGIR Forum **33** (1999) 6–12

# Evaluating Web Search Result Summaries

Shao Fen Liang, Siobhan Devlin, and John Tait

The University of Sunderland School of Computing and Technology,
Sunderland SR6 0DD, UK
{ShaoFen.Liang, Siobhan.Devlin, John.Tait}@sunderland.ac.uk

**Abstract.** The aim of our research is to produce and assess short summaries to aid users' relevance judgements, for example for a search engine result page. In this paper we present our new metric for measuring summary quality based on representativeness and judgeability, and compare the summary quality of our system to that of Google. We discuss the basis for constructing our evaluation methodology in contrast to previous relevant open evaluations, arguing that the elements which make up an evaluation methodology: the tasks, data and metrics, are interdependent and the way in which they are combined is critical to the effectiveness of the methodology. The paper discusses the relationship between these three factors as implemented in our own work, as well as in SUMMAC/MUC/DUC.

## 1 Introduction

Interest in the difficult topic of evaluation of automatic summarisation has been long standing [3]. The difficulties exist because evaluation procedures may depend on many variables such as intended purpose of the summaries, maximum acceptable length, type of texts being summarised and objective of the evaluation: in other words the data, task and metrics under consideration. Any changes in these variables can affect the outcome of the evaluation.

In this research, we have constructed a new methodology for evaluating web search result summaries. We consider that the manner of construction affects the whole evaluation process because of the interdependence of data, task and metrics. The metrics we employ are representativeness and judgeability, and we combine these measures to arrive at a third metric: summary quality. The related work of Berger and Mittal [2] states that query relevant summaries should include fidelity and relevance. It is important to note, however, that while our notion of representativeness equates to fidelity, we do not measure relevance but rather the user's ability to judge relevance or irrelevance.

Methods of evaluating automatic summarisation systems can be broadly classified into two types: intrinsic and extrinsic [1] [10]. Intrinsic evaluation assesses the quality of a summary *per se*, examining aspects such as coherence, readability, grammaticality, and fidelity. It does not consider the purpose of the system. Extrinsic evaluation, on the other hand, examines the quality of a system's output in relation to its purpose. So, for example if a summariser's purpose is to aid a user in making judgements about the summaries' usefulness then that is what is measured and this in turn can be the subject of intrinsic and extrinsic evaluation [12]. In the case of our system, our

M. Lalmas et al. (Eds.): ECIR 2006, LNCS 3936, pp. 96 – 106, 2006.
© Springer-Verlag Berlin Heidelberg 2006

representativeness score provides an intrinsic measurement of a summary's fidelity to an original source document, while the users' ability to judge relevance provides an extrinsic view of the system's fitness for purpose. Together these two factors determine our overarching extrinsic evaluation of the system's quality.

As it has proven especially difficult to find system based metrics for summarisation which genuinely reflect users' perceptions of search engine effectiveness, we decided to incorporate human judgement into our evaluation methodology and used Google to generate comparative baseline summaries. The paper examines how this decision affected the subsequent choice of data and metrics.

## 2   Relation to Earlier Work

The inter-relationship of the three factors pertinent to evaluation methodology construction: data, task and metrics, is key to our work and has also been apparent in recent related literature.

Of the early literature on automatic summarisation evaluation, the 1991 Message Understanding Conference (MUC-3) is important for its inclusion of evaluation methodology. The MUC-3 task was to extract data about terrorist incidents from newswire articles. These articles were analysed to create a standard template, which contained 18 slots for participant systems to fill in.  Answer keys were generated by humans for scoring purposes [4]. Finally, *recall, precision, overgeneration* and *fallout* were used as evaluation metrics [5].

In 1998, the U.S. government completed the first large-scale, developer-independent evaluation of automatic text summarisation systems: TIPSTER SUMMAC [13]. Three tasks were set in SUMMAC: 1. An ad hoc task to summarise a document as a topic description in for subjects to make relevance judgements; 2. A categorisation task: could subjects correctly categorise texts on the basis of the summary; 3. A question answering task which measured whether the summaries contained the answers to questions. News stories from newspaper sources were selected as data. The evaluation metrics of task 1 and 2 were based on *precision, recall* and *Fscore*. Task 3 was measured according to *Answer Recall Average* [9].

The Document Understanding Conference (DUC)[1] originated in 2001 and focuses on automatic summarisation. In 2004, the DUC competition had five tasks: 1. Very short single document summaries; 2. Short multi-document summaries; 3. Very short cross-lingual single-document summaries; 4. Short cross-lingual multi-document summaries, and 5. Short summaries focused by questions. Data used in Tasks 1 and 2 was English Newswire, in 3 and 4 Arabic document clusters and in 5 TREC English document clusters. These five tasks were evaluated using the ROUGE metric [8].

Most recent studies have focussed on news articles, perhaps driven by the available test data. MUC-3 restricted the data to terrorist stories from nine countries. The narrow range of documents allowed standard summary templates to be used, and the recall and precision metrics to be used to measure the match between system generated summaries and a human produced gold standard answer keys. SUMMAC, while still dealing only with news stories, dealt with more genres than MUC-3,

---

[1] Document   Understanding   Conference.   http://www-nlpir.nist.gov/projects/duc/guidelines/2004.html

making a template approach infeasible. Consequently using answer keys as the method of evaluation was not possible. The change in data collection led to SUMMAC setting different summarisation tasks and evaluation metrics. This varied approach was continued in DUC 2004 and DUC 2005.

In addition to the theoretical concerns behind this experimental methodology, namely the consideration of intrinsic and extrinsic motivation, we also took into account practical issues, so that rather than limiting the data to domain or genre independent data as did SUMMAC/MUC/DUC, we chose to use unrestricted English web pages. In this way we avoided the artificiality of the former tasks as well as word overlap issues. Of course the problem with using human based evaluations is that they are expensive in terms of time and sometimes in terms of the requirement for human expertise also. But while evaluations such as SUMMAC/MUC/DUC employ human expertise for producing the reference summaries, our methodology does not incur such an outlay as we simply require the human user to make a judgement.

## 3 Evaluation Method

The evaluation methodology was developed as part of a project to identify ways of improving internet search engine effectiveness from a searcher's point of view, and in particular to improve their ability to judge the relevance of pages by more effective presentation of search results, namely the presented page summaries. Our discussion focuses on the evaluation of our new summarisation algorithm, called Query Terms Order (QTO) [7], but the conclusions are generalisable.

We wished to answer two initial questions from our experimental evaluation: 1. How well do our summaries represent their corresponding page contents (*Representa-tiveness*)? 2. To what extent do the summaries help users judge the relevance of the original web page (*Judgeability*)? Having answered these questions we wished to determine a third aspect of the summaries: the *Quality*.

### 3.1 Data

The data for the task in hand was summaries of English language web documents. Summary length was set at a standardised 160 characters as this number is an average length derived from 1,000 Google returned summaries. We assume summary length is related to speed of relevance judgement but we are not investigating that here. We decided to work with TREC queries as they have standard descriptions of what constitutes a relevant page, which we hoped would help improve the constancy of inter subject relevance judgements [14]. Twelve TREC9[2] web track queries were selected and numbered Q1 to Q12. We arrived at this number because should the number be too small then we may not be able to get a significant result, while too large a figure might affect the quality of the test result. Twelve was deemed manageable in terms of how much a user could process without becoming tired of the tasks. The actual queries chosen were those from which both QTO and Google could produce useful summary data without producing error pages. Both Google and the QTO system produced 10 summaries from each of the twelve queries.

---

[2] Text TEtrieval Conference (TREC). http://trec.nist.gov/

## 3.2  Task

Having produced single short summaries for each page in the result set, our task was to evaluate them using the following criteria: the degree to which the summary represented its original page *(Representativeness)*, and the degree to which a user is able to judge a summary relevant to the input query *(Judgeability)*. Furthermore, we wished to derive a measure of *Summary Quality* by averaging *Representativeness* and *Judgeability*. We designed a user experiment to gather this data, and this is discussed below.

**Subjects.** To do a blind test between the baseline (ie. Google) and QTO systems, we required two groups of people, five in each, who fulfilled the following requirements. They should be:

- mature;
- native English speakers in order to reduce the difficulty of understanding summaries as much as possible;
- regular search engine users so that they all had an equal familiarity with search engine results;
- in a close range of English language proficiency (i.e. PhD students in a university computing school).

The sex of the participants was not considered relevant.

**Test Sheets.** The test was paper based in order to avoid possible confounding effects from the computer user interface. Two test sheets were required for the following tests:

- Representativeness

Subjects were presented with each summary on a separate single A4 sheet, followed by a five point table: 1 (very unrepresentative) to 5 (very representative). The actual web page was printed on each following sheet. Subjects were asked to read the summary, check the actual web page on the following sheet then select 1 to 5 from the table according to their judgement of the representativeness of the summary.

- Judgeability

Ten summaries were printed on a single sheet, and each of them was followed by three check boxes denoting *Relevant*, *Irrelevant* and *Unknown* for the subject's judgement. On the top of the sheet the related query and its narrative from TREC was printed. Subjects were asked to read each summary and check the related query then select a judgement of *Relevant*, *Irrelevant* or *Unknown* on the summary judgeability test sheets.

**Test Procedure.** The whole test was performed in four days: days 1 and 2 forming cycle 1 for Q1 to Q6, and days 3 and 4 forming cycle 2 for Q7 to Q12. Ten subjects were split equally into groups A and B. The *Representativeness* task was done in the first day, and the *Judgeability* task in the second day of each cycle. On each day, group A took the Google system and group B took QTO in the morning and they swapped their systems in the afternoon (see Table 1).

**Table 1.** Task timetable

|  | Morning | Afternoon |
|---|---|---|
| **Day 1 (Q1-Q6)**<br>( **Representativeness** ) | A -- Google<br>B -- QTO | A -- QTO<br>B -- Google |
| **Day 2 (Q1-Q6)**<br>( **Judgeability** ) | A -- Google<br>B -- QTO | A -- QTO<br>B -- Google |
| **Day 3 (Q7-Q12)**<br>( **Representativeness** ) | A -- Google<br>B -- QTO | A -- QTO<br>B -- Google |
| **Day 4 (Q7-Q12)**<br>( **Judgeability** ) | A -- Google<br>B -- QTO | A -- QTO<br>B -- Google |

Although each query in the Judgeability test took 5 minutes, the Representativeness test lasted 20 minutes. This was the justification for splitting the test into morning and afternoon sessions in order to ensure the maximum testing time did not exceed two hours. We used blind testing so that the subjects did not know which system they were assessing, and the test had no time restriction so that subjects did not feel pressured.

### 3.3 Metrics

The calculations used to determine the representativeness, judgeability and quality of the summaries are discussed below.

**Representativeness Score.** The formula (1) is used to calculate the summary representativeness score of each query and focuses on finding each subject's reaction to the summaries. The consistency of a subject while they are making the judgements is difficult to determine [6]. Therefore the variable of consistency is not taken into account in the formula.

$$\overline{R} = (\sum_{1}^{n} S_n) / 5n : \ 0 < \overline{R} \leq 1 \tag{1}$$

Where $\overline{R}$ represents the mean value among subjects' summary representativeness scores and is normalised to between 0 and 1, $S_n$ represents each summary's representativeness score determined by a subject, $n$ represents the number of retrieved links and the number 5 is used to normalise the result to between 0 to 1 because each representativeness score can be marked from 1 to 5.

**Judgeability Score.** The summary judgeability score is calculated according to the number of Unknown summaries. The more Unknown summaries the lower the summary judgeability score is.

$$J = \frac{Tj - Uj}{Tj} : 0 \leq J \leq 1 . \tag{2}$$

Where $J$ represents each subject's judgeability score, and the value of J is between 0 and 1, $Tj$ represents the total number of judgements (including *Relevant*, *Irrelevant* and *Unknown*) and $Uj$ represents the number of *Unknown* judgements.

**Summary Quality Score.** High representativeness or judgeability alone will not always mean positive searcher perception. We need to balance both scores from representativeness and judgeability in order to arrive a fair summary quality score. This is also the reason for setting both $\overline{R}$ and $J$ to between 0 and 1. Therefore, the summary's quality-SQ is averaged as formula (3) by the sum of formula (1) and formula (2).

$$SQ = (\overline{R} + J)/2. \tag{3}$$

## 4  Results

The *Representativeness* task results for both the QTO and Google systems are shown in Table 2. Each cell's entry represents a query's representativeness score, which is summed up from 10 subjects' representativeness judgements. Each subject's representativeness score is calculated according to Formula (1) which is not discussed in detail here.

Table 3 shows the judgements made by 10 subjects against each query. There is a total of 100 judgements from 10 subjects each being one of Relevant, Irrelevant and Unknown. Each judgement of Relevant, Irrelevant and Unknown is equally counted as *1*. For example, the 100 judgements of *Query1* from the 10 subjects are 43 of

**Table 2.** Representativeness task results

|        | QTO   | GOOGLE |
|--------|-------|--------|
| Q1     | 7.21  | 5.48   |
| Q2     | 8.07  | 5.77   |
| Q3     | 8.53  | 6.54   |
| Q4     | 5.52  | 4.28   |
| Q5     | 6.35  | 4.21   |
| Q6     | 6.39  | 5.09   |
| Q7     | 5.92  | 4.43   |
| Q8     | 5.73  | 4.56   |
| Q9     | 6.98  | 4.88   |
| Q10    | 7.00  | 5.11   |
| Q11    | 7.28  | 5.34   |
| Q12    | 8.12  | 5.37   |
| TOTAL  | 83.10 | 61.06  |

**Table 3.** Subjects' judgements of judgeability task

|       | QTO |     |     | GOOGLE |     |     |
|-------|-----|-----|-----|--------|-----|-----|
|       | R   | IR  | UN  | R      | IR  | UN  |
| Q1    | 43  | 32  | 25  | 19     | 36  | 45  |
| Q2    | 44  | 41  | 15  | 18     | 44  | 36  |
| Q3    | 64  | 23  | 13  | 35     | 23  | 42  |
| Q4    | 39  | 47  | 14  | 29     | 25  | 46  |
| Q5    | 36  | 40  | 24  | 24     | 24  | 52  |
| Q6    | 48  | 35  | 17  | 29     | 30  | 41  |
| Q7    | 50  | 27  | 23  | 22     | 23  | 55  |
| Q8    | 43  | 45  | 12  | 26     | 30  | 44  |
| Q9    | 50  | 35  | 15  | 29     | 28  | 43  |
| Q10   | 59  | 28  | 13  | 26     | 36  | 38  |
| Q11   | 72  | 22  | 8   | 29     | 25  | 46  |
| Q12   | 69  | 21  | 10  | 32     | 33  | 35  |
| TOTAL | 617 | 396 | 189 | 318    | 357 | 523 |

**Table 4.** Both systems' summary quality results

|      | QTO | | | GOOGLE | | |
|------|------------------|-------------------|--------------------|------------------|-------------------|--------------------|
|      | Represent-ativeness | Judge-ability | Summary Quality | Represent-ativeness | Judge-ability | Summary Quality |
| Q1   | 0.72 | 0.75 | 0.74 | 0.55 | 0.55 | 0.55 |
| Q2   | 0.81 | 0.85 | 0.83 | 0.58 | 0.62 | 0.60 |
| Q3   | 0.85 | 0.87 | 0.86 | 0.65 | 0.58 | 0.62 |
| Q4   | 0.55 | 0.86 | 0.71 | 0.43 | 0.54 | 0.48 |
| Q5   | 0.64 | 0.76 | 0.70 | 0.42 | 0.48 | 0.45 |
| Q6   | 0.64 | 0.83 | 0.73 | 0.51 | 0.59 | 0.55 |
| Q7   | 0.59 | 0.77 | 0.68 | 0.44 | 0.45 | 0.45 |
| Q8   | 0.57 | 0.88 | 0.73 | 0.46 | 0.56 | 0.51 |
| Q9   | 0.70 | 0.85 | 0.77 | 0.49 | 0.57 | 0.53 |
| Q10  | 0.70 | 0.87 | 0.79 | 0.51 | 0.62 | 0.57 |
| Q11  | 0.73 | 0.94 | 0.83 | 0.53 | 0.54 | 0.54 |
| Q12  | 0.81 | 0.90 | 0.86 | 0.54 | 0.65 | 0.59 |
| Mean | 0.69 | 0.84 | 0.77 | 0.51 | 0.56 | 0.54 |

Relevant, 32 of Irrelevant and 25 of Unknown for the QTO system.  QTO produced a total of 617, 396 and 189, Google produced 318, 357 and 523 Relevant, Irrelevant and Unknown judgements respectively.

Table 4 shows the summary quality results of the QTO and Google systems, where *R* represents the *Representativeness* score, *J* represents the *Judgeability* score and *SQ* represents the *Summary Quality* score. We used the data from Table 2 to convert the values in columns *J* by applying Formula (2). The values in *R* are also converted by using data in Table 1 and divided by 10 subjects. Finally, the values in *SQ* columns are derived from Formula (3). Both QTO's *Representativeness* and *Judgeability* scores are higher than Google's, therefore the *Summary Quality* score of the QTO system is demonstrably higher than Google's.

## 5  Discussion

Figures 1 and 2 provide a comparison between QTO and Google of representativeness and judgeability scores respectively. Clearly the curve for QTO is above the curve for Google in both figures, which means that QTO's summaries are more representative and more easily judged than Google's.

Figure 3 shows QTO and Google's summary quality.  Evidently QTO produced approximately 20% better summary quality than Google in our experiment. To determine if the result is significant we used a paired-samples t-test analysis [11] to compare representativeness, judgeability and summary quality respectively and obtained significant results in each case (df=11 p<0.05). We also determined that the correlation of the *Representativeness* results is .894, of the *Judgeability* results is.567, and of the *Summary Quality* is .880, therefore they are significant.  We suggest that

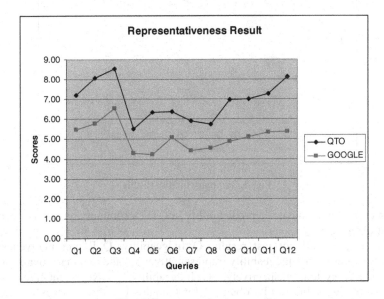

**Fig. 1.** Representativeness result

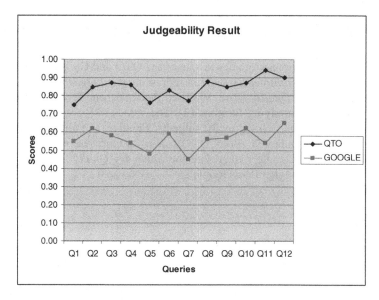

**Fig. 2.** Judgeability result

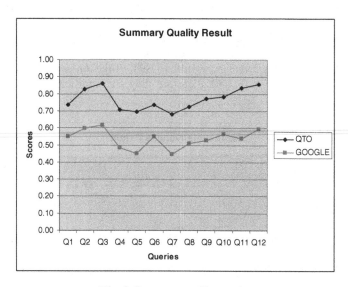

**Fig. 3.** Summary quality results

this high correlation indicates a predictability in QTO's summary quality performance over that of Google.

Figure 4 shows all our test results. Q_Judgeability, Q_Representativeness and Q_Quality represent the judgeability, representativeness and summary quality results of the QTO system respectively. G_Judgeability, G_Representativeness and G_Quality represent the results obtained for Google. The three curves of the QTO system have higher scores than those for Google.

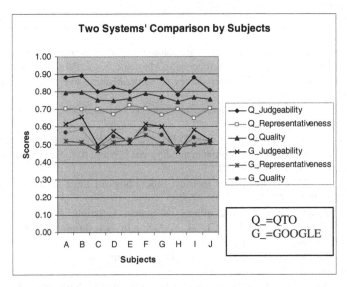

**Fig. 4.** Summary quality comparison by subjects

# 6  Conclusion

Automatic Summarisation evaluation is problematic due to the variety of factors that can be considered in any methodology and the interplay between these factors. In this paper we have discussed the factors that we believe influence the construction of an automatic summarisation evaluation methodology and referred to three salient works in the literature: namely SUMMAC, MUC and DUC. We have also presented our own evaluation methodology, which considers our end purpose i.e. why we are interested in producing summaries, the data we chose to use in response to the task, and the metric we have developed for evaluation purposes.

The experimental set up is the key point of this paper. Our evaluation methodology is not only task oriented but is also affected by end user considerations, namely: what is the system's role and who is it aimed at? The exponential rise in the numbers of people spending increasing amounts of time searching for information means that the problem ceases to be one just of the system efficiency and instead becomes one of enhancing the user experience. Therefore, real users' involvement is essential to ensure our summariser will help to reduce the people's search time. Also, by using real users in the evaluation procedure makes the test more realistic.   Although we realise that encapsulating human judgement is expensive and time consuming, users' perception cannot be ignored.

The fact that we chose real users for our extrinsic evaluation purpose influenced the data we used because we wished to avoid personal bias influencing the evaluation, hence we used TREC9 web track queries.  Moreover our metric then had to account for both representativeness and judgeability as independent measures and as a combined score of summary quality. Thus, while the order in which an evaluation methodology can be constructed is variable, it is not possible to ignore the impact that task, data and metric have on each other.

# References

1. Afantenos, S., Karkaletsis, V. and Stamatopoulos, P.: Summarization from medical documents: a survey. Artificial Intelligence in Medicine, 33, 2, February (2005), 157-177.
2. Berger, A. and Mittal, V.O.: Query-Relevant summarisation using FAQs. ACL (2000) 294-301.
3. Borko, H. and Bernier, C.L.: Abstracting concepts and methods. Academic Press, San Diego, Ca., USA (1975)
4. Chinchor, N. Hirschman, L. and Lewis, D.D.: Evaluating message understanding systems: An analysis of the third message understanding conference. Association for Computation Linguistics, 19, 3, (1993) 409-449.
5. Chinchor, N.: MUC-3 Evaluation metrics. Proceedings of third message understanding conference (1991) 17-24.
6. Harman, D. and Over P.: The effects of human variation in DUC summarisation evaluation. Proceedings of the ACL-04 Workshop in Text Summarization Branches Out (Barcelona, Spain, July, (2004) 10-17.
7. Liang, S.F., Devlin, S. and Tait, J.: Poster: Using query term order for result summarisation. SIGIR'05, Brazil (2005) 629-630.
8. Lin, C.Y.: ROUGE: a Package for Automatic Evaluation of Summaries. Proceedings of the Workshop on Text Summarization Branches Out, Barcelona, Spain, (2004) 25-26, July.
9. Mani, I., Firmin, T. and Sundheim, B.: The TIPSTER SUMMAC text summarisation evaluation. Proceedings of the ninth conference on European chapter of the Association ofr Computational Linguistics, Bergen, Norway (1999) 77-85.
10. Mani, I.: Automatic Summarization. John Benjamins, Amsterdam (2001).
11. Pagano, R.R.: Understanding statistics in the behavioural sciences. Wadsworth/Thomson Learning, USA (2001).
12. Sparck Jones, C. and Galliers, J.R.: Evaluating natural language processing systems: an analysis and review. Springer, New York (1996).
13. Tipster text phase III 18-month workshop notes, (1998), May, (1998) Fairfax, VA.
14. Voorhees, E.M.: Variations in Relevance Judgements and the Measurement of Retrieval Effectiveness. Information Processing & Management, 36, 5, (2000) 697-716, September.

# Measuring the Complexity of a Collection of Documents

Vishwa Vinay[1], Ingemar J. Cox[1], Natasa Milic-Frayling[2], and Ken Wood[2]

[1] Department of Computer Science, University College London, UK
v.vinay@cs.ucl.ac.uk, ingemar@ieee.org
[2] Microsoft Research Ltd, 7 J.J.Thomson Avenue, Cambridge, UK
{natasamf, krw}@microsoft.com

**Abstract.** Some text collections are more difficult to search or more complex to organize into topics than others. What properties of the data characterize this complexity? We use a variation of the Cox-Lewis statistic to measure the natural tendency of a set of points to fall into clusters. We compute this quantity for document collections that are represented as a set of term vectors. We consider applications of the Cox-Lewis statistic in three scenarios: comparing clusterability of different text collections using the same representation, comparing different representations of the same text collection, and predicting the query performance based on the clusterability of the query results set. Our experimental results show a correlation between the observed effectiveness and this statistic, thereby demonstrating the utility of such data analysis in text retrieval.

## 1   Introduction

In information retrieval (IR) it is often observed that the same set of design choices for data processing provides different effectiveness on different text collections. While some of the variation in performance can be attributed to user factors, there are algorithmic aspects that can be investigated in isolation from the user. Logically, we would expect the size of a data collection, the number of terms used in the representation of documents, the average number of relevant documents per query, the diversity amongst documents, and other related properties to affect retrieval performance. To the authors' knowledge, no systematic study has been conducted to evaluate the contribution of these factors to the effectiveness of retrieval techniques.

Ideally, we would like to be able to analyse a text collection in order to predict how well a particular algorithm will perform against it. While it appears reasonable to assume that the distribution of data points, i.e., document vectors, will affect performance, it has proven very difficult to identify a measure of this distribution that correlates with performance of a given algorithm. Amongst different properties that characterise the structure of a dataset, we concentrate on the clusterability of the set of points. This measure reflects the presence or absence of natural groups in the data and is closely tied with the choice of representation (the document feature set and feature weighting scheme) as well as the similarity metric used.

For measuring clusterability of text documents, a quantity based on the Cox-Lewis statistic is suggested (originally proposed in [1] and not related to one of the current authors). The use of this quantity is illustrated for three purposes. In Section 3 we

M. Lalmas et al. (Eds.): ECIR 2006, LNCS 3936, pp. 107–118, 2006.
© Springer-Verlag Berlin Heidelberg 2006

compare four different datasets and estimate their relative complexities. In Section 4 we use this statistic to compare two different representations of the same dataset, traditional tf-idf weighting and an entropy weighting described in [2]. We then apply Latent Semantic Indexing to these two representations and examine the retrieval performance before and after LSI by comparing the mean average precisions (MAP) of the corresponding retrieved sets. Experimental results show a correlation between the Cox-Lewis measure and the MAP results. Finally, in Section 5 we apply the Cox-Lewis statistic to predict the search performance for a given query based on the clusterability of the retrieved document set. We verify that the Cox-Lewis statistic of the query result set correlates with the average precision, calculated based on the query relevance judgments. While, in fact, our experiments focus on correlating the relative query rankings that result from the Cox-Lewis statistic and the average precision, respectively, the result has a much broader application. In particular, for any given query it enables us to predict, whether the query would be harder or easier than another query for which we may already have performance statistics based on the relevance judgments. We conclude with a summary of our results in Section 6.

## 2  Background

The main inspiration behind the work of this paper is provided in [3]. Section 4.6 of this book, entitled "Clustering tendency", examines the validity of the blind use of clustering algorithms on data. Most algorithms will create clusters regardless of the presence of *natural clusters* in the data. In order to make an informed decision as to whether or not to commit computing resources to data clustering, it is essential to estimate the predisposition of the data to coalesce into groups. Of course, a posterior analysis could be used to establish the quality of the clustering. However, it is interesting to ask whether the computational effort of applying the clustering algorithm would be justified at all. For that we would like to devise a measure of a data's clustering tendency. As we show in Sections 3, 4, and 5, such a measure exists and can be used with some success to predict the complexity of text collections and, explain the performance of methods that rely on structure in the data set.

Though it is difficult to define what it means for a data collection to be "easy" for processing, a uniformly distributed random set of points is likely to qualify as being difficult because of lack of structure that a suitably defined algorithm can take advantage of. An estimation of the uniformity of a set of points may therefore give an indication of "difficulty" for some tasks and this is the hypothesis we work on. We begin by reviewing a few measures aimed at characterizing the uniformity in the given data.

In application areas with very large dimensionalities, such as vector space representation of data in text retrieval, certain metrics may cause all data points to become almost equidistant from each other [4]. When the histogram of pairwise distances is plotted, a *complex* dataset is defined as one where there is a narrow and high peak with very light tails. Based on this intuition and some theoretical justification, Chavez and Navarro [5] propose the quantity $\rho = \mu^2 / 2\sigma^2$ as the intrinsic dimensionality of a set of points. Here, $\mu$ is the mean inter-point distance and $\sigma$ is the variance of the histogram of distances. When points are widely separated (which is one side-effect of increased dimensionality), the mean distance between points increases. Furthermore, since every point is approximately at the same distance from every other, the variance is low. Such a dataset, with large mean and low variance for inter-point distances, has a large intrinsic dimensionality and implies uniformity that may present difficulties for applications which rely upon structure in the data representations.

There are a few problems with the direct application of intrinsic dimensionality to text retrieval. The term-document matrix representing a text collection is very sparse, i.e., contains an extremely small fraction of non-zero entries since each document may contain only a small subset of terms from the term space of the collection. Due to the sparsity of individual document vectors, the mean inter-document similarity, as measured by the inner (dot) product of vectors, is almost always equal to 0, implying that most document vectors are orthogonal to each other in the high dimensional space. Moreover, the use of the inner product as a distance/similarity measure means that we are not in a metric space (the triangle inequality law does not necessarily hold). One way of converting the inner product similarity measure (with an upper bound of 1 for vectors normalized to be of unit length) into a distance function is by taking *1-simiarlity*. A similarity value that is almost always 0 would lead to an average distance close to 1 (see Table 1). A value of the intrinsic dimensionality calculated from such data would therefore not account for the possible structure in the set of points. Chavez and Navarro's measure might be more appropriate in situations where the data has lower sparsity and thus leads to non-zero values for inter-point distances.

Epter et al in [6] discuss the problem of measuring the clustering tendency of a given set of points. The authors suggest a visual method of examining the histogram of pairwise distances, the presence of multiple peaks in the histogram would indicate the presence of clusters. However, as we have just seen, this is likely to be ineffective in the text retrieval scenario because of minimal variance in inter-document similarity.

Another algorithm to measure the uniformity of a dataset is proposed in [7]. The authors begin with the null hypothesis that the given set of M points does not come from a multidimensional uniform distribution. N additional points are sampled from such a uniform distribution and are combined with the given set of M points. A minimal spanning tree (MST)[1] over the set of (M+N) points is then constructed. The number of links between the data points and the artificially generated points in the final tree is an estimate of the uniformity of the dataset – the larger the number of links, the more evidence to reject the null hypothesis. However, to build an MST requires the computation of a complete weighted graph whose nodes represent the points and the weights for the edges correspond to distances. In our case, the points would be documents, and the complexity of the algorithm would be $O(N^2)$, where N is the number of documents. This might be prohibitive for large collections.

Most relevant to our situation is [8]. The statistic recommended by the authors is a measurement of the density of the term-document matrix (i.e. the percentage of non-zero entries). The authors indicate that a higher density corresponds to highercluster-ability. While the sparsity/density is most definitely a factor, the exact nature of this dependence is not indicated. Further, the paper only deals with a binary representation and is therefore not suitable for comparing different representations of

---

[1] A minimal spanning tree can be defined as the sub-graph (more specifically, a sub-tree) of a given weighted undirected graph such that all the vertices are connected and the sum of the weights of the edges is the minimum.

documents. We wish to highlight the role of the *geometry* of the set of points, which would not only depend on the binary presence/absence of the features, but also on the weights associated with the features used in the representation.

Data analysis of this sort is usually performed as part of a larger application, most natural of which is clustering. In this paper, we look at query performance prediction – a problem that has recently received significant attention – and consider the influence of the clusterability of the retrieved set for a query in a given data representation. Properties of each query and its constituent terms are used to provide a prediction of the relative ranking amongst queries. The most successful results to date have been reported in [9] which defines a method of learning this prediction based on the agreement between the results to a query and each of its sub-queries.

We are interested in text retrieval, and converting a collection of documents to a set of points would involve the choice of a specific representation. Each such choice will lead to a dataset with different characteristics. The aim of our research is to define a property of these datasets that correlates with retrieval effectiveness, thereby providing us with a guideline for making the design choices.

## 3   Measuring the Clusterability of a Document Collection

In this section we define the statistic that we use to characterize the clusterability of data points and provide details of its calculation. The statistic is based on the Cox-Lewis measure, defined in [1]. Its multidimensional equivalent is given in [10]. For each of a number of randomly sampled points, we calculate the distance between the randomly generated point and its closest point within the dataset (called a 'marked point'). Then, we determine the distance between the marked point and its nearest neighbor within the given data. The ratio of these two distances, averaged over a number of samples, is the Cox-Lewis statistic.

A rigorous treatment of the calculation of this statistic requires the definition of a spatial point process which models the generation of the data and also provides a null

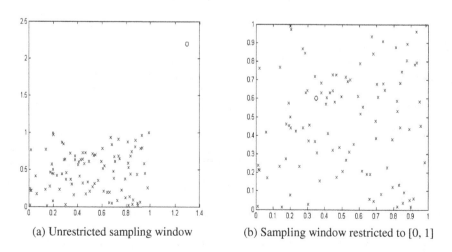

(a) Unrestricted sampling window          (b) Sampling window restricted to [0, 1]

**Fig. 1.** Effect of a wrongly chosen sampling window

*Calculate the minimum and maximum along each dimension*
*For every dimension j*
*{*

   *Calculate min_j representing the minimum along dimension j across all points*
   *Calculate max_j representing the maximum along dimension j across all points*
*}*


*Picking a random point*
*For a randomly chosen point i in the collection*
*{*

   *For all dimensions j*
   *{*

     *If (i, j) != 0*
       *Replace (i, j) by a randomly chosen value between max_j and min_j*
   *}*
*}*


*Calculating the statistic*
*Find the point p with similarity $s_{rand}$ that is closest to the random point*
*Find p's nearest neighbor with similarity $s_{nn}$ to p*
*Calculate $R = s_{rand} / s_{nn}$*
*Average R over a series of random points*

**Fig. 2.** Algorithm for the estimation procedure

hypothesis. Points can be sampled from this distribution to serve as pseudo data points. For the Cox-Lewis test, these points are used as the initial random points. The statistical significance of the value (after appropriate normalization) is then estimated. While generative models have been proposed for text documents [11], estimating the parameters of these models involves considerable computation. If we assume that two or more document collections share the same generative model, then it is possible to provide a basis for a relative comparison between the datasets that does not require normalization.

As has been noted in previous literature [3], the definition of a 'sampling window' from which a random point is generated is a critical factor for the Cox-Lewis statistic. Since we are trying to measure a property that is *internal* to the data, the generation of the random points needs to be done with care. In particular, we must sample data points from within a window of appropriate size. The effect of a wrongly chosen sampling window is illustrated in Figure 1.

In both cases, a set of 100 points were picked uniformly at random in the interval [0, 1] in 2 dimensions – these are illustrated as crosses in the figures and represent the dataset whose complexity we are attempting to measure. In case (a), the reference random point is chosen from an unrestricted sampling window (a circle in the top right hand corner) whereas in case (b), we impose a sampling window of [0, 1] in both dimensions. In the first figure, as seen from the reference point, the data would (wrongly) appear clustered. The presence of points all around the reference point in the second case would indicate randomness.

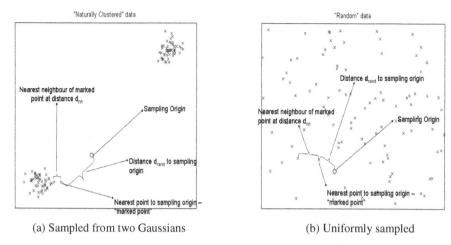

(a) Sampled from two Gaussians          (b) Uniformly sampled

**Fig. 3.** Behaviour of the Cox-Lewis statistic on clustered and random data

Given a document collection as a set of points in a vector space, we define the size of the sampling window by calculating the minimum and maximum for the vector component along each axis. This defines a hyper-rectangle. We pick a point by sampling values uniformly between the maximum and minimum along each dimension. In order to maintain the dependence on sparsity, we pick a point from within the dataset and replace its non-zero elements by randomly chosen values as described above. This provides all the details of our estimation algorithm which is described in Figure 2.

Figure 3 gives a visual illustration of the intuition behind this method. Figure (a) shows 50 points sampled from each of two Gaussians and figure (b) shows 100 points sampled from a uniform distribution. When the data contains inherent clusters, the distance $d_{rand}$ between the randomly sampled point and its closest neighbor in the dataset is likely to be much larger than the distance $d_{nn}$ between the marked point and its nearest neighbor. In other words, on average the similarity $s_{rand}$ is much smaller than $s_{nn}$, leading to a small ratio for $s_{rand}/s_{nn}$. On the other hand, data with no structure will have a larger average ratio $s_{rand}/s_{nn}$ and thus a larger Cox-Lewis statistic.

In our experiments we examine document sets using the vector space representation and retrieval (VSM). For calculating the Cox-Lewis statistics we define the multidimensional sampling window as above. Similar analysis can be performed using other IR models. For example, in the language model, the sampling origin could be obtained from the language model of the collection and the randomness statistic can be calculated by the use of an appropriate similarity metric.

Rather than provide an interpretation of the absolute value of the Cox-Lewis statistic for a given dataset, we use it as a basis for comparison of two or more datasets. The details of the experiments are provided in the following sections. As an illustration, we show in Table 1, the modified Cox-Lewis statistic and the intrinsic dimensionality statistics for four standard IR collections. These are the Financial Times collection (FT), the Congressional Record files (CR), the set of documents from the Foreign Broadcast Information Service (FB) and the Los Angeles Times material (LA) – all subsets of TREC disks 4 & 5.

All four datasets were indexed using the set of terms obtained after the removal of standard stopwords and application of the Porter stemmer and applying the tf-idf termweighting. The distance $d_{ij}$ between two documents i and j was calculated as 1-similarity, the dot product of unit document vectors being the similarity measure. The values for the Cox-Lewis statistic and the intrinsic dimensionality were both calculated from a random sample of 10% of documents in each dataset.

**Table 1.** Characteristics of the four IR collections considered

| | Number of documents | Number of unique terms (dimensionality) | Mean inter-document distance $(\mu)$ | Variance of pairwise distance computations $(\sigma^2)$ | Intrinsic Dimensionality $\rho = \mu^2 / 2\sigma^2$ | Cox-Lewis Statistic |
|---|---|---|---|---|---|---|
| FB | 130471 | 231574 | 0.999966 | 0.000008 | 61498.01 | 0.90789 |
| CR | 27922 | 166718 | 0.999869 | 0.000053 | 9387.21 | 3.91217 |
| FT | 210158 | 223468 | 0.999968 | 0.000007 | 75167.38 | 1.21419 |
| LA | 131896 | 187425 | 0.999978 | 0.000005 | 95537.22 | 1.29629 |

From Table 1 one observes the characteristics of the obtained data distributions in terms of the Cox-Lewis and intrinsic dimensionality. Columns 4 through 6 provide the mean, variance and intrinsic dimensionality as defined by Chavez and Navarro [5]. Based on this statistic, the four datasets are arranged in the order CR < FB < FT < LA in terms of increasing complexity as defined in [5]. However, as we can see from Columns 4 and 5, most documents are at a uniform distance of close to 1 from each other.

The Cox-Lewis statistic provides information about the clusterability of the data representations and clearly singles out the CR database as being more uniform in data distribution, with the value 3.9. We note that this coincides with the experimental evidence in TREC that CR data set has been most challenging for the retrieval systems from the retrieval performance point of view.

In our objective to find the means for characterizing clusterability of data sets, we aim at computationally efficient methods. The method should aid and supplement current practices, such as clustering, and thus be simpler than the most basic clustering algorithms themselves. Adopting a method that requires more sophisticated and involved calculations would therefore counter our aims. Positive results for our elementary procedure lend encouragement towards the use of such methods.

# 4   Studying the Effect of Representation on the Effectiveness of LSI

Given a text collection, there are many ways of converting it to its digital form depending on the choice of the retrieval model (e.g. vector space model, probabilistic model, language modeling, etc). Within the same model, there could be differences based on design choices, e.g. constants in the Okapi weighting scheme, the smoothing method in the language model, etc. Further, the choice of a similarity metric dictates the inter-document relationships. In this section, we consider the vector space model and examine the effect of the choice of weighting scheme (referred to here as "representation") on the success of Latent Semantic Indexing.

Latent Semantic Indexing (LSI) is a technique based in linear algebra that uses a low rank approximation of the original term-document matrix [12]. This is done by taking the Single Value Decomposition (SVD) of the matrix, which allows the arrangement of the space to reflect the major associative patterns in the data, and ignore the smaller, less important influences.

Though the success of LSI in text retrieval is unquestionable, the reasons for its improved performance have not been properly understood. Papadimitriou et al make an attempt towards this end by proving a theorem which is a weak form of the following logical statement - "LSI performs well if the corpus is a reasonably focused collection of meaningfully correlated documents" [13]. Amongst two representations of a given corpus, we would therefore expect LSI to perform better with the representation that better encapsulates the *meaningful correlations* between the documents. Since LSI can be seen as an unsupervised clustering algorithm, we hypothesize that the correlation amongst the documents in a corpus can be equated to the clustering tendency of this collection and that LSI would perform better using the representation that has a larger presence of natural groupings.

In [2], Dumais describes the following weighting scheme for use with LSI. The term j in document i was given the weight

$$w_{ij} = (t_{ij} + 1) * (1 - e_j)$$

where

$$e_j = 1 - \sum_{d=1}^{N} \frac{p_{jd} \log(p_{jd})}{\log(N)}$$

$$p_{jd} = \frac{t_{ij}}{g_j}$$

$g_j$ being the global frequency of term j, $t_{ij}$ the frequency of term j in document i and N is the number of documents in the collection. This weighting is referred to as "entropy" here. For comparison purposes, we consider a standard variant of the traditional tf-idf weighting given by:

$$w_{ij} = (t_{ij} / l_i) * \log(N / g_j)$$

where $t_{ij}$, $g_j$ and N are as before and $l_i$ is the length of document i. The documents are then normalized for length.

## 4.1 Experiments

We compare the two representations for two datasets – the CRAN and the MED collections – to estimate the potential benefits of LSI on the retrieval effectiveness. Each dataset comes with a set of queries which were issued against the set of documents before and after reduction by LSI (the dimensionality of the reduced space was 300). The dot product was used for scoring the documents with respect to the query. The mean average precision (MAP) was calculated in each case, the percentage change in the MAP gives us the improvement due to LSI. The results are provided in the following table.

**Table 2.** Comparing representations and their effect on LSI performance

| | Number of documents | Number of terms | Cox-Lewis Statistic | | % increase in MAP after LSI | |
|---|---|---|---|---|---|---|
| | | | tf-idf | entropy | tf-idf | entropy |
| CRAN | 1400 | 7234 | 1.112 | 0.668 | -1.47 | 41.36 |
| MED | 1033 | 10178 | 0.916 | 0.735 | -2.95 | 14.19 |

The last two columns of Table 2 indicate the improvement (degradation) in performance of using LSI given the two representations, tf-idf and entropy. We see that for the tf-idf case, the retrieval performance as measured by MAP actually degrades when LSI is applied. In contrast, there is a significant performance improvement when LSI is applied to the entropy representation. Interestingly, we observed that for both the datasets, the entropy representation has a lower value for the Cox-Lewis statistic (i.e. higher clustering tendency) than the corresponding value for the tf-idf scheme. This is in accordance with our intuition that the success of LSI is dependant on the choice of a representation that is more *clusterable*.

## 5  Predicting Query Performance

The task of any IR system is to satisfy a user's information need, as expressed in the form of a query, by providing a list of possible answers. It is almost inevitable that there will be queries which are difficult to answer by the system. Identifying such queries is extremely important in order to ensure adequate performance levels across queries. *Difficult queries* may need to be handled with extra care. The first task, however, is characterizing such queries before presenting the results to the user.

TREC has recognized the issue of 'difficult' queries and in 2003 established the Robust Track. A subset of older TREC queries and some new ones were used as the set of topics for this task. 50 queries from TREC 6-8 were chosen based on the fact that they had low average precision across participants but also had outliers in the form of participants who did perform well on this topic. This made the definition of the difficulty level of these queries dependant on the performance of systems of earlier years.

In this section, we demonstrate how the Cox-Lewis statistic can be used to characterize the 'difficulty' of the query by analyzing the clusterability of the query result set. We show a high correlation between the Cox-Lewis statistics and the average precision performance of the query.

We indexed TREC disks 4 & 5 by eliminating stopwords, applying Porter stemming, and using the tf-idf weighting scheme. For topics 301-450 and 601-700 we retrieved 100 top ranked documents using the inner dot product and calculated the average (non-interpolated) precision for each query based on the available relevance judgments.

From [14], we adopt the notion of the query-dependant extension to the dot-product to calculate the Cox-Lewis statistics for each query result set. It is the measure used to determine the closest point to the sampling origin and identify the nearest neighbor of this marked point. Amongst the alternatives suggested by Tombros and van Rijsbergen [14], we used "M1" where the final similarity between two documents is a product of their inner product and the query-dependant component:

$$Sim(d_i, d_j \mid q) = \frac{\sum_{k=1}^{N} d_{ik} d_{jk}}{\sqrt{\sum_{k=1}^{N} d_{ik}^2 \sum_{k=1}^{N} d_{jk}^2}} * \frac{\sum_{k=1}^{N} c_k q_k}{\sqrt{\sum_{k=1}^{N} c_k^2 \sum_{k=1}^{N} q_k^2}}$$

where $d_i$ and $d_j$ are the two documents, $q$ is the query and $c$ is the vector of terms common to both $d_i$ and $d_j$ with weights $c_k$ being the average of $d_{ik}$ and $d_{jk}$. We now associate the retrieved set of each query with a value of the Cox-Lewis statistic.

According to the cluster hypothesis [15], documents that are relevant to a given query are likely to be similar to each other. By evaluating the clustering tendency of a query result set, we measure the degree of randomness in the retrieved set. We rank the query result sets based on the Cox-Lewis statistic – the lower the value of the statistic, the larger the tendency for this set of results to cluster. We expect that queries whose result sets are more clusterable are those for which the retrieval system performed well, according to the user relevance judgment and the corresponding average precision. We compare this predicted ranking of queries with the ranking based on the corresponding average precision.

## 5.1 Experiments

Ordering based on the Cox-Lewis statistic provides us with a prediction of the retrieval performance over the given set of queries. The Kendall $\tau$ coefficient between this and the actual ranking of queries based on the average precision was found to be 0.349. If we use a simple dot product rather than query-specific dot product for Cox-Lewis calculation, the Kendall $\tau$ coefficient is slightly lower at 0.324.

As discussed in [16], the value of the Kendall $\tau$ metric alone is not sufficient. We measure the change in the MAP scores while eliminating successively increasing numbers of poorly performing topics. First, we take the predicted ranking of query performance and calculate the MAP over the whole set of topics. We then drop the topic which we expect to have performed worst, i.e., the topic with the largest Cox-Lewis statistic over the top 100 ranked documents, and calculate the MAP for the set of remaining topics. It should be expected that the MAP after removing the topic with the least average precision would be slightly higher than the MAP of the entire set. This procedure is continued by iteratively removing more and more queries. The procedure is repeated to generate a second curve, this time considering the actual ranking. The difference between the two curves (of changing MAP) that result from removing the worst performing topic at each step, provides information about the utility of the performance predicting method. As can be seen from figure 4, the two curves follow each other closely, indicating that the Cox-Lewis statistic was effective in distinguishing the poorly performing queries from the well performing ones. The value of the correlation coefficient also compares favorably to all but one other query difficulty prediction method found in the literature [9].

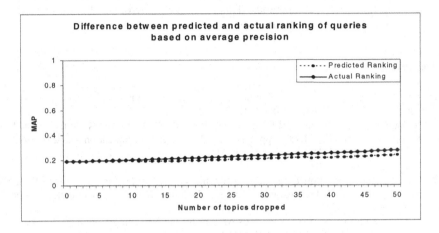

**Fig. 4.** Using the Cox-Lewis statistic to predict query performance using the Query-sensitive similarity measure. The two curves in the figure follow each other closely.

## 6  Conclusions

In this paper, we illustrated the need and the benefit of measuring the clustering tendency in a given set of points, as higher degrees of randomness in data typically implies a higher complexity from the processing point of view. We proposed the use of a statistic based on the Cox-Lewis measure to estimate the clustering tendency of a given data set. We used this statistic to compare four different subsets of the TREC collection, each of varying size and dimensionality. We concluded that the set of documents comprising the Congressional Record files would be most irresponsive to statistical algorithms due to its lower clusterability.

We use the same method to compare the effect of two distinct data representation schemes of the same data set on the retrieval performance, facilitated by LSI. The data representation that uses the entropy-based term weighting was found to have a lower complexity, i.e., it is characterized by a presence of more natural groupings than the tf-idf based representation. This was substantiated by the comparatively better retrieval performance when LSI was applied to the representation with the entropy-based weighting scheme.

Lastly, we addressed the question of predicting query performance. We showed that the clusterability of the top 100 results of a set of TREC topics is a good indicator of the query performance. More precisely, a relatively lower clustering tendency for the retrieved set indicates a query whose retrieval was ineffective. We found that the Cox-Lewis statistic performed favorably when predicting the ranking of the queries that results from their respective average precision measures.

Though the Cox-Lewis statistic proved useful, there are many open questions about the relationship between the complexity of the data representation and various other data properties, such as the number of data points (documents), the number of dimensions (terms), the degree of sparsity, etc. Understanding the exact nature of possible dependencies between the complexity and these factors would lead to better practices and more effective methods. This objective is therefore of great importance and will be the subject of our future work.

# References

[1] T.F. Cox and T. Lewis, "A conditional distance ratio method for analyzing spatial patterns", Biometrika 63, pp. 483-491, 1976
[2] S. Dumais, "LSI Meets TREC: A Status Report", In Proceedings of the First Text Retrieval Conference (TREC) , pp. 137--152, NIST Special Publication 500-207, 1993
[3] A.K. Jain and R.C. Dubes, "Algorithms for Clustering Data", Prentice-Hall Advanced Reference Series, 1988
[4] C.C. Aggarwal, A. Hinneburg and D.A. Keim, "On the Surprising Behavior of Distance Metrics in High Dimensional Space", Lecture Notes in Computer Science, Volume=1973, 2001
[5] E. Chavez and G. Navarro, "Towards Measuring the Searching Complexity of General Metric Spaces", Proceedings of ENC'01, 2001
[6] S. Epter, M. Krishnamoorthy, M. Zaki, "Clusterability Detection and Initial Seed Selection in Large Data Sets", Technical Report, Rensselaer Polytechnic Institute, 1999
[7] S.P. Smith and A.K. Jain, "Testing for Uniformity in Multidimensional Data", IEEE Transactions on Pattern Analysis and Machine Intelligence, Vol. PAMI-6, pp. 73-81, 1984
[8] A. El-Hamdouchi and P. Willett, "Techniques for the measurement of clustering tendency in document retrieval systems", Journal of Information Science, Volume 13 , Issue 6, pp 361-365, 1987
[9] E. Yom-Tov, S. Fine, D. Carmel, A. Darlow, "Learning to estimate query difficulty: including applications to missing content detection and distributed information retrieval." In Proceedings of the 28th annual international ACM SIGIR conference on Research and development in information retrieval. Salvador, Brazil, 2005
[10] E. Panayirci and R.C. Dubes, "A test for multidimensional clustering tendency", Pattern Recognition Volume 16, No. 4, pp. 433-444, 1983
[11] T. Minka and J. Lafferty, "Expectation-Propagation for the Generative Aspect Model", Proceedings of the 18th Conference on Uncertainty in Artificial Intelligence, pp. 352-359, 2002
[12] S. Deerwester, S.T. Dumais, T.K. Landauer, G.W. Furnas and R.A. Harshman, "Indexing by latent semantic analysis." Journal of the Society for Information Science, 41(6), pp. 391-407, 1990
[13] C.H. Papadimitriou, P. Raghavan, H. Tamaki, and S. Vempala, "Latent Semantic Indexing: A Probabilistic Analysis", In Proceedings of the ACM Conference on Principles of Database Systems (PODS), Seattle, 1998
[14] A. Tombros and C.J. van Rijsbergen, "Query-sensitive similarity measures for Information Retrieval", invited paper, Knowledge and Information Systems, 2004
[15] C.J. van Rijsbergen, "Information Retrieval", Butterworths, London, Second Edition, 1979
[16] E.M. Voorhees, "Overview of the TREC 2004 Robust Retrieval Track", Page 69, Proceedings of the 12th Text REtrieval Conference(TREC 2003), NIST Special Publication, 2003

# Sentence Retrieval with LSI and Topic Identification

David Parapar and Álvaro Barreiro

IR Lab, Department of Computer Science,
University of A Coruña, A Coruña, Spain
dparapar@udc.es, barreiro@udc.es

**Abstract.** This paper presents two sentence retrieval methods. We adopt the task definition done in the TREC Novelty Track: sentence retrieval consists in the extraction of the relevant sentences for a query from a set of relevant documents for that query. We have compared the performance of the Latent Semantic Indexing (LSI) retrieval model against the performance of a topic identification method, also based on Singular Value Decomposition (SVD) but with a different sentence selection method. We used the TREC Novelty Track collections from years 2002 and 2003 for the evaluation. The results of our experiments show that these techniques, particularly sentence retrieval based on topic identification, are valid alternative approaches to other more ad-hoc methods devised for this task.

## 1   Introduction and Motivation

In this work we understand the task of sentence retrieval in the way defined in the TREC Novelty Track. The Novelty Track was introduced for the first time in the TREC 2002 conference [1] and is composed of two main tasks. The first one is sentence retrieval: starting with a set of relevant documents for a query (topic in the TREC terminology), the system must extract from those documents the relevant sentences for that topic, removing the ones that do not contain significant information or that are related to different topics. The second task starts from the sentences retrieved in the first task or from the relevant sentences selected by human assessors. Taking in account this set, the system must retrieve only the novel sentences, i.e., sentences that contain new information with respect to the previous sentences in the set. In this paper we have focused only in the first task.

Among the applications of sentence retrieval we find query-biased text summarization and the presentation to the users of the most relevant sentences of the documents retrieved in a results list [2]. Furthermore, the novelty task would remove the redundant information in the extracted sentences. Another application could be the construction of question answering systems because query relevant sentences can be useful to obtain the user's query.

The research done for the Novelty Track can be divided in two groups. Some systems try to adapt classical document retrieval techniques to sentence retrieval with a different definition of the parameters of interest. For example,

M. Lalmas et al. (Eds.): ECIR 2006, LNCS 3936, pp. 119–130, 2006.
© Springer-Verlag Berlin Heidelberg 2006

the classical vector space model can be adapted with a new definition of term frequency, inverse document frequency and document length. On the contrary, some participants work with techniques specifically developed for related tasks like summarization or passage retrieval. Anyway, every retrieval model based on matching of query and sentence terms will have difficulties with the short length of sentences. For this reason most systems use pseudo-relevance feedback [3] and query and/or document expansion [4].

Despite of the research effort done, the effectiveness in the sentence retrieval task still can be improved. Our idea was to test Latent Semantic Indexing (LSI) because it had not been used before in this task and because it can lead to more general and less ad-hoc solutions and because only a small set of documents has to be analyzed in this task. Therefore, we expect effective and efficient solutions.

LSI [5, 6] is a retrieval model based on dimensionality reduction. An initial space of terms and documents is reduced to represent concepts instead of terms. With this transformation LSI claims to remove the noise produced for the variability in the use of terms, extracting the underlying semantic concepts in a document collection. Most retrieval models are based on the number of query and document matching terms with different weighting schemes. Therefore, for the sentence retrieval task, LSI can be appropriate because the query-sentence similarity measure is not obtained in the initial space of terms and sentences. In the TREC Novelty sentence retrieval task researchers are given a set of relevant documents for each query. This homogeneous set can facilitate the extraction of the latent semantic structure. LSI can be more effective than query expansion since this strategy introduces noise in the queries trying to increase term matching, and the expansion based on co-occurrence is going to be more difficult in the case of the sentences. Meanwhile LSI reduces the noise at the cost of a possible lost of information in the final reduced space. To achieve a good balance between noise filtering and information loss, the selection of the dimensions in the reduced space is crucial.

In this paper we also present another retrieval strategy based on topic identification. This strategy was devised starting from the Gong and Liu [7] summarization method. It uses Singular Value Decomposition (SVD) and topic identification for developing a generic summarization method for single documents. This process consists of two steps. First, the main topics of a document are identified from the SVD of the document text. Next, a sentence is selected for each main topic and added to the summary. In our case we need to produce a query-relevant set of sentences from a set of relevant documents for the query. Instead of identifying the main topics of a single document, we first identify the main topics of the query. In this last usage a topic is an aspect of the query and a query can be about several topics. Please note that in some sections we will use topic with the meaning of "TREC topic". Hereinafter the context is enough to distinguish between the two meanings of the word topic. The sentence selection process is also different. In the case of a generic summary of a single document, we intend to maximize the coverage of the document's main content by selecting one sentence for each main topic. On the other hand, to address the sentence

retrieval task, it is necessary to maximize the number of relevant sentences retrieved for each topic of the query. After the identification of the query topics,
we retrieve the set of relevant sentences for the topics.

We advance here that sentence retrieval based on topic identification outperforms the method based on LSI retrieval. In addition, it is competitive compared
with other more specific techniques.

The rest of the paper is organized as follows. In the next section we introduce
the LSI model and explain the alternative retrieval method proposed for sentence
retrieval. In section 3 the experimental setting is presented. In section 4 we show
and analyze the results. In section 5 different considerations and future research
lines are introduced. The paper ends with the conclusions section.

# 2   LSI and Topic Identification

## 2.1   LSI: Model

The LSI model [5, 6] is an extension of the the vector space model for information
retrieval based on a dimensionality reduction technique. LSI claims to capture
the latent semantic structure in the documents and represent them in function
of basic concepts and ideas instead of terms. This allows us to deal with the
polysemy and synonymy problems.

The first stage in LSI is the Singular Value Decomposition (SVD) in which
a matrix of terms by documents, obtained from the document collection, is
decomposed into three matrices and then truncated to a reduced space. In our
case we have a matrix A of terms by sentences (instead of documents) in which
the value of cell $ij$ is associated with the apparitions of term $i$ in sentence $j$
weighted with local and global weights. This matrix can be decomposed in the
following way:

$$A_{t \times s} = T_{t \times r} \Sigma_{r \times r} S_{r \times s}^t \qquad (1)$$

where,

   t: number of terms
   s: number of sentences
   r: rank of A
   T: matrix of left singular vectors
   S: matrix of right singular vectors
   $\Sigma$: diagonal matrix of singular values

The $\Sigma$ matrix is a diagonal matrix of singular values in decreasing order; the
singular values are the positive square roots of the eigenvalues of the matrix
$A \times A^t$, where $A^t$ is the transposed matrix of $A$. Each singular value represents
a dimension of the space, dimensions with higher singular values are more important in this space. The rows of the $T$ matrix are the term vectors and the
rows of the $S_{s \times r}$ are the sentence vectors. To avoid the noise in term usage and
to capture the latent structure in a document collection the SVD is truncated

to a reduced number of dimensions $k$. With this truncation, the $k$ higher singular values are kept with the correspondent dimensions in the $T_{t \times k}$ and $S_{s \times k}$ matrices:

$$\hat{A}_{t \times s} = T_{t \times k} \Sigma_{k \times k} S_{k \times s}^t \tag{2}$$

where $\hat{A}$ is the closest matrix of rank $k$ to $A$ in terms of $\| \cdot \|_2$ and $\| \cdot \|_F$ norms. In the sentence matrix $S_{s \times k}$ each sentence vector has $k$ components. The usual interpretation of this transformation is that each component now represents a concept extracted from some relationship between terms and sentences in the original space.

In this point it is worth to revisit the example given in one of the pioneer LSI works. In the example presented in [5], after a truncated SVD with $k = 2$ of an original space of 18 terms and 14 documents, it is clear that the documents pertaining to a certain topic are clustered above the x-axis which is associated with the first dimension of the final reduced space, while documents pertaining to another topic are clustered near the lower y-axis which is associated with the second dimension of the final reduced space.

## 2.2    Retrieval in LSI

Once we have this decomposition and truncation for an information retrieval system we must do the same transformation with the queries that arrive to the system. We need to project the queries to the same reduced space using the following formula:

$$\hat{q} = q^t T_{t \times k} \Sigma_{k \times k}^{-1} \tag{3}$$

With this transformation the query vector $\hat{q}$ is just like a pseudo-sentence vector that can be compared with the rows of $S_{s \times k}$ in a retrieval task. Actually, in order to make this comparison the rows of $S_{s \times k}$ and $\hat{q}$ are scaled multiplying them by $\Sigma$. Note that this scaling only produces a stretched version of the reduced space $S_{s \times k}$ giving more importance to the dimensions with higher singular values. Finally, query and sentences can be compared using the cosine or dot product. If the similarity measure is larger than a threshold $thr_{LSI}$ then the sentence is considered relevant.

## 2.3    Retrieval Based on Topic Identification

First we will give a brief description of the method and then we will provide a pseudo-code style description. Our intuition here is that a sentence contains a very low number of different concepts or topics, i.e., in most cases a sentence is only about one or two things. Considering that in the reduced space each dimension represents a concept, we can consider only a few dimensions of the sentence vector to determine its relevance. We considered that the most important topics in a query are those associated with the largest magnitude components, because they are the most discriminative in the space. So we take these dimensions as the representatives of the query and we select the sentences with the largest values for those dimensions.

In this method the query $\hat{q}$ and the sentences, rows of matrix $S_{s \times k}$, are not scaled with $\Sigma$ because this method is specifically devised for operating in the reduced space. The retrieval algorithm uses the $S_{s \times k}$ matrix and the projected query $\hat{q}$ as follows:

1. For a projected query $\hat{q} = (\hat{q}_1, \hat{q}_2, \ldots, \hat{q}_k)$ the $n$ components with the largest absolute values are chosen.
2. Let $\hat{q}_i$ be any of the selected components of $\hat{q}$ obtained in the previous step. Let $S_i = (s_{1i}, s_{2i}, \ldots, s_{si})$ be the column $i$ of matrix $S_{s \times k}$. Each element $s_{ji}$ represents the weight of the component $i$ in the sentence $j$ (row $j$ of $S_{s \times k}$). Let $thr_{TI}$ be a positive threshold.
   For each $\hat{q}_i$ selected in 1:
      For each j:1..s:
      If $\hat{q}_i$ and $s_{ji}$ are positive and $s_{ji} > thr_{TI}$ the sentence $j$ is selected.
      If $\hat{q}_i$ and $s_{ji}$ are negative and $|s_{ji}| > thr_{TI}$ the sentence $j$ is selected.
3. The union of sentences obtained in the previous step is returned.

Let us remark that in the inner loop of step 2 we only select those sentences that have components with values larger than the threshold and the same sign than the query component because we suppose that queries and sentences pertaining to a certain topic must be located in the same side of the axis associated to that dimension. It is possible to find an optimal number of retrieved sentences by changing the value of the threshold $thr_{TI}$ introduced in the algorithm.

Now we emphasize the differences with the algorithm exposed in [7] where the goal is to produce a generic summary of a document. First, in the algorithm presented here the goal is to obtain the set of relevant sentences to a query. Second, in [7] the first step obtains the singular values associated with the main concepts of a single document; in our algorithm the main concepts in the query are obtained in the first step. Third, in [7] for each important singular value, a sentence is selected trying to maximize the coverage of the document's main content; in the problem addressed in this paper we must cover the query topics but for each query topic we must retrieve not only a representative sentence but the set of relevant sentences.

The evaluation of the sentence retrieval task in the TREC Novelty track is set-based. The method for retrieval of sentences based on LSI described in section 2.1 produces a ranking. Therefore, it was necessary to define a similarity threshold to obtain a set. The method based on topic identification directly produces a set. For other tasks the algorithm based on topic identification could be modified to produce a ranking.

## 3   Experimental Settings

We used the collections of the TREC Novelty Track from years 2002 and 2003 for the evaluation of the two retrieval methods.

The 2002 collection consists of 49 topics selected from the ad-hoc task of TREC in the range from 300 to 450 [1]. For these topics a set of 25 relevant documents was provided. In fact, 25 is the upper limit, as for some topics the number of documents is lower. There are two relevance judgments for the relevant sentences in this track corresponding to the minimum and maximum assessor. The minimum assessor, the one with the lower number of relevant sentences, was taken as the official for this task. The average percentage of relevant sentences is very low, 2.54%.

The 2003 collection consists of 50 topics specifically created for the 2003 track [8]. Two kinds of topics were created: *events*, for news articles, and *opinions* for articles about controversial subjects. For each topic, 25 relevant documents were selected from the AQUAINT collection, composed of articles from New York Times News Service, Associated Press and Xinhua News Service. The authors of the topics, primary assessors, made the relevance judgments of their own topics and a secondary group of assessors provided a second set of judgments. The percentage of relevant sentences from the primary assessors, that was taken as the official for this task, was much higher than in 2002, 41.13%.

In both collections the sentences are previously identified in the documents and tagged separately to allow a quick processing of the documents. This separation is based in the points of the original text so the division in sentences is not part of the difficulties of the task.

We tested different stemmers; the best results were obtained with the Krovetz stemmer. The stop words were removed. All the experiments presented in the next section used the Krovetz stemmer and the same stop list.

In this task the relevant sentences only can be found in the set of 25 documents associated with each TREC topic. For this reason, the matrix $A$ of equation (1) was generated independently for each set of relevant documents associated with each TREC topic in both methods. This indexing scenario represents a real situation in which a standard IR system retrieves the top-ranked documents and these documents are analyzed to retrieve relevant sentences.

Retrieval was done with the programs provided by the LSI software package of Telcordia Technologies [9]. We used this software with the SVDLIBC [10] library to perform the SVD transformation.

The evaluation measures are the set-based precision, set-based recall, and the F measure for each topic and the average for the 50 topics. The metric taken as reference was the F measure given by the formula:

$$F = \frac{2 \times Precision \times Recall}{Precision + Recall} \tag{4}$$

This measure gives the same importance to precision and recall, so the goal of retrieval is a good trade-off between precision and recall.

## 4    Results

Different weighting schemes provided by the LSI software package of Telcordia were tested for local and global weights. For the local weights the best weight was the binary one. Anyway, if the log or raw term frequency option is used, the difference in the result obtained is small, since the information of the number of times a term appears in a sentence is usually not so important. The global weight *idf2*, which is the square of the logarithmic idf, also allows the best results in both methods and collections. For the LSI method the similarity measure chosen for the two collections was the dot product.

In figure 1 the best experiments for the 2002 collections with both methods are shown. For the 2002 collection the first method results were bad. The best results were obtained using 20 factors ($k = 20$) in the truncation of the SVD, although there are similar results with $k$ varying in the range from 15 to 25. With the dot product as the similarity measure we determined the value of the threshold $THR_{LSI}$ that produces the best F value. The higher F value was 0.06 with $THR_{LSI}$ in the range between 38 and 50. The F value is very low compared with the best runs submitted to the TREC track. Moreover, the groups participating in the track had only four topics for training while we used the full set of relevance judgments to adjust the used parameters. In fact, a random retrieval of sentences produces an F value of 0.04, so we can say that the LSI method is not able to work properly in this collection.

In the same collection the topic identification method improves substantially the performance. The best range for the number of factors is the same than in the LSI method, with the best value for $k = 15$. We used the same weighting scheme. The used threshold type is different: a minimun value for all of the components was fixed and only sentences with absolute values higher than that threshold were retrieved. The best results are obtained when the similarity threshold $THR_{TI}$ has a value of 0.05 and the parameter $n$ for the number of query components has a value of 1. In all experiments an increment in the number of query components produced a small decrement in the performance. The best F obtained was 0.141 which supposes a big improvement with respect to the LSI results. But these results still do not reach the ones obtained by the best runs submitted to the

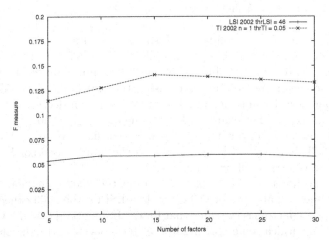

**Fig. 1.** F measure for the best runs in function of the number of factors ($k$), 2002 collection

track with an F value around 0.23. The F obtained with the second human judgments (maximum assessor) is 0.371.

In the evaluation of the two methods we only established the values of $k, THR_{LSI}, THR_{TI}$ and $n$ mentioned above to obtain the best results. Most systems participating in the TREC Novelty track applied specific techniques to improve performance: specific analysis of the queries or documents to be used in query or document expansion, query expansion with linguistic resources, pseudo-relevance feedback techniques, features extraction from the TREC topics or document clustering before sentence retrieval. For these reasons, it is difficult to compare our results with the results obtained for the runs submitted to the TREC tracks. The participants did not have the relevance judgments to find the best paremeters. Actually, in the 2002 track four training topics were provided. These topics were used for some participants to determine, for example, the percentage of sentences that should be retrieved. In the 2003 track no training topics were provided. However, since participants in the competition were allowed to send five runs, we presented here the comparison with the best results of TREC. Besides that, we presented the comparison of our results with the results of the secondary assessor, therefore this comparison gives an idea of the behavior of our methods with respect to a human performing the task.

The results of the LSI method with the 2003 collection were good. Parameter tuning has to be different for this collection so different experiments were repeated again to determine the best parameters. The optimal number of factors turned out to be $k = 5$. The reason of this could be that the 2003 collection is a bit smaller or more homogeneous than the 2002 collection. With the same weighting scheme and similarity measure, the value of the threshold $thr_{LSI}$ that achieves the best results is also different, in this case because the relevance judgments are very different and the percentage of relevant sentences is higher. As expected, the value of the threshold is lower than in the case of the 2002 collection and the range for the best results is between 16 and 20.

The best F with $k = 5$ factors and a threshold $thr_{LSI}$ of 16 is 0.593. This value is similar to those submitted for the best runs participating in the track. Indeed, the F value of the secondary assessor is 0.58. Our value is better in this case because our recall is very high 0.90, while the recall of the human assessor is 0.67. In terms of precision we obtain 0.5 while the human obtains 0.69. Results with better precision are obtained increasing the threshold value. With these increased values the F value decreases because the recall decreases faster than the precision increases. For example, for a value of $thr_{LSI} = 50$, a recall of 0.62 similar to the human is obtained, but the precision has a value of 0.55 and the F value is 0.533. It is a good F value close to the human assessor F value and more similar in the trade-off precision/recall.

Although the difference is not so large as in the 2002 collection, the topic identification method also performs better than LSI for the 2003 collection. The optimal number of factors is the same that for the LSI method ($k = 5$). Compared with the topic identification algorithm in the 2002 collection the threshold $thr_{TI}$ is also lower. The highest F value is 0.640 and it is obtained with $thr_{TI} = 0.02$.

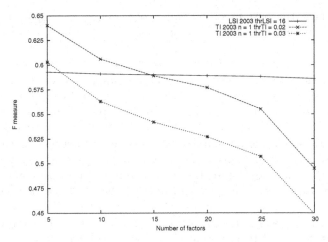

**Fig. 2.** F measure for the best runs in function of the number of factors ($k$), 2003 collection

This value is even better than the value provided by the secondary assessor and than the best runs submitted to the track, but it is obtained with a high recall (0.89) and a precision of 0.58; with $thr_{TI} = 0.03$ we obtain a recall of 0.73 (the secondary assessor obtains 0.67) and a precision of 0.62 (the secondary assessor obtains 0.69) and an F value of 0.603 which is still higher than the human assessor that obtains a 0.58. In figure 2 the changes of the best results in function of $k$ for the 2003 collection with both methods are shown.

In both collections, after selecting the best $k$, the topic identification method performs better than the LSI method. This is especially important in the 2002 collection where LSI simply does not work. An important fact is that in both methods the optimal number of factors is the same for the same collection. But, in the case of the topic identification method, the variation in the number of factors has a major influence in the performance of the system while in the LSI method the influence of the number of factors is quite soft. This variation can be seen in figures 1 and 2 but especially in the graphic from the 2003 collection where the performance of topic identification is lower than LSI for $k > 20$. So a previous statistical analysis to determine what number of factors is the best for a concrete collection will be more important in the topic identification than in the LSI algorithm.

## 5   Discussion and Future Work

In [11] different experiments with real relevance feedback and LSI were made. These experiments in several small collections achieved a big improvement in performance. For example, the use of the first relevant document retrieved as the new query is enough to improve the results in all the collections tested. We think that the use of pseudo-relevance feedback techniques can also improve the performance of LSI and, therefore, of our topic identification method in sentence retrieval. In fact, the best precision values obtained in the topic identification experiments can help to make the pseudo-relevance feedback more effective in this method.

The results presented here reinforce the hypothesis that each dimension in the reduced space of the truncated SVD represents a topic of the original documents. The algorithm proposed in [7] starts from the hypothesis that a pattern in the word usage in the original document space can be associated with a topic. LSI claims that it captures the variability in the word usage, reducing terms with similar usage pattern to the same dimension in the reduced space. If these associated terms represent a topic we can use each dimension in the reduced space as the representative of a concept in a document collection. Starting from these ideas Gong & Liu devised the algorithm for generic text summarization.

Following that research line, in our LSI sentence retrieval method each singular value is supposed to represent the importance of those topics, therefore the highest singular values represent the most important topics in the indexed text. In our topic identification approach the retrieval is not directly driven by the singular values. We projected the query in the truncated SVD space and the retrieval of relevant sentences is driven by the most important query components in this reduce space. Therefore, the good results of the method support the hypothesis that the algorithm finds query topics and can retrieve sentences about these topics.

The topic identification method always gets the best result using only one component of the query ($n = 1$). The main reason is that the best results are obtained with a small number of factors. Probably most queries are very focused in a single theme, so the use of one component can be the optimal. We made an individual query analysis, maintaining the same number of factors, and we observed that for some queries better results can be obtained for $n > 1$. This is an expected result because some queries can be about different related themes, in this case the selection of the same number of components as main themes is better. Obviously, this opens a research line whose goal is to produce a topic identification method in which the $n$ parameter could be established for each individual query. In fact this research line is related with some recent work in predicting query performance [12] [13]. In these works the objective is to predict the query difficulty. Weighting functions or query expansion parameters can be changed depending upon the prediction of query difficulty. In our case we are interested in prediction of query topicality but we believe that some of the predictors of query difficulty can be useful for query topicality. It is also interesting to mention another recent work analyzing the reasons of the failure of queries in different systems [14]: in many cases the query failure comes from the difficulty in determining the query topicality.

As we introduced in the first section, the sentence retrieval task can be seen like a type of summarization. Although the evaluated methods are presented to perform a query-relevant retrieval, they could be adapted to perform generic summaries using, for example, the full document to summarize instead of the query. If the summarization requires text modification, sentence retrieval can be simply the first step of the process, previous to the generation of a new summary.

Another application of sentence retrieval is the presentation of retrieval results. The traditional presentation strategies of web search engines usually include the title, the URL and the terms of the search in the context in which they appear. Some experiments with users [2] examined the effects of the presentation of relevant sentences instead of the documents surrogates. The main goal of using top-ranking sentences is the presentation of content to the users, encouraging users interaction and reducing the number of decisions that the users take to decide the relevance of a document an read it. Indeed, experiments of implicit feedback were developed changing the order of the sentences presented in function of the information extracted implicitly from the user. The experience of the users was positive with respect to these experiments, so the task of sentence retrieval has promising applications.

The novelty collections from the years 2002 and 2003 are very different. Due to the variability in the results obtained and the shifting of the parameters optimized to get these results we plan to repeat the evaluation for the 2004 Novelty track [15] collection. In the 2004 collection the major change is the inclusion of irrelevant documents into the documents sets associated with each topic, actually the irrelevant documents are close matches to the relevant ones, and not random irrelevant documents. After the evaluation with this collection we plan to research about the stability of these techniques given the variability in the input data.

# 6   Conclusions

Two methods were tested for the task of sentence retrieval. The LSI-based method had not been used before in sentence retrieval. The results of this method are very different for the two collections employed in the evaluation. For the 2002 TREC Novelty track collection the method has a performance only slightly better than a random retrieval, while in the 2003 TREC Novelty track collection the performance is competitive with the best systems tested with this collection.

The second method used is a new method based on topic identification. This method obtains better results than the previous one in the two evaluated collections. In the 2002 collection the performance is not as good as the performance of the best systems participating in the track. For the 2003 collection the results are among the best participant systems and the second human assessor, at least in terms of the F measure.

Most groups participating in the TREC Novelty track used techniques like query expansion or relevance feedback to address the difficulty of matching query and sentence terms. We have proposed two generic methods with a formal background getting good results and still being able to improve the performance.

## Acknowledgments

The work reported here was co-funded by "Ministerio de Educación y Ciencia" and FEDER funds under research projects TIC2002-00947 and TIN2005-08521-CO2-02.

## References

1. Harman, D.: Overview of the TREC 2002 Novelty Track. NIST Special Publication 500-251: The Eleventh Text REtrieval Conference. (2002) 17–28
2. White, R. W., Jose, J. M., Ruthven, I.: Using top-ranking sentences to facilitate effective information access. JASIST. **56**(10) (2005) 1113–1125
3. Larkey, L. S., Allan, J., Connell, M. E., Bolivar, A., Wade, C.: UMass at TREC 2002: Cross Language and Novelty Tracks. NIST Special Publication 500-251: The Eleventh Text REtrieval Conference. (2002) 721–732
4. Zhang, M., Song, R., Lin, C., Ma, S., Jiang, Z., Jin, Y., Liu, Y., Zhao, L.: THU TREC 2002: Novelty Track Experiments. NIST Special Publication 500-251: The Eleventh Text REtrieval Conference. (2002) 591–595
5. Berry, M. W., Dumais, S. T., Letsche, T. A.: Computational Methods for Intelligent Information Access. Supercomputing '95: Proceedings of the 1995 ACM/IEEE conference on Supercomputing. (1995)
6. Deerwester, S. C., Dumais, S. T., Landauer, T. K., Furnas, G. W., Harshman, R. A.: Indexing by Latent Semantic Analysis. JASIS. **41**(6) (1990) 391–407
7. Gong, Y., Liu, X.: Generic text summarization using relevance measure and latent semantic analysis. SIGIR '01, Proceedings of the 24th Annual International ACM SIGIR conference on Research and Development in Information Retrieval. (2001) 19–25
8. Soboroff, I., Harman, D.: Overview of the TREC 2003 Novelty Track. NIST Special Publication 500-255: The Twelfth Text REtrieval Conference. (2003) 38–53
9. Telcordia Technologies: LSI Software Home. http://lsi.research.telcordia.com
10. Rohde, D.: SVDLIBC. http://tedlab.mit.edu/~dr/SVDLIBC
11. Dumais, S.: Enhancing Performance in Latent Semantic Indexing. TM-ARH-017527 Technical Report, Bellcore. (1990)
12. Cronen-Townsend, S., Zhou, Y., Croft, W. B.: Predicting Query Performance. SIGIR '02, Proceedings of the 25th Annual International ACM SIGIR conference on Research and Development in Information Retrieval. (2002) 299–306
13. He, B., Ounis, I.: Inferring Query Performance Using Pre-retrieval Predictors. SPIRE '04, Proceedings of the 11th International Conference String Processing and Information Retrieval, LNCS 3246. (2004) 43–54
14. Buckley, C.: Why current IR engines fail. SIGIR '04, Proceedings of the 27th Annual International ACM SIGIR conference on Research and Development in Information Retrieval. (2004) 584–585
15. Soboroff, I.: Overview of the TREC 2004 Novelty Track. NIST Special Publication 500-261: The Thirteenth Text REtrieval Conference Proceedings. (2004)

# Ranking Web News Via Homepage Visual Layout and Cross-Site Voting

Jinyi Yao[1], Jue Wang[2], Zhiwei Li[1], Mingjing Li[1], and Wei-Ying Ma[1]

[1] Microsoft Research Asia, 49 Zhichun Road, Beijing 100080, China
{jinyi.yao, zli, mjli, wyma}@microsoft.com
[2] State Key Lab of Intelligent System and Technology, Tsinghua University,
Beijing 100084, China
wangyuanhao99@mails.tsinghua.edu.cn

**Abstract.** Reading news is one of the most popular activities when people surf the internet. As too many news sources provide independent news information and each has its own preference, detecting unbiased important news might be very useful for users to keep up to date with what are happening in the world. In this paper we present a novel method to identify important news in web environment which consists of diversified online news sites. We observe that a piece of important news generally occupies visually significant place in some homepage of a news site and import news event will be reported by many news sites. To explore these two properties, we model the relationship between homepages, news and latent events by a tripartite graph, and present an algorithm to identify important news in this model. Based on this algorithm, we implement a system TOPSTORY to dynamically generate homepages for users to browse important news reports. Our experimental study indicates the effectiveness of proposed approach.

## 1 Introduction

A survey conducted by Cerberian in May 2004 shows that news is one of the favorites for Internet users [1]. Specifically, 56% users rank "NEWS Sites" as one of the top 5 places they visit when surfing the Internet. The proliferation of many independent online news sources has created a sharp increase in news information channels available to us. What we are confronted with is the prohibitively huge amount of news information coming at us from multiple news sources. As us news readers are concerned, the important and latest news events can actually capture users' interest. Thus one key problem is to identify those pieces of news that report important events. We call this kind of news important news. However, not all the important news has the similar importance, how to rank them according to their importance becomes a key issue in IR field. In this paper, we mainly discuss the problem of detecting and ranking these publicly recognized important news, with no respect to user's personal interest preference.

It is not easy to distinguish important news, since each news source has its own preference in reporting events. But generally speaking, the following two properties can be utilized for identifying and ranking important news:

M. Lalmas et al. (Eds.): ECIR 2006, LNCS 3936, pp. 131–142, 2006.
© Springer-Verlag Berlin Heidelberg 2006

1. Important news usually occupies a visually significant place in the homepage. (Such as headline news);
2. Important news is usually reported by various news sources.

In this paper, we present a method to detect those pieces of news that possess these two properties. The visual significance of news in a homepage can be deemed as the recommendation strength to the news by the homepage. We notice that some homepages regularly recommend important news with proper strength, but others may have obvious local preference. We denote the term credibility to describe the extent to which we can believe a homepage's recommendation. Credibility of homepages and importance of news pages exhibit a mutual reinforcement relationship, which is similar to that between hub pages and authoritative pages in a hyperlinked environment [7]. Similarly, importance of news and importance of events also exhibit such a mutual reinforcement relationship. We model the relationship between homepages, news and events into a tripartite graph and present an algorithm to identify important news by seeking the equilibrium of those two mutual reinforcement relationships in this graph.

Related work can be classified into two categories. The first is important story detection that is mainly studied within the topic detection and tracking (TDT) community [4][5][6]. TDT tries to detect important stories from broadcast news. Our work differs from them in the way that we consider this problem in the web environment where more independent information sources are available. Another kind of related work is web object relationship mining, which has drawn widespread interest [8]. Especially, it has shown that taking the web as a graph has yielded valuable insight into various web algorithms [1][7]. Our work focuses on web news stories and our method is partially motivated by web relationship graphically modeling and mining.

The organization of this paper is as follows. In Section 2, we study the relationship between homepages, news and events and model it by a tripartite graph. In Section 3 we present the algorithm to identify the importance of news by exploiting two kinds of information in independent manner and combined manner respectively. In Section 4 we give an overview of the system TOPSTORY that implements our algorithm. Experiments are discussed in Section 5. Finally, we summarize our contributions and conclude in Section 6.

## 2  Observation and Formulation of Web News

To identify important news that follows the aforementioned properties, we investigate two kinds of information from homepages and news pages respectively.

News homepages not only provide a set of links to news pages, they also work as visual portals for users to read news. They are delicately designed to help user acquire information quickly. Examples include headline news, top story recommendation, etc. One of the most general forms is that all pieces of news are presented by homepages with different visual strength. The most important piece of news is often put in the top place, accompanied by some image or abstract text, while each of those less important ones is just a short sentence with a hyperlink. From another point of view, the visual layout of each homepage reflects its editor's viewpoint on important news at that time. Such kind of information is quite helpful to identify important news.

Each news article generally has a title, an abstract and the content etc. Thus we can compare the content of two news pages and estimate whether they are reporting the same event. Furthermore, from the corpus of multiple news sources, we may estimate how many pieces of news are reporting the same event.

## 2.1  Observations

Homepages vary in credibility. Each site generally contains two kinds of homepages: portal page and category pages. A portal page often summarizes important news from different classes, while each category page focuses on one kind of news, such as world, business, sports and entertainment etc.  The headline news in a category page is possibly important only within the corresponding class.  So generally speaking, portal pages are likely to be more credible within a site.  Besides, homepages of prestigious sites are averagely more creditable than those of non-famous sites. The later generally has obvious local preference. Credibility of homepages and importance of news exhibit a mutually reinforcing relationship as follows:

**Observation 1:** *Homepage and News*

- News presented by more creditable homepages with stronger visual strength is more likely to be important.
- More creditable homepages are expected to recommend important news more reliably.

All pieces of news are driven by the similar sets of events taking place in the world. Here we take the definition of event from topic detection and tracking community [4].

**Definition:** *Event*

Something that happens at a specific time and place. E.g. a specific election, accident, crime or natural disaster.

The importance of news and importance of events also exhibit a mutually reinforcement relationship.

**Observation 2:** *News and Events*

- Important events are likely to be reported by more pieces of news.
- A piece of news that reports an important event is important.

## 2.2  Tripartite Graph Model of Web News Relationship

We take a tripartite graph to model the aforementioned information and exploit our observations.  There are three objects here: homepages, news and events.  The graph is a five-tuple $G = \{F, N, E, Q, P\}$, where $F = \{F_1 \cdots F_m\}$, $N = \{N_1 \cdots N_n\}$, $E = \{E_1 \cdots E_d\}$ are three sets of vertices corresponding to homepages, news pages and events respectively. $Q$ is defined as an $m \times n$ matrix such that $Q_{ij}$ represents the recommendation strength of $N_j$ by $F_i$. We assume that the maximum recommendation strength equals for all homepages. Correspondingly, $Q$ is normalized along rows so that $\forall i, \max_j Q_{ij} = 1$.

$P$ is an $n \times d$ matrix such that $P_{jk}$ is the probability that $N_j$ is reporting

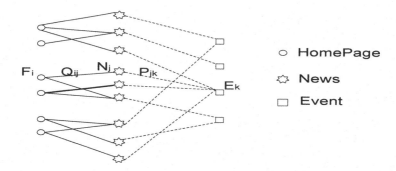

**Fig. 1.** A Tripartite Graph Model of Homepages, News Pages and Events

$E_k$. And $\forall j, \sum_k P_{jk} = 1$ holds. Here $P$ and $E$ are unobservable directly. A skeletal example is depicted in Figure 1.

Besides, we associate credibility weight $w_i^f$ for each homepage $F_i$, importance weight $w_i^n$ for each piece of news $N_i$ and importance weight $w_i^e$ for each event $E_i$. We maintain the invariant that the weights of each type are normalized:

$$\sum_{i=1}^{m} (w_i^f)^2 = 1, \ \sum_{i=1}^{d} (w_i^e)^2 = 1, \ \sum_{i=1}^{n} (w_i^n)^2 = 1.$$

## 3  Importance Propagation Model

Based on observation 1 and 2, we identify the credibility of homepages, importance of news by finding equilibriums in those relationships. It can be done by an iterative algorithm.

We first investigate these two kinds of relationships in independent manner. By further analysis, we find they are mutually beneficial. It is more advantageous to combine them and find a certain type of equilibrium in the two-level mutual reinforcement relationship.

### 3.1  Homepage Voting Model

Corresponding to observation 1, we can define the following operations: ($Q^T$ is the transpose of $Q$)

$$w^n \leftarrow Q^T \times w^f \tag{1}$$

$$w^f \leftarrow K_q \times Q \times w^n \tag{2}$$

Here $K_q$ is a diagonal matrix and $K_q(i,i) = 1 / \sum_j Q_{ij}^2$. The multiplier $K_q$ is necessary because the credibility of a homepage should not be biased by the number of piece of news it presents. Therefore when $w^n$ is given, we estimate $w^f$ as the following:

$$w_i^f = \frac{\sum_j Q_{ij} w_j^n}{\sum_j Q_{ij}^2}$$

These two operations are the basic means by which $w^f$ and $w^n$ reinforce one another. The equilibrium values for the weights can be reached by repeating (1) and (2) alternatively. Thus $w^f$ converges to $w^{f*}$, which is the unit principal eigenvector of $K_q \times Q \times Q^T$. And $w^n$ converges to $w^{n*}$, which is the unit principal eigenvector of $Q^T \times K_q \times Q$ and is proportional to $Q^T \times w^{f*}$.

It is based on the standard result of linear algebra that if $M$ is a symmetric $n \times n$ matrix, and $v$ is a vector not orthogonal to the principal eigenvector, then the unit vector in the direction of $M^k v$ converges to the principal eigenvector of $M$ as $k$ increases without bound. An assumption here is that the principal eigenvalue of $M$ is strictly greater than any other ones. But related analysis in this paper is not affected in any substantial way even if this assumption does not hold.

Define $B = Q^T \times K_q \times Q$. We note that $B_{ij} = \sum_{l=1}^m Q_{li} \times Q_{lj} \times K_l$. So if two pieces of news coexist in some homepage, their importance weights reinforce one another. The reinforce strength is proportional to the recommendation strength of both pieces of news by that homepage.

## 3.2  Cross-Site Similarity Model

Corresponding to the observation 2, we define the following operations:

$$w^n \leftarrow P \times w^e \tag{3}$$

$$w^e \leftarrow P^T \times w^n \tag{4}$$

The mathematical analysis of this process is totally same with that of the homepage model. Here we use $w^{n*}$ to denote the unit principal eigenvector of $P \times P^T$.

Define $A = P \times P^T$. We note that $A_{ij} = \sum_{l=1}^d P_{il} \times P_{jl}$. So $A_{ij}$ is exactly the probability that $N_i$ and $N_j$ are reporting the same events. We can approximate $A_{ij}$ by comparing the document similarity between these two pieces of news. The details are discussed in Section 4.2. Here we assume $A_{ij}$ is available without knowing $P$. Thus we can reach $w^{n*}$ without an explicit value of $E$ and $P$.

## 3.3  Hybrid Model

Both the homepage recommendation strength and multiple news similarity can help to identify news importance, however, the above two models have their shortcom-ings respectively. Improvement to the overall performance can be expected when combining them, to let them making up to each other. Here we investigate a simple combination rule:

$$w^n \leftarrow A \times w^n \leftarrow A \times Q^T \times w^f \tag{5}$$

$$w^f \leftarrow K_q \times Q \times w^n \tag{6}$$

Similarly we can repeat the above two steps alternatively to reach an equilibrium point. Here $w^{f*}$ is the principal eigenvector of $K_q \times Q \times A \times Q^T$, and $w^{n*}$ is the principal eigenvector of $A \times Q^T \times K_q \times Q$. The procedure to approximate the equilibrium values is in Figure 2. Generally $k = 20$ is sufficient to make it converge.

---

Iterate $(Q, A, k)$
         $Q$ : a frontpage-to-news matrix
         $A$ : a news-to-news matrix
         $k$ : the iteration count
         Let $z$ denote the vector $(1,1,\cdots,1) \in R^m$.
         Set $w_0^n = z$.
         For $i = 1, 2, \cdots, k$
         $w_i^n = A \times Q^T \times K_q \times Q \times w_{i-1}^n$.
         Normalize $w_i^n$
         End for
         Set $w_k^f = K_q \times Q \times w_n^f$.
         Normalize $w_k^f$
         Normalize $w_k^n$
         Return $(w_k^n, w_k^f)$

**Fig. 2.** Importance and Credibility Rank Algorithm

---

The tripartite graph is expected to be connected as a whole. Intuitively speaking, the sets of news pages from different sites are related via the same event set they report, the sets of news pages for different events are also related because they coexist in the same set of homepages. The exception is that all events reported by a set of homepages are not reported by any other homepage. It is quite impossible in reality and we ignore this kind of case.

Since the tripartite graph is connected and all edges are associated with positive values, we note that $w^{f*}$ and $w^{n*}$ have positive values in all coordinates. It means we can compare the importance of any two pieces of news. However, this is not the case for neither homepage model nor similarity model.

## 4   TOPSTORY System

We implement a system to verify our algorithm: TOPSTORY (See Figure 3). This system monitors a set of news sources and crawls their homepages and linked news pages in a certain frequency. By our algorithm, each piece of news gets a ranking score. We also implement a simple clusterer so that related news can be clustered into events. And these events are ranked by the most important news within them.

The system interacts with users in two ways. 1) It periodically detects latest important news and automatically generates homepage for users to browse. 2) It can be driven by users' queries, that is, it can dynamically detect important news during any given time period and generates corresponding homepage with top important events.

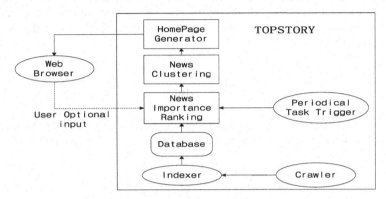

**Fig. 3.** An Overview of TOPSTORY System

### 4.1 Recommendation Strength in Homepage by Visual Importance

Each homepage is tracked by a set of snapshot pages $\{S_{t1}, S_{t2}, \cdots\}$. Here snapshot $S_t$ denotes the homepage at a specific time $t$. Each snapshot presents a set of news with different visual strength. We use a vision-based page segmentation algorithm (VIPS) [3] to analyze snapshot's content structure (See Figure 4).

**Fig. 4.** A Snapshot of Homepage

Figure 4 is an example of the result, where each framed red rectangle is a block of a piece of news. The visual strength of a block is decided by its size, position and whether it contains an image. We estimate it by:

$$q(S, N) = BlockSize / MaxBlockSize + (1 - top / PageHeight)$$
$$+ 0.5 * (ContainImage ? 1 : 0)$$

(7)

where $q(S, N)$ is the visual strength of news $N$ in $S$; $BlockSize$ is the block's size; $top$ is its top position; $ContainImage$ indicates whether it contains an image; $MaxBlockSize$ denotes the maximum size of all blocks in $S$; $PageHeight$ is the total height of the snapshot page.

The visual strength of a piece of news may evolve with time. We need to summarize these snapshots to have a global view that how the homepage recommends it. The summarization rule is actually determined by user's interest needs. If a user wants to browse important events during a week, all snapshots in this week are equal. In another case the user's interest decays with time, the latest snapshots should be more important than the older ones. Therefore we associate weights to snapshots according to their corresponding time. A sigmoid function is used to represent the decaying effect of user interest.

$$w(S_t) = \begin{cases} 1 & , \text{ for the first case} \\ \dfrac{1}{1 + e^{a(t-t_0)}} & , \text{ for the second case} \end{cases}$$

For each piece of news, its voting strength from a homepage is represented by a weighted combination of the visual strength it occupies at each snapshot.

$$q(F,N) = \frac{\sum\limits_{S_t} w(S_t) * q(S_t, N)}{\sum\limits_{S_t} w(S_t)}$$

where $w(S_t)$ is the weight of snapshot $S$ at time $t$. $q(F,N)$ is further normalized so that the maximum recommendation strength by each homepage equals 1.

## 4.2  News Document Similarity Measure

We use the Vector-Space Model (VSM) to represent each piece of news and compute their similarity by cosine similarity measure. For each piece of news, we distinguish two kinds of terms: name entities and general feature words. Name entities involve: *Name, Organization, Location, Time*, etc.

We consider three aspects to weight each word:

1. Traditional TF-IDF scheme.
2. Font information. Those with bold and bigger size font are of bigger weights.
3. Name entities are more relevant to the reported event.

We compute the weight of each term $e$ in a news page $N$ as the follows:

$$w(N,e) = \begin{cases} idf_e * \sum\limits_{w \in N \text{ and } w=e} f_N(w) & , \text{if e is a feature word} \\ idf_e * \sum\limits_{w \in N \text{ and } w=e} f_N(w) * 5 & , \text{if e is a name entity} \end{cases}$$

where $f_N(w)$ denotes the font weight of each occurrence of $w$ in $N$.

# 5  Experimental Results

In this section, we first explain how we collect data and set up the ground truth. Then a set of experiments were conducted to investigate our algorithms and evaluate the TOPSTORY system.

## 5.1 Data Sets Description

We monitor 8 online news sites for a week. All homepages are crawled in the frequency of ten minutes. We are especially interested in world news because it is popular and comparable among all sites. Statistics of crawled data are shown in Table 1.

**Table 1.** Statistics of Experimental Data

| News Sites | Homepage Num | News Page Num | World News Num |
|------------|--------------|---------------|----------------|
| BBC | 7 | 1262 | 348 |
| CNN | 8 | 331 | 133 |
| CBC | 5 | 498 | 258 |
| NEWSDAY | 6 | 922 | 336 |
| CBSNEWS | 5 | 197 | 50 |
| YAHOO | 8 | 1219 | 365 |
| ABCNEWS | 7 | 2601 | 463 |
| REUTERS | 6 | 624 | 289 |

It is quite difficult to give an importance value for each piece of news. The key problem is that users can only evaluate importance for each event instead of each piece of news. So it is necessary to associate each piece of news into some event for comparing our methods to the ground truth from users. We utilize a fixed clustering algorithm to deal with this task. We define three importance levels and their corresponding weight values. (See Table 2)

**Table 2.** Importance Label

| Importance Level | Weight |
|------------------|--------|
| Very important | 10 |
| Important | 5 |
| Normal | 0 |

We asked 5 users to label these clustered events. For each event, the average value is taken as its importance value.

## 5.2 Experiment Results

We conduct two experiments to compare the performance of the three proposed models. We hope to investigate the effect of information from homepages and news pages respectively and to see the effect of their combination as well.

### 5.2.1  Scope – Average Importance

We take a strategy like scope-precision, to evaluate the performance of the three models in TOPSTORY respectively. Here the scope is the number of top important events returned. Precision is the average importance value of these top events. We also define the ideal case for comparison. It represents the best performance we can expect from the user labelings. Figure 5 illustrates the result.

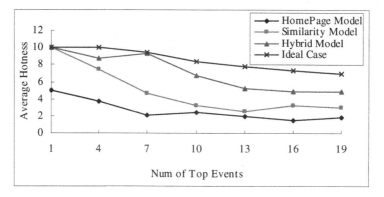

**Fig. 5.** Scope - Average Importance

The hybrid model outperforms both the similarity model and the homepage model remarkably. For the similarity model, some normal events contently similar to important events are wrongly identified as important, which degrades the final performance. For the homepage model, only one site determines its performance since the credibility converges to one site. Thus any less important news published on the homepage of this site will harm the scope – average importance.

### 5.2.2  Time Delay

Another criterion to evaluate their performance is time delay for reporting events. Given one event, its time delay is defined as the period from the earliest time when one piece of related news appears to the time we can identify it as important news. We hope the time delay should be as short as possible so that the system can report important news to users as soon as possible.

We randomly select a set of events from those that can be identified as important by all the three models. These events are listed as follows. The left column is the earliest time that our crawler found a piece of news corresponding to the event. The right column is a brief description of the events.

| | |
|---|---|
| 2005-01-02 14:44:39 | Car bomb attack kills 19 Iraqis |
| 2005-01-03 02:45:02 | Peru rebels surrend |
| 2005-01-02 23:39:46 | Powell warns of more Iraq attacks |
| 2005-01-04 06:53:55 | Governor of Baghdad assassinated |
| 2005-01-06 11:03:08 | Nelson Mandela's eldest son dies |
| 2005-01-05 05:35:40 | Aid plea for 'tsunami generation' |
| 2005-01-06 06:36:10 | Jordan rallies support for Iraq poll |
| 2005-01-02 14:36:06 | Peter Molyneux has been made an OBE. |
| 2005-01-03 14:47:06 | Uzbeks promise smelter clean-up |

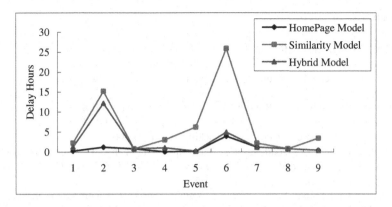

**Fig. 6.** Time Delay

The delays are illustrated in Figure 6. The average delays for three models are 1.0, 6.7 and 2.6 respectively (in hour). The time delay by the homepage model is very small because a piece of important news occupies significant importance as soon as it appears. While the similarity model requires a significant time delay and can hardly identify important events in the first time. It is because in this model an event can be identified as important only after many sites have reported it. The hybrid model is quite close to the homepage model for most cases.

## 6    Conclusion and Future Work

In this paper, we propose a method to identify and to rank important news in web environment. We investigate visual layout information in homepages and content similarity information in news pages. The relationship between homepages, events and news pages is modeled by a tripartite graph. Then we present an eigenvector-based algorithm to find the importance equilibrium in this graph. Based on this algorithm, we implement a system TOPSTORY to help users to read important news easily. Experiments show the whole framework is effective. We investigate these two kinds of information respectively by two different models. It turns out that they are mutually beneficial. The hybrid model can identify important news better.

Based on this work, there are three future directions worth further exploring. First, we have used the information of visual strength of blocks in homepages to identify news importance. The information in the web environment is much richer. How to dig out other kinds of information and exploit them for our task is an interesting problem. Second, we take the eigenvector-based method in this paper, but the power of such heuristics is not fully understood at an analytical level. One direction would be to consider it in a random graphic model. Finally, as the goal is to help users to browse important news rather than news events, the performance of event detection and clustering is also critical and need further study.

# References

1. 2004 Web Usage Survey Results. Sponsored by Cerberian and SonicWall
   http://www.cerberian.com/content/CerberianSonicWallSurveyResults.pdf
2. Andrei Broder. Graph Structure in the Web. In the Ninth International WWW Conference, 2000.
3. Deng Cai, Shipeng Yu, Ji-Rong Wen and Wei-Ying Ma. VIPS: a Vision-based Page Segementation Algorithm. Microsoft Technical Report, MSR-TR-2003-79, 2003.
4. J.Allan, etc.(Ed.) Topic Detection and Tracking. Springer 2002
5. Allan, J. Carbonell, G. Doddington, J. Yamron, and Y. Yang. Topic detection and tracking pilot study: Final report. In *Proceedings of the Broadcast News Understanding and Transcription Workshop*, pages 194{218, 1998.
6. Allan, V. Lavrenko, and H. Jin. First story detection in TDT is hard. In *Proceedings of the Ninth International Conference on Information and Knowledge Management*, pages 374{381, 2000.
7. J.M. Kleinberg. Authoritative Sources in a Hyperlinked Environment. *Journal of the ACM*, Vol. 46, No. 5, pp. 604-622,1999.
8. J.M. Kleinberg, R. Kumar, P. Raghavan, S. Rajagopalan and A.S. Tomkins. The Web as a graph: measurements, models and methods, In *Proc. 5th Int. Computing and Combinatorics.* 1999

# Clustering-Based Searching and Navigation in an Online News Source

Simón C. Smith and M. Andrea Rodríguez

Department of Computer Science, University of Concepción,
Center for Web Research, University of Chile,
Edmundo Larenas 215, 4070409 Concepción, Chile
{ssmith, andrea}@udec.cl

**Abstract.** The growing amount of online news posted on the WWW demands new algorithms that support topic detection, search, and navigation of news documents. This work presents an algorithm for topic detection that considers the temporal evolution of news and the structure of web documents. Then, it uses the results of the topic detection algorithm for searching and navigating in an online news source. An experimental evaluation with a collection of online news in Spanish indicates the advantages of incorporating the temporal aspect and structure of documents in the topic detection of news. In addition, topic-based clusters are well suited for guiding the search and navigation of news.

## 1 Introduction

The growing amount of online news posted on the WWW demands new algorithms that support topic detection, search, and navigation of news documents. This work explores the content of documents, the temporal evolution of news, and the structure of news documents to define an algorithm that creates topic-based clusters of documents (i.e., topic detection) and that uses these clusters for searching and navigating online news.

In this work, manifestations of events are seen as news. The proposed algorithm assigns news to previously detected or new events, a strategy called *single-link clustering* [16]. Basis for this work are the results from the TDT research initiative [13] that investigates new events in a stream of broadcast news stories. We consider a modification of the single-link topic detection algorithm (UMASS TDT2) that handles news as events in time [12]. Like the UMASS TDT2, the proposed algorithm assigns news to only one topic, which can also be extended to multiple topics. Such algorithm produces clusters of connected news that are then used for searching and navigating documents.

In the area of information systems, the concept of information navigation has been associated with visualization of retrieval results [11] [17] and with information access in an information space [10] [5]. This work uses a topic-based cluster as a semantic structure of connected news that can be used in a navigation process. In particular, this work has the following specific contributions:

M. Lalmas et al. (Eds.): ECIR 2006, LNCS 3936, pp. 143–154, 2006.
© Springer-Verlag Berlin Heidelberg 2006

- It implements an algorithm for Topic Detection of online news that modifies a previous algorithm (UMASS TDT2) by incorporating the structure of documents.
- It evaluates the proposed algorithm with respect to UMASS TDT 2 in a domain of news in Spanish.
- It presents a strategy for supporting the search and navigation of news. This strategy considers a cluster structure of connected news that embeds the temporal order and similarity in a stream of news.

The organization of the paper is as follows. Section 2 provides a review of related work concerning topic detection and navigation systems. Section 3 presents our algorithm for topic detection (CHILE TDT), which is compared to the UMASS TDT2 algorithm. Section 4 describes the use of clusters as a semantic structure for searching and navigation. Conclusions and further research issues are discussed in Section 5.

## 2   Related Work

Many advances on topic detection and tracking in online news sources are derived from the Topic Detection and Tracking (TDT) reseach initiative sponsored by DARPA [13]. Since its beginning in 1996, this research initiative has produced serveral important results. Most approaches to TDT use some sort of clustering strategy, such as single-link clustering or hierarchical group-average clustering [16]. The TDT developments started with the application of traditional clustering algorithm for topics detection [15]. Then, systems considered that topic detection and tracking of news are inherently related to the data flow in time [12]. Lately, methods considered that clusters of news may overlap; that is, a document may belong to different topics [2]. In addition, other studies have proposed algorithms that show improvements when using keyword based analysis of text documents; example of such studies are: relevance models for topic detection and tracking [15] and event tracking on domain dependency [6].

TDT2 proposes to incorporate the temporal dimension for clustering news documents with a single-link topic detection algorithm (UMASS TDT2) [12]. In this proposal the content of documents are represented as queries. If a new document triggers an existing query (i.e., the similarity between the document and the query exceeds the query's threshold), the document is considered to discuss the same topics (event) than the query; otherwise, it becomes a new event. This query's threshold is penalized by the temporal distance between the query and the new document.

A more recent work explores time and space with ontological information in the topic detection of online news [8]. This work uses semantic classes for locations, proper names, temporal expressions and general terms. Instead of representing news as a single document vector, this approach uses four vectors that reside in different spaces: spatial location, proper names, temporal dimension and general terms. It requires to extract terms with a grammar-based parser, a geographical ontology, and an automata for temporal expression pattern recognition. In this sense, this work goes beyond the simple syntactic analysis or keyword-based clustering strategy of information retrieval. An important effort goes to the grammar parsing, temporal analysis, and geographic association, but, unfortunately, no evaluation was found with respect to previous studies neither a complete description of the algorithm for its implementation and evaluation.

A topic-based cluster of news represents a collection of thematically related documents. Faced with a large collection of documents, the problem becomes to select and access the document to start with. A general idea for solving this problem is to use overviews of the information that guide users from general to more specific topics [3]. Implementations of this idea attempt to display overview information derived from the automatically extraction of most common themes in a collection. In many cases, these themes are associated with the centroids of clusters that group documents based on the similarity to one another. An innovative approach for clustering web documents uses web-snippet, which clusters the fragments of web pages that are returned by a search engine and summarizes the context of searched keywords [9] [5].

## 3   Topic Detection

### 3.1   Algorithm

This work models topics of news as events that occur in time. News has a temporal order. News that arrives at time instant $t_j$ may be thematically related to previously arrived news at time $t_i$, with $t_i \leq t_j$. Essentially, the topic detection algorithm includes the same steps as the single-link algorithm described in [12]:

- News documents define queries represented by using the $n-$most frequent terms (50 terms in our case) in a document query after eliminating stopwords.
- An initial threshold for a query is defined by comparing the query with respect to the document from where it was created (Equation 4).
- When a new document arrives, it is compared to previous queries (documents) (Equation 3) and linked to the query for which the similarity value between the document and the query most exceeds the query's threshold (Equation 4). In case a news document cannot be associated with any query, it is considered as the first document of a new cluster.
- The threshold of queries are adjusted by considering the arrival time of new documents.

The derived function of similarity takes as basic elements the *terms* in the documents, which are typically used in information retrieval systems to represent text documents. Each term in a document has a weight, which is determined by the number of occurrences in the document and in the set of documents. In particular, the weight of a term $k$ in a query $q_i$ is defined by $w_{q_{i,k}}$ (Equation 1), and the weight of a term $k$ in a new arriving document $d_i$ is defined by $w_{d_{i,k}}$ (Equation 2).

$$w_{q_{i,k}} = tf_{q_{i,k}} = \frac{t_{d_{i,k}}}{t_{d_{i,k}} + 0.5 + 1.5 \cdot \frac{dl_{d_i}}{avg\_dl}} \tag{1}$$

$$w_{d_{i,k}} = tf_{d_{i,k}} \cdot idf_{d_{i,k}} = tf_{d_{i,k}} \cdot \frac{log(\frac{C+0.5}{df_k})}{log(C+1)} \tag{2}$$

where

$t_{d_{i,k}}$ : frequency of the term in a document

$dl_{d_i}$ : size of the document

$C$ : number of documents in the corpus

$avg\_dl$ : average number of terms in a document

$df_k$ : number of documents that contain the term $k$

After eliminating stop-words, terms in a text document are separated in three sets: (1) terms in the title (2) terms extracted from a syntactic analysis of documents and (3) terms in the body of the news (general terms). The syntactic analysis of documents extracts all uppercase words in the body of the document, composite words in uppercase, and words between semicolon or parenthesis. By separating different components of the documents, the system aims to handle their relative importance in characterizing the information content.

A document $d_j$ is compared to a query $q_i$ with the Equation 3. In this definition, we assume that the comparison between a new arriving document and a query cannot exceed the similarity between a query and the document from which it was created.

$$sim(q_i, d_j) = \frac{\theta \sum_{k=1}^{N} w_{q_{i,k}}^{T} \cdot w_{d_{j,k}}^{T} + \gamma \sum_{k=1}^{N} w_{q_{i,k}}^{S} \cdot w_{d_{j,k}}^{S} + \delta \sum_{k=1}^{N} w_{q_{i,k}}^{B} \cdot w_{d_{j,k}}^{B}}{\sum_{k=1}^{N} w_{q_{i,k}}^{T} + \sum_{k=1}^{N} w_{q_{i,k}}^{S} + \sum_{k=1}^{N} w_{q_{i,k}}^{B}} \tag{3}$$

where

$q_{i,k}$ : term $k$ in the query $i$

$d_{j,k}$ : term $k$ in the document $j$

$T, S, B$ : terms in the title, extracted from the syntactic analysis, and in the body of the document, respectively

$\theta, \gamma, \delta$ : weights optimized with the training set

The threshold of a query represents the minimum possible value of similarity between a document and a query to consider the document to belong to the same topic of the query (Equation 4). The initial threshold is defined by a comparison between the query and the document from which it is created. As the temporal difference between a query and a document increases, the initial threshold also increases, making it more difficult that the document belongs to the same topic.

$$threshold(q_i, d_j) = belief(q_i, d_i) + \beta * (date_j - date_i) \qquad (4)$$

$$belief(q_i, d_j) = \frac{\sum_{k=1}^{N} w_{q_{i,k}}^{T} * w_{d_{j,k}}^{T} + \sum_{k=1}^{N} w_{q_{i,k}}^{S} * w_{d_{j,k}}^{S} + \sum_{k=1}^{N} w_{q_{i,k}}^{B} * w_{d_{j,k}}^{B}}{\sum_{k=1}^{N} w_{q_{i,k}}^{T} + \sum_{k=1}^{N} w_{q_{i,k}}^{S} + \sum_{k=1}^{N} w_{q_{i,k}}^{B}}$$

Time in this equation penalizes the similarity by the time distance in days between the query and the document. This penalization reflects the behavior of news stream where the frequency of related news tends to concentrate at the beginning of an event and decrease with the time [12]. This temporal behavior refers to the time when the news were posted, and not to the temporal content in the text of news, which requires a natural language processing and may not follow the same behavior used in this model. The weight of the time distance in Equation 4 ($\beta$) is determined by an optimization process over a set of training news.

Like for the temporal dimension, we initially explored the idea of using the spatial dimension of news by taking the geographic distance between news' publications. The analysis of news document shows, however, that there is a high geographic concentration of news that makes it inappropriate to consider geographic locations as data capable of distinguishing topics. From the total number of analyzed news of a Chilean site of online news, over 40% of them are related to the Chilean capital (Santiago) and, among Chilean news, more than 80% of their geographic associations are related to Santiago. This high concentration of news is due to the fact that documents were taken from online news services with bias to report news about one specific country (Chile).

Despite the high geographic concentration of news, we did a preliminary evaluation that considers the geographic association of news as a particular component of the similarity between document and query, such as we did with time in Equation 3, but the results were negative. Therefore, we have excluded this component from the model and from the results of the experimental evaluations.

## 3.2   Experimental Evaluation

The experimental evaluation of the topic detection algorithm uses a set of 60,000 news obtained from a Chilean web site of online news [4] between March 2003 and October 2004. Within this time period of data collection, 30 topics were selected, and each document of this collection was manually classified into one of the 30 topics or into a null-topic (i.e., a non identified event). Each of the selected topics was characterized with a title, a description of the starting event, an id of the initial event, a summary, and principles of interpretation. The selected topics vary in the length of the time interval they were relevant and the number of documents that appeared during this time interval (Table 1). In particular, topics cover time intervals from 8 days to one year and from 6 to 530 documents.

**Table 1.** A subset of the judged events in the dataset

| | Topic | Time interval | # documents |
|---|---|---|---|
| 0 | Caso MOP-GATE | 01/02/03-10/29/04 | 244 |
| 1 | Caso Inverlink | 02/03/03-10/29/04 | 191 |
| 2 | TLC entre Chile y Estados Unidos | 03/24/03-04/20/04 | 89 |
| 3 | Votación de Chile en la ONU acerca de Cuba | 04/10/03-05/05/03 | 11 |
| 4 | Nelson Mery Acusado de violaciones a DDHH | 04/16/03-09/25/04 | 71 |
| 5 | Chile campeón Mundial de Tenis 2003 | 05/16/03-09/24/03 | 14 |
| 6 | Publicación deudores crédito fiscal | 06/26/03-09/24/03 | 12 |
| 7 | Desafuero de Pinochet caso Berríos | 07/11/03-10/27/04 | 121 |
| 8 | Royalty a la gran Minería | 07/22/03-09/13/04 | 122 |
| 9 | Presos políticos en huelga de hambre | 07/26/03-10/28/03 | 69 |
| 10 | Incendios en Portugal | 08/03/03-08/12/03 | 6 |
| 11 | Caso Spinak | 10/06/03-10/27/04 | 531 |
| 12 | Asalto a consulado Argentino en Punta Arenas | 11/09/03-02/10/04 | 22 |
| 13 | Caso Matute Johns | 02/13/04-05/28/04 | 46 |
| 14 | Envío de tropas Chilenas a Haití | 03/02/04-09/21/04 | 50 |
| 15 | Atentados en Espanã del 11 de Marzo | 03/11/04-10/30/04 | 170 |

From the 60,000 documents, three different corpus were randomly created:

- Auxiliar Corpus. It consists of 1,500 documents used in the calculation of $tf$ and $idf$.
- Training corpus. it consists of 2,000 documents randomly selected.
- Evaluation corpus. It consists of 15,000 documents; 2,200 documents belonging to one of the identified topics and 12,800 documents randomly selected from the other 57,800 documents of the corpus (i.e., from all documents minus the 2,200 documents already selected).

A preprocessing of documents identified stop-words. Stop-words were not only prepositions or articles, but also all words whose high occurrence within the whole corpus makes them less significant for characterizing the topics of news. Examples of such words are *noticia* (news), *país* (country), and *internacional* (international).

To evaluate the performance of the algorithm, we calculated cases of *miss* and *false alarm*. *Miss* is the number of documents that are not, but should be, associated with a topic. *False alarm* is the number of documents that are wrongly associated with a topic. A cost function relates both measures by a weighted sum of the probabilities of *miss* ($P_{miss}$) and *false alarm* ($P_{false}$) (Equation 5) [1]. Like TDT2, we define $cost_{miss} = 0.02$ and $cost_{false} = 0.98$, giving more weight to assigning wrong documents to a cluster.

$$cost = cost_{false} * P_{miss} + cost_{miss} * P_{false} \tag{5}$$

The evaluation compares the results of our algorithm ( CHILE TDT) with the original algorithm in [12] (UMASS TDT2). For both algorithms, the experiment runs different settings with the goal of optimizing the cost function. The optimal

**Table 2.** Optimal settings and final cost values

| System | $\theta$ | $\beta$ | $\gamma$ | $\delta$ | $P_{miss}$ | $P_{false}$ | $Cost$ |
|---|---|---|---|---|---|---|---|
| UMASS TDT2 | 0.0767 | 0.0034 | | | 0.243 | 0.002 | 0.007 |
| CHILE TDT | 14.8 | 0.05 | 12.6 | 13.4 | 0.202 | 0.002 | 0.006 |

settings with the training corpus and the final cost evaluation are presented in Table 2.

The values of the parameters for the CHILE TDT algorithm indicates that terms in the title are more relevant than terms in the text of documents. The final values indicate a small advantage of CHILE TDT due to a less number of *miss*.

## 4   Navigation and Search

The characteristics of the topic-based clusters derived from the previous algorithm are used for navigating and searching among online news. The idea is that clusters provide means for finding related news based on users' queries with finer granularity.

The structure of clusters derived from the TDT algorithm is a hierarchical structure, starting with the first temporal document in the cluster. Time is implicit in the hierarchy, where up level news are earlier than bottom level news. Each news document within a cluster, with the exception of the starting document, is associated with the previous and most similar document. We represent such cluster as an acyclic, directed and weighted graph.

### 4.1   Navigation

A simple strategy to support the navigation in the information space defined by a cluster is to highlight nodes in the cluster with a strong thematic association, or inversely, to highlight nodes that are less connected to other nodes of the cluster. In this way, users may decide to access only nodes strongly connected or to look for different information contained in the same cluster. A basic approach to determining a strong association between news is to define a threshold that allows a binary classification between associations (strong or weak associations) based on the similarity value obtained from the topic detection algorithm. This threshold may be defined/modified by the users, but also may be initially proposed by the system.

This work proposes a threshold based on the percentage of *false alarm* detected in the evaluation process, which differs from the probability of false alarm used in Equation 5. The idea is to determine the number of nodes equivalent to the percentage of *false alarm* with the lowest association similarity, having that news belonging to the set of wrong assignments should have less association similarity. For example, if the percentage of *false alarm* for the system is 30% and we have a cluster with 100 news, the thirty news with the lowest association similarity are considered to have weak association, and the threshold is defined by the thirtieth lowest similarity value.

With a threshold for the classification between weak and strong associations, the classification process in the clusters is as follows. Starting from the root, if the association similarity between a child node and its corresponding parent node is larger than the threshold, the nodes are considered strongly associated with a same highlighting color. If the association similarity is less than the threshold, in contrast, the color of the child node will be set different to the parent node.

As an example, Figure 1 shows the original cluster and the cluster with further refinement that refer to the "Chile Campeón Mundial de Tenis 2003" (topic id 5, Table 1). In this figure, there are 4 changes of color that indicate weak associations of news. If we consider the path in the graph after the weak association, we have 6 different news that are separated from the main topic of the cluster. Based on the manual classification of news, this cluster obtained from the topic detection algorithm has 9 cases of false alarm, which include the 6 news graphically separated from the main topic of the cluster. Thus, three cases of false alarm (30% of cases of false alarm) were undetected by using the proposed threshold.

In our online implementation of the system, graphs, initially specified in Graph Description Language (GDL) [7], were translated into a Scalable Vector Graph (SVG) [14] format and visualized in a browser (Figure 2). In addition to the refinement by weak and strong associations, in this visualization the

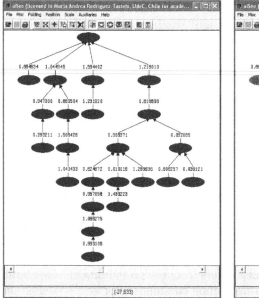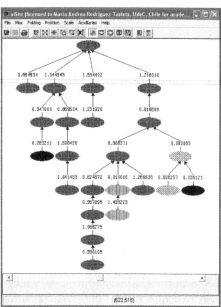

**Fig. 1.** Graph representation with highlighting similarity association for query "Chile Campeón Mundial de Tenis 2003"

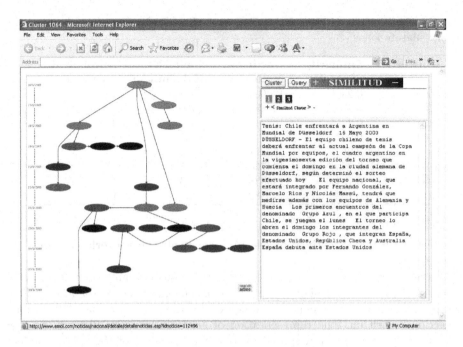

**Fig. 2.** Online implementation of the system using the SVG format

levels in the graph are associated with the temporal evolution of news, such that news that appear at the same level are concurrent. Other functionalities of the interface show the content of news as users move around the graph. We do not include a full description of the interface due to space constraints.

## 4.2  Search

In a search process, user queries and documents are compared for similarity. If no indexing of documents exists, the system has to do an exhaustive comparison with all documents. In this work, clusters of news provide a basic organization of documents such that it is possible to filter clusters that are not similar to the query. Even more, since clusters associate documents based not only by keyword occurrences, but also temporal proximity, it may be possible to find thematically relevant documents that, otherwise, would be excluded from the answer with a traditional model of information retrieval.

The strategy for retrieving news documents from topic-based clusters is as follows. A user query is compared with each cluster based on a common representation. If the value of similarity is positive, and all terms in the query appear in the representation of the cluster, the cluster is selected for a second comparison between the query and each document in the cluster. The system ranks the clusters and documents such that it returns the cluster with highest similarity and, within this cluster, the documents with highest similarity values. In case that the query includes a condition expressed by a time interval, time interval

**Table 3.** Most similar clusters and document in these clusters for a search with keywords "matute johns"

| Cluster ID | Similarity of cluster | Document in cluster | Similarity of document | Number of documents |
|---|---|---|---|---|
| 3090 | 0.286 | 138604 | 0.378 | 45 |
| 730 | 0.228 | 108452 | 0.430 | 3 |
| 447 | 0.208 | 105314 | 0.323 | 3 |
| 3769 | 0.202 | 146719 | 0.269 | 2 |
| 883 | 0.21 | 110321 | 0.214 | 1 |
| 3607 | 0.186 | 144766 | 0.287 | 1 |
| 3983 | 0.184 | 148938 | 0.333 | 1 |
| 3317 | 0.179 | 140882 | 0.152 | 1 |

of selected clusters, and then, of selected documents, must overlap the query's time interval.

A vector representation is applied to queries, clusters, and documents. The terms in the query are weighted by the same schema of the vector model. The terms in the news documents are weighted by the same schema of the topic detection algorithm. The representation of each cluster uses all terms in the documents of the cluster weighted by the *tf\*idf* schema of the vector model, but with respect to the clusters. Thus, the occurrence of terms in the cluster is the number of times the term appears in the documents of the cluster. The size of the cluster is the total number of different terms in the cluster. Like in the topic detection algorithm, the values of *idf* are taken from the auxiliary corpus.

As an example of a search, Table 3 shows the results of the search with a query expressed by the following keywords: matute johns. This table indicates the clusters with highest similarity values and, within these clusters, the document with the highest similarity value. In addition, the fifth column indicates the number of documents in the the the cluster. As additional information, the comparison with the manual classification of the topic "caso matute johns" (topic id 13) indicates that the cluster 3090 has 4 cases of *false alarm* and 5 cases of *miss*, the latter belonging to the other clusters in the table.

As the Table 3 shows, the similarity values of the clusters may be low, since they are determined by considering all terms that are present in the documents of a cluster. Although the first cluster has the most similar value with respect to the query, the second cluster contains the document with the highest similarity value. When comparing the search over the clusters with respect to a search with the traditional vector model, the cluster with the highest similarity value gives 86% of the best ranked document obtained from the vector model. The other 14% of documents obtained from the vector model are found within the other selected clusters of the cluster-based search. When considering all found news in the selected clusters, the cluster-based search gives more results than the vector model, including cases of documents that were associated with the topic, but with a lower weight for the query's keywords. Indeed, we obtained

17% of relevant news found by the cluster-based search that were not detected by the vector model.

## 5     Conclusions and Future Work

This work has presented a new topic detection algorithm for online news sources that includes text content, structure of documents and temporal content of news documents. The experimental results with the algorithm in a Spanish source of online news indicates a favorable improvement over a previous topic detection algorithm (UMASS TDT2). In addition to the topic detection algorithm, the work explored the use of this algorithm for search and navigation of news. It presents a graph-based navigation system that highlights the temporal and similarity association between news.

As future work, we expect to complete the implementation by handling updates of news in a online source. This is necessary if we expect to have good performance and avoid to compare arriving documents with all previous documents. Likewise, we expect to introduce indexing data structures that improve the search process. Within the context of future research, we want to explore the use of natural language techniques for analyzing explicit, implicit and vague temporal reference in the content of news documents. A broad domain of news with respect to geographic content would indicate whether or not the spatial content of news documents allows us to distinguish topics. Finally, we are exploring different strategies for navigating within a cluster such that a user could select, based on the information contribution of documents, what documents need to access.

**Acknowledgment.** This work has been funded by Nucleus Millenium Center for Web Research, Grant P04-067-F, Mideplan, Chile.

## References

1. J. Allan, J. Carbonell, G. Doddington, J.Yamron, and Y. Yang.   Topic detection and tracking pilot study: Final report.   In *DARPA Broadcast News Trasncription and Understanding Workshop*, pages 194–218. [http://citeseer.ist.psu.edu/article/allan98topic.html], September 1998.
2. J. Allan, A feng, and A.Bolivar. Flexible intrinsic evaluation of hierarchical clustering for TDT. In *Twelfth International Conference on Information and Knowledge Management*, pages 263–270. ACM press, 2003.
3. R. Baeza-Yates and B. Ribeiro-Neto. *Modern Information Retrieval*. ACM Press, 1999.
4. EMOL. El mercurio online [http://www.emol.com/].
5. P. Ferragina and A. Gulli. A perzonalized search engine based on web-snippet hierarchical clustering. In *International Conference in the World Wide Web WWW05*, pages 801–810, China, Japan, 2005. ACM Press.
6. F. Fukumoto and Y. Suzuki. Event tracking based on domain dependency. In *23rd Annual International ACM SIGIR Conference on Research and Development in Information Retrieval*, pages 24–28, Athens, Greece, 2000. ACM Press.

7. AbsInt Angewandte Informatik GmbH. GDL: aiSee graph visualization software: User manual unix version 2.2.07[http://www.aisee.com/manual/unix/], September 2005.

8. J. Makkonen, H. Ahonen-Myha, and M. Salmenkivi. Topic detection and tracking with spatio-temporal evidence. In Frabrizio Sebastini, editor, *Proceedings of 25th European Conference on Information Retrieval Research (ECIR 2003)*, pages 251–265. Springer-Verlag, 2003.

9. J. Mostafa. Seeking better web searches. *Scientific American Digital*, [ttp://www.sciam.com/], 2005.

10. S. Ram and S. G. Modeling and navigation of large information spaces: A semantic based approach. In *International Conference on System Science.* [http://computer.org/proceedings/hicss/0001/00016/00016020abs.htm], IEEE CS Press, 1999.

11. D. Roussinov and M. McQuaid. Information navigation by clustering and summary query results. In *International Conference on System Sciences*, page 3006. IEEE CS Press, 2000.

12. R.Papka, J. Allan, and V. Lavrenko. Umass approaches to detection and tracking at tdt2. In *Proceedings of the DARPA Broadcast News.* [http://www.nist.gov/speech/publications/darpa99/index.htm], 1999.

13. UMASS. *Topic Detection and Tracking TDT.* [http://ciir.cs.umass.edu/projects/tdt/index.html], 2005.

14. W3C. Scalable vector graphics (svg) 1.1 specification [http://www.w3.org/tr/svg/].

15. F. Walls, H. Jin, S. Sista, and R. Schwatz. Topic detection in broadcast news. In *Proceedings of the DARPA Broadcast News.* [http://www.nist.gov/speech/publications/darpa99/index.htm], 1999.

16. Y.Yang, J. Carbonelli, R. Brown, T. Pierce, B. Archibald, and X. Liu. Learning approaches for detection and tracking news events. *IEEE Intelligent Systems Special Isuue on Applications of Intelligent Information Retrieval*, 14:32–43, 1999.

17. Y. Zhang, X. Ji, C.-H Chu, and H. Zha. Correlating summarization of multi-source news with k-way graph bi-clustering. *ACM SIGKDD Explorations Newsletter*, 6(2):34–42, 2004.

# Mobile Clustering Engine

Claudio Carpineto[1], Andrea Della Pietra[2],
Stefano Mizzaro[2], and Giovanni Romano[1]

[1] Fondazione Ugo Bordoni, Rome, Italy
{carpinet, romano}@fub.it
[2] Dept. of Mathematics and Computer Science, University of Udine, Udine, Italy
andrea.dellapietra@gmail.com, mizzaro@dimi.uniud.it

**Abstract.** Although mobile information retrieval is seen as the next frontier of the search market, the rendering of results on mobile devices is still unsatisfactory. We present CREDINO, a clustering engine for PDAs based on the theory of concept lattices that can help overcome some specific challenges posed by small-screen, narrow-band devices. CREDINO is probably the first clustering engine for mobile devices freely available for testing on the Web. An experimental evaluation, besides confirming that finding information is more difficult on a PDA than on a desktop computer, suggests that mobile clustering engine is more effective than mobile search engine.

## 1  Introduction

The diffusion of high performance mobile phones and PDAs, together with the increasing willingness of mobile users to turn to their portable devices to find web content, products and services, are creating a new market (e.g., [10, 11]). However, mobile search must still face a number of technical limitations present in such devices, such as small screen, limited user input functionalities, and high cost connection. The result is that Information Retrieval (IR) by means of commercial search engines such as Google (http://mobile.google.com/) may become a tedious, long, and expensive process for mobile users.

In this paper we tackle the problem of mobile IR using a clustering engine approach, which consists of grouping the results obtained in response to a query into a hierarchy of labeled clusters. This approach is well known, especially due to the popularity of Vivisimo, which won the "best meta-search engine award" assigned by SearchEngineWatch.com from 2001 to 2003. The advantages of the cluster hierarchy can be summarized as follows: it makes for shortcuts to the documents of interest, it displays potentially good terms for query refinement, and it provides a higher level view of the topic, which is particularly useful for unknown domains. An additional benefit is that it helps disambiguating polysemous queries.

It is arguable that the features of a clustering engine approach appear even more suitable for mobile IR, where a minimization of user actions (such as scrolling and typing), device resources, and the amount of data to be downloaded are primary concerns. Furthermore, such features seem to nicely comply

M. Lalmas et al. (Eds.): ECIR 2006, LNCS 3936, pp. 155–166, 2006.
© Springer-Verlag Berlin Heidelberg 2006

with the recent changes in search behaviour, as observed in some recent user studies. For instance, according to [11], mobile users are more likely to enter shorter queries, less likely to scroll past the first few search results, both less able and less willing to access graphics-heavy web content. Despite such good potentials, however, the application of clustering engines to small mobile devices has not received much attention so far.

The first main objective of this paper is to help fill this gap. We build on CREDO, a clustering engine based on the theory of concept lattices described in [4, 5]. CREDO was developed for a desktop computer and does not scale to a small mobile device. We study which requirements must be met to extend desktop clustering engine to mobile search engine and then present CREDINO (small CREDO, in Italian), a version of the CREDO system for PDAs. CREDINO takes the cluster hierarchy produced in response to a query by CREDO and displays the cluster hierarchy on a PDA, handling the subsequent interaction with the user. CREDINO is available for testing at http://credino.dimi.uniud.it/. To the best of our knowledge, it is the first system of this kind on the Internet.

As a clustering engine offers a complementary view to the list of results returned by current search engines, it is interesting to compare the retrieval performance of the two approaches. Very few studies are available which do this for a desktop computer (one notable exception being [8]), let alone for mobile search. On the other hand, it is also useful to evaluate whether mobile IR is indeed less effective than desktop IR, in particular when using a search engine. This is one of the main hypotheses that motivate our research, although there is a lack of empirical observations.

The second main objective of this paper is to offer some insights into these somewhat overlooked issues. We compare the retrieval performance of CREDO and CREDINO to that of a conventional search engine on the respective device, through an experimental study involving external subjects searching a set of topics using the two retrieval methods on both devices. Our results suggest that mobile clustering engine can be faster and more accurate than mobile search engine, while confirming that mobile IR is less effective than desktop IR.

The rest of the paper is organized as follows. We begin by giving some background on concept lattices and CREDO, followed by a description of CREDINO. After discussing some related work, we turn to the experimental part, describing goals, design, and findings. Finally, the paper offers some conclusions and directions for future work.

## 2    Background: The Concept Lattice of Web Results

Our approach is based on concept data analysis, which combines a strong mathematical background with a set of efficient manipulation algorithms [4]. Here we recapitulate its main characteristics for IR applications.

In essence, any collection of documents described by a set of terms can be turned into a set of concepts, where each concept is formed by a subset of terms (the concept intent) and a subset of documents (the concept extent). The intent and extent of any concept are such that the intent contains all terms shared by the documents in the extent, and the extent contains all documents that share the terms in the intent.

More formally, consider a binary relation $I$ between a set of documents $D$ and a set of terms $T$. We write $dIt$ to mean that the document $d$ has the term $t$. For a set $X \subseteq T$ of terms and a set $Y \subseteq D$ of documents, we define:

$$X' = \{d \in D \mid dIt \ \forall t \in X\} \text{ and } Y' = \{t \in T \mid dIt \ \forall d \in Y\}.$$

A *concept* of $(D, T, I)$ is a pair $(X, Y)$ where

$$X \subseteq T, \ Y \subseteq D, \ X' = Y, \text{ and } Y' = X.$$

The set of concepts can be ordered by the standard set inclusion relation applied to the intent and extent that form each concept, i.e,

$$(X_1, Y_1) \le (X_2, Y_2), \text{if } X_1 \supseteq X_2 \text{ (which is equivalent to } Y_1 \subseteq Y_2),$$

with the resulting lattice yielding a subconcept/superconcept relation. The bottom concept is defined by the set of all terms and contains no documents, the top concept contains all documents and is defined by their common terms (possibly none). As an illustration, Figure 1 shows a very simple bibliographic collection consisting of four documents (1, 2, 3, 4) described by four terms (a, b, c, d), with the corresponding concept lattice.

The document lattice (i.e., the concept lattice built from the given document-term relation) can thus be seen as a particular form of hierarchical conceptual clustering. Thanks to its mathematical properties, it supports various tasks of text analysis based on inter-document similarity, including query refinement, browsing retrieval, document ranking, and text mining [4]. Most relevant to this paper, this approach has been implemented in the CREDO clustering engine to organize and explore web retrieval results. Here we give a brief overview of the system, which is best described in [5].

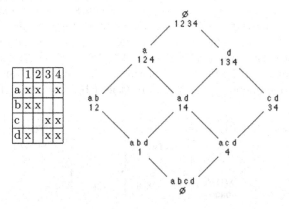

**Fig. 1.** The concept lattice of a simple collection

CREDO forwards a user query to an external Web engine and collects the first 100 results. Then it extracts a set of terms for each result and builds the corresponding concept lattice, the levels of which are displayed on demand using a simple hierarchical representation. In order to keep the number of top concepts small, the first level of the lattice is built using a narrower set of terms than those used to build the lower levels. CREDO can be tested at http://credo.fub.it.

## 3   Credino

Using a clustering engine approach for mobile search poses additional requirements compared to those which must be met in a desktop search. There are two main reasons why CREDO, like other clustering engines developed for a desktop computer, cannot be used on a PDA.

The first general requirement concerns usability and accessibility issues. Simply reproducing the frame-based CREDO interface would lead to a virtually unusable interface on a small screen, with an unacceptable amount of scrolling. In particular, users would be required to scroll horizontally, which is a very tedious way to see an entire CREDO screen.

A second constraint comes from bandwidth considerations. As the current implementation of CREDO is based on computing the whole hierarchy and sending out the results of all possible cluster selections at once, it is suitable for medium or broadband internet connections. By contrast, mobile devices connection to the Web usually has a low bandwidth (like GPRS) and is not free, the billing depending on the amount of data transmitted. Therefore it is important to choose, for CREDINO, an architecture that minimizes the amount of data transmitted to the mobile device.

The bandwidth constraint suggests to rely on an intermediate server (henceforth CREDINO server) to minimize both the amount of data sent to the mobile device and the load on the CREDO server (see Figure 2). The CREDINO server connects on one side to user's PDA and connects on the other side to (a slightly modified version of) the CREDO search engine.

CREDINO receives user's commands (query execution, cluster expansion, cluster contraction, visualization of the content of a cluster, visualization of a Web page) from a PDA. In some cases (e.g., for a query execution command), CREDINO forwards the command to the CREDO server, which processes it and returns the result as an XML data structure. The result of a query, consisting of clusters and documents, is then locally stored by CREDINO. Thus, in some

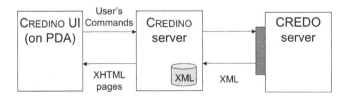

**Fig. 2.** Overall CREDINO architecture

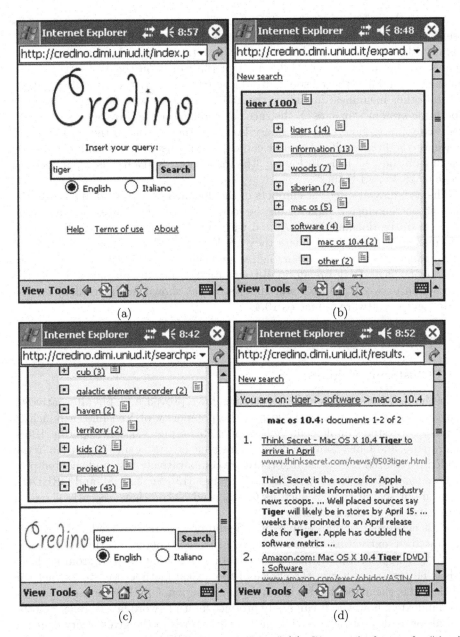

**Fig. 3.** CREDINO's home page with the query "tiger" (a); CREDINO's clusters for "tiger" (b) and (c), with the cluster "software" expanded; snippets of the documents associated with the path: tiger > software > mac os 10.4 (d)

cases, CREDINO can directly execute user's commands without connecting again to CREDO; i.e., after a query, CREDINO can deal with all subsequent user actions until the next query is issued or the visualization of a web page is requested.

To complete the description of CREDINO, we present some snapshots of its user interface. Figure 3(a) shows CREDINO's home page with the query "tiger". Figure 3(b) and (c) show the first-level clusters displayed by CREDINO in response to the query "tiger". Like most of the words on the Web, "tiger" has multiple meanings; the clusters, in addition to refer to the animal, highlight several other meanings, including the golf champion ("woods"), the computer operating system ("mac os"), the race car ("racing"), the Boy Scouts of America ("cub"), etc. Note that the query box is at the bottom of the page, to save space for the first results. The user can expand a cluster into its sub-clusters by clicking on the "+" icon. In Figure 3(b) the cluster "software" is expanded into "mac os 10.4" and "other".

The user may also see the snippets of the documents contained in a cluster by clicking on the cluster name or on the icon on the right. Figure 3(d) shows the snippets of the documents associated with the selected sub-cluster. To provide information to users as to where they are located within the hierarchy, we use the breadcrumb trail metaphor; i.e., a sequence of clusters from the root to the current page. Path breadcrumb trails are dynamically displayed during the interaction between the user and the system, as shown in Figure 3(d) for the path: tiger > software > mac os 10.4.

# 4 Related Work

## 4.1 Clustering Engines

Over the last few years, clustering engines have proved a viable alternative to conventional search engines. Following the popularity of Vivisimo, a bunch of commercial systems implement Web-snippet clustering: Mooter, Copernic, iBoogie, Kartoo, and Clusty, among others. This issue has also gained attention in the academic research field, although there are comparatively few implemented prototypes available on line (including CIIRarchies [13], SnakeT [8], and CREDO). Even major search engines such as Google and Yahoo! have recently shown a strong interest in this technology.

Most clustering engines employ a two-step procedure. Cluster labels are first generated by extracting short sequences of words (not necessarily contiguous) from the snippets, and then a cluster hierarchy is built with or from such labels. The systems differ in the choice of the lexical method used to extract the labels and in the algorithm for hierarchy construction. CREDO uses strict single-word indexing; however, it can easily produce multiple-word labels, reflecting the causal (or deterministic) associations between words in the given query context. For instance, for the query "tiger" (see Figure 3), CREDO returns some multiple-word concepts such as "mac os" and "galactic element recorder", reflecting the fact that, in the limited context represented by the results of "tiger", "mac" always co-occurs with "os", and "galactic" with "element" and "recorder".

A clustering engine based on concept lattices (this applies to both CREDO and CREDINO) presents some advantages over other clustering engines, which are more heuristic in nature, due to its reliance on a mathematical theory:

1) The clusters can be better justified, whereas the use of similarity metrics and heuristic decisions may result in the omission of clusters that are as plausible as those generated, or in a failure to include valuable clusters that are relatively rare. Figure 3, for instance, shows that even clusters formed by very few documents may easily appear at the top levels of the lattice. This can be useful to find unknown or less popular meanings of the given query; e.g., for the query "tiger", the concepts "tiger-cub" (related to the Boy Scouts of America), and "tiger-galactic element recorder" (related to a NASA program). Such meanings would probably go undetected by other clustering engines.

2) Cluster labeling is integrated with cluster formation, because a concept intent is univocally determined by a concept extent and viceversa. By contrast, cluster formation and cluster labeling are usually treated separately, thus implying that it may be difficult to find a good description for a given set of documents, or, symmetrically, a set of documents that fit a certain description.

3) The structure is a lattice instead of a tree, which facilitates recovery from bad decisions while exploring the hierarchy and can better adapt to the user. For instance, the document about the Mac OS Tiger software can be reached through two paths: *tiger - mac os - software* or *tiger - software - mac os*. Neither path is better than the other, but one may better fit a particular user's paradigm or need.

## 4.2   Search and Mobile Devices

Searching from small mobile devices has received quite a lot of attention, with dedicated publications and workshops in the main IR and human-computer interaction (see, e.g., [6, 7]). One of the central issues is the notion of search context, with its various forms: personalization and location are currently being exploited in a number of research and commercial efforts to filter and narrow retrieval results (see, e.g., [9]).

Other approaches have focussed on finding faster and more accurate decisions about the utility of the retrieved documents, using for instance keyphrases extracted from documents [15], summarization of Web pages and HTML forms [3], and related queries [12]. In [2], it is advocated that clustering helps to present information in a more dense and effective way on small devices, with a pilot study demonstrating small-screen access to a digital library system.

Speaking of mobile search, data organization and data visualization are obviously strictly interconnected. The use of specific data visualization schemes for small screens is discussed in [14], along with a set of guidelines to facilitate orientation and navigation, such as preferring vertical scrolling over page-to-page navigation and horizontal scrolling.

## 5   Experimental Evaluation

We have designed a comprehensive experiment aimed to evaluate how the choice of retrieval method (clustering engine or search engine) and device (PDA or desktop computer) affects retrieval performance. In particular, the main goals of our experiment are: (i) comparing the retrieval performance of clustering engine and search engine on both a PDA and a desktop computer, (ii) comparing the retrieval performance of PDA and desktop computer using both a clustering engine and a search engine approach.

We used 4 systems in the evaluation: 1) CREDINO (*PDA-Clustering*), 2) CREDO (*Desktop-Clustering*), 3) a mobile search engine obtained from CREDINO by switching off its clustering module (*PDA-Search*), 4) a desktop search engine obtained from CREDO by switching off its clustering module (*Desktop-Search*). We note by $\Delta$ followed by the initials of the two methods (devices) and the initial of one device (method) the differences in performance. For instance, $\Delta CS_D$ is the "Difference between Clustering and Search engine on Desktop computer". Figure 4 shows the scenario.

We tested 48 subjects in the experiment. They were computer science students or young faculty members at the University of Udine. As none of them was aware of CREDO and CREDINO systems before the experiment, and more than 90% of them were not users of any clustering engine, they were trained.

We used the four following topics, which represent various types of web searches (e.g., navigational, transactional, and informational) and are characterized by different levels of term ambiguity and difficulty:

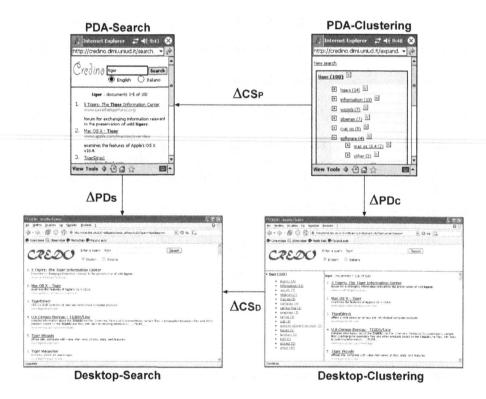

**Fig. 4.** The 4 systems tested in the experiment, and the 4 "$\Delta$s"

**T1.** "Your task is to find the Web site of the worldwide institution regulating the chess game".

**T2.** "Imagine you are a tourist going to visit Potenza.[1] You are interested in finding information about available accommodations, in particular you want to book a hotel room online".

**T3.** "You have to find a friend of yours which is on holidays in South Italy. You cannot reach him by phone, and you only know that he is in a place called 'Canasta' (and you do not know if it is a hotel, camping, village, etc.)."

**T4.** "Imagine that you have to find information concerning some athletes in the Boxing world. You are looking for an English-language web site that would allow you to search by name, weight, nationality, etc.".

It is well known that evaluating the effectiveness of interactive IR systems is a difficult task, for which there are no standard metrics available [1]. We took into account the two main aspects of the overall retrieval performance, namely, *success* and *speed*. *Success* represents the degree to which the goal has been accomplished and was measured using a four-point rating scale. *Speed* was computed as an inverse function of the time taken to complete the task, normalized by a task's maximum admissible execution time. A single numeric effectiveness value was then used by taking their product, i.e.:

$$\text{Performance} = \text{Success} * \text{Speed} \tag{1}$$

In our experimental setting there are two independent variables (device and method) and one dependent variable (the retrieval performance on the set of topics). The 48 subjects were randomly split into two groups with 24 subjects, each group being assigned to one device only (i.e., desktop computer or PDA), and each subject in either group used the two methods (clustering and search) to perform all four finding tasks. To minimize learning effects, each subject performed each task once, using one method for half of the topics and the other method for the second half of the topics. Furthermore, we varied the order of the two methods over the topic set.

We now turn to the results. In Table 1 we show the values of *Performance* (Equation 1) obtained for each topic by each retrieval method and device, normalized from 0 to 100 and averaged over the subgroup of subjects who performed the relative tasks. The subjects were in general able to successfully complete their tasks except for topic 4, where a substantial number of failures was observed ($success = 0$) and lower values of performance were thus achieved.

In Figure 5(a) we show the values of $\Delta CS_P$ and $\Delta CS_D$ averaged over the topic set. The figure shows that the clustering engine approach, on average, performed better than the search engine approach on both devices, with the difference being statistically significant for $\Delta CS_P$ (the non-parametric Mann-Whitney U test 1-tail gives $p = 0.016$).

A topic by topic analysis (Figure 5(b)) shows that while $\Delta CS_P$ was always positive, $\Delta CS_D$ presented considerable variations. Thus, at least in the case of

---

[1] Potenza is an Italian city.

**Table 1.** Performance by method and device on individual topics

|                   | T1    | T2    | T3    | T4    |
|-------------------|-------|-------|-------|-------|
| PDA-Clustering    | 67.60 | 62.28 | 51.68 | 32.47 |
| PDA-Search        | 54.77 | 49.94 | 41.91 | 27.57 |
| Desktop-Clustering| 63.49 | 65.77 | 61.16 | 37.66 |
| Desktop-Search    | 65.73 | 53.25 | 42.15 | 46.14 |

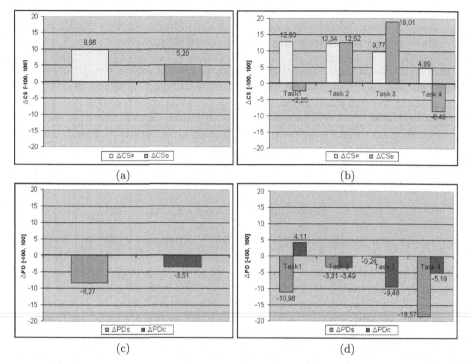

**Fig. 5.** Mean retrieval performance of clustering versus search for each device (a); Values of $\Delta CS_P$ and $\Delta CS_D$ on individual topics (b); Mean retrieval performance of PDA versus desktop computer for each retrieval methods (c); Values of $\Delta PD_S$ and $\Delta PD_C$ on individual topics (d)

desktop computer, the result depends on the specific topic being considered. This behavior is now analyzed more in depth. Topics 2 and 3 were characterized by some ambiguity and very useful clusters, so clustering was better than plain search both on PDA and desktop computer. For topics 1 and 4, the clusters produced by the system were pretty good, which explains the good performance of clustering on PDA. On the other hand, we found that, for topics 1 and 4, the subjects searching with search engine were able to detect good snippets and come up with effective query refinement strategies, whereas on the PDA device the screen size limitations and the typing constraints might have prevented them to do so in a fast and effective manner.

Figures 5(c) and 5(d) are the duals of Figures 5(a) and 5(b), obtained by swapping the roles of methods and devices. Figure 5(c) shows that the performance of PDA was on average lower than that of desktop computer across both retrieval methods, with the difference being statistically significant for $\Delta PD_S$ ($p < .05$). Figure 5(d) shows that $\Delta PD_S$ was negative for all topics and that $\Delta PD_C$ was always negative except for topic 1. The fact that on topic 1 clustering engine on PDA was better than clustering engine on desktop computer may seem somewhat surprising. As the cluster hierarchy produced for topic 1 was fine (see comment above), one possible explanation for the disappointing performance of desktop computer is that the presence of the snippets distracted the user away from the clustered results.

Overall, these findings represent an indication that (a) mobile clustering engine outperforms mobile search engine, whereas desktop clustering engine is not necessarily better than desktop search engine, and (b) mobile IR is worse than desktop IR, although it can be occasionally better for the clustering method.

## 6  Conclusions and Future Work

We showed that mobile clustering engine is not only feasible, as demonstrated by the system CREDINO, but also effective. We found that the retrieval performance of mobile clustering engine, while remaining in general inferior to that of desktop clustering engine, was better than mobile search engine.

Of course, more experiments are needed to support these findings. It is interesting to see what happens as we choose a larger set of more typical queries, referring to broader or better known domains. One possibility is to experiment with the test collection made available by [8], although it is not easy to evaluate the retrieval performance of a hierarchical clustering engine in a precision/recall style. Also, it would be useful to experimentally compare CREDO and CREDINO to some of the other few clustering engines that have been proposed, although a mobile version of the latter systems is not available at the moment.

CREDINO can be technically improved. We plan to re-implement the mobile device client as a complete application, to further reduce the amount of data transmitted to the mobile device and to improve the usability of the system by reducing the response time of the interface. Another direction for future work is to develop a version of CREDINO for cellular smart phones.

## References

1. E. Berenci, C. Carpineto, V. Giannini, and S. Mizzaro. Effectiveness of keyword-based display and selection of retrieval results for interactive searches. *International Journal on Digital Libraries*, 3(3):249–260, 2000.
2. G. Buchanan, M. Jones, and G. Marsden. Exploring small screen digital library access with the Greenstone digital library. In *Proceedings of the 6th European Conference on Research and Advanced Technology for Digital Libraries*, LNCS 2458, pages 583–596, Rome, Italy, 2003. Springer.

3. O. Buyukkokten, O. Kaljuvee, H. Garcia-Molina, A. Paepcke, and T. Winograd. Efficient web browsing on handheld devices using page and form summarization. *ACM Trans. Inf. Syst.*, 20(1):82–115, 2002.

4. C. Carpineto and G. Romano. *Concept Data Analysis — Theory and Applications*. Wiley, 2004.

5. C. Carpineto and G. Romano. Exploiting the potential of concept lattices for information retrieval with CREDO. *Journal of Universal Computer Science*, 10(8):985–1013, 2004.

6. F. Crestani, M. Dunlop, M. Jones, S. Jones, and S. Mizzaro, editors. *International Journal of Personal & Ubiquitous Computing, Special Issue on Interactive Mobile Information Access*. Springer-Verlag, 2006. In press.

7. F Crestani, M. D. Dunlop, and S. Mizzaro, editors. *Mobile and Ubiquitous Information Access, Mobile HCI 2003 International Workshop, Udine, Italy, September 8, 2003, Revised and Invited Papers*, volume 2954 of *Lecture Notes in Computer Science*. Springer, 2004.

8. P. Ferragina and A. Gulli. A personalized search engine based on web-snippet hierarchical clustering. In *WWW2005: The 14th World Wide Web Conference*, 2005. http://www2005.org/.

9. M. Halvey, M. Keane, and B. Smyth. Predicting navigation patterns on the mobile internet using time of week. In *Proceedings of the 14th International World-Wide Web Conference*, Chiba, Japan, 2005.

10. http://www.webpronews.com/insiderreports/searchinsider/wpn-49-20050708YahooAndTheQuestForMobileSearchSupremacy.html.

11. http://www.marketingvox.com/archives/2005/07/28/.

12. D. Kelly, F. Diaz, N. J. Belkin, and J. Allan. A user-centered approach to evaluating topic models. In *ECIR 2004*, pages 27–41, 2004.

13. D. J. Lawrie and W. B. Croft. Generating hiearchical summaries for web searches. In *Proceedings of SIGIR03*, 2003.

14. M. Noirhomme-Fraiture, F. Randolet, L. Chittaro, and G. Custinne. Data visualizations on small and very small screens. In *ASMDA 2005: Proceedings of Applied Stochastic Models and Data Analysis 2005*, 2005. http://asmda2005.enst-bretagne.fr/.

15. Jones S., Jones M., and Deo S. Using keyphrases as search result surrogates on small screen devices. *International Journal of Personal and Ubiquitous Computing*, 8(1):55–68, 2004.

# Improving Quality of Search Results Clustering with Approximate Matrix Factorisations

Stanislaw Osinski

Poznan Supercomputing and Networking Center,
ul. Noskowskiego 10, 61-704, Poznan, Poland
stanislaw.osinski@man.poznan.pl

**Abstract.** In this paper we show how approximate matrix factorisations can be used to organise document summaries returned by a search engine into meaningful thematic categories. We compare four different factorisations (SVD, NMF, LNMF and K-Means/Concept Decomposition) with respect to topic separation capability, outlier detection and label quality. We also compare our approach with two other clustering algorithms: Suffix Tree Clustering (STC) and Tolerance Rough Set Clustering (TRC). For our experiments we use the standard merge-then-cluster approach based on the Open Directory Project web catalogue as a source of human-clustered document summaries.

## 1 Introduction

Internet search engines have become an indispensable tool for people looking for information on the web. The majority of publicly available search engines adopt the so-called *query-list paradigm*, whereby in response to a user's query the search engine returns a linear list of short document summaries (*snippets*).

Despite its great popularity, the query-list approach has several deficiencies. If a query is too general, without a clear summary of different topics covered by the results, the users may have to go through a large number of irrelevant documents in order to identify the ones they were looking for. Moreover, especially in case of ill-defined queries, small groups of interesting but low-ranked outlier documents may remain unnoticed by most users.

One alternative to ranked lists is *search results clustering*. In this setting, in response to a query "london", for example, the user would be presented with search results divided into such topics as "London Hotels", "Weather Forecasts", "Olympic Games" or "London Ontario Canada". Users looking for information on a particular subject would be able to identify the documents of interest much quicker, while those who need a general overview of all related topics would get a concise summary of each of them.

Search results clustering involves a class of algorithms called post-retrieval document clustering algorithms [1]. A successful search results clustering algorithm must first of all identify the major and outlier topics dealt with in the results based only on the short document *snippets* returned by the search engine (most users are unwilling to wait for the full documents to download). Secondly,

M. Lalmas et al. (Eds.): ECIR 2006, LNCS 3936, pp. 167–178, 2006.
© Springer-Verlag Berlin Heidelberg 2006

in order to help the users to identify the results of interest more quickly, the algorithm must label the clusters in a meaningful, concise and unambiguous way. Finally, the clustering algorithm must group the results fully automatically and must not introduce a noticeable delay to the query processing.

Many approaches to search results clustering have been proposed, including Suffix Tree Clustering (STC) [2], Semantic On-line Hierarchical Clustering (SHOC) [3], Tolerance Rough Set Clustering (TRC) [4], and DisCover [5]. With their respective advantages such as speed and scalability, all these algorithms share one important shortcoming: none of them explicitly addresses the problem of cluster description quality. This, unfortunately, leads these algorithms to *knowing* that certain documents should form a group and at the same time being unable to concisely *explain* to the user what the group's documents have in common.

Based on our previous experiences with search results clustering [6], we proposed an algorithm called Lingo [7] in which special emphasis was placed on the quality of cluster labels. The main idea behind the algorithm was to *reverse* the usual order of the clustering process: Lingo first identified meaningful cluster labels using the Singular Value Decomposition (SVD) factorisation, and only then assigned documents to these labels to form proper clusters. For this reason this algorithm could be considered as an example of a *description-comes-first* approach. Although SVD performed fairly well as part of Lingo in our experiments [8], it had certain limitations in the context of the description-comes-first approach. For this reason, we sought to verify how alternative matrix factorisations, known from e.g. image processing, would perform in place of SVD.

The aim of this paper is to compare how different matrix factorisations perform as parts of a description-comes-first search results clustering algorithm. We compare the factorisations with respect to major topic identification capability, outlier detection and cluster labels quality. We evaluate four factorisation algorithms: Singular Value Decomposition (SVD), Non-negative Matrix factorisation (NMF) [9], Local Non-negative Matrix Factorisation (LNMF) [10] and Concept Decomposition (CD) [11]. To further verify the viability the description-comes-first approach, we compare Lingo with two other algorithms designed specifically for clustering of search results: Suffix Tree Clustering (STC) and Tolerance Rough Set Clustering (TRC). We perform our experiments using data drawn from a large human-edited directory of web page summaries called Open Directory Project[1].

## 2    Related Work

The idea of search results clustering was first introduced in the Scatter/Gather system [12], which was based on a variant of the classic K-Means algorithm. Scatter/Gather was followed by Suffix Tree Clustering (STC) [13], in which snippets sharing the same sequence of words were grouped together. The Semantic

---

[1] http://dmoz.org

On-Line Hierarchical Clustering (SHOC) [3] algorithm used Singular Value Decomposition to group search results in the Chinese language according to the latent semantic relationships between the snippets. Yet another algorithm called DisCover [5] clustered search results in such a way as to maximise the coverage and distinctiveness of the clusters. Finally, there exist algorithms that use matrix factorisation techniques, such as Non-negative Matrix Factorisation [14], for clustering full text documents.

# 3    Background Information

## 3.1    Lingo: Description-Comes-First Clustering

In this section we provide a brief description of the Lingo algorithm, placing emphasis on its relation to matrix factorisation. For an in-depth formalised description and an illustrative example we refer the Reader to [8] or [7].

The distinctive characteristic of Lingo is that it first identifies meaningful cluster labels and only then assigns search results to these labels to build proper clusters. The algorithm consists of five phases. Phase one is preprocessing of the input snippets, which includes tokenization, stemming and stop-word marking. Phase two identifies words and sequences of words frequently appearing in the input snippets. In phase three, a matrix factorization is used to induce cluster labels. In phase four snippets are assigned to each of these labels to form proper clusters. The assignment is based on the Vector Space Model (VSM) [15] and the cosine similarity between vectors representing the label and the snippets. Finally, phase five is postprocessing, which includes cluster merging and pruning.

In the context of this paper, phase three – cluster label induction – requires most attention. This phase relies on the Vector Space Model [15] and a term-document matrix $A$ having $t$ rows, where $t$ is the number of distinct words found in the input snippets, and $d$ columns, where $d$ is the number of input snippets. Each element $a_{ij}$ of $A$ numerically represents the relationship between word $i$ and snippet $j$. Methods for calculating $a_{ij}$ are commonly referred to as *term weighting schemes*, refer to [15] for an overview. The key component in label induction is an approximate matrix factorisation, which is used to produce a low-dimensional basis for the column space of the term-document matrix.

The motivation behind using the low-dimensional basis for label discovery is the following. In linear algebra, base vectors of a linear space can be linearly combined to create any other vector belonging that space. In many cases, base vectors can have interpretations that are directly related to the semantics of the linear space they span. For example, in [9] an approximate matrix factorisation called Non-negative Matrix Factorisation (NMF) applied to human face images was shown to be able to produce base vectors corresponding to different parts of a human face. It is further argued in [16] that low-dimensional base vectors can discover the latent structures present in the input data. Following this intuition, we believe that in the search results clustering setting each of the base vectors should carry some broader idea (distinct topic) referred to in the input collection of snippets. Therefore, in Lingo, each vector of the low-dimensional basis gives rise to one cluster label.

Unfortunately, base vectors in their original numerical form are useless as human-readable cluster descriptors. To deal with this problem, we use the fact that base vectors obtained from a matrix factorisation are vectors in the original term space of the term-document matrix. Moreover, frequent word sequences or even single words appearing in the input snippets can also be expressed as vectors in the same vector space. Thus, the well-known measures of similarity between vectors, such as the cosine similarity [15], can be used to determine which frequent word sequence or single word best approximates the dominant verbal meaning of a base vector. Bases produced by particular factorisation methods can have specific properties, discussed below, which can have an impact on the effectiveness of the label induction phase as a whole.

## 3.2   Matrix Factorisations

To introduce the general concept of matrix factorisation, let us denote a set of $d$ $t$-dimensional data vectors as columns of a $t \times d$ matrix $A$.[2] The task of factorisation, or decomposition, of matrix $A$ is to break it into a product of two matrices $U$ and $V$ so that $A \approx UV^T$, the sizes of the $U$ and $V$ matrices being $t \times k$ and $d \times k$, respectively. Columns of the $U$ matrix can be thought of as base vectors of the new low-dimensional linear space, and rows of $V$ as the corresponding coefficients that enable to approximately reconstruct the original data.

**Singular Value Decomposition.** Singular Value Decomposition (SVD) breaks a $t \times d$ matrix $A$ into three matrices $U$, $\Sigma$ and $V$ such that $A = U\Sigma V^T$. $U$ is a $t \times t$ orthogonal matrix whose column vectors are called the left singular vectors of $A$, $V$ is a $d \times d$ orthogonal matrix whose column vectors are termed the right singular vectors of $A$, and $\Sigma$ is a $t \times d$ diagonal matrix having the singular values of $A$ ordered decreasingly. Columns of $U$ form an orthogonal basis for the column space of $A$. Lingo uses columns of the $U$ matrix to induce cluster labels.

In the context of search results clustering, an important feature of SVD is that the $U$ matrix is orthogonal, which should lead to a high level of diversity among the induced cluster labels. On the other hand, to achieve the orthogonality, some components of the SVD-derived base vectors may have to be negative. This makes such components hard to interpret in terms of their verbal meaning. Moreover, although in practice the cosine distance measure seems to work well in the SVD-based cluster label induction phase, interpretation of the similarity between sequences of words and base vectors would be more straightforward if the latter contained only non-negative values.

**Non-negative Matrix Factorisation.** The Non-negative Matrix Factorisation (NMF) was introduced in [9] as a means of finding part-based representation of

---

[2] In the related literature the numbers of rows and columns are usually denoted by $m$ and $n$, respectively. In this paper, however, we have decided to adopt a convention that directly relates to a term-document matrix having $t$ rows and $d$ columns.

human face images. More formally, given $k$ as the desired size of the basis, NMF decomposes a $t \times d$ non-negative matrix $A$ into two nonnegative matrices $U$ and $V$ such that $A \approx UV^T$, the sizes of $U$ and $V$ being $t \times k$ and $d \times k$, respectively. An important property of NMF is that by imposing the non-negativity constraints it allows only additive, and not subtractive, combinations of base vectors. Lingo will use columns of the $U$ matrix as base vectors for discovering cluster labels.

The non-negativity of the base vectors enables us to interpret the verbal meaning of such vectors in an intuitive way, i.e. the greater value of a component in the vector, the more significant the corresponding term is in explaining its meaning. This also makes the interpretation of the cosine similarity between sequences of words and base vectors less ambiguous. On the other hand, the non-negativity of the NMF-derived basis is achieved at the cost of the base vectors not being orthogonal, which may cause some of the NMF-induced cluster labels to be more similar to each other than desired. In this paper we tested two slightly different variants of NMF described in [16]: NMF with Euclidean distance minimisation (NMF-ED) and NMF with Kullback-Leibler divergence minimisation (NMF-KL).

**Local Non-negative Matrix Factorisation.** Local Non-negative Matrix Factorisation (LNMF) is a variation of NMF introduced in [10] that imposes three additional constraints on the $U$ and $V$ matrices, which aim to expose the local features of the examples defined in the $A$ matrix. The constraints are: maximum sparsity in $V$ ($V$ should contain as many zero elements as possible), maximum expressiveness of $U$ (retain only those elements of $U$ that carry most information about the original $A$ matrix) and maximum orthogonality of $U$. Lingo will use columns of the $U$ matrix to discover prospective cluster labels.

Being a variant of NMF, Local Non-negative Matrix Factorisation inherits all its advantages, including the non-negativity of base vectors. Additionally, the fact that LNMF promotes sparseness of the base vectors should result in less ambiguous matching between these vectors and frequent phrases. The special emphasis on the orthogonality of $U$ is also desirable as it guarantees high diversity among candidate cluster labels. A possible disadvantage of LNMF in the context of search results clustering is its slow convergence [10].

**Concept Decomposition.** Concept Decomposition (CD) [11] is a factorisation method based on the Spherical K-Means clustering algorithm. For a $t \times d$ matrix $A$ and given $k$, Concept Decomposition generates a $t \times k$ matrix $U$ and a $d \times k$ matrix $V$ such that $A \approx UV^T$. In the CD factorisation, each column of the $U$ matrix directly corresponds to one centroid obtained from the K-Means algorithm. For cluster label induction Lingo will use the $U$ matrix.

Because K-Means is based around averaged centroids of groups of documents, it should be able to successfully detect major themes in the input snippets. However, it may prove less efficient in identifying topics represented by relatively small groups of documents.

There also exists a class of decomposition techniques based on random projections [17]. Even though these decompositions fairly well preserve distances and similarities between vectors, they are of little use in our approach. The reason is that they rely on randomly generated base vectors, which will directly lead to random labels being induced.

# 4    Experimental Setup

The primary aim of our experiment was to compare how four different matrix factorisations perform as parts of a description-comes-first search result clustering algorithm. We divided our tests into three parts: topic separation experiment, outlier detection experiment and subjective cluster label quality judgments. The aim of the topic separation experiment was to test the algorithms' ability to identify major topics dealt with in the input snippets. The outlier detection experiment aimed at verifying whether the algorithms can highlight a small topic that is clearly different from the rest of the test set. Finally, we subjectively analysed the properties of cluster labels produced by the algorithms.

## 4.1    Merge-Then-Cluster Approach Using Open Directory Project

We performed our experiments using data drawn from the Open Directory Project, which is a large human-edited hierarchical directory of the Web. Each branch of the ODP hierarchy, called a category, corresponds to some distinct topic (e.g. "Assembler Programming" or "Stamp Collecting") and contains links to Internet resources dealing with that topic. Every link in ODP is accompanied by a short (25–30 words) description, which in our setting emulates the contextual snippet returned by a search engine.

To implement the merge-then-cluster evaluation, we created 77 data sets, each of which contained a mixture of documents originating from 2 to 8 manually selected ODP categories. In 63 data sets, which were used in the topic separation experiment, each category was represented by an equal number of documents. The remaining 14 data sets, created for the outlier detection experiment, contained equal numbers of documents from 4 closely related ODP categories (major categories) plus documents from 1 or 2 categories dealing with a totally different subject (outlier categories). The numbers of documents representing the outlier categories varied from 100% to 10% of the number of documents representing one major category in that test set. In Table 1 we present an example outlier detection data set containing documents from one outlier category of size 30%. During the experiment, we fed all 77 data sets to the clustering algorithms and compared the contents of the automatically generated clusters with the reference categories defined in ODP.

Reliability of the merge-then-cluster approach largely depends on the way the correspondence between the automatically generated clusters and the original reference groups is measured. The similarity between two sets of clusters can be expressed as a single numerical value using e.g. mutual-information measures [18]. One drawback of such measures is that a smallest difference between the automatically generated clusters and the reference groups will be treated as the algorithm's mistake, even if the algorithm made a different but equally justified choice (e.g. split a large reference group into sub-groups).

**Table 1.** An example outlier detection test set (four major and one outlier topic)

| ODP CatId | Category path | Document count |
|---|---|---|
| 429194 | Computers/Internet/Abuse/Spam/Tracking | 28 |
| 397702 | Computers/Internet/Protocols/SNMP/RFCs | 28 |
| 791675 | Computers/Internet/Searching/.../Google/Web_APIs | 28 |
| 5347 | Computers/Internet/Chat/IRC/Channels/DALnet | 29 |
| 783404 | Science/Chemistry/Elements/Zinc (outlier) | 11 |

To alleviate this problem, we have decided to use alternative measures: Cluster Contamination, Topic Coverage and Snippet Coverage. Due to the limited length of this paper we can only afford an informal description of these measures, we refer the reader to [8] and [19] for formalised definitions.

### 4.2 Clustering Quality Measures

Let us define the Cluster Contamination (CC) measure to be the number of pairs of documents found in the same cluster $K$ but originating from different reference groups divided by the maximum potential number of such pairs in $K$. According to this definition, a cluster is *pure* if it contains documents belonging to only one reference group. Noteworthy is the fact that a cluster that consists of only a subset of some reference group is still pure. The contamination measure of pure clusters is 0. If a cluster contains documents from more than one reference group, its contamination measure falls within the 0..1 range. Finally, in the worst case, a cluster consisting of an equally distributed mixture of snippets representing different reference groups will be called *contaminated* and will have the CC measure equal to 1.

A simple example of a situation where the Cluster Contamination measure alone fails is when for a large number of reference groups the clustering algorithm generates clusters containing documents from only one reference group. In this case Cluster Contamination of all these clusters will be 0, and the algorithm will not get penalized for not detecting topics corresponding the remaining reference groups. To avoid such situations we have decided to introduce a complementary measure called Topic Coverage (TC). TC equal to 1 means that all reference groups have at least one corresponding cluster generated by the algorithm. Topic Coverage equal to 0 means that none of the clusters corresponds to any of the reference groups. Clearly, Topic Coverage promotes algorithms that can create clusters representing both major and outlier topics found in the input set. In our opinion, such behaviour is perfectly reasonable, as it helps the users to find the documents of interest more quickly, even if they come from a small outlier topic.

As clustering algorithms may omit some input snippets or put them in a group of unclustered documents, it is important to define the Snippet Coverage (SC) measure, which is the percentage of snippets that have been assigned to at least one cluster.

# 5   Experiment Results

## 5.1   Topic Separation Experiment

Figure 1(a) presents average[3] Topic Coverage, Cluster Contamination and Snippet Coverage for variants of Lingo employing different matrix factorisation algorithms. The NMF-like factorisations provide significantly[4] better average topic and snippet coverage, the difference between the NMF-like algorithms themselves being statistically insignificant. Interesting is the much higher value of cluster contamination in case of the LNMF algorithm compared to the other NMF-like factorisations. We explain this phenomenon when we analyse cluster labels generated by all the algorithms.

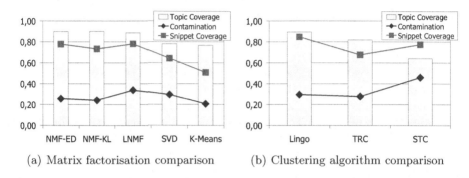

(a) Matrix factorisation comparison          (b) Clustering algorithm comparison

**Fig. 1.** Topic coverage, snippet coverage and cluster contamination measures in the topic separation experiment

Figure 1(b) shows how Lingo (NMF-ED) compares with two other search results clustering algorithms that do not follow the description-comes-first paradigm: Suffix Tree Clustering (STC) [13] and Tolerance Rough Set Clustering (TRC) [4]. Compared to TRC and STC Lingo achieves significantly better topic and snippet coverage. TRC produces slightly purer clusters, but the difference is not statistically significant. The above results prove that the description-comes-first approach to search results clustering is a viable alternative to the existing algorithms.

## 5.2   Outlier Detection Experiment

Table 2(a) summarises the number of outliers detected by variants of Lingo using different matrix factorisations. Interestingly, the base line K-Means-based factorisation did not manage to reveal any of the outliers, neither in the one-outlier data set nor in the two-outlier one. This may be because K-Means tends

---

[3] For full results, please refer to [19].

[4] Due to the fact that our data does not follow Gaussian distribution, differences marked hereafter as statistically significant have been tested using the Mann-Whitney non-parametric two-group comparison test at the significance level of 0.001.

**Table 2.** Numbers of detected outliers in the outlier detection experiment. For each matrix factorisation and each clustering algorithm we provide the numbers of detected outliers for data sets containing one and two outliers.

| Outlier size | Detected outliers | | | | | | | | | |
|---|---|---|---|---|---|---|---|---|---|---|
| | NMF-ED | | NMF-KL | | LNMF | | SVD | | K-Means | |
| | 1 | 2 | 1 | 2 | 1 | 2 | 1 | 2 | 1 | 2 |
| 100% | 1 | 2 | 1 | 2 | 1 | 2 | 1 | 1 | 0 | 0 |
| 50% | 1 | 2 | 1 | 1 | 1 | 1 | 1 | 1 | 0 | 0 |
| 40% | 1 | 2 | 1 | 2 | 1 | 2 | 0 | 0 | 0 | 0 |
| 30% | 1 | 1 | 1 | 1 | 1 | 1 | 0 | 1 | 0 | 0 |
| 20% | 1 | 2 | 1 | 2 | 1 | 2 | 1 | 1 | 0 | 0 |
| 15% | 1 | 1 | 0 | 1 | 0 | 1 | 1 | 2 | 0 | 0 |
| 10% | 1 | 0 | 1 | 0 | 1 | 0 | 1 | 1 | 0 | 0 |

(a) Matrix factorisation comparison

| Outlier size | Detected outliers | | | | | |
|---|---|---|---|---|---|---|
| | Lingo | | TRC | | STC | |
| | 1 | 2 | 1 | 2 | 1 | 2 |
| 100% | 1 | 2 | 1 | 1 | 1 | 0 |
| 50% | 1 | 2 | 0 | 1 | 0 | 0 |
| 40% | 1 | 2 | 0 | 2 | 0 | 0 |
| 30% | 1 | 1 | 0 | 1 | 0 | 0 |
| 20% | 1 | 2 | 0 | 0 | 0 | 0 |
| 15% | 1 | 1 | 0 | 0 | 0 | 0 |
| 10% | 1 | 0 | 0 | 0 | 0 | 0 |

(b) Clustering algorithms comparison

to locate its centroids in most dense areas of the input snippet space, which is usually not where the outliers lie. All NMF-like methods performed equally well, slightly better than SVD. SVD, however, was the only algorithm do discover one of the two smallest 10% outliers.

In Table 2(b) we show how Lingo (NMF-ED) compared with the Suffix Tree Clustering (STC) and Tolerance Rough Set Clustering (TRC) algorithms in the outlier detection task. Clearly, Lingo proves superior to the other two algorithms in this task for both one- and two-outlier data sets. This demonstrates the NMF's ability to discover not only the collection's major topics but also the not-so-well represented themes.

### 5.3   Subjective Label Quality Judgements

Figure 2 shows the labels of clusters produced by Lingo with different matrix factorisations for a data set containing documents from four ODP topics: Assembler Programming, Oncology, Collecting Stamps and Earthquakes. In the author's opinion, the majority of cluster labels, especially those placed at top positions on the cluster lists, are well-formed readable noun phrases (e.g. "Earthquake Prediction", "Oncology Conference", "Stamp Collecting", "Assembly Language Programming"). One interesting phenomenon is that two very similar labels appeared in the NMF-ED results: "Assembly" and "Assembler Programming". The reason for this is that the English stemmer we used did not recognise the words *assembly* and *assembler* as having the same stem.

A more careful analysis of the cluster labels created by the LNMF version of Lingo can reveal why this algorithm produces significantly more contaminated clusters (compare Figure 1(a)). The key observation here is that LNMF aims to generate highly sparse and localised base vectors, i.e. having as few non-zero elements as possible. This results in a high number of one-word candidate labels, such as "University", "Engineering", "World" or "Network", which in turn contributes to the high cluster contamination.

While cluster labels produced by the K-Means decomposition are generally readable and informative, they only cover the major topics of the test set, which

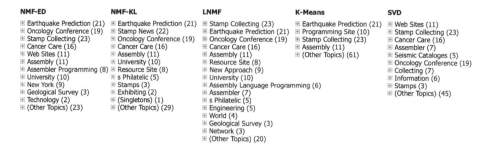

**Fig. 2.** Matrix factorisation comparison: cluster labels

**Lingo NMF-ED**
- ⊞ Search Engines (18)
- ⊞ Regular Graphs (13)
- ⊞ DIY Audio (14)
- ⊞ Independent Film (14)
- ⊞ Book Reviews (11)
- ⊞ Software Sites (19)
- ⊞ Senior Health (11)
- ⊞ Fitness Association (10)
- ⊞ Vacuum Tube (7)
- ⊞ Sample Chapters (5)
- ⊞ Current and Past Projects (6)
- ⊞ Color Theorem (4)
- ⊞ National Institute on Aging (5)
- ⊞ (Other Topics) (57)

**Suffix Tree Clustering (STC)**
- ⊞ search, software (26)
- ⊞ includes (28)
- ⊞ information (20)
- ⊞ site (18)
- ⊞ book (16)
- ⊞ resource (14)
- ⊞ article (11)
- ⊞ film (11)
- ⊞ projects (10)
- ⊞ offered (10)
- ⊞ free (10)
- ⊞ online (10)
- ⊞ seniors (9)
- ⊞ tube (9)
- ⊞ audio (8)

**Tollerance Rough Set (TRC)**
- ⊞ Search (30)
- ⊞ Software Search (21)
- ⊞ Tube (17)
- ⊞ Graph (11)
- ⊞ Books (16)
- ⊞ Senior (11)
- ⊞ Downloadable Software Directories (3)
- ⊞ Notes (1)
- ⊞ Film (19)
- ⊞ Other (65)

**Fig. 3.** Clustering algorithm comparison: cluster labels

further confirms poor performance of K-Means decomposition in the outlier detection test.

In Figure 3 we show cluster labels generated by Lingo, STC and TRC for a data set containing six ODP categories: Book Previews, Search Engines, Fitness, Do-It-Yourself, Graph Theory and Independent Filmmaking. Compared to STC and TRC Lingo seems to produce labels that are slightly more specific and probably easier to interpret, compare: "Search Engines" (Lingo) vs. "Search" (TRC), "Vacuum Tube" (Lingo) vs. "Tube" (STC and TRC) or "Independent Film" (Lingo) vs. "Film" (STC and TRC). Also, for this particular data set Lingo managed to avoid generating too general or meaningless labels such as "free", "online", "site", "includes", "information" (STC) or "Notes" (TRC).

## 6    Conclusions and Further Work

In this paper we have shown how a matrix factorisation can be used as part of a description-comes-first approach to search results clustering. We tested four factorisation algorithms (NMF, LNMF, SVD and K-Means/Concept Decomposition) with respect to topic separation, outlier detection and label quality. We also compared our approach with two other algorithms not based on matrix decompositions: Suffix Tree Clustering and Tolerance Rough Set Clustering.

Our experiments revealed that the Non-negative Matrix Factorisations significantly outperform both SVD and Concept Decomposition with respect to topic and snippet coverage, while maintaining almost the same level of cluster contamination. The reason for this is that, in contrast to SVD, NMF produces non-negative base vectors which can be better matched with the frequent phrases found in the input snippets. Another important observation is that due to high sparsity of base vectors, Local Non-negative Matrix Factorisation generates cluster labels that are shorter and more general compared to the other NMF methods. For this reason, contrary to our initial expectations, LNMF performed much worse with respect to average cluster contamination, and thus in the present form is not the best choice factorisation algorithm for Lingo. Finally, the description-comes-first approach to search results clustering implemented by Lingo significantly outperformed both STC and TRC in topic separation and outlier detection tests.

We feel that future experiments should investigate more complex matrix factorisations, such as [20]. It is also very interesting how our algorithm would perform for the full-text test collections such as REUTERS-21578 or OHSUMED. Such experiments would require efficient implementations of the factorisations taking advantage of e.g. the high sparsity of the term-document matrix or using subsampling.

## Acknowledgment

The author would like to thank anonymous reviewers for helpful suggestions. The experiments were performed within the Carrot$^2$ Search Results Clustering Framework. Carrot2 is available free of charge from *http://sf.net/projects/carrot2*.

## References

1. Zamir, O., Etzioni, O.: Web document clustering: a feasibility demonstration. In: SIGIR '98: Proceedings of the 21st annual international ACM SIGIR conference on Research and development in information retrieval, New York, NY, USA, ACM Press (1998) 46–54
2. Zamir, O.E.: Clustering Web Documents: A Phrase-Based Method for Grouping Search Engine Results. PhD thesis, University of Washington (1999)
3. Dong, Z.: Towards Web Information Clustering. PhD thesis, Southeast University, Nanjing, China (2002)
4. Lang, N.C.: A tolerance rough set approach to clustering web search results. Master's thesis, Faculty of Mathematics, Informatics and Mechanics, Warsaw University (2004)
5. Kummamuru, K., Lotlikar, R., Roy, S., Singal, K., Krishnapuram, R.: A hierarchical monothetic document clustering algorithm for summarization and browsing search results. In: Proceedings of the 13th international conference on World Wide Web, ACM Press (2004) 658–665
6. Stefanowski, J., Weiss, D.: Carrot$^2$ and language properties in web search results clustering. In: Proceedings of AWIC-2003, First International Atlantic Web Intelligence Conference. Volume 2663 of Lecture Notes in Computer Science., Madrid, Spain, Springer (2003) 240–249

7. Osiński, S., Stefanowski, J., Weiss, D.: Lingo: Search results clustering algorithm based on Singular Value Decomposition. In: Proceedings of the International IIS: Intelligent Information Processing and Web Mining Conference. Advances in Soft Computing, Zakopane, Poland, Springer (2004) 359–368
8. Osiński, S., Weiss, D.: A concept-driven algorithm for clustering search results. IEEE Intelligent Systems **20**(3) (2005) 48–54
9. Lee, D., Seung, S.: Learning the parts of objects by non-negative matrix factorization. Nature **401** (1999) 788–791
10. Li, S.Z., Hou, X.W., Zhang, H., Cheng, Q.: Learning spatially localized, parts-based representation. In: CVPR (1). (2001) 207–212
11. Dhillon, I., Modha, D.: Concept decompositions for large sparse text data using clustering. Machine Learning **42**(1) (2001) 143–175
12. Hearst, M.A., Pedersen, J.O.: Reexamining the cluster hypothesis: Scatter/gather on retrieval results. In: Proceedings of SIGIR-96, 19th ACM International Conference on Research and Development in Information Retrieval, Zürich, CH (1996) 76–84
13. Zamir, O., Etzioni, O.: Grouper: a dynamic clustering interface to Web search results. Computer Networks (Amsterdam, Netherlands: 1999) **31**(11–16) (1999) 1361–1374
14. Xu, W., Liu, X., Gong, Y.: Document clustering based on non-negative matrix factorization. In: Proceedings of the 26th annual international ACM SIGIR conference on Research and development in informaion retrieval, ACM Press (2003) 267–273
15. Salton, G.: Automatic text processing: the transformation, analysis, and retrieval of information by computer. Addison-Wesley Longman Publishing Co., Inc., Boston, MA, USA (1989)
16. Lee, D.D., Seung, H.S.: Algorithms for non-negative matrix factorization. In: Neural Information Processing Systems. Volume 13. (2000) 556–562
17. Bingham, E., Mannila, H.: Random projection in dimensionality reduction: applications to image and text data. In: KDD '01: Proceedings of the seventh ACM SIGKDD international conference on Knowledge discovery and data mining, New York, NY, USA, ACM Press (2001) 245–250
18. Dom, B.E.: An information-theoretic external cluster-validity measure. Technical Report IBM Research Report RJ 10219, IBM (2001)
19. Osiński, S.: Dimensionality reduction techniques for search results clustering. Master's thesis, The University of Sheffield (2004)
20. Xu, W., Gong, Y.: Document clustering by concept factorization. In: SIGIR '04: Proceedings of the 27th annual international ACM SIGIR conference on Research and development in information retrieval, New York, NY, USA, ACM Press (2004) 202–209

# Adapting the Naive Bayes Classifier to Rank Procedural Texts

Ling Yin[1] and Richard Power[2]

[1] Natural Language Technology Group (NLTG), University of Brighton,
Watts Building, Lewes Road, Brighton, BN2 4GJ, United Kingdom
Y.Ling@brighton.ac.uk
[2] Faculty of Mathematics and Computing, The Open University,
Walton Hall, Milton Keynes, MK7 6AA, United Kingdom
r.power@open.ac.uk

**Abstract.** This paper presents a machine-learning approach for ranking web documents according to the proportion of procedural text they contain. By 'procedural text' we refer to ordered lists of steps, which are very common in some instructional genres such as online manuals. Our initial training corpus is built up by applying some simple heuristics to select documents from a large collection and contains only a few documents with a large proportion of procedural texts. We adapt the Naive Bayes classifier to better fit this less than ideal training corpus. This adapted model is compared with several other classifiers in ranking procedural texts using different sets of features and is shown to perform well when only highly distinctive features are used.

## 1 Introduction

How-To questions constitute a large proportion of questions on the Web. Many how-to questions inquire about the procedure for achieving a specific goal. For such questions, typical information retrieval (IR) methods, based on key word matching, are better suited to detecting the content of the goal (e.g., installing a Windows XP server) than the general nature of the desired information (i.e., procedural, a series of steps for achieving this goal).

We suggest dividing the process of retrieving relevant documents for such questions into two stages: (1) use typical IR approaches for retrieving documents that are relevant to the specific goal; (2) use a text categorization approach to re-rank the retrieved documents according to the proportion of procedural text they contain. By 'procedural text' we refer to ordered lists of steps, which are very common in some instructional genres such as online manuals. This paper focuses on the second stage; the issue of integrating the text categorizer into a two-stage document retrieval system is addressed in [13].

Text categorization techniques are widely adopted to filter a document source according to a specific information need. In particular, extensive studies have been done on automatically filtering news releases. For instance, Stricker et al. [8] experiment on several news resources including the Financial Times, Los Angeles Times,

M. Lalmas et al. (Eds.): ECIR 2006, LNCS 3936, pp. 179–190, 2006.
© Springer-Verlag Berlin Heidelberg 2006

etc. They present a method for automatically generating for each topic "discriminant terms" [8] that are used as features to train a neural network classifier. In such studies, the specification of the information need is based on the topic of a document; much work has also been done on categorizing documents by focusing on the stylistic aspect (e.g., genre classification and authorship attribution). For instance, Santini [5] uses POS trigrams to categorize a subset of the BNC corpus into ten genres: four spoken genres (conversation, interview, public debate and planned speech) and six written genres (academic prose, advert, biography, instructional, popular lore and reportage). Despite the large amount of work done on text categorization, only a few studies have addressed the problem of automatically identifying procedural texts; these include [9], which uses word n-grams to classify (as procedural or non-procedural) list passages extracted using HTML tags. Our approach, instead, applies to whole documents, the aim being to measure the degree of *procedurality* — i.e., the amount of procedural text they contain.

Sebastiani [7] provides a detailed review of many machine-learning models for automatic text categorization. The Naive Bayes classifier, although shown to perform poorly in some comparative studies of classification models [11, 12], is commonly-used in text categorization. In this paper, we adapt the Naive Bayes classifier to better fit our less than ideal training corpus, which is built up by applying some simple heuristics to select documents from a large collection and only contains a few documents with a high proportion of procedural texts. We compare the performance of this model with several other state-of-the-art classification models when combined with different sets of features.

The features that are used to represent the documents, the training corpus and the adapted Naive Bayes classification model are presented in section 2, 3 and 4 respectively. Section 5 presents a few experiments on ranking document procedurality using different classification models and reports the results. Section 6 gives a detailed analysis of the experiment results and provides some tentative suggestions with regard to the characteristics of different classification models. A complementary experiment is also presented in section 6 for testing the suggestions. Section 7 provides a short summary and some future work.

## 2   Feature Selection and Document Representation

### 2.1   Linguistic Features and Cue Phrases

We targeted six procedural elements: actions, times, sequences, conditionals, preconditions, and purposes. These elements can be recognized using linguistic features or cue phrases. For example, an action is often conveyed by an imperative; a precondition can be expressed by the cue phrase 'only if'. We used Connexor's syntax analyzer[1] to preprocess documents and extracted all the syntactic and morphological tags excluding a few repetitive ones (34 surface syntactic tags and 34 morphological tags). We also handcrafted a list of relevant cue phrases (44), which were extracted from a document by using the Flex tool for pattern matching. Some sample cue phrases and the matching patterns are shown in Table 1.

---

[1] http://www.connexor.com/

**Table 1.** Sample cue phrases and matching patterns

| Procedural Element | Cue Phrase | Pattern |
|---|---|---|
| Precondition | 'only if' | [Oo]nly[[:space:]]if[[:space:]] |
| Purpose | 'so that' | [sS]o[[:space:]]that[[:space:]] |
| Condition | 'as long as' | ([Aa]s) [[:space:]]long[[:space:]]as[[:space:]] |
| Sequence | 'first' | [fF]irst [[:space:][:punct:]] |
| Time | 'now' | [nN]ow[[:space:][:punct:]] |

## 2.2 Modeling Inter-sentential Feature Cooccurrence

Some cue phrases are ambiguous and therefore cannot reliably suggest a procedural element. For example, the cue phrase 'first' can be used to represent a ranking order, a spatial relationship as well as a sequential order. However, it is more likely to represent a sequential order among actions if there is also an imperative in the same sentence. Indeed, sentences that contain both an ordinal number and an imperative are very frequent in procedural texts. We compared between the procedural training set and the non-procedural training set to extract distinctive feature cooccurrence patterns (limited to 2 features). Two schemas were used.

Chi-square was applied to measure the significance of the correlation between whether a sentence contains a particular feature cooccurrence pattern and whether it is in a procedural document. Table 2 is the contingency table for a cooccurrence pattern, where $p_{pro}$, $n_{pro}$, $p_{non}$ and $n_{non}$ stand for the total number of sentences of each category.

**Table 2.** The 2*2 contingency table for a feature cooccurrence pattern

|  | In procedural documents | In non-procedural documents |
|---|---|---|
| Contain the pattern | $p_{pro}$ | $p_{non}$ |
| Do not contain the pattern | $n_{pro}$ | $n_{non}$ |

Chi-square favors patterns that occur frequently. There are patterns that do not occur in every procedural document, but if they do occur, there is a high probability that the document is procedural. Such a pattern might have a low frequency of occurrence in the corpus and therefore cannot generate a significant chi-square value. To detect such patterns, another schema we used is the ratio between the number of sentences that contain a particular pattern in the procedural set ($p_{pro}$) and in the non-procedural set ($p_{non}$), normalized by the size of the two sets ($s_{pro}$ and $s_{non}$), i.e.,

$$R(p) = \frac{p_{pro} \times s_{non}}{p_{non} \times s_{pro}} . \tag{1}$$

Two ordered lists were acquired by applying the two schemas to rank the feature cooccurrence patterns. We cut the two lists at certain thresholds (which were decided empirically) and acquired two sets of top ranked patterns. Those patterns that were included in both sets were chosen as distinctive patterns.

## 2.3  Document Representation

Each document was represented as a feature vector $\vec{d} = \{x_1, x_2, ..., x_N\}$, where $x_i$ represents the proportion of sentences in the document that contains a particular feature. We compared the effectiveness of using individual features ($x_i$ refers to either a single linguistic feature or a cue phrase) and of using feature cooccurrence patterns ($x_i$ refers to a feature cooccurrence pattern).

# 3   Corpus Preparation

Pagewise[2] provides a list of subject-matter domains, ranging from household issues to arts and entertainment. We downloaded 1536 documents from this website (referred to hereafter as the Pagewise collection). We then used some simple heuristics to select documents from this set to build the initial training corpus. Specifically, to build the procedural set we chose documents with titles containing key phrases 'how to' and 'how can I' (209 documents); to build the non-procedural set, we chose documents which did not include these phrases in their titles, and which also had no phrases like 'procedure' and 'recipe' within the body of the text (208 documents).

Samples drawn randomly from the procedural set (25) and the non-procedural set (28) were submitted to two human judges, who assigned procedurality scores from 1 (meaning no procedural text at all) to 5 (meaning over 90% procedural text). The Kendall tau-b agreement between the two rankings is 0.821. Overall, the average scores for the procedural and non-procedural samples were 3.15 and 1.38. We used these 53 sample documents as part of the test set and the document remaining as the initial training set (184 procedural and 180 non-procedural).

This initial training corpus is far from ideal: first, it is small in size; a more serious problem is that many positive training examples do not contain a major proportion of procedural texts. In our experiments, we used this initial training set to bootstrap a larger training set. Details will be described in section 5.

# 4   Learning Method

As mentioned in section 1, we adapted the Naive Bayes classifier to better fit our suboptimal training corpus. Before describing the details of the adaptation, we first talk about another problem we came across while experimenting with the Naive Bayes classifier.

We used the Naive Bayes classifier from the Weka-3-4 package [10]. Some preliminary experiments showed that most documents were scored as either extremely procedural (i.e., the score is 1) or not procedural at all (i.e., the score is 0). Such scoring result does not enable us to rank the documents. We analyzed and modified the Naive Bayes classifier to solve the problem. Details are described as follows.

The Naive Bayes classifier scores the degree of procedurality using the probability that a document falls into the procedural category—i.e., $p\left(C = procedural \mid \vec{d_j}\right)$. Using the Bayes' theorem, the probability can be calculated as shown in

---

[2] Refer to http://www.essortment.com

$$p\left(C=c\mid\overrightarrow{d_j}\right)=\frac{p(C=c)p\left(\overrightarrow{d_j}\mid C=c\right)}{p\left(\overrightarrow{d_j}\right)}=\frac{p(C=c)p\left(\overrightarrow{d_j}\mid C=c\right)}{p(C=c)p\left(\overrightarrow{d_j}\mid C=c\right)+p(C=\neg c)p\left(\overrightarrow{d_j}\mid C=\neg c\right)},\qquad(2)$$

where c can represent any particular category (e.g., procedural) [3].

Assuming that any two coordinates in the document feature vector $\overrightarrow{d}=\{x_1,x_2,...,x_N\}$ are conditionally independent, we can then simplify the calculation by using

$$p\left(\overrightarrow{d_j}\mid C=c\right)=\prod_i p(X_i=x_i\mid C=c),\qquad(3)$$

where $p(X_i=x_i\mid C=c)$ represents the probability of randomly picking up a document in category c of which the feature $X_i$ has value $x_i$. The same simplification applies to $p\left(\overrightarrow{d_j}\mid C=\neg c\right)$.

Multiplying all the $p(X_i=x_i\mid C=c)$ together often yields an extremely small value that is difficult to represent in a computer; this is why the final procedurality score is either 1 or 0. To tackle this problem, we calculated the procedurality score by

$$\log\left(\frac{p\left(C=c\mid\overrightarrow{d_j}\right)}{p\left(C=\neg c\mid\overrightarrow{d_j}\right)}\right)=\log\left(\frac{p(C=c)p\left(\overrightarrow{d_j}\mid C=c\right)}{p(C=\neg c)p\left(\overrightarrow{d_j}\mid C=\neg c\right)}\right)\qquad(4)$$

$$=\log(p(C=c))-\log(p(C=\neg c))+\sum_i\log(p(X_i=x_i\mid C=c))-\sum_i\log(p(X_i=x_i\mid C=\neg c)).\qquad(5)$$

The above modification will be referred to hereafter as the first adaptation. It is worth to point out that the ranking order of any two documents remains the same when replacing (2) by (5).

As we can see from the above formulas, the Naive Bayes classifier scores a document according to whether it is a typical member of its set (i.e., $p(X_i=x_i\mid C=c)$) as well as how much it contrasts with members of other set (i.e., $\frac{1}{p(X_i=x_i\mid C=\neg c)}$). Specifically, the Naive Bayes classifier delivered in the Weka-3-4 package assumes that each feature follows a normal distribution and estimates $p(X_i=x_i\mid C=c)$ by

$$p(X_i=x_i\mid C=c)=\frac{1}{\sqrt{2\pi}\sigma}e^{-\frac{(x=\mu)^2}{2\sigma^2}},\qquad(6)$$

where $\mu$ and $\sigma$ are estimated from the training data. In figure 1, the solid curve and the dotted curve show the probability density functions estimated from the non-procedural training set and the procedural training set respectively.

As mentioned in section 3, the procedural documents in our initial training corpus have a low average procedurality score, which means many of them do not contain a large proportion of procedural elements. Since most of the features used represent some procedural elements, we suppose the actual population of procedural documents

---

[3] Note that formula (2), (3) and (6) are either extracted from [3] or inferred from the Java code in the Weka-3-4 package.

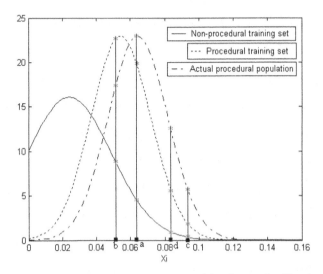

**Fig. 1.** An illustration of the problems in using the Naive Bayes classification algorithm

should have a higher mean value on such features compared to the procedural training set (as shown in Figure 1). In this case, point a, which obviously has a higher score than point b when using a training set that are representative of the actual population, is probably scored lower than b when using our training set.

Although the procedural training examples are not representative of the actual population of procedural documents, they are useful in indicating the difference between procedural documents and non-procedural documents. For example, we can infer from Figure 1 that feature $X_i$ is associated positively with the degree of proce-durality (since the positive training set has a higher mean value on this feature than the negative training set). However, the Naive Bayes classifier does not focus on modeling the difference between the two different classes. Therefore, point c, although larger than point d, is probably scored lower than d. We adjusted the formula to model the difference between the two different classes. Specifically, we replaced $p(X_i = x_i \mid C = c)$ in (5) by

$$
\begin{cases}
p(X_i \le x_i \mid C = c) = \int_{-\infty}^{x_i} \frac{1}{\sqrt{2\pi}\sigma} e^{-\frac{(x-\mu)^2}{2\sigma^2}} \, dx & \text{if} \quad mean(X_i \mid C = c) > mean(X_i \mid C = \neg c) \\
p(X_i \ge x_i \mid C = c) = \int_{x_i}^{\infty} \frac{1}{\sqrt{2\pi}\sigma} e^{-\frac{(x-\mu)^2}{2\sigma^2}} \, dx & \text{if} \quad mean(X_i \mid C = c) < mean(X_i \mid C = \neg c) \\
\hspace{3.5cm} 1 & \text{if} \quad mean(X_i \mid C = c) = mean(X_i \mid C = \neg c)
\end{cases}
\tag{7}
$$

where $mean(X_i \mid C = c)$ refers to the mean value of feature $X_i$ of the documents in category $c$. $p(X_i = x_i \mid C = \neg c)$ in (5) was replaced by a formula similar to (7), the only difference being that every $c$ in (7) is changed to be $\neg c$.

The new scoring curves are shown in figure 2. This way the score of a document is determined by the ratio of the probability of a document with a lower feature value being in the procedural class (represented by dotted curve) and the probability of a

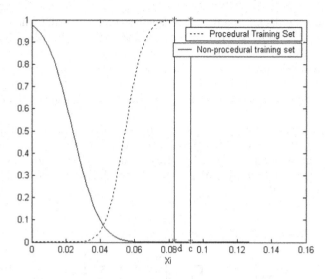

**Fig. 2.** An illustration of the Adapted Naive Bayes classification algorithm

document with a higher feature value being in the non-procedural class (represented by the solid curve). If feature $X_i$ is associated negatively with the degree of proce-durality (i.e., $mean(X_i \mid C = c) < mean(X_i \mid C = \neg c)$), then the word 'lower' and 'higher' in the last sentence should be reversed.

The new model will be referred to hereafter as the Adapted Naive Bayes classifier. It is worth to point out that, after the above modification, (5) is no longer equivalent to (4). This means, the core of the Naive Bayes classification approach — i.e., view-ing the "categorization status value" in terms of the probability that a document falls within a category [7] is changed.

## 5   Experiments

Our training and testing corpora were from two sources: the Pagewise collection and the SPIRIT collection. The SPIRIT collection contains a terabyte of HTML that are crawled from the web starting from an initial seed set of a few thousands universities and other educational organizations [1].

Our test set contained 103 documents, including the 53 documents that were sampled and then separated from the initial training corpus, another 30 documents randomly chosen from the Pagewise collection and 20 documents chosen from the SPIRIT collection. We asked two human subjects to score the procedurality for these documents, following the same instruction described in section 3. The correlation co-efficient (Kendall tau-b) between the two rankings is 0.725, which is the upper bound of the performance of the classifiers.

As mentioned before, the initial training corpus was used to bootstrap a larger training set. To do so, we first extracted 441 distinctive feature cooccurrence patterns based on the initial training corpus. These patterns were used to build document vectors to train an Adapted Naive Bayes classifier. We applied the classifier to rank the remaining documents from the Pagewise collection (the whole set excluding 83 documents that were added into the test set) and 500 web documents from the SPIRIT collection. 378 top ranked documents were selected to construct the positive training set and 608 lowest ranked documents were used to construct the negative training set. A random sampling of the procedural documents in this bootstrapped set suggests that their average procedurality score is slightly higher than those in the initial training set.

The bootstrapped training corpus was then used to reselect distinctive feature cooccurrence patterns and to train different classifiers. We compared the Adapted Naive Bayes classifier with the Naive Bayes classifier[4] and three other classifiers, including Maximum Entropy (ME)[5], Alternating Decision Tree (ADTree) [2] and Linear Regression [10].

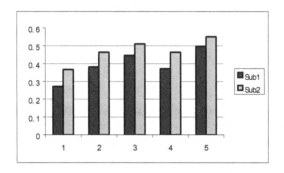

**Fig. 3.** Ranking results using individual features: 1 refers to Adapted Naive Bayes, 2 refers to Naive Bayes, 3 refers to ME, 4 refers to ADTree and 5 refers to Linear Regression

**Table 3.** Ranking results using individual features

| Ranking Method | Agreement with Subject 1 | Agreement with Subject 2 | Average |
|---|---|---|---|
| Adapted Naive Bayes | 0.270841 | 0.367515 | 0.319178 |
| Naive Bayes | 0.381921 | 0.464577 | 0.423249 |
| Maximum Entropy | 0.446283 | 0.510926 | 0.478605 |
| Alternating Decision Tree | 0.371988 | 0.463966 | 0.417977 |
| Linear Regression | 0.497395 | 0.551597 | 0.524496 |

Figure 3 and Table 3 show the kendall-tau b coefficients between human subjects' ranking results and the trained classifiers' ranking results on the test set when using individual features (112). Figure 4 and Table 4 show the kendall-tau b coefficients when using feature cooccurrence patterns (813).

---

[4] As mentioned in section 4, we cannot rank the documents based on the scoring result of the Naive Bayes classifier from the Weka-3-4 package. We therefore used the model acquired after the first adaptation instead.

[5] Refer to http://homepages.inf.ed.ac.uk/s0450736/maxent.html

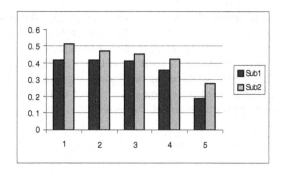

**Fig. 4.** Ranking results using feature cooccurrence patterns: 1 refers to Adapted Naive Bayes, 2 refers to Naive Bayes, 3 refers to ME, 4 refers to ADTree and 5 refers to Linear Regression

**Table 4.** Ranking results using feature cooccurrence patterns

| Ranking Method | Agreement with Subject 1 | Agreement with Subject 2 | Average |
|---|---|---|---|
| Adapted Naive Bayes | 0.420423 | 0.513336 | 0.466880 |
| Naive Bayes | 0.420866 | 0.475514 | 0.44819 |
| Maximum Entropy | 0.414184 | 0.455482 | 0.434833 |
| Alternating Decision Tree | 0.358095 | 0.422987 | 0.390541 |
| Linear Regression | 0.190609 | 0.279472 | 0.235041 |

As we can see from the figures, when using individual features, Linear Regression achieved the best result, Adapted Naive Bayes performed the worst, Naive Bayes, Maximum Entropy and Alternating Decision Tree were in the middle; interestingly, when using feature cooccurrence patterns, the order almost reversed, i.e., Adapted Naive Bayes performed the best and Linear Regression the worst. Comparing the results of using individual features and feature cooccurrence patterns, only Adapted Naive Bayes and Naive Bayes performed better when using feature cooccurrence patterns, all the other classifiers performed better when using individual features.

## 6 Discussion

The experiment results showed that two Naive Bayes classifiers fitted better with feature cooccurrence patterns while ME, ADTree and Linear Regression fitted better with individual features. In contrast to feature cooccurrence patterns, each of which is chosen as being very distinctive, individual features may contain many irrelevant features since all the morphological and syntactical taggers that the Connexor's Syntax Analyzer provides are included. This does not make much difference for ADTree and Linear Regression since they both have a feature selection process that can filter irrelevant features. However, the Adapted Naive Bayes classifier does not have such a function and it treats every feature as extremely distinctive. The Naive Bayes classifier and the ME classification model, although they do not have an explicit feature selection process, can estimate the degree of distinctiveness of each feature based on the training data. The above difference between the Naive Bayes classifier and the Adapted Naive Bayes classifier can be seen by comparing the scoring results at point d in Figure 1 (Naive Bayes classifier) and Figure 2 (Adapted Naive Bayes classifier).

To verify the above explanation with regard to why the Adapted Naive Bayes classifier performed poorly when using individual features, we applied the feature selection algorithms described in section 2.2 to select distinctive individual features (42 features were selected) and tested the classifiers again. Results are shown in Figure 5 and Table 5.

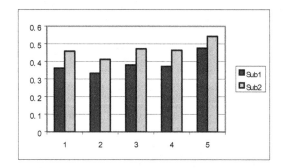

**Fig. 5.** Ranking results using selected individual features: 1 refers to Adapted Naive Bayes, 2 refers to Naive Bayes, 3 refers to ME, 4 refers to ADTree and 5 refers to Linear Regression

**Table 5.** Ranking results using selected individual features

| Ranking method | Agreement with Subject 1 | Agreement with Subject 2 | Average |
|---|---|---|---|
| Adapted Naive Bayes | 0.362007 | 0.458198 | 0.410103 |
| Naive Bayes | 0.332798 | 0.411717 | 0.372258 |
| Maximum Entropy | 0.380151 | 0.471868 | 0.426010 |
| Alternating Decision Tree | 0.371988 | 0.463966 | 0.417977 |
| Linear Regression | 0.476054 | 0.542832 | 0.509443 |

Compared to using all the individual features, the performance of Adapted Naive Bayes was greatly improved when only using a few selected ones; ADTree performed the same; but ME and Linear Regression performed slightly worse. This does support our thinking that the Adapted Naive Bayes classifier presumes every feature is extremely distinctive and therefore only distinctive features should be used with it.

Another important difference between feature cooccurrence patterns and individual features consists in their numbers. Because the number of feature cooccurrence patterns is huge, it is difficult for ADTree and Linear Regression to generalize and to select relevant features. This can be a reason why these two models performed poorly when using feature cooccurrence patterns.

As it was addressed in section 2.2, individual features are ambiguous and we expected modeling feature inter-sentential cooccurrence helps in disambiguate. However, this thinking is not supported by the results of the experiments. We believe this is because that most documents used in the experiments are from the Pagewise collection, which have a rather uniform style and ambiguities are greatly decreased.

## 7  Summary and Future Work

In this paper, we have presented an Adapted Naive Bayes classifier for ranking procedural documents and have compared it with several other classifiers when combined with different sets of features. We have shown that the Adapted Naive Bayes classifier performs well when only highly distinctive features are used and is better than many other classifiers when the number of relevant features is huge. Thinking individual features are ambiguous, we chose to use inter-sentential feature cooccurrence patterns instead. However, the result of the experiment did not show that the system gains better results by using feature cooccurrence patterns rather than using individual features. We believe this is because that most of the documents in our training and testing corpora have a rather homogenous style. As a future work we plan to test the Adapted Naive Bayes classifier and the method for modeling inter-sentential feature cooccurrence in a much broader context.

## References

1. Clarke, C., Cormack, G., Laszlo, M., Lynam, T., and Terra, E. (1998) The Impact of Corpus Size on Question Answering Performance. In *Proceedings of the 25th Annual International ACM SIGIR Conference on Research and Development in IR*, Tampere, Finland
2. Freund, Y. and Mason, L. (1999) The Alternating Decision Tree Learning Algorithm. In *Proceeding of the Sixteenth International Conference on Machine Learning*, Bled, Slovenia: 124-133
3. John, G. and Langley, P. (1995) Estimating Continuous Distributions in Bayesian Classifiers. *In Proceedings of the Eleventh Conference on Uncertainty in Artificial Intelligence.* Morgan Kaufmann, San Mateo: 338-345
4. Kelly, D., Murdock, V., Yuan, X.J., Croft, W.B., and Belkin, N.J. (2002) Features of Documents Relevant to Task- and Fact-Oriented Questions. In *Proceedings of the Eleventh International Conference on Information and Knowledge Management (CIKM '02)*, McLean, VA: 645-647
5. Santini, M. (2004) A Shallow Approach to Syntactic Feature Extraction for Genre Classification. In *Proceedings of the 7th Annual Colloquium for the UK Special Interest Group for Computational Linguistics (CLUK-04)*
6. Schwitter, R., Rinaldi, F., and Clematide, S. (2004) The Importance of How-Questions in Technical Domains. *Question-Answering workshop of TALN 04*, Fez, Morocco
7. Sebastiani, F. (1999) Machine Learning in Automated Text Categorisation. *ACM Computing Surveys*, 34(1): 1-47
8. Stricker, M., Vichot, F., Dreyfus, G. and Wolinski, F. (2000) Two Steps Feature Selection and Neural Network Classification for the TREC-8 Routing. *CoRR cs. CL/0007016*
9. Takechi, M., Tokunaga, T., Matsumoto, Y. and Tanaka, H. (2003) Feature Selection in Categorizing Procedural Expressions. *The Sixth International Workshop on Information Retrieval with Asian Languages (IRAL2003)*: 49-56
10. Witten, I. H., Frank, E. (2000) *Data Mining: Practical Machine Learning Tools and Techniques with Java Implementations*, Morgan Kaufmann, San Mateo, CA

11. Yang, Y. (1999) An Evaluation of Statistical Approaches to Text Categorization. *Journal of Information Retrieval 1(1/2)*: 67-88

12. Yang, Y. and Liu, X. (1999) A Re-Examination of Text Categorization Methods. In *Proceedings of ACM SIGIR Conference on Research and Development in Information Retrieval (SIGIR'99):* 42-49

13. Yin, L. (2006) A Two-Stage Approach to Retrieve Answers for How-To Questions. In *Proceedings of the 11th Conference of the European Chapter of the Association for Computational Linguistics*, Student session, Trento, Italy

# The Effects of Relevance Feedback Quality and Quantity in Interactive Relevance Feedback: A Simulation Based on User Modeling

Heikki Keskustalo, Kalervo Järvelin, and Ari Pirkola

Department of Information Studies, FIN-33014 University of Tampere, Finland

**Abstract.** Experiments on the effectiveness of relevance feedback with real users are time-consuming and expensive. This makes simulation for rapid testing desirable. We define a user model, which helps to quantify some interaction decisions involved in simulated relevance feedback. First, the relevance criterion defines the relevance threshold of the user to accept documents as relevant to his/her needs. Second, the browsing effort refers to the patience of the user to browse through the initial list of retrieved documents in order to give feedback. Third, the feedback effort refers to the effort and ability of the user to collect feedback documents. We use the model to construct several simulated relevance feedback scenarios in a laboratory setting. Using TREC data providing graded relevance assessments, we study the effect of the quality and quantity of the feedback documents on the effectiveness of the relevance feedback and compare this to the pseudo-relevance feedback. Our results indicate that one can compensate large amounts of relevant but low quality feedback by small amounts of highly relevant feedback.

## 1 Introduction

Selection of good search keys is crucial for successful text retrieval, yet users of information systems often find it difficult to find the best expressions for their information needs [3, 4, 11]. On the other hand, although users may have difficulties in expressing exactly their information needs, they are often able to identify useful information when they see it. This fact leads to the notion of relevance feedback (RF). In RF, the users mark documents as relevant to their needs and present this information to the system. This information can be used for automatically modifying better queries [8, 9].

Actually, users of information systems might best be served by systems that retrieve especially highly relevant documents [6, 15]. The results of a user study [14] indicate that the users are also able to identify highly relevant documents. Moreover, the textual characteristics of the documents at various relevance levels differ: [13] showed that in highly relevant documents a larger number of aspects of the request was discussed, and a larger set of unique expressions was used. These observations lead to our research questions: How effective is RF when we consider various levels of relevance in evaluation phase? How is the quality and quantity of the feedback documents related to the effectiveness? From the point in view of creating RF interfaces, we should learn what kind of evidence we should try to collect from the searchers. In this paper, we shall explore these questions through user

M. Lalmas et al. (Eds.): ECIR 2006, LNCS 3936, pp. 191–204, 2006.
© Springer-Verlag Berlin Heidelberg 2006

simulation in a laboratory setting. We use a test collection, a subset of TREC collection providing graded relevance assessments of documents for 41 topics [12]. The graded assessments are scaled from 0 (non-relevant) to 3 (highly relevant). We shall simulate the quantity of RF by the number of documents in the initial result marked as feedback by the user, and the quality by the relevance threshold set by the user. As an additional research question we ask whether the simulated relevance feedback may successfully compete with pseudo-relevance feedback (PRF), and if so, by what effort in terms of the amount and quality of the user feedback? We evaluate all cases using non-interpolated average precision (MAP) at three different relevance thresholds.

Our laboratory simulation provides a rapid means of exploring the limits of user feedback without laborious experiments with real users. For example, one may find out, as we will also report, what kind of user RF effort is most effective and how it compares with the PRF. One needs to verify these findings in real world situations. However, this may be done more efficiently when one has better insight into what to test.

The rest of the paper is organized as follows. In Section 2 we explain our experimental methodology – user modeling for simulations, the test collection, the retrieval system and the test runs. Section 3 presents our findings, Section 4 discusses the main result and Section 5 presents the conclusions.

## 2  Methods

### 2.1  User Modeling for Relevance Feedback Simulation

Pseudo relevance feedback is a highly parameterized process. For example, the number of documents used in the feedback, the methods for selecting and weighting the feedback keys, and the number of the feedback keys extracted may be varied.

Human relevance feedback has similar characteristics when one considers, as we do, user feedback based on document level judgments. The number of top documents the user is willing to examine varies. The user has also many methods for selecting and weighting the feedback keys. The number of feedback documents that the user actually selects may vary. In addition, importantly, the user may tolerate irrelevance, require relevance, or ignore marginal relevance to different degrees in the feedback documents. This is a characteristic of human feedback that escapes automatic methods of PRF. It might also provide a qualitatively better basis for RF, which leads to outperforming automatic PRF if the user is willing to provide the effort.

Since users vary greatly, we developed a simple user model to grab the parameters above. We use three concepts for modeling:

- requirement of document relevance (stringent, regular or liberal): relevance threshold $R$
- willingness to browse (patient/impatient): window size $B$
- willingness to provide feedback (eager/reserved): feedback set size $F$

The *requirement of document relevance, R,* is an important dimension since many users may want to focus on highly relevant documents only [6, 15]. Users can also identify them while marginal documents easily escape the user's attention [14]. We model the relevance threshold dimension by possible values of graded relevance

$R \in \{0,1,2,3\}$. In other words, $R = 3$ indicates that the user is capable and willing to recognize and accept only highly relevant documents for RF, whereas $R = 1$ indicates that the user liberally accepts even marginal documents for RF. As a special case, $R = 0$ models the case where all the documents considered are accepted, i.e., PRF (blind feedback).

The *willingness to browse*, $B$, models the user's capability and willingness to browse through the ranked retrieval result. The user's willingness to study retrieved sets is limited (futility point) [1]. We model the browsing dimension by the number of documents considered (window size $B$). For example, $B = 1$ indicates that the user is impatient and only willing to consider the first document and gives up after that, whereas $B = 30$ indicates a patient user willing to examine a long list of retrieval results. In the present study we shall only consider a limited set of values for $B$, i.e., $B \in \{1, 5, 10, 30\}$.

The *willingness to provide feedback*, $F$ ($\leq B$) models the user's willingness to mark documents as relevant. We separate this dimension from the previous one since even if the user is willing to browse through a long list, she may give up after finding the first or first few relevant documents. In this paper we examine only positive RF. This dimension is essential since, as [2] argues, users may be reluctant to provide feedback, and on the other hand the amount of feedback may be critical to success. We model the willingness to provide feedback by the maximum number of documents the user is willing to mark as relevant $F$. As an example, $F = 1$ indicates that the user is reserved and only willing to consider the first relevant document encountered as feedback and gives up marking after that, whereas $F \geq 10$ indicates an eager user willing to provide lots of feedback. In the present study we shall only consider a limited set of values for $F$, i.e. $F \in \{1, 5, 10, 30\}$ while $F \leq B$.

*User model* is a triplet $M = <R, B, F>$ which defines a three-dimensional space of user characteristics. Each triplet with specified values is a point in the space modeling a distinct type of user (*a user scenario*) or RF interaction. It is obvious that some regions of the space are more interesting than others. However, in general, relations between the more distant areas are of interest, e.g., can one compensate low quality feedback by giving it in large amounts. Moreover, how much user's effort, and what kind, is needed to outperform pseudo-relevance feedback, i.e., which scenarios $< R, B, F > (R > 0)$ provide better effectiveness than $<0, B', F' > ?$ (In PRF $R=0$ and $B' = F'$.)

## 2.2 The Test Collection

In this study the reassessed TREC documents from [12] are used including altogether 41 topics from TREC 7 and TREC 8 ad hoc tracks. The non-binary relevance judgments were obtained by re-judging documents judged relevant by NIST assessors together with about 5% of irrelevant documents for each topic. The selection of topics was based on the size of recall bases, i.e., each topic should have more than 30 relevant documents but the size of the pool to be reassessed should not exceed 200 documents (for details, see [5, 12]). The relevance judgment in the reassessment process was based on topicality. The new assessments were done on a four-point scale:

- (0) Irrelevant document - the document does not contain any information about the topic.
- (1) Marginally relevant document - the document only points to the topic and does not contain more or other information than the topic description.
- (2) Fairly relevant document - the document contains more information than the topic description but the presentation is not exhaustive. In case of multi-faceted topic, only some of the sub-themes or viewpoints are covered.
- (3) Highly relevant document - the document discusses the themes of the topic exhaustively. In case of a multi-faceted topic, all or most sub-themes or view-points are covered.

Altogether 6122 documents were reassessed (Table 1). Almost all of the originally irrelevant documents were also assessed irrelevant in reassessment (93.9%). Of the TREC relevant documents about 76% were judged relevant at some level and 24% irrelevant. This seems to indicate that the re-assessors have been somewhat stricter than the original judges. Among the relevant documents one half were marginal, a third fairly relevant, and a sixth highly relevant [5].

**Table 1.** The distribution of relevance assessments in the test collection (41 topics)

| Relevance Level | Total Number of Documents | % | % of Relevant | Avg number per Topic |
|---|---|---|---|---|
| Rel = 0 | 3719 | 62.1 | .. | .. |
| Rel = 1 | 1197 | 18.6 | 49.8 | 29.2 |
| Rel = 2 | 812 | 12.8 | 33.8 | 19.8 |
| Rel = 3 | 394 | 6.6 | 16.4 | 9.6 |
| Total | 6122 | 100.0 | 100.0 | 58.6 |

In the recall base there were on the average 29 documents of relevance level 1 per each topic, 20 documents at relevance level 2, and 10 documents at relevance level 3 per topic. In other words, on the there were on the average 59 relevant documents of some relevance level per each topic (Table 1).

The document collection contained 528155 documents organized under the retrieval system *InQuery* (see below). The database index is constructed by lemmatizing the document words (using ENGTWOL morphological analyzer by Lingsoft, Inc.).

### 2.3   The Retrieval System InQuery and the Feedback Key Extraction

The *InQuery* system was chosen for the test, because it has a flexible query language and it has shown good performance in several tests (see, e.g., [4]). *InQuery* is based on Bayesian inference networks. All keys are attached with a *belief value*, which is approximated by the following *tf.idf* modification:

$$0.4 + 0.6 * \left( \frac{tf_{ij}}{tf_{ij} + 0.5 + 1.5 * \left( \frac{dl_j}{adl} \right)} \right) * \left( \frac{\log\left( \frac{N + 0.5}{df_i} \right)}{\log(N + 1.0)} \right) \tag{1}$$

where $tf_{ij}$ = the frequency of the key $i$ in the document $j$

$dl_j$ = the length of document $j$ (as the number of keys)

$adl$ = average document length in the collection

$N$ = collection size (as the number of documents)

$df_i$ = number of documents containing key $i$.

The *InQuery* query language provides a large set of operators to specify relations between search keys. In the present paper we only need the typical probabilistic operator #sum and the synonym operator #syn. The probabilistic interpretations for these operators are given below:

$$P_{sum}(Q_1, Q_2, ..., Q_n) = (p_1 + p_2 + ... + p_n)/n \qquad (2)$$

where $P$ denotes probability, $Q_i$ is either a key or an InQuery expression, and $p_i$, $i = 1...n$, is the belief value of $Q_i$.

The probability for operands connected by SYN operator is calculated by modifying the tf.idf function as follows:

$$0.4 + 0.6 * \left( \frac{\sum_{i \in S} tf_{ij}}{\sum_{i \in S} tf_{ij} + 0.5 + 1.5 * \left( \frac{dl_j}{adl} \right)} \right) * \left( \frac{\log\left( \frac{N + 0.5}{df_s} \right)}{\log(N + 1.0)} \right) \qquad (3)$$

where $tf_{ij}$ = the frequency of the key $i$ in the document $j$

$S$ = the set of search keys within the SYN operator

$dl_j$ = the length of document $j$ (as the number of keys)

$adl$ = average document length in the collection

$N$ = collection size (as the number of documents)

$df_S$ = number of documents containing at least on key of the set $S$.

Our initial queries are based on the TREC topic wording, excluding the stop list words, and have the structure #sum(#syn(key_1, key_2, ...), #syn(..., key_n) ,...). The synonym structures are due to lemmatizing topic words. Some of them are ambiguous, and for a given word all its interpreted lemmas are included in one synonym set. The extracted expansion keys form a sum structure #sum(key_{e1}, key_{e2}, ...) and the revised feedback query has the structure #sum(#sum(#syn(key_1, key_2, ...), #syn(..., key_n) ,...) #sum(key_{e1}, key_{e2}, ...)).

Expansion keys were extracted from the feedback documents using the RATF weighting scheme [7]. The scheme computes *relative average term frequency* values for the keys of documents, as follows:

$$RATF(k) = (cf_k / df_k) * 10^3 / ln(df_k + SP)^p \qquad (4)$$

$cf_k$ = the collection frequency of the key $k$

$df_k$ = the document frequency of the key $k$

$SP$ = a collection dependent scaling parameter

$p$ = the power parameter

The scheme gives high values for the keys whose average term frequency (i.e., $cf/df$) is high and $df$ low. The scaling parameter $SP$ is used to down weight rare words.

For *SP* and *p* we used the values of *SP* = 3000 and *p* = 3. These values are based on a previous study using different topic sets but a corresponding database [7].

In the expansion key extraction, from each feedback document a word list containing the 50 best keys was extracted by the ranked order of their descending RATF values. When more than one document was given as feedback, the RATF key lists for each document were united followed by the extraction of 30 best keys (keys shared by the greatest number of word lists).

## 2.4  Experimental Set-Up

The overall experimental set-up consists of the following steps:

1. For each TREC topic (N=41) the title and description fields are processed and automatically formulated into the initial query.
2. Each initial query is run in the test collection and the initial result set (the top 50 documents for each topic) is retrieved.
3. By using the user scenario <*R, B, F*> together with the recall base, the set of feedback documents (defined uniquely by each user scenario) is extracted automatically from the initial result set.
4. The expansion keys are extracted from the set of feedback documents (among the relevant documents from the initial run). RATF weighting scheme is used here. The 30 best expansion keys are extracted and formed into a *#sum* –clause. This clause is combined with the initial query to form the feedback query.
5. Each feedback query is run in the test collection and the final result (document set) is retrieved.
6. Both the initial result and the final results are analyzed for their mean average precision (MAP), applying three different evaluation criteria: stringent, regular and liberal. The same evaluation criteria were also used for conceptualizing the feedback requirements as highly relevant (*Rel* =3), at least fairly relevant (*Rel* ≥ 2), or at least marginally relevant (*Rel* ≥ 1) documents, respectively.

The initial queries were formed automatically by excluding stop words, lemmatizing the content-bearing words and applying fuzzy matching from the database index in case of words which could not be lemmatized (two best matches were selected). Lemmatization leads to synonym sets of one or more components. These are combined by the *#sum* –operator into the initial query.

The evaluation of retrieval effects of RF methods when *real users* are involved has some special requirements. Admitting that users may be lazy to browse, an evaluation measure based on DCV (document cut-off values) or discounted cumulated gain [6] might be preferred over MAP. If only a small evaluation window is used, one may argue that only the unseen documents should be shown at the RF phase and the evaluation should not reward re-ranking of the feedback documents among the final document set [10]. This could be achieved by keeping the documents identified as relevant (within the browsing and feedback scope) "frozen" to their initial ranks. On the other hand, because there are no intermediate results seen by the user in the PRF, it is not possible to make an entirely fair comparison between the simulated user RF and the PRF case. In PRF, MAP or precision at 10 % recall are typical effectiveness measures.

In the present paper, we compare the user RF and PRF and want to find out how various user feedback scenarios are related to search effectiveness. We measure this by using MAP at various relevance thresholds. An inherent problem with using MAP this way is that the RF documents may be re-retrieved by the feedback query (although not necessarily) but with a better ranking, especially when the recall bases are small. On the other hand, we may think of a user situation where the user is collecting relevant documents at the end of the process and has not yet really read initial feedback documents. In this situation, re-retrieving the relevant documents is not problematic, as the user is simply interested in the quality of the *final* search result. In later studies, we shall apply DCV based measures and take specifically into account the role and effect of the feedback documents among the final result set considering the user view point differently.

## 3 Findings

### 3.1 Effect of User Scenario on the Amount of Feedback

The first obvious question is what is the relationship of user's relevance criteria and effort to the quantity and quality of relevance feedback available? In order to answer to that question, we first study the effect of selecting a specific user scenario to the number of feedback documents available (the third column in Tables 2-4), to the cases of no feedback (fourth column), to the maximum number of feedback documents available (fifth column), and to the actual window size used before the browsing window limit is reached (the last column). Table 2 presents the stringent user case, that is, the user accepts only highly relevant documents as feedback documents ($R = 3$) while we vary the values of the two effort thresholds ($B$ and $F$).

We can see that on the average, in case of stringent feedback threshold, the number of RF documents is very low even if both the browsing effort and the feedback effort thresholds are high (30). With a relatively small effort, e.g., $B=10$ and $F=5$, only 1.1 feedback documents on the average could be collected. Also, the number of topics

**Table 2.** Stringent user ($R = 3$): the effect of user effort on the availability of RF. All feedback documents are highly relevant.

| Browsing Effort B | Feedback Effort F | Average No of RF Docs Available | No of Topics with no RF Docs | Max No of RF Docs per Topic | Average Search Length |
|---|---|---|---|---|---|
| 30 | 30 | 2.3 | 11 | 11 | 30.0 |
| 30 | 10 | 2.2 | 11 | 10 | 29.6 |
| 30 | 5 | 1.9 | 11 | 5 | 27.4 |
| 30 | 1 | 0.7 | 11 | 1 | 15.0 |
| 10 | 10 | 1.2 | 21 | 8 | 10.0 |
| 10 | 5 | 1.1 | 21 | 5 | 9.9 |
| 10 | 1 | 0.5 | 21 | 1 | 6.7 |
| 5 | 5 | 0.8 | 23 | 4 | 5.0 |
| 5 | 1 | 0.4 | 23 | 1 | 3.9 |
| 1 | 1 | 0.3 | 29 | 1 | 1.0 |

with an empty feedback set increases as $B$ decreases. Yet for some topics a high number of feedback documents can be found even with low effort thresholds. For example, if browsing and feedback effort are set 5, for some topic 4 highly relevant threshold documents can be found. As one might expect, there is a weak connection between the relative sizes of $B$ and $F$ and the average window size actually used. As it is difficult to find enough highly relevant documents to fill up the size of $F$, in many instances the average search length is actually close to $B$. For example, with $B = 30$ and $F = 10$, the average search length is 29.6 – nearly the whole window of B=30.

Table 3 presents the case of a regular user accepting both fairly and highly relevant documents as feedback.

Compared to the previous table, in Table 3 the average number of RF documents reaches clearly higher values. Also, the number of topics with an empty RF set is much smaller here. It is still difficult to find enough highly or fairly relevant documents to

**Table 3.** Regular user ($R = 2$): the effect of user effort on the availability of RF. All feedback documents are at least fairly relevant.

| Browsing Effort B | Feedback Effort F | Average No of RF Docs Available | No of Topics with no RF Docs | Max No of RF Docs per Topic | Average Search Length |
|---|---|---|---|---|---|
| 30 | 30 | 6.3 | 4 | 21 | 30.0 |
| 30 | 10 | 5.5 | 4 | 10 | 27.6 |
| 30 | 5 | 3.9 | 4 | 5 | 21.6 |
| 30 | 1 | 0.9 | 4 | 1 | 7.3 |
| 10 | 10 | 3.2 | 8 | 10 | 10.0 |
| 10 | 5 | 2.6 | 8 | 5 | 9.3 |
| 10 | 1 | 0.8 | 8 | 1 | 4.4 |
| 5 | 5 | 1.8 | 11 | 5 | 5.0 |
| 5 | 1 | 0.7 | 11 | 1 | 3.1 |
| 1 | 1 | 0.6 | 18 | 1 | 1.0 |

**Table 4.** Liberal user ($R = 1$): the effect of user effort on the availability of RF. All feedback documents are at least marginally relevant.

| Browsing Effort B | Feedback Effort F | Average No of RF Docs Available | No of Topics with no RF Docs | Max No of RF Docs per Topic | Average Search Length |
|---|---|---|---|---|---|
| 30 | 30 | 9.4 | 3 | 26 | 30.0 |
| 30 | 10 | 7.2 | 3 | 10 | 25.2 |
| 30 | 5 | 4.4 | 3 | 5 | 15.6 |
| 30 | 1 | 0.9 | 3 | 1 | 5.3 |
| 10 | 10 | 4.2 | 4 | 10 | 10.0 |
| 10 | 5 | 3.4 | 4 | 5 | 9.1 |
| 10 | 1 | 0.9 | 4 | 1 | 3.4 |
| 5 | 5 | 2.4 | 5 | 5 | 5.0 |
| 5 | 1 | 0.9 | 5 | 1 | 2.7 |
| 1 | 1 | 0.7 | 12 | 1 | 1.0 |

fill up the size $F$, so in many instances the average search length is also actually very close to $B$. By selecting a regular threshold instead of the stringent threshold, more feedback documents become available within a selected threshold, but the price of this is that their quality varies more than in case of using a stringent threshold.

Table 4 presents the case where the user accepts even the marginally relevant documents (relevance level 1) as feedback documents.

Now the number of feedback documents is rather high (almost 10) when both the browsing effort and the feedback effort thresholds are set high (30). However, in this case the user could expect that many of the feedback documents are actually of low quality. On the other hand, there are clearly more feedback documents available. The relationship between the quantity and the quality of the feedback cannot be solved by looking at the quantity of the feedback data available only. Therefore, next we proceed on testing what happens to the retrieval effectiveness when various user scenarios are used.

### 3.2  Effect of User Scenario on Feedback Effectiveness

In this section, we study the effect of the quality and the quantity of the relevance feedback to the effectiveness of RF. The results using the stringent relevance evaluation threshold are presented in Table 5.

The baseline MAP figure 20.2 % corresponds to the search result for the 41 initial queries measured by stringent criteria. The differences with respect to the baseline are percentage units, not percentages. In case of every user feedback scenario the changes were positive with respect to baseline MAP. It seems that on the average, the searcher can expect good feedback results even pointing only one feedback document as long as it is highly relevant. This is shown in Table 5 as an improvement of

**Table 5.** Average precision of user feedback scenarios. Stringent relevance threshold is used in evaluation - baseline MAP = 20.2 %.

| | | MAP by Recognition of Relevance R, % | | | | | | |
|---|---|---|---|---|---|---|---|---|
| Browsing effort B | Feedback effort F | R = 3 | Diff. to baseline (% units) | R = 2 | Diff. to baseline (% units) | R = 1 | Diff. to baseline (% units) |
| 30 | 30 | 37.5 | +17.3 | 27.1 | +6.9 | 24.9 | +4.7 |
| 30 | 10 | 37.5 | +17.3 | 27.1 | +6.9 | 24.9 | +4.7 |
| 30 | 5 | 36.9 | +16.7 | 27.5 | +7.3 | 23.9 | +3.7 |
| 30 | 1 | 31.7 | +11.5 | 23.3 | +3.1 | 22.6 | +2.4 |
| 10 | 10 | 28.9 | +8.7 | 24.7 | +4.5 | 22.9 | +2.7 |
| 10 | 5 | 28.6 | +8.4 | 23.9 | +3.7 | 23.5 | +3.3 |
| 10 | 1 | 27.1 | +6.9 | 22.7 | +2.5 | 22.2 | +2.0 |
| 5 | 5 | 25.9 | +5.7 | 23.0 | +2.8 | 22.9 | +2.7 |
| 5 | 1 | 24.5 | +4.3 | 22.7 | +2.5 | 22.2 | +2.0 |
| 1 | 1 | 20.8 | +0.6 | 21.6 | +1.4 | 22.0 | +1.8 |

+11.5% units in case of a user scenario $M = <3, 30, 1>$. Notice, however, that if the relevance threshold for the feedback document is lower, such an improvement does not take place, even though we know that there are many feedback documents available (Tables 3 - 4). The improvement in average precision is only +3.1 % units in case of user scenario $<2, 30, 1>$ (the 6th column) even though the relevance feedback document may be highly relevant occasionally. This fact is probably due to the differences in the terminological properties of the documents at various relevance levels. Interestingly, the user strategy of a hard working user ($B = F = 30$) who collects lots of feedback documents using a liberal RF threshold ($R = 1$, 7th and 8th columns) is not as successful (+4.7 %-units). It seems to be essential that the user keeps the RF threshold high. As we can see from Table 5, the scenarios $<3, 30, 30>$, $<3, 30, 10>$, and $<3, 30, 5>$ give by far the best of all results (improvements of +16.7 to +17.3 % units), while the scenarios $<2, 30, 30>$, $<2, 30, 10>$, $<2, 30, 5>$ fall behind (improvements of +6.9 to +7.3 % units). Of course, for the scenario $<3, 30, 30>$ there are seldom RF documents available even close to F=30 in the window B=30. In conclusion, considering the relevance feedback quality, the quality of the input matters.

The results of the feedback effectiveness using the regular relevance evaluation threshold are presented in Table 6.

**Table 6.** Average precision of user feedback scenarios. Regular relevance threshold is used in evaluation - baseline MAP = 22.7.

| MAP by Recognition of Relevance R, % | | | | | | | |
|---|---|---|---|---|---|---|---|
| Browsing effort B | Feedback effort F | R = 3 | Diff. to baseline (% units) | R = 2 | Diff. to baseline (% units) | R = 1 | Diff. to baseline (% units) |
| 30 | 30 | **30.8** | +8.1 | **34.7** | +12.0 | **32.0** | +9.3 |
| 30 | 10 | **30.8** | +8.1 | **34.8** | +12.1 | **31.9** | +9.2 |
| 30 | 5 | **30.9** | +8.2 | **33.7** | +11.0 | **30.4** | +7.7 |
| 30 | 1 | **27.6** | +4.9 | **27.7** | +5.0 | **26.6** | +3.9 |
| 10 | 10 | **26.7** | +4.0 | **30.8** | +8.1 | **30.0** | +7.3 |
| 10 | 5 | **26.4** | +3.7 | **30.4** | +7.7 | **29.2** | +6.5 |
| 10 | 1 | **25.0** | +2.3 | **27.0** | +4.3 | **26.2** | +3.5 |
| 5 | 5 | **24.9** | +2.2 | **27.6** | +4.9 | **27.4** | +4.7 |
| 5 | 1 | **24.2** | +1.5 | **26.5** | +3.8 | **26.1** | +3.4 |
| 1 | 1 | **23.7** | +1.0 | **24.9** | +2.2 | **25.3** | +2.6 |

In Table 6 the baseline MAP of 22.7 % corresponds to the search result for the 41 initial queries measured by regular criteria. Also here, in every user feedback scenario the changes were positive with respect to baseline. An essential trend compared to the previous table seems to be that here the differences are smaller between the user scenarios having different threshold for accepting feedback documents. The scenarios $<2, 30, 30>$, $<2, 30, 10>$, and $<2, 30, 5>$ give the best results (improvements of +11.0 % units to +12.1 % units).

Table 7 presents the effectiveness figures when a liberal evaluation threshold is used. The baseline MAP figure 20.7 % corresponds to the search result for the 41 initial queries measured by liberal criteria. The trend noticed previously in Tables 5 and 6 is accentuated here: now the difference is very small between the user scenarios having different threshold for accepting feedback documents. If the final result set is evaluated by using a liberal threshold (Table 7), the results do not grow better by using a high threshold in selecting the RF documents. The situation is completely different if the final result set is evaluated by using a stringent threshold (Table 5) – in that case the user clearly should keep also high threshold in selecting the feedback documents.

**Table 7.** Average precision of user feedback scenarios. Liberal relevance threshold is used in evaluation - baseline MAP = 20.7 %.

| | | | MAP by Recognition of Relevance R, % | | | | |
|---|---|---|---|---|---|---|---|
| Browsing effort B | Feedback effort F | R = 3 | Diff. to baseline (% units) | R = 2 | Diff. to baseline (% units) | R = 1 | Diff. to baseline (% units) |
| 30 | 30 | **26.5** | +5.8 | **29.5** | +8.8 | **30.2** | +9.5 |
| 30 | 10 | **26.5** | +5.8 | **29.4** | +8.7 | **30.1** | +9.4 |
| 30 | 5 | **26.6** | +5.9 | **28.6** | +7.9 | **28.7** | +8.0 |
| 30 | 1 | **24.4** | +3.7 | **24.2** | +3.5 | **24.0** | +3.3 |
| 10 | 10 | **23.9** | +3.2 | **26.7** | +6.0 | **27.5** | +6.8 |
| 10 | 5 | **23.7** | +3.0 | **26.4** | +5.7 | **26.9** | +6.2 |
| 10 | 1 | **22.6** | +1.9 | **23.6** | +2.9 | **23.7** | +3.0 |
| 5 | 5 | **22.8** | +2.1 | **25.0** | +4.3 | **26.0** | +5.3 |
| 5 | 1 | **22.1** | +1.4 | **23.3** | +2.6 | **23.5** | +2.8 |
| 1 | 1 | **21.6** | +0.9 | **22.5** | +1.8 | **22.9** | +2.2 |

### 3.3  Comparison to PRF

We also tested the effectiveness of PRF by extracting terms from the top $B$ documents ($B \in \{1, 5, 10, 30\}$) and added them to the initial query as in RF (see Section 2.4). These results are presented in Table 8.

**Table 8.** Average precision of PRF scenarios evaluated by stringent, regular and liberal relevance thresholds

| PRF Set Size | PRF MAP (%) Stringent | Diff. to baseline (% units) | PRF MAP (%) Regular | Diff. to baseline (% units) | PRF MAP (%) Liberal | Diff. to baseline (% units) |
|---|---|---|---|---|---|---|
| 30 | 19.8 | -0.4 | 25.1 | +2.4 | 24.2 | +3.5 |
| 10 | 19.5 | -0.7 | 25.8 | +3.1 | 24.5 | +3.8 |
| 5 | 21.2 | +1.0 | 25.8 | +3.1 | 24.1 | +3.4 |
| 1 | 22.0 | +1.8 | 25.3 | +2.6 | 22.8 | +2.1 |

In Table 8, columns 2 to 3, we can see that our PRF method hardly improves the baseline results when stringent relevance threshold is used in evaluation. The improvements are small (at best only +1.8 % units) compared to the great improvements gained in the best user RF scenarios (+17.3 % units at scenario <3,30,10>) (Table 5).

The columns 4 to 5 show that PRF improves the baseline results slightly when the regular relevance threshold is used in evaluation. The best improvement is +3.1 % units compared to the baseline when the top 5 documents are used in pseudo-relevance feedback. This improvement is modest compared to the improvement in the best user RF scenarios (+12.1 % units using scenario <2,30,10>) (Table 6).

In columns 6 to 7, we can see that the same trend continues also when the liberal relevance threshold is used in evaluation. The improvements here are closer to the improvements of the user RF scenarios evaluated at the liberal relevance threshold, although the very best user RF scenario improvement of 9.5 % units is gained using scenario <1,30,30>. Here we can see that as the quality of the user RF sinks, it approaches PRF, and the effects become similar.

## 4 Discussion

Our original research questions were as follows:

1. How effective is RF when we consider various levels of relevance in evaluation?
2. How is the quality and quantity of the feedback documents related to the effectiveness?
3. Can the simulated relevance feedback successfully compete with pseudo-relevance feedback (PRF), and if so, by what effort in terms of the amount and quality of the user feedback?

For the first and the second research questions, our results indicate that RF can be effective at all three evaluation levels. When the stringent evaluation criterion for the final results is used (Table 5), if the user keeps also the feedback threshold high, as in scenario <3, 30, 30> the MAP of RF run improves from 20.2 % (baseline) to 37.5 %. However, if the user lowers the feedback threshold (user scenario <1, 30, 30>) the MAP of the RF run improves only from 20.2 % to 24.9 %. Also, the case of a single "pearl" feedback document (user scenario <3, 30, 1>) outperformed the case of several "mixed" documents (user scenario <1, 30, 5>); MAP values are 31.7 % and 23.9 %, respectively. Thus it seems that one cannot compensate even a small amount of high quality feedback by giving lots of low quality feedback if the stringent criterion is applied in the evaluation phase.

On the other hand, if the final evaluation criterion is liberal, the opposite happens (Table 7). For example, the RF scenario <3, 30, 30> performs worse (MAP = 26.5 %) than the scenario <1, 30, 30> (MAP = 30.2 %).

For the third research question, our PRF method improved the search results evaluated by any relevance level, but it was not very competitive with the best RF user scenarios when the stringent evaluation criterion was used. However, if the liberal evaluation criterion was used, PRF was close to the best RF user scenarios.

# 5  Conclusions

In real usage situations, the users of information systems would often be best served by enabling them to find the very best documents instead of collecting also marginally relevant documents. As the users are also able to identify highly relevant documents, it is natural to consider developing relevance feedback methods concentrating on finding especially the highly relevant documents. In this paper, we explore the effects of the quality and quantity of the relevance feedback documents to the effectiveness of the feedback measured at various relevance levels.

First we developed a simple user model which makes it possible to quantify three interaction decisions involved in relevance feedback: (1) the relevance criterion (threshold to accept documents used as the feedback), (2) the browsing effort, and (3) the feedback effort of the user. We measured the effectiveness of the final retrieved set after the RF by simulating the user behavior in a laboratory setting based on various user scenarios (three different relevance thresholds, ten different combinations of browsing and feedback efforts) and compared these RF methods to the pseudo-relevance feedback.

The best RF scenarios clearly outperformed all PRF scenarios, although PRF also improved the initial retrieval. When the stringent threshold was used in evaluation, the best user scenario clearly outperformed PRF, but instead, when a liberal evaluation threshold was used, the performance of the user scenarios in RF was close to the PRF results. This hints to the possibility that using binary relevance with a low relevance threshold hides meaningful variation caused by documents which actually belong to various relevance levels, as both marginally, regularly and highly relevant documents are seen as similar.

## Acknowledgements

The InQuery search engine was provided by the Center for Intelligent Information Retrieval at the University of Massachusetts. ENGTWOL (Morphological Transducer Lexicon Description of English): Copyright © 1989-1992 Atro Voutilainen and Juha Heikkilä. TWOL-R (Run-Time Two-Level Program): Copyright © Kimmo Koskenniemi and Lingsoft plc. 1983-1993.

This research was funded by the Academy of Finland under Project Numbers 177033 and 1209960. The authors thank the anonymous referees and members of the research groups FIRE and IRiX for useful suggestions.

## References

1. Blair, D.C. (1984) The Data-Document Distinction in Information Retrieval, *Communications of the ACM*, 4, Vol. 27, 1984, 369-374.
2. Dennis, S., McArthur, R. & Bruza, P.D. (1998). Searching the World Wide Web made easy? The cognitive load imposed by query refinement mechanisms. In: Proceedings of the 3rd Australian Document Computing Conference, Sydney, Australia. Sydney: University of Sydney, Department of Computer Science, TR-518: 65-71.

3. Efthimiadis, E.N. (1996). Query expansion. In: Williams, M.E. (Ed.), *Annual Review of Information Science and Technology, vol. 31 (ARIST 31).* Medford, NJ: Learned Information for the American Society for Information Science: 121-187.
4. Kekäläinen, J. (1999). *The effects of query complexity, expansion and structure on retrieval performance in probabilistic text retrieval.* Tampere, Finland: University of Tampere, Department of Information Studies, Ph.D. Thesis, Acta Universitatis Tamperensis 678. [Available at: http://www.info.uta.fi/tutkimus/fire/archive/QCES.pdf . Cited Oct. 31 2005.]
5. Kekäläinen, J. (2005). Binary and graded relevance in IR evaluations – Comparison of the effects on ranking of IR systems. *Information Processing & Management, 41*(5): 1019-1033.
6. Kekäläinen, J. & Järvelin, K. (2002). Using graded relevance assessments in IR evaluation. *Journal of the American Society for Information Science and Technology, 53*(13): 1120-1129.
7. Pirkola, A., Leppänen, E. & Järvelin, K. (2002). The RATF Formula (Kwok's Formula): Exploiting average term frequency in cross-language retrieval. *Information Research, 7*(2). Available at: http://InformationR.net/ir/7-2/infres72.html
8. Ruthven, I., Lalmas, M. (2003). A survey on the use of relevance feedback for information access systems. *Knowledge Engineering Review, 18*(2): 95-145.
9. Ruthven, I., Lalmas, M. & van Rijsbergen, K. (2003). Incorporating user search behaviour into relevance feedback. *Journal of the American Society for Information Science and Technology, 54*(6): 529-549.
10. Salton, G. (1989). *Automatic Text Processing: The Transformation, Analysis And Retrieval of Information by Computer.* Reading, MA: Addison-Wesley.
11. Sihvonen, A. & Vakkari, P. (2004). Subject knowledge, thesaurus-assisted query expansion and search success. In: RIAO 2004. *Coupling Approaches, Coupling Media And Coupling Languages for Information Retrieval, Proceedings of RIAO 2004 conference.* Paris: C.I.D: 393-404.
12. Sormunen, E. (2002). Liberal relevance criteria of TREC – Counting on negligible documents? In: Beaulieu, M. & Baeza-Yates, R. & Myaeng, S.H. & Järvelin, K. (Eds.) *Proceedings of the 25th Annual International ACM SIGIR Conference on Research and Development in Information Retrieval (ACM SIGIR 25),* Tampere, Finland, August 11-15, 2002. New York, NY: ACM Press: 320-330.
13. Sormunen, E., Kekäläinen, J., Koivisto, J., Järvelin, K. (2001). Document Text Characteristics Affect the Ranking of the Most Relevant Documents by Expanded Structured Queries. *Journal of Documentation, 57*(3):358-374.
14. Vakkari, P., Sormunen, E. (2004) The Influence of Relevance Levels on the Effectiveness of Interactive Information Retrieval. *Journal of the American Society for Information Science and Technology,* 55(11): 963-969.
15. Voorhees, E., (2001) Evaluation by Highly Relevant Documents, *Proceedings of the 24th Annual International ACM SIGIR Conference on Research and Development in Information Retrieval (ACM SIGIR 24),* New Orleans, Lousiana, USA, September 9-13, 2001. New York, NY: ACM Press: 74-82.

# Using Query Profiles for Clarification

Henning Rode and Djoerd Hiemstra

University of Twente, The Netherlands
{h.rode, d.hiemstra}@cs.utwente.nl

**Abstract.** The following paper proposes a new kind of relevance feedback. It shows how so-called query profiles can be employed for disambiguation and clarification.

Query profiles provide useful summarized previews on the retrieved answers to a given query. They outline ambiguity in the query and when combined with appropriate means of interactivity allow the user to easily adapt the final ranking. Statistical analysis of the profiles even enables the retrieval system to automatically suggest search restrictions or preferences. The paper shows a preliminary experimental study of the proposed feedback methods within the setting of TREC's interactive HARD track.

## 1 Introduction

When information retrieval left the library setting, where a user ideally could discuss her/his information need with a search specialist at the help-desk, many ideas came up how to imitate such interactive search scenario within retrieval systems. Belkin, among others, broadly sketches the system's tasks and requirements for interactive information seeking [1]. We do not want to further roll up the history of interactive information retrieval here, but to remind briefly its main aims.

In order to formulate clear queries, resulting in a set of useful, relevant answers, the user of a standard information retrieval system needs knowledge about the collection, its index, the query language and last but not least a good mental model of the searched object. Since it is unrealistic to expect such knowledge from an non-expert user, the system can assist the search process in a dialogue like manner. Two main branches of interactive methods try to bridge the gap between a vague information need and a precise query formulation:

*Relevance Feedback* helps the user refining the query without requiring sophisticated usage of the system's query language. Query terms are added or reweighted automatically by using the relevant examples selected by the user [2,3]. The examples shown to the user for judgement can either be documents, sentences out of those documents or even a loosely bundle of terms representing a cluster of documents. Experiments within TREC's interactive HARD track showed many variants of such techniques [4,5]. By presenting example answers to the user, relevance feedback can also refine the user's mental image of the searched object.

*Browsing techniques*, on the other hand, provide an overview on the existing document collection and its categorization (see e.g. the Open Directory Project [6]),

M. Lalmas et al. (Eds.): ECIR 2006, LNCS 3936, pp. 205–216, 2006.
© Springer-Verlag Berlin Heidelberg 2006

or visualize the relation among documents [7]. The user can restrict the search to certain categories. This can also be regarded as a query refinement strategy. It is especially helpful, when the selected categorical restriction cannot be expressed easily by a few query terms.

The query clarification technique, we are proposing in this paper, belongs mainly to the first type, the relevance feedback methods. However, it combines the approach with summarization and overview techniques from the browsing domain. This way it tries not only to assist formulating the query, but also provides information about the collection in a query specific preview, the so-called *query profile*. Following an idea of Diaz and Jones [8] to predict the precision of queries by using their temporal profiles, we analyzed the application of different query profiles as an instrument of relevance feedback. The main aim of the profiles is to detect and visualize query ambiguity and to ask the user for clarification if necessary. We hope to enable the user to give better feedback by showing him/her this summarized information about the expected query outcome.

The paper is structured as follows: After a short look on two related approaches, we start in Sec. 2 by giving a definition of query profiles and explain how they can be generated. Sec. 3 discusses their application for query classification. Sec. 4 shows a possible score computation and combination to make use of the user feedback for an improved final ranking. We further present a preliminary experimental study of our relevance feedback technique and finish with conclusions about the achieved results.

## 1.1   Related Approaches

In order to distinguish our approach from similar ones, we finish this introduction by looking at two comparable methods. The first one is a search interface based on clustering suggested by Palmer et al. [9][1]. It summarizes results aiming at query disambiguation, but instead of using predefined categories as we will suggest for our topical profiles, it groups the documents using a not specified clustering algorithm. Whereas the clustering technique shows more topical adaptiveness, our static categories ensure always a useful grouping.

Another search interface proposed by Sieg et al. [10] assists the user directly in the query formulation process. The system compares the initial query with a static topic hierarchy and presents the best matching categories to the user for selecting preferences. The chosen categories are then used for query expansion. In contrast, our query profiles are not based on the few given query terms directly but on the results of an initial search. This way, we get a larger base for suggesting appropriate categories and we involve the collection in the query refinement process.

The mentioned approaches exclusively consider the topical dimension of the query. We will further discuss the usage and combination of query profiles on other document dimensions, in this case temporal query profiles.

---

[1] The one-page paper briefly explains the concept also known from the *Clusty* web search engine (http://clusty.com) coming from the same authors.

## 2    Query-Profiles

Looking from the systems perspective, the set of relevant answers to a given query is the set of the top ranked documents. This set can unfortunately differ by far from the set of documents relevant to the user. The basic idea of query profiles is to summarize information about the system's answer set in a suitable way to make such differences obvious.

**Definition 1.** *A* query profile *is the distribution of the top X ranked documents in the result set along a certain property dimension, like time, topic, location, or genre. E.g. a temporal query profile shows the result distribution along the time dimension, a topical profile along the dimension of predefined topics the documents belong to.*

The underlying assumption of the profile analysis is that clear queries result either in a profile with one distinctive peak or show little variance in case the property dimension is not important for the query. In contrast, we expect ambiguous queries to have query profiles with more than one distinctive peak.

Whereas the general ideas stay the same for all kinds of query profiles, there are several domain specific issues to consider. We will thus take a closer look on generating temporal and topical profiles, the two types used in the later experimental study.

### 2.1    Generating Temporal Profiles

Having a date-tagged corpus, a basic temporal profile for a given query is simple to compute. We treat the 100 top ranked documents $D_j$ from the baseline run as the set of relevant answers and aggregate a histogram with monthly time steps $H_i$:

$$H_i = |\{D_j | month(D_j) = i\}| \ . \tag{1}$$

The decision for the granularity of one month is based on the overall time span of the corpus and the timeliness of news events. Other granularities, however, could be considered as well.

As a next step, we performed a *time normalization* on the profile. Knowing that the corpus articles are not evenly distributed over the total time span, the time profile should display the relative monthly frequency of articles relevant to the given topic rather than absolute numbers. Therefore, the frequency of each monthly partition $H_i$ is divided by the total number of corpus articles $C_i$ originating from month $i$. In order to avoid exceptional small numbers, the averaged monthly corpus frequency $avg(C)$ is used as a constant factor:

$$H_i^* = \frac{H_i}{C_i} * avg(C) \ . \tag{2}$$

Furthermore, we performed moving average smoothing on the histogram, a technique used for trend analysis on time series data [11]. It replaces the monthly frequencies of the profile by the average frequencies of a small time window around the particular month. We used here a window size of 3 months:

$$H_i^{**} = \frac{H_{i-1}^* + H_i^* + H_{i+1}^*}{3} \ . \tag{3}$$

The graph in Fig. 1 shows an example of a resulting temporal profile. There are two reasons for using such a smoothing technique. First, the time-line the search topic is discussed in the news will often overlap with our casual monthly partitioning. Second, although we want to spot peaks in the profile, we are not interested in identifying a high number of splintered bursts. If two smaller peaks are lying in a near timely neighborhood they should be recognized as one.

Finally, we want to determine the number, bounds, and the importance of peaks in the temporal profile. Diaz and Jones [8] tried several techniques for this purpose and decided to employ the so-called burst model from Kleinberg [12]. It assumes a hidden state machine behind the random events of emitting the specific word in certain frequencies. The assumed machine changes over time between its norm and peak state, corresponding to phases with normal and high emission of the word respectively. The aim is then to find the unknown state sequence with the highest probability to cause the observed random events of the time profile. Kleinberg employs for this task the Viterbi algorithm.

We have used for the generation of temporal profiles a two state automaton $\mathcal{A}_{1.5}^2$ with a very low value for $\gamma \approx 0.02^2$. The considerably different setting of parameters compared to Kleinberg's experiments can be explained by the fact that we analyzed profiles of word frequencies which are already averaged on the level of months. Hence bursts will remain smaller and less distinctive.

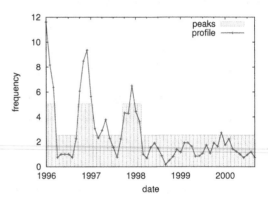

**Fig. 1.** Temporal Profile of Topic 363: *Transportation Tunnel Disasters*

When we also want to compute a measure for the importance of the found peaks $P_j$, the corresponding frequency values of the temporal profile can simply be summed up. A further division by the average of such frequency sums $avg(P)$ leads to a value for peak intensity better comparable among different temporal profiles:

$$P_j = \sum_{i \in range(P_j)} H_i^{**} \ , \qquad intensity(P_j) = \frac{P_j}{avg(P)} \ . \tag{4}$$

## 2.2 Generating Topical Profiles

Generating topical profiles faces different issues than the ones explained for the temporal dimension. First and most important, the corpus is not topic-tagged.

---

[2] See [12] for a detailed description of the automaton and its parameters.

A topic classification is therefore required. Secondly, the topical dimension is not continuous but divided in a discrete set of previously defined concepts. In principle, topics could have a hierarchical relation but there won't be any natural definition of an order. So the identification of peak bounds as in the temporal dimension ceases to apply here.

For topic classification we need to build abstract models for all different concepts, the classification should take into account. Language models can be applied as classifiers for this purpose. In order to demonstrate the idea, we used models built on a different training corpus to distinguish 12 different topical concepts similar to the main sections of common newspapers, like politics or sports. A more detailed description about the construction of these language models can be found in [13].

The required text classification for computing a topical profile differs slightly from the typical categorization task (described in [14]). We do not need to assign binary labels whether a document belongs to a certain category or not. A similarity measure showing to which extend an article belongs to a given category is already sufficient. Hence, the task falls back to the known domain of ranking a set of documents given a query. In fact, an abstract language model describing a topical

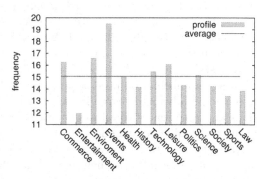

**Fig. 2.** Subject Profile of Topic 363: *Transportation Tunnel Disasters*

concept is nothing but an exceptional long query. We used in the experiments the NLLR measure (described in a later section) which is also applied to compute a score for the initial query. Only the smoothing factor $\lambda$ is set smaller in this case. Firstly, because the exceptional query length makes smoothing less important, and secondly, to increase differences between the models.

In order to speed up the computation of topical profiles as well as the later ranking procedure the score computation is performed off-line. For each classifier in the set of topical concepts a score vector is maintained, holding the individual scores for all documents within the collection. An example topical profile is displayed in Fig. 2.

After the classification task is done, topical profiles can be computed in the following way. Similar to temporal profiles explained previously, the set of the 100 top ranked documents given the query is determined. The score for a specific topic category $T_i$ is then defined by the sum of all document scores from $D$ for this category. The intensity value, as introduced in the last section, is computed accordingly:

$$T_i = \sum_{D_j} NLLR(T_i|D_j) \ , \qquad intensity(T_i) = \frac{T_i}{avg(T)} \ . \tag{5}$$

# 3   The Clarification Interface

After generating and analyzing the query profiles, we discuss in this section how the gained information can be presented to the user for query clarification. The user interface thereby has to fulfill two functions:

- It needs to present all necessary information to the user that allows her/him to take a decision.
- It should provide simple but powerful means to adapt the query in the intended way.

The second point needs further explanation. Not all search topics are easy to express by a few query terms. Although several articles contain the same keywords, their specific view on the topic or genre might not match the type of documents the user had in mind. If we allow the user to refine the query not only by further keywords but by selecting preferences to more abstract concepts or to restrict the search space to a certain location or time, the problem of expressing an information need accurately can be overcome. However, confronting a user in an advanced search interface with all possible combinations of restrictions and preferences to an in general unlimited number of concepts, dates, or locations, would overextend the searcher. Maybe he/she does not even know the correct query meta-data, e.g. the date or location of the event he/she is looking for. Query profiles can help here, since they allow to automatically find the most important meta-data concepts given the initial query terms. This way it is possible to provide the user with the necessary information to set preferences or restrictions and to limit the search dialog to the most interesting options.

Compared to the profiles shown in the last section (Fig. 1 and Fig. 2) a user does not need to see the whole spectrum of the profile. Instead it seems sufficient to cut out the most relevant part of it, which means the highest temporal or topical peaks. For the experiments, we just displayed the 5 top ranked topics, but all identified temporal peaks. In practice their number never exceeds 4. In order to demonstrate the usefulness of the profile information and to explain why we restrict the output to the top ranked parts of the profiles, let us distinguish three possible cases:

1. In case the initial query was clearly formulated, the user gets a positive confirmation by seeing the expected topic or time partition on top of the ranked profile list, succeeded by close related ones. The absence of non-matching topics will be enough information for the user here. He/she does not need to see a long list of minor ranking topics.
2. In case the query was ambiguous also unwanted topics or time partitions will populate the top of the ranked query profiles. In order to get an unambiguous output, it is now important to refine the query in a way that it excludes most of the unwanted answers, but keeps the relevant ones. Again, the end of the ranked profile list is less interesting, since the topics there are already efficiently excluded by the query.

3. In case the user does not even find the relevant topics or time partitions among the top part of the query profile, it won't help to just refine the query. Either the query needs to be reformulated entirely or the corpus does not include the documents the user is searching for.

The second case is the most interesting one since it requests appropriate query refinement strategies. Whereas a time restriction based on the profile can be expressed relatively easy, it is in general difficult for a user to find on his own additional keywords that allow to distinguish between the wanted and unwanted topics of the profiles. However, the system has already abstract classifiers at hand to perform such filtering. The simplest way to refine the query is thus to express preferences directly on the profile itself. For this reason we made our query profiles interactive by adding *prefer* and *dislike* buttons to the topic profiles and *restrict to* fields to the temporal profiles, refining the query in the obvious way. Their exact influence on the final ranking is discussed in the next section.

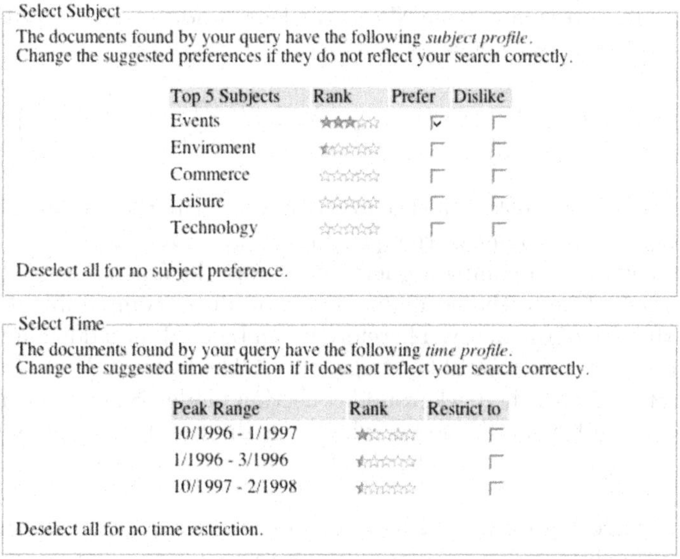

**Fig. 3.** Experimental Clarification Form of Topic 363: *Transportation Tunnel Disasters*

## 3.1 Automatic Preselection

We also looked, whether it is possible to make an automatic suggestion of an appropriate selection in the profiles. Obviously, the most high ranked topics or temporal peaks are good candidates, especially if they distinctively stand off from the lower ranked ones. The intensity measure defined in the last section explicitly addresses these characteristics. Using an intensity threshold, we can preselect all topics and temporal peaks above[3]. These values have been shown

---

[3] In the experiments an intensity threshold of 1.2 was used for the topical profiles, respectively 1.5 for the temporal profiles.

high enough to assure the selection of only distinctive peaks of the profile. An example clarification form with preselected items is shown in Fig. 3.

Automatic preselection is especially helpful in the first of the three scenarios above where the query is unambiguous. In such a case user feedback is not necessary and the query refinement could be performed as a sort of "blind feedback" procedure to sharpen the topical or temporal focus.

## 4    Retrieval Model and Score Combination

In this section we show a possible score computation and combination taking into account the initial query as well as the preferences and restrictions stated in the query refinement process. The focus lies thereby on the issues of score normalization and combination. We have chosen a language modeling approach, however, in principle the proposed feedback technique could also be used in the setting of other retrieval models.

In particular, we employed the NLLR, the length-normalized logarithmic likelihood ratio [15], as a score function:

$$NLLR(Q|D) = \sum_{t \in Q} P(t|Q) * \log \left( \frac{(1-\lambda)P(t|D) + \lambda P(t|C)}{\lambda P(t|C)} \right) . \qquad (6)$$

The additional factor $\lambda$ below the fraction does not harm the ranking but ensures that documents having none of the query terms get a zero score.

The NLLR is able to compare query terms and documents as well as entire language models. Due to the normalization it produces comparable scores independent of the size of the query. Therefore it can be used for a document ranking given either a query or a topical language model. The factor $\lambda$ determines the degree of smoothing with the background collection model. Since smoothing plays an important role for short queries, whereas it dilutes the score differences for large-scale query language models, this factor can be changed according to its application[4].

Next to the scoring itself, all single sources of relevance evidence need to be combined to one final ranking. We decided not to use query expansion techniques, but to combine the separately computed scores directly. This allows to make efficiently use of precomputed document scores for topic language models and avoids a second scoring of the initial query terms. When multiple preferences or dislikes have to be handled the logarithmic scores of their corresponding models $M_i$ are simply added, respectively subtracted for disliked models:

$$m\text{-}score(D) = \sum_{M_i} NLLR(M_i|D) . \qquad (7)$$

The final combination of the initial query score, called $q\text{-}score(D)$ now, and all summed up preference scores requires special attention. We have to ensure that

---

[4] We set $\lambda$ to 0.85 for queries, but to 0.5 for topic models.

the scores on both sides deliver "compatible" values or even more to guarantee still the dominance of the initial query in the final result. A minimum-maximum normalization solves such a task (among others described in [16]). It shifts the minimum of a score range $min\_s = \min\{score(D^*)|D^* \in C\}$ to 0 and its maximum to 1. We further stressed the initial query by doubling its score value in the final ranking:

$$norm(score(D)) = \frac{score(D) - min\_s}{max\_s - min\_s} \ , \tag{8}$$

$$final\text{-}score(D) = 2 * norm(q\text{-}score(D)) + norm(m\text{-}score(D)) \ . \tag{9}$$

## 5 Experimental Study

We tried to evaluate our relevance feedback based on query profiles in the setting of the HARD track 2005. A set of 50 queries, which are regarded as difficult[5], is evaluated on a $\approx$ 2GB newspaper corpus, the Aquaint corpus. The track set-up allows one-step user interaction with so-called clarification forms that have to fit one screen and have to be filled out in less than 3 minutes. In the original TREC setting the sent-in clarification forms were filled out by the same person who later does the relevance assessments for the specific query. We repeated the experiment ourselves, asking different users to state preferences or restrictions in the clarification forms after reading the query description and query narrative coming with the TREC search topics. This way, we inevitably lose the consistency between clarification and relevance assessment ensured by the HARD setting. However, we could study differences in the user behavior and their results.

The 4 test users [6] have been shortly introduced to their task by demonstrating one randomly picked out example clarification form. They needed on average 35 min to accomplish the task of clarifying all 50 queries. We want to remark here, that the conducted experiment have to be regarded preliminary. It was not the intention to carry out a fully qualified user study, but to gather first indication whether the proposed feedback technique is able to improve retrieval.

In order to compare the improvements, we performed a *baseline* run using just the up to 3 words from the query title, further one run with the automatically derived preferences only as explained in Sec. 3, referred to as *automatic* run. From the 4 evaluated user runs, we present here the two most different to keep the figures clear. Whereas *user1* selected almost no topic dislikes, *user2* had the highest fraction of dislike statements among his topic preferences. For comparison, the *user2** run refers to the same user, but ignores his dislikes.

A closer look at the set of the 50 search topics revealed, that they have not been distinctive with respect to their temporal profile. In fact, there was

---

[5] The query set was taken from the Robust track which tries to tackle selected difficult queries in an ad hoc retrieval setting.

[6] 1 female – 3 male students, one of them working in computer science but not in the same project.

almost no case where the user wanted to restrict the query to a certain time span. Therefore, we restricted our analysis to the improvements by topical query refinement and ignored all temporal restrictions.

Fig. 4(a) presents an overview on the main evaluation measures computed for all presented runs. At a first glance it is obvious that the refined queries, even in our non-optimal evaluation setting, show a considerable improvement over the baseline run. The precision gain is most visible at the $P@10$ measures, which is an interesting characteristic aiming at a high precision at the top of the ranked list. The precision recall graph (Fig. 4(b)) confirms the observation made with the $P@10$ values. The precision gain stays the highest at the top of the ranked list. On the right side, the runs with query refinement slowly converge to the baseline, but always stay on top of it.

The special run ignoring the topic dislikes of *user2* has a better general performance than its counterpart. Although it is not shown in the table, this observation holds for all four tested users. It indicates that topic dislike statements bear the risk to weaken the result precision in our current implementation.

Surprisingly, the values show also that the automatic run can compete with the user performed clarification. We cannot entirely explain this phenomenon, but can make two remarks on its interpre-

|  | base | auto | user1 | user2 | user2* |
|---|---|---|---|---|---|
| MAP | 0.151 | 0.187 | 0.204 | 0.187 | 0.201 |
| R-Prec | 0.214 | 0.252 | 0.268 | 0.255 | 0.265 |
| P@10 | 0.286 | 0.380 | 0.396 | 0.354 | 0.402 |

(a) Result Overview

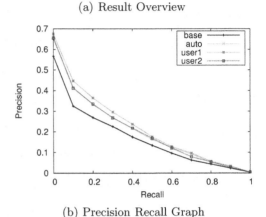

(b) Precision Recall Graph

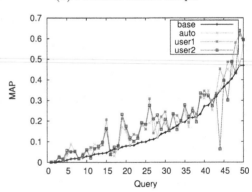

(c) MAP Improvements on Single Queries

**Fig. 4.** Evaluation Results

tation. First, the query set has not been designed to test disambiguation. If a query asking for "Java" expects documents about the programming language, automatic topic feedback will work perfectly. However, it fails if in fact the island was meant. Examples of the second type are necessary to compare user and automatic feedback, but are unlikely to be included in the test set. A further reason for the good performance of the automatic run might simply be the fact that it did not contain dislike statements.

For a more detailed view on the results, Fig. 4(c) presents the evaluation of all single queries sorted by increasing MAP value of the baseline run. Thus, the graphic shows the worst performing queries on the left, continued by a section with still relatively low quality response in the middle, up to acceptable or even good queries on the right. Although the improvement per query is not stable, it seldom happens that the user feedback deteriorates the results. The one extreme case on the right side of the figure is again caused by dislike statements. If we consider the relative improvement, the queries in the middle part of the figure apparently gain the most from query refinement. Within the distinction of queries from Sec. 3 these queries probably fall under the ambiguous category 2. The fact that we encounter the highest improvement in this category nicely demonstrates the usefulness of our method.

# 6   Conclusions and Outlook

The results show promising improvements for all runs that make use of query profiles even in our preliminary experimental study. With a query set designed to test how retrieval systems cope with ambiguity, we would probably be able to show even higher improvements using our feedback method. The same applies for queries that reward temporal restrictions. Also a finer grained topical "resolution", potentially in form of a topic hierarchy, could lead to a more focused query profile on the topic dimension.

Further analysis is needed, how to involve topical dislike statements in a way that they do not harm the results, but also contribute to the query refinement. Furthermore, we need to examine query profiles on other dimensions. The temporal profiles remained untested by the current HARD track query set, but also geographical or genre profiles - in order to name just two possible other parameters - might enable similar improvements as the topical query refinement.

The automatic feedback method turned out to be an interesting side product of the work with query profiles. It performed almost as good as the user feedback. It raises the question to which extend the system can decide based on query profile statistics, whether automatic feedback is reliable enough in a certain case to omit user interaction. Especially when profiles on more dimensions get involved in the analysis, the user should not be bothered by a multiple number of feedback questions. Instead an intelligent retrieval system might be able to select the most helpful dimension for explicit user feedback itself.

# References

1. Belkin, N.: Interaction with texts: Information retrieval as information-seeking behavior. In: Information Retrieval '93, Von der Modellierung zur Anwendung, Universitaetsverlag Konstanz (1993) 55–66
2. Salton, G., Buckley, C.: Improving retrieval performance by relevance feedback. JASIS **41**(4) (1990) 288–297

3. Harman, D.: Relevance feedback revisited. In Belkin, N., Ingwersen, P., Pejtersen, A., eds.: Proceedings of the 15th Annual International ACM SIGIR Conference on Research and Development in Information Retrieval. Copenhagen, Denmark, June 21-24, 1992, ACM (1992) 1–10

4. Allan, J.: Hard track overview in trec 2003: High accuracy retrieval from documents. In: TREC. (2003) 24–37

5. Allan, J.: Hard track overview in trec 2004: High accuracy retrieval from documents. In: TREC. (2004) 25–35

6. Netscape: Open directory project. http://www.dmoz.org (2005) Date retrieved: 03-11-2005.

7. Godin, R., Gecsei, J., Pichet, C.: Design of a browsing interface for information retrieval. In Belkin, N., Rijsbergen van, C., eds.: SIGIR'89, 12th International Conference on Research and Development in Information Retrieval, Cambridge, Massachusetts, USA, June 25-28, 1989, Proceedings, ACM (1989) 32–39

8. Diaz, F., Jones, R.: Using temporal profiles of queries for precision prediction. In Sanderson, M., Järvelin, K., Allan, J., Bruza, P., eds.: Proceedings of the 27th Annual International ACM SIGIR Conference on Research and Development in Information Retrieval. ACM, Sheffield, UK (2004) 18–24

9. Palmer, C., Pesenti, J., Valdés-Pérez, R., Christel, M., Hauptmann, A., Ng, D., Wactlar, H.: Demonstration of hierarchical document clustering of digital library retrieval results. In: ACM/IEEE Joint Conference on Digital Libraries, JCDL 2001, Roanoke, Virginia, USA, June 24-28, 2001, Proceedings, ACM (2001) 451

10. Sieg, A., Mobasher, B., Lytinen, S., Burke, R.: Using concept hierarchies to enhance user queries in web-based information retrieval. In: Proceedings of the IASTED International Conference on Artificial Intelligence and Applications. (2004)

11. Chatfiled, C.: The Analysis of Time Series. 3rd edition edn. Chapman and Hall (1984)

12. Kleinberg, J.: Bursty and hierarchical structure in streams. Data Mining and Knowledge Discovery 7(4) (2003) 373–397

13. Rode, H., Hiemstra, D.: Conceptual Language Models for Context-Aware Text Retrieval. In: Proceedings of the 13th Text REtrieval Conference Proceedings (TREC). (2005)

14. Sebastiani, F.: Text categorization. In Zanasi, A., ed.: Text Mining and its Applications to Intelligence, CRM and Knowledge Management. WIT Press, Southampton, UK (2005) 109–129

15. Kraaij, W.: Variations on language modeling for information retrieval. PhD thesis, University of Twente, Netherlands (2004)

16. Croft, B.: Combining approaches to information retrieval. In Croft, B., ed.: Advances in Information Retrieval : Recent Research From the Center for Intelligent Information Retrieval. Kluwer Academic Publishers, New York (2002) 1–36

# Lexical Entailment for Information Retrieval

Stéphane Clinchant, Cyril Goutte, and Eric Gaussier

Xerox Research Centre Europe,
6, chemin de Maupertuis, F-38240 Meylan, France
Cyril.Goutte@xrce.xerox.com

**Abstract.** Textual Entailment has recently been proposed as an application independent task of recognising whether the meaning of one text may be inferred from another. This is potentially a key task in many NLP applications. In this contribution, we investigate the use of various lexical entailment models in Information Retrieval, using the language modelling framework. We show that lexical entailment potentially provides a significant boost in performance, similar to pseudo-relevance feedback, but at a lower computational cost. In addition, we show that the performance is relatively stable with respect to the corpus the lexical entailment measure is estimated on.

## 1 Introduction

Textual Entailment has recently been proposed [7] as an application independent task of recognising whether the meaning of one text may be inferred from another text. As such, it plays a role in a variety of Natural Language Processing applications such as Question Answering or Machine Translation. Textual entailment may also impact Information Retrieval (IR) in at least two ways. First the notion of relevance bears strong similarities with the one of entailment. Second, the notion of entailment may offer a way to capture non-obvious dependencies between query and documents which are not captured by simple word-based similarities.

Although the general task of recognising textual entailment is potentially much broader, the practical probabilistic approach proposed for example in [11] relies on word based lexical probabilities. This amounts to assessing whether one lexical unit is entailed by another one. This approach is reminiscent of the lexical statistics used to characterize semantic domains or topics in IR. Most lexical statistics studies rely on standard similarity measures in order to derive affinities between words, affinities that can then be used to (a) create thesauri that can in turn be used for indexing or query enrichment purposes, or (b) compute an extended similarity between documents and queries.

Along the first line, one finds works pertaining to thesaurus construction, exemplified by the phrase construction procedure of [18] and the various similarity levels of [12]. Along the second line, one finds works that embed term similarities within the computation of the similarity between queries and documents. The *generalized vector space model* of [19], the *similarity thesaurus* of [17] or the *distributional semantics* approach of [4] illustrate this approach through the use of a term similarity matrix to map documents into a new vector space.

M. Lalmas et al. (Eds.): ECIR 2006, LNCS 3936, pp. 217–228, 2006.
© Springer-Verlag Berlin Heidelberg 2006

The goal of this work is to investigate whether the TE paradigm proposed in [7] leads to lexical measures which are better suited to the IR task than the ones previously studied. To this end, we will first review the new measures derived from TE using different IR collections, and assess their validity. We will then propose some adaptations of these measures for IR purposes.

The remainder of this document is organised as follows: Section 2 presents the various lexical entailment probabilities and similarities used in this work. Section 3 describes the language modelling approach to IR and how it may naturally take into account the entailment information. Section 4 summarises the experiments we carried out to test the use of textual entailment in IR. We discuss these results and their implications in section 5.

## 2   Lexical Entailment and Similarity

Given a mono-lingual collection $\mathcal{D}$, let us first introduce some notations. Let $u$ and $v$ be two terms from the vocabulary $\mathcal{V}$, and $\#(u, d)$ the number of occurrences of term $u$ in document $d \in D$. By analogy with the cross-lingual setting, we will call $u$ the source term, that is, the term for which we are interested to learn some entailment or similarities measures and $v$ is referred to as a target term.

Let us first recall the probabilistic lexical measure proposed in [11]:

$$P(v|u) = \frac{1 + \sum_{d \in \mathcal{D}:u \in d} \#(v, d)}{|\mathcal{V}| + \sum_{w \in \mathcal{V}} \sum_{d \in \mathcal{D}:u \in d} \#(w, d)}. \tag{1}$$

In fact, this model behaves as if we were merging all documents that contain the source term $u$ into a single large document, and then building a simple unigram language model with Laplace smoothing on this large document.

Because the notion of entailment is linked to that of lexical similarity, it makes sense to use a typical similarity measure for comparison. As a consequence, the second model we use is based on the Jaccard similarity.[1] In particular, let $U$ (resp. $V$) be the set of documents where $u$ (resp. $v$) occurs and $|U|$ (resp. $|V|$) the cardinal of this set:

$$jaccard(u, v) = \frac{|U \cap V|}{|U \cup V|}. \tag{2}$$

The similarity is normalised to provide a lexical entailment probability:

$$P(v|u) = \frac{jaccard(u, v)}{\sum_{w \in \mathcal{V}} jaccard(u, w)}. \tag{3}$$

Note that in that case, only the presence of a word in a document, not its frequency, is used. In other words, every document plays the same role, whether

---

[1] Note that this use of the Jaccard similarity is over the document space and is quite different from the traditional use in IR [13] for measuring the similarity between queries and documents, in the "vector space" model, which is over words.

the source term $(u)$ occurs one or ten times in a document. The context of a term is thus reduced to the set of documents in which this term occurs.

Instead of considering each document containing $u$ (or $v$) equally, we would like to take the frequencies of $u$ (or $v$) into account. Intuitively, a good measure of lexical similarity between $u$ and $v$ is that $v$ occurs often in documents that are typical of $u$ (meaning usually that $u$ also appears often). This leads us to the third model, which in fact is a simple application of the rules of probability:

$$P(v|u) = \sum_{d \in \mathcal{D}} P(v|d)P(d|u). \qquad (4)$$

Assuming that $P(d|u) = 0$ for all $d$ such that $u \notin d$, and assuming that $P(d)$ is uniform, the lexical entailment probability in equation 4 may be rewritten as:

$$P(v|u) \propto \sum_{d \in \mathcal{D}: u \in d} P(v|d)P(u|d). \qquad (5)$$

By analogy with the language modelling approach to Information Retrieval [16, 6], $P(u|d)$ and $P(v|d)$ is a simple unigram language model of document $d$.[2] In the experimental section we will call this third model "M3".

The textual entailment measure in equation 1 was used with some success for recognising textual entailment in a recent challenge [7] consisting of evaluating entailment between pairs of hypotheses and reference texts. In this work, we were interested in assessing whether a similar approach would be useful in a more "open" domain such as IR, where a query must be matched against a potentially large number of documents. This revealed a number of problems with the simple lexical entailment probabilities expressed in equations 1-5.

## 2.1 Dealing with Common Words

The first problem we encounter with these models is the presence of common words. Common words like 'year', 'make' or 'time' often get high scores, because they are present in large amounts in many documents, and tend to pollute the results. For example, the first model (eq. 1) acts as if it merges documents. When documents are quite long, the common words may become overwhelming. In order to decrease the influence of common words, the traditional IR countermeasure is to use a weighting such as the *inverse document frequency*, or *idf*. We found out however that this was not always effective in the context of the estimation of lexical entailment measures. In our experience, a more natural and effective technique was to first identify potentially related term pairs $(u, v)$ using the Information Gain (IG).[3] The Information gain measures the number of bits of information obtained on the presence of $v$ in a document by knowing that $u$ is or is not in the document. In the context of our study, given a term $u$, it seems natural to first identify which terms $v$ are related to $u$ before we estimate the probability that the former entails the latter. Overloading our notation some-

---

[2] Using an unsmoothed language model for which $P(u|d) = 0$ when $u \notin d$ implements the above assumption.

[3] The Information Gain, aka Generalised (or average) Mutual Information [5], has been used for selecting features in text categorisation [20, 9] or detecting collocations [8].

what, we denote by $u$ (resp. $\neg u$) the presence (resp. absence) of term $u$ in a document. The Information Gain measure is:

$$IG(u,v) = \sum_{X \in \{u, \neg u\}} \sum_{Y \in \{v, \neg v\}} P(X,Y) \ln \frac{P(X,Y)}{P(X)P(Y)}, \tag{6}$$

where the probabilities in eq. 6 are replaced by their empirical estimates: $P(X = u, Y = v) = \sum_{d \in \mathcal{D}} I(u \in d)I(v \in d)/|\mathcal{D}|$, etc. $I(\cdot)$ is the indicator function: it takes value one if the enclosed condition is true, and zero otherwise.

For each source term $u$, the information gain is computed for every other term $v$. The $N_{max}$ terms with the highest values of information gain are selected. Then, the lexical entailment probability defined in eqs. 1, 3 or 5 can be used on these $N_{max}$ terms (and possibly renormalised, if needed).

## 2.2  Estimating $P(u|u)$

The second problem is the estimation of the probability $P(u|u)$. Within the lexical entailment approach, $P(u|u)$ is the probability that a term entails itself. Intuitively, this probability should be high, because a source term is more likely to entail itself than any other term. However, in practice, using the lexical entailment probability defined in eqs. 1, 3 or 5 yields a value of $P(u|u)$ typically not so much larger than the probability obtained for the other terms. In the IR setting, this means that documents containing query terms may not be considered significantly more relevant than documents containing only "entailed" terms. As many words tend to have several, often quite different, meanings (polysemy), this means that the relevance tends to get "diluted" as we move away from query words.[4] In order to counter this effect, we increase the self-entailment probability $P(u|u)$ by interpolating the lexical entailment distribution obtained from eqs. 1, 3 or 5 with a Dirac distribution centred on $u$:

$$\tilde{P}(v|u) = \begin{cases} \alpha + (1-\alpha)P(v|u) & \text{if } v = u \\ (1-\alpha)P(v|u) & \text{otherwise.} \end{cases} \tag{7}$$

The additional parameter $\alpha$ enables us to modify the weight given to the self-entailment. The standard situation (no correction for $P(u|u)$) is obtained by $\alpha = 0$ and the extreme case of $\alpha = 1$ is the baseline situation which corresponds to using no lexical entailment. Accordingly, tuning this parameter is a way to check our hypothesis that reinforcing the entailment probability of the term itself is beneficial.

## 3  Language Modelling for Information Retrieval

Given a query $q$, the language model approach to IR [16] scores documents $d$ by estimating $P(q|d)$, the probability of the query according to a language model of the document. For a query $q = \{q_1, \ldots q_\ell\}$, we get:

---

[4] Of course there may be counter-examples where exact synonyms which are not polysemous may be perfectly acceptable, or even better than the original term.

$$P(q|d) = \prod_{i=1}^{\ell} P(q_i|d). \tag{8}$$

For each document $d$, a simple language model is obtained by considering the frequency of words in $d$, $P_{ML}(w|d) \propto \#(w, d)$ (this is the Maximum Likelihood, or ML, estimator). The probabilities are smoothed by the corpus language model $P_{ML}(w|\mathcal{D}) \propto \sum_d \#(w, d)$. The resulting language model is:

$$P(w|d) = \lambda\, P_{ML}(w|d) + (1 - \lambda)\, P_{ML}(w|\mathcal{D}). \tag{9}$$

In the simplest approach, we just assume that $P(q_i|d) = P(w = q_i|d)$, so the documents are scored according to:

$$\text{score}(q, d) = P(q|d) = \prod_{i=1}^{\ell} P(w = q_i|d). \tag{10}$$

Berger and Lafferty [3] later proposed an extension of the method, inspired by an analogy with translation. In this model, a word from the document may be translated into a different query term. Hence:

$$P(q_i|d) = \sum_w P(q_i|w)P(w|d), \tag{11}$$

where $P(q|w)$ is the probability of translating word $w$ into query term $q$, and $P(w|d)$ is again the language model of document $d$. This approach is especially useful in Cross-Lingual Information Retrieval (CLIR), where $P(q|w)$ is a genuine translation matrix which relates query terms written in one language to documents written in another. Such a matrix may be obtained using a machine-readable dictionary, or extracted from parallel or comparable corpora [10].

This framework is also convenient in order to take into account similarities between words and in particular, to formalise the use of textual entailment in IR. Given an entailment or similarity between words, expressed by a conditional probability $P(v|u)$, documents are scored according to:

$$P(q|d) = \prod_{i=1}^{\ell} \sum_w P(u = q_i|v = w)P(w|d). \tag{12}$$

$P(u|v)$ may be obtained by any of the methods described in section 2, and $P(w|d)$ is given by equation 9. In addition, the CLIR setting as implemented by the Lemur toolkit [2] introduces a background query-language smoothing. Instead of eq. 8 the document score is in fact:

$$P(q|d) = \prod_{i=1}^{\ell} \left(\beta P(q_i|d) + (1 - \beta)P(q_i|\mathcal{D})\right). \tag{13}$$

In order to use our lexical entailment probabilities within the Language Modelling approach, we must therefore set two extra parameters, $\lambda$ and $\beta$.

# 4   Experiments

Our experiments serve several purposes:

1. Evaluating the performance of various lexical entailment models (section 2);
2. Comparison with another query enrichment technique: pseudo-relevance feedback;
3. Assessing the stability of the lexical entailment probabilities by estimating them on a different, larger corpus than the IR collection.

## 4.1   Data

Our experiments were carried out on the English part of the CLEF-2003 corpus [15], which contains around 160,000 documents. The indexing was done using the Lemur toolkit [2] and the resulting vocabulary contains around 80,000 distinct terms (types). The indexing process only retained the following sections from the original documents: <TITLE>, <HEADLINE>, <LEAD>, <TX>, <LD>, <TI>, <ST>. Words occurring less than five times were removed from the index in order to limit its size.

In our evaluations, we used 54 queries of CLEF-2003, each with at least one relevant document, and the corresponding relevance judgments. The retrieval was also based on Lemur. When necessary, for example to implement the feature described in section 2.2, we used the Lemur API to implement new retrieval functions. The calculation of the lexical entailment probability tables also leveraged the Lemur API.

## 4.2   Evaluation of Lexical Entailment Models

In our first evaluation, we compared the performance of five models:

- Baseline: standard monolingual retrieval model from Lemur. It amounts to using an identity matrix as lexical entailment table, $P(v|u) = I(v = u)$.
- TE: this is the probabilistic lexical entailment model from [11] (equation 1).
- Jaccard: the model based on the jaccard similarity measure (equation 3)
- M3: this is our third model, equation 5.
- M3+IG: the third model, with an additional prefiltering step based on the information gain, as explained in section 2.1.

For each of the lexical entailment models, for each term $u$ in the corpus, the probability distribution $P(.|u)$ was computed and the top $Nbest = 20$ words were selected from this distribution. Then, a renormalisation of the score was done in order to obtain a new probability distribution. There are several parameters to set during these experiments: $\alpha$, $\beta$ and $\lambda$. Ideally, these should be optimised on a distinct validation set (for example a subset of queries). Then the optimised version may be used on the test queries. However, in order to get a better assessment of performance differences and help comparison with other results on the same data, we wish to keep our 54 queries for testing. As a consequence, we did not run an extensive optimisation of the parameters for each model. Instead, we ran a couple of preliminary experiments, and set parameter values to $\lambda = 0.5$ for the baseline and $\alpha = 0.5$, $\beta = 0.25$ and $\lambda = 0.8$ for the other methods. These values seem to provide reasonable performance in various situations. Note that the parameter values are therefore identical for all models, and not optimised for each model. This limits the optimistic bias resulting from a partial use of the test queries for deciding on reasonable global parameter values. Optimising $(\alpha, \beta, \lambda)$ for each model would yield better apparent performance but also a much larger optimistic bias.

We compare the various experimental results based on the mean average precision (MAP) over the 54 queries, as calculated by `trec_eval` [1]. In order to assess the significance of the differences in MAP observed between the different methods, we ran a (paired) Wilcoxon signed rank test [14] on the 54 average precision results for each method. We indicate results that are significantly better than the baseline at the 95% level, according to this test.

### Influence of Lexical Entailment Probabilities

Our first experimental results are presented in the top row of table 1. We observe that the lexical entailment models provide a small but significant improvement over the baseline. The use of the Information Gain to filter out common words provides an additional boost in performance. In conjunction with the M3 model, it yields the biggest improvement in performance (+3.19% absolute, highly significant). Note that because the paired Wilcoxon test is based on ranks, the significance is not a monotonous function of the average difference. With a MAP of 56.15%, the Jaccard similarity yields a slightly higher performance than the TE model, but this is due to a large gain on a single query, and is therefore not significant overall.

Figure 1 provides more information on the performance of TE and M3+IG using the average precision-recall curve at the 11 standard points of recall. This shows that the ranking in performance provided by the MAP is quite consistent over the whole spectrum of recall values.

### Comparison with Pseudo-relevance Feedback

Pseudo-relevance feedback (PRF) is a technique in which a first retrieval is carried out, and the query is enriched with typical words from the top retrieved

**Table 1.** Experimental results, expressed in mean average precision (in %), for the 5 models considered in the evaluation, with and without using pseudo-relevance feedback. Parameters are: $\lambda = 0.5$ for the baseline, and $\alpha = 0.5$, $\beta = 0.25$ and $\lambda = 0.8$ for the other 4 models. The pseudo-relevance feedback parameters are $NbDocs = 5$ and $NbTerms = 10$. Bold indicate significant improvement over the baseline (paired Wilcoxon test at 95% level).

| Model: | Baseline | TE | Jaccard | M3 | M3+IG |
|---|---|---|---|---|---|
| Without PRF | 54.34 | **55.99** | 56.15 | 55.94 | **57.52** |
| With PRF | 56.37 | **56.45** | 58.45 | 57.64 | **58.42** |

**P/R curve (standard retrieval)**

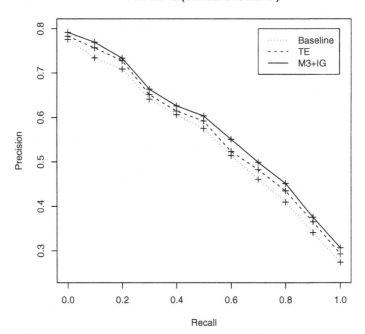

**Fig. 1.** Precision-recall curves for the standard retrieval results for the baseline method, the Textual Entailment model and the M3 model

documents. The rationale for this is that the top documents are more likely to contain relevant vocabulary. The intention is similar to the textual entailment problem: identify words which are different from query terms, but are somewhat related. It therefore makes sense to compare the lexical entailment approach to PRF.

PRF requires 2 additional parameters to be set: the number of top documents considered and the number of terms added to the query. In our experiments we consider the 5 highest ranked documents and enrich the query with the 10 most typical words.

The experimental results using pseudo-relevance feedback are presented in the second row of table 1. In our experiments, PRF provides an increase in performance around 1% to 2%, making all observed increases in performance significant or close to significant ($p = 5.45\%$ for M3, and $p = 7.89\%$ for baseline with PRF). The best results are obtained with the jaccard model and the (M3+IG) model, with a performance increase of around 4% (absolute). In fact, these two models are also significantly better than the baseline PRF.

Again, we present the precision/recall curves at the 11 standard points of recall for the baseline, the lexical entailment model, and the M3+IG model, all with PRF. These are displayed in figure 2. The results obtained by M3+IG with PRF are consistently above the other two. On the other hand, there is almost no

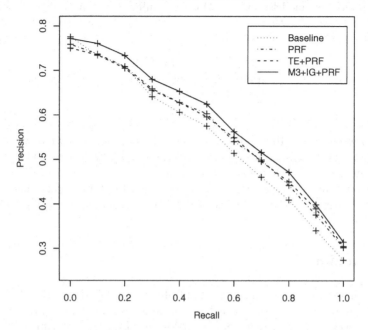

**Fig. 2.** Precision-recall curves using pseudo-relevance feedback on the baseline method, the Textual Entailment model and the M3 model

difference between TE and the baseline once PRF is applied. This is consistent with the MAP performance recorded in table 1.

## Dependency on the Corpus

The third issue we investigate is the dependency of the lexical entailment probabilities on the corpus. In the previous experiments, the probabilities $P(u|v)$ where estimated on the same collection they were tested on. This is perfectly "legal", because the estimation is carried out once and for all beforhands and does not use any relevance judgement. This leads to an important question: how corpus-specific are the estimated probabilities? In particular, would it be possible to estimate the lexical entailment probabilities once and for all on a large corpus, then apply the resulting estimates on every new collection?

In order to test this dependency, we use the Reuters RCV-1 corpus (used for example in the ad-hoc filtering track at TREC in 2002), which contains 800,000 documents, mostly from finance-related newswire stories. This corpus is much larger than the CLEF collection, and the two corpora differ somewhat thematically.

Table 2 summarises the MAP we obtained using two models, TE and M3, with entailment probabilities estimated on both corpora. Using the Reuters corpus degrades the results slightly. Most noticeably, the performance of the TE model is now below baseline, although the difference is not significant. The performance

**Table 2.** Performance using the Reuters corpus to estimate the lexical entailment probabilities for two models: TE and M3. All results are mean average precision (in %). Parameters are: $\alpha = 0.5$, $\beta = 0.25$ and $\lambda = 0.8$. No differences are significant (using a paired Wilcoxon test at 95% level).

| Model: | TE | M3 |
|---|---|---|
| using CLEF | 55.99 | 55.94 |
| using Reuters | 54.14 | 55.18 |

of the M3 model using Reuters is inbetween the baseline and what we obtained earlier (table 1), but again the differences are not significant ($p \approx 15\%$).

The conclusion from this experiment seems to be that although the entailment probabilities may be better estimated on the larger Reuters corpus, this does not offset the fact that these probabilities will be sub-optimal for querying the CLEF corpus, due to the different natures of the two corpora.

## 5 Discussion

Our investigation suggests that lexical entailment models do potentially provide significant improvements over the baseline language modelling system. Using our third model and a prefiltering based on the Information Gain, we obtain a significant improvement of 3.18% over a monolingual language modelling IR system, and even 4% by combining it with pseudo-relevance feedback.

Although the inspiration is entirely different, textual entailment models allow us to provide a kind of lexical query enrichment. The traditional pseudo-relevance feedback performs a different type of query enrichment. It yields improvements similar to our lexical entailment model. However, it should be noted that once the lexical entailment probability table is estimated, it may be used with any new query in one pass. In contrast, pseudo-relevance feedback requires two passes over the corpus: one for the original query and a second one for the enriched query. In our experiments, we showed that both techniques provide similar results and the use of PRF did not provide significant improvements over the best lexical entailment models.

Finally, we tested whether the entailment probabilities estimated on a large, independent corpus may compete with measures obtained on the queried collection itself. Our experiments show that performance seems to degrade slightly, but this effect is not significant.

One issue is the choice of lexical entailment model. The three models that we tried provide similar performance. In fact, we gain more from adding a prefiltering step than we do from switching models. This suggests that there may be additional work to do in developing new models that somehow incorporate this filtering. A related issue is that in the open domain of IR, we found it crucial to filter out common words. This is not so much an issue in the prototypical textual entailment evaluations which test a relatively small number of individual (*text*, *hypothesis*) pairs.

# 6    Conclusion

In this paper we have presented the results of our investigations into the use of lexical entailment models for IR. We have shown that lexical entailment potentially provides a significant boost to monolingual IR performance. It is at least comparable to what is achieved with pseudo-relevance feedback, and does so with a lower overhead.

Future works include the refinement of the models to further improve the estimation of the entailment probabilities. In addition, we would like to investigate the development of a query-specific entailment measure.

**Acknowledgements.** This work was supported in part by the IST programme of the European Community, through a "pump-priming" grant from the PASCAL network of excellence, IST-2002-506778. We thank our colleagues from this pump-priming project for useful discussions and feedback. This publication only reflects the author's views.

We also wish to acknowledge the many useful comments provided by the anonymous reviewers.

# References

1. http://trec.nist.gov/trec_eval/.
2. http://www.lemurproject.org/.
3. A. L. Berger and J. D. Lafferty. Information retrieval as statistical translation. In *Proceedings of the 22nd Annual International ACM SIGIR Conference on Research and Development in Information Retrieval*, pages 222–229. ACM, 1999.
4. R. Besançon, M. Rajman, and J.-C. Chappelier. Textual similarities based on a distributional approach. In *Proceedings of the Tenth International Workshop on Database and Expert Systems Applications (DEX'99)*, Florence, Italy, 1999.
5. B. Colin. Information et analyse des données. *Pub. Inst. Stat. Univ. Paris*, XXXVII(3–4):43–60, 1993.
6. W. Croft and J. Lafferty, editors. *Language Modeling for Information Retrieval*. Kluwer Academic Publishers, 2003.
7. I. Dagan, O. Glickman, and B. Magnini. The PASCAL recognising textual entailment challenge. In *PASCAL Challenges Workshop for Recognizing Textual Entailment*, 2005.
8. T. Dunning. Accurate methods for the statistics of surprise and coincidence. *Computational Linguistics*, 19(1):61–74, 1993.
9. G. Forman. An extensive empirical study of feature selection metrics for text classification. *Journal of Machine Learning Research*, 3:1289–1305, 2003.
10. É. Gaussier, J.-M. Renders, I. Matveeva, C. Goutte, and H. Déjean. A geometric view on bilingual lexicon extraction from comparable corpora. In *Proceedings of the 42nd Annual Meeting of the Association for Computational Linguistics*, pages 526–533, 2004.
11. O. Glickman, I. Dagan, and M. Koppel. A probabilistic classification approach for lexical textual entailment. In *Twentieth National Conference on Artificial Intelligence (AAAI-05)*, 2005.

12. G. Grefenstette. *Explorations in Automatic Thesaurus Construction*. Kluwer Academic Publishers, 1994.
13. D. A. Grossman and O. Frieder. *Information Retrieval*. Springer, 2nd edition, 2004.
14. M. Hollander and D. A. Wolfe. *Nonparametric Statistical Methods*. Wiley-Interscience, 2nd edition, 1999.
15. C. Peters, J. Gonzalo, M. Braschler, and M. Kluck, editors. *Comparative Evaluation of Multilingual Information Access Systems, 4th Workshop of the Cross-Language Evaluation Forum, CLEF 2003*, volume 3237 of *Lecture Notes in Computer Science*. Springer, 2004.
16. J. Ponte and W. Croft. A language modelling approach to information retrieval. In *Proceedings of the 21st Annual International ACM SIGIR Conference on Research and Development in Information Retrieval*, pages 275–281. ACM, 1998.
17. Y. Qiu and H. Frei. Improving the retrieval effectiveness by a similarity thesaurus. Technical report, Department of Computer Science, Swiss Federal Institute of Technology, 1994.
18. G. Salton and J. McGill. *Introduction to Modern Information Retrieval*. New York,McGraw-Hill, 1983.
19. S. K. M. Wong, W. Ziarko, and P. C. N. Wong. Generalized vector space model in information retrieval. In *Proceedings of the 8th Annual International ACM SIGIR Conference on Research and Development in Information Retrieval*, 1985.
20. Y. Yang and J. O. Pedersen. A comparative study on feature selection in text categorization. In *Proceedings of ICML-97, 14th International Conference on Machine Learning*, pages 412–420, 1997.

# A Hybrid Approach to Index Maintenance in Dynamic Text Retrieval Systems

Stefan Büttcher and Charles L.A. Clarke

School of Computer Science, University of Waterloo, Canada
{sbuettch, claclark}@plg.uwaterloo.ca

**Abstract.** In-place and merge-based index maintenance are the two main competing strategies for on-line index construction in dynamic information retrieval systems based on inverted lists. Motivated by recent results for both strategies, we investigate possible combinations of in-place and merge-based index maintenance. We present a hybrid approach in which long posting lists are updated in-place, while short lists are updated using a merge strategy. Our experimental results show that this hybrid approach achieves better indexing performance than either method (in-place, merge-based) alone.

## 1 Introduction

Traditional information retrieval systems deal with static text collections: Once indexed, no documents are ever added to or removed from the collection. Efficient index construction for static collections has been studied in detail over the last two decades. After contributions by Moffat and Bell [8, 9] and Heinz and Zobel [13, 5], the indexing problem for static collections seems solved. Following an inverted-file approach and combining the techniques described in the literature, it is possible to index text collections at a rate well above 50 GB per hour on a standard desktop PC, allowing the indexing of text collections in the terabyte range on a single PC (see section 4 for details).

For on-line index maintenance in dynamic search environments, the situation is different. Because index updates are interleaved with search queries, it is important that the index is *always* kept in a form that allows for efficient query processing. Traditional batch index construction techniques do not meet this criterion, as they do not make any guarantees about the contiguity of on-disk inverted lists during the index construction process. If queries have to be processed during index construction, this non-contiguity leads to a large number of disk seek operations and thus poor query processing performance.

In a truly dynamic environment, documents may be added to and removed from the collection at any point in time. For the purpose of this paper, we disregard deletions and focus exclusively on document insertions. It is possible, however, to integrate support for deletions into the methods described in this paper (see [1], for example).

Many index maintenance strategies that deal with document insertions in dynamic search systems have been examined in the past. The two dominant

M. Lalmas et al. (Eds.): ECIR 2006, LNCS 3936, pp. 229–240, 2006.
© Springer-Verlag Berlin Heidelberg 2006

families are *in-place* update and *merge-based* index maintenance. When new documents are added to the collection, in-place strategies update the index by adding new postings at the end of existing on-disk inverted lists, relocating the lists if necessary. Merge-based strategies update the index by merging the existing on-disk inverted file with the new postings, resulting in a new inverted file that replaces the old one.

The main disadvantage of merge-based update is that, whenever an on-disk inverted file is updated, the entire file has to be read/written, even though most parts of the index remain unchanged and only a relatively small number of postings are added to the file. For large indices, this leads to a substantial decrease in index update performance. In-place strategies try to overcome this problem by leaving a certain amount of free space at the end of every on-disk inverted list. If, during an index update, there is enough space for the new postings, they are simply appended to the existing list. If not, the entire list has to be moved to a new location in order to make enough room for the new postings. These relocations make it impossible to keep the on-disk lists in any given order (e.g., lexicographical order), as the order is destroyed every time a list is relocated. This leads to a large number of non-sequential disk accesses during index updates, the main shortcoming of in-place update strategies.

We propose a hybrid approach to index maintenance, based on the idea that for long lists it takes more time to copy the whole list than to perform a single disk seek operation, while for short lists a disk seek is more expensive than copying the list as part of a longer, sequential read/write operation. Our approach exhibits an amortized indexing performance superior to that of existing merge-based strategies, while providing an equivalent or even slightly better level of query processing performance.

The remainder of this paper is organized as follows: The next section gives an overview of related work, divided into techniques for off-line and on-line index construction; the on-line part covers both merge-based and in-place strategies. In section 3, we present our hybrid approach to index maintenance, explain how in-place updates are realized, and which merge strategies are used for the merge part of the hybrid update. We present an experimental evaluation in section 4 and compare our new approach to existing merge-based maintenance strategies. The evaluation is done in terms of both indexing and query processing performance.

## 2   Related Work

This section gives an overview of existing work on index construction techniques for retrieval systems based on inverted lists. We first cover the case in which a static collection is indexed, using an off-line method, and then explain how the off-line construction method can be adapted to deal with dynamic environments.

### 2.1   Off-Line Index Construction

Inverted files have proved to be the most efficient data structure for high performance indexing of large text collections [14]. For every term that appears in

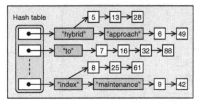
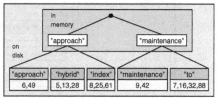

(a) In-memory index with hash table and linked lists.     (b) On-disk index with 2-level search tree.

**Fig. 1.** Basic structure of in-memory index and on-disk inverted file. Vocabulary terms in memory are arranged in a hash table, using linked lists to organize the individual posting lists. Terms on disk are sorted in lexicographical order, allowing for efficient index access at query time.

the given collection, the inverted file contains a list of all positions at which the term occurs (the term's *posting list*).

The process of creating this inverted file can be roughly described as follows: Input documents are read, one at a time, and postings are accumulated in an in-memory index, using a hash table with move-to-front heuristics [13] to look up vocabulary terms. Postings for the same term are stored in memory in compressed form, either in an augmentable bitvector [5] or in a linked list [2]. When the entire collection has been indexed, all terms are sorted in lexicographical order and the in-memory data are written to disk, forming an inverted file. In order to decrease disk I/O, the data in the inverted file are stored in compressed form. A two-level search tree is used to access on-disk posting lists during query processing later on. The general structure of the in-memory and the on-disk index can be seen in Figure 1.

If the amount of main memory available is not sufficient to index the whole collection at a single blow, the process is repeated several times, each time creating an inverted file for a part of the total collection. The size of these subcollections depends on the available main memory. It is determined on-the-fly during the indexing process and does not require multiple passes over the collection.

After the whole collection has been indexed, all sub-indices created so far are brought together through a multi-way merge process, resulting in the final index. Since the posting lists in the sub-indices are stored in lexicographical order, this can be done very efficiently by organizing the input indices in a priority queue and employing standard input buffering techniqes (read-ahead). For a given term, its final posting list is created by concatenating the sub-lists from the individual sub-indices. This does not require the decompression of the postings and thus allows for a very efficient creation of the final index.

## 2.2   On-Line Index Construction

It is possible to use the same techniques employed for off-line index construction in a dynamic retrieval system in which update operations are interleaved with search queries. Whenever a query is being processed and a posting list has to be fetched from the (incomplete) index, sub-lists are retrieved from the existing

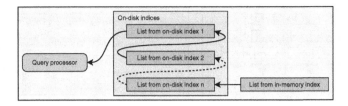

**Fig. 2.** Query processing during batched index construction. A term's posting list is constructed by concatenating sub-lists from all on-disk indices and the in-memory index containing the postings for the sub-index currently being created.

on-disk indices and the in-memory index. By concatenating these sub-lists, the whole posting list is constructed, and the query can be processed (shown in Figure 2). We refer to this method as the *No Merge* strategy.

Although, in principle, *No Merge* does solve the problem of dealing with a dynamic text collection, it is not a good solution. Because the point at which the whole collection has been indexed is never reached in a dynamic environment, the final index is never created and all the on-disk inverted files have to be queried individually. Since the number of these files can be quite large, this severely harms query processing performance, as it requires a large number of disk seeks – at least one per inverted file.

In order to avoid these disk seeks, the on-disk indices should be re-organized in some way whenever a new sub-index is created. Unfortunately, this requires additional disk operations and can be quite time-consuming. Büttcher and Clarke [1] characterize this as a trade-off between indexing performance and query processing performance; maximum indexing performance is obtained by following the off-line index construction strategy described above, while query performance is optimized by immediately merging the in-memory postings with the existing on-disk index, creating a new, optimized on-disk index whenever main memory is exhausted. Depending on the ratio of document insertions and search queries, different strategies lead to optimal overall system performance.

**In-Place Index Maintenance**

In-place index update techniques were examined very early in the history of dynamic information retrieval systems. In general, two different flavors of in-place update exist: those that keep each posting list in a contiguous part of the on-disk index and those that allow posting lists to be split up by index update operations. Keeping posting lists in a contiguous part of the inverted file maximizes query performance, but requires frequent relocations of most lists in the index. If lists have to be kept contiguous, and no free space is reserved at the end of an existing list, it has to be relocated every time an update is applied to the index. Preallocation strategies, such as predictive overallocation [10], reduce the number of times a posting list has to be relocated, but do so at the cost of increased disk space consumption.

Tomasic, Shoens, and García-Molina [12, 11] present a very thorough discussion of in-place index maintenance and propose a system that is based on the distinction between short and long posting lists, storing short lists in fixed-size buckets together with other short lists and long lists in (not necessarily contiguous) sections of the inverted file.

The main problem of in-place strategies is the very high number of disk seeks necessary to update an inverted file. Relocating inverted lists means destroying the original ordering of the lists on disk. This has two important implications:

1. Accessing the index terms in a pre-defined order (e.g., in lexicographical order) does not lead to a sequential disk access pattern during index updates and thus requires a large number of disk seek operations.
2. Since on-disk index terms are unordered, a second index structure is necessary, mapping terms to the positions of their posting lists. For large collections, this map cannot be kept in memory, but has to be stored on disk.

Because random disk accesses are very slow, compared with sequential access patterns, in-place strategies might reduce the number of read/write operations necessary to perform an index update, but this is not really reflected by their effective indexing maintenance performance.

One possible implementation of the in-place strategy is to keep each posting list in a separate file inside the file system. Whenever in-memory postings have to be combined with the on-disk index, the respective file is opened and the in-memory postings are appended to the existing on-disk list. Fragmentation management etc. are deferred to the file system. This is the implementation we are using in our experiments.

## Merge-Based Index Maintenance

Merge-based update strategies share the common idea that disk read/write operations are most efficient when they are carried out in a sequential manner, minimizing disk head movement. The most popular form of merge update is the *Immediate Merge* strategy: Whenever main memory is exhausted, the in-memory postings are merged with the existing on-disk index, processing the on-disk index in a sequential fashion, resulting in a new on-disk index that immediately replaces the old one. Since, at any given time, there is only a single active on-disk index, this strategy minimizes the number of disk head movements necessary to fetch a posting list from disk and thus maximizes query processing performance.

The Immediate Merge strategy was first described by Cutting and Pedersen [4]. In their work, they present an index structure based on a B-tree and give a comparison of leave node caching (a form of in-place update) and index re-merging. Using the same amount of memory, the merge approach exhibits vastly superior performance. Lester et al. [7] conducted similar experiments, comparing Immediate Merge with more recently developed in-place strategies, and obtained similar results, indicating that merge-based index maintenance is usually more efficient than in-place update.

The main problem of Immediate Merge is that, whenever main memory is exhausted, the entire on-disk index has to be re-processed. Hence, after $N$ tokens have been added to the collection, the total number of postings that have been transferred from/to disk is:

$$\sum_{i=1}^{\lfloor \frac{N}{M} \rfloor} (2i - 1) \cdot M \ \in \ \Theta\left(\frac{N^2}{M}\right),$$

where $M$ is the available main memory (the number of postings that can be kept in memory at a time). This quadratic time complexity renders Immediate Merge infeasible for text collections much larger than the available main memory.

Recently, Büttcher and Clarke [1] and Lester et al. [6] have proposed merge-based update strategies that do not share this shortcoming. By allowing a controlled number of on-disk indices to exist in parallel, indexing efficiency is greatly increased, while query processing performance remains almost unchanged compared to the Immediate Merge strategy. The basic idea is to maintain a set of sub-indices of exponentially growing size. If $M$ is the amount of main memory available to the indexing system, then on-disk indices can be of size $M$, $k \cdot M$, $k^2 \cdot M$, ..., for some small value of $k$ (usually, $k = 2$ or $k = 3$ is chosen). For any given index size, there can be at most $k - 1$ indices of that size at the same time. Whenever the creation of a new on-disk index leads to a situation where there are $k$ indices of the same size $k^n \cdot M$, they are merged into a new index of size $k^{n+1} \cdot M$. This process is repeated until, for every integer $n$, there are at most $k - 1$ indices of the same magnitude $k^n \cdot M$.

This strategy is referred to as *geometric partitioning* or *Logarithmic Merge*. At any given time, the number of on-disk sub-indices is bounded by $\lceil \log_k \left( \lfloor \frac{N}{M} \rfloor \right) \rceil$, where $N$ again is the number of input tokens processed so far. The total number of postings that have been transferred from/to disk is $\Theta\left(N \cdot \log\left(\frac{N}{M}\right)\right)$. Limiting the number of sub-indices to the logarithm of the collection size keeps query performance at a very high level, but allows the retrieval system's indexing complexity to decrease dramatically from $\Theta(N^2)$ to $\Theta(N \cdot \log(N))$ disk operations. However, although this is a great improvement, Logarithmic Merge shares the same basic problem of all merge-based maintenance strategies: When a new sub-index is created, posting lists (or parts thereof) have to be transferred from/to disk even though they have not been changed.

## 3    A Hybrid Approach to Index Maintenance

In the previous section, we have discussed the advantages and disadvantages of merge-based and in-place index update schemes. In merge-based index maintenance strategies, especially for Immediate Merge, a great amount of time is spent copying postings from an old index to the new one. In-place strategies avoid this overhead by leaving unchanged portions of a posting list untouched during an index update operation, at the cost of many, possibly too many, disk seek operations.

It seems obvious that there is a certain system-specific number $X$ such that for posting lists shorter than $X$ postings it is faster to read the list (as part of a longer, sequential read operation) than to perform a disk seek, while for lists longer than $X$ a disk seek is faster than reading the list. In other words, a hybrid index maintenance strategy, in which short lists are maintained using a merge-based update method, while long lists are updated in-place, seems promising. It can be expected that such a method performs better than either pure merge-based or pure in-place index maintenance.

We first explain how in-place updates are realized in our retrieval system and then present two different hybrid strategies. The first is a combination of in-place update and Immediate Merge. The second is a combination of in-place update and Logarithmic Merge.

### 3.1  In-Place and the File System

Some of the optimizations for the in-place index update scheme, such as pre-allocation strategies, have been used in file systems for a long time. Other techniques, such as keeping very short posting lists inside dictionary data structure instead of allocating separate space in the index file, are more recent, but have their analoga in file system implementations as well: The Reiser4[1] file system stores very small files within the directory tree itself, avoiding the overhead that is associated with allocating a separate block for every file.

Since implementing an in-place strategy and fine-tuning it so that it delivers good indexing performance is a time-consuming task, we chose to realize the in-place portion of our hybrid strategy by using existing file system services. Whenever we refer to an in-place-updatable posting list in the remainder of this paper, this means that the list is stored in an individual file. Updates to the list are realized by appending the new postings to the existing file data.

We rely on the file system's ability to avoid relocations and fragmentation by using advanced pre-allocation strategies and hope that several decades of file system research have resulted in file system implementations that are no worse at this than a custom implementation of the in-place index update scheme. Since in our hybrid approach only long lists are updated in-place, this seems like a reasonable assumption.

### 3.2  In-Place + Immediate Merge

The combination of in-place update and Immediate Merge is straightforward. Whenever a new on-disk index is created by merging the in-memory data with the existing on-disk index, terms are divided into two categories:

1. Terms whose posting list contains less than $X$ postings (*short lists*).
2. Terms whose posting list contains at least $X$ postings (*long lists*).

The merge process is performed as usual. The only modification is that, whenever a term with a long list is encountered during the merge, its postings are appended to a file that contains the postings for that term (the file is created if it does not exist yet) instead of being added to the new index that results from the merge process. Short lists do not have their own files. They are added to the new index, following the standard Immediate Merge strategy.

---

[1] http://www.namesys.com/v4/v4.html

### 3.3  In-Place + Logarithmic Merge

Integrating in-place update into the Logarithmic Merge strategy is slightly more complicated than the combination with Immediate Merge. This is for two reasons:

- Most sub-index merge operations do not involve all existing on-disk indices, but only a subset. Therefore, the total number of postings for a given term is unknown at merge time.
- Even if we always knew the the total number of postings for a term, it is not clear what implications the total size of a term's posting list has for a merge operation that only involves a small part of that list.

We address these problems by choosing a very conservative strategy. When main memory is exhausted for the very first time and the first on-disk inverted file is created, the predefined long list threshold value $X$ is used to divide the posting lists of all terms into short lists and long lists. Once this decision has been made, it will never be changed. From the indexing system's point of view, a posting list that does not make it into the set of long lists when the first index is created will always remain a short list, regardless of how many postings it actually contains.

Clearly, this solution is not optimal, as it does not take into account possible changes in the term distribution that take place after the first on-disk index has ben created. More adaptive strategies fall into the category "future work".

### 3.4  Partial Flush

The main rationale behind our hybrid approach is to avoid the unnecessary disk transfers that are caused by reading/writing unchanged portions of posting lists during merge operations. Therefore, it makes sense to defer the merge part of the hybrid update for as long as possible. This is achieved by the *partial flush* strategy: When main memory is exhausted and postings have to be transferred to disk, the indexing system only writes those postings to disk that belong to long lists (i.e., postings whose list resides in an individual file and is updated in-place). If, by doing so, the total memory consumption of the indexing system is decreased below a certain threshold, the system does not perform the merge part of the update, but continues its normal operation. Only if the total memory consumption cannot be decreased below the predefined threshold value, the merge part is performed and all postings are transferred from memory to disk.

For our experiments, we set the partial flush threshold value to 85% of the available memory. Depending on the value of the long list threshold $X$, this made the system perform 2-3 in-place update sequences per re-merge operation.

## 4  Experimental Evaluation

In this section, we give an experimental evaluation of our hybrid index maintenance strategy. We compare it with the *Immediate Merge* and *Logarithmic Merge* strategies, paying attention to both index maintenance and query processing performance. We also compare it with *No Merge* (the dynamic variant

**Table 1.** Comparing indexing and query processing performance of the off-line method, Immediate Merge, Logarithmic Merge, and the best hybrid strategy (In-Place + Log. Merge). The indexing time for the No Merge strategy does not include the final merge operation that is part of the off-line method. Including the final merge, the total indexing time is 5h30m (77.6 GB/h).

|                        | No Merge   | Imm. Merge | Log. Merge | Hybrid (IP+LM) |
|------------------------|------------|------------|------------|----------------|
| Total indexing time    | 4h01m      | 40h14m     | 7h14m      | 6h08m          |
| Indexing throughput    | 106.1 GB/h | 10.6 GB/h  | 59.0 GB/h  | 69.5 GB/h      |
| Average time per query | 5.028 sec  | 2.840 sec  | 3.011 sec  | 2.940 sec      |

of off-line index construction, described in section 2.2) and show that the hybrid update strategy achieves indexing performance very close to that of the off-line method.

### 4.1   Experimental Setup

For our experiments, we employed the GOV2 collection used in the TREC Terabyte track [3]. GOV2 contains 25.2 million documents with a total uncompressed size of about 426 GB. The collection was indexed using 1024 MB of main memory for the in-memory index. As query set, we used 100 Okapi BM25 queries derived from the topics of the 2004 and 2005 TREC Terabyte ad-hoc retrieval tasks. After stopword removal, the average query length was 3.0 terms.

For all experiments, the same update/query sequence was used. It contained 1360 search queries, interleaved with update commands (document insertions). Queries were randomly drawn from the query set described above, with each query occurring 13-14 times in the entire sequence. No caching is performed by the search engine itself. Since the average amount of data read from the input documents between two consecutive search queries is approximately 325 MB, the entire content of the file system cache is replaced after about 6 queries. This means that cache effects are negligible, and repeating each query 13-14 times does not affect the experimental results.

The experiments were conducted on a PC based on an AMD Athlon64 3500+ (2.2 GHz) with a 7200-rpm SATA hard drive. The input files were read from a RAID-0 built on top of two 7200-rpm SATA drives.

### 4.2   Results

Our first series of experiments consists of indexing the entire collection using the *No Merge* strategy and two pure merge-based strategies (1. Immediate Merge; 2. Logarithmic Merge for base $k = 2$). The results (reported in Table 1) are consistent with earlier findings [6, 1] and show that the off-line method really should not be used in a dynamic environment. Logarithmic merge exhibits indexing performance close to off-line index construction and query processing performance close to Immediate Merge.

The next series of experiments evaluates the indexing performance of the two hybrid strategies described in the previous section. The long list threshold

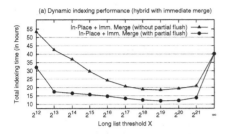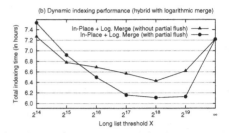

**Fig. 3.** Dynamic indexing performance of the two hybrid index maintenance strategies (In-Place + Immediate Merge and In-Place + Logarithmic Merge) with different long list threshold values $X$. The rightmost data points ($X = \infty$) represent pure Immediate Merge and pure Logarithmic Merge, respectively.

$X$, used to determine which posting lists are updated in-place and which are maintained by the merge strategy, is varied in order to study the effects of different values and to find the optimal configuration. The results presented in Figure 3 show that hybrid index maintenance achieves a huge improvement over the pure merge-based methods. For the hybridization of Immediate Merge (Figure 3a), the time needed to index the whole collection can be reduced by roughly 50% if $X$ values between $2^{18}$ and $2^{20}$ are used to realize the split. With partial flush enabled, the improvement is even greater; the total indexing time drops by 70% – from 40 hours to just under 12 hours.

As expected, the improvements achieved by hybridizing Logarithmic Merge are not as dramatic as in the case of Immediate Merge. Still, our experimental results (depicted in Figure 3b) show that the combination of in-place update and Logarithmic Merge reduces the total indexing time by 11% (15% with partial flush), compared with pure Logarithmic Merge. For $X$ around $2^{18}$ and partial flush turned on, the hybrid Logarithmic Merge indexes the whole collection in 367 minutes, only 37 minutes slower than off-line index construction. This represents an indexing throughput of 69.5 GB/h.

Since all these improvements are worthless unless the hybrid strategies exhibit query processing performance similar to their pure merge-based counterparts, we also measured average query time for both hybrid strategies and different threshold values $X$. The average query times depicted in Figure 4 show that both hybrid Immediate Merge and hybrid Logarithmic Merge exhibit query processing performance very close to the pure merge strategies. Figure 4a indicates that the large number of in-place-updatable lists associated with small $X$ values overburdens the file system. Fragmentation increases, and as a consequence query performance drops. For hybrid Immediate Merge, greater $X$ values mean less fragmentation and thus better query performance. The effect that file fragmentation has on query processing performance is quite substantial. For $X = 2^{10}$, average query time increases by 25%, from 2.84 seconds to 3.55 seconds. The lowest query time is achieved when $X = \infty$ (pure Immediate Merge).

For the hybridized Logarithmic Merge, the situation is different. Threshold values between $2^{16}$ and $2^{20}$ actually increase query performance (compared to

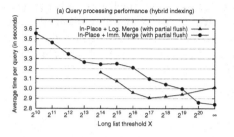
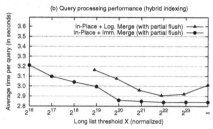

**Fig. 4.** Query processing performance of the two hybrid index maintenance strategies (In-Place + Immediate Merge and In-Place + Logarithmic Merge) with different long list threshold values $X$. The rightmost data points ($X = \infty$) represent pure Immediate Merge and pure Logarithmic Merge, respectively. Small $X$ values lead to high file fragmentation and thus poor query performance.

pure Logarithmic Merge) because in this interval the negative effect of file fragmentation is smaller than the impact of having to fetch partial posting lists from different on-disk indices, as it is the case for Logarithmic Merge. This leads to a query time reduction of up to 4% ($X \approx 2^{17}$).

The reader might be surprised that the query times reported in Figure 4a are lower for Logarithmic Merge than for Immediate Merge. The reason for this is that in the case of Logarithmic Merge, the $X$ value is used to split up short lists and long lists when the first on-disk index is created, while with Immediate Merge it is possible for a list initially classified as short to change its status to *long* later on. This asymmetry is taken into account in Figure 4b in which the $X$ values for hybrid Logarithmic Merge are adjusted, pretending the decision whether a list is long or short is made after 50% of the collection has been indexed. Figure 4a shows the expected situation, where Logarithmic Merge has slightly higher query times than Immediate Merge – due to the greater number of disk seeks.

## 5   Conclusion and Future Work

We have presented a novel family of index maintenance strategies to be used in dynamic information retrieval systems. These strategies are combinations of merge-based and in-place index maintenance methods and offer better indexing performance than either in-place or merge-based index maintenance alone, while providing an equivalent level of query processing performance.

In our experiments, using optimal parameter settings, the combination of in-place update and Logarithmic Merge achieved an indexing throughput of 69.5 GB/h on a typical desktop PC – only 10% less than the 77.6 GB/h of our off-line index construction method. This demonstrates that on-line index construction, in which update operations and search queries are interleaved, can be performed very efficiently and almost as fast as the traditional batched index construction.

One of the shortcomings of our results is that the work being done within the file system is completely invisible to us. We do not know the preallocation strategy used by the file system, we do not know how much internal fragmentation there is in the individual files, and we do not know how often files are relocated in order to avoid fragmentation. The main focus of our future work in this area will be to investigate other implementations of hybrid index maintenance that take these issues into account.

# References

1. S. Büttcher and C. L. A. Clarke. Indexing Time vs. Query Time Trade-offs in Dynamic Information Retrieval Systems. In *Proc. of the 14th ACM Conf. on Information and Knowledge Management (CIKM 2005)*, Bremen, Germany, 2005.
2. S. Büttcher and C. L. A. Clarke. Memory Management Strategies for Single-Pass Index Construction in Text Retrieval Systems. UW-TR-CS-2005-32. Technical report, University of Waterloo, Canada, October 2005.
3. C. Clarke, N. Craswell, and I. Soboroff. The TREC Terabyte Retrieval Track. *SIGIR Forum*, 39(1):25–25, 2005.
4. D. R. Cutting and J. O. Pedersen. Optimization for Dynamic Inverted Index Maintenance. In *Proceedings of the 13th Annual International ACM SIGIR Conference on Research and Development in Information Retrieval (SIGIR 1990)*, pages 405–411, New York, USA, 1990. ACM Press.
5. S. Heinz and J. Zobel. Efficient Single-Pass Index Construction for Text Databases. *Journal of the American Society for Information Science and Technology*, 54(8):713–729, 2003.
6. N. Lester, A. Moffat, and J. Zobel. Fast On-Line Index Construction by Geometric Partitioning. In *Proceedings of the 14th ACM Conference on Information and Knowledge Management (CIKM 2005)*, Bremen, Germany, 2005.
7. N. Lester, J. Zobel, and H. E. Williams. In-Place versus Re-Build versus Re-Merge: Index Maintenance Strategies for Text Retrieval Systems. In *CRPIT '26: Proceedings of the 27th Conference on Australasian Computer Science*, pages 15–23. Australian Computer Society, Inc., 2004.
8. A. Moffat. Economical Inversion of Large Text Files. *Computing Systems*, 5(2): 125–139, 1992.
9. A. Moffat and T. C. Bell. In-Situ Generation of Compressed Inverted Files. *Journal of the American Society of Information Science*, 46(7):537–550, 1995.
10. W.-Y. Shieh and C.-P. Chung. A Statistics-Based Approach to Incrementally Update Inverted Files. *Inf. Processing and Management*, 41(2):275–288, 2005.
11. K. A. Shoens, A. Tomasic, and H. García-Molina. Synthetic Workload Performance Analysis of Incremental Updates. In *Proceedings of the 17th Annual International ACM SIGIR Conference on Research and Development in Information Retrieval (SIGIR 1994)*, pages 329–338, 1994.
12. A. Tomasic, H. García-Molina, and K. Shoens. Incremental Updates of Inverted Lists for Text Document Retrieval. In *Proceedings of the 1994 ACM SIGMOD Conference*, pages 289–300, New York, USA, 1994. ACM Press.
13. J. Zobel, S. Heinz, and H. E. Williams. In-Memory Hash Tables for Accumulating Text Vocabularies. *Information Processing Letters*, 80(6), 2001.
14. J. Zobel, A. Moffat, and K. Ramamohanarao. Inverted Files versus Signature Files for Text Indexing. *ACM Trans. on Database Systems*, 23(4):453–490, 1998.

# Efficient Parallel Computation of PageRank

Christian Kohlschütter, Paul-Alexandru Chirita, and Wolfgang Nejdl

L3S Research Center/University of Hanover,
Deutscher Pavillon, Expo Plaza 1,
30539 Hanover, Germany
{kohlschuetter, chirita, nejdl}@l3s.de

**Abstract.** PageRank inherently is massively parallelizable and distributable, as a result of web's strict host-based link locality. We show that the Gauß-Seidel iterative method can actually be applied in such a parallel ranking scenario in order to improve convergence. By introducing a two-dimensional web model and by adapting the PageRank to this environment, we present efficient methods to compute the exact rank vector even for large-scale web graphs in only a few minutes and iteration steps, with intrinsic support for incremental web crawling, and without the need for page sorting/reordering or for sharing global rank information.

## 1 Introduction

Search engines are the enabling technology for finding information on the Internet. They provide regularly updated snapshots of the Web and maintain a searchable index over all retrieved web pages. Its size is currently reaching several billions of pages from about 54 million publicly accessible hosts, but these amounts are rapidly increasing [19]. When searching such huge datasets, one would usually receive quite a few pages in response to her query, some of them being much more relevant than others. This gave birth to a lot of ordering (or ranking) research, the most popular algorithm being Google's PageRank [20], which recursively determines the importance of a web page by the importance of all the pages pointing to it.

Although improvements for a centralized computation of PageRank have been researched in detail [1, 5, 9, 11, 12, 16, 13, 18], approaches on distributing it over several computers have caught researchers' attention only recently. In this paper we introduce a new approach to computing the exact PageRank in a parallel fashion. We obtain exact results faster than all the other existing algorithms, improving by orders of magnitude over the other algorithms generating exact Page-Rank scores. We achieve this by modeling the web graph in a two-dimensional fashion (with the URL's hostname as the primary criterion), thus separating it into reasonably disjunct partitions, which are then used for distributed, incremental web crawling [6] and PageRank computation.

The remainder of the paper is organized as follows. After reviewing the PageRank algorithm, common web graph representation techniques and existing parallel versions of PageRank in Section 2, we introduce our two-dimensional

M. Lalmas et al. (Eds.): ECIR 2006, LNCS 3936, pp. 241–252, 2006.
© Springer-Verlag Berlin Heidelberg 2006

web graph model in Section 3. We then present a refined PageRank algorithm in Section 4, and show that the convergence improvements of the Gauß-Seidel method for solving linear systems [1] can also be efficiently applied in a parallelized PageRank scenario. Experimental results are discussed in Section 5. Finally, Section 6 concludes with discussion of further work.

## 2   Related Work

### 2.1   PageRank

The main concept behind the PageRank paradigm [20] is the propagation of importance from one Web page towards others, via its out-going (hyper-)links. Each page $p \in P$ (P is the set of all considered pages) has an associated rank score $r(p)$, forming the rank vector $\vec{r}$. Let $L$ be the set of links, where $(s, t)$ is contained iff page $s$ points to page $t$ and $L(p)$ be the set of pages $p$ points to ($p$'s outgoing links). The following iteration step is then repeated until all scores $r$ stabilize to a certain defined degree $\delta < \varepsilon$:

$$\forall t \in P : r^{(i)}(t) = (1 - \alpha) \cdot \tau(t) + \alpha \sum_{(s,t) \in L} \frac{r^{(i-1)}(s)}{|L(s)|} \tag{1}$$

The formula consists of two portions, the jump component (left side of the summation) and the walk component (right side), weighted by $\alpha$ (usually 0.85). $r^{(i-1)}(s) \cdot |L(s)|^{-1}$ is the uniformly distributed fraction of importance a page $s$ can offer to one of its linked pages $t$ for iteration $i$. Intuitively, a "random surfer" follows an outgoing link from the current page (walk) with probability $\alpha$ and will get bored and select a random page (jump) with probability $1 - \alpha$. The main utility of $\alpha$ is however to guarantee convergence and avoid "rank sinks" [3].

This "random-walk" is in fact the interpretation of the Markov chain associated to the web graph, having $\vec{r}$ as the state vector and $A$ (see Equation 2) the transition probability from one page to another. We can therefore also write Equation 1 in matrix terms as follows:

$$\vec{r} = (1 - \alpha) \cdot \vec{\tau} + \alpha A \vec{r} \tag{2}$$

Equation 1 also represents the linear system representation of this matrix computation using the Jacobi iterative method. This enables the consideration of using other stationary iterative solvers, such as the Gauß-Seidel method, which converges two times faster than Jacobi but was said not to be efficiently parallelizable here [1, 5, 18]. Actually, there already are parallel Gauss-Seidel implementations for certain scenarios such as the one described in [14], using block-diagonally-bordered matrices; however, they all admit their approach was designed for a static matrix; after each modification, a specific preprocessing (sorting) step is required, which can take longer than the real computation. Because the web is highly dynamic, almost 40% of all links change in less than one week [6], disregarding this preparation step would veil the real overall processing time. Steady reorganization of coordinates in a huge link matrix simply imposes an unjustified management overhead.

## 2.2    Web Graph Representation

Computing the PageRank vector for a large web graph using a materialized in-memory matrix $A$ is definitely not feasible. A common solution is to store the links in a format like "Destination Page ID, Out-degree, Source Page IDs..." (which resembles $L$). Because pages only link to a few others (the link matrix is sparse), this results in much lower memory requirements of the link structure, in the magnitude of $\mid L \mid \cdot \overline{n}^{-1} \cdot c$ bytes ($\overline{n}$ = average outdegree; $c = const.$)

Of course, compression techniques [15] or intelligent approaches to disk-based "swapping" [9, 5, 18] can improve the space requirements even further (e.g. by relying on a particular data order, or on the presence of caches). But with the permanent growth of the web, even such techniques will soon hit memory limits of a single computer, or unacceptably slow down the computation process. See [18] for a thorough discussion of these optimizations.

In this paper, we thus propose a new strategy for keeping the web graph and rank information completely in RAM of several networked machines, based on the separation between global (host) and local information about each page.

## 2.3    Other Parallel PageRank Algorithms

Existing approaches to PageRank parallelization can be divided into two classes: Exact Computations and Approximations.

**Parallel Computations.** In this scenario, the web graph is initially partitioned into blocks: grouped randomly [21], lexicographically sorted by page [17, 22, 26] or balanced according to the number of links [8].

Then, standard iterative methods such as Jacobi (Equation 1) or Krylov subspace [8] are performed over these pieces in parallel. The partitions periodically must exchange information: Depending on the strategy this can expose suboptimal convergence speed because of the Jacobi method and result in heavy inter-partition I/O (e.g., in [17], computing the rank for a page $t$ requires access to all associated source page ranks $r(s)$ across all partitions).

**PageRank Approximations.** The main idea behind these approaches is that it might be sufficient to get a rank vector which is comparable, but not equal to PageRank. Instead of ranking pages, higher-level formations are used, such as the inter-connection/linkage between hosts, domains, server network addresses or directories, which is orders of magnitudes faster. The inner structure of these formations (at page level) can then be computed in an independently parallel manner ("off-line"), as in BlockRank [10], SiteRank [25], the U-Model [4], ServerRank [24] or HostRank/DirRank [7].

We will try to take the best out of both approaches: the exactness of a straight PageRank computation but the speed of an approximation, without any centralized re-ranking.

# 3  The Two-Dimensional Web

## 3.1  Host-Based Link Locality

Bharat et al. [2] have shown that there are two different types of web links dominating the web structure, "intra-site" links and "inter-site" ones. A "site" can be a domain (.yahoo.com), a host (geocities.yahoo.com) or a directory on a web server (http://www.geocities.com/someuser/). In general, we can define a site as an interlinked collection of pages identified by a common name (domain, host, directory etc.), and under the control of the same authority (an authority may of course own several sites).

Due to web sites' hypertext-navigable nature, it is supposable that a site contains more internal than external links. In fact, about 93.6% of all non-dangling links are intra-host and 95.2% intra-domain [10]. This assumed block structure has been visualized by Kamvar et al. [10] using dotplots of small parts (domain-level) of the "LargeWeb" graph's link matrix [23]. In these plots, the point $(i, j)$ is black, if there is a link from page $p_i$ to $p_j$, clear otherwise.

We performed such a plot under the same setting, but on whole-graph scale. The outcome is interesting: a clear top-level-domain (TLD) dominant structure (see Figure 1a). For example, the .com TLD represents almost 40% of the complete structure and has high connectivity with .net and .org, whereas the .jp domain shows almost no interlinkage with other TLDs. However, if we only inspect the .com domain (see Figure 1b, the dotplot depicts a diagonally dominant structure. The diagonal represents links from target pages near by the source page (which are *inter-host* pages). Both results are primarily caused by the lexicographical order of URLs (with hostnames reversed, e.g. http://com.yahoo.www/index.html).

But is this costly *sorting* over all URLs necessary at all? To further analyze the impact of hostname-induced link locality, we redraw the LargeWeb dotplot in a *normalized* (histographical) fashion, where a dot's greyscale value depicts the cumulative percentage of links in a specific raster cell. In addition, we do not sort the pages lexicographically, but only group them per host and permute all hosts randomly to avoid any lexicographical or crawl-order-dependent

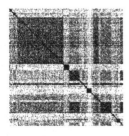 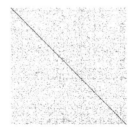

(a) LargeWeb, sorted    (b) .com subgraph of (a)    (c) LargeWeb, normalized

**Fig. 1.** Linkage dotplots

relationship between them. The clear diagonal dominance now also becomes visible on whole-graph scale (Figure 1c).

## 3.2 From Numbers to Tuples

It should be obvious that the web was already designed to be two-dimensional: Hostnames are "namespaces" aimed to disambiguate different local contexts (i.e., paths like "/dir/index.html"). Previous approaches to web graph partitioning always resulted in having *one* unique ID associated to each page, eventually sorted lexicographically [10, 17, 22] or in crawling order to exploit specific graph properties [18].

Such a single page ID provides a very compact representation of the web graph, which can be visualized in a matrix dotplot as shown above. But it also requires continuous reorganization (sorting) for newly added or removed pages in the course of incremental crawling. Otherwise, a mixture of hosts along the URL IDs would render a host no longer characterizable by a closed interval of IDs, thereby losing the advantage of link locality. One may introduce gaps in the numbering to reduce the sorting costs, but still, all subsequent pages will have to be renumbered once the gap is filled. In a distributed scenario, this can cause extensive network I/O by repeatedly moving pages from one partition to another.

We therefore propose a different page identification scheme, based on the affiliation of each page to a specific host and independently of pages from other hosts. More specifically, we propose using a *tuple* consisting of two independent, positive integers, a HostID (only dependent on the URL's hostname) and a LocalID (only identifying the remaining local components – path and query string). The addition of new local pages to a specific host, as well as of new hosts, is very easy, since renumbering is no longer necessary.

As an implementation-specific note, we expect that for current web graphs, it is sufficient to store the tuples as two `uint32` four-byte integers. We then can address a maximum of 4.29 billion hosts and a maximum of 4.29 billion pages per host in 8 bytes. For small hosts, we could even reduce the local part to 16 bit, thereby further cutting down memory footprint.

# 4    Partitioned PageRank

We will now consider the impact of such a partitioning scheme on the PageRank algorithm. We will first present an analysis that unifies two of the most common algorithms for solving linear systems, Gauß-Seidel and Jacobi. Then, we will apply this analysis to propose an improved parallel PageRank algorithm, and finally we will discuss several optimization issues.

## 4.1    Unifying Jacobi and Gauss-Seidel

It has been observed that the Gauß-Seidel iteration method compared to the Jacobi method can speed-up PageRank convergence by a factor of 2, as it uses scores of the current iteration as soon as they become available [1]:

$$\forall(s,t) \in L: \quad r^{(i)}(t) = (1-\alpha)\,\tau(t) \,+\, \alpha \left( \sum_{s<t} \frac{r^{(i)}(s)}{|L(s)|} + \sum_{s>t} \frac{r^{(i-1)}(s)}{|L(s)|} \right) \qquad (3)$$

As opposed to the Jacobi iteration, the Gauß-Seidel variant requires iterating over the links $(s,t) \in L$ in a strictly ascending order. At first glance, this seems to be a major drawback when we want to apply it to a distributed, partitioned web graph. To clarify the impact of the restriction of link order, we derive a common base algorithm for both, Jacobi (equation 1) and Gauß-Seidel (equation 3) algorithms: We define an intermediate ranking vector $r^{(i-1,i)}$ that combines the vectors of the previous and the current iteration, depending on the state of a ranked page $p$ in the set of available pages $P$ ($P = P' \cup P''$; $\nexists\, p : p \in P' \wedge p \in P''$; $P'$ contains all pages which have already been ranked for iteration $i$; $P''$ contains all other pages, whose score has not been touched since iteration $i-1$):

$$r^{(i-1,i)}(p) := \begin{cases} r^{(i)}(p) & \text{if } p \in P' \\ r^{(i-1)}(p) & \text{if } p \in P'' \end{cases}; \; r^{(i)}(t) = (1-\alpha)\,\tau(t) + \alpha \sum_{(s,t)\in L} \frac{r^{(i-1,i)}(s)}{|L(s)|} \quad (4)$$

Under this setting, for the Gauß-Seidel method, $P' = \{\, p \mid p < k \,\}$ and $P'' = \{\, p \mid p \geq k \,\}$, with $k \in \{1, 2, ..., |P|\}$, whereas for the Jacobi method, we have $P' = \emptyset$ and $P'' = P$. Both iteration methods, Jacobi and Gauß-Seidel, can then be simplified to this joint formula:

$$r^{(\star)}(t) = (1-\alpha)\,\tau(t) + \alpha \sum_{(s,t)\in L} \frac{r^{(\star)}(s)}{|L(s)|}, \text{ with } r^{(\star)}(t) = r^{(i-1,i)}(t) \qquad (5)$$

From Equation 4, we know that before each iteration $i$, $\vec{r}^{(\star)} = \vec{r}^{(i-1)}$ and after the iteration $\vec{r}^{(\star)} = \vec{r}^{(i)}$. The state of $\vec{r}^{(\star)}$ during the iteration then only depends on the order of links $(s,t) \in L$ (the way how $P'$ and $P''$ are determined). This iteration method has worst-case convergence properties of Jacobi and best-case of Gauß-Seidel, depending on the order of elements, random order vs. strictly ascending order, while always providing the same per-iteration running time as the Jacobi iteration.

We further generalize the impact of the rules for $P'$ and $P''$: We argue that if only a small fraction $F$ of all links concerned ($|F| \ll |L|$) is not in strictly ascending order, the overall convergence speed still remains in the magnitude of standard Gauß-Seidel. In our case, in order to be able to parallelize the Gauß-Seidel algorithm, we will assign inter-host/inter-partition links (about 6%) to this small fraction.

### 4.2   Reformulating PageRank

For such an optimization, let us reformulate our above mentioned unified PageRank equation using our new two-dimensional page numbering scheme. Thus, page variables "$p$" will be replaced by page tuples $\mathsf{p} = (p_x, p_y)$, with $p_x$ representing the page's HostID, $host(\mathsf{p})$, and $p_y$ its LocalID, $local(\mathsf{p})$. To account for the separation of inter- and intra-host links, the formula now reads as follows:

$$r^{(*)}(t) = (1 - \alpha)\,\tau(t)\; + \alpha\; \left( v_I^{(*)}(t) + v_E^{(*)}(t) \right)$$

$$v_I^{(*)}(t) = \sum_{(s,t) \in L} \frac{r^{(*)}(s)}{|L(s)|} \quad \forall\; host(s) = host(t) \tag{6}$$

$$v_E^{(*)}(t) = \sum_{(s,t) \in L} \frac{r^{(*)}(s)}{|L(s)|} \quad \forall\; host(s) \neq host(t)$$

Since $v_I^{(*)}(t)$ solely requires access to *local* (intra-host) rank portions, it can efficiently be computed from scores stored in RAM. The local problem of ranking intra-host pages is solvable via a fast, non-parallel Gauß-Seidel iteration process. There is no need for intra-host vote parallelization – instead, we parallelize on the host-level, thus necessitating only inter-host communication, which is limited to the exchange of external votes.

Our approach produces the same ranks as the original PageRank, while being more scalable than the other parallel PageRank algorithms. This is mainly due to the parallelization of the Gauß-Seidel algorithm, in which we take advantage of web's host-oriented block structure.

### 4.3   Reaching Optimal Performance

**Communication Cost Optimization.** While votes between hosts of the same partition (server) can easily be conveyed in RAM, votes across hosts of different partitions require network communication. The gross total for exchanging external votes over the network must not be underestimated. With the LargeWeb graph setup, almost 33 million are exchanged between partitions. For bigger web graphs, this could rise up to a few billion and can easily lead to network congestion if too much information is transmitted per vote.

As opposed to other approaches, where a vote consisted of target page ID (sometimes along with source page ID) and score, we simply reduce this to transmitting a single value per page (the score), because the link *structure* does not change during the iteration cycle. More generally, the link structure of all the pages that exchange votes between two partitions pages only needs to be determined whenever the graph changes (in the case of incremental web crawling) and then to be sent to the specific target partition. Moreover, the source page does not need to be specified in order to compute the PageRank score, but only the target page ID (see Equation 6). Additionally, by grouping the list of target pages by host, we need to transmit each target host ID only once.

Most notably, each partition has to transmit only one single value per target page, not per link to that page, since all votes from local pages that link to a specific page can be aggregated to a single value (surprisingly, this simple but very effective approach did not appear in any previous work):

$$v_E^{(*)}(t) = \sum_{\beta \in \Pi} \sum_{(s,t) \in L_\beta} \frac{r^{(*)}(s)}{|L|} = \sum_{\beta \in \Pi} v_\beta^{(*)}(t) \quad \forall\; host(s) \neq host(t) \tag{7}$$

**Table 1.** LargeWeb Inter-Partition links and votes

| Type | Amount | Percent |
|------|-------|---------|
| Total Links | 601,183,777 | 100% |
| Inter-Partition Links | 32,716,628 | 5.44% |
| Inter-Partition Votes | 3,618,335 | 0.6% |

with $\Pi$ being the set of partitions containing links towards $t$, and $\beta$ each one of these partitions.

Transferring $v_\beta(t)$ (the sum of votes from partition $L_\beta$ to $t$) as a single value reduces the network load dramatically. Using this optimization, we can show a reduction of vote exchanges by 89% with the DNR-LargeWeb graph. Table 1 depicts the difference between inter-partition links and votes and their quota of all links.

**Computational Load Balancing.** In order to keep the convergence behavior of the centralized PageRank in our parallel scenario, inter-partition votes must be exchanged after every iteration (see [17] for a discussion of consequences of not doing so). To keep the overall computation time still low, all intra-partition computations and after that all network communication should terminate isochronously (at the same time). Because intra-partition computation is directly proportional to the number of pages per partition (see Equation 6), this either means that all available servers must be equally fast, or the graph has to be at least partitioned adequately to the performance of the servers. Moreover, other slow-down factors could also influence the running time, such as different network throughput rates of cheap NICs and system boards (even with the same nominal speed).

A good strategy to load-balancing Parallel PageRank in a heterogeneous environment could be running a small test graph on all new servers, measure computation speeds, and balance the real graph accordingly. In any case, memory overflows due to bad balancing parameters like in [8] are avoided, and no manual interaction to find these parameters is necessary.

## 5   Experiments

We first converted the Stanford DNR-LargeWeb graph [23] into the new tuple representation, resulting in 62.8M pages and 601M links distributed over 470,000 hosts with averaged 137.5 pages each (maximum was 5084 pages per host); the inter-host link percentage[1] is 6.19% (see Table 2).

For our PageRank experiments, we sorted the available hosts by their page count in descending order and distributed the pages host-wise in a round-robin manner over 8 partitions of equal size ($\frac{1}{8}$ of the graph just fitted into our smallest server's RAM).

---

[1] Unfortunately, the last 8 million pages of DNR-LargeWeb could not be converted, since there was no URL associated with them – thus, our numbers slightly differ from the ones in [10].

**Table 2.** LargeWeb link distribution

| Type | Amount | Percent |
|---|---|---|
| Total | 601,183,777 | 100% |
| Intra-Host | 563,992,416 | 93.81% |
| Inter-Host | 37,191,361 | 6.19% |
| Inter-Partition | 32,716,628 | 5.44% |
| Intra-Partition | 4,474,733 | 0.74% |

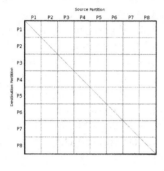

**Fig. 2.** Partitioned LargeWeb-Dotplot

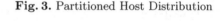

**Fig. 3.** Partitioned Host Distribution

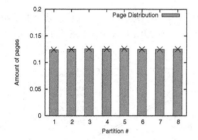

**Fig. 4.** Pages per Partition

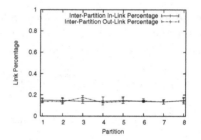

**Fig. 5.** Inter-partition link distribution

Although the pages-per-host distribution was not strictly exponential, it resulted in an equal page and link distribution (see Figures 2, 3, 4, 5). Remarkably, the intra-partition ratio (inter-host links inside the same partition) is negligible, as the inter-partition link rate nearly equals to the inter-host ratio. This means that hosts can arbitrarily be shifted from one partition to another one (which is necessary for fast re-balancing with incremental web crawling).

### 5.1 Implementation

We have implemented Partitioned Parallel PageRank in Java using a P2P-like network with a central coordinator instance. This coordinator is only responsible for arranging the iteration process at partition-level and does not know anything about the rank scores or the link structure (it is much simpler than the coordinator in [26]). Before the computation, all nodes announce themselves to the coordinator, communicating the hosts they cover. The iteration process is started as soon as all nodes are ready. The coordinator then broadcasts the global host structure to all known nodes and instructs them to iterate. Whenever a node's subgraph changes, it sends lists of external outgoing link targets to the corresponding nodes.

For every iteration step, a node will compute its votes using our reformulated PageRank (Equation 6); the partition itself is again divided into subpartitions processed in parallel. The nodes then aggregate all outgoing inter-partition votes by target page and send them directly to the other nodes responsible for these target pages, in the order specified beforehand. Finally, each node reports its local rank status (using the sum and number of its PageRank scores) to the coordinator, in order to compute the global residual $\delta$. As soon as all nodes have succeeded, the coordinator decides whether to continue iterating, by broadcasting another "iterate" command unless the residual reached the threshold $\varepsilon$.

The addition of new pages during incremental crawling may happen at any time. If the addition covers new hosts, the coordinator selects a node according to the current balancing. From then on, this node is responsible for all pages of that host. The assignment is broadcasted to all nodes in case that there were dangling links to that (previously uncovered) host.

## 5.2   Results

We conducted most of the experiments on four Linux machines, an AMD Dual Opteron 850 2.4 GHz, 10GB RAM ("A"), an Intel Dual Xeon 2.8 GHz, 6GB

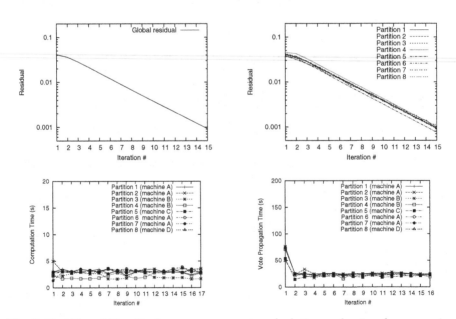

**Fig. 6.** Partitioned PageRank convergence, vote calculation and network communication times using 8 partitions on 4 machines; $\varepsilon = 0.001$

RAM ("B") and two Intel Xeon 3.0 GHz, 1.5GB RAM ("C" and "D"). They were connected via 100MBit Ethernet LAN and not under load before our experiments. We divided the LargeWeb graph into eight partitions and distributed them among the four servers according to available memory (Machine A holds four partitions, B two, C and D one) and performed unbiased PageRank computations.

We examined the convergence behavior, rank distribution and elapsed time both globally and per-partition. All per-partition results matched almost perfectly with the global counterpart and therefore confirmed our assumptions (see Figure 6). The PageRank computation converged below $\varepsilon = 10^{-3}$ after 17 iterations, and the entire computation took less than 9 minutes, with only 66 seconds accounted for rank computation, the rest being network I/O. With a Gigabit-Ethernet connection, network communication costs would probably go down to the same magnitude as computation costs.

Compared to the running times of a centralized PageRank computation with disk I/O, using our networked servers, Parallel PageRank is about 10 times faster per iteration. The recomputation itself (ignoring network transmission) was about 75 times faster. Thus, for further experiments, it might be interesting how our algorithm performs on a massive parallel machine.

## 6    Conclusions and Further Work

In this paper, we have presented an efficient method to perform the PageRank calculation in parallel over arbitrary large web graphs. We accomplished this by introducing a novel two-dimensional view of the web, having the host ID as the only discriminator, as well as by adapting the Gauß-Seidel method for solving linear systems in this scenario. Additionally, we have presented optimizations for the distributed computation, such as vote aggregation and utilizing the partitioning scheme for fast re-balancing in the course of incremental crawling.

Our next goal is to combine our approach with other PageRank specific enhancements that reduce convergence time, under extensive memory demanding scenarios.

## References

1. Arvind Arasu, Jasmine Novak, Andrew Tomkins, and John Tomlin. PageRank computation and the structure of the web: Experiments and algorithms, 2001.
2. Krishna Bharat, Bay-Wei Chang, Monika Rauch Henzinger, and Matthias Ruhl. Who links to whom: Mining linkage between web sites. In *Proc. of the IEEE Intl. Conf. on Data Mining*, pages 51–58, 2001.
3. Sergey Brin, Rajeev Motwani, Lawrence Page, and Terry Winograd. What can you do with a web in your pocket? *Data Engineering Bulletin*, 21(2):37–47, 1998.
4. Andrei Z. Broder, Ronny Lempel, Farzin Maghoul, and Jan Pedersen. Efficient pagerank approximation via graph aggregation. In *Proc. of the 13th International World Wide Web Conference*, pages 484–485, 2004.

5. Yen-Yu Chen, Qingqing Gan, and Torsten Suel. I/o-efficient techniques for computing pagerank, 2002.
6. Junghoo Cho and Hector Garcia-Molina. The evolution of the web and implications for an incremental crawler. In *Proceedings of the 26th International Conference on Very Large Databases*, 2000.
7. Nadav Eiron, Kevin S. McCurley, and John A. Tomlin. Ranking the web frontier. In *Proc. of the 13th Intl. Conf. on the World Wide Web*, pages 309–318, 2004.
8. David Gleich, Leonid Zhukov, and Pavel Berkhin. Fast parallel PageRank: A linear system approach. Technical report, Yahoo! Research Labs, 2004.
9. Taher H. Haveliwala. Efficient computation of PageRank. Technical Report 1999-31, Stanford Library Technologies Project, 1999.
10. Sepandar Kamvar, Taher Haveliwala, Christopher Manning, and Gene Golub. Exploiting the block structure of the web for computing PageRank. Technical report, Stanford University, 2003.
11. Sepandar D. Kamvar, Taher H. Haveliwala, and Gene H. Golub. Adaptive methods for the computation of PageRank. Technical report, Stanford University, 2003.
12. Sepandar D. Kamvar, Taher H. Haveliwala, Christopher D. Manning, and Gene H. Golub. Extrapolation methods for accelerating PageRank computations. In *Proc. of the 12th Intl. Conf. on the World Wide Web*, pages 261–270, 2003.
13. Sung Jin Kim and Sang Ho Lee. An improved computation of the PageRank algorithm. In *Proc. of the European Conference on Information Retrieval (ECIR)*, pages 73–85, 2002.
14. D. P. Koester, S. Ranka, and G. C. Fox. A parallel gauss-seidel algorithm for sparse power system matrices. In *Proc. of the ACM/IEEE Conf. on Supercomputing*, pages 184–193, 1994.
15. Amy N. Langville and Carl D. Meyer. Deeper inside PageRank, 2004.
16. Chris P. Lee, Gene H. Golub, and Stefanos A. Zenios. A fast two-stage algorithm for computing PageRank. Technical report, Stanford University, 2003.
17. Bundit Manaskasemsak and Arnon Rungsawang. Parallel PageRank computation on a gigabit pc cluster. In *Proc. of the 18th International Conference on Advanced Information Networking and Application (AINA'04)*, 2004.
18. Frank McSherry. A uniform approach to accelerated pagerank computation. In *Proc. of the 14th international conference on World Wide Web*, pages 575–582, New York, NY, USA, 2005. ACM Press.
19. Netcraft. Web server survey, 2005.
20. Lawrence Page, Sergey Brin, Rajeev Motwani, and Terry Winograd. The PageRank citation ranking: Bringing order to the web. Technical report, Stanford Digital Library Technologies Project, 1998.
21. Karthikeyan Sankaralingam, Simha Sethumadhavan, and James C. Browne. Distributed pagerank for p2p systems. In *Proc. of the 12th IEEE Intl. Symp. on High Performance Distributed Computing (HPDC)*, page 58, 2003.
22. Shu-Ming Shi, Jin Yu, Guang-Wen Yang, and Ding-Xing Wang. Distributed page ranking in structured p2p networks. In *Proc. of the 2003 International Conference on Parallel Processing (ICPP'03)*, pages 179–186, 2003.
23. Taher H. Haveliwala et al. 2001 Crawl of the WebBase project, 2001.
24. Yuan Wang and David J. DeWitt. Computing PageRank in a distributed internet search system. In *Proceedings of the 30th VLDB Conference*, 2004.
25. Jie Wu and Karl Aberer. Using SiteRank for P2P Web Retrieval, March 2004.
26. Yangbo Zhu, Shaozhi Ye, and Xing Li. Distributed pagerank computation based on iterative aggregation-disaggregation methods. In *Proc. of the 14th ACM international conference on Information and knowledge management*, 2005.

# Comparing Different Architectures for Query Routing in Peer-to-Peer Networks

Henrik Nottelmann and Norbert Fuhr

Department of Informatics, University of Duisburg-Essen, 47048 Duisburg, Germany
{nottelmann, fuhr}@uni-duisburg.de

**Abstract.** Efficient and effective routing of content-based queries is an emerging problem in peer-to-peer networks, and can be seen as an extension of the traditional "resource selection" problem. Although some approaches have been proposed, finding the best architecture (defined by the network topology, the underlying selection method, and its integration into peer-to-peer networks) is still an open problem. This paper investigates different building blocks of such architectures, among them the decision-theoretic framework, CORI, hierarchical networks, distributed hash tables and HyperCubes. The evaluation on a large testbed shows that the decision-theoretic framework can be applied effectively and cost-efficiently onto peer-to-peer networks.

## 1 Introduction

Peer-to-peer (P2P) networks have emerged recently as an alternative to centralised architectures. The major problem in such networks is query routing, i.e. deciding to which other peers the query has to be sent for high efficiency and effectiveness. In contrast to the traditional resource selection problem, this process is inherently decentralised in peer-to-peer networks and based on local knowledge.

The decision-theoretic framework (DTF) [10, 6] computes an optimum selection based on cost estimations (including retrieval quality, time or money). Most other (centralised) resource selection methods follow a heuristic approach and compute a ranking of the digital libraries (DLs), e.g. CORI [4] or the language modelling approach [15]. The latter has been extended towards hierarchical peer-to-peer networks [8, 9], where a hub also stores language models ("hub descriptions") of the hubs directly connected to it. A fixed number of hubs is selected, while unsupervised learning is employed for learning a threshold for the number of selected DL peers. A modified version of the semi-supervised learning algorithm [14] is used for result merging.

This paper presents an extensive discussion of resource selection architectures for peer-to-peer networks. The architectures are classified based on the underlying resource selection approach (in our case, DTF and CORI as a baseline), design choices like the locality of knowledge (e.g. IDF values) and selections (centralised vs. decentralised), as well as the network topology (hierarchical networks with DLs and hubs, distributed hash tables and HyperCubes).

This paper is structured as follows: Section 2 briefly describes DTF and CORI. Then, different topologies are introduced, and the resource selection frameworks are extended towards P2P networks in section 4. The proposed approaches for resource selection in P2P networks have been evaluated in section 5.

M. Lalmas et al. (Eds.): ECIR 2006, LNCS 3936, pp. 253–264, 2006.
© Springer-Verlag Berlin Heidelberg 2006

## 2    Resource Selection Approaches

This section only sketches the decision-theoretic framework (DTF) and CORI.

### 2.1    The Decision-Theoretic Framework (DTF)

In contrast to other resource selection approaches (e.g. CORI, see section 2.2) which only consider the similarity of the DL to a query, the decision-theoretic framework (DTF) [10, 6] estimates retrieval "costs" from different sources (e.g. monetary costs, computation and communication time, retrieval quality). As the actual costs are unknown in advance, expected costs (for digital library $DL_i$ when $s_i$ documents are retrieved for query $q$) are regarded instead:

$$EC_i(s_i,q) := E[r_i(s_i,q)] \cdot C^+ + [s_i - E[r_i(s_i,q)]] \cdot C^- + C^t \cdot EC^t(s_i) + C^m \cdot EC^m(s_i) , \quad (1)$$

where $E[r_i(s_i,q)]$ is the expected number of relevant documents among the $s_i$ top-ranked documents and $s_i - E[r_i(s_i,q)]$ is the expected number of non-relevant documents, $EC^t(s_i)$ denotes the expected "time" costs, and $EC^m(s_i)$ the expected monetary costs. In addition, $C^+$, $C^-$, $C^t$ and $C^m$ are user-specific parameters which allow a user to specify her own selection policy, e.g. cheap and fast results. Non-relevant documents have higher costs (wasted time) than relevant ones, thus $C^+ < C^-$.

A user also specifies the total number $n$ of documents to be retrieved out of $m$ libraries, and the task is to compute an optimum solution (employing the algorithm presented in [6]):

$$s := \operatorname*{argmin}_{\sum_{i=1}^m s_i = n} \sum_{i=1}^m EC_i(s_i,q). \quad (2)$$

Relevance costs are computed in two steps:

1. First, the expected number $E(\mathrm{rel}|q,DL)$ of relevant documents in $DL$ is computed based on statistical aggregations (called "resource description") of the DL.
2. Then, a linearly decreasing approximation of the recall-precision function is used for computing the expected number $E[r_i(s_i,q)]$ of relevant retrieved documents.

For the first step, the resource descriptions store the DL size $|DL|$ and the average (expectation) $\mu_t = E[w(d,t)|d \in DL]$ of the indexing weights $w(d,t)$ (for document $d$ and term $t$). For a query with term weights $a(q,t)$ (summing up to one) and a linear retrieval model, the expected number $E(\mathrm{rel}|q,DL)$ of relevant documents in $DL$ w.r.t. query $q$ can be estimated as:

$$E(\mathrm{rel}|q,DL) = \sum_{d \in DL} Pr(\mathrm{rel}|q,d) \approx \sum_{d \in DL} \sum_{t \in q} a(q,t) \cdot w(d,t) = |DL| \cdot \sum_{t \in q} a(q,t) \cdot \mu_t , \quad (3)$$

where $Pr(\mathrm{rel}|q,d)$ denotes the probability that document $d$ is relevant.

In a second step, $E(\mathrm{rel}|q,DL)$ is mapped onto the expected number $E[r_i(s_i,q)]$ of relevant retrieved documents employing a linearly decreasing recall-precision function:

$$\frac{E[r_i(s_i,q)]}{s} = precision(recall) := 1 - recall = 1 - \frac{E[r_i(s_i,q)]}{E(\mathrm{rel}|q,DL)} . \quad (4)$$

For DTF, the libraries have to return the probabilities of relevance of the result documents, thus no further normalisation step is required.

## 2.2   CORI

CORI [4, 5] only considers retrieval quality, by ranking the DLs w. r. t. their similarity to the query. This scheme can efficiently be implemented using a traditional IR system, where documents are replaced by "meta-documents" which are created by concatenating all documents in the DL.

CORI uses a $df \cdot icf$ weighting scheme instead of $tf \cdot idf$, based on the number $m$ of involved libraries, the document frequency $df$, the collection frequency $cf$ (the number of libraries containing the term) and the collection length $cl$ (the number of terms in the DL). Thus, the belief in a DL due to observing query term $t$ (the "indexing weight" of term $t$ in the "meta-document" DL) is determined by:

$$w(DL,t) := 0.4 + 0.6 \cdot \frac{df}{df + 50 + 150 \cdot \frac{cl}{avgcl}} \cdot \frac{\log(\frac{m+0.5}{cf})}{\log(m+1)} . \tag{5}$$

Similar to DTF, a linear retrieval function is used based on $w(DL,t)$. CORI then selects a fixed number of top-ranked libraries, and retrieves an equal number of documents from each selected DL.

CORI also covers the data fusion problem. The library scores $C$ and the document scores $D := Pr(q|d)$ are normalised to $[0,1]$, and then combined for computing the final normalised document score $D''$:

$$C' := \frac{C - C_{min}}{C_{max} - C_{min}}, \quad D' := \frac{D - D_{min}}{D_{max} - D_{min}}, \quad D'' := \frac{1.0 \cdot D' + 0.4 \cdot C' \cdot D'}{1.4} , \tag{6}$$

where $C_{min}$ and $C_{max}$ are the minimum and maximum DL scores for that query, and $D_{min}$ and $D_{max}$ the minimum and maximum document score in the DL.

## 3   Network Topologies

This section introduces different topologies of the peer-to-peer network, which will be evaluated in section 5. In any topology, a direct neighbour of a peer is another peer if and only if there is a (direct) connection link. All other peers are called remote peers. The distance between two peers is the minimum number of hops (i.e., messages) required to go from one peer to the other.

### 3.1   Hierarchical Networks

Most of the work reported in this paper—including the two other topologies—is based on a partition of peers into DL peers (sometimes also called "leaves") and hubs. DLs are typically end-user machines which answer but do not forward queries, while hubs are responsible for routing and, thus, high-end computers with high bandwidth which are nearly permanently online. Each DL peer is connected to at least one hub but not to other DL peers, which reduces the number of messages during query routing (i.e., resource selection). This results in a simple yet reasonable and efficient topology, called hierarchical peer-to-peer networks (see figure 1(a)).

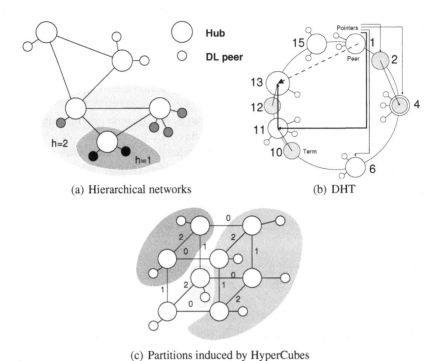

(a) Hierarchical networks                    (b) DHT

(c) Partitions induced by HyperCubes

**Fig. 1.** Different peer-to-peer network topologies

## 3.2  Distributed Hash Tables

Distributed hash tables (DHTs) are similar to traditional hash tables, which provide fast insert and lookup functionality for keys based on hash functions. The DHT system Chord [16] (see figure 1(b)) maps peers and keys onto numbers using the same hash function. Peers are ordered in a ring according to the hash values, and each peer is responsible for storing the values for all keys mapped onto its hash value (and all values lower than the following peer). Each peer maintains a list of peers in exponentially increasing distance, which allows for efficient routing in $O(\log m)$ hops for $m$ peers.

DHT have already been used for storing the complete index (of all documents) [7]. Here, the keys are terms, and the values are inverted lists (pairs comprised of document identifiers and the indexing weight). Thus, all documents form a single (but distributed) collection.

Similarly, DHTs can be employed for storing resource descriptions, Keys are terms, and the values are inverted lists (pairs of DL identifiers and e.g. average indexing weights). Once the inverted lists are fetched, a centralised selection can take place (see section 4.1). This contrasts other DHT approaches, where either the whole document index is kept in the DHT [7], or DHTs are used for resource selection in unstructured networks (Minerva [1]).

### 3.3   HyperCubes

Hierarchical networks can contain cycles, which decrease efficiency as peers are contacted multiple times. In addition, estimating the quality of a hub connection is more difficult. HyperCube graphs (HyperCubes for short) [13] can be used to overcome this problem. A (binary) HyperCube is a regular $d$-dimensional structure, where each peer is connected to exactly $d$ other peers (one per dimension, see figure 1(c)). Messages arriving via a connection on dimension $l \in \{0, 1, \ldots, d - 1\}$ can only be forwarded to peers on strictly higher dimensions $l' > l$. A consequence is that the dimensions define (starting from an arbitrary peer) a spanning tree on the network, which ensures that there is exactly one path from one peer to another peer. It also corresponds to a clearly defined partition of the whole network. Positions of missing peers are filled with "virtual peers" (see [13] for details), which are then replaced by "shortcuts" to all original peers which can be contacted through virtual peers only. As a consequence, peers can be connected to more or less than $d$ neighbours.

## 4   Query Routing in Peer-to-Peer Networks

Query routing (i.e., resource selection) is a crucial task in peer-to-peer networks, as contacting all connected peers does not scale [11]. This section introduces several competing approaches for resource selection in peer-to-peer networks, which all can be used with DTF or CORI.

### 4.1   Centralised Selection

A simple selection strategy is to use the P2P network for a "cost estimation collection phase", where the query is flooded in a Gnutella-like way through the hub network. Each hub computes cost estimations of its neighbour DLs, and sends them to the hub starting the routing process. Then, DTF or CORI are employed for a single central selection, and the selected DL peers are notified directly. As the hub starting the routing process can only compute a selection when all cost estimations have arrived, synchronous messages are employed. This centralised selection strategy yields a global optimum, but is rather inefficient (see [11] for Gnutella, and section 5.2 for hierarchical networks).

DHTs can significantly reduce the cost estimation collection phase in centralised selection. Instead of flooding the hub network, the resource descriptions of all DLs are extracted from the DHT with one lookup for each query term. In contrast to earlier approaches, we combine DHTs with hierarchical networks, thus the DHT ring is formed by the (fast and high-bandwidth) hubs only. The DHT contains resource descriptions in the form of inverted lists (DL identifiers plus average indexing weight), either for DLs (like in Minerva [1]) or for hubs. In the latter case, the inverted lists are much shorter; however, the quality of hub descriptions is lower than for DL descriptions, and a second selection step would be required for selecting DLs without the DHT. Costs are estimated based on the returned inverted lists. Centralised selection in hierarchical networks involves each hub. In contrast, $O(l \cdot \log m)$ hops for $l$ terms and $m$ peers are required for the DHT, which is in most cases much more efficient. Effectiveness is not affected, as the same cost estimations are computed in both strategies.

An alternative solution is to leverage the hierarchical network topology in a two-step selection algorithm, where the DHT stores only descriptions of all hubs, and DLs are still connected to hubs (topology "dht-hubs"). A queried peer first computes a selection of hubs, and then calls the selected hubs which themselves compute a local selection, considering only the directly connected DL peers. The advantage is that the inverted lists are much smaller now and consume less bandwidth (remember that the full inverted lists have to be transferred to the queried hub).

A last approach is to exploit the spanning tree property of HyperCubes: As no cycles exist, each hub is contacted exactly once (not multiple times as for "cmu"), thus centralised selection with a HyperCube is more efficient (24 hops vs. 72 hops for the cost estimation collection phase in our case).

## 4.2 Decentralised Selection

In contrast to the approaches mentioned in section 4.1, decentralised selection computes a local optimum selection on every hub receiving the query, by considering locally available descriptions of all DL and hubs in a predefined distance. Coordinating this decentralised routing approach is easier, as no responses have to be collected before a selection can be started; thus, asynchronous messages are sufficient. This decentralised selection method produces an overhead as a cost estimation and selection has to be performed on every hub. On the other hand, this method cuts down the number of hubs that are traversed, and thus saves time and bandwidth. Section 4.3 describes how hub descriptions can be obtained.

Decentralised selection also is the major application area for HyperCubes, as problems with cycles are avoided, in particular for "hc-1", where there is exactly one path from any hub to any DL. The selection should be improved by disjoint hub descriptions, where each DL is included in at most one hub description.

## 4.3 Computing Hub Descriptions

A hub description is a representative of the neighbourhood of a hub. Its statistical characteristics are defined by combining the resource descriptions of a set of DL peers.[1] Given the average term weights $\mu_{t,i}$ for each involved $DL_i$, the average term weights $\mu_{t,H}$ in the description of hub $H$ can efficiently be computed as:

$$\mu_{t,H} = \frac{1}{\sum_j |DL_j|} \cdot \sum_i \sum_{d \in DL_i} w(d,t) = \frac{1}{\sum_j |DL_j|} \cdot \sum_i |DL_i| \cdot \mu_{t,i}. \tag{7}$$

The horizon $h$ defines the maximum distance between the hub $H$ and the DLs to be considered for its hub description (see figure 1(a)). In the simplest case, only neighbour DLs are considered (horizon $h = 1$). With a horizon $h = 2$, also DLs directly connected to a neighbour hub of $H$ have to be considered, and so on.

---

[1] In peer-to-peer networks, co-operative peers can be assumed, so query-based sampling is not considered here; each DL returns its description upon request.

## 4.4   Locality of Knowledge

Often retrieval and resource selection methods rely on some "global" statistics, e.g. inverse document frequencies (IDF). Early experiments have shown that DL-local IDFs (i.e., each DL computes its own values) are not accurate enough. Two alternatives are investigated, system-wide and hub-global IDF values. System-wide DL values are derived by combining all documents in all DL peers, and thus yield accurate estimates. In a large peer-to-peer network, they are too expensive to acquire, and hub-global IDFs (computed by combining all documents from all peers in a hub's neighbourhood) can be used as an approximation. A similar scheme is applied to CORI with its collection frequencies (CF values).

# 5   Evaluation

The methods proposed in the previous sections have been evaluated on a large test-bed. This sections describes the setup of the experiments and results in terms of efficiency and effectiveness.

## 5.1   Experimental Setup

The WT10g collection is used as a basis for our experiments. The topology "cmu" (taken from [8]) employs a hierarchical P2P network, where the WT10g collection is divided into 11,485 collections according to the document URLs; 2,500 collections (containing in total 1,421,088 documents) were chosen randomly, each of them forming one DL peer. Hubs are formed by similarity of the DL peers, each hub is connected to 13-1,013 DLs (379.8 on average). Neighbour hubs are selected randomly so that each hub has 1-7 hub neighbours (3.8 on average). The "dht-dl" and "dht-hubs" topology organise the hubs as a DHT ring (dismissing the "cmu" hub subnetwork). All DLs are kept in the hash table in "dht-dl", while "dht-hubs" stores hub descriptions only (which requires an additional local DL selection step).

The constructed HyperCube topologies "hc" and "hc-1" comprise of 25 hubs as in "cmu" (with dimension $d = 5$); each hub is connected to 4-14 other hubs (5.8 on average). For "hc", DLs are connected to these 25 hubs as in "cmu". As an alternative, each DL is connected to exactly one hub, randomly chosen out of the "cmu" connections[2] in the "hc-1" topology, so that each hub is connected to 3-254 DLs (100 on average). Thus, "hc-1" completely avoids cycles and yields disjoint hub neighbourhoods, in contrast to "cmu" and "hc".

The WT10g collection only provides 100 topics with relevance judgements. For large P2P networks, more queries are required. Thus, we use 1,000 random queries (from the test set) generated from title fields of documents. Each query contains up to 6 terms, the average is 2.9 terms per query. Unless otherwise noted, $n = 50$ documents are requested. As these queries were created artificially, no relevance judgements are

---

[2] An alternative solution would be to choose the hub which is most similar to the DL, using a suitable similarity measure.

available. Pseudo-relevance judgements[3] were obtained by combining all 2,500 collections into one centralised collection (using system-wide IDF values), and marking the 50 top-ranked documents for each query as "relevant". Thus, the experiments measure how well distributed retrieval approximates the centralised collection. As the same linear retrieval function with the same indexing weights is used for the centralised collection, the DTF and the CORI experiments, these pseudo-relevance judgements form a fair baseline.

BM25[12] indexing weights are used for terms $t$ in documents $d$:

$$w(d,t) := \frac{tf(t,d)}{tf(t,d) + 0.5 + 1.5 \cdot \frac{dl(d)}{avgdl}} \cdot \frac{\log \frac{|DL|}{df(t)}}{\log |DL|}, \tag{8}$$

with term frequency $tf(t,d)$, document length $dl(d)$ and its average $avgdl$, the library size $|DL|$ and document frequency $df(t)$.

Peer-to-peer networks form graphs, thus it is possible for a query to arrive at the same peer multiple times for the topologies "cmu" (DLs and hubs) and "hc" (only DLs). When this happens to a hub, it can only select DL peers which have not been selected before. A DL has to return additional documents when it is contacted multiple times. In earlier experiments, this approach has proven to be superior to other approaches like ignoring queries which reach a node for the second time, or preventing infinite loops by disallowing selections of a single hub.

All CORI variants select 5 peers (DLs and/or hubs) in each selection step, and retrieve an equal amount of documents for each selected peer. As the CORI-inherent result merging (section 2.2) performs poorly, documents are re-ranked w.r.t. probabilities of relevance, estimated in the same way as for DTF.

Only relevancy costs are investigated, as a good model for measuring time in peer-to-peer networks is missing yet; we defer this to future work.

## 5.2  Results

Due to space restrictions, we only show tables for hub-global IDF/CF values which can efficiently be computed in peer-to-peer networks, and report results on system-wide values in the text where necessary.

First we set $h = 1$, and compare centralised with decentralised resource selection (Table 1). DTF-d, the decentralised DTF variant, has lower effectiveness than DTF-c, the centralised counterpart with its global knowledge (5-10% worse). Surprisingly, CORI-d performs slightly better than CORI-c. The drawback of the centralised selection is its inefficiency; DTF-d needs about 40% less hops[4], CORI-d 22% less hops compared to their centralised counterparts, mainly due to the cost estimation collection phase. Table 1 also shows that CORI is outperformed by DTF in both variants: Set-based precision is 30% (26%), MAP and recall are 40% (30%) lower for centralised (decentralised, respectively) selection. CORI-c is more efficient compared to DTF-c, while there is virtually no difference for decentralised DTF and CORI.

---

[3] Queries and pseudo-relevance judgements are available at http://www.is.informatik. uni-duisburg.de/projects/pepper/p2p-wt10g-testbed.zip.

[4] Hops are the only efficiency measure investigated in this work.

**Table 1.** Centralised vs. decentralised selection, DTF vs. CORI, topology "cmu", $h = 1$

|           | DTF, cent.    | DTF, decent.     | CORI, cent.      | CORI, decent.    |
|-----------|---------------|------------------|------------------|------------------|
| P@5       | 0.8032 / 0.0% | 0.7058 / -12.1%  | 0.6760 / -15.8%  | 0.6902 / -14.1%  |
| P@10      | 0.6630 / 0.0% | 0.5721 / -13.7%  | 0.6144 / -7.3%   | 0.5663 / -14.6%  |
| P@15      | 0.5562 / 0.0% | 0.4896 / -12.0%  | 0.4672 / -16.0%  | 0.4705 / -15.4%  |
| P@20      | 0.4793 / 0.0% | 0.4295 / -10.4%  | 0.3693 / -23.0%  | 0.3859 / -19.5%  |
| P@30      | 0.3792 / 0.0% | 0.3456 / -8.9%   | 0.2520 / -33.5%  | 0.2705 / -28.7%  |
| MAP       | 0.2586 / 0.0% | 0.2391 / -7.5%   | 0.1558 / -39.8%  | 0.1660 / -35.8%  |
| Precision | 0.2706 / 0.0% | 0.2515 / -7.1%   | 0.1839 / -32.0%  | 0.1859 / -31.3%  |
| Recall    | 0.2582 / 0.0% | 0.2417 / -6.4%   | 0.1562 / -39.5%  | 0.1665 / -35.5%  |
| #Hops     | 103.3 / 0.0%  | 59.9 / -42.0%    | 77.8 / -24.7%    | 60.2 / -41.7%    |

DTF is used in the remainder for resource selection on a hub.

Two different research questions for decentralised selection—the influence of different hub description horizons, and the effect of different topologies, namely "cmu", "hc" and "hc-1"—are covered by table 2. Effectiveness and efficiency dramatically decreases for "cmu" when the horizon $h$ increases. This counter-intuitive result is caused by the large hub neighbourhoods which contain half of the DLs in the network on average; thus it is more difficult to distinguish between good and bad hubs. For the two HyperCube topologies "hc" and "hc-1", however, effectiveness increases while efficiency decreases for larger hub horizons; as each hub (and for "hc-1", each DL) is contained in at most one neighbourhood, hubs can better identify good neighbours. The HyperCube topology "hc" outperforms "hc-1" for all investigated horizons, probably because the accuracy of the IDF values is higher (as more DLs are considered). For system-wide (high-accuracy) IDFs and $h = 3$, also smaller neighbourhoods are useful, thus results for "hc-1" are better than "hc". In addition, "hc" also performs better than "cmu" for $h \geq 2$; there is virtually no difference for $h = 1$.

Table 3 finally compares centralised resource selection in hierarchical networks ("cmu") and in distributed hash tables ("dht-dl" and "dht-hubs"). Effectiveness for "cmu" and "dht-dl" are the same, as the same DL descriptions and therefore the same cost estimations, are used. The different way of acquiring them in this "cost estimation collection" phase determines overall effectiveness: 72 hops are required for "cmu" (as each hub is reached multiple times due to cycles), compared with 6.7 hops (on average) for the DHT. When only hub descriptions are stored in the DHT (i.e., "dht-hubs") and 5 hubs/DLs are selected in each selection step, precision in the first 10 ranks decreases while set-based precision and recall as well as precision in lower ranks are improved. The drawback of this method, however, is the lower efficiency: The cost estimation collection phase requires the same number of hops as for "dtf-all", but about 15 hops to selected hubs have to be added, and the number of overall selected DLs is 25% higher. This result for "dtf-hubs" cannot be replicated for system-wide IDFs: Here, effectiveness is 10-13% worse w. r. t. all measures.

Indexing and retrieval for the 1,000 queries requires transmitting about 120 million inverted list entry hops [5] for "cmu", about 75 million entry hops for "dht-dl" (38% less), as the latter topology lacks any redundancy (which is an disadvantage if a hub and all

---

[5] When an entry is transmitted over multiple hops, each hop is counted individually.

**Table 2.** DTF, decentralised selection, Hierarchical networks vs. HyperCubes

(a) Topologies "cmu" and "hc"

|  | cmu, $h=1$ | cmu, $h=2$ | cmu, $h=3$ | hc, $h=1$ | hc, $h=2$ | hc, $h=3$ |
|---|---|---|---|---|---|---|
| P@5 | 0.7058 / 0.0% | 0.6260 / -11.3% | 0.5874 / -16.8% | 0.6990 / -1.0% | 0.7440 / 5.4% | 0.7528 / 6.7% |
| P@10 | 0.5721 / 0.0% | 0.4891 / -14.5% | 0.4475 / -21.8% | 0.5772 / 0.9% | 0.6306 / 10.2% | 0.6411 / 12.1% |
| P@15 | 0.4896 / 0.0% | 0.4021 / -17.9% | 0.3601 / -26.5% | 0.4937 / 0.8% | 0.5501 / 12.4% | 0.5622 / 14.8% |
| P@20 | 0.4295 / 0.0% | 0.3389 / -21.1% | 0.2989 / -30.4% | 0.4357 / 1.4% | 0.4944 / 15.1% | 0.5079 / 18.3% |
| P@30 | 0.3456 / 0.0% | 0.2492 / -27.9% | 0.2167 / -37.3% | 0.3539 / 2.4% | 0.4156 / 20.3% | 0.4309 / 24.7% |
| MAP | 0.2391 / 0.0% | 0.1601 / -33.0% | 0.1411 / -41.0% | 0.2500 / 4.6% | 0.3310 / 38.4% | 0.3554 / 48.6% |
| Precision | 0.2515 / 0.0% | 0.1679 / -33.2% | 0.1468 / -41.6% | 0.2584 / 2.7% | 0.3104 / 23.5% | 0.3254 / 29.4% |
| Recall | 0.2417 / 0.0% | 0.1565 / -35.2% | 0.1345 / -44.4% | 0.2479 / 2.6% | 0.3077 / 27.3% | 0.3256 / 34.7% |
| #Hops | 59.9 / 0.0% | 89.9 / 50.2% | 95.1 / 58.7% | 49.2 / -17.9% | 56.8 / -5.2% | 57.1 / -4.6% |

(b) Topologies "hc" and "hc-1"

|  | hc, $h=1$ | hc, $h=2$ | hc, $h=3$ | hc-1, $h=1$ | hc-1, $h=2$ | hc-1, $h=3$ |
|---|---|---|---|---|---|---|
| P@5 | 0.6990 / 0.0% | 0.7440 / 6.4% | 0.7528 / 7.7% | 0.5916 / -15.4% | 0.7120 / 1.9% | 0.7574 / 8.4% |
| P@10 | 0.5772 / 0.0% | 0.6306 / 9.3% | 0.6411 / 11.1% | 0.4488 / -22.2% | 0.5743 / -0.5% | 0.6157 / 6.7% |
| P@15 | 0.4937 / 0.0% | 0.5501 / 11.4% | 0.5622 / 13.9% | 0.3585 / -27.4% | 0.4831 / -2.1% | 0.5277 / 6.9% |
| P@20 | 0.4357 / 0.0% | 0.4944 / 13.5% | 0.5079 / 16.6% | 0.2965 / -31.9% | 0.4150 / -4.8% | 0.4633 / 6.3% |
| P@30 | 0.3539 / 0.0% | 0.4156 / 17.4% | 0.4309 / 21.8% | 0.2182 / -38.3% | 0.3239 / -8.5% | 0.3750 / 6.0% |
| MAP | 0.2500 / 0.0% | 0.3310 / 32.4% | 0.3554 / 42.2% | 0.1334 / -46.6% | 0.2099 / -16.0% | 0.2543 / 1.7% |
| Precision | 0.2584 / 0.0% | 0.3104 / 20.2% | 0.3254 / 26.0% | 0.1579 / -38.9% | 0.2310 / -10.6% | 0.2673 / 3.5% |
| Recall | 0.2479 / 0.0% | 0.3077 / 24.1% | 0.3256 / 31.3% | 0.1409 / -43.2% | 0.2197 / -11.4% | 0.2614 / 5.4% |
| #Hops | 49.2 / 0.0% | 56.8 / 15.4% | 57.1 / 16.2% | 42.9 / -12.8% | 50.6 / 2.9% | 51.3 / 4.4% |

**Table 3.** Topologies "cmu", "dht-dl" and "dht-hubs", $h=1$

|  | cmu, cent. | cmu, decent. | dht-dl | dht-hubs |
|---|---|---|---|---|
| P@5 | 0.8032 / 0.0% | 0.7058 / -12.1% | 0.8032 / 0.0% | 0.7546 / -6.1% |
| P@10 | 0.6630 / 0.0% | 0.5721 / -13.7% | 0.6630 / 0.0% | 0.6468 / -2.4% |
| P@15 | 0.5562 / 0.0% | 0.4896 / -12.0% | 0.5562 / 0.0% | 0.5723 / 2.9% |
| P@20 | 0.4793 / 0.0% | 0.4295 / -10.4% | 0.4793 / 0.0% | 0.5186 / 8.2% |
| P@30 | 0.3792 / 0.0% | 0.3456 / -8.9% | 0.3792 / 0.0% | 0.4405 / 16.2% |
| MAP | 0.2586 / 0.0% | 0.2391 / -7.5% | 0.2586 / 0.0% | 0.3670 / 41.9% |
| Precision | 0.2706 / 0.0% | 0.2515 / -7.1% | 0.2706 / 0.0% | 0.3326 / 22.9% |
| Recall | 0.2582 / 0.0% | 0.2417 / -6.4% | 0.2582 / 0.0% | 0.3328 / 28.9% |
| #Hops | 103.3 / 0.0% | 59.9 / -42.0% | 38.1 / -63.1% | 60.6 / -41.4% |

inverted lists on it disappears) while each DL is connected to multiple hubs in "cmu". In "dht-hubs", 250 million hops are required. In the retrieval phase, "dht-hubs" is the best performing approach with about 127,000 entry hops, compared to 4,9 million entry hops for "dht-dl" and 8,6 million entry hops for "cmu".

For $n = 100$ documents to be retrieved using "cmu", set-based precision decreases (more irrelevant documents are retrieved, and at most 50 of the retrieved 100 documents can be relevant at all), while recall (25-30%) and precision in the top ranks (up to 30%) dramatically improves. For centralised selection, it is close to the optimum; for decentralised selection, it performs about as well as centralised selection for $n = 50$.

**Table 4.** Evaluation summary and suggestions

| Policy | Best method |
| --- | --- |
| High precision in top ranks (5-10) | "cmu", centralised DTF; "dht-dl" |
| High precision in lower ranks (15-30) | "dht-hubs" |
| High MAP, set-based precision/recall, higher efficiency | "hc", decentralised DTF, $h = 3$ |
| High MAP, set-based precision/recall, lower efficiency | "dht-hubs" |
| High efficiency (lowest number of hops) | "dht-dl" |

With full knowledge (i.e., actual number of relevant documents and system-wide knowledge), centralised DTF performs close to the optimum, with precision and recall >99% (even if only the relevant documents in the DL are known). For decentralised selection, precision drops to 72.8% and recall to 62.6%; the top ranking, however, is still close to the optimum (e.g. P@15 is still >0.9). Thus, further work should concentrate on improvements in estimating the number of relevant documents in the collections.

The evaluation has shown that no method outperforms all others for all measures (efficiency, precision in top ranks, MAP, set-based precision and recall). Table 4 summarises the most important results and suggests the best method for a given policy.

## 6 Conclusion and Outlook

This paper investigates different architectures of peer-to-peer information retrieval systems. The architectures are based on the DTF or CORI resource selection approaches and use different strategies for extending them towards peer-to-peer networks (e.g. centralised vs. decentralised selection, system-wide or hub-global statistics). Five different topologies, namely hierarchical networks, HyperCubes (with two variants) and distributed hash tables (DHTs, also with two variants) are investigated.

The extensive evaluation showed that there is no clear winner. Centralised DTF selection in the "dht-dl" topology minimises the number of hops. Set-based precision and recall and precision in the lower ranks can be maximised by switching to HyperCubes ("hc" with $h = 3$, slightly better efficiency) and the DHTs storing only hub descriptions ("dht-hubs", slightly better effectiveness). Thus, the final goals (high efficiency or effectiveness) designate the choice of the selection approach.

The major drawback of this approach is that hub descriptions are created by considering a hub as a single large library which is created by merging all documents of all DLs in a neighbourhood. This does not take the distance of the involved DLs into account (prohibiting cost estimations w. r. t. time), and ignores DLs in a larger distance. Future work will concentrate on better descriptions for hubs and methods for approximating unknown distant DLs.

## Acknowledgements

This work is supported by the DFG (grant BIB47 DOuv 02-01, PEPPER).

# References

[1] M. Bender, S. Michel, C. Zimmer, and G. Weikum. Bookmark-driven query routing in peer-to-peer web search. In Callan et al. [3].

[2] J. Callan, G. Cormack, C. Clarke, D. Hawking, and A. Smeaton, editors. *Proceedings of the 26st Annual International ACM SIGIR Conference on Research and Development in Information Retrieval*, New York, 2003. ACM.

[3] J. Callan, N. Fuhr, and W. Nejdl, editors. *SIGIR Workshop on Peer-to-Peer Information Retrieval*, 2004.

[4] J. P. Callan, Z. Lu, and W. B. Croft. Searching distributed collections with inference networks. In E. A. Fox, P. Ingwersen, and R. Fidel, editors, *Proceedings of the 18th Annual International ACM SIGIR Conference on Research and Development in Information Retrieval*, pages 21–29, New York, 1995. ACM. ISBN 0-89791-714-6.

[5] J. French, A. Powell, J. Callan, C. Viles, T. Emmitt, K. Prey, and Y. Mou. Comparing the performance of database selection algorithms. In *Proceedings of the 22nd International Conference on Research and Development in Information Retrieval*, pages 238–245, New York, 1999. ACM.

[6] N. Fuhr. A decision-theoretic approach to database selection in networked IR. *ACM Transactions on Information Systems*, 17(3):229–249, 1999.

[7] M. Harren, J. M. Hellerstein, R. Huebsch, B. T. L. Loo, S. Shenker, and I. Stoica. Complex queries in DHT-based peer-to-peer networks. In *Electronic Proceedings for the 1st International Workshop on Peer-to-Peer Systems (IPTPS)*, 2002.

[8] J. Lu and J. Callan. Content-based retrieval in hybrid peer-to-peer networks. In D. Kraft, O. Frieder, J. Hammer, S. Qureshi, and L. Seligman, editors, *Proceedings of the 12th International Conference on Information and Knowledge Management*, New York, 2003. ACM.

[9] J. Lu and J. Callan. Federated search of text-based digital libraries in hierarchical peer-to-peer networks. In Callan et al. [3].

[10] H. Nottelmann and N. Fuhr. Evaluating different methods of estimating retrieval quality for resource selection. In Callan et al. [2].

[11] J. Ritter. Why Gnutella can't scale. No, really., 2001. http://www.darkridge.com/~jpr5/doc/gnutella.html.

[12] S. E. Robertson, S. Walker, M. Hancock-Beaulieu, A. Gull, and M. Lau. Okapi at TREC. In *Text REtrieval Conference*, pages 21–30, 1992.

[13] M. Schlosser, M. Sintek, S. Decker, and W. Nejdl. Digital libraries. In *1st Workshop on Agents and P2P Computing*, 2005.

[14] L. Si and J. Callan. A semi-supervised learning method to merge search engine results. *ACM Transactions on Information Systems*, 24:457–49, 2003.

[15] L. Si, R. Jin, J. Callan, and P. Ogilvie. Language modeling framework for resource selection and results merging. In C. Nicholas, D. Grossman, K. Kalpakis, S. Qureshi, H. van Dissel, and L. Seligman, editors, *Proceedings of the 11th International Conference on Information and Knowledge Management*, New York, 2002. ACM.

[16] I. Stoica, R. Morris, D. Karger, F. Kaashoek, and H. Balakrishnan. Chord: A scalable peer-to-peer lookup service for internet applications. In *ACM SIGCOMM*, 2001.

# Automatic Document Organization in a P2P Environment

Stefan Siersdorfer and Sergej Sizov

Max-Planck Institute for Computer Science
{stesi, sizov}@mpi-sb.mpg.de

**Abstract.** This paper describes an efficient method to construct reliable machine learning applications in peer-to-peer (P2P) networks by building ensemble based meta methods. We consider this problem in the context of distributed Web exploration applications like focused crawling. Typical applications are user-specific classification of retrieved Web contents into personalized topic hierarchies as well as automatic refinements of such taxonomies using unsupervised machine learning methods (e.g. clustering). Our approach is to combine models from multiple peers and to construct the advanced decision model that takes the generalization performance of multiple 'local' peer models into account. In addition, meta algorithms can be applied in a restrictive manner, i.e. by leaving out some 'uncertain' documents. The results of our systematic evaluation show the viability of the proposed approach.

## 1 Introduction

**Motivation.** Text processing using machine learning algorithms (e.g. using supervised methods such as classification or unsupervised algorithms like clustering) is an important part of many Web retrieval applications. As an example, we may consider a focused crawler [7] that starts with the sport-related topics 'ball games', 'track and fields', and 'swimming' that are initially filled by the user with some training data. Based on these training data the parameters of a mathematical decision model can be derived, which allows the system to automatically classify web pages gathered during the crawl into the topic taxonomy. In the next step, a large crawl would populate the topics of interest. In the postprocessing phase, unsupervised machine learning methods (e.g. clustering) may be applied for automatic organization of the 'ball games' documents by partitioning this class into appropriate subtopics (say 'soccer', 'basketball', and 'handball').

The key to success for the classification step clearly lies in the selection of an appropriate amount of human labeled training samples, being the intellectual bottleneck of the system. The clustering step should provide high accuracy in the sense that whatever subclasses it forms should indeed be reasonably homogeneous.

In the context of a peer-to-peer (P2P) network that puts together multiple users with shared topics of interest, it is natural to aggregate their knowledge and construct better machine learning models that could be used by every network

M. Lalmas et al. (Eds.): ECIR 2006, LNCS 3936, pp. 265–276, 2006.
© Springer-Verlag Berlin Heidelberg 2006

member. The naive solution would be to share available data (training samples and/or results of the focused crawl) along a higher number of peers with others. However, the following reasons may prevent the peer from sharing all of its data with other members of the overlay network:

- significantly increased network costs for downloads of additional training data on every peer
- increased runtimes for the training of the decision models
- privacy, security, and copyright aspects of the user's personal information sources

**Contribution.** To overcome the limitations of single-peer models, we propose the application of *meta methods*. Our objective is to combine multiple independently learned models from several peers and to construct the advanced decision model that utilizes the knowledge of multiple P2P users.

In addition we show how meta learning can be applied in a *restrictive* manner, i.e. leaving out some documents rather than assigning them to inappropriate topics or clusters with low confidence, providing us with significantly more accurate classification and clustering results on the remaining documents.

**Related Work.** Focused Web exploration applications were intensively studied in the recent literature. The idea of focused crawling [7] was recently adopted for P2P systems. However, this work was mainly focused on sharing crawling results from particular peers (e.g. using distributed indexes) rather than improving the underlying crawler and its components.

On the other hand, there is a plethora of work on text classification and clustering using all kinds of probabilistic and discriminative models [7]. The machine learning literature has studied a variety of meta methods such as bagging, stacking, or boosting [5, 29, 19, 13], and even combinations of heterogeneous learners (e.g., [30]). There are also methods available for combining different clustering methods [26, 12, 24]. The approach of intentionally splitting a training set for meta classification has been investigated by [8, 25]. However, these techniques were not considered in the context of P2P systems.

Algorithms for distributed clustering are described in [16, 18], but here document samples must be provided to a central server, making these solutions inconsistent with our requirements. The distributed execution of k-means was discussed in [11]. However, this method requires multiple iterations that must be synchronized among the peers and causes a considerable amount of coordination overhead. Privacy-preserving distributed classification and clustering were also addressed in the prior literature: In [27] a distributed Naive Bayes classifier is computed; in [20] the parameters of local generative models are transmitted to a central site and combined, but not in a P2P system.

## 2   System Architecture

The implementation of a peer in our distributed system consists of two layers. The *lower (network) layer* determines the communication among the peers. The peers form an autonomous agent environment: the exact way one particular peer solves its Web retrieval problem (e.g. crawling the Web, sending queries to 'Deep Web' portals, analyzing recent newsgroup discussions or publications in electronic journals, etc.) is not restricted in any way. We assume that all peers share the same thematic taxonomy such as *dmoz.org* [2]. The *upper (application) layer* is the distributed algorithm that utilizes results from particular peers to construct improved learning models (e.g. classification and/or clustering models) that can be used to continue the focused crawl with higher accuracy and to adjust the topics of a user-specific personalized ontology.

In our model, the peers use the epidemic-style communication [10]. Every peer maintains an incomplete database about the rest of the network. This database contains entries (e.g. addresses) on some other peers (neighbors) together with timestamps of the last successful contact to that neighbor. The neighbor list is refreshed using a push-pull epidemic algorithm.

To connect a new peer to the network one needs only one living address. The database of the new peer is initialized with the entry containing this living address only, and the rest is taken care of by the epidemic algorithm. Removal of a peer does not require any administration at all.

When new data becomes available, the peer initiates the building of a new meta learning method together with its direct neighbors as described in Section 3.1. With the next epidemic messages, it is broadcast to all neighboring peers.

## 3   Properties of the Application Layer

In this section we first describe a general framework for aggregating information from $k$ peers in meta models, and then consider two typical applications for such a framework: classification and clustering for document collections.

### 3.1   Exchanging Data Models Among Peers

In our framework we are given a set of $k$ peers $P = \{p_1, \ldots, p_k\}$. Each peer $p_i$ maintains its collection of documents $D_i$. In the first step, each peer $p_i$ builds a model $m_i(D_i)$ using its own document set $D_i$. Next, the models $m_i$ are propagated among the $k$ peers as described in Section 2. To avoid high network load, it is crucial for this step that the models $m_i$ are a very compressed representation of the document sets $D_i$. Each peer $p_i$ uses the set of received models $M = \{m_1, \ldots, m_k\}$ to construct a meta model $Meta_i(m_1, \ldots, m_k)$. From now on, $p_i$ can use the new meta model $Meta_i$ (instead of the 'local' model $m_i$) to analyze its own data $D_i$.

We notice that the dynamic nature of P2P overlay networks has no direct impact on the construction of meta models. If the participating nodes do not receive models $M^F = \{m_{f_1}, \ldots, m_{f_u}\}$ from some (failed) neighbors, they are still able to construct the meta model $Meta_i^*(M - M^F)$ on models obtained from the remaining live peers. When the number $k$ of required models is explicitly given by estimators or tuning parameters of the framework (Section 3.2), the multicast capability of the network layer can be combined with advanced scheduling methods [14] in order to reach the desired number of live nodes in presence of failures.

## 3.2  Application to Automatic Document Organization

**Meta Classifiers on $k$ Peers.** In the context of classification algorithms, the introduced general approach 3.1 can be substantiated as follows. Each peer $p_i$ contains a document collection $D_i$, consisting of a set of labeled training documents $T_i$ and unlabeled documents $U_i$. The peer's goal is to automatically classify the documents in $U_i$. In the first step, every peer $p_i$ builds its own feature vectors of topic labeled text documents $T_i$ (e.g., capturing $tf \cdot idf$ weights of terms). The model $m_i$ corresponds to the classifier obtained by running a supervised learning algorithm on the training set $T_i$.

Now, instead of transferring the whole training sets $T_i$, only the models $m_i$ need to be exchanged among the peers. For instance, linear support vector machines (SVMs) [6] construct a hyperplane $w \cdot x + b = 0$ that separates the set of positive training examples from a set of negative examples with maximum margin. For a new, previously unseen, document $d$ the SVM merely needs to test whether the document lies on the "positive" side or the "negative" side of the separating hyperplane. The classifiers $m_i$ can represented in a very compressed way: as tuples $(w, l, b)$ of the normal vector $w$ and bias $b$ of the hyperplane and $l$, a vector consisting of the encodings of the terms (e.g. some hashcode) corresponding to the dimensions of $w$.

In the next step, every peer $p_j$ considers the set $M = \{m_1, \ldots, m_k\}$ of $k$ binary classifiers with results $R(m_i, d)$ in $\{+1, -1\}$ for a document $d \in U_j$, namely, $+1$ if $d$ is accepted for the given topic by $m_i$ and -1 if $d$ is rejected. These results can be easily combined into a meta result:

$$Meta(d) = Meta(R(m_1, d), \ldots, R(m_k, d)) \in \{+1, -1, 0\} \qquad (1)$$

A family of such meta methods is the linear classifier combination with thresholding [25]. Given thresholds $t_1$ and $t_2$, with $t_1 > t_2$, and weights $w(m_i)$ for the $k$ underlying classifiers we compute $Meta(d)$ as follows:

$$Meta(d) = \begin{cases} +1 \text{ if } \sum_{i=1}^{n} R(m_i, d) \cdot w(m_i) > t_1 \\ -1 \text{ if } \sum_{i=1}^{n} R(m_i, d) \cdot w(m_i) < t_2 \\ 0 \quad \text{otherwise} \end{cases} \qquad (2)$$

The important special cases of this meta classifier family include voting [5] ($Meta()$ returns the result of the majority of the classifiers), unanimous decision (if all classifiers give us the same result), and weighted averaging [28] ($Meta()$ weights the classifiers using some predetermined quality estimator, e.g., a leave-one-out estimator for each $v_i$).

The restrictive behavior is achieved by the choice of the thresholds: we dismiss the documents where the linear result combination lies between $t_1$ and $t_2$. For real world data there is often a tradeoff between the fraction of dismissed documents (the *loss*) and the fraction of correctly classified documents (the *accuracy*).

If a fixed set $U$ of unlabeled documents (that does not change dynamically) is given, we can classify the documents with a user-acceptable loss of $L$ as follows:

1. for all documents in $U$ compute their classification confidence $\sum_{i=1}^{n} R(m_i, d) \cdot w(m_i)$
2. sort the documents into decreasing order according to their confidence values
3. classify the $(1 - L)|U|$ documents with the highest confidence values according to their sign and dismiss the rest

In our experiments we assigned equal weights to each classifier, and instead of $R(m_i, d)$, we considered a "confidence" value $conf(m_i, d)$ for the classification of document $d$ by the classifier. For SVM we chose the SVM scores, i.e., the distance of the test points from the hyperplane. A more enhanced method to map SVM outputs to probabilities is described, e.g., in [21].

Note that meta classifiers can be, similar as base classifiers, easily transferred between peers as tuples

$$(m_1, \ldots, m_k, w(m_1), \ldots w(m_k), t_1, t_2). \tag{3}$$

**Meta Clustering Algorithms on $k$ Peers.** Clustering algorithms partition a set of objects, text documents in our case, into groups called *clusters*. In the introduced scenario, each peer $p_i$ contains a document collection $U_i$ of unlabeled data. Every peer wants to cluster its unlabeled data. Analogously to the classification task every peer $p_i$ can execute a clustering algorithm on its own data $U_i$ to build the model $m_i$; a representation of the resulting clustering models $m_i$ can be propagated to the other peers.

A simple, very popular member of the family of partitioning clustering methods is *k-means* [15]: $k$ initial centers (points) are chosen, every document vector is assigned to the nearest center (according to some distance or similarity metric), and new centers are obtained by computing the means (centroids) of the sets of vectors in each cluster. After several iterations (according to a stopping criterion) one obtains the final centers, and one can cluster the documents accordingly. For the k-means algorithm, the clustering model $m_i$ can be represented as $(z_1, \ldots, z_l, l)$, where the $z_i$ are vector representations of the computed centroids, and $l$ contains encodings of the feature dimensions as described above for the supervised case.

After propagating the models, every peer contains a set $M = \{m_1, \ldots, m_k\}$ of different clustering models. Document $d$ is assigned to one of $l$ clusters with labels $\{1, \ldots, l\}$ by each model: $m_i(d) \in \{1, \ldots, l\}$. In the case of k-means this is the label of the centroid most similar to the document. The goal of meta clustering is now to combine the different clustering results in an appropriate way.

To combine the $m_i(d)$ into a meta result, the first problem is to determine which cluster labels of different methods $m_i$ correspond to each other (note that cluster label 3 of method $m_i$ does not necessarily correspond to the same cluster label 3 of method $m_j$, but could correspond to say cluster label 1). With perfect clustering methods the solution would become trivial: the documents labeled by $m_i$ as $a$ would be exactly the documents labeled by $m_j$ as $b$. However, real clustering results exhibit certain fuzziness so that some documents end up in clusters other than their perfectly suitable cluster. Informally, for different clustering methods we would like to associate the clusters which each other which are "most correlated".

Formally, for every method $m_i$ we want to determine a bijective function $map_i : \{1, \ldots, l\} \rightarrow \{1, \ldots, l\}$ which assigns all labels $a \in \{1, \ldots, l\}$ assigned by $m_i$ a meta label $map_i(a)$. By these mappings the clustering labels of the different methods are associated with each other and we can define the clustering result for document $d$ using method $m_i$ as:

$$result_i(d) := map_i(m_i(d)) \tag{4}$$

One way to obtain the $map_i$ functions is to take correlation of clusters from different clusterings into account. We want to maximize the correlation between the cluster labels. For sets $A_1..A_x$, we can define their *overlap* as

$$overlap(A_1, .., A_x) := \frac{|A_1 \cap .. \cap A_x|}{|A_1| + .. + |A_x| - |A_1 \cap .. \cap A_x|} \tag{5}$$

Now using

$$A_{ij} := \{d \in U | res_i(d) = j\} \tag{6}$$

we can define the *average overlap* for a document set $U$ and the set of clustering methods $M$ as

$$\frac{1}{l} \sum_{j=1}^{l} \frac{1}{\binom{k}{2}} \sum_{(i,m) \in \{1,\ldots,l\}^2, i<m} overlap(A_{ij}, A_{mj}) \tag{7}$$

We choose the mappings $map_i$ which maximize the average overlap.

After having computed the mapping we are given a set $M = \{m_1, \ldots, m_k\}$ of $k$ binary clustering methods with results $res_i(d)$. For simplicity we consider here the case of $k = 2$ clusters and choose $res_i(d) \in \{+1, -1\}$ for a document $d$, namely, $+1$ if $d$ is assigned to cluster 1, and -1 if $d$ is assigned to cluster 2. We can combine these results into a meta result: $Meta(d) = Meta(res_1(d), \ldots, res_k(d))$ in $\{+1, -1, 0\}$ where 0 means abstention. A family of such meta methods is the linear combination with thresholding [24]. Given thresholds $t_1$ and $t_2$, with $t_1 > t_2$, and weights $w(m_i)$ for the $l$ underlying clustering methods we compute $Meta(d)$ as follows:

$$Meta(d) = \begin{cases} +1 \text{ if } \sum_{i=1}^{k} res_i(d) \cdot w(m_i) > t_1 \\ -1 \text{ if } \sum_{i=1}^{k} res_i(d) \cdot w(m_i) < t_2 \\ 0 \quad \text{otherwise} \end{cases} \tag{8}$$

Thus by an intermediate meta mapping step we have a completely analogous situation to the one for the supervised case described in Section 3.2. Confidence values $conf(v_i, d)$ for the clustering of a document $d$ by the base methods $v_i$ can be obtained, say for k-means clustering, by computing the similarity (e.g., using the cosine measure) to the nearest centroid. The restrictive behavior can be obtained in exactly the same way as for the supervised case.

**Estimators and Tuning.** For a restrictive meta classifier, we are interested in its behavior in terms of *accuracy* and *loss* (fraction of unclassified documents). A typical scenario could be a number of users in different peers accepting a loss up to fixed bound, to obtain a higher classification accuracy for the remaining documents. In [25] the tuning of the number $k$ of classifiers for a user-acceptable loss threshold was described. We will not repeat this here and will instead focus on the P2P specific aspects.

The main ingredients of the estimation and tuning process are:

1. estimators for base classifiers (based on cross-validation between the training subsets $T_i$)
2. estimators for the pairwise correlations between the base classifiers $\{m_1, \ldots, m_k\}$
3. probabilistic estimators for loss and error based on 1. and 2.

For the cross-validation, at least two peers, $p_i$ and $p_j$, must cooperate: $p_i$ sends a tuple $(m_i, IDs(T_i))$, consisting of its classifier $m_i$ and a list of IDs (not contents!) of its training documents, to $p_j$. The peer $p_j$ uses the list of submitted IDs to identify duplicates in both collections and performs cross-validation by $m_i$ on $T_j - T_i$. (In the Web context, the IDs of $T_i$ can be easily obtained by computing content-based 'fingerprints' or 'message digests' (e.g. MD5 [23])). The resulting error estimator (a simple numerical value) for $m_i$ can be forwarded from $p_j$ back to $p_i$ or to other peers.

For the computation of pairwise covariance, at least three peers, $p_i, p_j$ and $p_m$, must cooperate: $p_i$ and $p_j$ send their classifiers and document IDs to $p_m$ and $p_m$ cross-validates in parallel both classifiers on $T_m - T_i - T_j$. By this procedure we get also accuracy estimators.

Finally, the estimators for *covariance* and *accuracy* (numerical values) can be distributed among the peers and estimators for the overall meta classifier can be built. When the estimated quality of the resulting meta classifier does not meet the application-specific peer requirements (e.g. the expected accuracy is still below the specified threshold), the initiating peer may decide to invoke additional nodes for better meta classification. Note that for meta clustering, estimators *cannot* be built in the same easy way, because for the unsupervised case we cannot evaluate base methods by cross-validation.

## 4 Experiments

**Setup.** To simulate different P2P Web retrieval scenarios (crawling the Web, sending queries to 'Deep Web' portals, analyzing recent newsgroup discussions or publications in electronic journals) we performed multiple series of experiments with real-life data from

1. The academic WebKB dataset [9] containing 8282 HTML Web pages from multiple universities, manually classified into the categories 'student', 'faculty', 'staff', 'department', 'course', 'project', and 'other'.
2. Newsgroups collection at [1]. This collection contains 17847 postings collected from 20 Usenet newsgroups. Particular topics ('rec.autos', 'sci.space', etc.) contain between 600 and 1000 documents.
3. The Reuters articles [17]. This is the most widely used test collection for text categorization research. The collection contains 21578 Reuters newswire stories, subdivided into multiple categories ('earn', 'grain', 'trade', etc.).
4. The Internet Movie Database (IMDB) at [3]. Documents of this collection are articles about movies that include the storyboard, cast overview, and user comments. The collection contains 6853 movie descriptions subdivided into 20 topics according to particular genres ('drama', 'horror', etc.).

We used the Porter stemming algorithm [22] in combination with stopword elimination to transform documents into the vector space model. In all discussed experiments, the standard bag-of-words approach [4] (using term frequencies to build L1-normalized feature vectors) was used for document representation.

**Experiments with Supervised Learning Methods (Classification).** For each data set we identified all topics with more than 200 documents. These were 20 topics for Newsgroups, 6 for Reuters, 12 for IMDB, 4 for WebKB. Among these topics we randomly chose 100 topic pairs from Newsgroups and all possible combinations for the others, i.e. 66 topic pairs from IMDB, 15 for Reuters, and 6 for WebKB. For each topic pair we randomly chose 200 training documents per class and kept - depending on the available topic sizes in particular collections - a distinct and also randomly chosen set of documents for the validation of the classifiers.

In each experiment, the training data was distributed over 16 peers (data collections in sizes suitable for larger network experiments are hard to get for our scenarios) using equal-sized subsets with approximately 15% overlap (corresponding to peers that contain non-disjoint training data). Among these peers we randomly chose 1,2,4,8, and all 16 peers to simulate various P2P classification scenarios. The configuration with 1 peer corresponds to the 'local' classification that does not involve sharing of classifiers. As discussed in Section 3.2, we also compared the *restrictive* form of meta classification, where we dismissed at each peer exactly the same amount of documents with worst classification confidence using confidence values as discussed in Section 3. Our quality measure is the fraction of correctly classified documents (the *accuracy*) among the documents not dismissed by the restrictive algorithm. The *loss* is the fraction of dismissed documents.

Finally, we computed micro-averaged results along with their 95% confidence intervals for all groups of topic pairs. Figure 1 shows the observed dependencies between the numbers of cooperating peers, the induced loss, and the resulting accuracy for various reference collections. It can be observed that the meta classification and restrictive meta classification by multiple cooperating peers

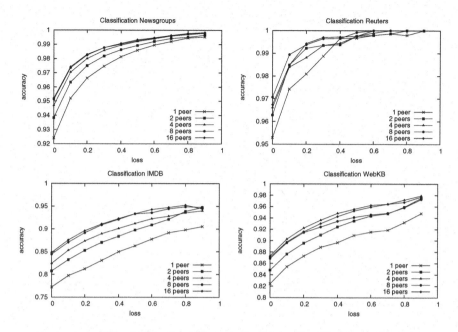

**Fig. 1.** Results of Restrictive Meta Classification

clearly outperforms the single-peer solution for all settings of the user-defined
*loss*, including the non-restrictive meta classification with *loss* = 0. The quality
of the meta algorithm clearly increases with the number of participating peers.
In general, the difference between the one-peer solution and the meta solution is
statistically significant for 4 and more participating peers and all values of the
induced loss. The only exceptions are the results for Reuters with *loss* > 0.7
(the accuracy of all peer combinations, including one-peer experiment, becomes
nearly 1.0) and the WebKB collection (due to the very limited number of possible
topic combinations).

**Experiments with Unsupervised Learning Methods (Clustering).** The
same collections and topics were used to evaluate distributed meta clustering.
All documents from randomly combined selections of 3 or 5 topics were considered as unlabeled data and distributed among peers analogously to classification
experiments from the previous section, with approximately 15% overlap. The
goal of the clustering algorithm was to reproduce the partitioning into topics on
each peer with possibly high accuracy. Our quality measure describes the correlation between the actual topics of our datasets and the clusters found by the
algorithm. Let $k$ be the number of classes and clusters, $N_i$ the total number of
clustered documents in $class_i$, $N_{ij}$ the number of documents contained in $class_i$
and having cluster label $j$. We define the clustering accuracy as follows:

$$accuracy = \max_{(j_1,...,j_k)\in perm((1,...,k))} \frac{\sum_{i=1}^{k} N_{i,j_i}}{\sum_{i=1}^{k} N_i} \qquad (9)$$

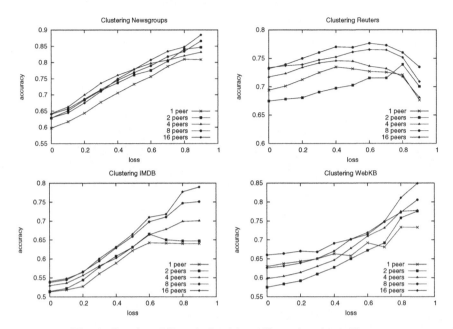

**Fig. 2.** Results of Restrictive Meta Clustering, k=3 Clusters

The *loss* is the fraction of documents dismissed by the restrictive algorithm.

For all peers, k-means was used as the underlying base method. We compared the one-peer clustering (i.e. clustering that can be executed by one peer on its local dataset without cooperation with others) with meta clustering, exchanging centroids from cooperating peers and correlation-based mapping (Section 3.2) of the final clusters. Analogously to classification experiments, we considered restrictive meta clustering, dismissing exactly the same number of documents with the worst clustering confidence [24] on each peer.

The results are summarized in Figure 2. The main observations are similar to the ones discussed for the supervised case:

– The quality of the meta clustering results is consistently higher than for isolated one-peer solutions.
– The quality of the meta algorithm tends to increase with the number of participating peers and is in almost all cases statistically significant. For the Reuters collection, the difference between one-peer solution and the meta result is statistically significant for 8 and more participating peers and all values of the induced loss. For the IMDB and Newsgroups collections, the difference between the one-peer solution and the meta result is statistically significant for 4 and more participating peers and all loss values.

In the experiments with the Reuters dataset, the accuracy decreases for high loss values (greater 0.7). Possibly this can be explained by the fact that the Reuters topics - unlike the other considered reference collections - are very different in size (e.g. the topics '*earn*' and '*grain*' contain about 3900 and 280 documents, respectively). The in-depth analysis of such artifacts is subject of our future work.

# 5    Conclusion

In this paper, we proposed a new methodology to construct distributed machine learning meta models for P2P Web exploration applications. The results of the evaluation clearly show the advantages of cooperation between nodes for building meta decision models. Our method does not require the comprehensive exchange of private data collections between peers and thus provides substantial advantages for aspects of privacy, network bandwidth, storage, and computational expense. Furthermore, in terms of accuracy our restrictive meta methods clearly outperform the models that can be separately built on training sources of isolated peers and - more importantly - also the restrictive variant of such one-peer solutions with the same induced loss.

# References

1. The 20 newsgroups data set. *http://www.ai.mit.edu/ jrennie/20Newsgroups/*.
2. dmoz - open directory project. *http://dmoz.org/*.
3. Internet movie database. *http://www.imdb.com*.
4. R. Baeza-Yates and B. Ribeiro-Neto. *Modern Information Retrieval*. Addison Wesley, 1999.
5. L. Breiman. Bagging predictors. *Machine Learning*, 24(2):123–140, 1996.
6. C. Burges. A tutorial on Support Vector Machines for pattern recognition. *Data Mining and Knowledge Discovery*, 2(2), 1998.
7. S. Chakrabarti. *Mining the Web*. Morgan Kaufmann, 2003.
8. P. Chan. An extensible meta-learning approach for scalable and accurate inductive learning. *PhD thesis, Department of Computer Science, Columbia University, New York*, 1996.
9. M. e. a. Craven. Learning to extract symbolic knowledge from the World Wide Web. *15th National Conference on Artificial Intelligence (AAAI)*, 1998.
10. A. e. a. Demers. Epidemic algorithms for replicated database management. *6th Annual ACM Symposium on Principles of Distributed Computing (PODC'87)*, 1987.
11. I. S. Dhillon and D. S. Modha. A data-clustering algorithm on distributed memory multiprocessors. In *Large-Scale Parallel Data Mining, Lecture Notes in Artificial Intelligence*, pages 245–260, 2000.
12. A. Fred and A. K. Jain. Robust data clustering. In *Proc. Conference on Computer Vision and Pattern Recognition, CVPR*, 2003.
13. Y. Freund. An adaptive version of the boost by majority algorithm. *Workshop on Computational Learning Theory*, 1999.
14. Gorunova,K. and Merz,P. Reliable Multicast and its Probabilistic Model for Job Submission in Peer-to-Peer Grids. *WISE, New York, USA*, 2005.
15. J. Hartigan and M. Wong. A k-means clustering algorithm. *Applied Statistics, 28:100-108*, 1979.
16. H. Kargupta, W. Huang, K. Sivakumar, and E. L. Johnson. Distributed clustering using collective principal component analysis. *Knowledge and Information Systems*, 3(4):422–448, 2001.

17. D. D. Lewis. Evaluating text categorization. In *Proceedings of Speech and Natural Language Workshop*, pages 312–318. Defense Advanced Research Projects Agency, Morgan Kaufmann, Feb. 1991.
18. T. Li, S. Zhu, and M. Ogihara. Algorithms for Clustering High Dimensional and Distributed Data. *Intelligent Data Analysis Journal*, 7(4), 2003.
19. N. Littlestone and M. Warmuth. The weighted majority algorithm. *FOCS*, 1989.
20. S. Merugu and J. Ghosh. Privacy-preserving distributed clustering using generative models. In *International Conference on Data Mining (ICDM'03), Melbourne, FL*, 2003.
21. J. Platt. Probabilistic outputs for support vector machines and comparisons to regularized likelihood methods. *Advances in Large Margin Classifiers, MIT Press*, 1999.
22. M. Porter. An algorithm for suffix stripping. *Automated Library and Information Systems*, 14(3).
23. R. Rivest. The MD5 message digest algorithm. *RFC 1321*, 1992.
24. S. Siersdorfer and S. Sizov. Restrictive Clustering and Metaclustering for Self-Organizing Document Collections. In *SIGIR*, 2004.
25. S. Siersdorfer, S. Sizov, and G. Weikum. Goal-oriented methods and meta methods for document classification and their parameter tuning. In *CIKM, Washington, USA*, 2004.
26. A. Strehl and J. Gosh. Cluster ensembles - a knowledge reuse framework for combining multiple partitions. *Journal of Machine Learning Research 3, pp. 583-617*, 2002.
27. J. Vaidya and C. Clifton. Privacy preserving naïve bayes classifier for vertically partitioned data. In *SDM*, 2004.
28. H. Wang, W. Fan, P. Yu, and J. Han. Mining concept-drifting data streams using ensemble classifiers. *SIGKDD*, 2003.
29. D. Wolpert. Stacked generalization. *Neural Networks, Vol. 5, pp. 241-259*, 1992.
30. H. Yu, K. Chang, and J. Han. Heterogeneous learner for Web page classification. *ICDM*, 2002.

# Exploring URL Hit Priors for Web Search

Ruihua Song, Guomao Xin, Shuming Shi, Ji-Rong Wen, and Wei-Ying Ma

Microsoft Research Asia, 5F, Sigma Center, No.49 Zhichun Road,
100080 Beijing, P.R. China
{rsong, guomxin, shumings, jrwen, wyma}@microsoft.com

**Abstract.** URL usually contains meaningful information for measuring the relevance of a Web page to a query in Web search. Some existing works utilize URL depth priors (i.e. the probability of being a good page given the length and depth of a URL) for improving some types of Web search tasks. This paper suggests the use of the location of query terms occur in a URL for measuring how well a web page is matched with a user's information need in web search. First, we define and estimate URL **hit** types, i.e. the priori probability of being a good answer given the type of query term hits in the URL. The main advantage of URL hit priors (over depth priors) is that it can achieve stable improvement for both informational and navigational queries. Second, an obstacle of exploiting such priors is that shortening and concatenation are frequently used in a URL. Our investigation shows that only 30% URL hits are recognized by an ordinary word breaking approach. Thus we combine three methods to improve matching. Finally, the priors are integrated into the probabilistic model for enhancing web document retrieval. Our experiments were conducted using 7 query sets of TREC2002, TREC2003 and TREC2004, and show that the proposed approach is stable and improve retrieval effectiveness by 4%~11% for navigational queries and 10% for informational queries.

## 1 Introduction

When searching the World Wide Web, "end users want to achieve their goals with a minimum of cognitive load and a maximum of enjoyment."[11] Some recent studies [4] [17] [10] found that the goal of a user can be classified into at least two categories: navigational and informational. A user searches a navigational query to reach a particular Web page in mind, whereas an informational query is usually short and broad where the user intends to visit multiple pages to learn about a topic. Actually, real Web search is to deal with the mixed query stream. Therefore, finding robust evidence which works well for various types of queries has been one challenging interest of Web IR community.

As a workshop that provides the infrastructure necessary for large-scale evaluation of text retrieval methodologies, Text Retrieval Conference (TREC) has set up 3 tasks, namely homepage finding, named page finding and topic distillation, in Web track to encourage research on Web information retrieval. Homepage finding (HP) and named page finding (NP) is to model two types of navigational queries. The difference is that a homepage finding query is the name of a site while a named page finding query is the name of a non-homepage that the user wishes to reach. Topic distillation (TD), on the other hand, is to model informational queries. It was first proposed by Bharat and

M. Lalmas et al. (Eds.): ECIR 2006, LNCS 3936, pp. 277–288, 2006.
© Springer-Verlag Berlin Heidelberg 2006

Henzinger [3] to refer to the process of finding quality document on a query topic. They argued that it is more practical to return quality documents related to the topic than to exactly satisfy the users' information need since most short queries do not express the need unambiguously. In TRECs, a topic distillation query describes a general topic and requires retrieval systems to return homepages of relevant sites. Until now, these three types of queries are acknowledged and TRECs cumulated valuable data through years for related research.

URL, as a Uniform Resource Locator [19] for each Web page, usually contains meaningful information for measuring the relevance of the Web page to a query. Related works can be roughly grouped into 3 categories: one is to use the length or depth of a URL as query-independent evidence in ranking [9][21][12][6]; another is to use URL-based sitemap to enhance topic distillation [20][18]; the other addresses the issue of word break in URLs [5][12].

Kraaij et al [9] found that the probability of being an entry page, i.e. homepage, seems to inversely related to the depth of the path in the corresponding URL. They classified URLs into four types in terms of the depth, estimated prior relevance probability for each type, and integrated the priors in the language model. Their experimental results verified that the depth is a strong indicator for homepages. By doing some extension, Ogilvie and Callan [12] reported improvements on mixed homepage/named-page finding task. However, by closely observing the URL priors in [12], we found that the priors for homepage finding queries are quite different from those for named page finding queries (see Section 2 for details). Thus the priors may hurt named-page finding while improving homepage finding.

In this paper, we aim to find a kind of stable priors to enhance retrieval performance for various kinds of queries. We observe that the occurrence location of the query terms in a URL is an effective indicator of the quality and relevance of a Web page. Especially, a URL with some query term appearing near to its tail promises to be a relevant domain, directory or file. Our statistics on queries of past TREC experiments verify this observation. Therefore, we treat the occurrence location of the query terms in a URL as a good prior for the relevance of a page. We call this kind of priors the URL hit priors as a hit refers to a query term occurrence.

The effectiveness of URL hit priors relies on the capability of detecting the hits of query terms in URLs. To increase the hit rates of query terms, we explore three successive methods to recognize terms in URLs. First, a simple rule is used to recognize most of acronyms in URLs. Second, the recognition of concatenations is formulated as a search problem with constraints. Third, prefix matching is used to recognize other fuzzily matched words. With this 3-step approach, it is shown on the TREC data that the recall of URL hits is doubled from 33% to 66% while the precision is close to 99%.

We integrate the URL hit priors into the probabilistic model. Experimental results, on seven TREC Web Track datasets, indicate that, with the URL hit priors and URL hit recognition methods, the performance is consistently improved across various types of queries.

The rest of the paper is organized as follows. Section 2 introduces the related work. In section 3, we give the details of URL hit priors, URL hit recognition methods, and how to combine URL hit priors into the probability model. We conduct experiments to verify the proposed methods in Section 4. Conclusion and future work are given in Section 5.

## 2  Related Work

As mentioned in the introduction, several URL-related approaches have been proposed to enhance Web search or recognize more query terms. In this section, we will briefly review four latest and representative works.

Kraaij et al found that the URL depth is a good predictor for entry page search [9]. Four types of URLs are defined in their work [21] as follows:

> *"ROOT*: a domain name, optionally followed by 'index.html'.
> *SUBROOT*: a domain name, followed by a single directory, optionally followed by 'index.html'.
> *PATH*: a domain name, followed by a path with arbitrarily deep, but not ending with a file name other than 'index.html'.
> *FILE*: any other URL ending with a filename other than 'index.html'."

The priori probability of being an entry page is elegantly integrated in the language model. As a result, the performance is improved by over 100%. About 70% of entry pages are ranked at No.1. The TREC2001 evaluation confirmed some successful exploitation of URL depth in entry page search [7][13].

Ogilvie and Callan extends the usage of URLs in TREC2003 [12]. A character-based trigram generative probability is computed for each URL. A shortened word or a concatenation of words is handled by treating a URL and a query term as a character sequence. Another extension is that they include named page in the estimation of URL depth priors.

Based on the TREC2003 data, we did some statistics about the distributions of URL depth types for different retrieval tasks. The results are shown in Table 1. It is clear that most of the relevant documents for HP queries have the ROOT type URLs, while the majority of NP queries tend to have the FILE type URLs for their relevant documents. For TD queries, more than half of relevant documents' URLs are with the FILE type, whereas the distributions in the other three URL types are quite even. Therefore, the computed priors based on URL depth are unlikely to benefit all query types.

Craswell et al [6] use URL length in characters as query independent evidence and propose a function to transform the original depth for effective combination. Their results show a significant improvement on a mixed query set. And their finding is that the average URL length of relevant pages is shorter than that of the whole collection.

Chi et al [5] reported that over 70% URL words are "compound word", that means multiple words are concatenated to form one word. Such phenomenon is caused by the special of URLs. Some of the most frequent delimiters, such as spaces, in a document are not allowed to appear in URLs [19]. Consequently, webmasters have to

**Table 1.** Distributions of URL depth types (TREC2003)

| URL Depth Type | HP | NP | TD |
|:---:|:---:|:---:|:---:|
| ROOT | 103 | 1 | 79 |
| SUBROOT | 33 | 8 | 65 |
| PATH | 13 | 11 | 77 |
| FILE | 45 | 138 | 295 |

concatenate multiple words when creating a URL. These compound words cannot be found in the ordinary dictionaries. Thus they proposed to exploit maximal matching, a Chinese word segmentation mechanism, to segment a "compound word". An interesting idea is that title, anchor text and file names and alternated text of embedded objects are used as a reference base to help disambiguate segmentation candidates. Although the authors aim to recover the content hierarchy of Web documents in terms of URLs, the approach is also a good solution for recognizing URL hits. We have not implemented their approach because this paper focuses on the effectiveness of URL hit priors for search and their approach does not handle individual shortened words. In addition, our recognition methods do not use any dictionary but the query only. Another solution worth mention was proposed by Ogilvie and Callan [12]. They treat a URL and a query term as a character sequence and compute a character-based trigram generative probability for each URL.

## 3  Our Approach

In this section, we first define a new classification of URL types and the related URL priors called URL hit priors. Then three methods are described to recognize URL hits. Finally, we introduce how to combine the URL hit priors into the probabilistic model and for improving retrieval performance.

### 3.1  URL Hit Priors

A query term occurrence in a URL is called a URL hit. We assume that the location of a URL hit may be a good hint to distinguish a good answer from other pages. For example, when a user is querying "wireless communication" and 2 URLs below are returned, U2 is more probably to be a better answer because it seems to be a good entry point, neither too general nor too narrow.

*U1: cio.doe.gov/wireless/3g/3g_index.htm*
*U2: cio.doe.gov/wireless/*

When "ADA Enforcement" is queried, U3 looks like a perfect answer as a URL hit occurs in the file name.

*U3: http://www.usdoj.gov/crt/ada/enforce.htm*

Given the query of "NIST CTCMS", U4 is easy to beat other pages like U5 and again the URL hits appear in a good position.

*U4: http://www.ctcms.nist.gov/*
*U5:http://www.ctcms.nist.gov/people/*

Given a URL, slashes can easily split the URL into several segments (the last slash will be removed if there is no character followed by it). U2, U3 and U4 are similar for the last URL hit occurs in the last segment. Therefore, we define four kinds of URL hit types:

   ***Hit-Last***: A URL, in which the last URL hit occurs in the last segment;
   ***Hit-Second-Last***: A URL, in which the last URL hit occurs in the second last segment;

**Hit-Other**: A URL, in which all the URL hits occur in other segment than the last two;

**Hit-None**: A URL, in which no URL hit is found.

In our examples, U2, U3 and U4 belong to the type of "Hit-Last", U5 is of the type "Hit-Second-Last", while U1 is of the type "Hit-Other".

We perform a statistical analysis base on the TREC2003 data. The distribution of URL hit types is shown in Table 2. There are two important observations from the statistics. First, a large portion of good answers have query term hits in their URLs. Second, the distributions of good answers in different types are quite consistent across different query types. Except for the "Hit-None" type, most of the good answers fall into the URL type "Hit-Last" for all the three query types HP, NP and TD. Also, type "Hit-Second-Last" has more good answers than type "Hit-Other". Thus, we expect to find a stable prior relevance probability for the URL hit types, which can be uniformly used in various tasks.

**Table 2.** Distribution of URL hit types (TREC2003)

| URL Hit Type | HP | NP | TD |
|---|---|---|---|
| Hit-Last | 136 | 86 | 129 |
| Hit-Second-Last | 21 | 17 | 21 |
| Hit-Other | 8 | 12 | 6 |
| Hit-None | 29 | 43 | 360 |

Based on the above observations, we target to assign each URL a prior relevance probability. Given a hit type $t$, this prior is consistently used for HP, NP and TD queries. Given a query $q$ and a page with URL $u$, we denote $P(t)$ as the probability of URL $u$ having hit type $t$ for the query. We denote $P(R)$ as the probability of $u$ being relevant to query $q$. And $P(TD)$, $P(HP)$, and $P(NP)$ are denoted respectively as the probability of query $q$ being a TD, HP, and NP query. Since NP, HP and TD are disjoint, we can estimate the prior for hit type $t$ by the following formula,

$$P(R|t) = P(R, TD \vee HP \vee NP | t)$$
$$= P(R, TD|t) + P(R, HP|t) + P(R, NP|t)$$

By applying Bayes' formula [2], we get

$$P(R|t) = \frac{P(R, t|TD) \cdot P(TD)}{P(t)} + \frac{P(R, t|HP) \cdot P(HP)}{P(t)} + \frac{P(R, t|NP) \cdot P(NP)}{P(t)}$$

As $P(t) = P(t, TD \vee HP \vee NP) = P(t, TD) + P(t, HP) + P(t, NP)$, we have

$$P(R|t) = \frac{P(R, t|TD) \cdot P(TD) + P(R, t|HP) \cdot P(HP) + P(R, t|NP) \cdot P(NP)}{P(t, TD) + P(t, HP) + P(t, NP)}$$
$$= \frac{P(R, t|TD) \cdot P(TD) + P(R, t|HP) \cdot P(HP) + P(R, t|NP) \cdot P(NP)}{P(t|TD) \cdot P(TD) + P(t|HP) \cdot P(HP) + P(t|NP) \cdot P(NP)}$$

By applying a training query set, the values of $P(R,t|TD)$, $P(t|TD)$, and $P(TD)$ can be roughly estimated by maximal likelihood estimation (the probabilities for HP and NP can be estimated in a similar way) as follows,

$$P(R,t|TD) \approx \frac{c_r(t,TD)}{n_{td} \cdot K}$$

$$P(t|TD) \approx \frac{c(t,TD)}{n_{td} \cdot K}$$

$$P(TD) \approx \frac{n_{td}}{n}$$

where $n_{td}$ and $n$ are the numbers of TD queries and all queries respectively. We denote $c_r(t,TD)$ as the total number of *relevant* pages in top $K$ with hit type $t$ for all TD queries in the training data and $c(t,TD)$ denotes the number of all pages (relevant or irrelevant) in top $K$ for all TD queries. Please note that only top $K$ query result pages are considered in counting the number of Web pages.

Consequently, the estimated priors for different URL hit types are shown in Table 3.

**Table 3.** Estimated URL hit priors

| Type | Prior |
|---|---|
| Hit-Last | 0.03273 |
| Hit-Second-Last | 0.00382 |
| Hit-Other | 0.00056 |
| Hit-None | 0.00349 |

### 3.2  URL Hit Recognition

The key of estimating and applying URL hit priors is to correctly identify URL hits. However, the way of word usage in forming a URL is very different from word usage in composing a document. Our investigation shows that only about 30% URL hits are recognized by an ordinary word break method (see Section 4.2 for details). Therefore, we use three URL hit recognition methods to detect acronym hits, concatenation hits and fuzzy hits sequentially.

**Step 1: Acronym Hits Recognition**
Similar to [5], this method was used to recognize acronyms. The assumption is that an acronym is often the concatenation of the first character of each word in the full name. For example, "fdic" is the acronym of "Federal Deposit Insurance Corporation" in the following URL:

*http://www.fdic.gov/*

Given an ordered list of query terms $Q = <q_1,...,q_n>$, when eliminating functional words, such as "of", "and" and "the", in $Q$, we get $Q' = <q'_1,...,q'_m>$. The first characters of all words in $Q$ are concatenated as $s$, and the first characters of all words of $Q'$ are concatenated as $s'$. Then $s'$ or $s$ is matched against the URL to see if any URL word is a substring of $s'$ or $s$. If matched, the URL word is mapped to the set of query terms.

### Step 2: Concatenation Hits Recognition

This method aims at recognizing the URL word that is concatenated by the whole or prefix of query terms. For example, the query 185 in known-item task of TREC2003 is "Parent's Guide to Internet Safety" and the target URL is as below:

*http://www.fbi.gov/publications/pguide/pguide.htm*

"pguide" concatenates the first character "p" of "Parent's" and the word "guide".

The concatenated query terms are required to appear continuously and in the same order as in $Q'$ or $Q$. A dynamic programming algorithm is used in this step.

### Step 3: Fuzzy Hits Recognition

In some other URL words, only parts of them match with the whole or parts of query terms. We call such a hit as a fuzzy hit. For example, given a query of "FDA Human Gene Therapy" and a target document URL:

*http://www.fda.gov/cberlinfosheets/genezn.htm*

"gene" is a partial of the URL word of "genezn", which is a fuzzy hit.

Given strings $a$ and $b$, the operation $|a|$ returns the count of characters in the string $a$. The operation of prefix match $a \cap b$ is defined as the longest prefix of $a$ that is also a substring of $b$. Therefore, for each query term $q$ and a URL word $u$, $u$ will be recognized as a fuzzy hit if it satisfies two conditions as follows.

1)  $|q \cap u| > Threshold_1$

2)  $\dfrac{\sum\limits_{q_j \in Q} |q_j \cap u|}{|u|} > Threshod_2$

In our latter experiments, $Threshold_1$ is set to 3 and $Threshold_2$ is set to 0.6.

A more complex way of abbreviating may omit some characters in the middle. For example, "standards" is shortened as "stds". In this paper, we will not address this complex case that occurs less often in our investigations.

### 3.3  Combining URL Hit Priors into Retrieval Models

A classic probability model is the *binary independent retrieval* (BIR) model, which has been introduced by Robertson and Sparck Jones [15]. Please refer to [1] for more details. The ranking function, well-known as BM25, is derived from such a model and has shown its power in TRECs [14]. For our experiments, we choose BM25 as our basic ranking function, in which the retrieval status value (RSV) is computed as follows.

$$RSV(D,Q) = \sum_{i \in Q} \frac{(k_1 + 1)tf_i}{k_1((1-b) + b\dfrac{dl}{avdl}) + tf_i} \log \frac{N - df_i + 0.5}{df_i + 0.5}$$

Where, $i$ denotes a word in the query $Q$, $tf_i$ and $df_i$ are term frequency and document frequency of the word $i$ respectively, $N$ is the total number of documents in the collection, $dl$ is document length, $avdl$ is average document length, and $k_1$, $b$ are parameters.

In our experiments, a document $D$ is represented as all of the texts in the title, body and anchor (i.e. the anchor text of its incoming links), while URL is treated as a special field that is labeled as $U$. We linearly interpolate two scores based on $D$ and $U$ to get the final.

$$S_{combi} = S_D + w \cdot S_U$$

Here, $w$ is combination weight for the URL score.

To make the combination easy, it is necessary to transform the original scores on $D$ and $U$ to the same scale and also to eliminate the query dependent factors. The original score on $D$ is $RSV(D,Q)$, we divide $RSV(D,Q)$ by the query dependent factor below to get $S_D$ as Hu et al did in [8].

$$\sum_{i \in Q} (k_1 + 1) \log \frac{N - df_i + 0.5}{df_i + 0.5}$$

$S_U$ is the URL hit priors that we have estimated in section 3.1. Such a score is a probability and thus needs no transformation.

# 4 Experiments

In this section, we report the results of four kinds of experiments: a) by using the URL hit recognition methods, how many new query term hits can be found; b) the effectiveness of using URL hit priors in the probabilistic model; and c) the performance comparison between using the URL hit recognition methods and not using them.

## 4.1 Experimental Settings

Our experiments are conducted on the Web track datasets of TREC2002, TREC2003 and TREC2004. All of them use the ".GOV" Web page set, which is crawled in 2002. Topic distillation task of TREC2002 is not used because its relevance judgments are not consistent with the guidelines of TREC2003 and TREC2004 [10].

In order to evaluate the performance for different types of queries, we separate queries of the known item finding task of TREC2003 into HP and NP queries, and queries of the mixed query task of TREC2004 into HP, NP and TD queries. Totally seven query sets used. The numbers of queries are 300, 150, 150, 50, 75, 75 and 75 respectively.

In our retrieval experiments, the mean reciprocal rank (MRR) is the main measure for named-page finding and homepage finding tasks, while the mean average precision (MAP) is the main measure for topic distillation tasks.

## 4.2 Experiments on URL Hit Recognition

The experiments on URL hit recognition are conducted on the URLs that are judged as relevant for the TREC data. Two volunteers labeled all the pairs that a query term occurs in a URL word. Then we applied the ordinary method and our 3-step method respectively to automatically recognize URL hits and output the pairs. The ordinary method breaks words in a URL based on delimiters, and then stems the words with the Porter stemmer. Finally precision and recall is calculated. The ordinary method achieves 100% precision but low recall, about 33.2% only. Our 3-step method doubles the recall while the precision is high, about 98.5%.

### 4.3   Experiments on Retrieval Performance

As described in Section 3.3.1, we use computed on all the texts in the title, body and anchor by BM25 formula as the baseline. In our experiments, parameters are trained on TREC2003. The optimized parameters of BM25 formula are $k_1 = 1.1, b = 0.7$. And Figure 1 shows the tuning curves on the training set. The start point at the left is the baseline. The improvements are significant and it is easy to find a common and stable wide range of the optimal parameter for three types of queries.

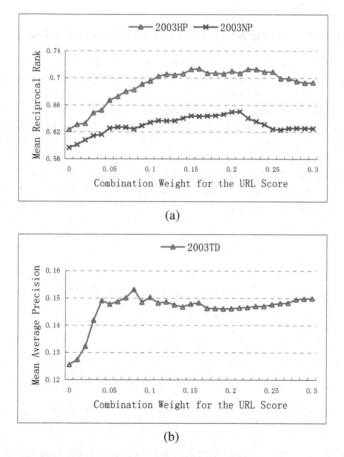

(a)

(b)

**Fig. 1.** Tuning the combination weight on TREC2003 data. (a) shows the results for HP and NP task in terms of MRR and (b) shows the result for TD in terms of MAP.

**Table 4.** Integrating URL Hit Priors in the Probability Model

| Query | $S_D$ | $S_{combi}$ | Improve |
|-------|-------|-------------|---------|
| 2002NP | 0.6294 | 0.6529 | +3.73% |
| 2004NP | 0.557 | 0.5818 | +4.45% |
| 2004HP | 0.5404 | 0.6002 | +11.07% |
| 2004TD | 0.13 | 0.1436 | +10.46% |

On the test set, the URL hit priors improve MRR by about 4% for named page finding queries and by about 11% for homepage finding queries. And it also improves MAP by about 10% for topic distillation queries (See Table 4). Therefore, it is safe to conclude that the improvement with the usage of URL hit priors is stable for different types of queries. In addition, the improvement for NP tasks are less than those for the HP and TD tasks, which may be caused by the relatively rare occurrences of query terms in file names.

### 4.4 Experiments on Using 3-Step Recognition Method vs. Not Using

It is necessary to evaluate how the URL hit recognition affects URL hit priors and the retrieval performance. Therefore, we use the ordinary word break method to recognize URL hits and apply the same approach to estimate the URL hit priors. And we redo the retrieval experiments of combining the priors with the basic content score. Figure 2 shows the results on HP task of TREC2003. There is a big gap between priors based on different recognition methods. The same gaps are also found for other query sets and data sets. We omit the figures due to space limitation. In summary, the URL hits recognition methods are essential for fully taking advantage of the URL hits priors. If not sufficient URL hits are detected, the URL hit priors are less useful for improving retrieval performance.

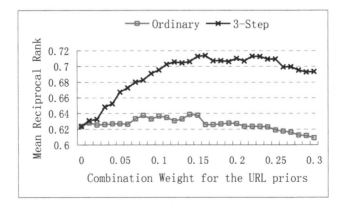

**Fig. 2.** Comparison of priors based on the ordinary word break method and our 3-step method

# 5 Conclusion and Future Work

Through observation and statistics, we found that the location of a query term appearing in a URL is closely related to whether the corresponding document is a good answer for homepage finding, named-page finding and topic distillation queries. However, shortening and concatenating make it difficult to match a URL word with query terms. We proposed three steps together to recognize URL hits. Such method improves the recall of URL hits from 33% to 66% for relevant URLs of TREC data of three years. Based on recognized URL hits, URL hit priors are estimated and integrated into the probability model. Experiments conducted on the TREC datasets show that the URL hit priors can achieve stable improvement across various types of queries.

In the current implementation, URL hits are detected when a query is submitted to the search engine. This requires additional time in processing the query, which could be an issue when the approach is used in a real large-scale search engine. We will leave offline URL hit recognition as our future works. Our current experiments are based on TREC dataset which have little spam. As a next step, more experiments can be done for current real Web data to further test the effectiveness of our approach.

# References

1. R. Baeza-Yates, B. Ribeiro-Neto, Modern Information Retrieval., ACM Press, 1999.
2. J. Berger. Statistical decision theory and Bayesian analysis. New York: Springer-Verlag, 1985.
3. K. Bharat and M. Henzinger. Improved algorithms for topic distillation in a hyperlinked environment. In 21st Annual International ACM SIGIR Conference, pages 104--111, Melbourne, Australia, August 1998.
4. A. Border. A taxonomy of Web search. SIGIR Forum, 36(2), 2002
5. C.-H. Chi, C. Ding and A. Lim. Word segmentation and recognition for web document framework. CIKM'99, 1999
6. N. Craswell, S. Robertson, H. Zaragoza and M. Taylor. Relevance weight for query independent evidence. In Proceedings of ACM SIGIR'05, Salvador, Brazil, 2005
7. D. Hawking, E. Voorhees, N. Craswell, and P. Bailey. Overview of the TREC-8 web track. In The Eighth Text Retrieval Conference (TREC8), NIST, 2001
8. Y. Hu, G. Xin, R. Song, G. Hu, S. Shi, Y. Cao and H. Li. Title extraction from bodies of HTML documents and its application to Web page retrieval. In Proceedings of SIGIR'05, Salvador, Brazil, 2005
9. W. Kraaij, T. Westerveld and D. Hiemstra. The importance of prior probabilities for entry page search. SIGIR'02, 2001
10. U. Lee, Z. Liu and J. Cho. Automatic identification of user goals in Web search. In the Proceedings of the Fourteenth Int'l World Wide Web Conference (WWW2005), Chiba, Japan, 2005
11. G. Marchionini. Interfaces for End-User Information Seeking. Journal of the American Society for Information Science, 43(2):156-163, 1992.
12. P. Ogilvie and J. Callan. Combining structural information and the use of priors in mixed named-page and homepage finding. TREC2003, 2003

13. D.-Y. Ra, E.-K. Park, and J.-S. Jang. Yonsi/etri at TREC-10: Utilizing web document properties. In The Tenth Text Retrieval Conference (TREC-2001), NIST, 2002

14. S. E. Robertson and S. Walker. Okapi/Keenbow at TREC-8. In the Eighth Text REtrieval Conference (TREC 8), 1999, pp. 151-162.

15. S. E. Robertson and K. Sparck Jones. Relevance weighting of search terms. Journal of the American Society of Information Science, Vol. 27, No. May-June, 1976, pp. 129-146.

16. TREC-2004 Web Track Guidelines. http://es.csiro.au/TRECWeb/guidelines_2004.html

17. D. E. Rose and D. Levinson. Understanding user goals in Web search. In Proceedings of the Thirteenth Int'l World Wide Web Conference (WWW2004), New York, USA, 2004

18. T. Qin, T.-Y. Liu, X.-D. Zhang, Z. Chen and W.-Y. Ma. A study on relevance propagation for Web search. In Proceedings of the 28th Annual International ACM SIGIR Conference on Research and Development in Information Retrieval (SIGIR 2005), Salvador, Brazil, 2005

19. Universal Resource Identifiers. http://www.w3.org/Addressing/URL/URI_Overview.html

20. J.-R. Wen, R. Song, D. Cai, K. Zhu, S. Yu, S. Ye and W.-Y. Ma, Microsoft Research Asia at the Web Track of TREC 2003. In the Twelfth Text Retrieval Conference, 2003

21. T. Westerveld, W. Kraaij, and D. Hiemstra. Retrieving web pages using content, links, URLs and anchors. TREC2001, 2001

# A Study of Blog Search

Gilad Mishne and Maarten de Rijke

ISLA, University of Amsterdam,
Kruislaan 403, 1098 SJ Amsterdam, The Netherlands
{gilad, mdr}@science.uva.nl

**Abstract.** We present an analysis of a large blog search engine query log, exploring a number of angles such as query intent, query topics, and user sessions. Our results show that blog searches have different intents than general web searches, suggesting that the primary targets of blog searchers are tracking references to named entities, and locating blogs by theme. In terms of interest areas, blog searchers are, on average, more engaged in technology, entertainment, and politics than web searchers, with a particular interest in current events. The user behavior observed is similar to that in general web search: short sessions with an interest in the first few results only.

## 1 Introduction

The rise on the Internet of blogging—the publication of journal-like web page logs, or blogs—has created a highly dynamic and tightly interwoven subset of the World Wide Web [10]. The blogspace (the collection of blogs and all their links) is giving rise to a large body of research, both concerning *content* (e.g., Can we process blogs automatically and find consumer complaints and breaking reports about vulnerabilities of products?) and *structure* (e.g., What is the dynamics of the blogspace?). A variety of dedicated workshops bear witness to this burst of research activity around blogs; see e.g., [20].

In this paper we focus on another aspect of the blogspace: searching blogs. The exponential rise in the number of blogs from thousands in the late 1990s to tens of millions in 2005 [3, 18, 19] has created a need for effective access and retrieval services. Today, there is a broad range of search and discovery tools for blogs, offered by a variety of players; some focus exclusively on blog access (e.g., Blogdigger [2], Blogpulse [3], and Technorati [18]), while web search engines such as Google, Yahoo! and AskJeeves offer specialized blog services.

The development of specialized retrieval technology aimed at the distinct features of the blogspace is still in its early stages. We address a question whose answer should help inform these efforts: How does blog search differ from general web search? To this end we present an analysis of a blog search engine query log. We study the intent of blog searches, find out what the user behavior of blog searchers is, and determine the profile of blog searchers in terms of query types.

In the next section we briefly survey related work that guided us in our study. In Section 3 we describe the data used for our analysis and provide basic descriptive statistics about it. In Section 4 we analyze the queries in terms of user

M. Lalmas et al. (Eds.): ECIR 2006, LNCS 3936, pp. 289–301, 2006.
© Springer-Verlag Berlin Heidelberg 2006

intent. Then, in Section 5 we classsify queries by category, and Section 6 is devoted to an analysis of the sessions in our data. Section 7 wraps up the paper with conclusions, discussions, and future work.

## 2   Related Work

At the time of writing, no published work exists on blog search engine logs. However, work on search engine log analysis is plentiful: a recent survey paper describes a large body of related work in this area published during the last 10 years [5]. Our work was particularly inspired by some of this work. Most notably, work by Broder [4] on classifying search requests of web users using the (then popular) AltaVista search engine, as well as the follow-up work by Rose and Levinson [13] with Yahoo! data, inspired our attempts at classifying the hidden intents behind blog searches.

In terms of statistical analysis, our work is influenced by one of the first large-scale studies of search logs available to the public, performed by Silverstein et al. [16], and the numerous analyses published by Jansen, Spink et al., which targeted various angles of search engine usage (e.g., [4, 7, 8]), analyzing data not accessible to the majority of the research community.

Finally, our query categorization work was influenced by work done by Pu and Chuang [12], and by Beitzel et al. [1]. Some of the query categorization methods used for the 2005 KDD Cup [9] (which targeted query classification) are similar to our categorization approach, which was developed in parallel.

## 3   Dataset

Our data consists of the full search log of Blogdigger.com for the month of May 2005. Blogdigger.com is a search engine for blogs and syndicated content feeds (such as RSS and ATOM feeds) that has been active since 2003, being one of the first fully-operational blog search engines. Recently, as major web search engines introduced their capabilities for blog search, it is gradually becoming a second-tier engine. Nevertheless, Blogdigger.com provides some unique services such as local-based search and media search, which attract a relatively large number of users to it. Our log contains both queries sent to Blogdigger's textual search engine and queries sent to its media search engine—a service for searching blog posts (and additional syndicated content) containing multimedia files or links.

Blogdigger.com—like other major blog search engines—serves both ad-hoc queries and filtering queries. Ad-hoc queries originate from visitors to the search engine's web site, typing in search terms and viewing the result pages, in a similar manner to the typical access to web search engines. A user who is interested in continuous updates about the results of a specific query can subscribe to its results: in practice, this means she is adding a request for a machine-readable version of the query results to a syndicated content aggregator (e.g., an RSS reader) she is running. The query results will then be periodically polled; each of these polls is registered as a filtering query in the search log.

**Table 1.** Search log size and breakdown

|  | All queries | Unique queries |
| --- | --- | --- |
| Number of queries | 1,245,903 | 116,299 |
| Filtering queries | 1,011,962 (81%) | 34,411 (30%) |
| Ad-hoc queries | 233,941 (19%) | 81,888 (70%) |
| Text queries | 1,016,697 (82%) | 50,844 (44%) |
| Media queries | 229,206 (18%) | 65,455 (56%) |
| Link queries | 2,967 (<1%) | 562 (<1%) |
| Mean terms/filtering query | 1.96 | 1.98 |
| Mean terms/ad-hoc query | 2.44 | 2.71 |

Table 1 contains statistics about our log file. Due to the large percentage of duplicates typical of query logs, we provide statistics separately for all queries and for the set of unique queries in the log (i.e., exact repetitions removed). While filtering queries make up the bulk of all queries, they constitute a relatively small amount of unique terms, and the majority of unique queries originate from ad-hoc sessions. The mean terms/query number for (all) ad-hoc queries is comparable to the mean terms/query numbers reported in the literature for general web search (2.35 [16], 2.21 [6], 2.4–2.6 [17], and 2.4 [7]); while the mean terms/query number for filtering queries appears somewhat smaller (1.96), a closer examination reveals that this difference is caused to a large extent by two specific clients; excluding these outliers, the mean terms/query for filtering queries is 2.5, similar to that of ad-hoc ones.[1]

## 4   Types of Information Needs

Next, we analyze the information needs in the blogspace, partitioning the queries into two broad classes.

Following Broder's influential work [4], queries submitted to web search engines are generally grouped into three classes: *informational* (find information about a topic), *navigational* (find a specific web site), and *transactional* (perform some web-mediated activity). This may not be an appropriate classification for queries submitted to blog search engines—clearly, transactional queries are not a natural category for blog search, and a user searching for a particular site, or even a particular blog (i.e., submitting a navigational query) would not necessarily use a blog search engine, but rather a general-purpose web engine. Our working hypothesis, then, is that the majority of blog queries are *informational* in nature, and a scan of the search log confirms this.

Given this assumption, is it possible to identify different types of informational queries submitted to a blog search service? Ideally, this would be done using a user survey—in a manner similar to the one performed by Broder [4]. Unfortunately, we only have retrospective access to the submitted queries, with

---

[1] The two clients issued large amounts of queries in fixed, short intervals; the queries appear to have been taken from a dictionary in alphabetical order and are all single words, pushing down the mean number.

no possibility of conducting such a survey. However, Broder's work shows a fairly good correlation between the results of his survey and manual classification of a subset of the queries, leading us to assume that an analysis of the query types based on an examination of the queries in our data is worthwhile.

First, we examined a random set of 1000 queries, half of which were ad-hoc queries and half filtering ones, so as to discover likely query types. We observed that the majority of the queries—52% of the ad-hoc ones and 78% of the filtering ones—were named entities: names of people, products, companies, and so on. Of these, most belonged to two types: either very well-known names ("Bush", "Microsoft", "Jon Stewart"), or almost-unheard-of names, mostly names of individuals and companies.[2] An additional popular category of named entities was location names, mostly American cities. Of the non-named-entity queries, most queries—25% of the ad hoc queries and 18% of the filtering ones—consisted of high-level concepts or topics, such as "stock trading", "linguists", "humor", "gay rights", "islam" and so on; the filtering queries of this type were mostly technology-related. The remainder of the queries consisted of adult-oriented queries (almost exclusively ad-hoc queries), URL queries, and other queries for which we could not find specific characteristics.

Next, we examined the 400 most common queries (again, half ad-hoc and half filtering), to find out whether the query types there differ from those found in "the long tail." While the types remained similar, we witnessed a different distribution: 45% of the ad-hoc queries and 66% of the filtering queries were named entities; concepts and technologies consisted of an additional 30% of top ad-hoc queries and 28% of filtering ones. Adult-oriented ad-hoc queries were substantially more common in top ad-hoc queries than in the random set.

Consequently, our hypothesis regarding the intents of blog searchers divides the searches into two broad categories:

– **Context Queries:** The purpose of these queries is to locate contexts in which a certain name appears in the blogspace: what bloggers say about it. Most of the named entity queries have this intent; the well-known names might be entities in which the searcher has an ongoing interest (such as politicians) or products she is researching, whereas the lesser-known names are typically vanity searches, or searches for contexts of entities which constitute part of the searcher's closer environment (an employer, organization in which the searcher is a member, etc).
– **Concept Queries:** With these queries the searcher attempts to locate blogs or blog posts which deal with one of the searcher's interest areas, or with a geographic area that is of particular interest to the searcher (such as blogs authored by people from his home town). Typical queries of this type are the various high-level concepts mentioned earlier, as well as location names.[3]

---

[2] The prevalence of the named entity was established using Google hit counts: well-known names typically had millions of hits; unknown names had few if any.

[3] These queries are somewhat similar to distillation queries as defined by TREC, with target results being blogs rather than websites.

**Table 2.** Query classes: the top 400 queries vs. a random sample of 1000 queries

| | Top queries | | Random queries | |
| Class | Ad-hoc | Filtering | Ad-hoc | Filtering |
|---|---|---|---|---|
| *Context* | 39% | 60% | 47% | 73% |
| *Concept* | 36% | 34% | 30% | 23% |
| *Other* | 25% | 6% | 23% | 4% |

Table 2 shows a breakdown of both the random set and the top-query set according to query type, for ad-hoc and filtering queries separately. For this breakdown, named-entity queries (except location names) were considered as context queries; high-level areas of interest and location names were considered concept queries.

As an aside, while examining the top queries, we observed an interesting phenomenon which we did not witness in the random set: many of the queries were related to events which were "in the news" at the time of the log. This supports the assumption that blogs are conceived as a source of information and commentry about current events [11]. To quantify the number of news-related queries, we used two independent methods. First, a human decided, for each query, whether it was news-related. This was done by studying the terms in the query, and attempting to locate events related to it that happened during May 2005, the period covered by the log. The second method was an automated one: we obtained daily word frequencies of the terms appearing in the query as reported by Technorati, for the entire year of 2005. Terms which had substantial peaks in the daily frequency counts during May 2005 were considered related to news; sample daily frequencies over the entire year of 2005 are shown in Figure 1. The agreement between our two methods (kappa) was 0.72.

In total, we found that 20% of the top ad-hoc queries and 15% of the top filtering ones are news-related; in the random set, news-related queries were substantially less frequent, amounting to 6–7% of both ad-hoc and filtering queries.

In sum, blog searches have different intents than typical web searches, suggesting that the primary targets of blog searchers are tracking references to named

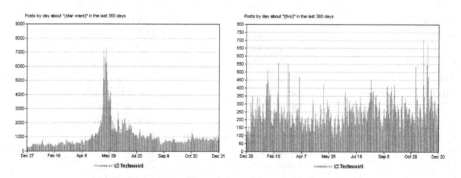

**Fig. 1.** Sample daily frequency counts in 2005. (Left): a news-related query ("Star Wars"). (Right): a non-news-related query ("Tivo").

entities and identifying blogs or posts which focus on a certain concept; in addition, searches related to current events are substantially more common in blog searches than in web searches, in particular in the popular queries.

# 5  Popular Queries and Query Categories

Next, we provide a brief overview of the top queries posted, describe a categorization method, and apply this method to the queries in the log, trying to construct the profile of topics blog searchers are interested in.

Simply counting the number of times a query appears in our log yields misleading results regarding the most popular queries. This is due to the fact that the majority of the search requests are automated, and are repeated at regular intervals; agents issuing these queries with high refresh rates will create a bias in the query counts. As a result, we measure the popularity of a query not according to the number of occurrences, but according to the number of different users submitting it. As a key identifying a user we use a combination of the IP address and the user agent string (more details on user identification are given in Section 6).

The most popular queries in the log are shown in Table 3, columns 1 and 2, separately for ad-hoc and filtering queries.

**Table 3.** Top 20 queries. (Left): Ad-hoc blog queries. (Center): Filtering blog queries. (Right): Web queries.

| Ad-hoc | Filtering | Web |
|---|---|---|
| filibuster | Lotus Notes | American Idol |
| Blagojevich | Daily Show | Google |
| sex | microcontent | Yahoo |
| porn | information architecture | eBay |
| blogdigger | MP3 | Star Wars |
| Madagascar | Streaming | Mapquest |
| RSS | Google | Hotmail |
| adult | Wayne Madsen | Valentine's day |
| Google | Tom Feeney | NASCAR |
| nude | Clint Curtis | hybrid cars |
| MP3 | digital camera | MP3 players |
| Los Angeles | DMOZ | NFL |
| test | desktop search | dictionary |
| China | manga | Paris Hilton |
| 3G | RSS | Michael Jackson |
| Star Wars | Abramoff | Hillary Clinton |
| IBM | knowledge management | heartburn |
| blog | government | Lohan |
| music | restaurant | flowers |
| Bush | information management | Xbox 360 |

## 5.1   Comparison to Web Queries

To compare the popular queries submitted to blog search engines with those sent to general web search engines, we obtained a set of 3.5M queries submitted to Dogpile/Metacrawler, a second-tier general web search engine,[4] during May 2005—the same timespan as our blog search log. The top 20 queries from this source are listed in Table 3, column 3.

Some differences between the query lists are clear: the web queries contain many large web sites (Yahoo!, eBay, Hotmail, and so on), perhaps because for some users, the distinction between the search input box and the browser's address bar is unclear. Additionaly, the top blog queries seem to contain a somewhat higher percentage of political and technology-related queries; this strengthens our findings in Section 5.2 regarding the top interests of bloggers.

Other differences between blog queries and web queries require examining more than a small number of top queries. Comparing the most popular 400 queries from both sources, we observed a substantially higher rate of named-entity queries within blog queries than in web queries. As mentioned in Section 4, 45% of ad-hoc blog queries and 66% of the filtering queries were named entities; in comparison, only 33% of the top 400 web queries were named entities, many of which were website names. This suggests that blog searchers—especially those registering filtering queries—are more interested in references to people, products, organizations or locations than web searchers.

As noted earlier, we found a relatively large amount of new-related queries among top blog queries; this type of queries proved to be fairly uncommon in general web search engines, accounting for less than 8% of the top 400 queries, and less than 2% of 400 random ones.

An additional difference between the query lists is the presence of very detailed information needs (such as factoid questions) in the web query log: such queries were not found among the blog queries. Finally, as is the case with web searches, adult-oriented queries are an important area of interest for ad-hoc blog searchers; however, these are nearly non-existent in filtering queries.

## 5.2   Query Categories

Current approaches to automatic categorization of queries from a search log are based on pre-defining a list of topically categorized terms, which are then matched against queries from the log; the construction of this list is done manually [1] or semi-automatically [12]. While this approach achieves high accuracy, it tends to achieve very low coverage, e.g., 8% of unique queries for the semi-automatic method, and 13% for the manual one.

We take a different approach to query categorization, substantially increasing the coverage but (in our experience) sustaining high accuracy levels: our approach relies on external "categorizers" with access to large amounts of data. We submit every unique query in our corpus as a search request to two

---

[4] This is a metasearch engine, submitting queries to a number of other engines such as Google and Yahoo! and aggregating the results.

category-based web search services: Yahoo! Directory (`http://dir.yahoo.com`) as well as Froogle (`http://froogle.google.com`). The former is a manually-categorized collection of web pages, including a search service for these web pages; the latter is an online sales search service. We use the category of the top page retrieved by the Yahoo! Directory as the "Yahoo! Category" for that query, and the top shopping category offered by Froogle as its "Froogle Category;" while the Yahoo! Category is a topical category in the traditional sense, the Froogle Category is a consumer-related one, possibly answering the question "if there is potential commercial value in the query, what domain does it belong to?" In spirit, this is similar to the usage of the Open Directory Project to classify web pages by category (e.g., in [15]), except that we classify terms, not URLs (similar methods for query classification have been developed in parallel for the KDD 2005 Cup [14]).

The coverage achieved with this method is fairly high: in total, out of 43,601 unique, non-media queries that were sent to Yahoo! and Froogle, 24,113 (55%) were categorized by Yahoo! and 29,727 (68%) by Froogle. Some queries were not categorized due to excessive length, non-standard encodings, and other technical issues, so the coverage over common queries is even higher. An examination of the resulting categories shows high accuracy, even for queries which are very hard to classify with traditional methods, using the query words only. Table 4 lists some examples of queries along with their corresponding categories.

**Table 4.** Example queries and categories

| |
|---|
| *Query*: **24** |
| *Yahoo! category*: /Entertainment/Television Shows/Action and Adventure/24 |
| *Froogle category*: /Books, Music and Video/Video/Action and Adventure |
| *Query*: **Atkins** |
| *Yahoo! category*: /Business and Economy/Shopping and Services/Health/Weight Loss/Diets and Programs/Low Carbohydrate Diets/Atkins Nutritional Approach |
| *Froogle category*: /Food and Gourmet/Food/Snack Foods |
| *Query*: **Evolution debate** |
| *Yahoo! category*: /Society and Culture/Religion and Spirituality/Science and Religion/Creation vs. Evolution/Intelligent Design |
| *Froogle category*: /Books, Music and Video/Books/Social Sciences |
| *Query*: **Vioxx** |
| *Yahoo! category*: /Health/Pharmacy/Drugs and Medications/Specific Drugs and Medications/Vioxx, Rofecoxib |
| *Froogle category*: /Health and Personal Care/Over-the-Counter Medicine |

Figure 2(Left) shows a breakdown of the top Yahoo! categories for ad-hoc and filtering queries. Taking into account that "Regional" queries often refer to news-related events, we witness again that current events are a major source of interest for blog searchers. A similar breakdown of the top Froogle categories is given in Figure 2(Right), indicating that most queries which can be related to products deal with intellectual property, such as movies and books. An added benefit of the Yahoo! and Froogle categories is their hierarchical nature: this enables us to not only examine the most frequent category, but also to evaluate the breakdown of subcategories within a given category. For space reasons, we do not include an analysis of these subcategories here, and plan to do so in future work.

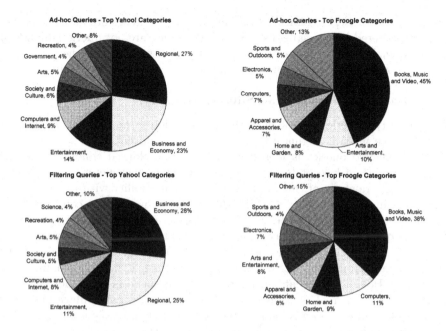

**Fig. 2.** (Left): Top Yahoo! categories. (Right): Top Froogle categories.

As is the case for general web searches, adult-oriented searches are the top category for commercial queries, followed by technology-related queries and financial issues. In the entertainment domain, music clearly dominates the scene.

We conclude that in terms of interest areas, blog searchers are more engaged in technology and politics than web searchers, with a noticeable interest in named entities: names of people, brands, companies, and so on.

## 6   Session Analysis

Next we analyze the query sessions in the log, examining issues such as the amount of queries submitted in a session and the number of viewed results.

Our log does not contain full session information: we do not know how long the user spent examining the results, and which result links she followed. However, since some identification of the user is given for each query in the log in the form of IP address and user agent string, it is possible to group the queries by sessions and to perform a basic analysis of these.

Before describing our approach to session recovery and discussing characteristics of the extracted sessions it is important to note the difference between sessions that contain ad-hoc searches and sessions that contain filtering searches. The former are similar to standard web search sessions, and consist of different queries that a user submitted to the search engine during her visit. These different queries include, in many cases, reformulations of a query, or highly-related terms which indicate the user is trying to collect more information regarding her interest. In contrast, "sessions" containing filtering searches are actually sets of queries registered by the same user: in practice, they are not queries submitted during a single visit to the search engine, but a list of queries the same user expressed ongoing interest in, possibly added over a long period of time.

## 6.1    Recovering Sessions and Subscription Sets

We assume two queries to belong to the same session if the following conditions hold: (1) The queries originate from the same IP address; (2) The user agent string of the two queries is identical, and (3) The elapsed time between the queries is less than $k$ seconds, where $k$ is a predefined parameter.

The main drawback of this method is its incompatibility with proxy servers: queries originating from the same IP address do not necessarily come from the same user: they can also be sent by different users using the same proxy server; this is a common scenario in certain environments, such as companies with a single internet gateway. While the usage of the user agent string reduces the chance of mistaking different users for the same one, it does not eliminate it completely. Having said that, anecdotal evidence suggests that the recovered sessions are in fact "real" sessions: the conceptual and lexical similarity between queries in the same session is high for the vast majority of sessions we examined. Additional evidence for the relative robustness of this method can be seen in the fact that, when used on the set of all queries, it produces less than 0.5% "mixed sessions" – sessions containing both ad-hoc and filtering queries, which are unlikely to be a real session.

We performed our analyses independently for ad-hoc and filtering queries; to avoid confusion, we use the term "sessions" only for ad-hoc sessions—which are indeed sessions in the traditional sense; for filtering sessions, we use the term "subscription sets" (which denotes lists of filtering queries done by the same user within a short timeframe).

## 6.2    Sessions and Subscription Sets

We experimented with various values of $k$; manual examination of the recovered sessions suggests that values between 10 and 30 seconds yield the most reliable sessions for ad-hoc queries. For filtering queries, the session time is much shorter, in-line with intuition (since the queries are automated): reliable sessions are found with $k$ values of 2–5 seconds. The thresholds were set to 20 seconds for sessions and 5 seconds for subscription sets; this produces 148,361 sessions and 650,657 subscription sets.

Many sessions and subscription sets contain simple reformulations such as different uses of query operators; others are composed of related terms, and yet others consist of seemingly unrelated queries, matching different interests of the same user. Table 5 provides example sessions and subscription sets, and Table 6(Top) details statistics about the session length (the number of unique queries per session), comparing our findings to those for general web searches [16].

The short session length is similar to the one observed in web search engines, e.g., in [16]. While subscription sets also exhibit a short length on average, the

**Table 5.** Example sessions and subscription sets; queries belonging to the same session or subscription set are separated by semicolons

| Type | Queries |
|---|---|
| Session | autoantibodies ; autoantibodies histamine ; histamine |
| Session | firmware dwl 2000 ap+ ; dwl 2000 ap+ ; dwl-2000 ap+ |
| Subscription set | "XML Tag Monitor Report" ; "XML Search Selector" |
| Subscription set | imap ; imap gmail ; Thunderbird IMAP ; imap labels ; rss email ; thunderbird label ; imap soap |

**Table 6.** (Top): Session and subscription set lengths (number of unique queries). (Bottom): Result page views for ad-hoc queries, per session.

| | | Blog queries | | Web queries |
|---|---|---|---|---|
| | | Sessions | Subscriptions | Sessions [16] |
| **Length** | Mean | 1.45 | 1.53 | 2.02 |
| | Length 1 | 70.2% | 75.8% | 77.6% |
| | Length 2 | 20.9% | 13.7% | 13.5% |
| | Length $\geq$3 | 8.8% | 10.4% | 9.9% |
| **Page views** | Mean | 1.09 | N/A | 1.39 |
| | 1 result page | 94.9% | N/A | 85.2% |
| | 2 result pages | 3.4% | N/A | 7.5% |
| | 3 or more pages | 1.7% | N/A | 7.3% |

actual lengths of the sets vary much more than those of sessions—as can be seen from the much higher variance (5.10 for subscriptions vs. 0.87 for sessions). Users may subscribe to any amount of queries, and, in our data, some users registered as much as 20 queries.

For ad-hoc queries, an additional interesting aspect is the number of result pages the user chooses to view (each containing up to 10 matches). As with web searches, we find that the vast majority of users view only the first result page: see the detailed breakdown in Table 6(Bottom), again comparing our findings to those presented for general web searches in [16]. While there is a statistically significant difference between the two samples (blog sessions vs web sessions), the bottom line is similar: most users do not look beyond the first set of results.[5]

In sum, while we found that query types in the blogspace differ from the types of queries submitted to general web search engines, we discovered a very similar user behavior for issuing queries and viewing their results.

## 7   Conclusions

We presented a study of a large blog search engine log, aimed at analyzing the type of queries issued by users in this domain, the user behavior in terms of

---

[5] Also, the number of page views for web searches is constantly decreasing, as search engine technology is improving and more relevant documents appear in the first few results.

amount of queries and page views, and the categories of the queries. The query log covers an entire month, and contains both ad-hoc and filtering queries.

Our main finding in terms of query types is that blog searches fall into two broad categories—context queries, attempting to track the references to various named entities within the blogspace, and concept queries, aimed at locating blogs and blog posts which focus on a given concept or topic. The distribution of these types differs between ad-hoc and filtering queries, with the filtering ones being more context-oriented. In addition, we found that blog searches tend to focus on current events more than web searches.

As to user behavior, the behavior observed is similar to that in general web search engines: users are typically interested only in the first few results returned, and usually issue a very small number of queries in every session.

Finally, using external resources to categorize the queries, we uncovered a blog searcher profile which is substantially more concentrated on news (particularly politics), entertainment, and technology than the average web searcher. Hence, it may be useful for blog search engines to identify and exploit named entities (and parts of them), especially in the domains mentioned above.

**Acknowledgments.** We thank Blogdigger.com, and especially Greg Gershman and Michael Miller for generously providing the data set without which this research could not have been conducted. Many thanks also to our anonymous reviewers for useful suggestions. This work was supported by the Netherlands Organization for Scientific Research (NWO) under project number 220-80-001.

# References

[1] S. M. Beitzel, E. C. Jensen, A. Chowdhury, D. Grossman, and O. Frieder. Hourly analysis of a very large topically categorized web query log. In *Proceedings SIGIR '04*, pages 321–328, New York, NY, USA, 2004. ACM Press.

[2] Blogdigger, 2005. Search engine for RSS and blogs. URL: http://blogdigger/, accessed January 2006.

[3] Blogpulse, 2005. Automated trend discovery system for blogs. URL: http://blogpulse.com/, accessed January 2006.

[4] A. Broder. A taxonomy of web search. *SIGIR Forum*, 36(2):3–10, 2002.

[5] F. M. Facca and P. L. Lanzi. Mining interesting knowledge from weblogs: a survey. *Data Knowl. Eng.*, 53(3):225–241, 2005.

[6] B. Jansen and U. Pooch. Web user studies: a review and framework for future work. *J. American Society of Science and Technology*, 52(3):235–246, 2001.

[7] B. Jansen and A. Spink. An analysis of Web searching by European AlltheWeb.com users. *Inf. Process. Manag.*, 41(2):361–381, 2005.

[8] B. J. Jansen, A. Spink, and T. Saracevic. Real life, real users, and real needs: a study and analysis of user queries on the web. *Inf. Process. Manag.*, 36(2): 207–227, 2000.

[9] KDD Cup, 2005. URL: http://kdd05.lac.uic.edu/kddcup.html, accessed January 2006.

[10] R. Kumar, J. Novak, P. Raghavan, and A. Tomkins. On the bursty evolution of blogspace. In *WWW '03: Proceedings of the 12th international conference on World Wide Web*, pages 568–576, New York, NY, USA, 2003. ACM Press.

[11]  M. Ludtke, editor. *NIEMAN REPORTS: Journalist's Trade - Weblogs and Journalism*, volume 57,3. Bob Giles, 2003.

[12]  H. T. Pu and S. L. Chuang. Auto-categorization of search terms toward understanding web users' information needs. In *ICADL 2000: Intern. Conference on Asian Digital Libraries*, 2000.

[13]  D. E. Rose and D. Levinson. Understanding user goals in web search. In *Proceedings WWW '04*, pages 13–19, New York, NY, USA, 2004. ACM Press.

[14]  D. Shen, R. Pan, J.-T. Sun, J. J. Pan, K. Wu, J. Yin, and Q. Yang. Q2c@ust: Our winning solution to query classification in kdd cup 2005. *SIGKDD Exploration*, 2006.

[15]  X. Shen, S. Dumais, and E. Horvitz. Analysis of topic dynamics in web search. In *WWW '05: Proceedings of the 14th intern. conf. on World Wide Web*, 2005.

[16]  C. Silverstein, H. Marais, M. Henzinger, and M. Moricz. Analysis of a very large web search engine query log. *SIGIR Forum*, 33(1):6–12, 1999.

[17]  A. Spink, B. Jansen, D. Wolfram, and T. Saracevic. From e-sex to e-commerce: Web search changes. *IEEE Computer*, 35(3):107–111, 2002.

[18]  Technorati, 2005. Blog tracking service. URL: `http://technorati.com/`, accessed January 2006.

[19]  Technorati, 2005. State of the Blogosphere according to Technorati. URL: `http://www.sifry.com/alerts/archives/000298.html/`, accessed January 2006.

[20]  Weblogging Ecosystem, 2005. WWW 2005 2nd Annual Workshop on the Weblogging Ecosystem: Aggregation, Analysis and Dynamics. URL: `http://www.blogpulse.com/www2005-workshop.html`, accessed January 2006.

# A Comparative Study of the Effectiveness of Search Result Presentation on the Web

Hideo Joho and Joemon M. Jose

Department of Computing Science, University of Glasgow,
17 Lilybank Gardens, Glasgow, G12 8QQ, UK
{hideo, jj}@dcs.gla.ac.uk

**Abstract.** Presentation of search results in Web-based information retrieval (IR) systems has been dominated by a textual form of information such as the title, snippet, URL, and/or file type of retrieved documents. On the other hand, document's visual aspects such as the layout, colour scheme, or presence of images have been studied in a limited context with regard to their effectiveness of search result presentation. This paper presents a comparative evaluation of textual and visual forms of document summaries as the *additional* document surrogate in the search result presentation. In our study, a sentence-based summarisation technique was used to create a textual document summary, and the thumbnail image of web pages was used to represent a visual summary. The experimental results suggest that both have the cases where the additional elements contributed to a positive effect not only in users' relevance assessment but also in query re/formulation. The results also suggest that the two forms of document summary are likely to have different contexts to facilitate user's search experience. Therefore, our study calls for further research on adaptive models of IR systems to make use of their advantages in appropriate contexts.

## 1 Introduction

The Internet has transformed into a main source of information for many and as a consequence web search engines have become an essential tool in our day to day life. Web search engines such as Google, Yahoo!, and MSN Search are processing millions of queries a day. The interaction paradigm of such engines follows more or less the same style assuming that this is the best for all users. However, recent user behaviour studies on commercial search engines challenge such assumptions [1]. In this paper, we conduct a comparative evaluative study assessing the effectiveness of various forms web search interfaces.

Most web search engines operate on a general principle of retrieval. Users' provide a set of query terms as a representative of their underlying information need. In response systems, after comparing the query to the documents in the collection, provide a list of potential documents which might contain useful information to satisfy the users' information need [2].

However, a number of issues are overlooked in such a simplistic view. The first one is that formulating a good query is proved to be cognitively challenging task for users [3]. Often queries are approximations of their underlying need and hence the

M. Lalmas et al. (Eds.): ECIR 2006, LNCS 3936, pp. 302–313, 2006.
© Springer-Verlag Berlin Heidelberg 2006

whole information seeking process is iterative in nature [4]. The second issue is in interpreting and assessing the relevance of documents in the returned list [5]. It has been shown that users of web search engines are reluctant to examine a large number of individual documents or even past the first page of the result list [1]. The users decision to view a document or not depend on the information in the document surrogates such as title, URLs and abstracts (often snippets extracted form the documents). The third issue is in the matching of the submitted query with the documents (or their indexes) with the intention of selecting a set of documents that contain information on the query. The first two issues make the development of information seeking interfaces a non-trivial task.

The major thrust of this paper is related to the first two issues. That is pertaining to user interaction which includes issues related to query formulation and judging the usefulness of each document in the list. In this paper we propose and evaluate a number of interfaces which facilitate the relevance (usefulness) judgement issues differently. The results of the experiments demonstrate the effectiveness of our proposed interfaces and demonstrate the inadequacy of current interfaces.

## 2 Background and Motivation

The main purpose of search engines is to help people find information that is useful or relevant to completing a task. Search interfaces are the means through which users interact with search systems and control all aspects of their search.

The results from information seeking studies point to the fact that users look for information to complete a task. From a cognitive perspective, it has been termed that there is a gap in users' knowledge and the information is needed to fill this gap [3]. Finding relevant information may require running several queries, making judgments on the usefulness of documents returned, and reading many documents. Considering the importance of this task to many users, it is imperative to design interfaces that maximize the amount of information users can obtain during a search.

Submitted user queries are often an approximation of his/her underlying information need [6]. Since the system returns documents based on such queries, the usefulness of such documents are not certain. The documents in the result list might be not relevant, or partially relevant. Often documents contain partial information or redundant information from a previously seen document. In order to conduct an effective search it is imperative that users be able to make reasonably correct judgements about the documents in the result list.

Novel result visualisation techniques were proposed to address this problem [5]. Another techniques tried out are various summarisation techniques [7]. It has shown that the use of query-based summarisation techniques in improving the search effectiveness. Recently, new approaches to web page result presentation were tried. Most of these systems present the user with an unfamiliar, graphical interface that imposes an increased cognitive burden on the user or consider documents as finest level of granularity for result presentation [8].

Users' assessment of relevance of documents in the result list is based on the surrogates displayed (e.g., title, URL and snippets). It has been shown that such information is inadequate to provide effective search sessions [9]. For example, the quality of title information can vary mainly because of the casual approach to generating a title at the time of web-page creation. The document snippets shown by many web search engines are fragments extracted from the whole document. Often such snippets are incomplete sentences extracted from the documents and as such inadequate to aid effective relevance judgements. The role of query-based sentences in assisting on making proper relevance assessments has been reported [9].

An aspect that affects information seeking process is the task at hand. For some tasks, it is important to know the genre of document. Often users may search for same information again and again. In this case, a thumbnail of the document would aid in judging the usefulness of the document [10].

In this work, we device three alternative forms of search result presentations. We use Google result presentation as a baseline. As additional surrogates we use query-based document summary called top ranking sentences, or TRS [11] and thumbnails of documents retrieved. While the previous study used the TRS as a replacement of Google snippet, in our interface, the TRS was used as additional information to the snippet. In addition, we make use of document thumbnails as a surrogate. We believe it is useful in judging the relevance and assessing the genre of a document. We augment information on the Google interface with thumbnails of documents. In the following session we will introduce these interfaces briefly.

The purpose of the experiment is to find the effectiveness of these interfaces in web information seeking tasks. We designed an experiment with real users, real tasks on the live Internet.

## 3    Interfaces for Search Result Presentation

We augment web search system Google with 3 new interfaces. Our interfaces collect user queries and forward to the Google search system using Google API[1]. The result list from Google collected and processed. Information needed for new interfaces were created at this time. Like in web search result pages, user can peruse ten document records at a time. After this, they can either reformulate the query or peruse the next ten records.

As a baseline we use the Google interface. Three layouts of search results presentation were designed and compared to the baseline layout. All layouts were designed to show ten records per page as Google's default setting did. The rest of this section will present the layouts used in our experiment.

**Layout 1: Baseline** – The baseline layout was designed to provide an almost identical interface to the search result of Google. For each record, it had a title, snippet, URL, size, and the hyperlinks of cached page and similar page.

**Layout 2: Baseline + TRS** – The second layout integrated up to three top ranking sentences (TRS) into the baseline layout. The sentences were inserted below the snippet as a list, and background was highlighted to clarify the distinction between the TRS and snippet. The query terms were highlighted in bold in the same manner as it would have been in the title and snippet. There was some run-time overhead in generating TRS for retrieved documents. In order to minimise the difference of response

---

[1] http://www.google.com/apis/

time among the layouts, TRS was always created when a new query was submitted to the interface, but it was only displayed in Layout 2 and 4.

**Layout 3: Baseline + Thumbnail** – The third layout integrated a thumbnail image of the web page screenshot into the baseline layout. The thumbnails were fetched from the Alexia's thumbnail archive[2]. The thumbnail was placed on the left side of the other document surrogates, and it was linked to the URL of the pages. The size of thumbnails was 112 (width) and 82 (height) pixels which was perhaps too small to read the texts, but we considered that it should be large enough to grasp the visual aspects of pages such as the layout, colour scheme, or the presence of images.

**Layout 4: Baseline + TRS + Thumbnail** – The last layout was the combination of Layout 2 and 3 (See Fig. 1). While this layout took up the largest space in the screen, it was designed to provide the largest amount of information per record among the four layouts.

**Fig. 1.** Search result with TRS and thumbnail (Layout 4)

As can be seen, we designed the four layouts so that the different variable between layouts remained to be a single element. This was due to our consideration for minimising the difference between layouts to evaluate the effectiveness of TRS and thumbnails in a systematic way. The next section will discuss the detail of our experiment based on the four layouts.

## 4 Experiments

A comparative user study was carried out to evaluate the effectiveness of the four search result layouts described above. This section will discuss the methodology adopted in our experiment.

A total of twenty-four people (6 female and 18 male) were recruited for our experiment. Most participants were the research students of the University of Glasgow. The rest was affiliated members of the University. The entry questionnaire established that the range of age varied from 20 to 37 with an average of 27.7. Their experience

---

[2] The Alexa archive (www.alexa.com) did not always contain the thumbnail of the web pages retrieved during our experiment. Our understanding was that a missing thumbnail was replaced by a parent site when it was available. Otherwise it showed the Alexa's logo image to indicate the absence of thumbnails. In our experiment, a missing thumbnail was treated as a similar case to a dead link on the web.

with search engines varied from 4.5 to 11 years with an average of 7.1 years. All participants carried out several searches every day, and 91.6% of them used Google most frequently.

Participants were asked to carry out four search tasks in the experiment. The tasks were designed based on the simulated work task approach [12]. The simulated work task described a task as a form of short scenario. The scenario explained the contexts and motivation of the search with the sufficient information about the relevance of pages. The details of the tasks used in our experiment were as follows.

**Task 1: Background search task** – This task asked participants to find general background information on a topic. In our experiment, participants were asked to find the pages which provide the information about the recent change of student populations. Task 1 and the following Task 2 were originally used and replied by [13].

**Task 2: Decision making task** – This task asked participants to make a decision about a topic. In our experiment, participants were asked to find the best Hi-Fi speakers available in a target price. Participants were encouraged to compare the speakers' details in the decision making.

**Task 3: Known item search task** – This task asked participants to find the information about a topic which was previously known by the searcher. In out experiment, participants were asked to find the current whereabouts of a person who assumed to be a previous colleague of the searcher.

**Task 4: Topic distillation task** – This task asked participants to find a list of key resources for a topic. The definition of key resources was based on the instruction of the Web Track of TREC[3]. The main criteria for being a key resource was that the website was principally devoted to the topic. In our experiment, participants were asked to find the key resources for designer handbags.

One of our intentions behind the selection of these tasks was to investigate a different level of documents' textual and visual elements that were likely to be significant to complete the tasks. For example, Task 1 was likely to involve more textual information than visual while Task 4 was likely to involve visual aspects of documents in a greater degree than other tasks. Task 2 and 3 were supposed to involve both aspects in a similar degree.

The user study was carried out in the following manner. At arrival time participants were asked to read an information sheet which described the guideline for the participation and goal of the experiment. Upon the agreement of participation, participants were asked to fill in an entry questionnaire to indicate their age, sex, and search experience. Then they were presented with a training topic and explained the nature of simulated-work task. They were given approximately 10 minutes to familiarise with the search interfaces and task activity. During the training session, the four layouts were introduced to participants and the questions regarding the interface and tasks were answered.

During the tasks, participants were asked to bookmark the pages they thought relevant. However, no explicit instruction was given to participants regarding the number of bookmarks required to complete the tasks. We asked participants to bookmark pages

---

[3] http://es.csiro.au/TRECWeb/guidelines_2004.html

to ensure their engagement to search tasks. Participants were given up to 15 minutes to complete a task, but allowed to end it when they felt they completed the tasks.

After the first task was completed, participants were asked to fill in a post-search questionnaire to provide subjective assessments about their search. Then a new task was given to them and change of layout was informed. The same procedure was repeated four times. The presentation order of topic and layout was rotated according to a Latin-Square arrangement to reduce bias from participants performing the same tasks with the same system in the same order.

After the completion of four tasks, participants were asked to fill in an exit questionnaire to indicate their overall preference of layouts, followed by an open-end interview to capture their feedback and comments of the result presentation and experiment.

## 5   Experimental Results

This section presents the results of our experiment. A total of 96 search sessions were performed by participants and analysed in our investigation. Due to the nature of study concerning search results presentation, both quantitative and qualitative data were equally important to our study. The quantitative data such as participants' interactions with the interface were based on the system logs recorded during the experiment. The qualitative data such as participants' subjective assessments of search were established by the post-search questionnaires and exit interview. We used a 7 point scale to capture participants' assessments where a positive assessment was represented by a low score in the analysis.

The results of our experiment were analysed from four perspectives as follows: user interaction, relevance assessment, contribution of layout features, and finally, layout preference. In this section, the discussion about the results is often based on the comparison to our *baseline layout* (Layout 1). For simplicity, we sometimes use the term *summary layouts* to refer to Layout 2, 3, and 4. In addition, one of the aspects we were interested in this investigation was participants' decision of which document to visit from search results. We refer such decisions as to an *initial relevance assessment* in this section.

For most differentials presented in this section, the Kruskal Wallis Test was applied to the data to establish statistical significance of the results. When a statistical significance was found between groups, Dunn's post hoc test was applied to determine the significant pairs. Due to the size of cases and arguably large variance of layouts' performance across the tasks, we did not find a statistical significance in many cases. We only report it when the significance was found in this section.

### 5.1   User Interaction

Table 1 shows participants' interactions with the four layouts evaluated in our experiment. The second column shows the average number of queries submitted to the interface per search session. The third column shows the number of words used in the queries. The fourth column shows the number of result pages viewed during the tasks. The fifth column shows the number of pages viewed per iteration. The sixth

**Table 1.** User interaction

| Layout | Iteration | Query Length | Page | Page / Iteration | Click / Page | Bookmark | Time (min) |
|---|---|---|---|---|---|---|---|
| 1 | 5.6 (3.9) | 3.6 (2.6) | 7.7 (5.7) | 1.5 (0.7) | 2.2 (1.6) | 4.0 (2.8) | 13.5 (2.8) |
| 2 | 8.5 (6.3) | 3.4 (1.6) | 10.1 (6.4) | 1.3 (0.6) | 1.6 (1.3) | 3.4 (2.2) | 13.3 (3.0) |
| 3 | 7.4 (4.7) | 3.9 (1.5) | 10.1 (5.7) | 1.9 (1.5) | 1.3 (0.8) | 3.6 (3.3) | 13.6 (2.5) |
| 4 | 7.6 (5.6) | 3.2 (1.4) | 10.0 (6.1) | 1.7 (1.1) | 1.6 (1.4) | 4.0 (3.7) | 13.7 (2.5) |
| Total | 7.3 (5.2) | 3.5 (1.7) | 9.6 (6.0) | 1.6 (1.0) | 1.7 (1.3) | 3.7 (3.0) | 13.6 (2.6) |

*n=24 (Layout 1-4), n=96 (Total)*

column shows the number of retrieved records clicked per result page. The seventh column shows the number of bookmarked URLs. The eighth column shows the time taken to complete the tasks. The numbers in 2nd to 5th rows are a mean value across 24 sessions, and the standard deviation of the value is shown in the brackets.

One of the noticeable differences in Table 1 is the number of iterations. Participants tended to submit more queries to the interface in the summary layouts compared to the baseline layout. We also examined the presence of phrases in the queries. The number of queries that had at least one phrase was six in Layout 1, while 31, 21, and 30 queries contained at least one phrase in Layout 2, 3, and 4, respectively. This suggests that participants were more engaged in query re/formulation with the summary layouts compared to the baseline layout.

More iteration in the summary layouts led to a greater number of result pages viewed by participants to find relevant documents. However, the click per page ratio shown in the sixth column of Table 1 suggests that participants tended to click fewer records in the summary layouts. Given that an underlying search engine was identical across the layouts, this suggests that participants made more relevance judgements based on the document surrogates in the summary layouts, thus, they did not have to visit the retrieved pages as much as they did with the baseline layout. This suggests that the additional information offered by TRS or thumbnails appears to facilitate participants' relevance assessments.

A statistical significance was found in the query length between Layout 1 and Layout 3. No statistical significance was found for other differentials.

Figure 1 shows the distribution of click-through documents' ranking positions. Two trends can be found for the summary layouts in this figure. Firstly, more clicks were found in the top ranking positions which can be due to the larger number of iterations. Secondly, the clicks were stretched across a wider range of the ranking position compared to the baseline layout. This suggests that the TRS and thumbnails can contribute to an increasing level of exhaustively in relevance assessments.

## 5.2 Relevance Assessments

The previous results indicated that the initial relevance assessment might be more focused and exhaustive when TRS and/or thumbnails were added to the document surrogates. Table 2 presents participants' perception of relevance assessment from

**Table 2.** Relevance assessment

| Layout | Ease of finding | New information | Contents prediction |
|--------|-----------------|-----------------|---------------------|
| 1 | 3.6 (1.7) | 3.9 (1.6) | 3.3 (1.5) |
| 2 | 3.6 (2.1) | 3.1 (1.4) | 4.1 (1.7) |
| 3 | 2.8 (1.5) | 3.3 (1.4) | 3.8 (1.9) |
| 4 | 2.5 (1.6) | 3.2 (1.1) | 3.1 (1.8) |
| Total | 3.2 (1.8) | 3.3 (1.4) | 3.6 (1.8) |

*n=24 (Layout 1-4), n=96 (Total)*

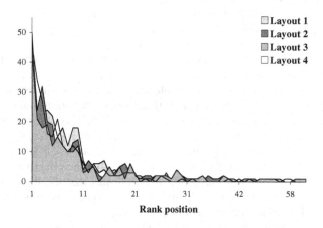

**Fig. 2.** Rank positions of click-through pages (n=1039)

three perspectives. The second column is the score given to the question regarding the ease of finding relevant documents from search results. The third column is the score regarding the ease of finding the documents which contained new information. Finally, the third column is the score regarding how often the documents contained the contents they expected to find in the full text. A positive assessment is represented by a low score (i.e., Score 1 = Very easy or very often, 7 = Not at all). The numbers are the average of 24 sessions, and the standard deviation of the mean value is shown in the brackets.

As can be seen, a similar or more positive average score was found in Layout 2, 3, and 4 compared to Layout 1 with regard to the ease of finding relevant documents as well as of finding new information. While Layout 4 was given the best score among them in the ease of finding relevant documents, Layout 2 was given a better score than the others in the ease of finding new information. This suggests that both a textual and visual presentation of document's summary had the cases where user's relevance assessments were facilitated by them.

A slightly contradicting result was found in the expectation of document's contents. While Layout 4 was given a better score than Layout 1, participants tended to give a lower score to the other two layouts. It is not clear why participants found Layout 2 and 3 less predictable for document's contents, but there might be an unfamiliarity factor of TRS or thumbnails causing confusion in user's contents prediction.

## 5.3  Contribution of Layout Features

The previous sections highlighted the advantages and disadvantages of adding new elements to the baseline presentation. The overall results suggested that Layout 4 were likely to offer a better support in user's information seeking process than Layout 1. However, the difference between Layout 2 and 3 was less clear in several aspects. This section compares TRS and thumbnails by analysing the contribution of layout features in initial relevance assessments.

The document surrogates are some of the primary sources for the searchers to decide which documents to view from the search results. A typical document surrogate in search engines consists of the title, snippet, URL, size, and/or file type. In our experiment, after each task, participants were asked to indicate to what extent each of the layout features contributed to their decisions of viewing documents from the search results. Like the previous section, a 7 point scale was used for the assessments. The result is shown in Table 3 where a stronger contribution is represented by a low score. The numbers are the average, and the standard deviation of the mean value is shown in the brackets. Note that the sample size differs across the layout features.

The bottom row of the table suggests that participants often found the title of retrieved documents the strongest factor in deciding which document to view from the search result. This echoes the finding of [13]. When we compare TRS and thumbnail to Google's snippet, TRS was given a stronger score in Task 1 while the thumbnail was given a stronger score in Task 4. This suggests that the effectiveness of TRS and thumbnail can vary across the tasks. Also it indicates that the benefits of TRS and thumbnails might be mutually exclusive. In other words, the thumbnails might be useful where TRS are less effective, and vice versa.

We were also interested in the correlation of the layout features contribution. Table 4 shows Spearman correlation coefficient of seven layout features measured in our experiment. The correlations that are statistically significant ($p < .05$) are highlighted in italic in the table. As can be seen, TRS was found to have a positive correlation with both the title and snippet of the retrieved documents. On the other hand, the thumbnails had a small but significant negative correlation with the snippet and a positive correlation with URLs. The negative correlation with the snippet again suggests that the usefulness of textual information might be mutually exclusive to the visual information in user's initial relevance assessments. Also, thumbnails' positive correlation with URLs indicates that the thumbnails can be more influential when the genre or category of web pages is an important factor in the search tasks.

**Table 3.** Contribution of layout features

| Task | Title | Snippet | TRS | Thumb. | URL | Size | Type |
|---|---|---|---|---|---|---|---|
| 1 | 1.6 (1.1) | 2.4 (1.7) | 2.1 (1.2) | 4.4 (2.2) | 4.3 (1.9) | 6.7 (0.8) | 5.8 (1.7) |
| 2 | 1.9 (1.5) | 2.7 (1.8) | 2.7 (1.4) | 4.8 (2.0) | 3.5 (2.3) | 6.5 (1.0) | 6.4 (1.2) |
| 3 | 2.1 (1.6) | 2.0 (1.3) | 2.6 (1.7) | 4.3 (1.8) | 4.4 (2.0) | 6.8 (0.5) | 5.8 (1.7) |
| 4 | 1.8 (1.2) | 2.5 (1.5) | 3.3 (1.7) | 2.3 (1.5) | 3.0 (2.0) | 6.4 (1.3) | 5.8 (1.7) |
| Total | 1.8 (1.4) | 2.4 (1.6) | 2.6 (1.5) | 4.0 (2.1) | 3.8 (2.1) | 6.6 (0.9) | 5.9 (1.6) |

*n=12 (TRS and Thumb. in Task 1-4), n=24 (the rest in Task 1-4), n=48 (TRS and Thumb. in Total), n=96 (the rest in Total)*

**Table 4.** Correlation of layout features contribution

|        | Title | Snippet | TRS | Thumb. | URL | Size | Type |
|--------|-------|---------|------|--------|------|------|------|
| **TRS**   | .410 | .314 | 1.000 | -.175 | -.202 | .010 | .147 |
| **Thumb.** | .210 | -.265 | -.175 | 1.000 | .284 | .247 | .051 |

*n=48*

### 5.4 Layout Preference and Participants' Comments

Upon the completion of four tasks, participants were asked to rank the four layouts in their order of preference. In the exit open-ended interview, participants had an opportunity to provide any comments and feedback regarding the layouts and overall experiment. We asked participants to rank the layouts based on the search experience with the given tasks. The most preferred layout was given Score 1 and the least was given Score 4. The counts of participant's ranking are presented in Table 5, along with the average ranking. As can be seen, nearly half of participants preferred Layout 4 over the other layouts. Layout 1 was give the largest votes as the least preferred layouts. There appeared to be a slight preference towards Layout 2 compared to Layout 3.

**Table 5.** Layout preference

| Preference | Layout 1 | Layout 2 | Layout 3 | Layout 4 |
|------------|----------|----------|----------|----------|
| 1 (Most) | 4 | 6 | 3 | 11 |
| 2 | 6 | 8 | 8 | 2 |
| 3 | 2 | 7 | 10 | 5 |
| 4 (Least) | 12 | 3 | 3 | 6 |
| Average rank | 2.92 | 2.29 | 2.54 | 2.25 |

## 6 Implications

The results of our study have several implications for the design of search interface on the web. First of all, adding the new elements that are designed to support user's information seeking activity are likely to increase the level of interaction with a search interface. Our results suggest that query re/formulation and initial relevance assessments are likely to be facilitated by adding TRS and thumbnails to the result presentation. Given that many search engine users are reluctant to offer their effort in search [1], it is encouraging to see the cases where the proposed presentation of search results can contribute to the enhancement of search experience. Our results indicate that the additional information might have a positive effect for increasing the number of iterations. Participants often found it easier to find relevant documents and new information when TRS and thumbnails were added to the document surrogate. This suggests that the current search engine's result presentation is not necessarily optimised and there is a room for improving the presentation.

Our study also provided additional insight into the nature of textual and visual forms of documents' summary. Previous study shows that, for example, TRS can be useful for supporting users of interactive IR systems [7], and the effectiveness of thumbnails can vary across the types of search tasks [14]. Our experiment with the four types of layouts allowed us to compare the effectiveness of these two forms of additional information in a systematic way. Moreover, TRS and thumbnails were evaluated as an additional element as opposed to a replacement of some of layout features used in the current search engines. Our results suggest that the textual and visual presentation of documents' summary is likely to offer additional information in a different context. Therefore, the effectiveness of TRS and thumbnails is often task dependent, but also their usefulness can be mutually exclusive in the search tasks. The overall positive performance of Layout 4 appears to be due to the fact that it could offer a support in a wider range of tasks than Layout 2 or 3.

One of our conclusions, therefore, might be that it is *safer* to show both the textual and visual summaries of documents in the result presentation. It might offer some searchers a greater degree of control in the selection of useful information to carry out searches. However, it is also likely that user's cognitive load will be increased when more elements are added to the search interface. Therefore, we suggest that the search interface should be able to offer a right form of document's summary in an appropriate context or task. Consequently, this study calls for more research on the understanding of users' search contexts and adaptive technique to capture their needs in an appropriate context. This study presented the cases where such advance can be used to improve several aspects of search experience.

## 7  Conclusion

This paper presented a user study investigating the effectiveness of search result presentation on the web. Both the textual and visual forms of document's summary were evaluated as additional information that can be integrated into the current search engine interface. Our evaluation investigated a wider range of aspects of information seeking behaviour than those previously carried out. Our results presented the cases where the additional elements of result presentation were likely to have a positive effect not only in the relevance assessment but also in query re/formulation. Therefore, it was suggested that the typical result presentation used in the major search engine was not necessarily optimised and had a room for improving searching experience. The textual and visual forms of document summaries were likely to have different contexts to facilitate user's search experience. However, we will need more progress on adoptive models of information retrieval systems to make use of their advantages in an appropriate context.

## Acknowledgements

The authors thank to the participants of our experiment for their time and valuable feedback. This work was funded by the EPSRC (Grant ref: EP/C004108/1). Any opinions, findings, and conclusions described here are the authors and do not necessarily reflect those of the sponsor.

# References

1. Jansen, B.J., et al., *Real Life Information Retrieval: A Study of User Queries on the Web.* ACM SIGIR Forum: A Publication of the Special Interest Group on Information Retrieval, 1998. **32**(1): p. 5-17.
2. Ingwersen, P. and K. Järvelin, *The Turn - Integration of Information Seeking and Retrieval in Context.* The Information Retrieval Series. Vol. 18. 2005: Springer.
3. Belkin, N.J., R.N. Oddy, and H.M. Brooks, *ASK for information retrieval: Part I. Background and theory.* Journal of Documentation, 1982. **38**(2): p. 61-71.
4. Belew, R., *Finding Out About- Search Engine Technology from a Cognitive Perspective.* 2000: Cambrdige University Press.
5. Hearst, M.A. and J.O. Pederson. *Re-examining the Cluster Hypothesis: Scatter/Gather on Retrieval Results.* in *Proceedings of the 19th Annual International ACM SIGIR Conference on Research and Development in Information Retrieval.* 1996. Zurich, Switzerland: ACM.
6. Taylor, R.S., *Question negotiation and information seeking in libraries.* College and Research Libraries, 1968. **29**: p. 178-194.
7. White, R., J.M. Jose, and I. Ruthven, *Using Top-Ranking Sentences to Facilitate Effective Information Access.* Journal of the American Society for Information Science and Technology, 2005. **56**(10): p. 1113-1125.
8. Chen, H. and S. Dumais. *Bringing Order to the Web: Automatically Categorizing Search Results.* in *Proceedings of the CHI 2000 Conference on Human factors in computing systems.* 2000. The Hague Netherlands: ACM.
9. White, R., J.M. Jose, and I. Ruthven, *A task oriented-study on the influencing effects of query-biased summarisation in web searching.* Information Processing and Management, 2003. **9**(5): p. 707-733.
10. Dziadosz, S. and R. Chandrasekar. *Do thumbnail previews help users make better relevance decisions about web search results?* in *Proceedings of the 25th annual international ACM SIGIR conference on Research and development in information retrieval.* 2002. Tampere, Finland: ACM.
11. Tombros, A. and M. Sanderson. *Advantages of query-biased summaries in information retrieval.* in *Proceedings of the 21st Annual International ACM SIGIR Conference on Research and Development in Information Retrieval.* 1998. Melbourne, Australia: ACM.
12. Borlund, P., *Experimental components for the evaluation of interactive information retrieval systems.* Journal of Documentation, 2000. **56**(1): p. 71-90.
13. Tombros, A., I. Ruthven, and J.M. Jose, *How Users Assess Web Pages for Information Seeking.* Journal of the American Society for Information Science and Technology, 2005. **56**(4): p. 327-344.
14. Woodruff, A., et al., *A comparison of the use of text summaries, plain thumbnails, and enhanced thumbnails for Web search tasks.* Journal of the American Society for Information Science and Technology, 2002. **53**(2): p. 172 - 185.

# Bricks: The Building Blocks to Tackle Query Formulation in Structured Document Retrieval

Roelof van Zwol[1], Jeroen Baas[2], Herre van Oostendorp[1], and Frans Wiering[1]

[1] Utrecht University, Centre for Content and Knowledge Engineering,
Utrecht, The Netherlands
{roelof, herre, fransw}@cs.uu.nl
[2] Elsevier, User Centered Design, Amsterdam, The Netherlands
j.baas@elsevier.com

**Abstract.** Structured document retrieval focusses on the retrieval of relevant document fragments for a given information need that contains both structural and textual aspects.

We focus here on the theory behind Bricks, a visual query formulation technique for structured document retrieval that aims at reducing the complexity of the query formulation process and required knowledge of the underlying document structure for the user, while maintaining full expression power, as offered by the NEXI query language for XML retrieval.

In addition, we present the outcomes of a large scale usability experiment, which compared Bricks to a keyword-based and a NEXI-based interface. The results show that participants were more successful at completing a search assignments using Bricks. Furthermore, we observed that the participants were also able to successfully complete complex search assignments significantly faster, when using the Bricks interface.

## 1 Introduction

The focus in this article is on the query formulation process for structured document retrieval. The large scale search engines available on the Internet allow easy access to large quantities of on-line information. Using a few keywords a user can formulate the information need and retrieve a list of relevant documents. This approach is satisfactory for most users; but for digital libraries and large intranets, where the information need is usually more specific and large amounts of information on a particular subject are available, more sophisticated query formulation techniques are desired.

Current approaches in structured document retrieval allow a user to either specify the information need using keywords (content only), or by using a combination of structural constraints and keywords. This is formalized in the NEXI query language [1], where a user can specify the information request through an XPath-like expression [2], that combines both the structural and content-based aspects of the user information need.

Using such a query language for retrieval provides powerful expression mechanisms, but also has its impact on the query formulation process. The user should then be able to express the information need using the syntax of the

M. Lalmas et al. (Eds.): ECIR 2006, LNCS 3936, pp. 314–325, 2006.
© Springer-Verlag Berlin Heidelberg 2006

query language. In addition, the user should have knowledge of the structure of the document. Consider the information need of Example 1, where a user visiting the Lonely Planet Web-site wants to:

*Example 1.* Find <u>historical</u> information about *revolutions* for <u>destinations</u> with a *constitutional monarchy* as <u>government</u>.

Using a (NEXI-CO) content-only approach, the user is likely to use the following keyword combination to formulate the user information need: *history revolutions destination government "constitutional monarchy"*. Without any path directives in the information request a structured document retrieval system can literally retrieve any document fragment that contains one or more of the given terms. For example, this can be a piece of text that is emphasized, or the entire document.

Taking a closer look at the information need, we can see that the objective in the example is to retrieve historical information. Furthermore suppose that the user is familiar with the (semantical) structure of the document collection, the user is then able to identify the structural conditions of the information need.

In Example 1 the structural conditions of the information request are underlined, while the emphasized terms form the content-based aspects of the information need. If we make the transition from the information need to a formal specification, the following NEXI content and structure (NEXI-CAS) query is derived:

*//destination[about(.//government,     "constitutional     monarchy")]//history[about (., revolutions)]*

The NEXI query language provides the necessary expression power for structured document retrieval. Although the syntax of the NEXI query language is relatively simple, a user needs to learn the syntactical features. This makes it hard, if not impossible, for the average user to express their information need in NEXI.

To overcome these limitations we have developed *Bricks*, a visual query formulation technique for structured document retrieval that aims at:

1. Reducing the complexity of the query formulation process.
2. Reducing the required knowledge of the document structure.
3. Maintaining maximum expression power, as offered by the NEXI query language.

To realize this, Bricks uses a graphical approach that allows the user to specify the information need using small building blocks ('bricks'), starting with the specification of the desired element of retrieval. As a result, Bricks guides the user in a more natural way through the query formulation process. Not only does it solve the syntactical formulation issues, it also prevents possible information overload, when the document structure is large and complex. This is realized by using a priority for the different XML elements. Elements with a low priority are not visible for the user early in the query formulation process. In Figure 1 the information need of Example 1 is expressed with Bricks.

To validate our ideas, we have designed and implemented the Bricks interface on top of the structured document retrieval system that was developed for

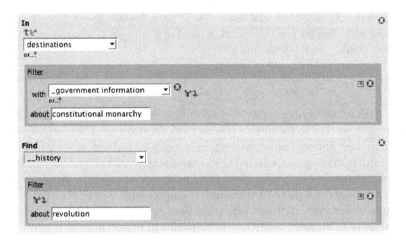

**Fig. 1.** Example information request in Bricks

participation in INEX, the INitiative for the Evaluation of XML retrieval [3]. INEX provides an international platform for the evaluation of structured document retrieval strategies, allowing researchers to measure the retrieval performance of their system.

Furthermore, we have set-up and performed a usability experiment to evaluate our ideas. In the experiment, we used the Lonely Planet document collection[1] to compare Bricks with a keyword-based (NEXI-CO) approach and the 'content and structure'-based (NEXI-CAS) approach. We will discuss the outcome of the experiment in terms of effectiveness, efficiency and user satisfaction [4].

## 2   Related Work

In general an information retrieval system consists of three components: a query formulation interface, a retrieval strategy (engine), and an interface for the result presentation. Below we will discuss the impact of various research approaches on structured document retrieval for each of the three components.

**Query Formulation.** The research on query formulation, presented in this article is using the NEXI query language as a starting point. NEXI [1] is an XPath-based query language that primarily focusses on the extraction of relevant information, using a combination of path directives and content-based filters. This makes NEXI an excellent query language for structured document retrieval, providing a powerful expression mechanism to the user.

Alternative XML query languages, such as XQuery[5] and XSLT[6], do not focus on the retrieval task. They provide additional functionality that lays outside the scope of structured document retrieval, like for example transformations on the extracted XML document structure.

---

[1] We would like to thank the Lonely Planet organization for provided the XML document collection, based on their WorldGuide that is used for our experiments.

A more trivial query formulation technique is adopted by Lucene [7]. Information that is found within a specific field, i.e. an XML element, can be specifically targeted, like: *government: "constitutional monarchy"*. The downside of this approach is that it is not possible to retrieve anything other than the document containing the requested field and content, or to specify more complex paths.

Of course one should not neglect the power of keyword-based information retrieval. It is still the driving force behind all popular search engines, allowing literally anyone to specify the user's information need with just a simple keyword combination. The NEXI query language therefore allows for the specification of keyword combinations, including the usage of phrases. This is referred to as NEXI-CO (Content Only), while a NEXI query that contains a path specification is referred to as a NEXI-CAS query (Content and Structure).

**Retrieval Strategy.** The success of a structured document retrieval system also depends heavily on the retrieval strategy. It executes the (structural) information request and derives a ranked list of relevant document fragments. In INEX, the INitiative for the Evaluation of XML Retrieval [3], the retrieval performance of structured document retrieval strategies is evaluated. Within INEX a number of user-related issues are topic of discussion. With respect to query formulation it is the question whether the structural conditions of the information request should be strictly interpreted, or whether these conditions should be seen as merely hints of where the user expects to find the relevant information [8]. For our experiment, we have used a semi-strict interpretation of the path directives, which penalizes retrieved document fragments that do not exactly fulfill the structural conditions of the information request [9].

**Result Presentation.** Another issue within INEX refers to result presentation. It deals with the question of finding the most specific and exhaustive element of retrieval for a given information need. Therefore, it is possible that the list of document fragments returned by the retrieval strategy contains overlapping results [10]. When an XML fragment is considered relevant, its parent is by definition also relevant, and probably more exhaustive. From a user perspective, however, it is undesirable to have redundant items in the ranking of the document fragments.

Since relatively small document fragments are derived by the system, it is possible to use alternative techniques to present the retrieved information to the user. This is also the scope of the INEX interactive track [11], where the interaction of the user with a result presentation interface for structured document retrieval is evaluated, using a content-only approach for query formulation.

For our experiment we use a commonly accepted presentation technique, which provides a link to the relevant fragment, a short summary of the fragments content, and some additional statistical information that help the users to judge the relevancy of the retrieved information. Nearly all main search engines use this presentation format, therefore we can safely assume that the result presentation is not of significant influence to the outcome of our experiment.

# 3 Theoretical Foundation for Bricks

The theoretical foundation for Bricks is derived from the three objectives that are identified in the introduction.

**A Graphical Approach.** The use of a graphical interface reduces the burden of syntactical formulation issues related to the NEXI query language. Although NEXI uses a relatively simple syntax based on XPath, it still allows users to submit malformed queries to the retrieval system. This is not possible with the graphical approach adopted by Bricks, apart from submitting incomplete queries. This feature is referred to as direct manipulation of the query language [4].

Furthermore, the underlying structure that is present in the document collection can be integrated into the query interface. Several approaches can be imagined, but for Bricks we have chosen to work with pull-down lists, allowing the user to select structural elements into the query. Alternatively, a tree-based approach can be used to visualize the structure to the user. However, this is a more complex structure that needs to be interpreted by the user.

**Construction of a Mental Model for Query Formulation.** When formulating a specific information request, the user has a mental model of the information he is looking for [12]. Research on information seeking behavior [13, 14] has shown that the effectiveness of the task performance can be increased if the interface and offered functionality is closely related to the mental model of the user. When focussing on query formulation for structured document retrieval the task is more complex. The user also has to specify what the structural and content-based conditions of the information need are. If a user is asked to express the information need in natural language, it is likely that a sentence is formulated, such as: *"Find historical information about revolutions, for destinations ..."*.

A logical first step is to specify the requested element of retrieval, *"Find historical information"*. Next, a limited number of iterative steps are possible. The user either specifies a content-based constraint, *"about revolutions"*, using the filter that is associated with the request path, or adds additional path directives to the request path, *", for destinations"*. If needed the user can add one more content-based filter, and simultaneously introduce a support path to the information request. This allows the users enough flexibility to follow their intuition, and to perform intermediate checks on the specified information request.

To further stimulate the construction of a mental model, words are added to illustrate the relation between the bricks (see Figure 1), such as 'in', 'with' or 'about'. As a result, the composed query can be read back in natural language: *"In destinations with government information about* 'constitutional monarchy', *find historical information about* revolution(s).".

**Step-by-Step Formulation of the Information Need.** Bricks uses small building blocks to formulate the information request (query). Each block represents a small step in the formulation process, that needs to be completed, before another block is added to the query. After specifying the requested element of retrieval, the user can add an *about* clause to the request filter, or specify additional path directives to the request path. By adding an about clause, the user can specify a text constraint to the current context and specifiy a sub path for this text constraint.

Based on the document structure and the syntax of the NEXI query language, the possible actions are controlled by the Bricks interface. This prevents the specification of malformed and unmeaningful (with respect to the document structure) queries. On the other hand we aim at preserving full expression power, as offered by the NEXI query language.

**Avoiding Information Overload.** It is important that the user is not overwhelmed with options and possible next steps. In a sense, the gradual building of a mental model is one approach to avoid information overload. Using a wizard-based approach is a proven technique to reduce the learning curve of a task that needs to be accomplished. However, expert users can experience a limitation in the provided functionality, causing them to get frustrated [15]. In our case, we are not focussing on the high-end experts, such as programmers and database administrators, but on users with a complex information need that goes beyond the average profile of a user on the Internet. Although Bricks is more flexible than a wizard-based approach, the aim is similar: by reducing the number of options that are available, it becomes easier to complete (more efficiently) the query formulation task.

In an attempt to reduce the required knowledge of the document structure, Bricks provides lists of structural elements that allow the user to select path elements into their query. However, the Lonely Planet XML document collection contains 271 unique element and attribute names. This can easily cause an information overload for the user, and lower the efficiency of the task performance. But it appears that not all elements are meaningful from a retrieval perspective. For instance, the retrieval of a highlighted (italic) text fragment, containing just a few keywords, will probably not satisfy the user's information need, since all context is missing.

In general, it is possible to define a structure for a document collection that consists of three layers, as is presented in Figure 2. The top layer is formed by a semantical markup that provides a high level description of the content that is contained. The middle layer provides a logical markup, containing elements that

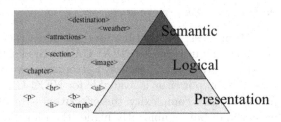

**Fig. 2.** Three layer structure for XML document collections

have a logical function/meaning to the user. I.e. a chapter and its sections form logical containers of information. At the bottom layer the presentation markup is found, which is used for visual layout and presentation of the content. Any XML document can be seen as a tree. When using such a three-layer structure, the semantical element will naturally appear in the top of the tree, while the presentation element as usually found near the leaves to the tree. The mid-section of the XML document will then contain the logical elements.

Bricks exploits this three layer structure in the retrieval process by adding a priority to each of the structural elements. Semantical elements will receive a high priority, followed by the logical elements, while the presentation elements are given a low priority. Early in the query formulation process, only the high priority elements can be selected in the query. Elements with a lower priority will become available once the user has made a first selection of the elements that should be retrieved. In a sense the user is traversing down the tree structure of the document collection, and narrowing down the possible elements that can be added to the query.

For the experiment a threshold of 20 elements is used, which limits the number of structural elements that can be presented to the user at once. Alternative presentation techniques with sub-lists are possible, to allow the user to explore a larger set of structural elements that can be included in the query.

## 4    Usability Experiment

We evaluated three different query formulation techniques: keyword-based (NEXI-CO), content and structure-based (NEXI-CAS), and Bricks. First we will discuss the hypotheses, then present the setup and methodology used for the experiment and finally discuss the results and some observations. A more detailed discussion of the experiment, including the results of a retrieval performance experiment can be found in [16].

### 4.1    Hypotheses

Based on the three objectives for query formulation that are discussed in Section 1 we have formulated three hypotheses.

**Hypothesis 1.** *The use of advanced query formulation techniques will lead to a higher effectiveness of the task performance.*

The intuition behind Hypothesis 1 is that if a user can add structural conditions to the information request, by using either NEXI-CAS or Bricks, the user is more successful in completing a given complex task. Furthermore we designed Bricks to provide similar expression power as is available for NEXI-CAS. Therefore we expect that regardless of task complexity the effectiveness of NEXI-CAS and Bricks will be almost equal, but significantly higher than for NEXI-CO.

When taking task complexity into account, we expect to find that for tasks with a low complexity the three approaches will have a similar performance, however if the task complexity increases, the effectiveness of NEXI-CO will drop. The effectiveness of NEXI-CAS and Bricks should remain more or less constant, or slightly decrease.

To validate our expectations we adopt two measures that express the effectiveness of the user: *correctness* and *positioning*. Correctness (scale: [0..1]) expresses the ability of the user to find a correct answer for a given task. The positioning measure (scale: [0..10]) defines the ability to rank the relevant fragment selected by the user at a high position. E.g. if the user-selected relevant fragment is retrieved at the first position in the ranking, the maximum score (10) is given. If an answer is incorrect, or found below the first ten hits, the minimum score is assigned (0) [17].

**Hypothesis 2.** *The Bricks approach for query formulation will increase the efficiency of the user for a given task.*

When taking the time factor into account, we expect to see a different picture. If our assumptions for Bricks are correct, a user should be able to successfully complete a search task in a shorter period of time, compared to NEXI-CAS. It is difficult to predict how this will relate to NEXI-CO, because we expect that in this case the user behavior will be focussed more on query refinement and a quick scan of the list with retrieved document fragments. This corresponds with normal search behavior of users on the Internet [17]. We will measure the efficiency of the systems using the following formula: $efficiency = correctness/time$.

**Hypothesis 3.** *Bricks will achieve a higher overall satisfaction among users that perform a (complex) search, when compared to both NEXI-based approaches.*

We expect that users who are offered sophisticated query formulation techniques (Bricks and NEXI-CAS) will be more satisfied, than users working with a keyword-based interface. Furthermore, the reduction of both the syntactical and structural obstacles at the user interface will have a positive influence on the user satisfaction. Together this will result in higher overall satisfaction, when working with Bricks.

## 4.2   Methods

For the usability experiment we have used the following method, as implemented in TERS, the testbed for the evaluation of Retrieval Systems [17]:

*Document Collection.* For the experiment we used the Lonely Planet WorldGuide,which consists of XML documents with interesting facts and background information about destinations on our planet.

*Systems.* Three systems were prepared for the experiment: NEXI-CO, NEXI-CAS, and Bricks. To eliminate undesirable side-effects all three systems used the same retrieval engine and result presentation technique.

*Users.* The user pool consisted of 52 students, who participated in the course 'Multimedia Information Retrieval'. During the course they were taught the basic principles of structured document retrieval, and they followed a lecture on the NEXI query language. Prior to the experiment, they had to complete an assignment where they were asked to create both NEXI-CO and NEXI-CAS queries for fifteen representative information needs, based on the Lonely Planet WorldGuide. The users were divided randomly over the three systems in three groups of 18 participants.

*Experience.* The first 30 minutes of the experiment the participants performed training tasks using the retrieval system and assigned interface. This reduces the learning effects, and familiarizes the user with the setup of the experiment.

*Topics.* A pool of 27 topics is used that represent the specific information need of travelers planning their next holiday or business trip. The topics can be sorted in three complexity groups, ranging from low to high complexity. The groups were formed by counting the syntactical and structural elements of the ideal NEXI-CAS query that represents the information need expressed in the topic [16]. Based on this classification, we equally distributed the topics over the complexity groups. Each user carried out all topics.

*Survey.* Prior to and directly after the experiment we have presented the participants a survey to examine their expertise and experiences with the systems.

### 4.3   Results of the Usability Experiment

First we will give a brief overview of the overall results, and then discuss the influence of task complexity on the performance.

**Overall Results.** In Table 1 the overall results of the experiment are presented for the three systems based on the measures that we used for the experiment: *time, correctness, positioning, efficiency,* and *satisfaction.* The effectiveness measures (correctness and positioning), which are used to test Hypothesis 1 show that a significant difference ($p < .001$) is found between the systems, where Bricks is more effective than both NEXI-CO and NEXI-CAS. Therefore we can support Hypothesis 1.

When the time factor is taken into account, it becomes apparent that users need significantly ($p < .001$) more time to formulate their information need in NEXI-CAS expressions. But also query formulation in Bricks takes longer than for NEXI-CO. With the focus on efficiency, NEXI-CO and Bricks are performing best ($p < 0.04$), which partly supports Hypothesis 2.

Inspection of the outcome of the experiment for user satisfaction shows that users appreciate the additional query formulation power, but have a marginal preference for Bricks. Given that the satisfaction scale goes from 1 to 7, we conclude that the users were content with both the Bricks and NEXI systems.

**Table 1.** Overall performance for the three systems

| System | Time (sec.) | Correctness avg. (std.) | Positioning avg. (std.) | Efficiency avg. (std.) | Satisfaction avg. (std.) |
|---|---|---|---|---|---|
| **NEXI-CO** | 197 | 0.58 (0.49) | 4.42 (4.62) | **0.72** (1.03) | 4.62 (1.69) |
| **NEXI-CAS** | 245 | 0.65 (0.48) | 6.07 (4.63) | 0.48 (0.55) | 4.96 (1.43) |
| Bricks | 214 | **0.73** (0.45) | **6.32** (4.29) | **0.72** (0.80) | **5.25** (1.42) |

The differences are however not significant, therefore we are inconclusive with respect to Hypothesis 3.

**Including Task Complexity.** A more detailed insight in the results can be obtained when task complexity is also considered an influencing factor.

**Correctness and Positioning:** Figure 3.a and 3.b show the influence of task complexity on the effectiveness of the performance. An increase in complexity of the information need results in a linear decline of correctness for Bricks, where both NEXI-based approaches show a sudden drop in correctness when the task complexity is shifting from low- to mid-level complexity. Focussing on the positioning measure, it becomes apparent that the NEXI-CO lacks the necessary query formulation power, forcing users to browse more often to the lower ranked results. With respect to our expectations, we see a sudden drop in effectiveness for Bricks and NEXI-CAS, which was not predicted. The overall picture however, supports our expectations.

**Time:** When comparing the task complexity with respect to the average time needed to complete a task, we see that time increases with the task complexity, regardless of the system (Figure 3.c). However, on average the users need more time to formulate NEXI-CAS queries, compared to the other systems.

**Efficiency:** Figure 3.d illustrates the combination of correctness and time into the efficiency measure. It shows that the highest efficiency for tasks with a low complexity is achieved with NEXI-CO, closely followed by Bricks.

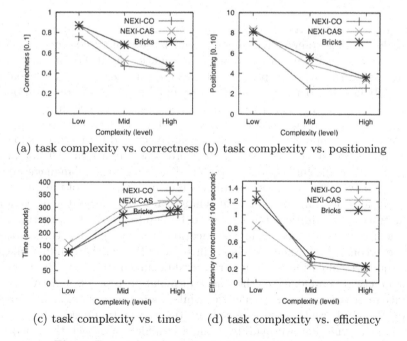

(a) task complexity vs. correctness (b) task complexity vs. positioning

(c) task complexity vs. time    (d) task complexity vs. efficiency

**Fig. 3.** Experimental results, including task complexity

However, for mid-level complexity Bricks is more efficient, and for highly complex tasks the results converge to an almost equal low point of efficiency. Comparing the results for efficiency with our expectations, we are mildly positive with the outcome. We had not anticipated the significant increase in time needed to complete more complex tasks.

### 4.4  Observations

The search behavior of the users working with the different systems was completely different. Users working with the NEXI-CO interface used many iteration steps to formulate a query and inspect the top of the ranking. If the results were unsatisfactory, they refined their previous query and tried again.

The participants working with the NEXI-CAS interface showed a different strategy: they constructed the NEXI query in several steps. After each step, they submitted the query, to check the syntax and the intermediate results. Then continued extending the query, until they were satisfied with the results. Manual inspection of the submitted queries, showed numerous syntax errors, and misinterpretation of the document structure.

Finally, we observed that the participants working with Bricks hardly used any refinement steps. They continued working until they fully created a representation of the information need in Bricks, and only then inspected the results.

## 5  Conclusions

Structured document retrieval has gained popularity due to the use of XML in digital libraries, intranet environments, and large structured web-sites, where users have a specific and often complex information need. For structured document retrieval to work in practice, it is important that users are capable to adequately use the structure of a document in all facets of the retrieval process.

In this article we have identified three aspects that influence the query formulation process for structured document retrieval: (1) adequate expression power, (2) syntactical complexity of the query formulation, and (3) required knowledge of the document structure. Using a keyword-based approach will not provide the user with sufficient expression power. The NEXI query language allows a user to specify both the structural and content-based aspects of the information need, but also burdens the user with syntactical issues during the query formulation process. In addition, the user must be familiar with the structure of the document collection to avoid the specification of ill-formed structural paths.

To overcome these issues, we have introduced Bricks, the building blocks to tackle query formulation issues in structured document retrieval. Bricks reduces the syntactical complexity of the query formulation process, and the required knowledge of the document structure, while maintaining maximum expression power. Bricks allows the user to formulate the information need, while avoiding a possible information overload, by using a graphical approach that follows the construction of a mental model for query formulation.

Based on the results of the usability experiment we conclude that sophisticated query formulation techniques, such as offered by Bricks, will increase the effectiveness (correctness) of the task performance. For simple tasks the content-only approach is most efficient. However when task complexity increases, Bricks turns out to be a better choice.

# References

1. Trotman, A., Sigurbjörnsson, B.: NEXI, now and next. In: Advances in XML Information Retrieval. LNCS 3493, Springer (2005) 42–53
2. Clark, J., DeRose, S.: XML Path Language (XPath). Technical report, World-Wide-Web Consortium (W3C) (1999)
3. Fuhr, N., Lalmas, M., Malik, S., Szlávik, Z., eds.: Advances in XML Information Retrieval. Number 3493 in LNCS, Schloss Dagstuhl, Germany, INitiative for the Evaluation of XML Retrieval, Springer (2005)
4. Preece, J., Rogers, Y., Sharp, H., Benyon, D., Holland, S., Carey, T.: Human Computer Interaction: Concepts and Design. Addison Wesley (1994)
5. Boag, S., et al.: Xquery 1.0: An XML query language. Working draft, W3C: World-Wide-Web Consortium (2005)
6. Adler, S., et al.: Extensible stylesheet language (XSL). W3c recommendation, W3C: World-Wide-Web Consortium (2001)
7. Hatcher, E., Gospodnetic, O.: Lucene in Action. Manning Publications Co. (2005)
8. Lalmas, M., Roelleke, T.: Modelling vague content and structure querying in XML retrieval with a probabilistic object-relational framework. In: 6th International Conference On Flexible Query Answering Systems, Lyon, France (2004)
9. Zwol, v.R., Dignum, V., Wiering, F.: The Utrecht Blend: Basic ingredients for an XML retrieval system. In: Advances in XML Information Retrieval. LNCS 3493, Springer (2005) 140–152
10. Kazai, G., Lalmas, M., Vries, A.d.: The overlap problem in content-oriented XML retrieval evaluation. In: Proceedings of the 27th Annual International ACM SI-GIR Conference on Research and Development in Information Retrieval. Number ISBN:1-58113-881-4, Sheffield, UK, ACM Press (2004) 72 – 79
11. Tombros, A., Larsen, B., Malik, S.: The interactive track at INEX 2004. In: Advances in XML Information Retrieval. LNCS 3493, Springer (2005) 410–423
12. Ingwersen, P., Järvelin, K.: The Turn: Integration of Information Seeking and Retrieval in Context. Volume 18 of The Information Retrieval Series. Springer (2005)
13. Meho, L., Tobbo, H.: Modelling the information-seeking behaviour of social scientists; Elly's study revisited. Journal of American Society for Information Science and Technology 4(6) (2003) 570–587
14. Muramatsu, J., Pratt, W.: Transparent queries: Investigating users' mental models of search engines. In: proceedings of the 24th International ACM SIGIR Conference on Research and Development in Information Retrieval, ACM Press (2001) 217–224
15. Dryer, D.: Wizards, guides, and beyond: Rational end empirical methods. In: proceedings of the International Conference on Intelligent User Interfaces, New York, NY, ASU, ACM Press (1997) 265–286
16. Baas, A.J.: Structured document retrieval from a user perspective. Master's thesis, Department of Information and Computing Sciences, Utrecht University, Utrecht, the Netherlands (2005)
17. Zwol, v.R., Oostendorp, H.v.: Google's "I'm feeling lucky", truly a gamble? In: Web Information Systems - WISE 2004, Brisbane, Australia, Springer (2004) 378–390

# Structural Feedback for Keyword-Based XML Retrieval

Ralf Schenkel and Martin Theobald

Max-Planck-Institut für Informatik, Saarbrücken, Germany
{schenkel, mtb}@mpi-inf.mpg.de

**Abstract.** Keyword-based queries are an important means to retrieve information from XML collections with unknown or complex schemas. Relevance Feedback integrates relevance information provided by a user to enhance retrieval quality. For keyword-based XML queries, feedback engines usually generate an expanded keyword query from the content of elements marked as relevant or nonrelevant. This approach that is inspired by text-based IR completely ignores the semistructured nature of XML. This paper makes the important step from pure content-based to structural feedback. It presents a framework that expands a keyword query into a full-fledged content-and-structure query. Extensive experiments with the established INEX benchmark and our TopX search engine show the feasibility of our approach.

## 1   Introduction

### 1.1   Motivation

XML has seen increasing importance recently to represent large amounts of semistructured or textual information in digital libraries, intranets, or the Web, so information retrieval on XML data is growing more and more important. XML search engines employ the ranked retrieval paradigm for producing relevance-ordered result lists rather than merely using XPath or XQuery for Boolean retrieval. An important subset of XML search engines uses keyword-based queries [2, 8, 31], which is especially important for collections of documents with unknown or highly heterogeneous schemas. However, simple keyword queries cannot exploit the often rich annotations available in XML, so the results of an initial query are often not very satisfying.

Relevance Feedback is an important way to enhance retrieval quality by integrating relevance information provided by a user. In XML retrieval, existing feedback engines usually generate an expanded keyword query from the content of elements marked as relevant or nonrelevant. This approach that is inspired by text-based IR completely ignores the semistructured nature of XML. This paper makes the important step from content-based to structural feedback. We extend the well-established feedback approach by Robertson and Sparck-Jones [21] to expand a keyword-based query into a possibly complex content-and-structure query that specifies new constraints on the structure of results, in addition to "standard" content-based query expansion. The resulting expanded query has

M. Lalmas et al. (Eds.): ECIR 2006, LNCS 3936, pp. 326–337, 2006.
© Springer-Verlag Berlin Heidelberg 2006

weighted structural and content constraints and can be fed into a full-fledged XML search engine like our own TopX engine [25, 26].

As an example, consider the keyword query (query 204 from the INEX benchmark [12]) `moldovan semantic networks`. Without additional knowledge, it is unclear that the term "moldovan" actually refers to the author of a paper about semantic networks. Additionally, it is very unlikely that the author name and the terms "semantic network" occur in the same element, as author names are usually mentioned in different places than the content of articles. A query with constraints on both content and structure would probably yield a lot more relevant results, but it is impossible to formulate a query like the following without knowledge of the underlying schema:

`//sec[about(.//au, ''moldovan") and about(., ''semantic networks")]`

The techniques presented in this paper automatically construct a content-and-structure query from a keyword-based query, exploiting relevance feedback by a user. This paper makes the following important contributions: (1) It presents a formal framework to integrate different classes of query expansions, beyond content-based feedback, into XML retrieval, (2) it presents the implementation of four expansion classes, and (3) it evaluates the performance of the techniques, showing a huge gain in effectiveness with the established INEX benchmark [12].

The primary goal of this paper is to show that structural feedback helps to enhance result quality. The paper does not claim to present the ultimately best implementation of structural feedback, but opens a whole design space and presents variants that give reasonably good results.

## 1.2   Related Work

Relevance feedback has already been considered for document retrieval for a long time, starting with Rocchio's query expansion algorithm [22]. Ruthven and Lalmas [23] give an extensive overview about relevance feedback for unstructured data, including the assessment of relevance feedback algorithms.

Relevance feedback in XML IR is not yet that popular. Of the few papers that have considered it, most concentrate on query expansion based on the content of elements with known relevance [5, 14, 24, 30]. Some of these focus on blind ("pseudo") feedback, others on feedback provided by users. Pan et al. [16] apply user feedback to recompute similarities in the ontology used for query evaluation.

Even fewer papers have considered structural query expansion [9, 10, 15, 18, 19]. Mihajlovic et al. [15, 18, 19] proposed deriving the relevance of an element from its tag name, but could not show any significant gain in retrieval effectiveness. Additionally, they considered hand-tuned structural features specific for the INEX benchmark (e.g., the name of the journal to which an element's document belongs), but again without a significant positive effect. In contrast, we propose a general approach for feedback that can be applied with the INEX data, but does not rely on any INEX-specific things.

Hlaoua and Boughanem [9] consider common prefixes of relevant element's paths as additional query constraints, but don't provide any experimental evaluation of their approach.

The work of Hsu et al. [10] is closest to our approach. They use blind feedback to expand a keyword-based query with structural constraints derived from a neighborhood of elements that contain the keywords in the original query. Our approach considers the whole document instead of only a fragment, can generate constraints with negative weight, and integrates also content-based constraints.

## 2    Formal Model and Notation

### 2.1    Data Model

We consider a fixed corpus of $D$ XML documents with $E$ elements. For such a document $d$, $E(d)$ denotes the set of elements of the document; for an element $e$, $T(e)$ denotes its tag name and $d(e)$ the document to which it belongs.

The *content* $c(e)$ of an element $e$ is the set of all terms (after stopword removal and optional stemming) in the textual content of the element itself and all its descendants. (Note that XML retrieval engines usually use this content model, while boolean languages like XPath or Xquery typically only use the content of the element itself.) For each term $t$ and element $e$, we maintain a weight $w_e(t)$. This can be a binary weight ($w_e(t) = 1$ if the term occurs in $e$'s content and 0 otherwise), a tf-idf style [13] or a BM25-based [1, 29] weight that captures the importance of $t$ in $e$'s content. The *content* $c(d)$ of a document $d$ is defined as the content $c(r)$ of its root element $r$.

We maintain a number of statistics about the occurrence of terms in documents and elements: The *document frequency* $df_t$ of a term $t$ is the number of documents in which the term appears in the content. Analogously, the *element frequency* $ef_t$ of a term $t$ is the number of elements in which the term appears in the content.

### 2.2    Queries and Relevance of Results

We use an extended version of INEX's query language NEXI [27]. NEXI basically corresponds to XPath restricted to the `descendants-or-self` and `self` axis and extended by an IR-style `about` predicate to specify conditions that relevant elements should fulfil. The wildcard symbol '*' matches any tag and can be used to formulate keyword queries in NEXI. We extend NEXI with additional weights for each content constraint. A typical extended NEXI query looks like the following:

`//article[about(.,''0.8*XML")//*[about(//p,''0.4*IR -0.2*index")]`

The result granularity of such a query are elements. The relevance of an element with respect to a query relevance model is measured binarily, i.e., an element is either relevant or nonrelevant.

## 3    Expanding Keyword-Based Queries

We studied the content-and-structure queries from INEX to find patterns that are regularily used in such queries to describe relevant elements, in addition to content conditions on the result element. A canonical example for such a query is the following:

`//article[about(.,''XML") and about(//bib,''numbering")]//sec[about(.,IR)` `and about(//par,index)]`

that is a content-and-structure version of the simpler keyword query "XML IR index numbering". In contrast to the keyword query, the structured query specifies a tag (or, more generally, a set of tags) that relevant elements should have ("I am interested in sections about 'IR'"). Additionally, this query contains constraints on the content of descendants of relevant elements ("sections with a paragraph about 'index'"), the content of ancestors ("sections in articles about 'XML'"), and the content of descendants of ancestors ("sections in articles that cite a paper about 'numbering'").

As such a content-and-structure query specifies much more precisely the conditions that relevant elements must satisfy, we can expect that a search engine will return more relevant results for a content-and-structure query than for the keyword query, provided that the content-and-structure query correctly captures the same information need as the keyword query.

Our feedback framework aims at generating a content-and-structure query from a keyword query, exploiting relevance feedback provided by a user for some results of the keyword query. This section presents the core elements of our feedback framework. We start with the formal model for relevance feedback, discuss possible expansions of a query, show how the possibly best expansions can be selected, and how an expanded query is generated.

## 3.1   Feedback Model

We consider a keyword query $q = \{q_1, \ldots, q_p\}$ with a set $E = \{e_1, \ldots, e_l\}$ of results with known relevance, i.e., elements for which a user has assigned an exhaustivness value $e(e)$ and a specificity value $s(e)$. We say that an element $e$ is *relevant* for the query if both $e(e)$ and $s(e)$ are maximal (i.e., have the value 3 in INEX), yielding a set $E^+ = \{e_1^+, \ldots, e_R^+\}$ of relevant elements and a set $E^- = \{e_1^-, \ldots, e_N^-\}$ of nonrelevant elements.

Note that even though this paper considers only binary relevance, it is possible to extend the mechanism presented here to approaches where relevance is measured with a probability-like number between 0 and 1, for example by representing $E^+$ and $E^-$ as probabilistic sets.

## 3.2   Candidates for Query Expansion

Following the discussion in the beginning of this section, we derive the following classes of candidates for query expansion from an element with known relevance:

- all terms of the element's content together with their score (C candidates),
- all tag-term pairs of descendants of the element in its document, together with their score (D candidates),

- all tag-term pairs of ancestors of the element in its document, together with their score (A candidates), and
- all tag-term pairs of descendants of ancestors of the element in its document, together with their score and the ancestor's tag (AD candidates).

The system can be extended with additional classes of candidates like tags, twigs, or paths, which is subject to future work.

Formally, we consider for an element $e$

- the set $C(e) = \{t \in c(e)\}$ of its C candidates, i.e., the terms in its content,
- the sets $A(e)$ of A and $D(e)$ of D candidates, i.e., all triples $(a, T(e'), t)$ where $e'$ is an element in $e$'s document that is an ancestor/a descendant of $e$, $a$ is the relative position of $e$ and $e'$ (ancestor or descendant), $T(e')$ is the tag name of $e'$, and $t$ is a term in the content of $e'$, and
- the set $AD(e)$ consists of its AD candidates, i.e., triples $(T(e'), T(e''), t)$ where $e'$ is an ancestor of $e$, $e''$ is a descendant of $e'$, and $t \in c(e'')$.

The candidate set $\Gamma(e) := C(e) \cup A(e) \cup D(e) \cup AD(e)$ is the set of all candidates for element $e$. We extend the notion of frequencies from terms to candidates as follows: The element frequency $ef(c)$ of a candidate $c$ is the number of elements $e$ for which $c \in \Gamma(e)$, and its document frequency $df(c)$ is the number of documents that contain at least one element $e$ with $c \in \Gamma(e)$.

## 3.3 Weights for Expansion Candidates

To weight the different candidates, we apply a straight-forward extension of the well-known Robertson-Sparck-Jones weight [21] to element-level retrieval in XML. The weight $w_{RSJ}^+(c)$ of a candidate $c$ is computed analogously to Robertson and Sparck-Jones with binary weights:

$$w_{RSJ}^+(c) = \log \frac{r_c + 0.5}{R - r_c + 0.5} + \log \frac{E - ef_c - R + r_c + 0.5}{ef_c - r_c + 0.5}$$

Here, for a candidate $c$, $r_c$ denotes the number of relevant elements which contain the candidate $c$ in their candidate set, $R$ denotes the number of relevant elements, and $E$ the number of elements in the collection. As the RSJ weights do not yield useful values if there are no relevant results at all, we additionally compute another weight for each term that captures its importance within the nonrelevant results:

$$w_{RSJ}^-(c) = \log \frac{n_c + 0.5}{N - n_c + 0.5} + \log \frac{E - ef_c - N + n_c + 0.5}{ef_c - n_c + 0.5}$$

where $n_c$ denotes the number of nonrelevant elements which contain the candidate $c$ in their candidate set and $N$ denotes the number of nonrelevant elements. The weight $w_{RSJ}(c)$ of the candidate is then $w_{RSJ}^+(c)$ if $R > 0$ and $-w_{RSJ}^-(c)$ otherwise, so we consider our new weight only if there are no relevant results at all.

### 3.4 Selecting Expansion Candidates

The set of all possible expansion candidates is usually very large and contains many unimportant and misleading expansions, so we have to select the best $b$ of them for generating the expanded query. This problem already exists for content-based expansion of keyword queries, and several possible weights have been proposed in the literature that go beyond naively ordering terms by their weight, like prefering terms that occur in many relevant elements [6], Porter's Algorithm [17], and the expected mutual information measure EMIM [28]. We use the so-called Robertson Selection Values (RSV) proposed by Robertson [20]. For a candidate $c$, its RSV has the form $RSV(c) = w_{RSJ}(c) \cdot (p - q)$, where $p = r_c/R$ is the estimated probability of the candidate occurring in a relevant element's candidate set and $q$ is the probability that it occurs in a nonrelevant element's set. Unlike Robertson who assumed $q$ to be negligible, we estimate $q = n_c/N$ as there are usually a lot more nonrelevant than relevant elements in the top results. We ignore candidates that occur only within the documents of elements with known relevance as they have no potential to generate more relevant results outside these documents. We order the union of the remaining candidates by their RSV and choose the top $b$ of them, where $b$ is a configuration parameter of the system. To be able to generate a valid NEXI query in the next step, we have to limit the A and AD candidates chosen to contain the same ancestor tag.

### 3.5 Generating an Expanded Query

Using the top-$b$ candidates, we generate a content-and-structure query from the original keyword query. This expansion is actually straight-forward, and the generated query has the following general structure:

```
//ancestor-tag[A+AD constraints]//*[keywords+C+D constraints]
```

As an example, if the original query was 'XML' and we selected the A candidate (anc,article,'IR'), the AD candidate (article,bib,'index') and the D candidate (desc,p,'index'), the expanded query would be

```
//article[about(.,'IR') and about(//bib,'index')]//*[about(.,'XML')
and about(//p,'index')]
```

Each of the expansions is weighted, where the weight is the candidate's RSJ weight adjusted by a factor that depends on the candidate's class. C and D candidates help finding new relevant results, so they should get a high weight; we allow for C and D conditions at most the weight of all original keywords (to make sure that the new constraints don't dominate the query's results). As an example, for a query with four keywords and six C and D expansions, the factor for each expansion is $\frac{4}{6}$. On the other hand, A and AD conditions are satisfied by most – if not all – elements of a document, so they generate a huge amount of new result elements, most of which will be nonrelevant. Their weight should therefore be smaller than the weight of C and D conditions. We choose a fraction $\beta$ of the accumulated weight of existing keyword conditions, with $\beta = 0.2$ in our experiments.

## 4   Architecture and Implementation

Figure 1 shows the high-level architecture of our extensible feedback framework. Each candidate class is implemented with a standard interface that allows a simple integration of new classes:

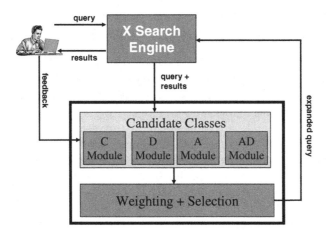

**Fig. 1.** Architecture of the feedback engine

The initial results of a query are presented to the user who gives positive or negative feedback to some of the results. This feedback is sent together with the query and its initial results to the feedback framework which forwards them to the available candidate classes. For each class, all possible candidates are computed for the results with known relevance. Out of all those candidates, the best $b$ candidates are selected and used to build the expanded query that is sent back to the engine which evaluates it and presents the results to the user. The user may now again submit feedback for some of the new results, triggering another feedback cycle. To facilitate an automatic assessment of the feedback approach, the system can additionally import queries and results from INEX (see Section 5.1) and automatically generate feedback for the top-$k$ results, using the existing INEX assessments.

We have implemented the framework in Java with the candidate classes shown in Section 3.2 and the TopX search engine. Our implementation requires that important information about elements is precomputed: unique identifiers for the element (eid) and its document (did), its pre and post order to facilitate the evaluation of structural query conditions like the XPath axes [7] or any other similar information, its tag, and its terms (after stemming and stopword removal), together with their score. This information is stored in a database table with schema (did,eid,pre,post, tag,term,score) that contains one tuple for each distinct term of an element. We can reuse an existing inverted file of an XML search engine that typically captures similar information, possibly after some transformation. On the database side, we provide indexes on (eid,did) to efficiently find $d(e)$ for an element $e$ and on (did) to efficiently collect all elements of a document. Inverse element and document frequencies of the different candidate classes are precomputed (e.g., while initially parsing the collection) and stored in database tables, too.

For each element with known relevance, the implementation of the feedback engine first loads the complete content of the element's document and computes all possible expansions in memory with the ief for the candidate loaded from the database. The additional constraint on the candidate's document frequency is then only checked for the best candidates that are considered for expanding the query.

# 5    Experimental Results

## 5.1    Settings

We use the *INEX* [12] benchmark for XML IR that provides a set of 12,107 XML documents (scientific articles from IEEE CS), a set of NEXI queries together with a manually assessed set of results for each query, and an evaluation environment to assess the effectiveness of XML search engines. INEX provides a Relevance Feedback Track [11, 4] that aims at assessing the quality of different feedback approaches. As this paper concentrates on keyword-based queries (*content-only topics* or *CO* for short in INEX), we used the set of 52 CO queries from the 2003 and 2004 evaluation rounds with relevant results together with the *strict* quantization mode, i.e., an element was considered as relevant if it exactly answers the query.

A *run* is the result of the evaluation of all topics with a search engine, it consists of 1500 results for each topic that are ranked by expected relevance. The measure of effectiveness is the *mean average precision* (MAP) of a run. Here, we first compute for each topic the average precision over 100 recall points (0.01 to 1.00) and then take the macro average over these topic-wise averages. Note that absolute MAP values are quite low for INEX (with 0.152 being the best MAP value of any participating engine in 2004). This reflects the fact that XML retrieval is inherently more complex than document retrieval as not only relevant documents, but also relevant elements within these documents have to be identified. In addition to MAP values, we also measured precision at different positions for each run.

To assess the quality of feedback algorithms, we use the residual collection technique [23] that is also used in the INEX 2004 Relevance Feedback Track. In this technique, all XML elements that are used by the feedback algorithm, i.e., those whose relevance is known to the algorithm, must be removed from the collection before evaluation of the results with feedback takes place. This includes all $k$ elements "seen" or used in the feedback process regardless of their relevance. Under INEX guidelines, this means not only each element used or observed in the RF process but also all descendants of that element must be removed from the collection (i.e., the residual collection, against which the feedback query is evaluated, must contain no descendant of that element). All ancestors of that element are retained in the residual collection.

**Table 1.** Precision at $k$ for the baseline run

| $k$ | 5 | 10 | 15 | 20 |
|---|---|---|---|---|
| prec@$k$ | 0.231 | 0.204 | 0.191 | 0.174 |

For all experiments we used the TopX engine that fully supports the evaluation of weighted content-and-structure queries. The baseline for all experiments is a run for all 52 INEX topics, with 1500 results for each topic. Table 1 shows the macro-averaged precision for this run for the top-$k$ ranked elements per topic, for different $k$; this corresponds to the average fraction of relevant results among the elements used for top-$k$ feedback.

To select the candidates for query expansion, we tried using the plain weight, the number of relevant elements with the feature, and RSV. In our experiments, all of these gave similar results with a small advantage for RSV, so we report only the results for experiments with RSV for feature selection.

## 5.2   Results

Table 2 shows the MAP values of our experiments with different combinations of candidate classes for query expansion, providing relevance feedback for a different number of top elements of the baseline run and selecting the best 10 candidates for expansion. Note that all values, including those for the baseline, are computed for the residual collection. It is evident that using only candidates of class D consistently outperforms the established content-based feedback (candidates of class C), with an increase over the baseline run of almost 150% for top-15 feedback. Candidates of classes A and AD did not perform too well if used alone, but this could be expected as using these candidates potentially adds a lot of nonrelevant elements to the result of the expanded query (see Section 3.3). However, if they are combined with the other classes and relevance for at least 10 elements is provided, the combination outperforms all other combinations.

We also measured the precision of the feedback runs at different positions; the results are depicted in Table 3. Again, using class D candidates outperformed traditional content-based feedback and gained up to 100% increase over the baselines' precision values. The combination of all candidate classes was again best if feedback for more than 10 results was available.

**Table 2.** MAP values for top-$k$ feedback runs with different configurations and different values of $k$

| $k$ | baseline | C | D | C+D | A | AD | A+AD | A+C+D+AD |
|---|---|---|---|---|---|---|---|---|
| 5 | 0.0493 | 0.0727 | 0.0757 | **0.0772** | 0.0520 | 0.0540 | 0.0497 | 0.0647 |
| 10 | 0.0544 | 0.0748 | **0.0784** | 0.0778 | 0.0584 | 0.0528 | 0.0547 | 0.0777 |
| 15 | 0.0290 | 0.0659 | 0.0717 | 0.0709 | 0.0574 | 0.0560 | 0.0575 | **0.0742** |
| 20 | 0.0498 | 0.0644 | 0.0725 | 0.0721 | 0.0555 | 0.0594 | 0.0579 | **0.0759** |

**Table 3.** Precision@p values for top-$k$ feedback runs with different configurations and different values of $k$

| $k$ | baseline | C | D | C+D | A | AD | A+AD | A+C+D+AD |
|---|---|---|---|---|---|---|---|---|
| | | | | p=5 | | | | |
| 5 | 0.1529 | 0.1804 | 0.2118 | **0.2157** | 0.1725 | 0.1686 | 0.1765 | 0.2000 |
| 10 | 0.1373 | 0.2078 | **0.2471** | 0.2392 | 0.1686 | 0.1752 | 0.1451 | 0.2391 |
| 15 | 0.0980 | 0.1804 | **0.1922** | 0.1843 | 0.1412 | 0.1529 | 0.1490 | **0.1922** |
| 20 | 0.1120 | 0.1800 | 0.1960 | **0.2160** | 0.1360 | 0.1600 | 0.1360 | 0.2000 |
| | | | | p=10 | | | | |
| 5 | 0.1411 | 0.1569 | 0.1588 | **0.1667** | 0.1549 | 0.1490 | 0.1412 | 0.1569 |
| 10 | 0.1275 | 0.1647 | 0.1765 | 0.1745 | 0.1373 | 0.1471 | 0.1451 | **0.1843** |
| 15 | 0.1039 | 0.1569 | 0.1627 | 0.1647 | 0.1235 | 0.1294 | 0.1314 | **0.1667** |
| 20 | 0.1040 | 0.1480 | 0.1720 | 0.1700 | 0.1140 | 0.1320 | 0.1200 | **0.1820** |
| | | | | p=15 | | | | |
| 5 | 0.1333 | 0.1412 | 0.1412 | **0.1464** | 0.1373 | 0.1399 | 0.1373 | 0.1346 |
| 10 | 0.1163 | 0.1438 | **0.1634** | 0.1621 | 0.1280 | 0.1307 | 0.1294 | 0.1608 |
| 15 | 0.1033 | 0.1333 | **0.1529** | 0.1490 | 0.1124 | 0.1216 | 0.1176 | 0.1490 |
| 20 | 0.0933 | 0.1307 | 0.1360 | 0.1360 | 0.0987 | 0.1147 | 0.1080 | **0.1467** |
| | | | | p=20 | | | | |
| 5 | 0.1255 | 0.1373 | 0.1363 | **0.1412** | 0.1255 | 0.1275 | 0.1245 | 0.1245 |
| 10 | 0.1108 | 0.1314 | **0.1431** | 0.1412 | 0.1186 | 0.1245 | 0.1225 | 0.1373 |
| 15 | 0.0902 | 0.1245 | **0.1382** | 0.1343 | 0.0980 | 0.1078 | 0.1029 | 0.1343 |
| 20 | 0.0830 | 0.1170 | 0.1150 | 0.1190 | 0.0890 | 0.1080 | 0.0990 | **0.1260** |

# 6    Conclusion and Future Work

This paper has made important steps from content-based to structural feedback in XML retrieval. It presented an integrated solution for expanding keyword queries with new weighted content and structure constraints as a part of an extensible framework and showed huge performance gains with the established INEX benchmark of up to 150% for MAP and up to 100% for precision under the evaluation method used in the INEX 2004 relevance feedback track.

Our future work will contentrate on adding new candidate classes (like twigs, tags and paths) and extending this work to queries with content and structural constraints. We also plan to evaluate the effectiveness of our approach with pseudo relevance feedback.

# References

1. G. Amati, C. Carpineto, and G. Romano. Merging XML indices. In *INEX Workshop 2004*, pages 77–81, 2004.
2. A. Balmin et al. A system for keyword proximity search on XML databases. In *VLDB 2003*, pages 1069–1072, 2003.
3. H. Blanken, T. Grabs, H.-J. Schek, R. Schenkel, and G. Weikum, editors. *Intelligent Search on XML Data*, volume 2818 of *LNCS*. Springer, Sept. 2003.

4. C. Crouch. Relevance feedback at the INEX 2004 workshop. In *SIGIR 2005 Forum*, 2005.
5. C. J. Crouch, A. Mahajan, and A. Bellamkonda. Flexible XML retrieval based on the extended vector model. In *INEX 2004 Workshop*, pages 149–153, 2004.
6. E. N. Efthimiadis. A user-centred evaluation of ranking algorithms for interactive query expansion. *SIGIR Forum (USA), special issue*, pages 146–159, 1993.
7. T. Grust. Accelerating XPath location steps. In *SIGMOD 2002*, pages 109–120, 2002.
8. L. Guo et al. XRANK: ranked keyword search over XML documents. In *SIGMOD 2003*, pages 16–27, 2003.
9. L. Hlaoua and M. Boughanem. Towards context and structural relevance feedback in XML retrieval. In *Workshop on Open Source Web Information Retrieval (OSWIR)*, 2005. http://www.emse.fr/OSWIR05/.
10. W. Hsu, M. L. Lee, and X. Wu. Path-augmented keyword search for XML documents. In *ICTAI 2004*, pages 526–530, 2004.
11. INEX relevance feedback track. http://inex.is.informatik.uni-duisburg.de:2004/tracks/rel/.
12. G. Kazai et al. The INEX evaluation initiative. In Blanken et al. [3], pages 279–293.
13. S. Liu, Q. Zou, and W. Chu. Configurable indexing and ranking for XML information retrieval. In *SIGIR 2004*, pages 88–95, 2004.
14. Y. Mass and M. Mandelbrod. Relevance feedback for XML retrieval. In *INEX 2004 Workshop*, pages 154–157, 2004.
15. V. Mihajloviè et al. TIJAH at INEX 2004 modeling phrases and relevance feedback. In *INEX 2004 Workshop*, pages 141–148, 2004.
16. H. Pan, A. Theobald, and R. Schenkel. Query refinement by relevance feedback in an XML retrieval system. In *ER 2004*, pages 854–855, 2004.
17. M. Porter and V. Galpin. Relevance fedback in a public access catalogue for a research library: Muscat at the Scott Polar Research Institute. *Program*, 22(1): 1–20, 1988.
18. G. Ramirez, T. Westerveld, and A. de Vries. Structural features in content oriented xml retrieval. Technical Report INS-E0508, CWI,Centre for Mathematics and Computer Science, 2005.
19. G. Ramírez, T. Westerveld, and A. P. de Vries. Structural features in content oriented XML retrieval. In *CIKM 2005*, 2005.
20. S. Robertson. On term selection for query expansion. *Journal of Documentation*, 46:359–364, Dec. 1990.
21. S. Robertson and K. Sparck-Jones. Relevance weighting of search terms. *Journal of the American Society of Information Science*, 27:129–146, May–June 1976.
22. J. Rocchio Jr. Relevance feedback in information retrieval. In G. Salton, editor, *The SMART Retrieval System: Experiments in Automatic Document Processing*, chapter 14, pages 313–323. Prentice Hall, Englewood Cliffs, New Jersey, USA, 1971.
23. I. Ruthven and M. Lalmas. A survey on the use of relevance feedback for information access systems. *Knowledge Engineering Review*, 18(1), 2003.
24. B. Sigurbjörnsson, J. Kamps, and M. de Rijke. The University of Amsterdam at INEX 2004. In *INEX 2004 Workshop*, pages 104–109, 2004.
25. M. Theobald, R. Schenkel, and G. Weikum. An efficient and versatile query engine for TopX search. In *VLDB 2005*, pages 625–636, 2005.
26. M. Theobald, R. Schenkel, and G. Weikum. TopX & XXL at INEX 2005. In *Preproceedings of the 2005 INEX Workshop*, Dagstuhl Castle, Germany, 2005.
27. A. Trotman and B. Sigurbjörnsson. Narrowed Extended XPath I (NEXI). available at http://www.cs.otago.ac.nz/postgrads/andrew/2004-4.pdf, 2004.

28. C. van Rijsbergen, D. Harper, and M. Porter. The selection of good search terms. *Information Processing and Management*, 17(2):77–91, 1981.

29. J.-N. Vittaut, B. Piwowarski, and P. Gallinari. An algebra for structured queries in bayesian networks. In *INEX Workshop 2004*, pages 58–64, 2004.

30. R. Weber. Using relevance feedback in XML retrieval. In Blanken et al. [3], pages 133–143.

31. Y. Xu and Y. Papakonstantinou. Efficient keyword search for smallest LCAs in XML databases. In *SIGMOD 2005*, pages 537–538, 2005.

# Machine Learning Ranking for Structured Information Retrieval

Jean-Noël Vittaut and Patrick Gallinari

Laboratoire d'Informatique de Paris 6,
8, rue du Capitaine Scott, F-75015 Paris, France
{vittaut, gallinari}@poleia.lip6.fr

**Abstract.** We consider the Structured Information Retrieval task which consists in ranking nested textual units according to their relevance for a given query, in a collection of structured documents. We propose to improve the performance of a baseline Information Retrieval system by using a learning ranking algorithm which operates on scores computed from document elements and from their local structural context. This model is trained to optimize a Ranking Loss criterion using a training set of annotated examples composed of queries and relevance judgments on a subset of the document elements. The model can produce a ranked list of documents elements which fulfills a given information need expressed in the query. We analyze the performance of our algorithm on the INEX collection and compare it to a baseline model which is an adaptation of Okapi to Structured Information Retrieval.

## 1 Introduction

Structured document collections, with documents encoded into a structured representation standard such as XML, XHTML, RDF, RSS are now becoming available and the IR community has started to develop search engines specifically dedicated to this type of documents [1] [2]. Document structure offers many new possibilities such as answering queries with structural constraints (Content and Structure queries in the INEX context[1] [1]), or simply providing the user with a list of relevant units with different granularities (Content Only queries in INEX (CO)). These units may correspond to different types of document elements in a structured document. In this paper, we consider the latter (CO) problematic. One difficulty of this task is to compare and rank document elements with very different characteristics such as their length, their redundancy, their thematic homogeneity, etc. Traditional search engines have been developed for ranking similar documents and are not adapted to this ranking task. Different frameworks have been developed for scoring elements in structured documents. For example theory of evidence has been used for aggregating evidence from sub-documents elements [3] [4]. Bayesian networks [5] or language models [6] are other formal paradigms for combining evidence from sub-elements in order

---

[1] INEX is the "INitiative for the Evaluation of XML Retrieval of the DELOS network of excellence".

M. Lalmas et al. (Eds.): ECIR 2006, LNCS 3936, pp. 338–349, 2006.
© Springer-Verlag Berlin Heidelberg 2006

to score a containing document element. In the Machine Learning community, ranking algorithms have recently motivated different studies and developments. In the field of textual documents, they have been successfully used to combine features or preferences relations in task such as meta search [7] [8] [9], automatic summarization [10] and recently for the combination of different sources of evidence in IR [11]. One of the difficulties of this paradigm is its complexity which is in the general case quadratic in the number of examples. Linear solutions have been proposed by some authors [9] [10]. Our approach extends the work of [10] to multiclass problems whereas most of experiments of ranking are based on two-classes problems, with a small class of relevant elements, and a large class of irrelevant elements. Under some conditions, fast rates of convergence are achieved with this class of methods [12].

We propose here to develop and use ranking methods adapted to a particular task of Structured Information Retrieval (SIR) which consists in producing a list of ordered documents elements which fulfills a content oriented query. Ranking can be particularly useful for SIR due to the intrinsic difficulty of this task, as already mentioned above, and because traditional search engines are not well adapted to this ranking task. It is hoped that ranking algorithms may help to improve the performance of existing techniques. Ranking algorithms work by combining features which characterize the data elements to be ranked. In our case, these features will depend on the document element itself and on its structural context. Ranking algorithms will learn to combine these different features in an optimal way according to a specific loss Function using a set of examples.

The paper is organized as follows, in section 2 we present the ranking model, in section 3 we show how it can be adapted to Structured Information Retrieval. In section 4 we describe some experiments with content-based queries on a semi-structured database and compare the algorithm to a baseline Okapi method adapted for SIR.

## 2   Framework

We present in this section a general model of ranking which can be adapted to IR or SIR. The idea of the ranking algorithms proposed in the Machine Learning community is to learn a total order on a set $\mathcal{X}$, which allows to compare any element pair in this set. Given this total order, we are able to order any subset of $\mathcal{X}$ in a ranking list. For instance in IR, $\mathcal{X}$ can be the set of documents which are relevant to a given query, and the total order is the natural order on the document scores.

As for any Machine Learning technique, one needs a training set of labeled examples in order to learn how to rank. This training set will consist in ordered pairs of examples. This will provide a partial order on the elements of $\mathcal{X}$. The ranking algorithm will use this information to learn a total order on the elements of $\mathcal{X}$ and after that will allow to rank new elements. For plain IR, the partial ordering may be provided by human assessments on different documents for a given query.

We introduce below some notations which will be used to compare the different subsets of a partially ordered set $\mathcal{X}$.

## 2.1   Notations

Let $\mathcal{X}$ be a set of elements with a partial order $\prec$ defined on it. This means that some of the element pairs in $\mathcal{X}$ may be compared according to the $\prec$ relation. If there is no preference between two element $x$ and $x'$, this is denoted by $x \perp x'$. For Structured Information retrieval $\mathcal{X}$ will be the set of couples (doxel[2], query) for all doxels and queries in the document collection. This set is partially ordered according to the existing relevance judgments for each query.

The set of all couples of $\mathcal{X} \times \mathcal{X}$ which are comparable according to $\prec$ is denoted:

$$\mathcal{A}(\mathcal{X}) = \{(x, x') \in \mathcal{X} \times \mathcal{X} / x \prec x' \text{ or } x' \prec x\}.$$

## 2.2   Ranking

Let $f$ be a Function from $\mathcal{X}$ to the set of real numbers. We can associate a total order to $f$ such that:

$$x \prec x' \Leftrightarrow f(x) < f(x') . \tag{1}$$

Clearly, learning the $f$ Function is the same as learning the total order.

An element of $\mathcal{X}$ is represented by a real vector of features $x = (t_1, t_2, ..., t_d)$. In our case, the features will be local scores computed on different contextual elements of a doxel (label, parent, children, document...). In the following, $f$ will be a linear combination of $x$'s features:

$$f_\omega(x) = \sum_{j=1}^{d} \omega_j t_j \tag{2}$$

where $\omega = (\omega_1, \omega_2, ..., \omega_d)$ are the parameters of the combination to be learned.

**Ranking Loss.** $f_\omega$ is said to respect $x \prec x'$ if $f_\omega(x) < f_\omega(x')$. In this case, couple $(x, x')$ is said to be well ordered by $f_\omega$. The ranking loss [9] measures how much $f_\omega$ respects $\prec$.

By definition, the ranking loss measures the number of mis-ordered couples in $\mathcal{A}(\mathcal{X})$:

$$R(\mathcal{A}(\mathcal{X}), \omega) = \sum_{\substack{(x,x') \in \mathcal{A}(\mathcal{X}) \\ x \prec x'}} \chi(x, x') \tag{3}$$

where $\chi(x, x') = 1$ if $f_\omega(x) > f_\omega(x')$ and 0 otherwise.

Ranking aims at learning $\omega$ for minimizing Function 3. This approach is different from previous Machine Learning approaches to IR such as Logistic Regression [13], since we do not try to classify elements into relevant group and irrelevant groups. Here, we are only interested in producing a well ordered list. That is why the criterion we use is only based on the relative position of elements in the

---

[2] Doxel means *document element*, a subpart of the document.

ranking list rather than on an absolute probability of belonging to a relevant or irrelevant class.

**Exponential loss.** In practice, this expression is not very useful since $\chi$ is not differentiable, ranking algorithms use to optimize an approximation of this loss criterion called the exponential loss:

$$R_e(\mathcal{A}(\mathcal{X}), \omega) = \sum_{\substack{(x,x') \in \mathcal{A}(\mathcal{X}) \\ x \prec x'}} e^{f_\omega(x) - f_\omega(x')} \tag{4}$$

It is straightforward that $R(\mathcal{A}(\mathcal{X}), \omega) \leq R_e(\mathcal{A}(\mathcal{X}), \omega)$. Function 4 is differentiable and convex, and then can be minimized using standard optimization techniques. Minimizing Function 4 will allow to minimize $R(\mathcal{A}(\mathcal{X}), \omega)$.

**Properties.** Some properties may be inferred from Function 4 which will allow us to reduce the complexity of the learning algorithm. In the general case, the complexity is quadratic in the number of examples and this does not allow us to learn with more than a few thousands of examples, which is not sufficient for most of real tasks.

Let us introduce on the subsets of $\mathcal{X}$, $\mathcal{P}(\mathcal{X})$, a derived strict partial order $\prec_{\mathcal{P}(\mathcal{X})}$ from $\prec$. For two subsets $\mathcal{X}_i$ and $\mathcal{X}_j$ of $\mathcal{X}$ :

$$\mathcal{X}_i \prec_{\mathcal{P}(\mathcal{X})} \mathcal{X}_j \Leftrightarrow \begin{cases} \forall x_i \in \mathcal{X}_i, \forall x_j \in \mathcal{X}_j : x_i \prec x_j \text{ and} \\ \forall (x_i, x_i') \in \mathcal{X}_i \times \mathcal{X}_i : x_i \perp x_i' \text{ and} \\ \forall (x_j, x_j') \in \mathcal{X}_j \times \mathcal{X}_j : x_j \perp x_j' \end{cases}$$

We derive similarly $\perp_{\mathcal{P}(\mathcal{X})}$ from $\perp$ as :

$$\mathcal{X}_i \perp_{\mathcal{P}(\mathcal{X})} \mathcal{X}_j \Leftrightarrow \forall x_i \in \mathcal{X}_i, \forall x_j \in \mathcal{X}_j : x_i \perp x_j.$$

Using these definitions, we can deduce elementary properties for $R_e(\mathcal{A}(\mathcal{X}), \omega)$.

*Property 1.* We denote $\mathcal{A}_i = \mathcal{A}(\mathcal{X}_i)$ and $\mathcal{A}_j = \mathcal{A}(\mathcal{X}_j)$. If any element of $\mathcal{X}_i$ is not comparable to any element of $\mathcal{X}_j$, the ranking loss can be expressed as the sum of two sub-ranking losses over $\mathcal{A}(\mathcal{X}_i)$ and $\mathcal{A}(\mathcal{X}_j)$:

$$\mathcal{X}_i \perp_{\mathcal{P}(\mathcal{X})} \mathcal{X}_j \Rightarrow R_e(\mathcal{A}(\mathcal{X}_i) \cup \mathcal{A}(\mathcal{X}_j), \omega) = R_e(\mathcal{A}(\mathcal{X}_i), \omega) + R_e(\mathcal{A}(\mathcal{X}_j), \omega). \tag{5}$$

*Property 2.* If any element of $\mathcal{X}_i$ is superior to any element of $\mathcal{X}_j$, and elements inside $\mathcal{X}_i$ or $\mathcal{X}_j$ are not ordered, the ranking loss can be expressed as the product of two summations over $\mathcal{X}_i$ and $\mathcal{X}_j$:

$$\mathcal{X}_i \prec_{\mathcal{P}(\mathcal{X})} \mathcal{X}_j \Rightarrow R_e(\mathcal{X}_i \times \mathcal{X}_j, \omega) = \left( \sum_{x \in \mathcal{X}_i} e^{f_\omega(x)} \right) \left( \sum_{x' \in \mathcal{X}_j} e^{-f_\omega(x)} \right) \tag{6}$$

**Reduction of the complexity.** Using these properties, we will now propose a way for reducing the complexity of minimizing Function 4. It is based on

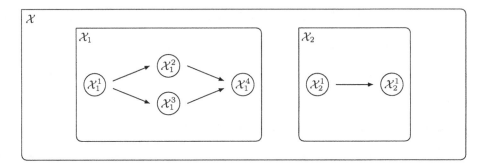

**Fig. 1.** Representation of a partition of $\mathcal{X}$. There is no order between an element of $\mathcal{X}_1$ and an element of $\mathcal{X}_2$. Inside $\mathcal{X}_1$, the arrow $\mathcal{X}_1^1 \to \mathcal{X}_1^2$ means that an element of $\mathcal{X}_1^1$ must be higher ranked than an element of $\mathcal{X}_1^2$. Inside any $\mathcal{X}_i^j$, there is no order.

a decomposition of $R_e(\mathcal{A}(\mathcal{X}), \omega)$ according to the greatest subsets of $\mathcal{X}$ which verify either of the conditions expressed in the left hand side of Equations 5 or 6 ($\mathcal{X}_i \perp_{\mathcal{P}(\mathcal{X})} \mathcal{X}_j$ or $\mathcal{X}_i \prec_{\mathcal{P}(\mathcal{X})} \mathcal{X}_j$). These subsets are denoted $\mathcal{X}_i^j$ in the following.

Let $\mathcal{X}_1, \mathcal{X}_2, ..., \mathcal{X}_n$ be a partition of $\mathcal{X}$ such that:

$$\forall (i, j) \in \{1, ..., n\}^2 : \mathcal{X}_i \perp_{\mathcal{P}(\mathcal{X})} \mathcal{X}_j. \tag{7}$$

The subsets used for the decomposition of the error Function, $\mathcal{X}_k^1, \mathcal{X}_k^2, ..., \mathcal{X}_k^{n_k}$, will be a partition of $\mathcal{X}_k$ such that:

$$\forall (i, j) \in \{1, ..., n_k\}^2 : \begin{cases} \mathcal{X}_k^i \perp_{\mathcal{P}(\mathcal{X})} \mathcal{X}_k^j \text{ or} \\ \mathcal{X}_k^i \prec_{\mathcal{P}(\mathcal{X})} \mathcal{X}_k^j \text{ or} \\ \mathcal{X}_k^j \prec_{\mathcal{P}(\mathcal{X})} \mathcal{X}_k^i \end{cases} \tag{8}$$

An example of possible partition is represented in figure 1.

According to property 1 and property 2, the exponential loss (4) can be rewritten:

$$R_e(\mathcal{A}(\mathcal{X}), \omega) = \sum_{k=1}^{n} \sum_{i=1}^{n_k} \left\{ \left( \sum_{x \in \mathcal{X}_k^i} e^{f_\omega(x)} \right) \left( \sum_{\substack{j \in [1, n_k] \\ \mathcal{X}_k^j \prec \mathcal{X}_k^i}} \sum_{x' \in \mathcal{X}_k^j} e^{-f_\omega(x')} \right) \right\}. \tag{9}$$

The complexity for computing this expression is $O(n \cdot K \cdot |\mathcal{X}|)$ whereas it is $O(n \cdot |\mathcal{X}|^2)$ for Function 4 where $K$ is the total number of subsets $\mathcal{X}_j^i$ in the partition of $\mathcal{X}$. The worst case occurs when $K = |\mathcal{X}|$.

**Gradient descent.** Since Function 9 is convex, we can use a gradient descent technique to minimize it. The components of the gradient has the following form:

$$\frac{\partial R_e(\mathcal{A}(\mathcal{X}))}{\partial \omega_p} = \sum_{k=1}^{n} \sum_{i=1}^{n_k} \left\{ \left( \sum_{x \in \mathcal{X}_k^i} t_p e^{f_\omega(x)} \right) \left( \sum_{\substack{j \in [1,n_k] \\ \mathcal{X}_k^j \prec \mathcal{X}_k^i}} \sum_{x' \in \mathcal{X}_k^j} e^{-f_\omega(x')} \right) \right.$$

$$\left. + \left( \sum_{x \in \mathcal{X}_k^i} e^{f_\omega(x)} \right) \left( \sum_{\substack{j \in [1,n_k] \\ \mathcal{X}_k^j \prec \mathcal{X}_k^i}} \sum_{x' \in \mathcal{X}_k^j} -t'_p e^{-f_\omega(x')} \right) \right\} . \tag{10}$$

The complexity for computing the gradient is the same ($O(n \cdot K \cdot |\mathcal{X}|)$) as that of Function 9.

## 3 Application to Structured Information Retrieval

### 3.1 Definitions

Suppose we have a collection of hierarchically structured documents. Each document $d$ can be represented by a tree $T$. Each node of the tree has a "type" (or tag) and a textual content. $\mathcal{L}$ will denote the set of node types.

For each node $n$ of $T$, the doxel at node $n$ is the subtree $T_n$ of $T$ rooted at $n$.

We use the following notations, $\mathcal{D}$ is the set of doxels for all the documents in the collection, $\mathcal{Q}$ is a a set of information needs and $\mathcal{X} = \mathcal{Q} \times \mathcal{D}$ is the set of elements we want to order.

We suppose that there exists a partial order $\prec$ on $\mathcal{X} = \mathcal{Q} \times \mathcal{D}$, this partial order will reflect for some information needs, the evidence we have about preferences between doxels. It is provided via user feedback or manual assessments of the SIR corpus. Note that these relevance assessments are needed only on a subpart of the collection We consider here the task which consists in producing a ranked list of doxels which fulfill an information need $q \in \mathcal{Q}$. For that, we will train the ranking model to learn a total strict order on $\mathcal{X}$.[3]

### 3.2 Representation

Each element $x \in \mathcal{X}$ is represented by a vector $(t_1, t_2, ..., t_d)$ were $t_i$ represents some feature which could be useful to order elements of $\mathcal{X}$.

To take into account the structural information, we will use the information provided by the context of the doxel and the information given by the node type of the doxel. For the former, we will use features characterizing the doxel, its parent, and the whole document. For the latter, label information can be used by ranking doxels with the same node type which leads to learn a $f_{\omega|l}$ for each node type $l$, and then using all $f_{\omega|l}(x)_{l=1..|\mathcal{L}|}$ as features in a second ranking step.

---

[3] For simplification, we consider here a total strict order on the doxels, and not the case where different doxels may have the same rank.

These two steps can be reduced to one using the following vector representation. If we denote $x^l = (t_0^l, t_1^l, t_2^l, ..., t_d^l)$, where $t_0^l = 1$ is a bias term, the vector representing $x$ for node type $l$, we have $t_i^l = t_i$ if $l$ is the node type of the root of $x$ and $t_i^{(l)} = 0$ if not. We will consider the ranking of global vectors defined as follows:

$$x = \left( (t_0^{l_1}, t_1^{l_1}, t_2^{l_1}, ..., t_d^{l_1}), (t_0^{l_2}, t_1^{l_2}, t_2^{l_2}, ..., t_d^{l_2}), ..., (t_0^{l_{|\mathcal{L}|}}, t_1^{l_{|\mathcal{L}|}}, t_2^{l_{|\mathcal{L}|}}, ..., t_d^{l_{|\mathcal{L}|}}) \right).$$

Where $|\mathcal{L}|$ is the number of different labels in the collection. In the above expression all vector components of the form $(t_0^{l_i}, t_1^{l_i}, t_2^{l_i}, ..., t_d^{l_i})$ will be equal to $(0, 0, ..., 0)$ except for one which corresponds to $x$ label. This representation allows computing in one step the ranking of nodes from different types.

## 3.3   Reduction of Complexity

In order to reduce the complexity, we have to find the subsets $\mathcal{X}_1, \mathcal{X}_2, ..., \mathcal{X}_n$ of $\mathcal{X}$ which verify the condition (7) in section 2.2. We can easily find such subsets, if we denote $(q_i)_{i=1..|\mathcal{Q}|}$ the elements of $\mathcal{Q}$, there are at least for each $q_i$:

$$\mathcal{X}_i = \{x = (d, q) \in \mathcal{X}/q = q_i\}$$

$\mathcal{X}_i$ is the set of couples (doxel, information need) which corresponds to the same information need. A corollary of this property is that it is useless to compare scores of doxels from different queries. For each $\mathcal{X}_i$'s, the preferences among doxels may be expressed according to several discrete dimensions. For example in INEX, we have:

- an information of exhaustivity, which measures how much a doxel answers the totality of an information need (0 not exhaustive, ..., 3 fully exhaustive)
- an information of specificity, which measures how much a doxel answers only the information need (0 not specific, ..., 3 means fully specific)

A doxel labeled $E_3 S_3$ (which means fully exhaustive and specific) is greater than one labeled $E_1 S_3$ (which means marginally exhaustive and fully specific).

If such a discrete multidimensional scale exists, we can find a partition according to (8) by considering for each $\mathcal{X}_i^j$ a set of doxels whose assessments share the same values along all dimensions. For instance, we can choose $\mathcal{X}_i^0$ to be the set of doxels assessed $E_0 S_0$ for the information need $q_i$.

# 4   Experiments

## 4.1   Test Collection

To evaluate our method, we used the INEX document, topic and assessment collection. This collection contains 16819 XML documents representing the content of the articles of the IEEE Computer Society's journal publications from 1995 to 2004. These documents are represented in the same DTD. In the year 2003, 36 content-oriented topics with the corresponding assessments on doxels were produced. In 2004, 40 topics and assessments were added. The assessments for 2003

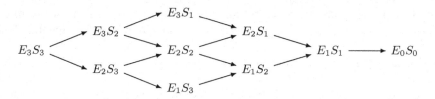

**Fig. 2.** Graph representing the order between elements for a given information need, according to the two dimensional discrete scale of INEX. Doxels labeled $E_3S_3$ must be the highest ranked, and doxels labeled $E_0S_0$ the lowest ranked.

and 2004 only concern 12107 documents from 1995 to 2002, since the rest of the collection was not available at this time. In 2005, the database has been extended with document from 2003 to 2004 and 40 topics and assessments were added.

A content-oriented topic is a list of words representing an information need.

An assessment is an evaluation of how much a particular doxel of the document collection answers the information need. In INEX, assessments are expressed in a two dimensional discrete scale which has been described above in section 3.3. The assessments and the trellis giving the partial ordering between these assessments are described in Figure 2.

### 4.2   Representation

For computing features, we used an Okapi model[4] [14], which is one of the reference models on flat documents. Okapi was adapted so as to reach good performance on the collection of structured documents. This adaptation consists in using doxels rather than documents for computing the term frequencies, and using as normalization factor for each doxel, the mean size of the doxels with the same node type.

In the experiments, we used three features for the combination:

- $t_1 = $ the Okapi score of the doxel
- $t_2 = $ the Okapi score of the parent of the doxel
- $t_3 = $ the Okapi score of the whole document

these features provide some information about the structural context of a doxel. Sets of node types were defined according to the DTD of the document collection: article, abstract, sections, paragraphs, lists... Node type was introduced according to the method described in section 3.2.

We used the series of topics and assessments from the INEX 2003 and 2004 collections as a learning base and those from 2005 as a test base.

### 4.3   Filtering

For some SIR systems, returning overlapping doxels could be an undesirable behaviour, which means for example that it should not return a section, and

---

[4] With parameters $k_1 = 2.0$, $k_3 = 7.0$ and $b = 0.75$.

one of its paragraphs. In order to suppress all overlapping elements from an existing list, we used a strategy which consists in removing all elements which are overlapping with an element ranked higher in the list. This is the simplest way to remove overlap and this allows us to focus on the efficiency of the ranking algorithm rather than the filtering technique. Other ways of limiting overlapping can be found in [15]. Two kinds of experiences have been carried out : 2 without removing overlap, and 2 where overlap was removed.

### 4.4   Evaluation

We used two metrics to evaluate our approach:

- a precision recall metric which does not take into account overlapping elements;
- a cumulated gain based metric [16]. This metric, developed for the evaluation of INEX [17], considers the dependency of XML elements, and will penalize ranked lists with overlapping elements.

### 4.5   Results

**With filtering.** We have plotted in figures 3 and 4 the evaluation of the lists produced by the ranking algorithm and by the modified Okapi where overlap was removed. We can see for both metrics that the ranking algorithm performs better than Okapi. The difference for the precision/recall metric is not large: this is due to the post filtering of the lists. The ranked lists had not been optimized for non overlapping elements since there is no notion of overlapping in the exponential loss.

**Without filtering.** Figures 5 and 6 show the evaluation of the lists produced by the ranking algorithm and modified Okapi where overlap was removed. We can see for both metrics that the ranking algorithm performs clearly better than

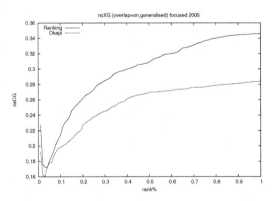

**Fig. 3.** Performance of Ranking and Okapi models with filtering evaluated with the cumulated based metric ncXG

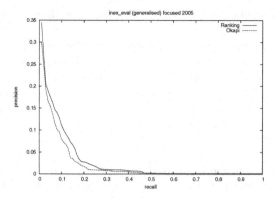

**Fig. 4.** Performance of Ranking and Okapi models with filtering evaluated with the precision/recall metric

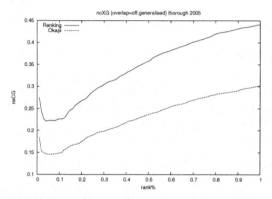

**Fig. 5.** Performance of Ranking and Okapi models without filtering evaluated with the cumulated based metric ncXG

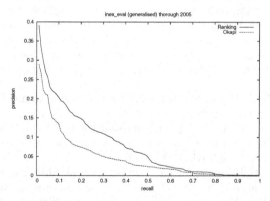

**Fig. 6.** Performance of Ranking and Okapi models without filtering evaluated with the precision/recall metric

Okapi and the difference in performance is superior than in the non overlapping case.

For both experiments, the ranking algorithm has been able to increase the performance of the baseline Okapi. Ranking methods thus appear as a promising direction for improving SIR search engine performance. It remains to perform tests with additional features (for example the scores of additional IR systems).

## 5    Conclusion

We have described a new model for performing Structured Information Retrieval. It relies on a combination of scores from the Okapi model and takes into account the document structure. This score combination is learned from a training set by a ranking algorithm. We have shown that learning to rank document elements improves a baseline model Okapi, which is known to be effective on IR on flat documents.

## Acknowledgements

This work was supported in part by the IST Programme of the European Community, under the PASCAL Network of Excellence, IST-2002-506778. This publication only reflects the authors' views.

## References

1. Fuhr, N., Lalmas, M., Malik, S., Szlávik, Z., eds.: Advances in XML Information Retrieval, Third International Workshop of the Initiative for the Evaluation of XML Retrieval, INEX 2004, Dagstuhl Castle, Germany, December 6-8, 2004, Revised Selected Papers. In Fuhr, N., Lalmas, M., Malik, S., Szlávik, Z., eds.: INEX. Volume 3493 of Lecture Notes in Computer Science., Springer (2005)
2. Baeza-Yates, R., Maarek, Y.S., Roelleke, T., de Vries, A.P.: Third edition of the "XML and Information Retrieval" workshop. first workshop on integration of ir and db (wird) jointly held at sigir'2004, sheffield, uk, july 29th, 2004. SIGIR Forum (2004) 24-30
3. Lalmas, M.: Dempster-shafer's theory of evidence applied to structured documents: Modelling uncertainty (1997)
4. Lalmas, M., Moutogianni, E.: A dempster-shafer indexing for the focussed retrieval of hierarchically structured documents: Implementation and experiments on a web museum collection (2000) RIAO, Paris, France.
5. Piwowarski, B., Gallinari, P.: A bayesian network for XML Information Retrieval: Searching and learning with the INEX collection. Information Retrieval (2004)
6. Ogilvie P., Callan J.: Using Language Models for Flat Text Queries in XML Retrieval. In Proceedings of INEX 2003 (2004) 12-18
7. Cohen, W.W., Schapire, R.E., Singer, Y.: Learning to order things. In Jordan, M.I., Kearns, M.J., Solla, S.A., eds.: Advances in Neural Information Processing Systems. Volume 10., The MIT Press (1998)

8. Bartell, B.T., Cottrell, G.W., Belew, R.K.: Automatic combination of multiple ranked retrieval systems. In: Research and Development in Information Retrieval. (1994) 173–181

9. Freund, Y., Iyer, R., Schapire, R.E., Singer, Y.: An efficient boosting algorithm for combining preferences. In Shavlik, J.W., ed.: Proceedings of ICML-98, 15th International Conference on Machine Learning, Madison, US, Morgan Kaufmann Publishers, San Francisco, US (1998) 170–178

10. Amini, M.R., Usunier, N., Gallinari, P.: Automatic text summarization based on word-clusters and ranking algorithms. In: ECIR. (2005) 142–156

11. Craswell, N., Robertson, S., Zaragoza, H., Taylor, M.: Relevance weighting for query independent evidence. In: SIGIR '05: Proceedings of the 28th annual international ACM SIGIR conference on Research and development in information retrieval, New York, NY, USA, ACM Press (2005) 416–423

12. Auer, P., Meir, R., eds.: Learning Theory, 18th Annual Conference on Learning Theory, COLT 2005, Bertinoro, Italy, June 27-30, 2005, Proceedings. In Auer, P., Meir, R., eds.: COLT. Volume 3559 of Lecture Notes in Computer Science., Springer (2005)

13. Cooper, W.S., Gey, F.C., Dabney, D.P.: Probabilistic retrieval based on staged logistic regression. In Belkin, N.J., Ingwersen, P., Pejtersen, A.M., eds.: Proceedings of the 15th Annual International ACM SIGIR Conference on Research and Development in Information Retrieval. Copenhagen, Denmark, June 21-24, 1992, New York, ACM (1992) 198–210

14. Robertson, S.E., Walker, S., Hancock-Beaulieu, M., Gull, A., Lau, M.: Okapi at TREC. In: Text REtrieval Conference. (1992) 21–30

15. Kazai, G., Lalmas, M., Rölleke, T.: A model for the representation and focussed retrieval of structured documents based on fuzzy aggregation. In: SPIRE. (2001) 123–135

16. Järvelin, K., Kekäläinen, J.: Cumulated gain-based evaluation of ir techniques. ACM Trans. Inf. Syst. (2002) 422–446

17. Kazai, G., Lalmas, M.: Inex 2005 evaluation metrics. Technical document (2005)

# Generating and Retrieving Text Segments for Focused Access to Scientific Documents

Caterina Caracciolo and Maarten de Rijke

ISLA, University of Amsterdam,
Kruislaan 403, 1098 SJ Amsterdam, The Netherlands
{caterina, mdr}@science.uva.nl

**Abstract.** When presented with a retrieved document, users of a search engine are usually left with the task of pinning down the relevant information inside the document. Often this is done by a time-consuming combination of skimming, scrolling and Ctrl+F. In the setting of a digital library for scientific literature the issue is especially urgent when dealing with reference works, such as surveys and handbooks, as these typically contain long documents. Our aim is to develop methods for providing a "go-read-here" type of retrieval functionality, which points the user to a segment where she can best start reading to find out about her topic of interest. We examine multiple query-independent ways of segmenting texts into coherent chunks that can be returned in response to a query. Most (experienced) authors use paragraph breaks to indicate topic shifts, thus providing us with one way of segmenting documents. We compare this structural method with semantic text segmentation methods, both with respect to topical focus and relevancy. Our experimental evidence is based on manually segmented scientific documents and a set of queries against this corpus. Structural segmentation based on contiguous blocks of relevant paragraphs is shown to be a viable solution for our intended application of providing "go-read-here" functionality.

## 1 Introduction

The growing number of scientific publications available in electronic format has changed the way people relate to documents. Working within the scientific domain, Tenopir and King [32] observe that researchers now tend to read more articles than before, but that, on average, the time dedicated to each article has shrunk and readers very rarely read an entire article—instead, they browse and skim the document, possibly doing attentive reading of only some parts of it. Increasingly, people use a "locate-and-read" strategy instead of the more traditional "read-and-locate" typical of a paper environment.

Currently, there are several examples where a kind of "go-read-here" functionality is available or being explored. For example, some general web search engines help users in their search "within" retrieved documents by providing links labeled "HTML version" (for non-HTML documents) and "In cache" (which takes the user to a cached version of the document where query words are highlighted). In the setting of document-centric XML retrieval, the search engine looks inside the document for relevant information, and selects small relevant elements ("sub-documents") to be returned to the user [17].

M. Lalmas et al. (Eds.): ECIR 2006, LNCS 3936, pp. 350–361, 2006.
© Springer-Verlag Berlin Heidelberg 2006

Our setting is that of scientific literature digital libraries, and, more specifically, reference works such as surveys and handbooks in such libraries. Within this setting our aim is to provide "go-read-here" functionality of the following kind: given a query, suggest to the reader short, highly relevant segments from retrieved documents. How should we identify and retrieve appropriate segments for a "go-read-here" type of facility, using only query-independent information? Put differently, how should we create potential targets for hypertext links prior to knowing the link source (i.e., the query). Since every text has an internal structure [35], corresponding to the topics the author of the text wants to present, one obvious approach to identify the kind of segments we seek to identify is to adopt a so-called *structural* view on text segments, and take segments to be nothing but paragraphs. How does this strategy compare to so-called *semantic* segments, as produced by state-of-the-art segmentation algorithms such as Text-Tiling [13, 14] and C99 [6, 7]? These are the research questions that have guided much of the research on which we report in this paper.

Our main contributions are the following. First, we present an analysis of query independent text segmentation techniques applied to scientific texts. Second, we investigate the use of segments within a "go-read-here" retrieval task; in the process we define two new evaluation measures and also define a variation of precision to meet our needs. Our experimental evaluation is based on the *Handbook of Logic and Language* [34], a collection of 20 essays on the interface between logic and linguistics; each chapter (65 pages long, on average) is written by a different author and with varying internal organization and writing style. Our main finding is that structural segmentation based on contiguous blocks of relevant paragraphs is a simple but viable solution for our intended application of providing "go-read-here" functionality.

The rest of the paper is structured as follows. In Section 2 we present related work on "within document navigation." In Section 3 we survey relevant aspects of text segmentation methods. In Section 4 we describe experiments concerning document segmentation, and in Section 5 we present experiments concerning the use of these segments in a retrieval setting. We conclude in Section 6.

## 2   Related Work

Work related to this paper comes from research into hypertext link generation, information retrieval, information visualization, and digital libraries. The relations between two linked hypertext documents have been analyzed extensively [3, 9, 11, 33]. Information retrieval techniques have been used to generate hypertexts [1], and also text passages have played a role in generating links among documents [2]. In IR, passage retrieval refers to approaches that either return passages to the reader [27], or make use of evidence obtained from passages to improve the performance of full document retrieval [5, 18], or to select excerpts to index independently [14]; we follow the latter route.

Information visualization techniques have provided important means for improving the way in which documents are accessed, and especially the way in which *focused* retrieval is increasingly being facilitated. For example, TileBars [15] is a visualization paradigm for boolean retrieval, where documents are represented in their relative size, and passages within them are highlighted in color depending on the distribution of the query terms. SmartSkim [12] is a content-based browsing and skimming tool that divides a document deemed relevant by a user into fixed length sections represented by histograms whose height corresponds to the computed relevance of that section to a query.

In the context of digital libraries there has been considerable work on digitizing both content and metadata. Increasingly, methods are considered that integrate ideas building on traditional classification techniques developed over the centuries by librarians and information specialists with "free text" search technology, thus bringing in modern document retrieval technology [19].

Relatively little research has been aimed at providing focused access to *scientific* documents. Our work differs from the work carried out on generating hypertext in that we do not split the document into hyperlinked snippets, but, instead, provide the reader with a passage where she is to start reading, without missing out relevant text. In this sense, our work also differs from SmartSkim, in that we do not use fixed size passages. Finally, like TileBars, we presuppose that the document segmentation takes place offline, at indexing time, but unlike TileBars we aim at performing a comparison to understand which segmentation better suits the type of documents at hand.

## 3   Methods for Text Segmentation

Recall that our overall aim is to provide "go-read-here" functionality: return a highly relevant text segment from a long document in return to a user's query. Our first steps, then, will be to identify suitable text segments.

A segmentation is called *semantic* if segments are defined using a notion of the semantics of the text, *structural* if defined on the basis of structural information, e.g., paragraphs or sections, and *fixed size* if segments are identified through a fixed number of words or characters [30]. Many authors have proposed algorithms for semantic segmentation [16, 23, 25, 28, 29], either to achieve more accurate indexing [16] or to detect topic shifts in streams of news [31].

One of our core questions in this paper is to find out whether semantic methods offer an advantage over and above structural methods. Rather than implementing a new semantic segmentation method, or providing an exhaustive experimental comparison of all existing ones, we selected two well-known semantic methods for our experiments: *TextTiling* and *C99*. Both perform linear segmentation, the former based on cosine similarity between sliding windows of text, the latter based on divisive clustering. We chose TextTiling because of its established position in the literature (and because many other methods build on it); C99 was chosen because of the good results reported in the literature [6]. Below, we outline both segmentation methods; after that we compare the quality of the outputs of the two algorithms against the quality of structural methods (Section 4), and examine the effectiveness of segments identified using either of the two methods for information access, again in comparison with structural methods (Section 5).

*TextTiling* [13, 14] tokenizes the document and performs stopword removal and morphological normalization. TextTiling divides texts into *pseudo-sentences* of a fixed length, which are grouped into pseudo-paragraphs, or *blocks*, of a fixed size, sliding along the text. Hearst [14] suggests that pseudo-sentences of twenty words and blocks of six pseudo-sentences work best in practice.

Each *gap* in between pseudo-sentences is assigned a cosine similarity value between pairs of adjacent blocks, computed with a sliding window mechanism. These values are then smoothed with a simple median smoothing algorithm [24] with a window of size 3, to eliminate small local minima, and the smoothed similarity values are then plotted against the sequence of gaps. The resulting plot is analyzed for peaks and valleys. Each gap is assigned a *depth score*, indicating how strong the evidence is that it is a candidate topic break. The depth score at gap $g$, $ds(g)$, is computed as $ds(g) = (a_s - g_s) + (b_s - g_s)$, where $g_s$ is the smoothed similarity value at gap $g$ and $a_s$ and $b_s$ are the smoothed similarity values at gaps $a$ and $b$, to the left and to the right of $g$, respectively, each being a peak with respect to $g$. The deeper $g$ is with respect to the closest valleys to the left and to the right, the more likely it is that the gap is a candidate break. Finally, TextTiling takes the gaps with the highest depth scores as candidate subtopic boundaries, but only places topic boundaries at (real) paragraph breaks.

*C99* [6, 7] differs from TextTiling in that it takes real sentences as units and identifies topic boundaries by means of a divisive clustering method. First, the text is divided into tokenized sentences, then stop word removal and stemming follow. The algorithm then computes a similarity matrix at the sentence level, where the adopted similarity measure is the usual cosine similarity. Since the cosine measure is sensitive to the length of the sentences, Choi [6] applies a *ranking scheme* [22] to the similarity matrix to avoid using absolute values. Finally, a hierarchical divisive clustering method (based on [25]) is applied, where segment boundaries are selected to maximize a measure of internal segment cohesion. If the number of desired segments is not given up front, the clustering process is continued until no further segmentation is possible.

TextTiling has a clear intuitive interpretation in terms of text structure, while this is not the case for C99 (consider, e.g., the ranking scheme and the lack of references to specific textual or linguistic features). The experiments reported in [6] were performed on an artificially generated corpus of 700 samples, where a sample is a concatenation of ten text segments, where each segment consists of the first $n$ lines extracted from a random document from the Brown Corpus.

# 4    Splitting Documents into Topic-Oriented Segments

Having introduced the two semantic text segmentation methods that we consider in this paper, our first aim is to see to how the segments they produce compare against a structural segmentation. Recall that structural segmentations in terms of paragraphs exploit the topic shifts (implicitly) marked by authors through their paragraph boundaries.

When applied to our data, consisting of long scientific documents, do Text-Tiling and C99 produce segments that are topically coherent? And: do they add anything when compared against two structural segmentations, into paragraphs and sections respectively? To answer these questions we developed a gold standard segmentation using two documents from our corpus, and used it to assess and compare the outputs of both the semantic and structural segmentation, as we will now describe.

## 4.1 Experimental Setting

First, a manually annotated corpus was created, containing "gold standard" topic breaks, to be used as the ground truth for evaluating the output of the structural and semantic segmentation algorithms. Two annotators independently annotated the text for topic breaks, and then discussed their results between them to come to a single annotation. The annotators were given basic guidelines:

1. a topic segment is a text snippet smaller than the original text and of homogeneous content;
2. segments do not overlap;
3. there are no topic breaks within paragraphs; and
4. no segment should span more than an entire section.

The corpus consists of two chapters—[36] and [21]—from the *Handbook of Logic and Language*, here called Chapter $A$ and Chapter $B$, respectively (see Table 1, left-hand side, for details), with different internal structure and writing styles.[1] Chapters were in LaTeX format, which necessitated some preprocessing.

**Table 1.** (Left): Details about the corpus. (Right): Details about the ground truth for segmentation. Average paragraph length is given in number of words.

| | Chapter $A$ | Chapter $B$ | | Chapter $A$ | Chapter $B$ |
|---|---|---|---|---|---|
| # pages | 55 | 54 | # segments | 102 | 90 |
| # section | 13 | 3 | # paragraphs/segm | 1.6 | 2.5 |
| # subsections | 0 | 9 | $\kappa$ (inter-annotator | 0.69 | 0.84 |
| # paragraphs | 168 | 223 | agreement) | | |
| avg. par. length | 458 | 320 | | | |

The right-hand side of Table 1 contains details about the annotators' output. The inter-annotator agreement, $\kappa$ [8], indicates tentative reliability for Chapter $A$ and high reliability for Chapter $B$ (third row, right-hand side). The low $\kappa$ score for Chapter $A$ is probably due to the presence of long lists of examples and properties. This caused the annotators to have different perceptions about where an appropriate break between segments could be placed. The annotators agreed on a rather fragmented segmentation in case of Chapter $A$ and on an only slightly more aggressive annotation in case of Chapter $B$.

---

[1] We counted as paragraph blocks of text separated by indentation, independently of the non-textual elements they can include (e.g., figures, tables, equations, ...).

**Table 2.** Results for the two structural segmentations, and the best performing versions of TextTiling and C99. The highest values are in boldface.

|  | Chapter $A$ | | | | Chapter $B$ | | | |
|---|---|---|---|---|---|---|---|---|
|  | P | R | F | # Segm. | P | R | F | # Segm. |
| Paragraphs | 0.61 | **1** | 0.76 | 168 | 0.41 | **1** | 0.58 | 223 |
| Sections | **1** | 0.10 | 0.18 | 13 | **1** | 0.02 | 0.04 | 3 |
| TT default | 0.62 | **1** | **0.77** | 165 | 0.42 | 0.98 | **0.59** | 212 |
| TT s5-w20 | 0.61 | **1** | 0.76 | 169 | 0.42 | **0.99** | **0.59** | 215 |
| TT s5-w30 | 0.61 | **1** | 0.76 | 166 | 0.42 | **0.99** | **0.59** | 215 |
| TT s20-w30 | **0.64** | 0.83 | 0.72 | 132 | **0.46** | 0.79 | 0.58 | 157 |
| TT s20-w40 | **0.64** | 0.80 | 0.71 | 128 | 0.43 | 0.71 | 0.54 | 150 |
| C99 default | 0.57 | 0.08 | 0.14 | 14 | 0.57 | 0.14 | 0.22 | 24 |
| C99 r9 | 0.54 | 0.07 | 0.12 | 13 | **0.62** | 0.11 | 0.19 | 17 |
| C99 r57 | **0.72** | **0.13** | 0.22 | 18 | 0.60 | 0.16 | 0.25 | 25 |

## 4.2   Evaluation

We compared the segmentations produced by TextTiling and C99 with two structural segmentations: one in which each paragraph is a segment, and one in which each section is a segment. We used the implementations of TextTiling and C99 made available by Choi. We exhaustively explored the parameter settings for TextTiling (the number of smoothing cycles $s$, default $= 5$, and the window size $w$, default $= 30$ words) and for C99 (the size of the rank mask, default $= 11 \times 11$, and the number of segments to find). Table 2 reports the results obtained with default values and with the best performing parameter settings. We report on precision (P), recall (R), and F-scores; P and R were computed on segment breaks, as opposed to entire segments.[2]

As expected, segments that are one paragraph long score best in recall but much less in precision, while sections do the opposite. C99 and the segmentation based on sections produce a similar number of segments and recall figures for Chapter $A$. In the case of Chapter $B$, they both score very low. This suggests that the quality of a segmentation is strictly related to the number and size of segments in the reference annotation.

C99 performs worst. When default parameters are used, the algorithm returns a few very long segments, too long to be of use in our intended focused retrieval application; varying the rank mask size does not yield significant change in the resulting segmentation. The stopping criterion used by the algorithm seems unsuitable to the type of text we deal with, and the good results achieved by C99 in the experiments reported in [6] do not carry over to our corpus.

TextTiling performs better on Chapter $A$ than on Chapter $B$, and for C99 it is the other way around. This is related to the type of text and the type of segmentation they perform: TextTiling is more like a splitter (which matches with the

---

[2] In this way we look at how many segment boundaries are correctly identified, and we obtain a slightly more forgiving measure, with respect to counting how many entire segments are correctly identified.

Chapter $A$ gold standard), while C99 is more like a lumper (matching with the gold standard for Chapter $B$).[3] The precision of C99 improves greatly when using a large rank mask (57) in the case of Chapter $A$, although recall remains very low.

We set out to find out whether TextTiling and C99 produce segments that are topically coherent, and whether they add anything when compared against two structural segmentations, into paragraphs and sections, respectively. The segments produced by C99 do not seem to be usable, given their low F-score. TextTiling and paragraph-based structural segmentation are on a par, both producing segments with reasonable F-score for one chapter ($A$) and mediocre F-score on another ($B$).

## 5    Retrieving Segments

Now that we have examined different ways of generating topically coherent segments from long scientific documents, our next aim is to use these segments in a retrieval setting. If we return relevant segments to users' queries, do we obtain segments that are "on target?" Do we obtain segments that are both relevant and a good starting points for reading? Are semantic segments better than structural segments?

To address these questions, we asked a single annotator (different from the two that created the gold standard segmentation described in Section 4) to create topics and mark up paragraphs in Chapters $A$ and $B$ for relevancy with respect to these topics. A baseline retrieval system was used to return ranked lists of segments for each of the segmentation methods and parameter settings listed in Table 2), and the outcomes were compared against the gold standard relevancy annotation. Below, we provide details about the development of the gold standard, the evaluation measures used, and the outcomes of our experiments.

### 5.1    The Gold Standard

We created a manually annotated corpus based on the same two chapters used in Section 4. A new annotator (different from the ones used for the gold standard creation in the previous section) developed a set of 37 queries and marked paragraphs in both Chapter $A$ and Chapter $B$ with respect to relevancy to each of the queries. The annotator was told to think of the annotation task in the following terms: you are helping to create a hypertext environment, with (possibly multiple) links from your topics into the corpus; you have to identify good link targets for your topics. The annotator was given the following constraints:

1. targets are non-empty sets of paragraphs;
2. the minimal target, i.e., the minimal unit of relevancy, is a single paragraph;

---

[3] The distinction between 'lumpers' and 'splitters' is used in lexicography to distinguish different behaviors in building of dictionary definitions. Lumpers look at similarities and tend to provide fewer definitions, broad enough to cover several cases; splitters look at differences and tend to provide more specific definitions, each covering a smaller set of cases.

3. if there are cross-references within a paragraph, do not also mark the text
   the cross-reference refers to (the text will be accessed in a hyperlinked form).

The annotator was given the chapters with no indication of the segmentation(s)
produced in Section 4. The annotation resulted in an average of 2.1 and 7.1
relevant paragraphs per query, for Chapter $A$ and Chapter $B$, respectively. In
Chapter $A$ relevant paragraphs are grouped in a single "block" per query, while
in Chapter $B$ there are, on average, 2.3 segments per query.

## 5.2    Evaluation Measures

We are interested in obtaining segments that are both relevant and good starting
points for reading. Our task is similar to INEX in that we need to assess the
relevancy of a document excerpt with respect to a topic, but arguably in our
setting exhaustivity is less important than specificity, nor do we have the problem
of document overlapping. Since we compare segments of varying length against
a corpus where the unit for relevance assessment is the paragraph, we base our
evaluation measures on paragraphs. In view of these considerations, we developed
three measures: C-presision to determine the relevancy of a retrieved segment,
and early onset error (EoE) and late onset error (LoE) to capture appropriateness
of the start of the segment with respect to the distribution of the relevancy in the
document. While C-precision corresponds to the (binary) notion of specificity in
INEX, the two error measures were loosely inspired by [10].

*C-precision* is the proportion of relevant paragraphs included in a segment.

*Early onset Error* (EoE) measures the *proportion of non-relevant paragraphs*
before the first relevant paragraphs in the segment. For a paragraph $P$, let $r_P$
denote its rank in the document order (i.e., 1 for the first paragraph in the
document, 2 for the second, etc.); by extension, for a segment $S$, $r_S$ denotes the
rank of the first paragraph in $S$. Then, for a query $q$ and a retrieved segment $S$,
$EoE(S) = 1$ if there is no block $R$ of relevant paragraphs for $q$ that overlaps with
$S$, and otherwise $EoE(S) = \min\{1, (r_R - r_S)/|S| : r_R \geq r_S$ and $R$ is relevant to
$q$ and overlaps with $S\}$, where $|S|$ is its size in number of paragraphs.

*Late onset Error* (LoE) measures the *proportion of missed relevant paragraphs*
at the beginning of the segment. Using the same notation as in the definition
of EoE, assuming that $q$ is a query, and $S$ is a retrieved segment, we define
$LoE(S) = 1$ if there is no block $R$ of relevant paragraphs that overlaps with
$S$, and otherwise we put $LoE(S) = \min\{1, (r_S - r_R)/|R| : r_R \leq r_S$ and $R$ is a
relevant segment for $q$ that overlaps with $S\}$.

A segment $S$ with a perfect entry point, i.e., coinciding with the beginning of
a relevant block $R$, will have $LoE(S) = EoE(S) = 0$.

A few quick remarks are in order. C-Precision depends on the size of the
segment, as a segment consisting of only one relevant paragraph scores 1. The
number of irrelevant paragraphs before the first relevant paragraph in a segment
gives an indication of the effort required by the reader to reach relevant text.
EoE has a bias for longer documents, since it divides the number of non-relevant
paragraphs by the total number of paragraphs in the segment.

**Table 3.** Summary values for all algorithms considered, across all queries. Highest scores per measure are in boldface.

| Segm. method | NoE[††] | Prop. NoE[†] | C-prec.[†] | Non-rel. segm.[††] | Non-rel. par. begin[†] | EoE[†] | Rel. par. missed[†] | LoE[†] |
|---|---|---|---|---|---|---|---|---|
| Paragraphs | **22** | **1.08** | **0.36** | 69 | 0.00 (0) | **0.64** | 2.11 (17) | 0.71 |
| Sections | 13 | 0.83 | 0.07 | 78 | 7.77 (13) | 0.72 | 3.00 (1) | 0.67 |
| TT default | **22** | 1.06 | 0.35 | 70 | 0.00 (0) | 0.65 | 2.12 (16) | 0.71 |
| TT s5-w20 | 21 | 1.00 | 0.33 | 72 | 0.00 (0) | 0.67 | 2.05 (15) | 0.73 |
| TT s5-w30 | 21 | 1.03 | 0.34 | 71 | 0.00 (0) | 0.66 | 2.12 (16) | 0.72 |
| TT s20-w30 | **22** | 1.06 | 0.32 | 71 | 1.00 (3) | 0.67 | 2.05 (12) | 0.70 |
| TT s20-w40 | **22** | 1.06 | 0.31 | 71 | 3.50 (2) | 0.67 | **1.78 (12)** | 0.69 |
| C99 default | 6 | 0.92 | 0.09 | 78 | 6.44 (16) | 0.75 | 4.88 (5) | **0.66** |
| C99 r9 | 4 | 0.83 | 0.06 | **81** | 10.78 (19) | 0.81 | 6.00 (1) | 0.67 |
| C99 r57 | 7 | 0.97 | 0.10 | 77 | 6.00 (17) | 0.76 | 4.88 (5) | 0.67 |

([†]) results averaged over all queries. ([††]) total number.

## 5.3   Evaluating the Retrieval of Segments

We will now evaluate the retrieval of segments, using the 37 topics developed. We use a basic retrieval engine based on the vector space model, with tf.idf term weighting and settings that are known to be beneficial for the retrieval of short documents [26]. In Table 3 we report on the following measures: total number of topics for which an exact entry point was returned (no onset error, NoE); average proportion of retrieved segments with no onset error, average C-precision; total number of non-relevant segments; average number of non-relevant paragraphs at the start of segments returned; average EoE; average number of relevant paragraphs missed at the start of segments; and average LoE.

The measures described above are applied at cut-off three; i.e., we capture the situation where we are returning three targets per query. Results are reported in Table 3, where columns 2–8 correspond to the measures listed above.

When a segment only contains one non-relevant paragraph, the entire segment can only be counted as non-relevant, Similarly, the longer a segment is, the more likely it is that it also contains non-relevant paragraphs, possibly placed at the beginning of the segment. The number of non-relevant segments retrieved when segments are as long as entire sections suggests that tf.idf tends to discriminate short documents better than long ones.

As in the previous section, the results for TextTiling are similar to those of the single paragraph structural segmentation. This is due to the length of the segments, which is similar in the two cases. Analogously, when C99 is used, the retrieval algorithm finds approximately as many non-relevant segments as in the case of segments one section long.

All C99 versions perform only slightly better than segmentation by sections. The single paragraph segmentation has lowest average EoE, a fact that is explained by the high precision: since a single paragraph can only be either totally relevant or totally irrelevant, it follows that in case of many relevant segments, there will be many zeros in the average. This is also witnessed by the fact that C-precision and EoE sum to one for this system. C99 with default settings scores the highest EoE, due to the large size of the segments. Concerning the LoE, this time the lower error rate is scored by C99 with default parameters, immediately followed by the baseline based on paragraphs.

*Discussion.* The experiments on which we reported in this section were aimed at investigating the use of structural vs. semantic text segmentation as a basis for providing "go-read-here" functionality. Structural segmentation (in terms of single paragraphs) scores best according to many of the measures adopted: in some cases this is due to the length of the segments (e.g., C-precision and EoE), in other cases it is due to the sparsity of the relevant text in the reference corpus. The fact that LoE is higher for the single paragraph structural segmentation and TextTiling suggests that, in case of documents with more dense relevancy, it is useful to retrieve longer segments than just paragraphs. This issue could also be addressed by aggregating paragraphs after the retrieval phase, which will also help in case of documents with sparse relevancy with respect to the query. In order to address this issue, it could be good to aggregate paragraphs after the retrieval phase, and only then form the segment to return to the user.

# 6   Conclusions and Future Work

In this paper we reported on an analysis of query-independent text segmentation methods aimed at supporting "go-read-here" type of functionality in the setting of scientific literature digital libraries. We focused on two aspects: generating segments and retrieving segments as focused responses to user queries. For both aspects we had to develop ground truth data and evaluation measures.

For the generation of segments our main finding was that the presence of formulas, tables and long list of examples, together with the presence of different kinds of internal references, made the annotators divide the documents in a very fragmented way, which resulted in very competitive scores for the structural segmentation into paragraphs. As to retrieving segments, we found that the structural segmentation into paragraphs is hard to beat using the semantic segmentation methods that we considered. We conjecture that it may be beneficial to aggregate paragraphs after retrieving them.

Now, a number of caveats apply. First, we only worked with one corpus, albeit with chapters authored by different people. It remains to be seen to what extent our findings generalize to other corpora. Second, we treated the issue of search within a document as a passage retrieval task, where we assume that the passages are independent: relevancy of one paragraph does not imply relevancy of earlier or later paragraphs. It would be interesting to see whether a more sophisticated model that captures dependencies between paragraphs improves the retrieval scores. Third, we assumed that segmentation can be done off-line, independent of user queries. We have not investigated whether text segments can best be established with respect to the question one intends to ask, in which case it is worthwhile integrating the segmentation and the retrieval phases so that segments can be defined on the basis of the query posed.

For future work, it is interesting to see to which extent some level of discourse semantics might be used to improve both the identification of segments and their retrieval. Along similar lines, we suggest looking in more detail at cue phrases, even though there is mixed evidence in the literature (they have been shown to be misleading in [4] but useful in [20]).

**Acknowledgments.** This research was supported by Elsevier and by the Netherlands Organization for Scientific Research (NWO) under project numbers 017.001.190, 220-80-001, 264-70-050, 365-20-005, 612.000.106, 612.000.207, 612.013.001, 612.066.302, 612.069.006, 640.001.501, and 640.002.501.

# References

[1] M. Agosti and J. Allan, editors. *Methods and Tools for the Automatic Construction of Hypertext.* Elsevier Science Ltd, March 1997. Special Issue of *Information Processing and Management* Volume 33.

[2] J. Allan. Building hypertext using information retrieval. *Information Precessing and Management*, 33(2):145–159, March 1997.

[3] L. Baron, J. Tague-Sutcliffe, M. T. Kinnucan, and T. Carey. Labeled, typed links as cues when reading hypertext documents. *Journal of the American Society for Information Science*, 47(12):896–908, 1996.

[4] G. Brown and G. Yule. *Cambridge Textbooks in Linguistics Series.* Cambridge University Press, 1983.

[5] J. P. Callan. Passage-level evidence in document retrieval. In *Proc. of the 17th Annual International ACM SIGIR Conference on Research and Development in Information Retrieval, Dublin, Ireland*, pages 302–310, July 1994.

[6] F. Choi. Advances in independent linear text segmentation. In *Proc. of the 1st Meeting of the North American Chapter of the Association for Computational Linguistics (ANLP-NAACL-00)*, pages 26–33, 2000.

[7] F. Choi. Linear text segmentation: approaches, advances and applications. In *Proc. of CLUK3*, 2000.

[8] J. Cohen. The coefficient of agreement for nominal scales. *Educational and Psychological Measurement*, 21(1):37–46, 1960.

[9] J. Conklin. Hypertext: An introduction and survey. *Computer*, 20(9):17–41, 1987.

[10] A. P. de Vries, G. Kazai, and M. Lalmas. Tolerance to irrelevance: A user-effort oriented evaluation of retrieval systems without predefined retrieval unit. In *Recherche d'Informations Assistee par Ordinateur (RIAO 2004)*, April 2004.

[11] S. J. DeRose. Expanding the notion of links. In *Proc. of Hypertext'99*, pages 249–257, 1989.

[12] D. J. Harper, S. Coulthord, and S. Yixing. A language modeling approach to relevance profiling for document browsing. In *Proc. of JCDL*, 2002.

[13] M. A. Hearst. *Context and Structure in Automated Full-text Information Access.* PhD thesis, University of California at Berkeley, 1994.

[14] M. A. Hearst. Multi-paragraph segmentation of expository text. In *Proc. 32nd ACL*, 1994.

[15] M. A. Hearst. Tilebars: visualization of term distribution information in full text information access. In *Proc. of CHI'95*, 1995.

[16] M. A. Hearst and C. Plaunt. Subtopic structuring for full-lenght document access. In *Proc. of the 16th Annual International ACM SIGIR Conference on Research and Development in IR*, pages 59–68, 1993.

[17] INEX. INitiative for the Evaluation of XML Retrieval, 2004. `http://inex.is.informatik.uni-duisburg.de:2004/`.

[18] M. Kaszkiel and J. Zobel. Passage retrieval revisited. In *Proc. of SIGIR 97*, pages 178–185, 1997.

[19] M. Lesk. *Understanding Digital Libraries*. The Morgan Kaufmann series in multimedia information and systems. Morgan Kaufmann, second edition, 2005.

[20] C. Manning. Rethinking text segmentation models: An information extraction case study. Technical Report SULTRY-98-07-01, University of Sydney, 1998.

[21] R. Muskens, J. van Benthem, and A. Visser. Dynamics. In *Handbook of Logic and Language*. Elsevier, 1997.

[22] M. O'Neill and M. Denos. Practical approach to the stereo matching of urban imagery. *Image and Vision Computing*, 10(2):89–98, March 1992.

[23] J. M. Ponte and W. B. Croft. Text segmentation by topic. In *European Conference on Digital Libraries*, pages 113–125, 1997.

[24] L. W. Rabiner and R. W. Schafer. *Digital processing of speech signals*. Prentice-Hall, Inc., 1978.

[25] J. C. Reynar. *Topic Segmentation: Algorithms and Applications*. PhD thesis, University of Pennsylvania, 1998.

[26] G. Salton and C. Buckley. Term-weighting approaches in automatic text retrieval. *Information Processing and Management*, 25:513–523, 1988.

[27] G. Salton, J. Allan, and C. Buckley. Approaches to passage retrieval in full text information systems. In *Proc. of the 16th Annual International ACM/SIGIR Conference, Pittsburgh, USA*, pages 49–58, 1993.

[28] G. Salton, J. Allan, and A. Singhal. Automatic text decomposition and structuring. *Information Processing and Management*, 32(2):127–138, 1996.

[29] G. Salton, A. Singhal, C. Buckley, and M. Mitra. Automatic text decomposition using text segments and text themes. In *Proc. of the 7th ACM Conference on Hypertext, Washington D.C., USA*, 1996.

[30] E. Skorochod'ko. Adaptive method of automatic abstracting and indexing. *Information Processing*, 71:1179–1182, 1972.

[31] N. Stokes, J. Carthy, and A. F. Smeaton. Segmenting broadcast news streams using lexical chaining. In T. Vidal and P. Liberatore, editors, *Proc. of STAIRS 2002*, volume 1, pages 145–154. IOS Press, 2002.

[32] C. Tenopir and D. W. King. Reading behaviour and electronic journals. *Learned Publishing*, 15(4):159–165, October 2002.

[33] R. Trigg. *A network approach to text handling for the online scientifc community*. PhD thesis, University of Maryland, 1983.

[34] J. van Benthem and A. ter Meulen, editors. *Handbook of Logic and Language*. Elsevier, 1997.

[35] T. van Dijk. *Some Aspects of Text Grammar*. Mouton, 1972.

[36] J. van Eijck and H. Kamp. Representing discourse in context. In *Handbook of Logic and Language*. Elsevier, 1997.

# Browsing Personal Images Using Episodic Memory (Time + Location)

Chufeng Chen, Michael Oakes, and John Tait

School of Computing and Technology, University of Sunderland
{chufeng.chen, michael.oakes, john.tait}@sunderland.ac.uk

**Abstract.** In this paper we consider episodic memory for system design in image retrieval. Time and location are the main factors in episodic memory, and these types of data were combined for image event clustering. We conducted a user studies to compare five image browsing systems using searching time and user satisfaction as criteria for success. Our results showed that the browser which clusters images based on time and location data combined was significantly better than four other more standard browsers. This suggests that episodic memory is potentially useful for improving personal image management.

## 1 Introduction

As digital images are becoming increasingly popular, it becomes necessary to support users of digital cameras with software tools for personal image management. Most digital cameras time stamp each photograph at the time the image is created. More recently, digital cameras with the Global Positioning System (GPS) function have been developed. These cameras record the geographical coordinates at which each picture file is taken, and then using gazetteers, annotate each picture with location data. In this paper we describe a system which combines time and location data for the automatic identification of episodes or events, since these are the main factors in human episodic memory [4]. We perform user studies to show that this identification of events helps users to browse their personal collections of digital photographs. Graham et al. [10] and Platt et al. [15] have previously shown that browsing and retrieving images arranged by time is quicker than for unindexed images. Graham [10] also suggested that the use of GPS location data could be used to assist browsing. Naaman et al [14], built a time and location hierarchy clustering system, but did not evaluate it on real users.

In section 2, this paper will review some previous studies related to human episodic memory. Section 3 describes the development of our time and location clustering system. Section 4 describes our experimental design, where subjects were asked to perform both general and specific scenario image retrieval tasks using five different image browsing systems, and retrieval performance was assessed by speed of searching and user satisfaction questionnaires. Both user and system centre evaluation results are given in Section 5, and our analysis is in Section 6 concludes that the use of episodic memory (time and location) is one way of improving personal browsing.

M. Lalmas et al. (Eds.): ECIR 2006, LNCS 3936, pp. 362–372, 2006.
© Springer-Verlag Berlin Heidelberg 2006

## 2  Background and Related Work

Within the field of image retrieval, the focus of research has been on the development of image processing techniques rather than measuring the usability of the search tools. Previous studies [7] [9] [11] [17] [18] [19] have suggested that images can be indexed in a variety of ways. We currently know relatively little about the image search process and the factors which affect this process. However, Chan & Wang [3] found that human factors strongly affect the search results of image retrieval. Specifically, human episodic memory has been considered in system design in a number of areas of Human-Computer Interaction (HCI) - see for example, [1] [5] [10] [14] [15]. Baddeley [2] described episodic memory as people's memory of events and experience, sometimes referred to as personal memory. Episodic memory is about special events and episodes, such as a birthday, or a meeting which took place a week ago. For example: I remember the conversation between you and me yesterday, and I remember what I was doing and what were my feelings during the conversation. Episodic memory can be general or specific, it can also involve either long-term memory or short-term memory. Episodic memory has been used to support system design in a number studies. Abrams et al. [1] used episodic memory for helping users retrieve web pages and web documents in a bookmark management system. Users used the "my history" (an implementation of episodic memory) tool for navigating the web [1]. User feedback indicated that the use of episodic memory could help them keep track of what they had browsed before. Platt et al. [15] developed an image browsing system based on time and colour histogram clustering called PhotoTOC. Graham et al. [10] developed two photo browser systems for collections of thousands of time-stamped digital photographs. Their first browser was called the calendar browser, which had a very simple interface which included only the date line and time line to enable browsing and summarisation. Users could browse images by year or month. They called their second system a hierarchical browser which allowed users to browse a hierarchy of year, month, date, and time. Their experimental results showed that time (a component of episodic memory) can improve both the retrieval performance and user satisfaction of image searching. Naaman et al. [14] developed a time and location hierarchy clustering system. They also discuss episodic memory, particularly the location component, but did not perform any user studies of this interface. Cooper et al. [5] are also interested in the specific events associated with images, but because they feel that GPS cameras are still not widespread, their image browsing system concentrates on time and visual content clustering. However, Content-Based Image retrieval relies on low-level features of the images such as colour, texture and shape. The term "semantic gap" [7] refers to the mismatch between the meaning humans assign to images, and these low-level feature descriptions. For example, images interpreted by humans as being of "sailing boat" and "pyramid" might both be interpreted as "triangle" using shape alone. In contrast, human episodic memory is concerned with high-level semantic concepts, so the use of time and location does not suffer from the semantic gap problem.

## 3 Development of the Time and Location Clustering System

A personal image browsing system which relates to human episodic memory by using both time and location for identifying different events has been developed [4]. This system includes the database shown in Figure 1 and the user interface shown in Figure 2. The database contains all the data for date and time, latitude, longitude and location names automatically provided for each image by the GPS digital camera (mobile phone cameras also can do this). Our starting point was the time clustering model for event identification by [15], which we have modified to enable images to be clustered into events according to both time and location.

### 3.1 Time Clustering

Time-based clustering can detect obvious gaps in the creation time of digital images. A cluster is then defined as those photographs falling between two such obvious time gaps. These gaps are assumed to identify different events. Following Platt et al. [15], we separate different events by comparing the average time gap in a fixed length window of successive images with the local time gap between two successive images. When the local time gap is much longer than the average time gap, a boundary between two separate events has been found. Platt et al. [15] provided an algorithm which operates on logarithmically transformed gap times, as follows:

$$Log\ (gN) \geq K + 1/(2d + 1)\sum_{i=-d}^{d} Log\ (gN + i)$$

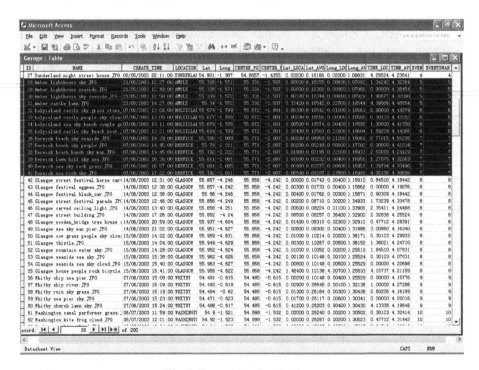

**Fig. 1.** Data processing database

**Fig. 2.** Example of the user interface

where $gN+i$ is the time gap between the image $i$ and image $i+1$, $gN$ is the local time gap between two successive images, $d$ is the window size of images (Platt et. al. used $d = 10$, the value used in our experiments). $K$ is a suitable threshold (we also followed Platt et al. who used $K = log17$). If the local time gap $gN$ is much greater than the average gap $K + 1/(2d+1)\sum_{i=-d}^{d} Log\ (gN+i)$, then a time event has been located. We call this condition 1.

## 3.2 Location Clustering

Location clustering can detect obvious gaps in the location coordinates, latitude and longitude. A cluster is defined as those photographs falling between two obvious latitude or longitude gaps. Like time gaps, latitude and longitude gaps are also assumed to identify different events. Just as two different events can be identified by comparing the local time gap and the average time gap, two separate events can also be located by comparing the local latitude or longitude gap with the average latitude or longitude gap. We use an analogous formula for our location clustering model, separated into a latitude clustering algorithm model and a longitude clustering algorithm model.

**Latitude Clustering:** $LatgN \geq 1/(2d+1)\sum_{i=-d}^{d} LatgN + i$

$LatgN+i$ is the latitude distance gap between, image $i$ and $i+1$, $LatgN$ is the local latitude distance gap, $d$ (we used $d=10$) is the window size of images. If the local latitude distance gap is much greater than the average gap $1/(2d+1)\sum_{i=-d}^{d} LatgN+i$, then a new location event has been located. We call this condition 2.

**Longitude Clustering:** $LonggN \geq 1/(2d+1)\sum_{i=-d}^{d} LonggN + i$

$LonggN+i$ is the longitude distance gap between, image $i$ and $i+1$, and $LonggN$ is the local longitude distance gap. If the local longitude distance gap is much bigger than the average gap, then a new location event has been located. We call this condition 3. Log and $K$ are not included in the location models because the location gaps tend to be very small numbers of latitude and longitude degrees.

### 3.3   Time – Latitude and Longitude Clustering Model

The relationship of time, latitude and longitude is shown on a three dimensional x-y-z-coordinate (figure 3). If any one of the above conditions (1 to 3) occurs, a new event has been located. Thus events are not only located by time, but also by location. For example, I might take some pictures in London in the morning, then take some pictures in Oxford in the afternoon. In this case the local time gap between these two sets of photos is small, suggesting that they could not be separated on the basis of time alone. However, the large gaps in latitude and longitude between the sets of photographs clearly show that they belong to separate events.

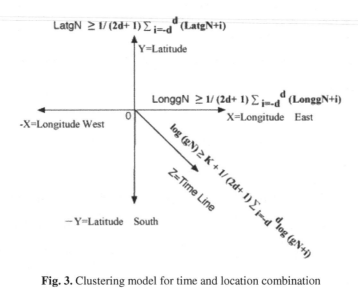

**Fig. 3.** Clustering model for time and location combination

## 3.4 User Interface

We have produced a user interface, so users can browse their personal images which have been grouped into discrete events. The browser allows users to browse their entire collection on a scrollable panel as shown in Figure 2. The images follow the time line (the earliest taken photo in the top left corner, the last taken in the bottom right hand corner). Events are separated by the symbol "event".

# 4   Main Experiment

The main experiment was designed to test the time and location combination browser described in this paper against the four other, more standard, browsers: BR's PhotoArchiver®, Canon ZoomBrowserEX®, the WinXP® image folder browser, and our own time alone clustering browser (using Platt et al.'s original model). BR's PhotoArchiver allows EXIF metadata extraction, so users can browse images using the metadata such as time and place name in a classified hierarchy browsing interface. It hierarchically classifies images by year, month and place name, but unlike our system, does not use this data to automatically cluster the images by event. Canon ZoomBrowserEX is a time base line browser, but does not have the function of clustering. We use the Microsoft windows XP folder browser for unindexed photos. The time alone clustering browser is similar to the time and location clustering combination browser, except in that it does not have the function of location clustering.

## 4.1 Hypothesis and Aim

The hypothesis of this study was that the browsing features related to episodic memory, incorporated into our time and location combination browser would improve image searching of personal collections. To confirm this hypothesis, we needed to show that the time and location clustering combination browser performed better than the other four browsers with real experimental subjects.

## 4.2 Subjects

Six volunteers, three male and three female, all with normal colour vision, participated in this study. They were all staff and students at the University of Sunderland, and all had experience in managing their own digital photos. Each subject was asked to provide a personal collection of about 200 images, as shown in Table 1. This modest number was comparable with the sizes of the subjects' entire personal photograph collections, since 5 subjects estimated that they had collected between 250 and 400 photographs, and just one subject had over 2000 photographs. Some subjects did not want to give us all their personal photographs.

**Table 1.** The photo collection size for each subject

|  | Subject1 | Subject2 | Subject3 | Subject4 | Subject5 | Subject6 |
|---|---|---|---|---|---|---|
| Collections | 202 | 199 | 200 | 202 | 208 | 199 |

In a future experiment we will require the subjects to annotate the collections they submitted, and we felt that 200 photographs would be a manageable number.

### 4.3  Scenario Tasks

We gave each subject four general and four specific tasks for image searching. They were each asked to read each the scenario description beforehand, and then in the timed phase of the experiment, find out the image which best matched each scenario description.

The **General search tasks** involved non-specific scenarios, so that every collection would contain at least one image answering that description. No time limit was set for any of the searching tasks, but for each task the time spent searching was recorded. The general search tasks were as follows: 1. Please find a photo where you were with one or two of your friends (or family members), at an outdoor sunny place on your last holiday. 2. Please find a photo where you were standing in a crowded city centre. 3. Please find a Photo where you were with your families in an indoor environment. 4. Please find a photo of the most famous building of the city which you last visited.

The **Specific search tasks** were based on the contents of each subject's personal collection, so were different for each subject. For example, one subject was asked to perform the following four search tasks: 1. please find the photo where your girl friend was sitting on the grass with flowers in the background in sunny weather. 2. Please find out the photo where your were sitting with your girl friend in front of your new house in your hometown. 3. Please find the photo where in good weather, you were on the way to Sunderland air show, and there was a river next to you. 4. Please find the photo with a rainbow over the river and docks. All the subjects performed four general scenario tasks and four specific scenario tasks for all five browsers under test.

### 4.4  The Experimental Method

The experiment used the repeated measures design. In order to overcome the problems of practice and order effects inherent in repeated measures experiments, we used a Latin square design. Half of the subjects did the general tasks first followed by the specific tasks, and the other half did the specific tasks first followed by the general tasks. Each subject also used the different browsing tools in Latin square design order.

We used five Likert scale questionnaires to determine the degree of user satisfaction for each browser, using the same questions as [15], as follows: 1. I like this image browser. 2. This Browser is easy to use. 3. This Browser feels familiar. 4. It is easy to find the photo I am looking for. 5. A month from now, I would still be able to find these photos. 6. I was satisfied with how the pictures were organized.

### 4.5  System-Centred Evaluation

System performance, in terms of how closely the event clusters suggested by the users match the event clusters produced automatically, were evaluated quantitatively using Recall and Precision. We found the number of image pairs in the collection which fall into each of the following categories:  1. user and machine place the image pair in the same event; 2. user places the image pair in the same event, but the machine places them in different events; 3. user places the image pair in different events but the machine places them in the same event; 4 user and machine both place the image pair into separate events. Recall = (pairs in 1) / (pairs in 1 + pairs in 2), while Precision = (pairs in 1) / (pairs in 1 + pairs in 3). The overall effectiveness measure, F, was the harmonic mean of Recall and Precision, 2PR / (P + R). We compared the performance of time-based clustering alone with time and location-based clustering.

# 5   Results

## 5.1   Completion Time of the General Scenario Searching Tasks

The searching times (averaged over all 6 subjects) for the general scenario tasks using each of the five browsers are shown in Table 2. Although the average searching time was less when using the time and location combination browser than for any of the other browsers, a one-way ANOVA test showed that this difference was not significant at the $p = 0.05$ level ($F_{(4, 25)} = 2.44$, $p = 0.0733$).

## 5.2   Completion Time of the Specific Scenario Searching Tasks

Table 3 shows the subjects' average searching time for the specific scenario tasks when using the five different browsers. As was the case for the general scenarios, the time and location combination browser required the shortest average searching time. Once again, the one way ANOVA analysis was not significant at the $p=0.05$ level ($F_{(4, 25)} = 2.38$, $p = 0.0787$). However, when taking the average total search time for the general and specific scenarios combined, the time and location combination browser was again the fastest overall. This time the one-way ANOVA test showed that this difference was significant at the $p = 0.05$ level ($F_{(4, 25)} = 2.99$, $p = 0.0381$).

## 5.3   Questionnaires

The user satisfaction questionnaires were filled in immediately after the timed searching tasks had been performed, and the average satisfaction ratings for the six subjects are shown in Table 3. The time and location combination browser was rated more highly than the other browsers according to all six criteria, except for question 5, where

**Table 2.** System searching time for five browsers

| | Time & location combined | BR's Photo-Archiver | Canon Zoom-Browser-EX | Un-indexed browser | Time alone | ANOVA $F_{(4, 25)} =$ |
|---|---|---|---|---|---|---|
| 1. Average searching time general scenario tasks | 54.67 | 112.33 | 96.83 | 104 | 78.83 | 2.44, $p = 0.0733$ |
| 2. Average searching time specific scenario tasks | 46.17 | 91.5 | 86.5 | 82.33 | 51.5 | 2.38, $p = 0.0787$ |
| 3. Average total finish time | 100.83 | 203.83 | 183.33 | 186.33 | 130.33 | **2.99, $p = 0.0381$** |

**Table 3.** User satisfaction for five different browsers

| | Time & location combined | BR's Photo-Archiver | Canon Zoom-Browser-EX | Un-indexed browser | Time alone | ANOVA $F(4, 25) =$ |
|---|---|---|---|---|---|---|
| 1. I like this image browser | *3.83* | 2.67 | 3.17 | 2.5 | 3.67 | **4.4,** **p= 0.0079** |
| 2. This browser is easy to use | *4.17* | 2.84 | 3.5 | 3.33 | 3.84 | **2.87,** **p=0.0436** |
| 3. This browser feels familiar | *4.17* | 2.84 | 3.5 | 3.5 | 3.67 | 2.14, p= 0.1062 |
| 4. It is easy to find the photo I am looking for | 4 | 2.5 | 3.34 | 2 | 3.67 | **10.16,** **p< 0.0001** |
| 5. A month from now, I would still be able to find these photos | *4.17* | 3.17 | 3.84 | 3.67 | 4.17 | 2.04, p= 0.1194 |
| 6. I was satisfied with how the pictures were organized | *4.5* | 3 | 3.17 | 1.83 | 3.67 | **13.61,** **p< 0.0001** |
| Average | *4.14* | 2.84 | 3.42 | 2.81 | 3.78 | **8.18,** **p= 0.0002** |

**Table 4.** Recall and precision results

| | Time and location clustering. | | | Time Alone clustering | | |
|---|---|---|---|---|---|---|
| | Recall | Precision | $F_1$ measure | Recall | Precision | $F_1$ measure |
| Subject1 | 0.7289 | 1.0000 | 0.8432 | 0.9419 | 0.6965 | 0.8008 |
| Subject2 | 0.9927 | 0.9647 | 0.9785 | 0.6903 | 0.6071 | 0.6551 |
| Subject3 | 0.7956 | 0.9290 | 0.8571 | 0.9962 | 0.2757 | 0.4319 |
| Subject4 | 0.8826 | 0.9449 | 0.9127 | 0.8832 | 0.9422 | 0.8976 |
| Subject5 | 0.8435 | 0.9747 | 0.9044 | 0.9979 | 0.3555 | 0.5242 |
| Subject6 | 0.8847 | 0.9956 | 0.9369 | 0.8847 | 0.9956 | 0.9369 |
| Average | 0.8547 | 0.9681 | 0.9079 | 0.8990 | 0.6454 | 0.7514 |

it was rated equal to the time alone clustering browser. One way ANOVA tests for each question showed that the differences between the browsers were significant at p = 0.5 for questions 1, 2, 4, 6 and the overall average, but not for questions 3 and 5.

## 5.4 Recall and Precision

The results for Recall, Precision and the F measure for both the time and location combination system and the time alone system are shown in table 4:

The results show that precision for the time and location combined clustering is better than for time alone clustering, while the recall for time alone clustering is higher than time and location clustering. The overall effectiveness, as estimated by the F measure, was better for the time and location combined clustering.

## 6  Discussion and Conclusion

Although we could not find a significant improvement with the time and location browser in searching time at the 5% level for either the general scenario searching tasks or specific scenario searching tasks alone, the total system searching time (searching time for the general and specific searching tasks combined) was significantly better for the time and location browser. In the user satisfaction analysis, the time and location combination browser received significantly more favorable questionnaire responses than the other browsers. For the two important questions 4 and 6 (see table 3), the time and location combination browser had strong scores on the one way ANOVA. Our system-centered evaluation showed that the time and location combination browser had greater retrieval effectiveness than the time alone browser, as measured by the F measure. All these results support our hypothesis that factors related to human episodic memory, time and location, can be used to help users search their personal photograph collections more easily.

We have shown that the time and location browser is helpful for users with collections of about 200 photographs, but it remains to be seen whether our experiments will scale up to very large collections.

In future we plan to continue our experiments with a larger number of subjects. Some subjects suggested that we should modify the system to label each event with its location and time, rather than using a standard label "event" to signal the beginning of each new event, so this feature will be incorporated into future versions. We also intend to develop a prototype system which can automatically caption personal images by location using gazetteers, and to make use of short captions for each image provided by the subjects themselves. We will devise quantitative studies of system performance and qualitative studies of human satisfaction for this new prototype personal image browser.

## References

1. Abrams, D., Baecker, R., Chignell, M.: Information Archiving with Bookmarks: Personal Web Space Construction and Organization, CHI98, ACM (1998) 41 – 48.
2. Baddeley A.: Human Memory, Theory and Practice, LEA Publishers (1990).
3. Chan H. & Wang Y.: Human factors in colour-based image retrieval: an empirical study on size estimate accuracies, Journal of visual communication & Image Representation 15 (2004) 113-131.
4. Chen, C., Oakes, M. and McDonald, S.: Using a time and location combination clustering model for browsing personal images. Proceedings of British HCI 2005, Edinburgh (2005) Volume 2, 244-246.
5. Cooper, M., Foote, J., Girgensohn, A., and Wilcox, L.: Temporal event clustering for digital photo collections, ACM Transactions on Multimedia Computing, Communications, and Applications (TOMCCAP), Volume 1, Issue 3, (2005) 269–288.

6. Dix, A.J., Finlay, J.E., Abowd, G. D., Beale, R.: Human-Computer Interaction. 2nd ed. London Prentice Hall (1998).
7. Eakins, J. P.: Automatic image content retrieval--are we getting anywhere? In: Proceeding of Third International on Conference of Electronic Library and Visual Information Research, Research, De Montfort University. (1996) 123-135.
8. Eakins, J.P., Graham, M.E.: Content-Based Image Retrieval: A Report to the JISC Technology Applications Programme. Institute for Image Data Research, University of Northumbria at Newcastle, UK (1999). Available at http://www.unn.ac.uk/iidr/report.html.
9. Fidel, R.: Image Retrieval task: Implications for the Design and Evaluation of Image Databases. The New Review of Hypermedia and Multimedia, 3 (1997) 181-199.
10. Graham, A., Molina, H., Paepcke, A. & Winograd T.: Time as essence f or photo browsing through personal digital libraries, submitted to ACM (2002). http://dbpubs.stanf ord.edu: 8090/pub/2002-4.
11. Jose, J.,.M., Furner, J., Harper, D., J.: Spatial querying for image retrieval: a user-oriented evaluation, Proceedings of the 21st annual international ACM SIGIR conference on Research and development in information retrieval, Melbourne, Australia, (1998) p.232-240.
12. Holink, L., Schreiber, A., Wielinga, B., Worring, M.: Classification of user image descriptions, Human-Computer Studies (2004) 601-626.
13. McDonald, S. and Tait, J.: Search Strategies in Content-Based Image Retrieval. Proceedings of the 26th ACM SIGIR Conference, Toronto, (2003) 80-87.
14. Naaman, M., Song, Y. J., Paepcke, A., and Garcia-Molina, H.: Automatic organization for digital photographs with geographic coordinates. In Proceedings of the Joint Conference on Digital Libraries. ACM Press, New York, NY, (2004) 326--35.
15. Platt, J.C., Czerwinski, M. & Field, B.: PhotoTOC: Automatic clustering for browsing personal photographs, Microsoft Research Technical Report MSR-TR-2002-17 (2002).
16. Rodden K.: Evaluating similarity-based visualisations as interfaces for image browsing, Ph.D. dissertation. Univeristy of Cambridge, Cambridge, U.K (2002).
17. Rodden, K., Wood, R. K.: How Do People Manage Their Digital Photographs, proceedings of SIGCHI'03 ACM press, (2003) 409-416.
18. Tait, J I, McDonald, S, Lai, T-S.: CHROMA: An experimental Image retrieval System. In Isaias, Proceedings of the first international workshop on new developments in digital libraries (2001) 141-153.
19. Venters, C., C., Hartley, R., J., Cooper, .M., D., Hewitt, W., T.: Query by Visual Example: Assessing the Usability of Content-Based Image Retrieval System User Interfaces, Proceedings of the Second IEEE Pacific Rim Conference on Multimedia: Advances in Multimedia Information Processing, (2001) 514-521.

# An Information Retrieval System for Motion Capture Data

Bastian Demuth[1], Tido Röder[1], Meinard Müller[1], and Bernhard Eberhardt[2]

[1] Universität Bonn, Institut für Informatik III,
Römerstr. 164, 53117 Bonn, Germany
{demuth, roedert, meinard}@cs.uni-bonn.de
[2] Hochschule der Medien, Fachhochschule Stuttgart,
Nobelstr. 10, 70569 Stuttgart, Germany
eberhardt@hdm-stuttgart.de

**Abstract.** Motion capturing has become an important tool in fields such as sports sciences, biometrics, and particularly in computer animation, where large collections of motion material are accumulated in the production process. In order to fully exploit motion databases for reuse and for the synthesis of new motions, one needs efficient retrieval and browsing methods to identify similar motions. So far, only ad-hoc methods for content-based motion retrieval have been proposed, which lack efficiency and rely on quantitative, numerical similarity measures, making it difficult to identify logically related motions. We propose an efficient motion retrieval system based on the query-by-example paradigm, which employs qualitative, geometric similarity measures. This allows for intuitive and interactive browsing in a purely content-based fashion without relying on textual annotations. We have incorporated this technology in a novel user interface facilitating query formulation as well as visualization and ranking of search results.

## 1 Introduction

In the past two decades, motion capture systems have been developed that allow to track and record human motions at high spatial and temporal resolutions. The resulting motion capture data, typically consisting of 3D trajectories of markers attached to a live actor's body, is used to analyze human motions in fields such as sports sciences and biometrics (person identification), and to synthesize realistic motion sequences in data-driven computer animation. Even though there is a rapidly growing corpus of motion data, there still is a lack of efficient motion retrieval systems that allow to identify and extract user-specified motions.

Previous retrieval systems often require manually generated textual annotations, which roughly describe the motions in words. Since the manual generation of reliable and descriptive labels is infeasible for large data sets, one needs efficient *content-based* retrieval methods such as techniques based on the query-by-example paradigm. The crucial point in such an approach is the notion of *similarity* used to compare the query with the documents to be searched. For the motion scenario, two motions may be regarded as similar if they represent

M. Lalmas et al. (Eds.): ECIR 2006, LNCS 3936, pp. 373–384, 2006.
© Springer-Verlag Berlin Heidelberg 2006

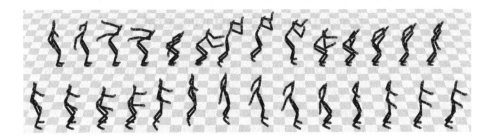

**Fig. 1.** Top: 14 poses from a forceful jump. Bottom: 14 poses from a weak jump.

| Input: | Short query motion clip. |
|---|---|
| | Feature selection. |
| | Fault tolerance settings. |
| Procedure: | Automatic conversion of query motion into a sequence of geometric |
| | configurations (with respect to the selected features). |
| | Index-based retrieval, post-processing, and ranking. |
| Output: | Ranked list of hits. |

**Fig. 2.** Overview of the retrieval process based on the query-by-example paradigm

variations of the same action or sequence of actions, see [4]. These variations may concern the spatial as well as the temporal domain. For example, the jumps shown in Fig. 1 describe the same kind of motion even though they differ considerably with respect to timing, intensity, and execution style (note, e.g., the arm swing). In other words, *logically similar* motions need not be *numerically similar*, as is also pointed out in [4].

In this paper, we present a motion retrieval system that allows for efficient retrieval of *logically* related motions based on the query-by-example paradigm, see Fig. 2 for an overview. As opposed to previous approaches that are based on *quantitative, numerical features*, our approach is based on *qualitative, relational features*, which describe certain geometric constellations between specified points of the body. As will be described in Sect. 2, such relational features are not only robust to spatio-temporal variations (thus providing a basis for the identification of logically related motions) but are also ideally suited for indexing (speeding up the retrieval process considerably). The front end of our retrieval system consists of a graphical user interface facilitating intuitive query formulation as well as visualization and ranking of search results, see Sect. 3. Finally, we report on some of our experiments in Sect. 4. For more experimental details and result videos, we refer to http://www-mmdb.iai.uni-bonn.de/projects/mocap/RetrievalGUI.html.

We close this section with a discussion of related work. So far, only little work has been published on motion capture indexing and retrieval based on the query-by-example paradigm. To account for spatio-temporal variations, most previous approaches rely on the technique of *dynamic time warping* (DTW), see [2, 4, 8].

However, major drawbacks to DTW are its quadratic running time and storage requirements, making DTW infeasible for large data sets. To speed up similarity search, Keogh et al. [3] use an index structure based on bounding envelopes, allowing to identify similar motion fragments that differ by some uniform scaling factor with respect to the time axis. In comparing individual frames of the data streams, all of these approaches rely on *numerical* cost measures. As a first step towards logical similarity, Liu et al. [5] compare motions based on a so-called cluster transition signature that is immune to temporal variations. To bridge the semantic gap between logical similarity as perceived by humans and computable numerical similarity measures, Müller et al. [6] introduce a new type of qualitative geometric features and induced motion segmentations, yielding spatio-temporal invariance as needed to compare logically similar motions.

The main contribution of the present paper is to extend the concepts from [6] in the following ways: we define new classes of generic relational features grasping important aspects of an actor's motion patterns, which prove to be well-suited for content-based motion retrieval. A novel Feature Design GUI allows to instantiate the generic features into semantically meaningful feature sets, supported by suitable optimization and visualization tools. As a further contribution, we present a Retrieval GUI based on the query-by-example paradigm that includes a novel ranking strategy and facilitates merging operations on hits.

## 2   Relational Motion Features

The most common recording technology for motion capture data uses an array of digital cameras to three-dimensionally track reflective markers attached to a live actor's body, see, e.g. [7]. The tracking data can then be post-processed to obtain a multi-stream of 3D trajectories corresponding to the joints of a fixed skeletal *kinematic chain* as indicated by Fig. 3. A full set of 3D coordinates describing the joint positions of a kinematic chain for a fixed point in time is also referred to as a *pose*. A motion capture data stream is thought of as a sequence of poses or *frames*, typically sampled at 30–600 Hz.

In a sense, motion capture data has a much richer semantic content than, for example, pure video data of a motion, since the position and the meaning of all joints is known for every pose. This fact can be exploited by considering *relational features* that describe (boolean) geometric relations between specified points of a pose or short sequences of poses, see [6]. We explain the main idea of such features by means of some typical examples. Consider the test whether the right foot lies in front of (feature value one) or behind (feature value zero) the plane spanned by the center of the hip (the root), the left hip joint, and the left foot, cf. Fig. 3 (a). Interchanging left with right, one obtains the analogous feature for the other leg. A combination of these features is useful to identify locomotion such as walking or running. A similar feature is defined by the oriented plane fixed at the left and right shoulders and the root, shifted one humerus length to the front: checking whether the left hand is in front of or behind this plane, one obtains a feature suitable to identify left punches, see Fig. 3 (b). The feature indicated by Fig. 3 (c) checks whether the right hand is moving into the direction

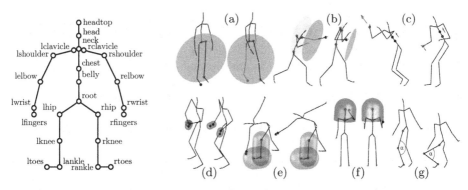

**Fig. 3.** Left: skeletal kinematic chain model consisting of rigid *body segments* flexibly connected by *joints*, which are highlighted by circular markers and labeled with joint names. Right: qualitative features describing geometric and kinematic relations between the body points of a pose that are indicated by thickened markers.

determined by the belly-chest segment. Other types of relational features express whether specified points of the body are close together, yielding, for example, "touch" detectors for the two hands, a hand and a leg, or a hand and the head (Fig. 3 (d)–(f)). We also use relational features to check if certain parts of the body such as the arms or the legs are bent or stretched (Fig. 3 (g)).

By looking at maximal runs of consecutive frames yielding the same feature values for a fixed combination of frame-based relational features, one obtains a temporal segmentation of motion data streams, see Fig. 4. In order to compare two different motions, each motion data stream is coarsened by transforming it into a segment-based progression of feature values. Two motion clips are then considered as similar if they possess (more or less) the same progression of feature values. For further details, we refer to [6]. The main point is that relational features are invariant under global orientation and position, the size of the

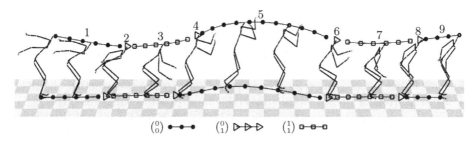

**Fig. 4.** Segmentation of a parallel leg jumping motion with respect to a combination of the feature "left knee bent" and the feature "right knee bent". Here the nine segments correspond to the sequence $\left(\binom{0}{0},\binom{0}{1},\binom{1}{1},\binom{0}{1},\binom{0}{0},\binom{0}{1},\binom{1}{1},\binom{0}{1},\binom{0}{0}\right)$ of feature values. Poses assuming the same feature values are indicated by identically marked trajectory segments. The trajectories of the joints 'headtop' and 'rankle' are shown.

skeleton, and local spatial deformations, whereas the induced segmentation introduces robustness to temporal variations.

## 2.1   Feature Design

To facilitate retrieval in large motion databases containing a great variety of motions, it is essential to provide the end-user of our retrieval system with a semantically rich set of features covering different body parts and various aspects of motions. Of course, the requirements to such a feature set will heavily depend on the intended application. The goal of our retrieval system is to search for motion clips in view of their rough course of motion. In this paper, we describe an exemplary system based on a set of 22 features, see Table 1.

In constructing such a feature set, we started with a small set of *generic* boolean features, which encode certain joint constellations in 3D space and time. In particular, we used the following generic features:

$$F_{\alpha,\text{plane}}^{(j_1,j_2,j_3;j_4)}, \quad F_{\alpha,\text{nplane}}^{(j_1,j_2,j_3;j_4)}, \quad F_{\alpha,\text{touch}}^{(j_1;j_2)}, \quad F_{\alpha,\text{bent}}^{(j_1,j_2,j_3)}, \quad F_{\alpha,\text{fast}}^{(j_1;j_2)}, \quad F_{\alpha,\text{move}}^{(j_1,j_2;j_3)}, \quad F_{\alpha,\text{nmove}}^{(j_1,j_2,j_3;j_4)}.$$

Each of these features assumes either the value one or the value zero and depends on a set of joints, denoted by $j_1, j_2, \ldots$, and on a threshold value $\alpha \in \mathbb{R}$. The first generic feature assumes the value one iff joint $j_4$ has a signed distance greater than $\alpha$ from the oriented plane spanned by the joints $j_1, j_2$ and $j_3$. For example, setting $j_1 =$ 'root', $j_2 =$ 'rhip', $j_3 =$ 'rankle', $j_4 =$ 'lankle', and $\alpha = 0.3$, one obtains the feature of Fig. 3 (a). The same test is described by $F_{\alpha,\text{nplane}}^{(j_1,j_2,j_3;j_4)}$, but here we define the plane in terms of a normal vector (given by $j_1$ and $j_2$), and fix it at $j_3$. The generic feature $F_{\alpha,\text{touch}}^{(j_1;j_2)}$ assumes the value one iff the two joints $j_1$ and $j_2$ are closer than $\alpha$. Similar generic touch detectors can also be defined for two body segments, or a joint and a body segment, see Fig. 3 (d)–(f). The generic feature $F_{\alpha,\text{bent}}^{(j_1,j_2,j_3)}$ assumes the value one iff the angle between the segments determined

**Table 1.** The feature set used in our experiments. All described features pertain to the right half of the body. Analogous versions for the left body parts exist and are assigned the even IDs $F_2, F_4, \ldots F_{22}$. The abbreviation "hl" denotes the relative length unit "humerus length", which is used to handle differences in absolute skeleton sizes.

| gen. feature | ID | set | $j_1$ | $j_2$ | $j_3$ | $j_4$ | $\alpha$ | description |
|---|---|---|---|---|---|---|---|---|
| $F_{\alpha,\text{plane}}^{(j_1,j_2,j_3;j_4)}$ | $F_1$ | $\ell$ | root | lhip | ltoes | rankle | 0.3 hl | foot in front |
| $F_{\alpha,\text{nplane}}^{(j_1,j_2,j_3;j_4)}$ | $F_3$ | $\ell$ | lhip | rhip | rhip | rankle | 0.5 hl | leg sideways |
| $F_{\alpha,\text{bent}}^{(j_1,j_2,j_3)}$ | $F_5$ | $\ell$ | rhip | rknee | rankle | | 110° | knee bent |
| | $F_7$ | u | rshoulder | relbow | rwrist | | 110° | elbow bent |
| $F_{\alpha,\text{fast}}^{(j_1;j_2)}$ | $F_9$ | $\ell$ | root | rankle | | | 6 hl/s | foot fast |
| | $F_{11}$ | u | rshoulder | rwrist | | | 6 hl/s | hand fast |
| | $F_{13}$ | $\ell$ | root | belly | rankle | | 2 hl/s | hand moves up |
| $F_{\alpha,\text{move}}^{(j_1,j_2;j_3)}$ | $F_{15}$ | u | belly | chest | rwrist | | 3 hl/s | hand moves up |
| | $F_{17}$ | u | chest | belly | rwrist | | 3 hl/s | hand moves down |
| | $F_{19}$ | u | neck | rshoulder | rwrist | | 3 hl/s | hand moves sideways |
| $F_{\alpha,\text{nmove}}^{(j_1,j_2,j_3;j_4)}$ | $F_{21}$ | u | root | lshoulder | rshoulder | rwrist | 3 hl/s | hand moves forward |

by $(j_2, j_1)$ and $(j_2, j_3)$ is below the threshold $\alpha$. For example, in Fig. 3 (g), we set $j_1 =$'lhip', $j_2 =$'lknee', $j_3 =$'lankle', and $\alpha = 110°$. The generic feature $F_{\alpha,\text{fast}}^{(j_1,j_2)}$ assumes the value one iff joint $j_2$ has a relative velocity with respect to $j_1$ that is above $\alpha$. Similarly, the feature $F_{\alpha,\text{move}}^{(j_1,j_2;j_3)}$ considers the velocity of joint $j_3$ relative to joint $j_1$ and assumes the value one iff the component of this velocity in the direction determined by $(j_1, j_2)$ is above $\alpha$. For example, setting $j_1 =$'belly', $j_2 =$'chest', $j_3 =$'rwrist', one obtains the feature of Fig. 3 (c). $F_{\alpha,\text{nmove}}^{(j_1,j_2,j_3;j_4)}$ has the same semantics, but the direction is given by the normal vector of the oriented plane spanned by $j_1, j_2$ and $j_3$. Of course, there are numerous other ways to define semantically meaningful generic features.

To determine reasonable joint combinations as well as suitable thresholds $\alpha$ for the generic features, we implemented a Feature Design GUI, which provides tools for visual feedback, statistical evaluations, and optimization. In designing our features, we incorporated most parts of the body, in particular the end effectors, so as to create a well-balanced feature set. One guiding principle was to cover the space of possible end effector locations by means of a small set of pose-dependent space "octants" defined by three intersecting planes each (above/below, left/right, in front of/behind the body). Obviously, this subdivision is only suitable to capture the rough course of a motion, since the feature function would often yield a constant output value for small-scaled motions. Here, our new features of type $F_{\alpha,\text{move}}$ turned out to effectively grasp finer motion details. In general, our boolean features are designed to be zero for large portions of time (e.g., for a standing pose, all features assume the value zero), but still manage to capture important motion characteristics. Threshold specification is a delicate issue, since improper thresholds $\alpha$ may significantly degrade retrieval quality. To determine a suitable $\alpha$ for a given feature, we proceed as follows: we supply the system with a training set $A$ of "positive" motions that should yield the feature value one for most of its frames and a training set $B$ of "negative" motions that should yield the feature value zero for most of its frames. The threshold $\alpha$ is then determined by a one-dimensional optimization algorithm, which iteratively maximizes the occurrences of the output one for the set $A$ while maximizing the occurrences of the output zero for the set $B$. Visual feedback about the resulting feature values aids the designer in fine-tuning $\alpha$. Further boolean features can then be derived—supported by a textual editor—by taking boolean expressions (AND, OR, XOR) of previously designed features.

## 2.2    Indexing

A major advantage of our approach is that all involved retrieval and indexing algorithms are time and space efficient. Here, the crucial point is that by incorporating spatio-temporal invariance in the relational features and induced segments, one can employ standard information retrieval techniques for fast content-based and fault-tolerant retrieval based on inverted lists, see [6]. In our system, we have divided the 22 features from Table 1 into two subsets $F^\ell$ (10 features) and $F^u$ (12 features), as denoted by the column marked "set".

$F^\ell$ expresses properties of the lower part of the body (mainly of the legs), while $F^u$ expresses properties of the upper part of the body (mainly of the arms).

Given a motion database (w.l.o.g. consisting of a single motion), we create an index $I^\ell$ for $F^\ell$, which consists of the inverted list representation of the temporal segmentation of the motion, see Sect. 2. Analogously, we create a second index $I^u$ for the feature set $F^u$. Note that in this approach, a feature set containing $n$ features leads to $2^n$ possible feature vectors, each of which may give rise to an inverted list in the index. Thus, we restrict the maximum number of features per index to 12, corresponding to a maximum of 4,096 inverted lists. Efficient retrieval can then be done by suitable union and intersection operations on the inverted lists, see [6] for further details.

# 3   User Interaction

Recall from Fig. 2 that a query specification consists of an example motion together with some fault tolerance settings and a suitable selection from the relational features listed in Table 1. In this section, we illustrate the typical workflow in our query-by-example system by means of a "jump" query as shown in Fig. 4, while presenting the corresponding elements of our Retrieval GUI.

*Step 1: Specifying an example motion.* In our system, a query motion is specified by selecting a frame range from a motion capture file, see Fig. 5 (a). Here, the selected jumping motion is a small excerpt from a sequence of pre-recorded sports movements, corresponding to segments 3–9 in Fig. 4. Note that in principle, it would also be possible to provide an example motion by *keyframing*, a process widely used in computer animation. Here, a motion is sketched by a few characteristic poses that are then interpolated. In a further input mode, the example motion could be generated on-line using suitable motion capturing hardware.

To get a better feeling for our query motion from Fig. 4, let us first focus on the movement of the legs. Both legs are kept parallel throughout the jump sequence and are stretched during the initial phase of arm-swing (segment 1 in Fig. 4). The legs are then bent into a half-squatting position (segments 2–3), preparing the following push-off (starting shortly before segment 4), during which the legs are stretched once more. In the landing phase (starting shortly before segment 6), the legs absorb the energy of the jump by bending as deep as before push-off. The jump sequence is concluded by stretching the legs into a normal standing position (segments 8–9). This sequence of bending and stretching the knees is characteristic for many kinds of parallel-leg jumping motions.

*Step 2: Selecting suitable features.* The above considerations show that it is reasonable to choose the features as in Fig. 4, where `kneeLeftAngle` and `kneeRightAngle` (corresponding to $F^5/F^6$ in Table 1) were selected. This is indicated in our GUI by a '+' mark, see Fig. 5 (b). In general, the strong semantics of geometric relations makes feature selection an intuitive process: the user can often anticipate which features will grasp important aspects of the query.

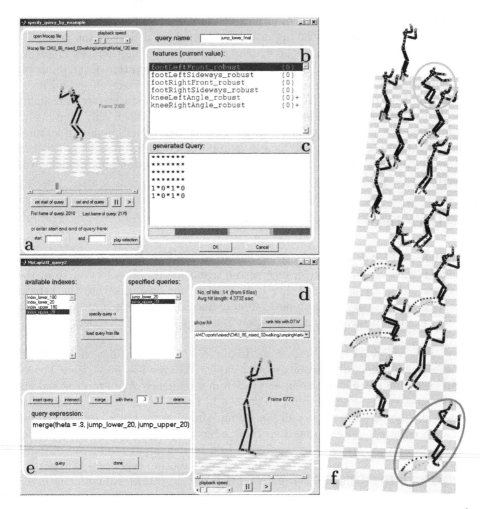

**Fig. 5.** Left: query interface; for a better overview, only 6 of the 10 features in $I^\ell$ are shown in (b). Right: fourteen hits for a "jump" query on $\mathcal{D}^{20}$. The query motion (foreground) and a false positive hit (background) are highlighted.

Since in Step 1, we only selected the frames corresponding to segments 3–9, we obtain the sequence $\left(\binom{1}{1},\binom{0}{1},\binom{0}{0},\binom{0}{1},\binom{1}{1},\binom{0}{1},\binom{0}{0}\right)$ with respect to $F_5$ and $F_6$, which is a subsequence of the feature progression given in the caption of Fig. 4. In our GUI, we represent this feature progression as a *query matrix* $Q$, where each column corresponds to a segment, each row corresponds to a feature, and where features from the chosen index that were not selected by the user are marked by rows of asterisks, e.g.,

$$Q = \begin{pmatrix} * & * & * & * & * & * & * \\ * & * & * & * & * & * & * \\ * & * & * & * & * & * & * \\ * & * & * & * & * & * & * \\ 1 & 0 & 0 & 0 & 1 & 0 & 0 \\ 1 & 1 & 0 & 1 & 1 & 1 & 0 \end{pmatrix} \begin{matrix} F_2 \\ F_4 \\ F_1 \\ F_3 \\ F_6\ + \\ F_5\ + \end{matrix}$$

For the sake of simplicity, we omitted the features $F_9, F_{10}, F_{13}$, and $F_{14}$, which are constituents of $F^\ell$. The features corresponding to each row are given to the right of $Q$, and the user-selected features are once more marked by a '+'. Such a query matrix is automatically generated by our system as soon as the frame range and the features have been selected (cf. Fig. 5 (c)). We visualize the structure of the current segmentation as a multicolored bar, as shown in the lower part of Fig. 5 (c). Here, each color corresponds to a feature vector, and the lengths of the colored bars are proportional to the segment lengths in frames.

*Step 3: Setting up fault tolerance.* The query matrix shown in Fig. 5 (c) differs from $Q$ in that the user has inserted asterisks in columns 2, 4, and 6. These asterisks mask out irrelevant transitions between the alternating vectors $\binom{1}{1}$ and $\binom{0}{0}$ from the original feature sequence. In more detail, the feature vectors $\binom{0}{1}$ arise because the actor does not bend or stretch both legs at the same time. Instead, he has a tendency to keep the right leg bent a bit longer than the left leg. There are many possible transitions from, e.g., $\binom{1}{1}$ (legs bent) to $\binom{0}{0}$ (legs stretched), such as $\binom{1}{1} \to \binom{0}{0}$, $\binom{1}{1} \to \binom{0}{1} \to \binom{0}{0}$, or $\binom{1}{1} \to \binom{1}{0} \to \binom{0}{1} \to \binom{0}{0}$. This is the reason why we inserted the asterisk columns in Fig. 5 (c): each of the aforementioned transitions encodes the motion "stretching the legs", which is all that matters to our query. Our system automatically translates the asterisk notation into a suitable query.

*Step 4: Querying, ranking and result presentation.* Once the user has finalized the query matrix, the system starts the retrieval and then presents the hits to the user, who can browse the corresponding motion fragments in a graphical display, see Fig. 5 (d). The hits can be post-processed by means of a new DTW-based ranking strategy: a hit's ranking value is determined by the cost of a cheapest path in a cost matrix $(c_{ij})$, where each entry $c_{ij}$ is the hamming distance between the $i$-th vector in the feature progression of the query and the $j$-th vector in the feature progression of the hit. At this stage, we use a segmentation that is induced by a compound feature function containing all features from Table 1, regardless of the features that were selected for the query. Note that DTW is only applied to a generally very small number of hits that were efficiently retrieved by our index-based approach and not to the entire database, as for most previous DTW-based methods. Furthermore, the cost matrices are typically very small because the query and the hits are compared at the segment level instead of the frame level, thus working on strongly downsampled motion representations.

*Step 5: Combining queries.* Our example query as it has been discussed so far yields a relatively large number of false positive hits on our test database. For example, many squatting motions exhibit the same progression of knee bending and stretching as found in a jump. To further refine our query, we can incorporate additional constraints regarding the upper part of the body, i.e., the index $I_u$. To this end, the user may specify several independent queries (on different indexes or even on the same index), which can then be combined in a query expression by means of *merge* and *intersect* operations, cf. Fig. 5 (e). Merging two sets of hits $H_1$ and $H_2$ means that a hit $h_1 \in H_1$ is reported as a result if there is a hit $h_2 \in H_2$ that overlaps $h_1$ by more than a fraction of $\theta \in (0, 1]$ (relative to the length of $h_1$, measured in seconds). Our intersection operator coincides with the set theoretical intersection of the hits interpreted as time intervals. The results of a combined "jump" query, which uses merging to incorporate a query that focuses on the arm motion, are discussed in Sect. 4 and visualized in Fig. 5 (f).

*Step 6: Iteratively refining the query.* Assisted by the system's feedback, a user can modify his query at several points in the query process. Initially, he may modify the frame range and feature selection so as to achieve a segmentation that is characteristic, but not too specific. Here, the query matrix and the segmentation bar support the user's decisions. Short segments in the segmentation bar hint at transitions that may be masked out by means of an asterisk column, cf. Step 3. After inspecting the hits for the initial query, the user may reconsider the current query settings. If, for instance, many false positive hits have been retrieved, it often helps to extend the query motion or to incorporate additional features that discern the query motion from the false positives. If, on the other hand, only few hits are retrieved, the user may decrease the complexity of the induced segmentation by reducing the number of selected features, by reducing the length of the example motion, or by decreasing the merging parameter $\theta$.

## 4  Experimental Results

Our motion retrieval system was implemented in Matlab, and experimental results were obtained on a 3.6 GHz Pentium 4 with 1 GB of main memory. We evaluated the system on a subset $\mathcal{D}^{180}$ of the CMU database [1], which contains about one million frames of motion capture data ($\sim$180 minutes sampled at 120 Hz) and covers a wide range of motions.

The columns of Table 2 show the results for five exemplary queries: a forceful jump, a cartwheel, the gymnastics motions "elbow-to-knee" and "jumping

**Table 2.** Summary of representative query results. See Sect. 4 for a discussion.

|  | jump | cartwheel | elbow-to-knee | jumping jack | punch |
|---|---|---|---|---|---|
| recall on $\mathcal{D}^{20}$ | 13/16 | 4/4 | 14/14 | 19/19 | 24/24 |
| precision on $\mathcal{D}^{20}$ | 13/14 | 4/4 | 14/15 | 19/19 | 24/37 |
| precision on $\mathcal{D}^{180}$ | 17/27 | 4/59 | 14/27 | 19/29 | 83/153 |
| $p_5^{180}$ \| $p_{10}^{180}$ \| $p_{20}^{180}$ | 5 \| 10 \| 16 | 4 \| 4 \| 4 | 5 \| 9 \| 14 | 5 \| 10 \| 18 | 5 \| 10 \| 20 |
| query time on $\mathcal{D}^{180}$ (s) | 0.87 | 0.06 | 0.39 | 0.60 | 0.08 |
| ranking time on $\mathcal{D}^{180}$ (s) | 4.42 | 5.87 | 1.04 | 1.54 | 4.46 |
| total length of hits in $\mathcal{D}^{180}$ (s) | 136.45 | 125.89 | 15.08 | 37.87 | 128.53 |

jack", and a punch with the right fist. Further information and result videos for these queries can be found at http://www-mmdb.iai.uni-bonn.de/projects/ mocap/RetrievalGUI.html. In order to determine the recall (proportion of relevant hits that were retrieved) of our queries, we manually annotated a subset $\mathcal{D}^{20}$ of $\mathcal{D}^{180}$ consisting of about 145,000 frames ($\sim$20 minutes). $\mathcal{D}^{20}$ includes a diverse range of about 15 different gymnastics motions, some walking, jogging, jumping, climbing sequences, several martial arts moves, pantomime, and basketball motions. The precision (proportion of retrieved hits that are relevant) of query results was evaluated on both $\mathcal{D}^{20}$ and $\mathcal{D}^{180}$. Our retrieval concept focuses on maximizing the recall for any given query, which may lead to a relatively low precision. However, we improve the quality of our retrieval results by applying DTW-based ranking as explained in Sect. 3. In order to evaluate this ranking, we counted the number of relevant hits within the top 5, top 10, and top 20 positions of the ranked hit list, denoted in Table 2 by $p_5^{180}$, $p_{10}^{180}$, and $p_{20}^{180}$, respectively.

Our query for parallel-leg jumps (first column of Table 2) successfully retrieved 13 of the 16 jumping motions that were contained in $\mathcal{D}^{20}$, leading to a recall of 13/16. The three remaining jumps were missed because the actors' knees were not bent far enough to trigger our features. The total number of hits was 14 (cf. Figure 5 (f)), only one of which was a false positive, namely, the squatting motion that is highlighted in Figure 5 (f). This leads to a precision of 13/14 on $\mathcal{D}^{20}$. On $\mathcal{D}^{180}$, four additional jumps and nine additional false positives were found, leading to a precision of 17/27. There were no false positives in the top 5 and top 10 positions of the ranked hit list, and only one of the 17 relevant hits did not appear in the top 20. Only 136.45 seconds of $\mathcal{D}^{180}$, or 1.26%, had to be inspected by the DTW-based ranking procedure. The index-based retrieval step took 0.87 seconds for the $\mathcal{D}^{180}$ database, whereas the ranking consumed another 4.42 seconds. Note that in general, the running time for the ranking step correlates with the total length of the retrieved hits.

The query for right cartwheels uses only two different features, $F_9$ and $F_{10}$, which test whether the feet move with a high velocity. The resulting feature sequence $\left(\binom{0}{0},\binom{0}{1},\binom{1}{1},\binom{1}{0},\binom{0}{0}\right)$ reflects how the left leg is kicked up in the air, quickly followed by the right leg. The left leg touches the ground first, leading to a low velocity in this phase, again followed by the right leg. This query is characteristic enough to lead to perfect precision and recall values on $\mathcal{D}^{20}$. Its precision on $\mathcal{D}^{180}$ is very low, as there are 55 false positive hits, but our ranking strategy places the cartwheels among the top 5 hits. In contrast to the three other examples, the cartwheel and punch queries operated on one index only, which makes merging superfluous—hence the low retrieval times of 0.06 and 0.08 seconds, respectively.

For the gymnastics motions "elbow-to-knee" and "jumping jack", a larger number of spurious hits was returned on $\mathcal{D}^{180}$, but our ranking succeeds in placing the relevant hits at the top of the list. The queries "cartwheel", "elbow-to-knee", and "jumping jack" achieve perfect recall values on $\mathcal{D}^{20}$. No additional relevant hits for these queries appear in the results for $\mathcal{D}^{180}$ because to our knowledge, all of these rather specific motions are already contained in the subset $\mathcal{D}^{20}$ of $\mathcal{D}^{180}$. For characterizing right-handed punches, we used $F_7$, $F_{11}$, $F_{21}$, and, to improve precision, $F_{22}$. Once again, the recall on $\mathcal{D}^{20}$ is perfect, while the precision is 24/37. On $\mathcal{D}^{180}$, the precision decreases to roughly 50%, but this is successfully compensated for by our ranking.

## 5   Conclusions and Future Work

In this paper, we presented a Retrieval GUI for content-based motion retrieval, where the query consists of a motion clip as well as a user-specified selection of motion aspects to be considered in the retrieval process. Based on the concept of quantitative relational features as introduced in [6], we suggested several generic boolean features, which can then be used—aided by our Feature Design GUI— to determine a set of semantically meaningful features covering a wide range of motion aspects. Being in a way conceptually orthogonal to computationally expensive DTW-based strategies, our technique is ideally suited to efficiently cut down the search space in a pre-processing step, thus making DTW-based techniques applicable to large data sets. This finding is supported by our experimental results, see Sect. 4.

Motion reuse based on morphing and blending as used in computer animation may require batch techniques to automatically retrieve suitable motion fragments. To this end, we plan to automate the feature selection step using statistical methods. Furthermore, we are developing and analyzing DTW-based ranking strategies based on different cost measures. First experiments showed that our relational approach to motion description not only constitutes a possible framework for flexible and efficient retrieval mechanisms, but also for automatic classification and annotation of motion data.

## References

1. CMU, *Carnegie-Mellon MoCap Database.* Created with funding from NSF EIA-0196217. http://mocap.cs.cmu.edu, 2003.
2. K. FORBES AND E. FIUME, *An efficient search algorithm for motion data using weighted PCA*, in SCA '05: Proc. 2005 ACM SIGGRAPH/Eurographics Symposium on Computer Animation, New York, NY, USA, 2005, ACM Press, pp. 67–76.
3. E. J. KEOGH, T. PALPANAS, V. B. ZORDAN, D. GUNOPULOS, AND M. CARDLE, *Indexing large human-motion databases*, in Proc. 30th VLDB Conf., Toronto, 2004, pp. 780–791.
4. L. KOVAR AND M. GLEICHER, *Automated extraction and parameterization of motions in large data sets*, ACM Trans. Graph., 23 (2004), pp. 559–568.
5. G. LIU, J. ZHANG, W. WANG, AND L. MCMILLAN, *A system for analyzing and indexing human-motion databases*, in SIGMOD '05: Proc. 2005 ACM SIGMOD Intl. Conf. on Management of Data, New York, NY, USA, 2005, ACM Press, pp. 924–926.
6. M. MÜLLER, T. RÖDER, AND M. CLAUSEN, *Efficient content-based retrieval of motion capture data.*, ACM Trans. Graph., 24 (2005), pp. 677–685.
7. VICON, *3D optical motion capture.* http://www.vicon.com.
8. M.-Y. WU, S. CHAO, S. YANG, AND H. LIN, *Content-based retrieval for human motion data*, in 16th IPPR Conf. on Computer Vision, Graphics and Image Processing, 2003, pp. 605–612.

# Can a Workspace Help to Overcome the Query Formulation Problem in Image Retrieval?

Jana Urban and Joemon M. Jose

Department of Computing Science, University of Glasgow,
Glasgow G12 8RZ, UK
{jana, jj}@dcs.gla.ac.uk

**Abstract.** We have proposed a novel image retrieval system that incorporates a workspace where users can organise their search results. A task-oriented and user-centred experiment has been devised involving design professionals and several types of realistic search tasks. We study the workspace's effect on two aspects: task conceptualisation and query formulation. A traditional relevance feedback system serves as baseline. The results of this study show that the workspace is more useful with respect to both of the above aspects. The proposed approach leads to a more effective and enjoyable search experience.

## 1 Introduction and Motivation

Content-based image retrieval (CBIR) systems have still not managed to find favour with the public even after more than a decade of research effort in the field. There are two main reasons for their lack of acceptability: first, the low-level features used to represent images in the system do not reflect the high-level concepts the user has in mind when looking at an image (*semantic gap*); and—partially due to this—the user tends to have major difficulties in formulating and communicating their information need effectively (*query formulation problem*).

We are seeking to find a solution to these problems by supporting an alternative search strategy. We have designed a system, *EGO*, that combines the search and the management process [1]. This is accomplished by introducing a workspace and rec-ommendation system. While searching for images, the creation of groupings of related images is supported, encouraging the user to break up the task into related facets to or-ganise their ideas and concepts. The system can then assist the user by recommending relevant images for selected groups. This way, the user can concentrate on solving spe-cific tasks rather than having to think about how to create a good query in accordance with the retrieval mechanism.

Although a workspace has been introduced in a few IR systems before, e.g. Sketch-Trieve [2], its usefulness—especially for *image retrieval*—has not been evaluated for-mally yet. To remedy this shortcoming, we have designed a user experiment to evaluate the effectiveness of our approach for solving realistic image search tasks. We compare *EGO*'s performance to that of a traditional relevance feedback system as a baseline. In the relevance feedback system, the user is given the option of selecting relevant images from the search results in order to improve the results in the next iteration. Our aim is

M. Lalmas et al. (Eds.): ECIR 2006, LNCS 3936, pp. 385–396, 2006.
© Springer-Verlag Berlin Heidelberg 2006

to collect evidence on the systems' effectiveness as perceived by the users. More importantly, however, we would like to determine the workspace's role in helping the user to both conceptualise their search tasks and overcome the query formulation problem.

The experiment has been completed in two stages. Experiment 1 involved 12 participants using the two systems for category search tasks and a design task. A summary of the results has been published elsewhere [3]. This previous study only provided indicative conclusions on our research hypotheses. The results of the system's effectiveness were ambiguous: people performed better (using quantitative measures) in the category search tasks on the baseline while they were generally more satisfied with the workspace system. On the other hand, it indicated that the organisation did indeed help to conceptualise the tasks. However, we only studied two kinds of tasks from which the design task was only performed on the workspace system. So to be able to further study the effect of task on searching and organisation behaviour we need to investigate a larger variety of tasks. Above all, we failed to capture the grouping process' effect on the query formulation process, which we address in this paper.

In addition, the retrieval mechanism based on visual features only was limiting: the results were generally poor, the recommendation system was even more affected as it only returned the top 10 results, and the users were often swamped by irrelevant images due to not being able to provide negative feedback. We have decided to remedy these problems and introduce a different set of tasks for the second stage of the experiment. With this improved evaluation setup, Experiment 2 should help to clarify the validity of our research hypotheses. These results are presented in this paper. We look at the results from slightly different angles, such as a detailed analysis of the users' perception of task performance and user effort to complete the tasks. In particular, a direct comparison between the relevance feedback process and the grouping and recommendation system finally enables us to compare their impact on query formulation.

## 2   The Interfaces

We describe the main characteristics of both interfaces used in the evaluation, followed by an overview of the underlying retrieval system in this section.

### 2.1   Workspace Interface – WS

The interface used in the evaluation is a simplified version of that of the *EGO* system [1]. *EGO* has some additional features for personalisation and can, in principle, accommodate any sort of query facility. Since our main objective in these experiments is to evaluate the usefulness of the workspace, this interface is referred to as the Workspace Interface (*WS*). The WS interface depicted in Figure 1 comprises the following components:

1. Query Panel: This provides a basic query facility to search the database by allowing the user to compose a search request by entering search terms or adding example images to the query-by-example (QBE) panel provided here. Clicking on the "Search" button in this panel will issue a search.

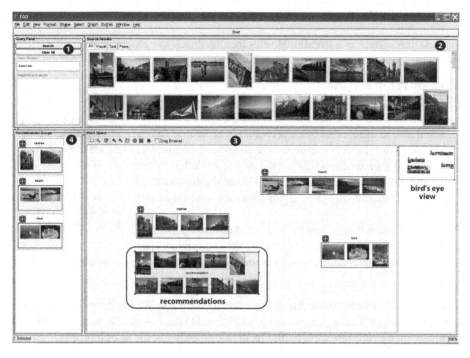

**Fig. 1.** Annotated WS interface

2. Results Panel: The search results from a query constructed in the Query Panel will be displayed in this panel. Any of the returned images can be dragged onto the workspace to start organising the collection or into the QBE panel to change the current query.

3. Workspace Panel: The workspace holds all the images added to it by the user, and serves as an organisation ground for the user to construct groupings of images. Groupings can be created by right-clicking anywhere on the workspace, which opens a context menu in which the option can be selected. Traditional drag-and-drop techniques allow the user to drag images into (or out of) a group or reposition the group on the workspace. An image can belong to multiple groups simultaneously. Panning and zooming techniques are supported to assist navigation in a large information space. The top 10 recommendations will be displayed close to the selected group on the workspace (see centre of workspace in Figure 1). In addition, the complete recommendation results are also displayed in the Results Panel.

4. Group Results Panel: For each query or recommendations issued the existing groups will be ranked in order of similarity to the current query/group and the five top matching groups will be displayed in this panel. Each returned group contains a link to the original group on the workspace.

To recapitulate, the query facilities available in the WS interface are: (1) manually constructed queries by providing keywords and/or one or more image examples (QBE), and (2) user-requested recommendations.

## 2.2   Relevance Feedback Interface – CS

The baseline system is a traditional relevance feedback system, referred to as *CS* (for Checkbox System). The interface contains the following components:

1. Query Panel: as above.
2. Results Panel: As above, but instead of dragging a relevant image onto the workspace the user has the choice of marking it as one of relevant (+), irrelevant (-), or neutral (=) by checking the respective combo box underneath the image. After images have been marked the user can ask the system to update the current search results (based on the feedback provided) by clicking the "Update Results" button in this panel.
3. Selected Items Panel: Any item selected relevant during the course of the search session will be added to this panel. The user can manually delete images from this panel if they change their mind at a later change.

**Fig. 2.** Relevance feedback in CS (image is marked "neutral")

To summarise, the look-and-feel of the interface is similar to WS (without the workspace facility). Finally, CS supports two query facilities: (1) manual queries as above, and (2) automatic query reformulation by the feedback provided in the search results.

## 2.3   Retrieval System

The underlying retrieval system is the same in both interfaces and is described in [1]. Images are represented by a set of low-level visual features and modelled according to the hierarchical object model [4]. The distance between an object in the database and a given query representation is computed in two steps: computing the individual feature distances by the generalised Euclidean distance; then combining the individual distances linearly with a set of feature weights. The relevance feedback algorithm is implemented by an optimised framework for updating the retrieval parameters as proposed in [4]. It attempts to learn the best query representation and feature weighting for a selected group of images (positive training samples).

After the results obtained from the first set of participants, the experimental systems were scrutinised and consequently redesigned to take into account the lessons learnt. The main changes made were:

– The recommendation system in WS was not used to its full potential, due to its inability to recommend relevant images. This has been addressed in two ways. First, instead of just showing the top 10 recommendations on the workspace, the results panel now also shows the complete results (limited to 100 images). Second, a textual search facility has been introduced, because the visual features seemed not sufficient to solve more abstract tasks providing a more realistic search experience. Textual annotations obtained from [5] were incorporated and implemented according to the vector-space model [6]. Visual and textual features are combined using a rank-based list aggregation method [7].

– The retrieval mechanism was further improved by allowing negative feedback, as people complained about the inability to continue a search when the majority of returned images were irrelevant. Since incorporating negative feedback is a difficult endeavour [8], we have opted for a quick and safe approach: irrelevant images are added to a negative filter excluding them to be returned for the same search. It was straight-forward to implement this in CS where negative feedback can easily be provided explicitly. In WS however, we have chosen an implicit feedback strategy, whereby an image is automatically added to a negative filter for a group when it has been ignored (i.e. not dragged into this group) after having been returned 3 times amongst the top 10 recommendations.

## 3   Evaluation Methodology

It has been argued that traditional IR evaluation techniques based on precision-recall measures are not suitable for evaluating adaptive systems [9, 10]. Thus, we adopted a task-oriented, user-centred approach [10]. We have designed the experiments to be as close to real-life usage as possible: we have chosen participants with a design-related background and have set tasks that are practical and relevant.

We employed a subset of the Corel collection (CD 1, CD 4, CD 5, and CD 6 of the Corel 1.6M dataset), containing 12800 photographs in total. 12 searchers used two systems in a randomised within-subjects design. The independent variable was system type; two sets of values of a variety of dependent variables indicative of acceptability or user satisfaction were to be determined through questionnaires. In addition, users' actions were logged and analysed.

**Participants.** Since we wanted to test the system in a realistic usage scenario, our sample user population consisted of post-graduate design students and young design professionals. There were 12 participants, 7 male and 5 female, with a wide variety of ages in the range of 20-50 years. The average age was 28 years. The participants had on average 5 years experience in a design-related field (graphic design, architecture, photography). Most people dealt with digital images at least once a day as part of their course or work. The user profile in the current experiment is similar to Experiment 1.

**Tasks.** The tasks in Experiment 1 consisted of: category search tasks where participants had to find as many images as possible for a specific topic such as "elephants" (Task A) and a complex topic such as "underwater world" (Task B); and a design-task in which participants chose 3-5 images for designing a leaflet with a very open topic (Task C). We felt that more tasks were needed in order to draw definitive conclusions on the workspace's usefulness in helping to conceptualise tasks. We have devised a variety of realistic tasks, with different levels of complexity, abstraction and creativity. The tasks in Experiment 2 are:

**Theme search task (Task D).** In this task people were asked to find an image fitting into a specified theme ("people in national costumes" and "seasons in the country"). The theme was illustrated by three example images and the task involved searching for and selecting *one further image* complementing this set.

**Illustration task (Task E).** The task was to illustrate a piece of text for publication on the WWW, or an advertising slogan with *three images*. There were four tasks in total from which the participants had to choose two (one on each system).

**Abstract search task (Task F).** Here people were asked to select *at least one image* representing a given abstract topic ("cute" and "dynamic"). The simulated work task situation prescribed to select an image for a photo competition.

The level of abstraction grows from Task D to F: Task D has a very specified theme as defined by the three example images; the theme in Task E is specified by the given text or slogan but leaves more room for choosing the appropriate images; Task F finally leaves both the interpretation of the topic as well as the choice of images illustrating that topic open to the individual. Tasks A and B would be found before Task D on this scale, while Task C is a little more abstract and creative than Task E (since there was no text for illustration purposes). The complexity of a task is influenced by the coherence of its topic: if a topic is composed of several concepts or interpretations we regard it as complex. When we talk about facets of a task, we mean the concepts or interpretations that an individual filtered out when pursuing the task.

In Tasks D and F, the participants were assigned a specific topic, which was rotated based on a Latin-square design. The 4 topics of Task E were very similar in nature (level of complexity and available choice of suitable images). We have not found any significant variations between these topical alternatives within this search task group.

No time limits were set on the new tasks, as was learnt from Experiment 1 that this adversely affected people's performance.

**Hypothesis.** Evidence was to be collected for the following sub-hypotheses:

1. The workspace leads to an increased effectiveness and user satisfaction.
2. The workspace helps to conceptualise and diversify tasks.
3. The grouping process helps to overcome the query formulation problem.

**Procedure.** Each participant performed four search sessions, using each system twice, completing two tasks with a different topic per system. The procedure involved a pre-search questionnaire, the four search sessions followed by a post-search questionnaire each time, and finally an exit questionnaire/interview comparing the systems. A search session was preceded by a training session if the system was used for the first time. The whole procedure lasted approximately two hours. Tasks and systems were rotated according to a Latin-square design in order to compensate the learning bias.

## 4   Results Analysis

The systems are compared according to (a) their effectiveness, and (b) user satisfaction. The following results are based on 48 ($12 \times 4$) searches in total.

The results for Likert-scales and semantic differentials are in the range $[1, 5]$, the higher the value the better. Statistically significant differences are provided where appropriate with $p \leq .05$ using the two-tailed version of the non-parametric Wilcoxon Paired-Sample test. $\overline{CS}$ and $\overline{WS}$ denote the means for CS and WS respectively, while $\widetilde{CS}$ and $\widetilde{WS}$ denote the medians.

## 4.1    Effectiveness

The systems' effectiveness is investigated from two sides: objectively from the perspective of the required effort as determined from the usage logs and subjectively from the perspective of the participants.

**User Effort.** Due to the lack of ground truth for the tasks in Experiment 2, we provide an analysis of the number of images selected per task and the amount of user effort required to select them. These include: total search time and number of queries issued. People can issue either manual queries—constructed in textual form, by providing image examples or a combination of both—or relevance feedback queries. The latter correspond to relevance feedback iterations in CS or group recommendations in WS.

Table 1 reveals that less queries were issued and more images were selected on WS. In particular, more *relevance feedback* queries were requested on WS, while more *manual queries* were constructed on CS (with the exception of Task F). The RF queries were particular useful for Tasks E and F. The search session lasted on average longer on WS. By contrast, Task E stands out for being completed in less time on WS (with a difference of about 4 minutes) but still achieving a slightly larger selection of images in the end. This indicates that WS is particularly useful for design-oriented tasks.

**Table 1.** User effort indicators per task and system in Experiment 2

|          | $D_{CS}$ | $D_{WS}$ | $E_{CS}$ | $E_{WS}$ | $F_{CS}$ | $F_{WS}$ | $\overline{CS}$ | $\overline{WS}$ |
|----------|---------|---------|---------|---------|---------|---------|---------|---------|
| time     | 9'55"   | 12'02"  | 18'26"  | **14'18"** | 9'40"   | 14'31"  | 12'40"  | 13'35"  |
| #images  | 9.6     | 12.3    | 17.9    | **18.6** | 13.6    | 17.8    | 13.7    | 16.2    |
| #queries | 11.9    | 9.8     | 21.5    | 19.1    | 15.9    | 17.1    | 16.4    | 15.3    |
| manual   | 8.4     | 7.6     | 15.8    | 12.2    | 11.4    | 12.0    | 11.9    | 10.6    |
| RF       | 3.4     | 2.1     | 5.8     | 6.9     | 4.5     | 5.1     | 4.6     | 4.7     |

**User Perception of Performance.** After each task the users were asked if they thought they had succeeded in their performance of the task and also rate potential problems that might have affected their performance. Performing a task on WS was more successful, as can be seen in Table 2. In comparison to CS, people had a slight difficulty in

**Table 2.** User perception of task performance per task and system (performance:higher=better, problems:lower=more problematic)

|                            | $D_{CS}$ | $D_{WS}$ | $E_{CS}$ | $E_{WS}$ | $F_{CS}$ | $F_{WS}$ | CS | WS | p |
|----------------------------|---------|---------|---------|---------|---------|---------|-----|-----|---|
| performance success        | 4.2     | 4.6     | 4.1     | 4.2     | 4.3     | 4.4     | 4.2 | **4.4** | - |
| did not understand task    | 5.0     | 4.8     | 5.0     | 4.9     | 4.9     | 4.6     | 5.0 | **4.8** | - |
| images not in collection   | 4.2     | 4.4     | 3.5     | 3.5     | 4.1     | **3.4** | 3.9 | 3.8 | - |
| no relevant images returned| **4.0** | 4.4     | 3.6     | 3.5     | 4.5     | 4.4     | 4.0 | 4.1 | - |
| not enough time            | 4.8     | 4.9     | 4.4     | **4.1** | 4.9     | 4.6     | 4.7 | **4.5** | - |
| unsure of next action      | **4.1** | 4.5     | 4.4     | 4.4     | **4.0** | 4.3     | 4.2 | 4.4 | - |

understanding the search task. Also, time was more of an issue on WS than CS[1]. This reflects the increased cognitive effort required to perform a task on WS.

On the other hand, people's performance was hindered more by an uncertainty of what action to take next on CS. Together with the user comments presented below this indicates that—though a simple concept in principle—providing relevance feedback brings uncertainty as to which images to select for feedback in order to achieve better results. This corroborates similar results in textual information retrieval [11].

## 4.2 User Satisfaction

In this section we first present the user satisfaction with the particular interface features—the grouping and recommendation system in WS and the relevance feedback process in CS. After that, we discuss the responses concerning user satisfaction with the system in general.

**Interface Support.** People were asked how effective they found the interface and rated the contributing features. Table 3 summarises these results. Overall, WS was regarded significantly more *effective*. The three top rated features on WS were that it helped to *organise images*, *explore the collection*, and *analyse the task*. The ordering of features on CS was: *find relevant images*, *explore the collection*, and *detect/express different task aspects*. Apart from *find relevant images*, all features are rated significantly higher on WS.

Table 4 compares the adaptive querying mechanisms: the relevance assessment in CS and the grouping in WS. It turns out that the grouping was considered significantly more *effective* and *useful*. It is also interesting to note that the relevance assessment was even considered more *difficult* than the grouping.

In open-ended questions the participants were asked to state the most and least useful tools of the interface. The most useful tools in CS were stated as, in order of frequency of responses: textual query (10 responses[2]), QBE (9), and relevance feedback facility (7). The least useful tools were: result filters for various features (5), relevance feedback (4), and lack of storing facility/overview of selected images (4). Users who thought the relevance feedback was a useful tool stated it as helping them to improve and/or narrow down their search. The problems with relevance assessment were mainly that it returned unexpected results and that it was difficult to keep track of what the system was doing.

In WS, people unanimously liked the grouping facility on the workspace. The three most useful tools in WS included the grouping of images (14), group recommendations (10) and textual queries (5), and the least useful tools were: QBE (4), top 10 window of recommendations (3) and text search (2). This shows that using groups and recommendations was considered more useful than the manual search facilities; especially the query-by-example facility was superfluous in this system. The grouping's only disadvantage that became apparent was that it was difficult to remove images from existing groups.

These results support our view that WS, with its grouping and recommendation facility, assists the user in the query formulation process, while removing the need to

---

[1] In Experiment 1, people also tended to agree more with the statement that they had enough time to complete their task in CS: $\overline{CS} = 4.6$, and $\overline{WS} = 4.3$.

[2] This question was asked after each search, thus 24 responses are possible per system.

**Table 3.** Interface effectiveness

| Statement | $\tilde{CS}$ CS $\tilde{WS}$ WS | p |
|---|---|---|
| effective | 3.7 4 **4.4** 5 | 0.032 |
| analyse task | 2.8 3 **4.3** 5 | 0.001 |
| explore collection | 3.5 4 **4.6** 5 | 0.001 |
| find relevant images | 4.2 4 4.2 4 | - |
| organise images | 2.7 3 **4.7** 5 | 0.001 |
| detect/express task aspects | 3.0 3 **4.2** 4 | 0.003 |

**Table 4.** Relevance assessment on CS vs. grouping on WS

| Differential | $\tilde{CS}$ WS | p |
|---|---|---|
| easy | 3.8 **4.4** | - |
| effective | 3.3 **4.3** | 0.019 |
| useful | 3.7 **4.4** | 0.017 |

**Table 5.** Results for system part

| Differential | $\tilde{CS}$ CS $\tilde{WS}$ WS | p |
|---|---|---|
| wonderful | 3.3 3 **4.1** 4 | - |
| satisfying | 3.2 3 **4.0** 4 | - |
| stimulating | 3.5 3 **4.3** 4 | - |
| easy | **4.0** 4 3.8 4 | - |
| flexible | 2.9 3 **4.2** 4 | 0.004 |
| efficient | 3.3 3 **3.9** 4 | - |
| novel | 3.7 4 **4.4** 5 | - |

| | $\tilde{CS}$ CS $\tilde{WS}$ WS | p |
|---|---|---|
| in control | 3.6 4 3.6 4 | - |
| comfortable | 3.7 4 **4.3** 5 | - |
| confident | 3.1 3 **3.8** 4 | - |
| learn to use | **4.1** 4 3.9 4 | - |
| use | 3.9 4 3.9 4 | - |

manually reformulate queries. The picture in CS is quite different: people were divided on the usefulness of the relevance assessments and some still relied heavily on the manual query facilities. On average, people selected 2.4, 3.2, and 3.8 images per relevance feedback iteration for Task D, E, and F, respectively. Compared to that, the groups in WS contained 4.9, 4.6, and 4.4 images. So the manual selection process was less productive than collecting the images in groups. Moreover, the grouping process has the additional benefit of supporting a diversifying search by allowing to declare and pursue various task aspects simultaneously.

**System.** In the post-search questionnaires, the participants considered CS more *easy* than WS, while they considered WS to be significantly more *flexible*. The scores for the remaining differentials, *wonderful, satisfying, stimulating, efficient*, and *novel* were generally higher for WS as well (see Table 5). While using the system, people felt more *comfortable* and *confident*. However, WS was more difficult to *learn to use*.

After completing all four search tasks, the users were asked to determine the system that was (a) easiest to learn to use, (b) easiest to use, (c) most effective, and (d) they liked best overall in the exit questionnaire. They could choose between WS, CS, and no difference as responses to these questions. 67% liked WS best and the majority also thought it was more effective (46% compared to 26% for CS). CS was clearly easier to learn to use (58%), whereas the ranking for using the systems was relatively balanced (46% for WS and 42% for CS).

Finally, the participants were asked for their opinion on what they liked or disliked about each system. The responses reconfirmed most advantages and disadvantages already identified in the previous experiment. The advantages listed for CS were that it was easy to use, fast and efficient especially for specific searches. Its disadvantages included that the users felt they did not have enough control over the search and that its interface and search process was less intuitive.

People appreciated WS as an organising tool. The workspace enabled them to plan their tasks and pursue alternative search threads, without losing the overview of intermediate results and searches. Once more, the system was regarded as more flexible and offering better control over the search process. In Experiment 1, the disadvantages were mainly concerned with the poor quality of the recommendations and that the handling of groups was sometimes cumbersome. Both of these issues are not inherent in the interaction paradigm of the proposed system itself, and were consequently improved for Experiment 2. The recommendation quality was improved by taking textual annotations into account. The handling of the groups and images within groups was changed so that the system now automatically arranges the layout of the images in a group. Consequently, none of these issues resurfaced in Experiment 2.

**Organisation Analysis.** A further objective of this study was to see if there is any correlation between task characteristics and the way people organise images on the workspace. Due to space restrictions we can only briefly provide our conclusions here. We observed that the more open or complex a task is, the more groups were created on the workspace (1.5, 2.9, and 2.6 for Task D, E, and F, respectively). For these types of tasks the organisation was deemed most useful and recommendations were requested more often.

The groups the participants created for any given task often overlapped in the overall themes of the groups, but not necessarily the images themselves. This shows that groups are to a great extent task-dependent and hence people would possibly benefit from using and working with other people's groups. We briefly list some examples of the facets created by the participants for two topics. For Task D, topic "seasons in the country", people created groups for "autumn" images (the image that was missing from the set) mainly displaying leafy, red forests; other groups created were "colourful fields", "close-up of plants", "boats", "country houses". The abstract topic "dynamic" of Task E was illustrated by the following groups: "animals" (sometimes split into "flying birds", "tigers/leopards", etc.), "sports", "mountains", "waterfalls", "sunsets/landscapes", "boats/water".

## 5   Discussion

In this section, we explore the benefits of the workspace system in comparison to the traditional relevance feedback approach. Our observations are based on the overall results of the two-stage experiment involving 24 participants on a variety of realistic search tasks.

First, we investigated the systems' ability to support the users in solving their tasks. The questionnaire responses indicated that the workspace helped them to analyse and explore their tasks better. This is most likely as a result of it allowing them to explore the facets of the search task they were performing. Together with the recommendation facility, this has increased the effectiveness of the system. The required effort to complete a task was lower on WS: less queries were issued to find a larger selection of images.

In particular, users created less manual queries but issued more system recommendations. The participants also perceived their performance as more successful on WS and the interface was perceived significantly more effective for completing the tasks. This shows that the workspace helped to *conceptualise and diversify the task* better and as a result *increased the effectiveness of the search.*

Moreover, the grouping facility was not only considered easier, more effective and useful than the relevance feedback approach in CS, but was praised unanimously in open-ended questions. In addition, the relevance feedback facility caused more confusion. It became apparent that providing relevance feedback brings uncertainty as to which images to select for feedback in order to improve the results. Hence, people relied more on the manual query facilities on CS than WS. Although both systems have the same underlying retrieval mechanism, the workspace approach is more successful at eliciting constructive feedback while hiding the internals of the retrieval mechanism. It is more natural to the user to provide feedback in a structured form by creating groups on the workspace instead of indicating relevant and irrelevant images indiscriminately. The groups allowed users to see which images contributed to the result list. Consequently, people selected more images for feedback and requested more recommendations on WS than RF iterations on CS. Thus, one can conclude that the grouping process is *better at overcoming the query formulation problem.*

We also found a link between task and the use of the workspace. The more complex or open the task, the more useful the workspace was perceived to be. For these tasks, the organisation was regarded more useful and recommendations were consulted more often. With growing task complexity, users created more groups which allowed them to explore the task and collection by following up on various facets (trains of thought). On the other hand, CS was better for tasks that required selection of a large number of images for a very specific topic.

These observations have led us to accept all three experimental hypotheses. However, this study also helped to identify the limitations of the workspace. WS was more difficult to use and the cognitive effort required to solve a task was higher. This was reflected in the questionnaire responses; in particular users had more difficulty in understanding the task and it took longer to complete it. However, the longer learning period and increased cognitive effort is not perceived as a disadvantage of WS; after all, 16 people preferred WS over CS. More importantly, we found evidence that attributed the prolonged search session to the system's ability to support the user in exploring the tasks from different perspectives. As mentioned before, people were able to diversify their search better and follow up on multiple trains of thought simultaneously. Still, one has to keep in mind that it takes longer to become familiarised with this interface, although we strived to make its operation as intuitive as possible by using standard commands which the user may already be familiar with wherever possible.

Finally, we did not explore the use of WS for collaborative image retrieval. On the workspace, people leave footprints of their activities behind for later usage. We also observed that people's groups overlapped in their overall themes, which could be exploited in a collaborative context. Such a feature will be explored in future studies.

## 6  Conclusion

In this paper, we have established the usefulness of the workspace system for image retrieval. We have created a realistic experimental study, in which design professionals performed a variety of realistic search tasks. Based on the results of this experiment, we argue that the workspace is an indispensable tool in an image retrieval system. It is used for organising the results according to the different aspects or facets of the task. This helps users greatly in analysing and exploring the task as well as the collection. Moreover, the workspace supports a more intuitive search process and helps to overcome the query formulation problem. All these factors lead to a more effective and enjoyable search experience.

## References

1. Urban, J., Jose, J.M.: EGO: A personalised multimedia management and retrieval tool. International Journal of Intelligent Systems (IJIS), Special Issue on 'Intelligent Multimedia Retrieval' (2005) to appear.
2. Hendry, D.G., Harper, D.J.: An informal information-seeking environment. Journal of the American Society for Information Science **48** (1997) 1036–1048
3. Urban, J., Jose, J.M.: An explorative study of interface support for image searching. In: Proc. of the 3rd Int. Workshop on Adaptive Multimedia Retrieval. (2005)
4. Rui, Y., Huang, T.S.: Optimizing learning in image retrieval. In: IEEE Proc. of Conf. on Computer Vision and Pattern Recognition (CVPR-00), IEEE Computer Society Press (2000) 236–245
5. Berkley's Digital Library Project: http://elib.cs.berkeley.edu/photos/corel/ (2005)
6. Salton, G., McGill, M.J.: Introduction to Modern Information Retrieval. McGraw-Hill, Tokio (1983)
7. Urban, J., Jose, J.M.: Evidence combination for multi-point query learning in content-based image retrieval. In: Proc. of the IEEE Sixth Int. Symposium on Multimedia Software Engineering (ISMSE'04). (2004) 583–586
8. Zhou, X.S., Huang, T.: Relevance feedback in image retrieval: A comprehensive review. ACM Multimedia Systems Journal **8** (2003) 536–544
9. Jose, J.M., Furner, J., Harper, D.J.: Spatial querying for image retrieval: A user-oriented evaluation. In: Proc. of the Annual Int. ACM SIGIR Conf. on Research and Development in Information Retrieval (SIGIR'98), ACM Press (1998) 232–240
10. Ingwersen, P.: Information Retrieval Interaction. Taylor Graham, London (1992)
11. Beaulieu, M., Jones, S.: Interactive searching and interface issues in the Okapi best match probabilistic retrieval system. Interacting with Computers **10** (1998) 237–248

# A Fingerprinting Technique for Evaluating Semantics Based Indexing

Eduard Hoenkamp and Sander van Dijk

Nijmegen Institute for Cognition and Information
hoenkamp@acm.org, a.h.vandijk@gmail.com

**Abstract.** The quality of search engines depends usually on the content of the returned documents rather than on the text used to express this content. So ideally, search techniques should be directed more toward the semantic dependencies underlying documents than toward the texts themselves. The most visible examples in this direction are Latent Semantic Analysis (LSA), and the Hyperspace Analog to Language (HAL). If these techniques are really based on semantic dependencies, as they contend, then they should be applicable across languages.

To investigate this contention we used electronic versions of two kinds of material with their translations: a novel, and a popular treatise about cosmology. We used the analogy of fingerprinting as employed in forensics to establish whether individuals are related. Genetic fingerprinting uses enzymes to split the DNA and then compare the resulting band patterns. Likewise, in our research we used queries to split a document into fragments. If a search technique really isolates fragments semantically related to the query, then a document and its translation should have similar band patterns.

In this paper we (1) present the fingerprinting technique, (2) introduce the material used, and (3) report results of an evaluation for two semantic indexing techniques.

## 1 Introduction

Users searching the web for on-line documents are usually looking for content, not words. So it is at least remarkable that the user's information need can be satisfied with search results based on keywords. This may stem from the user's ability to quickly learn to formulate an effective query, and the possibility to refine it. Or perhaps it is due to statistical properties of large corpora. Yet, most IR researchers would agree that trying to target the semantics underlying documents more directly could lead to better search results. One argument is that it may obviate or circumvent the lexicon problem (the influence of synonymy and polysemy) and another argument is the growing interest in retrieval of material other than text. Regarding textual material, there are already several proposals that contend to target the semantics underlying documents. For the present paper we selected two particular techniques that, first, seem more than an isolated proposal, second, have been under experimental scrutiny, and third, represent two different IR paradigms. Our proposal is to investigate the claim

M. Lalmas et al. (Eds.): ECIR 2006, LNCS 3936, pp. 397–406, 2006.
© Springer-Verlag Berlin Heidelberg 2006

about the semantics underlying a document by applying the same technique to the document and its translation. If a technique really operates on the underlying semantics, than it should be invariant under translation. We will first look at research that pertains to the experiment in this paper.

## 2   Cross-Language Information Retrieval

As we will talk about language pairs, we should mention up front that we don't want to study cross-language information retrieval (CLIR). Researchers in CLIR have pursued a variety of goals (e.g. [1] mentions five goals) that are different from ours. Yet we borrow the method of using a corpus in one language aligned with one in another language. An example that can stand for several others is Yang et al.'s [2] study of bilingual corpora. It is an experiment in the vector space paradigm, and it compares traditional IR approaches such as the Generalized Vector Space Model (GVSM), Latent Semantic Analysis (LSA), relevance feedback, and term in context translation. The evaluation is based on the usual recall/precision metrics. In contrast to this inquiry and others, our interest here is not so much in *which* is the most effective IR system, but *why* is it the most effective. More precisely, we are interested to discern whether a system is successful because it handles the underlying concepts that were communicated, or because it excels in statistical sophistication. Hence, we shift the focus from comparing how well techniques work for CLIR, to using the CLIR paradigm to compare which ones best handle underlying concepts. If the success of a technique for a corpus can be attributed to its handling of the underlying concepts, then it should (1) also be successful for a translation of the corpus, and (2) show similar search results for a query and its translation. We will describe a technique to assess the degree of invariance under translation, with an illustration from two approaches to IR: the traditional vector space model, and the more recent probabilistic language modeling approach.

## 3   Paradigms of Semantics Based Indexing: LSA and HAL

One approach in the vector space model that tries to target the underlying semantics of a corpus, is Latent Semantic Analysis (LSA). LSA performs a lossy compression [3] of the high dimensional document space spanned by the terms, and empirical evidence suggests that this results in a lower dimensional space spanned by *latent* semantic factors [4]. The same technique has been applied in CLIR experiments such as the one mentioned above [2]. The approach we will compare it with, and which tries to incorporate *manifest* semantic relationships in the corpus, is the 'Hyperspace Analog to Language' (HAL). It is related to early attempts in psycho-linguistics to measure a 'semantic distance' between words [5]. The HAL approach is based on the observation that distance between words in text is an indicator of how related the words are in meaning [6]. The representation for HAL is computed as follows: (1) a window slides over the documents, and (2) for each window position, and each word-pair in the window, a weight is assigned inversely related to the distance between the pair of words. (So a high weight means that the words are semantically close, and semantic closeness decreases with distance in the text.) Accumulating the weights produces a matrix of word pairs with weights in the cells. The weights can be mapped to probabilities [7] used for experiments in probabilistic language modeling. The latter is a more recent development in IR, which views documents as samples from a source that stochastically produces terms (e.g. [8]).

In the remainder we will report on our experiments in the two distinct paradigms of HAL and LSA. The paradigms differ in their actual representation of the semantics (latent versus manifest), but their claims are similar. The claims that (1) similar words appear in similar contexts, (2) cross-document relationships emerge from shared contexts, and (3) that their formalisms in some way represent the semantics underlying texts. Both techniques allow for the fingerprinting technique we are about to describe.

## 4   Cross-Language Fingerprinting

CLIR experiments in the literature have often used multilingual, document-aligned corpora, where documents in one language are paired with their translations in the other.

To study the semantic relationship between an original and its translation, we developed a fingerprinting technique inspired by the kind of comparison made between fingerprints (RFLP's) in case of a paternity dispute. To explain the fingerprint analogy, figure 1 shows the DNA fingerprints of pairs of twins. Identical twins have band patterns that are much more alike than fraternal twins (who are genetically less strongly connected). Now imagine documents in one language stacked on a pile. For a given query, a search technique will assign a relevance weight to each document. Suppose we translate the weights into a grayscale from black (highly relevant) to white (not relevant) and we paint the spine of the documents accordingly. Then the pile will show bands reminiscent of the bands in a DNA fingerprint. We do the same for the translation, keeping the same order of documents. If the search technique is invariant under translation, than we expect the bands for both piles to be in the same place. And the less invariance, the less the band patterns will look alike.

In our experiment we did not use a document aligned corpus, but instead we used books and their translations. For the experiment, a book takes the role of a corpus, and passages from the book take the role of documents. We aimed for heterogeneous material, to wit: a novel, a popular science book, and a technical data base. For all three we had electronic versions of the original in English with translations in German and Italian. In the experiment for the present paper, we used the English-German pairs of the novel and the popular science book.

The advantage of using books was twofold. Having read the books, we could easily determine the relevance of search results for a query (would the need for such a judgement arise). It also allowed us to make more qualitative judgments, such as that the answer to a query would be in the beginning of a book or more toward the end. For example, if the answer to a query is at the beginning of

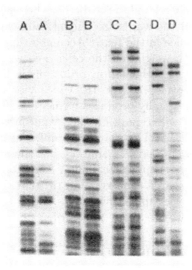

**Fig. 1.** The figure shows DNA fingerprints for four pairs of twins. B's and C's are identical twins, and their band patterns are much more alike then those of the other (fraternal) twins A and D. The "twins" in our retrieval experiment are books and their translations. With grayscale indicating relevance of a passage to a query, band patterns should in that case also approximately align.

the original, it should be at the beginning of the translation as well. And so in that case both fingerprints would be expected to have dark bands at the top that approximately align. Note that they need not align exactly, as first, the human translator may need more words, or perhaps fewer words, to render the original sentence in the target language. And second, the translator may take some liberty in the arrangement of sentences. If we construct queries by hand, and verify search results by hand, such variations can be accommodated. But automated query construction and result verification requires a more careful design, as we will explain in a moment.

### 4.1   Computing Relevance Values for LSA and HAL

LSA and HAL use different document representations, and the relevance values have to be computed appropriately. For LSA the traditional vector space approach was used. After lossy compression of the document space, the relevance of a document was its cosine distance from the query. The same procedure does not work for HAL, as it does not represent the document as a vector, but as a distance matrix of the words it contains. We used a variant of HAL, that maps the distance matrix to a distribution over terms [7] called epi-HAL (ergodic process interpretation of HAL). This way, the epi-HAL representation of a document becomes an instance of probabilistic language modeling. This means that to compute a relevance ranking, two probability distributions must be compared: the term distribution of the query and that of the documents. The Kullback-Leibler divergence between these distributions was used to compute the relevance of a document given the query.

## 4.2   An Experiment Comparing Semantic Indexing Techniques

*Preparation of the material.* We chose two kinds of material with their paired translations:

- Hemingway. *The old man and the sea* and its German translation *Der alte Mann und das Meer,*
- Hawking. *A brief history of time* and its German translation *Eine kurze Geschichte der Zeit.*

We wanted to split the books into segments of about equal size, segments taking the role of documents in a corpus, so they could be aligned. We could not take a fixed number of words to define segments, because the number of words in the original segment will likely be different in the translation. Therefore, a segment was defined relative to the length of the book, and we took the same percentage of text for original and translation. For a workable absolute length, we checked a series of segments by hand, to find that around 1000 words gives sufficient overlap in the stories. Queries were formed by picking random samples of text of approximately 100 words. This number was large enough to guarantee a contiguous meaningful passage with enough overlap in both languages.

*Procedure.* We compared retrieval results for HAL and LSA. As queries we selected fragments from the book itself, as exemplified in figure 2, where the example fragments are located at the arrows. Using fragments from the book as query has several advantages: (1) it gives an overall measure for quality of the search, as at least this fragment should be located as relevant (i.e. there should be a dark band at the place of the query), (2) we will not have to manually translate the query into the target language. (So in principle the technique could even be repeated for a language we don't have a command of.) This way for each fragment in the original language the corresponding fragment in the translation can be found.

Invariance under translation was computed as follows:

1. Select a random fragment (100 word contiguous text) from the original book. This will be the query.
2. For each segment of the book compute its relevance value (as per section 4.1). This produces the fingerprint for the query.
3. Repeat the previous steps for the translation. (Using the corresponding fragment in the translation.) This produces a pair of fingerprints for the given query.
4. Compute the similarity of the pair of fingerprints[1].
5. Repeat the previous steps 500 times, and compute the average correlation. The resulting value is taken as the measure of invariance under translation.

---

[1] Obviously the values themselves are retained, the band pattern is just a visual representation of these values.

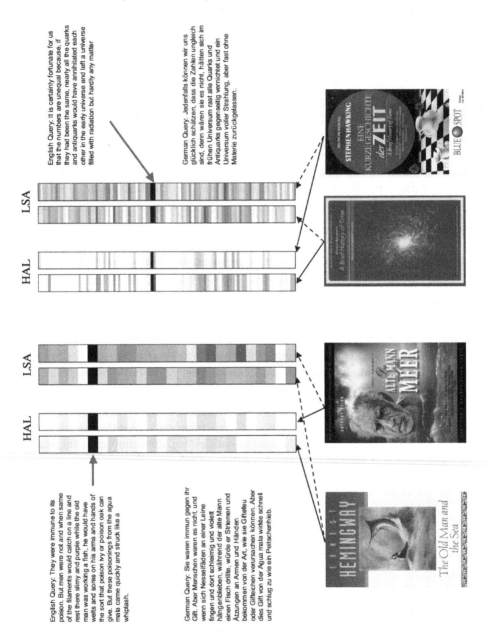

**Fig. 2.** Two examples of fingerprinting. The gray-level indicates the relevance for the query, with black most relevant. The black band indicates here the position of the query (which is obviously relevant to itself). The vertical axis is the location of passages in the book, page 1 at the top. Fingerprints were collected for 500 passages from the original, used as queries, in parallel with their translations. Relevance was calculated for HAL and for LSA. Fingerprints and queries are taken from the actual, but reduced here to keep the example readable.

For step (4), of course we looked for such measures in forensics. But the measures employed there are derived from specific knowledge about the fragments produced in RFLP digests of real DNA material, and they can therefore not be used. Instead, especially given the large number of relevance values per fingerprint (the number of bands) we chose to simply use the *correlation between the fingerprints of the original and its translation*. In step (5) we chose the value 500 because the *Old Man and the Sea* contains about 500 segments of 1000 words, and the statistical significance of the result would be guaranteed (as the sample covers the whole population). Yet the sampling was done randomly so we could use the same value for *A Brief History of Time*.

*Results.* There are several variables in the query matching procedure that have to be controlled for. For example, for both LSA and HAL it is important to look at the influence of stemming, stop-word removal, and query expansion. Both paradigms have also their own variables to control for. In the case of LSA this is the degree of dimension reduction. For HAL it is the window size. In the literature about HAL we only found a window size of 10. Yet we wanted to control for the influence of window size because it may give different values depending on the grammar and spelling of the target language. For example, in the spelling of compound nouns, The German spelling of a compound is usually as one word whereas English usually puts spaces between the nouns. This may influence the accumulated distances between words in the HAL matrix. The window size may also have to be greater for languages with freer word order (such as Italian). For an impression of how these variables influence the fingerprint correlations, we included Table 3 which summarizes the values for the (epi-)HAL approach. We constructed the same table for LSA to study the influence of the degree of dimension reduction, using reduction to 5, 10, 15, and 20 dimensions (beyond 20 the data changed too little). Table 1 shows the average results for the paradigms. We could take this outcome as a rough indication of the quality of the search technique. If we do, HAL seems more effective for the given corpora. Note, however, that we would need a more sophisticated measure to cover all the variables in-

**Table 1.** The number of original fragments recovered in the matching process

|       | The Old Man and the Sea | A Brief History of Time |
|-------|-------------------------|-------------------------|
| HAL   | 99-100%                 | 99-100%                 |
| LSA   | 28-40%                  | 40-45%                  |

**Table 2.** The average correlation of the fingerprints over 500 queries

|       | The Old Man and the Sea | A Brief History of Time |
|-------|-------------------------|-------------------------|
| HAL   | .99 %                   | .98%                    |
| LSA   | .69%                    | .68%                    |

**Table 3.** Average fingerprint correlations between English and German for *The Old Man and the Sea* for the HAL paradigm, depending on the controlled variables. As the query was always a part of the text itself, the last column shows how well the search technique locates this original part.

| window size | stemming | stopword removal | query expansion terms | fingerprint correlation | original segment most relevant |
|---|---|---|---|---|---|
| 5 | no | no | 0 | 0.66 | 100 % |
| 5 | no | no | 10 | 0.73 | 100 % |
| 5 | no | no | 20 | 0.95 | 100 % |
| 5 | no | yes | 0 | 0.75 | 96 % |
| 5 | no | yes | 10 | 0.76 | 95 % |
| 5 | no | yes | 20 | 0.76 | 94 % |
| 5 | yes | no | 0 | 0.63 | 100 % |
| 5 | yes | no | 10 | 0.70 | 100 % |
| 5 | yes | no | 20 | 0.94 | 100 % |
| 5 | yes | yes | 0 | 0.69 | 95 % |
| 5 | yes | yes | 10 | 0.69 | 93 % |
| 5 | yes | yes | 20 | 0.69 | 92 % |
| 10 | no | no | 0 | 0.97 | 100 % |
| 10 | no | no | 10 | 0.97 | 100 % |
| 10 | no | no | 20 | 0.97 | 100 % |
| 10 | no | yes | 0 | 0.95 | 99 % |
| 10 | no | yes | 10 | 0.95 | 99 % |
| 10 | no | yes | 20 | 0.95 | 99 % |
| 10 | yes | no | 0 | 0.96 | 100 % |
| 10 | yes | no | 10 | 0.96 | 100 % |
| 10 | yes | no | 20 | 0.96 | 99 % |
| 10 | yes | yes | 0 | 0.92 | 97 % |
| 10 | yes | yes | 10 | 0.92 | 97 % |
| 10 | yes | yes | 20 | 0.92 | 97 % |
| 15 | no | no | 0 | 0.98 | 99 % |
| 15 | no | no | 10 | 0.97 | 99 % |
| 15 | no | no | 20 | 0.97 | 99 % |
| 15 | no | yes | 0 | 0.97 | 99 % |
| 15 | no | yes | 10 | 0.97 | 99 % |
| 15 | no | yes | 20 | 0.97 | 99 % |
| 15 | yes | no | 0 | 0.96 | 99 % |
| 15 | yes | no | 10 | 0.96 | 99 % |
| 15 | yes | no | 20 | 0.96 | 99 % |
| 15 | yes | yes | 0 | 0.97 | 99 % |
| 15 | yes | yes | 10 | 0.97 | 99 % |
| 15 | yes | yes | 20 | 0.97 | 99 % |

volved. Note also that LSA may still have a better relevance ranking on average. We did not investigate this further as evaluating the search technique is not the aim of the present paper. In addition, LSA could still have a good average fingerprint correlation, as long the correct and incorrect relevance judgments are in the same place for original and translation. And this would corroborate the translation invariance of the search technique. So an independent assessment is needed for fingerprint correlations. This is presented in Table 2, where HAL performs much better than LSA on average. But these are two completely different search paradigms, and the difference in evaluation can have many causes. To give the LSA data an advantage, we also compared the average values for HAL with the best correlations for LSA. That is, we took an instance where the combination of controlled variables such as stemming, dimension reduction, etc. gave the best overall results for LSA. Still HAL outperformed LSA on fingerprint correlation.

## 5    Conclusion

In this paper we accomplished several things.

First, precision and recall can be boosted for monolingual retrieval in clever ways that may or may not pertain to the meaning underlying the documents. We introduced a fingerprinting technique that seems orthogonal to the usual precision and recall evaluation. It can be used for document aligned bilingual (or multilingual) corpora, and we constructed the method such that it might be useful even in the absence of human relevance judgments. Note, that although it was is not our goal to study cross-language IR, we think it could easily contribute to CLIR as evaluations tool.

Second, we applied fingerprinting to techniques that seem to explicitly target underlying semantics: HAL and LSA. In a cross-language study using two different kinds of material, we found that HAL was considerably more invariant under translation than LSA. Note however, that this does *not* show that one or the other derives its results from being based on semantics, because either technique could be conducive to translation invariance for other reasons. It does show however that if there is a claim that the search technique is based on underlying semantics, then HAL is much more justified to this claim than LSA.

Third, if information retrieval would benefit from using semantics underlying the documents to be retrieved, then it is important to look at approaches that explicitly target semantics. We postulated that such an approach would be invariant under translation, and that fingerprinting can be used to assess this, by using the correlation between the fingerprints, which can be easily obtained.

## References

1. Hull, D.A., Grefenstette, G.: Querying across languages: A dictionary-based approach to multilingual information retrieval. In: 19th Annual ACM Conference on Research and Development in Information Retrieval. (1996) 49–57
2. Yang, Y., Carbonell, J.G., Brown, R.D., Frederking, R.E.: Translingual information retrieval: Learning from bilingual corpora. Artificial Intelligence **103** (1998) 323–345
3. Hoenkamp, E.: Unitary operators on the document space. Journal of the American Society for Information Science and Technology **54** (2003) 314–320
4. Deerwester, S.C., Dumais, S.T., Landauer, T.K., Furnas, G.W., Harshman, R.A.: Indexing by latent semantic analysis. Journal of the American Society of Information Science **41** (1990) 391–407

5. Osgood, C.E., Suci, G.J., Tannenbaum, P.H.: The measurement of meaning. Urbana: University of Illinois Press (1957)
6. Burgess, C., Livesay, K., Lund, K.: Explorations in context space: Words, sentences, discourse. Discourse Processes **25** (1998) 211 – 257
7. Hoenkamp, E., Song, D.: The document as an ergodic markov chain. In: Proceedings of the 27th Conference on Research and Development in Information Retrieval. (2004) 496–497
8. Lafferty, J., Zhai, C.: Document language models, query models, and risk minimization for IR. In: Proceedings of the 24th Conference on Research and Development in Information Retrieval. (2001) 111–119

# A Cross-Language Approach to Historic Document Retrieval

Marijn Koolen[1,2], Frans Adriaans[1,3], Jaap Kamps[1,2], and Maarten de Rijke[1]

[1] ISLA, University of Amsterdam, The Netherlands
[2] Archives and Information Studies, University of Amsterdam, The Netherlands
[3] Utrecht Institute of Linguistics OTS, Utrecht University, The Netherlands

**Abstract.** Our cultural heritage, as preserved in libraries, archives and museums, is made up of documents written many centuries ago. Large-scale digitization initiatives make these documents available to non-expert users through digital libraries and vertical search engines. For a user, querying a historic document collection may be a disappointing experience: queries involving modern words may not be very effective for retrieving documents that contain many historic terms. We propose a cross-language approach to historic document retrieval, and investigate (1) the automatic construction of translation resources for historic languages, and (2) the retrieval of historic documents using cross-language information retrieval techniques. Our experimental evidence is based on a collection of 17th century Dutch documents and a set of 25 known-item topics in modern Dutch. Our main findings are as follows: First, we are able to automatically construct rules for modernizing historic language based on comparing (a) phonetic sequence similarity, (b) the relative frequency of consonant and vowel sequences, and (c) the relative frequency of character n-gram sequences, of historic and modern corpora. Second, modern queries are not very effective for retrieving historic documents, but the historic language tools lead to a substantial improvement in retrieval effectiveness. The improvements are above and beyond the improvement due to using a modern stemming algorithm (whose effectiveness actually goes up when the historic language is modernized).

## 1 Introduction

Natural languages evolve over time. In Europe, almost all languages are part of the Indo-European language family [25]; they have evolved gradually, changing in pronunciation and spelling. To a large extent, our cultural heritage, as preserved in libraries, archives, and museums, consists of documents written many centuries ago. Many cultural heritage institutions are currently exploring ways of digitizing their document collections [13], which has resulted in a number of collaborative projects on digital cultural heritage, including DigiCULT [7].

Having digital versions of old, fragile documents is a good way of preserving them, and it makes them easily accessible to a multitude of users over the web. Browsing through such documents, one can probably recognize the language they are written in as a historical variant of a modern European language, although

M. Lalmas et al. (Eds.): ECIR 2006, LNCS 3936, pp. 407–419, 2006.
© Springer-Verlag Berlin Heidelberg 2006

one may run into significant differences with today's spelling rules and vocabulary. What if a vertical search engine is created that gives access to the historic documents? One that "knows" about changes in spelling and vocabulary? Consider a user that searches for 300 year old documents about, for instance, Central European politics. Her query will consist of modern words, and hence will not be very effective for retrieving documents containing historic terms. In order to make historic documents accessible to modern users, our vertical search engine should be able to bridge the gap between the historic language of the document and the modern language of a user's query. This is the focus of the present paper.

We define Historic Document Retrieval (HDR) as the retrieval of relevant historic documents given a modern query. Earlier research [18, 17, 3] dealt with spelling differences between a modern language and a historical variant in a collection of old documents. We continue research on this spelling problem and propose a cross-language approach to HDR. Using historic Dutch as a concrete example, we argue that the gap between modern and 17th century Dutch is substantial, and that effective retrieval therefore requires a mapping between the two languages.

A cross-language approach to HDR raises a number of questions. Manually constructing historic language tools is an unattractive option, because of the large number of spelling variants. These variants are caused by the absence of strict spelling rules and by various regional differences. Is it possible to automatically construct translation resources for historic languages? In Cross-Language Information Retrieval (CLIR, [2]), stemming algorithms have proved to be effective in modern monolingual retrieval. Are these also effective in HDR? Our research identifies HDR as a new cross-language IR problem and consists of two main parts. The first is the construction of resources for our CLIR approach to HDR. We have developed tools to automatically construct translation resources. In the second part we test the effectiveness of these translation resources on historic documents in a CLIR experiment. Since these methods are data-driven, they can be straightforwardly applied to new HDR problems.

The article is outlined as follows: Section 2 discusses Historic Document Retrieval, and details the historic documents used. Section 3 describes the automatic construction of translation tools for historic languages. Then, Section 4 focuses on HDR proper, and evaluates the effectiveness of the constructed translation tools. Finally, in Section 5 we discuss the results and our main findings.

## 2   Historic Document Retrieval

Robertson & Willett [17] tested spelling correction methods to find historic variants of modern word-forms in historic English documents. They also tested the effectiveness of a list of manually constructed phonetic substitutions to preprocess historic words before applying the spelling correction methods to see if preprocessing decreases the gap between 17th century and modern English. For instance, the phonetic substitution $YGHT \rightarrow IT$ (**ME**), replaces all occurrences of *yght* in the middle or at the end of a word to *it*. They find that preprocessing has very little effect. However, the spelling correction methods themselves are very effective in finding historic word-forms. The use of the same correction techniques on old French confirmed these results [16].

Braun [3] tested the effectiveness of preprocessing 17th century Dutch documents by applying rewrite rules in a document retrieval experiment. Rewrite rules take a sequence of characters out of a word and replaces it with a new sequence. After rewriting, historic words, especially their pre- and suffixes, are closer in spelling to modern Dutch words, making the Dutch variant of the Porter Stemmer more effective. Rewrite rules are thus an effective way of decreasing the spelling gap between 17th century and modern Dutch.

The main problem with the rewrite rules in [17, 3] is that manual construction takes a lot of time and requires intimate knowledge of the specific historic language. Moreover, the rewrite rules for 17th century Dutch work for 17th century Dutch, but probably not for 17th century English, nor for 14th century Dutch. In the next section we propose data-driven methods for constructing rewrite rules using only a historic and modern document collection. Because of their data-driven nature, these methods can be applied to historic and modern document collections in other languages as well. Their output—sets of rewrite rules—can be used to construct translation dictionaries for a specific historic document collection, thus providing the resources required for our CLIR approach to HDR.

As mentioned before, we take historic Dutch as a case study. Dutch cultural heritage institutions possess large collections of old books, newspapers and other documents, and many of these are written in historic variants of modern Dutch. Uniformity in the Dutch language is a relatively new phenomenon. *Middelnederlands* is a predecessor of the modern Dutch language that was spoken during the Middle Ages and can best be thought of as a collection of different dialects. Moreover, whereas modern Dutch spelling is based on strict spelling rules, spelling in *Middelnederlands* was based on pronunciation [11]. Since pronunciations can have different orthographic representations, spelling was highly inconsistent. Each region had its own pronunciation, and hence its own spelling conventions. Although the Dutch language became more uniform in the 17th century, mainly through the nation-wide use of the first official Dutch Bible translation, the lack of spelling rules still resulted in the occurrence of many spelling variations throughout documents.

In our tool development and retrieval experiments we use the same historic corpus as [3]. It contains two 17th century collections of legal texts: the *Antwerpse Compilatae* (1609) and the *Gelders Land- en Stadsrecht* (1620). Although they are written in different dialects (southern and eastern, respectively), they are written in the same legal idiom. Hence, they contain many technical law terms and long sentences. This contrasts with other idioms from that period, such as the language of sailors. The *Antwerpse Compilatae* are part of a collection of legal texts called the *Costumen van Antwerpen* [1]. The collection consists of four parts: the Anitiquissimae (1547), the Antiquae (1571), the Impressae (1582), and the Compilatae (1609). OCR errors were manually corrected. Each section was treated as a separate document. This resulted in 222 documents. The *Gelders Land- en Stadsrecht* [9] is very similar to the *Antwerpse Compilatae*. It contains parts on the same subjects as the Compilatae, with the only difference that substantive and formal criminal law are covered in one part. This collection was digitized by manually entering the text into the computer. The *Gelders Land- en Stadsrecht* collection contains 171 documents.

To clarify the differences between the historic language of the corpus and modern Dutch, we took a random sample of 500 words from the historic collection. Each word was assigned to one of three categories: modern, spelling variant, or historic. The overlap between historic and modern Dutch is significant (177 words, 35%). These words are spelled in accordance with modern Dutch spelling rules. An example is the word *ik* (English: I) which is often found in historic texts, but it has not changed over time. It turns out that most of the words (239 words, about 48%) are historic spelling variants of modern words. These words can still be recognized as a modern word, but are spelled in a non-modern way. An example is the word *heyligh* which is easily recognized as a historic spelling of the modern word *heilig* (English: holy) The remaining words (84 words, 17%) have a non-modern morphology, or cannot be recognized as a modern word at all. An example is the word *beestlijck*. Even adjusting its historic spelling, producing *beestelijk*, it is not a correct modern Dutch word. Taking a look at the context makes it possible to identify this word as a historic translation of the modern word *beestachtig* (English: bestial or beastly).

All documents in our collection were transformed into the standard TREC document format, resulting in 393 documents, with an average length of 912 words. In total, the corpus contains 17,794 distinct word tokens. We created a topic set consisting of 25 modern Dutch known-item topics. The topic creators are non-experts in the field of historical law texts, and are therefore unfamiliar with specific historical law terms. This is an important criterion for a HDR topic set, since this leaves the linguistic difficulties to the system. Here is an example topic (description field):

(Q25) *Welke methoden zijn geoorloofd ter ondervraging van gevangenen?*
     (English: *Which methods are allowed in the interrogation of prisoners?*)

Topics were given the familiar TREC topic format: title, description, and narrative.

## 3   Tools for Historic Document Retrieval

Our goal is to design algorithms for mapping historic spelling variations of a word into a single modern form. Below, we describe three tools for creating rewrite rules for 17th century Dutch. One of these tools exploits the phonological overlap (i.e., how words are pronounced) to find sequences that are spelled differently but sound the same. The other two algorithms exploit the orthographical overlap in a historic and a modern word to find the most probable modern version of a historic sequence. These two algorithms use *only* a corpus of 17th century Dutch documents and a corpus of modern Dutch documents. Since the corpus described in the previous section is rather small, for the construction of the rewrite rules, the corpus was expanded with a number of 17th century literary works taken from the DBNL [6]. To make sure that they were written in roughly the same period as our main corpus, we used texts written between 1600 and 1620. The literary texts from DBNL are not suitable for a document retrieval experiment because it is hard to determine the topic of such a text, but they do contain the same spelling variations, so they can be used for devising rewrite rules. As a modern corpus, we used the Dutch newspaper *Algemeen Dagblad*, part the Dutch corpus of CLEF [4].

The three techniques are related to spelling correction techniques such as isolated-word error correction [12, 20]. Since the context of a historic word is also historic text, context dependent (semantically or syntactically informed) error correction techniques are no option in the case of cross-language HDR.

**PSS.** The Phonetic Sequence Similarity (PSS) algorithm finds historic spelling variants of modern words by comparing the phonetic transcriptions of historic and modern words.[1] If the phonetic transcription of a historic word $W^{hist}$ is equal to the phonetic transcription of a modern word $W^{mod}$, but their spelling is different, then $W^{hist}$ is a spelling variant of $W^{mod}$. All words in the historic corpus and the modern corpus are converted to phonetic transcriptions by the grapheme-to-phoneme converter tool in NeXTeNS, a text-to-speech generation system for Dutch [15]. $W^{hist}$ and $W^{mod}$ are then split into sequences of vowels and consonants, and these sequences are aligned. If sequence $S_i^{hist}$ is orthographically different from sequence $S_i^{mod}$, $S_i^{hist}$ is a historic spelling variant of $S_i^{mod}$. The resulting rewrite rule is: $S_i^{hist} \rightarrow S_i^{mod}$.

Take the following example. The 17th century Dutch verb *veeghen* (English: to sweep) is pronounced the same as its modern counterpart *vegen*; their phonetic transcriptions are both $v\ e\ g\ @\ n$ according to Nextens. Splitting both words into sequences and aligning these, results in:

| historic: | v | ee | gh | e | n |
|-----------|---|----|----|---|---|
| modern:   | v | e  | g  | e | n |

At positions 2 and 3 we find differences between the historic sequences and the modern counterparts. This results in the rewrite rules: $ee \rightarrow e$ and $gh \rightarrow g$. Each rewrite rule is assigned a value $N$, where $N$ is the number of times the rule was generated. If $N$ is high, there is a high probability that the rule is correct.

**RSF.** The Relative Sequence Frequency (RSF) algorithm exploits orthographic overlap between historic and modern words, to construct rewrite rules for the parts that do not overlap. First, all words in the historic corpus are split into sequences of consonants and sequences of vowels. An index is made, containing the corpus frequency $F(S_i^{hist})$ of each unique sequence $S_i^{hist}$. The same is done for all words in the modern corpus.

---

[1] This requires a tool to transform the orthographic form into a phonetic transcription. For a number of European languages, such a tool exists, making the PSS algorithm useful for several languages.

The relative frequencies $RF(S_i^{hist})$ and $RF(S_i^{mod})$ of a sequence $S_i$ are given by:

$$RF(S_i^{hist}) = \frac{F(S_i^{hist})}{N^{hist}} \quad \text{and} \quad RF(S_i^{mod}) = \frac{F(S_i^{mod})}{N^{mod}},$$

where $N^{hist}$ is the total number of sequences in the historic corpus, and $N^{mod}$ is the total number of sequences in the modern corpus. The relative sequence frequency $RSF(S_i)$ of sequence $S_i$ is then defined as

$$RSF(S_i) = \frac{RF(S_i^{hist})}{RF(S_i^{mod})}.$$

In words, $RSF(S_i)$ is the frequency of $S_i$ in the historic corpus compared to its frequency in the modern corpus. If $S_i$ is relatively more frequent in the historic corpus than in the modern corpus, its RSF value will be greater than 1. Sequences with a high RSF-value are sequences with *typical historic spelling*. The RSF-algorithm tries to find modern spelling variants for these typical historic sequences.

RSF proceeds as follows. The sequence $S^{hist}$ in a historic word $W^{hist}$ is replaced by a wildcard. Vowel sequences are replaced by vowel wildcards, consonant sequences by consonant wildcards. These wildcard words are matched with words from the modern corpus, and the modern sequence $S^{mod}$ matching the wildcard sequence is considered a possible modern spelling variant of $S^{hist}$. Consider the 17th century Dutch word *volck* (English: people). This is split into the following consonant/vowel sequences: v o lck. The sequences *v* and *o* are fairly frequent in modern Dutch, but *lck* is *much* more frequent in 17th century Dutch than in modern Dutch: it is a typical historic sequence. It is replaced by a consonant wildcard *C*, so the wildcard word becomes: v o C. The *C* wildcard can be matched with any sequence of consonants. In the modern Dutch corpus, *voC* is matched with *vol* (English: full), *volk* (English: people), and *vork* (English: fork), among others. Thus, the rewrite rules *lck* → *l*, *lck* → *lk* and *lck* → *rk* are created and receive score 1. (If one of these rules has already been created by another wildcard word, its score is increased by one.) After all wildcard words containing *lck* have been processed, the rule with the highest score is the most probable.

**RNF.** A variant of the RSF algorithm is the Relative N-Gram Frequency (RNF) algorithm. Instead of splitting words into sequences of consonants and sequences of vowels, the RNF algorithm splits words into n-grams of a certain length, and tries to find typically historic n-gram sequences. With an n-gram length of 3, the word *volck* is split into the following n-grams: #vo vol olc lck ck#, where # denotes a word boundary.

Since the restriction on consonants and vowels is dropped, another restriction on the wildcard is necessary to prevent overly productive matches. If the *lck* sequence is considered typically historic, the wildcard word *voW* (with *W* being the wildcard) can be matched with any modern Dutch word starting with *vo*, including *voorrijkosten* (English: initial driving charge). Clearly the length of the modern sequence replacing *lck* should be similar, we allow a maximal difference in length of 2. The rest of the algorithm is the same as RSF.

## 3.1  Evaluation

The algorithms PSS, RSF, and RNF construct a large amount of rules; not all of them make sense. Pruning of rewrite rules can be done in several ways. Simply selecting the highest scoring rule for each typical historic sequence is one way. Another way is to test the rules on a small test set containing historic Dutch words from the collection and their modern Dutch counterparts. First, the edit distance $D(W^{hist}, W^{mod})$ between the historic word $W^{hist}$ and its modern form $W^{mod}$ is calculated, similar to [24]. Next, the rewrite rule $R_i$ is applied to $W^{hist}$, resulting in $W^{rewr}$. $D(W^{rewr}, W^{mod})$ is the distance between $W^{rewr}$ and $W^{mod}$. The test score $S$ for rule $R_i$ is:

$$S(R_i) = \sum_{j=0}^{N} D(W_j^{hist}, Wj^{mod}) - D(W_j^{rewr}, W_j^{mod}),$$

where $j$ ranges over all $N$ word pairs in the test set. If $S(R_i)$ is positive, applying the rewrite rule on $W^{hist}$ has decreased the edit distance between the historic words and their modern forms. In other words, the historic spelling is more similar to the modern spelling after rewriting. The test set contains 1600 manually constructed word pairs. For each typical historic sequence $S^{hist}$, the rule with the highest test score is selected. By setting a threshold, rules that have a negative score can be filtered since they do not bring the historic word and its modern variant closer to each other.

To compare the three rule construction algorithms PSS, RSF and RNF, another test set with 400 new word pairs (historic Dutch words and their modern spelling) was used; the historic words were fed to the various algorithms, and their outputs were compared against the corresponding modern word.

The first column in Table 1 shows the method used (for RNF, the suffixes indicate the n-gram length); the second column shows the number of selected rewrite rules; the third gives the total number of words from the test set that were affected, while the fourth column gives the number of historic words that are rewritten to their correct modern form (edit distance is 0). This is used as an extra measure to compare the rule sets. The last column gives the average edit distance between the rewritten historic words and the modern words, plus the difference with the baseline in parentheses.

**Table 1.** Results of evaluating the different sets of rewrite rules

| Method | number of rules | total rewrites | perfect rewrites | new distance |
|--------|-----------------|----------------|------------------|--------------|
| *none* | – | – | – | 2.38 |
| *PSS* | 104 | 253 | 101 | 1.66 (−0.72) |
| *RSF* | 62 | 252 | 140 | 1.33 (−1.05) |
| *RNF-2* | 12 | 271 | 152 | 1.29 (−1.09) |
| *RNF-3* | 127 | 274 | 162 | 1.19 (−1.19) |
| *RNF-4* | 276 | 269 | 166 | 1.20 (−1.18) |
| *RNF-5* | 276 | 153 | 97 | 1.79 (−0.59) |
| *RNF-all* | 691 | 315 | 207 | 0.97 (−1.41) |
| *RNF-all + RSF + PSS* | 753 | 337 | 224 | 0.86 (−1.52) |

The RNF algorithm clearly outperforms the other 2 algorithms with almost all n-gram lengths, except for n-gram length 5. The rule set for $N = 3$ gives the best results. Compared to the baseline (no rewriting at all), this rule set reduces the average edit distance between the historic words and the modern words in the test set by 50%. However, by combining the rule sets of all n-gram lengths, even better results are obtained. This shows that the rule sets have a complementary effect on the test set.

Finally, a combination of all 3 algorithms was used. First creating and applying these rules using one algorithm, then constructing and applying rules using the second algorithm, then the third algorithm was used. These 3 sets of rules were then combined and tested again on the 400 word pair test set (in Table 1, only the best order of application is given). We see that the combination of methods scores best on all of the measures.

Which of our rewrite methods is most effective in bridging the spelling gap between 17th century and modern Dutch? A bigger reduction in edit distance does not always lead to a better rule. The modern Dutch spelling for the historic sequence $cx$ should be $ks$. The rule $cx \rightarrow k$ leads to a bigger reduction than the rule $cx \rightarrow cs$, but also leads to a change in pronunciation and often a change in word meaning as well. The number of perfect rewrites provides additional information. A larger reduction in edit distance leads to a larger number of perfect rewrites, leading to more direct matches between historic and modern Dutch. Together, these measures give a fair indication of the effectiveness of the rule sets. For now, this suffices: our aim is to enable the retrieval of historic documents. Does the rewrite method with the biggest reduction in edit distance and/or the largest number of perfect rewrites give rise to the best retrieval performance?—This is the topic of the next section.

## 4    CLIR Approaches to Historic Document Retrieval

Finally, we turn to retrieval, and investigate the effectiveness of the translation tools developed in the previous section for the retrieval of historic documents. Our main issue is whether the translation resources help the user in retrieving historic documents. For comparison, we take a monolingual approach as our baseline; here, no mapping between the languages takes place. For comparison with earlier research on historic English [18], we also apply the SoundEx algorithm that translates words into codes based on phonetic similarity [19]; based on preliminary experiments we use code length 7.

Also based on preliminary experiments, we found that document translation outperforms query translation. In the case of HDR, translating the historic documents into modern Dutch provides additional advantages over query translation. An advantage for the user is that the "modernized" documents are easier to read. Also, since no stemming algorithm exists for historic Dutch, document translation enables us to use tokenization techniques that have proven to be useful in modern Dutch. This is important because successful cross-language retrieval requires both effective translation and tokenization [22, 10]. In addition to the performance of the translation tools, we investigate the effectiveness of a stemming algorithm for modern Dutch [23].

Our third set of questions concerns the use of long versus short topic statements. Since the spelling bottleneck may have an especially detrimental impact on retrieval effectiveness for short queries, we conjecture that our translation tools will be more effective for short topics than for long topics.

## 4.1 Experimental Setting

We used the corpus in historic Dutch, and the topic set in modern Dutch described in Section 2 above. All runs were of the following form: query in modern Dutch, with relevant document in 17th century Dutch. All runs used out-of-the-box Lucene [14] with the default vector space retrieval model and the Snowball stopword list for Dutch [23]. In addition to our monolingual baseline run, we generated runs using the outputs of the various tools described in the previous section, runs with and without the use of stemming, and runs using only the title field of the topic statement as well as runs that use the description field. The measure used for evaluation purposes is mean reciprocal rank (MRR), a natural (and standard) measure for known-item retrieval [5]. To determine whether the observed differences between two retrieval approaches are statistically significant, we used the bootstrap method, a non-parametric inference test [8, 21]. We take 100,000 resamples, and look for significant improvements (one-tailed) at significance levels of 0.95 (*) and 0.99 (**).

## 4.2 Results

Table 2 shows the results for runs produced without invoking a stemmer. First, restricting our attention to the title queries in the top half of the table, we see that all translation resources (except RSF) improve retrieval effectiveness. SoundEx is surprisingly effective, almost on a par with the combination of all

**Table 2.** Evaluating translation effectiveness, using the title of the topic statement (top half) or its description field (bottom)

| Method | MRR | % Change |
|---|---|---|
| Baseline (titles) | 0.1316 | – |
| Soundex7 | 0.2600* | +97.6 |
| PSS | 0.2397* | +82.1 |
| RSF | 0.1299 | -1.3 |
| RNF-all | 0.2114* | +60.6 |
| RNF-all + RSF + PSS | 0.2780** | +111.2 |
| Baseline (descriptions) | 0.1840 | – |
| Soundex7 | 0.1890 | +2.7 |
| PSS | 0.2556 | +38.9 |
| RSF | 0.1861 | +1.1 |
| RNF-all | 0.2025 | +10.1 |
| RNF-all + RSF + PSS | 0.2842* | +54.5 |

**Table 3.** Does the stemming of modern translations further improve retrieval? Using the title of the topic statement (top half) or its description field (bottom)

| Method | MRR | % Change |
|---|---|---|
| *Baseline (titles)* | 0.1316 | – |
| *Stemming* | 0.1539 | +16.9 |
| *RNF-all + RSF + PSS* | 0.2780** | +111.2 |
| *RNF-all + RSF + PSS + Stemming* | 0.2766** | +110.2 |
| *Baseline (descriptions)* | 0.1840 | – |
| *Stemming* | 0.1870 | +1.6 |
| *RNF-all + RSF + PSS* | 0.2842* | +54.5 |
| *RNF-all + RSF + PSS + Stemming* | 0.3410** | +85.3 |

translation resources. The results for runs that use the description field of the topic statement, shown in the bottom half of Table 2, are somewhat different. Here, Soundex only makes a minor difference. How can this behavior be explained? Soundex transforms all words into codes of a certain length. Many short words that start with the same letter are transformed into the same code, matching the short (and often irrelevant) words in the description with many other short Dutch words. Soundex adds much more of these short words to the query than the rewrite rules. The titles contain only content words, which are often longer than non-content words, and are matched far less by other, irrelevant words. While still impressive, the relative gain in MRR produced by the combination of all translation resources (on the description field of the topic statement) is only about half the gain on the title topics.

Next, to find out whether there is an added benefit of performing stemming on top of the translated documents, we turn to the results in Table 3. Note that the SoundEx algorithm generates codes rather than human readable text, defying the application of further linguistic tools. On title-only topic statements (see the top half of Table 3) stemming improves effectiveness, but it does not add anything to the combination of the translation resources. In contrast, on the description topics (see the bottom half of Table 3), the grand combination of all translation resources plus stemming leads to further improvements over stemming and over the translation resources.

The previous section showed that the resulting rule set of a combination of the RNF, RSF, and PSS algorithms produced the largest reduction in edit distance and the largest number of perfect rewrites. The question was whether these measures provide a reliable indication of the retrieval effectiveness. The success of the combination is reflected in the retrieval results: all individual algorithms are outperformed by the combined method. It should be noted, however, that the contribution of the RSF algorithm seems minimal. This is likely caused by the relatively small number of rewrite rules it produces: of the 17,794 unique words in the corpus, somewhat more than 4,000 words are rewritten by the RSF rule set, while the PSS rule set rewrites over 8,000 words. The RNF rule set and the combined rule sets rewrite over 11,000 words.

# 5   Discussion and Conclusions

We proposed a cross-language approach to Historic Document Retrieval, and investigated (1) the automatic construction of translation resources for historic languages, and (2) the retrieval of historic documents using cross-language information retrieval techniques. Our experimental evidence was based on a collection of 17th century Dutch documents and a set of 25 known-item topics in modern Dutch. Our main findings are as follows: First, we are able to automatically construct rules for modernizing a historic language based on comparing (a) phonetic sequence similarity, (b) the relative frequency of consonant and vowel sequences, and (c) the relative frequency of character n-gram sequences, of historic and modern corpora. Second, modern queries are not very effective for retrieving historic documents, but the historic language tools lead to a substantial improvement of retrieval effectiveness. The improvement is above and beyond the improvement due to using a modern stemming algorithm. In fact, modernizing the historic language generally has a beneficial impact on the effectiveness of the stemmer. In sum, our translation resources reduce the spelling gap between 17th century and contemporary Dutch, showing that a cross-language approach to HDR is a viable way of bridging the gap between the historic language of the document and the modern language of a user's query.

Following Braun [3], one can identify two bottlenecks for retrieving documents written in a historic language. The *spelling bottleneck* is caused by differences in spelling between the modern and historic language. The highly inconsistent spelling also resulted in the existence of multiple spelling variations of a word within a single document. A second problem is caused by vocabulary changes. As languages evolve, new words are introduced, while others disappear over time. Yet other words remain part of the language, but their meanings shift. This problem forms the *vocabulary bottleneck*. Our CLIR approach to HDR implies the use of translation resources for retrieval purposes. At present, we make no distinction between different linguistic relations that may hold between translations. The automatically produced rewrite rules exploit the fact that there are common elements in the different orthographic forms of words. Hence, they are an effective method for addressing the spelling bottleneck. The vocabulary bottleneck is a much harder problem. We are currently exploring methods that address the vocabulary bottleneck both directly and indirectly. First, we address it indirectly by using query expansion techniques that specifically expand queries with words not occuring in a modern corpus. Second, we address it directly by mining annotations to historic texts published on the web. This exploits the fact that these words require explanation for modern readers, frequently leading to annotations that explain the historic meaning of a term.

All resources used for the experiments in this paper (the corpus, the topics, and the qrels) are available from `http://ilps.science.uva.nl/Resources/`.

**Acknowledgments.**   Thanks to Margariet Moelands (National Library of the Netherlands) for drawing our attention to historic document retrieval. Thanks to Loes Braun for making available the *Antwerpse Compilatae* and *Gelders stad-en landrecht* corpus.

This research was supported by the Netherlands Organization for Scientific Research (NWO) under project numbers 016.054.616, 017.001.190, 220-80-001, 264-70-050, 365-20-005, 612.000.106, 612.000.207, 612.013.001, 612.066.302, 612.-069.006, 640.001.501, and 640.002.501.

# References

1. Brabants recht. Costumen van Antwerpen, 2005.
   `http://www.kulak.ac.be/facult/rechten/Monballyu/Rechtlagelanden/Brabantsrecht/brabantsrechtindex.htm`.
2. M. Braschler and C. Peters. Cross-language evaluation forum: Objectives, results, achievements. *Information Retrieval*, 7:7–31, 2004.
3. L. Braun. Information retrieval from Dutch historical corpora. Master's thesis, Maastricht University, 2002.
4. CLEF. Cross language evaluation forum, 2005. `http://www.clef-campaign.org/`.
5. N. Craswell and D. Hawking. Overview of the TREC 2004 web track. In *The Thirteenth Text REtrieval Conference (TREC 2004)*. National Institute for Standards and Technology. NIST Special Publication 500-251, 2005.
6. DBNL. Digitale bibliotheek voor de Nederlandse letteren, 2005. `http://www.dbnl.nl`.
7. DigiCULT. Technology challenges for digital culture, 2005. `http://www.digicult.info/`.
8. B. Efron. Bootstrap methods: Another look at the jackknife. *Annals of Statistics*, 7:1–26, 1979.
9. Gelders recht. Gelders Land- en Stadsrecht, 2005. `http://www.kulak.ac.be/facult/rechten/Monballyu/Rechtlagelanden/Geldersrecht/geldersrechtindex.htm`.
10. V. Hollink, J. Kamps, C. Monz, and M. de Rijke. Monolingual document retrieval for European languages. *Information Retrieval*, 7:33–52, 2004.
11. M. Hüning. Geschiedenis van het Nederlands, 1996. `http://www.ned.univie.ac.at/publicaties/taalgeschiedenis/nl/`.
12. K. Kukich. Technique for automatically correcting words in text. *ACM Computing Surveys*, 24:377–439, 1992.
13. M. Lesk. *Understanding Digital Libraries*. The Morgan Kaufmann series in multimedia information and systems. Morgan Kaufmann, second edition, 2005.
14. Lucene. The Lucene search engine, 2005. `http://jakarta.apache.org/lucene/`.
15. NeXTeNS. Text-to-speech for Dutch, 2005. `http://nextens.uvt.nl/`.
16. A.J. O'Rourke, A.M. Robertson, P. Willett, P. Eley, and P. Simons. Word variant identification in old french. *Information Research*, 2, 1996. `http://informationr.net/ir/2-4/paper22.html`.
17. A.M. Robertson and P. Willett. Searching for historical word-forms in a database of 17th-century English text using spelling-correction methods. In *Proceedings ACM SIGIR '92*, pages 256–265, New York, NY, USA, 1992. ACM Press.
18. H.J. Rogers and P. Willett. Searching for historical word forms in text databases using spelling-correction methods. *Journal of Documentation*, 7:333–353, 1991.
19. R.C. Russell. *Specification of Letters*, volume 1,261,167 of *Patent Number*. United States Patent Office, 1918.

20. D. Sankoff and J. Kruskal. *Time Warps, String Edits, and Macromolecules: The Theory and Practice of Sequence Comparison.* Addison-Wesley Publishing Co., Reading, Massachusetts, USA, 1983.
21. J. Savoy. Statistical inference in retrieval effectiveness evaluation. *Information Processing and Management*, 33:495–512, 1997.
22. J. Savoy. Combining multiple strategies for effective monolingual and cross-language retrieval. *Information Retrieval*, 7:121–148, 2004.
23. Snowball. A language for stemming algorithms, 2005. `http://snowball.tartarus.org/`.
24. R.A. Wagner and M.J. Fischer. The string-to-string correction problem. *Journal of the ACM*, 21:168–173, 1974.
25. Wikipedia. Indo-european languages, 2005. `http://en.wikipedia.org/wiki/Indo-European_languages`.

# Automatic Acquisition of Chinese–English Parallel Corpus from the Web

Ying Zhang[1], Ke Wu[2], Jianfeng Gao[3], and Phil Vines[1]

[1] RMIT University, GPO Box 2476V, Melbourne, Australia
`yzhang@cs.rmit.edu.au`, `phil@cs.rmit.edu.au`
[2] Shanghai Jiaotong University, Shanghai 200030, China
`wuke@sjtu.edu.cn`
[3] Microsoft Research, Redmond, Washington 98052, USA
`jfgao@microsoft.com`

**Abstract.** Parallel corpora are a valuable resource for tasks such as cross-language information retrieval and data-driven natural language processing systems. Previously only small scale corpora have been available, thus restricting their practical use. This paper describes a system that overcomes this limitation by automatically collecting high quality parallel bilingual corpora from the web. Previous systems used a single principle feature for parallel web page verification, whereas we use multiple features to identify parallel texts via a $k$-nearest-neighbor classifier. Our system was evaluated using a data set containing 6500 Chinese–English candidate parallel pairs that have been manually annotated. Experiments show that the use of a $k$-nearest-neighbors classifier with multiple features achieves substantial improvements over the systems that use any one of these features. The system achieved a precision rate of 95% and a recall rate of 97%, and thus is a significant improvement over earlier work.

## 1 Introduction

Parallel corpora provide a rich source of translation information. In the past, they have been used to train statistical translation models [1, 2, 3], translation disambiguation systems [4], out-of-vocabulary term translation [5], and multilingual thesaurus construction [6]. However, some parallel corpora are subject to subscription or licence fee and thus not freely available, while others are domain specific. For example, parallel corpora provided by the Evaluations and Language resources Distribution Agency [7], the Linguistic Data Consortium [8], and the University Centre for Computer Corpus Research on Language [9], all require subscription or fee. There are several large manually constructed parallel corpora available on the web but they are always domain specific, thus significantly limiting their practical usage. For instance, the biblical text [10] in a number of languages (collected by the University of Maryland) and the European parliament proceedings parallel corpus (1996-2003) [11] in eleven European languages.

In order to make use of the ever increasing number of parallel corpora, a robust system is needed to automatically mine them from the web. This paper presents a

M. Lalmas et al. (Eds.): ECIR 2006, LNCS 3936, pp. 420–431, 2006.
© Springer-Verlag Berlin Heidelberg 2006

system to automatically collect parallel Chinese–English corpora from the web — Web Parallel Data Extraction (WPDE). Similar to previous systems that have been developed for the same purposes, WPDE uses a three stage process: first, candidate sites are selected and crawled; second, candidate pairs of parallel texts are extracted; finally, we validate the parallel text pairs. Compared to previous systems, WPDE contains improvements at each stage. Specifically, in stage one, in addition to anchor text, image ALT text (the text that always provides a short description of the image and is displayed if an image is not shown) is used to improve the recall of candidate sites selection. In stage two, candidate pairs are generated by pattern matching and edit-distance similarity measure, whereas previous systems only applied one or the other of these. In stage three, where previous systems used a single principle feature to verify parallel pages, WPDE applies a KNN classifier to combine multiple features. Experiments on a large manually annotated data set show that each of the methods leads to improvements in terms of the overall performance in each step, and that the combined system yields the best overall result reported.

The structure of the paper is as follows. In Section 2, we consider other related work. Section 3 lays out the WPDE architecture. In Section 4 we detail our experiments and present the results we obtained; and Section 5 concludes the paper.

## 2   Related Work

The amount of information available on the web is expanding rapidly, and presents a valuable new source of parallel text. Recently, several systems have been developed to exploit this opportunity.

Nie et al. [1, 12] developed the PTMiner to mine large parallel corpora from the web. PTMiner used search engines to pinpoint the candidate sites that are likely to contain parallel pages, and then used the URLs collected as seeds to further crawl each web site for more URLs. The pairs of web pages were extracted on the basis of manually defined URL pattern-matching, and further filtered according to several criteria, such as file length, HTML structure, and language character set. Several hundred selected pairs were evaluated manually. Their results were quite promising, from a corpus of 250 MB of English–Chinese text, statistical evaluation showed that of the pairs identified, 90% were correct.

STRAND [13] is another well-known web parallel text mining system. Its goal is to identify pairs of web pages that are mutual translations. Resnik and Smith used the AltaVista search engine to search for multilingual websites and generated candidate pairs based on manually created substitution rules. The heart of STRAND is a structural filtering process that relies on analysis of the pages' underlying HTML to determine a set of pair-specific structural values, and then uses those values to filter the candidate pairs. Approximately 400 pairs were evaluated by human annotators. STRAND produced fewer than 3500 English–Chinese pairs with a precision of 98% and a recall of 61%.

The Parallel Text Identification System (PTI) [14] was developed to facilitate the construction of parallel corpora by aligning pairs of parallel documents

**Table 1.** Summarized Results from PTMiner, STRAND, and PTI

|         | Precision | Recall | Parallel text size | Number of pairs evaluated |
|---------|-----------|--------|--------------------|---------------------------|
| PTMiner | 90%       | –      | 250 MB             | 100–200 (randomly picked) |
| STRAND  | 98%       | 61%    | 3500 pairs         | 400 (randomly picked)     |
| PTI     | 93%       | 96%    | 427 pairs          | all                       |

from a multilingual document collection. The system crawls the web to fetch (potentially parallel) candidate multilingual web documents using a web spider. To determine the parallelism between potential document pairs, a filename comparison module is used to check filename resemblance, and a content analysis module is used to measure the semantic similarity. The results showed that the PTI system achieves a precision rate of 93% and a recall rate of 96%. PTI is correct in 180 instances among a total of 193 pairs extracted. Our later evaluation showed that WPDE is able to produce 373 correct pairs with a precision of 97% and a recall of 94% on the same domain, using the file length feature-based verification only.

The summarized results from above studies are tabulated in Table 1.

## 3   The WPDE Architecture

WPDE is an automatic system for large scale mining of parallel text from existing English–Chinese bilingual web pages in a variety of domains. In summary, our procedure consists of three steps: candidate sites selection and crawling, candidate pairs extraction, and parallel pairs verification.

### 3.1   Candidate Sites Selection and Crawling

Rather than using search engines to identify the candidate sites, we started with a snapshot of two million web pages from Microsoft Research. We noticed that images representing the language types are almost always accompanied by their text equivalents — ALT text. One of the major differences between WPDE and previous systems is that the candidate sites are selected on the basis of both anchor text and image ALT text. For a given web page, we extract the hypertext links when the anchor text or the image ALT text matches a list of pre-defined strings that indicate English, simplified Chinese, and traditional Chinese (see Appendix A). If a website contains two or more hypertext links to the different versions, we select these as candidate websites. 1598 candidate websites were selected based on the anchor text and 211 extra candidate websites were obtained using the image ALT text.

Once candidate sites were extracted from the snapshot, we used Wget[1] to fetch all documents from each site on the live web and create local copies of remote directory hierarchies.

---

[1] http://www.gnu.org/software/wget/

## 3.2   Candidate Pairs Extraction

We then extract candidate parallel pairs from the crawled web pages. URLs consist of a protocol prefix, a domain name, a pathname, and a filename. Webmasters tend to name the pages with similar names if they are the translation of each other. The only difference between these two URLs is the segments that indicate the language type. For example, given the URLs of an English–Chinese parallel pair,

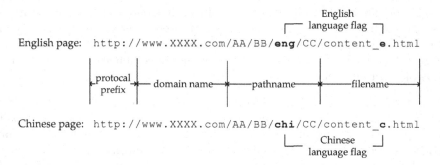

where **eng** and **e** are used to indicate the English version and **chi** and **c** are used to indicate the Chinese version. We observed that there are only five patterns **e,en,eng,engl,english** that are utilized to indicate the English version. Whereas, the patterns employed to indicate the Chinese version are quite unpredictable, and it is unrealistic to expect a "complete" pattern list. Therefore, previously employed language flag matching approaches [1, 12], that replace one language prefix/suffix/infix with all possible prefixes/suffixes/infixes in the other language based on a static pre-defined pattern list, will not work on a large scale URL matching process.

An improved approach combining pattern matching and edit-distance similarity measure [15] has been exploited in our work. For example, if an English pattern is detected in the pathname of an URL, we first extract the candidate Chinese URLs with the same protocol prefix, the same domain name, and the same pathname, except for the language flag segment. If the Chinese URL contains a language pathname segment that is in our standard Chinese pattern list — **c,ch,chi,chinese**, we select this URL. Otherwise we use an edit distance metric to find the nearest match to one of these Chinese patterns, for example **tc,sc,tchi,schi**, etc. If the filenames are the same, the process is finished. Sometimes this is not the case, and an additional filename matching step is required. In the simplest case the filename will differ by one of the standard language flag patterns, otherwise we again use the same edit distance function to find the filename closest to the one of these Chinese patterns.

We have extracted a total of 7894 candidate pairs. Later evaluation showed that in isolation, this approach has a precision of 79%. Among a total of 606 pages, which are in *.pdf*, *.doc*, *.rtf*, and *.cfm* format, 558 of them are parallel pages with a high quality. We would suggest the web documents in these specific formats as a reliable parallel text source.

### 3.3  Parallel Pairs Verification

The candidate pairs extracted in the previous steps are further filtered based on three common features of parallel pages: the file length, the file structure, and the translation of the web page content. To filter out the pairs that are not similar enough, a threshold is set to each feature score. The experimental results are shown in Section 4.

**File length.** We assume the files sizes of Chinese–English parallel texts are roughly proportional. Additionally, files of length 40 bytes or less are discarded. Using these metrics, 323 candidate pairs (5%) were filtered out. For the candidate pairs that remain, we then calculate the ratio of the two file lengths $S_{len} =$ length($f_{ch}$) / length($f_{en}$). This ratio is then used in combination with other features as described below.

**File structure.** The HTML structures of two parallel pages should be similar. We extract the linear sequences of HTML tags from each candidate pair, then apply case-folding and remove noise, such as *meta*, *font* and *scripts*. Unix sdiff[2] is used to find differences between these two sequences of HTML tags obtained. For example, as shown in Figure 1, consider the two sequences of HTML tags on the left, the aligned sequence generated by sdiff is shown on the right.

The feature score of the file structure is calculated using $S_{struct} = N_{diff} / N_{all}$, where $N_{diff} = 4$ is the number of unaligned lines in the given example above, and $N_{all} = 12$ is the total number of the lines, and is used to normalize the score. Thus, the lower the score the better, with 0 being ideal.

**Content translation.** To consider the content translation of a candidate parallel pair, we align the two pages using the Champollion Tool Kit[3], which provides ready-to-use parallel text sentence alignment tools. Champollion depends heavily on lexical information, but uses sentence length information as well. Past experiments indicate that champollion's performance improves as the translation lexicon becomes larger. We therefore compiled a large English–Chinese lexicon, which contains 250,000 entries. The score of the content translation feature is calculated using $S_{trans} = N_{aligned} / N_{(ch,en)}$, where $N_{aligned}$ is the number of aligned sentences and $N_{(ch,en)}$ is the total number of lines in the two pages.

**K-nearest-neighbors classifier.** After investigating the recall-precision results of each single feature verification, we observed that although the file length feature produced the highest precision, the file structure feature can achieve a relatively high recall when lower precision is acceptable. Intuitively, it is possible to achieve better overall performance if multiple features can be combined using an appropriate model. To observe the data distribution in a 2-dimensional feature space, we generated the scatter plot matrix shown in Figure 2. The file length feature score is plotted in the X axis, while the file structure feature score is plotted on the Y axis. The 'true' pair is marked by triangle and the 'false'

---

[2] http://linuxcommand.org/man_pages/sdiff1.html
[3] http://champollion.sourceforge.net/

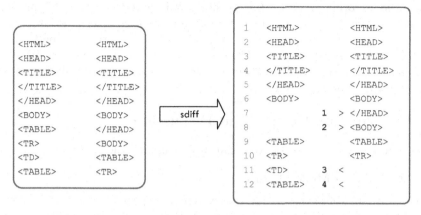

**Fig. 1.** An example of file structure comparison using sdiff

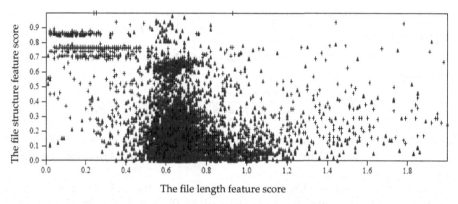

The file length feature score

**Fig. 2.** A scatter plot of the 2-feature dimensions. The x-axis shows the file length feature score. The y-axis shows the file structure feature score.

pair is represented by cross. As we can see, in the case of mixture of tightly clustered 'true and false' data, a linear decision boundary is unlikely to be optimal. $k$-nearest-neighbors method would be more appropriate for the mixture.

KNN has been successfully used for pattern classification on many applications [16]. Being a non-parametric classification method, it is a simple but effective method for classification. It labels an unknown sample with the label of the majority of the $k$ nearest neighbors. A neighbor is deemed nearest if it has the smallest distance. The distance is usually calculated using the Euclidean distance.

Using a total of 6500 English-Chinese candidate pairs, we carried out tenfold cross-validation experiments using a KNN classifier to predict the correctness of a candidate pair. Specifically, the data is randomly split into 10 disjoint validation subsets, each with 650 pairs. In each fold, we then select one of those subsets as a test set with 650 test items and use the rest 5850 pairs as its training set; the fraction of true and false pairs in each fold's test and training sets approximates the overall division, 80% to 20%, respectively. The choice of $k$

affects the performance of a KNN classifier. Wilson and Martinez [17] proposed that the $k$ is typically a small integer that is odd and often determined from cross-validation. Therefore we choose the optimal $k$ value with the best performance in cross-validation experiments. Through our experiments, we determined that the best results are generally obtained with $k = 15$ for 3-feature dimension, and $k = 7$ for 2-feature dimensions.

# 4    Experiments Results and Discussion

In this section, we describe the experimental setup and the experimental results.

## 4.1    Evaluation Methodology

The performance of a system that finds web parallel pages can be evaluated using standard IR measures of precision and recall. Precision represents the proportion of candidate parallel pages retrieved that are correct, thus:

$$Precision = \frac{Number\ of\ correctly\ aligned\ pairs}{Total\ number\ of\ aligned\ pairs}$$

Whereas recall represents the proportion of parallel pages that the system actually found:

$$Recall = \frac{Number\ of\ correctly\ aligned\ pairs}{Total\ number\ of\ parallel\ pairs\ in\ the\ collection}$$

Recall can be calculated for a test collection since the total number of parallel pairs can be determined by inspection, but cannot be calculated for the entire web.

We used three Chinese–English bilingual speakers (none of whom are authors of this paper) to evaluate the correctness of all the parallel pairs we extracted from the web. Only if the English and Chinese pages contain entirely the same meaning, the pair is annotated as a 'correct pair'. While previous systems have been evaluated on relatively small data set (about a few hundreds of pairs), we created a large manually annotated test collection containing around 6500 English–Chinese pairs.

## 4.2    Web Crawling Results

A total of 61 web sites, which include 26 .hk sites and 35 .cn sites, were randomly selected from the candidate websites obtained in Section 3.1. We have crawled about 2.7 GB of web data, comprising approximately 53, 000 web pages. We noticed that the quality of the parallel data provided by the .hk sites is seemingly better than that provided by the .cn sites, and therefore we strongly suggest that more importance should be attached to the .hk web sites in candidate website selection.

## 4.3    Parallel Pairs Mining Results

We then tested the effect of the features, both separately and in various of combinations.

**Single feature effect.** We have run three experiments to separately gauge the effectiveness of each of these features — the file length, the file structure, and the content translation features in $\text{RUN}_{len}$, $\text{RUN}_{struct}$, and $\text{RUN}_{trans}$, respectively. The evaluation results with the highest average precision achieved using tenfold cross-validation are shown in Table 2.

Surprisingly, the file length feature, the simplest and thus the most efficient, is clearly superior. When $0.55 \leq S_{len} < 0.75$, we are able to achieve a precision of 97% and a recall of 70%. This compares favorably to the results of STRAND and PTMiner (see Table 1), which while not directly comparable because of the the differing corpora, suggests that our system performs reasonably well.

Our utilization of linear sequence of HTML tags to determine whether two pages are parallel, is similar to that of STRAND and PTMiner. The file HTML structure feature provides a relatively high precision; meanwhile, it greatly impairs the recall.

The content translation feature has produced mediocre results. Given Champollion depends heavily on lexical information (previously described in Section 3.3), we suspect the main reason is that the majority of the candidate pairs we have generated in Section 3.2 are in traditional Chinese, where the bilingual lexicon we have compiled is based on simplified Chinese. Although there are no differences between the basic vocabularies or grammatical structures of simplified and traditional Chinese, different Chinese communities translate English terms in different ways. Due to the limited communication between mainland China (using simplified Chinese) and Taiwan, Hong Kong and the overseas areas (using traditional Chinese), there are some differences in terminology, especially new cultural or technological nouns. For instance, the English computer phrase "cross-language information retrieval" is commonly translated in simplified Chinese as "跨语言信息检索" while in traditional Chinese it is "跨語言資訊檢索". This suggests that better results might be obtained if specially tailored lexicons were used for mainland and overseas Chinese text.

**Feature fusion effect.** This set of experiments allowed us to test whether using feature fusion in the parallel pairs verification is likely to provide any benefit, as well as the effect of the number of the features of fusion on the overall performance. As shown in Figure 3, three types of feature combinations are investigated: the direct intersection, the linear phase filtering, and a KNN classifier.

**Table 2.** Effect of the features separately. For the file length feature, ratios between 0.55 and 0.75 achieved the best precision. For the file structure feature, pairs with scores $\leq 0.1$ performed best, whereas for the translation feature, attribute scores $\geq 0.1$ provided the best precision.

| RUN ID | Precision | Recall |
|---|---|---|
| $\text{RUN}_{len}$ $(0.55 \leq S_{len} < 0.75)$ | 97% | 70% |
| $\text{RUN}_{struct}$ $(S_{struct} \leq 0.1)$ | 95% | 46% |
| $\text{RUN}_{trans}$ $(S_{trans} \geq 0.1)$ | 90% | 53% |

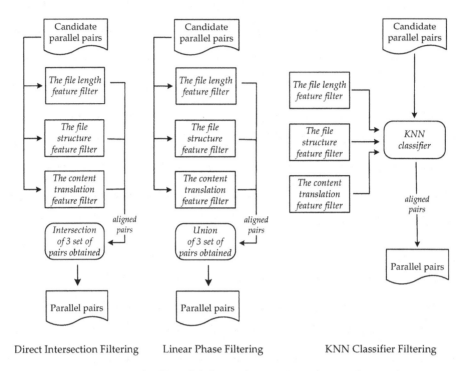

Direct Intersection Filtering      Linear Phase Filtering      KNN Classifier Filtering

**Fig. 3.** Outline of different feature fusion methods

In the direct intersection run $RUN_{inters}$, we evaluated a direct intersection of the pair sets aligned by each of the features. In the linear phase filtering run $RUN_{linear}$, the candidate pairs were passed through the linear phase filters. The pairs that are unable to be detected by the first feature filter were aligned using the second feature filter, the pairs left were piped to the last feature filter and processed. In other words, this process produces the union of the sets of pairs aligned by each filter. In the $RUN_{knn}$, we experimented with a KNN classifier previously described in Section 3.3. For example, using a feature space of three dimensions each pair instance $x$ is represented as a vector $\langle S_{len}(x), S_{struct}(x), S_{trans}(x) \rangle$. $RUN_{len}$ provided the best results for a single feature run, and thus is used to establish a reference by which we can measure our feature fusion results. The results reported are obtained after selecting an optimal threshold for each of the feature scores. The experimental results with the highest average precision achieved using tenfold cross-validation are shown in Table 3.

The results of the direct intersection combination method ($RUN_{inters}$) were disastrous. This suggests a large proportion of correct pairs only satisfy some of the above three features. The result of this was often that many correct pairs were omitted. This outcome is corroborated by the results of $RUN_{linear}$. Using the liner phase filtering feature fusion, we are able to achieve a precision of 96% and a recall of 90%. The KNN classifier further improved the recall to 97%. We used the Wilcoxon ranked signed test to test the statistical significance of the

**Table 3.** Effect of the different types of feature fusion. (All values are percentages).

| RUN ID | Features | | | Precision | Recall |
|---|---|---|---|---|---|
| | $F_{len}$ | $F_{struct}$ | $F_{trans}$ | | |
| $RUN_{len}$ (Baseline) | √ | | | 97 | 70 |
| $RUN_{inters}$ | √ | √ | | 97 | 30 |
| | √ | | √ | 97 | 64 |
| | | √ | √ | 97 | 27 |
| | √ | √ | √ | 98 | 20 |
| $RUN_{linear}$ | √ | √ | | 95 | 85 |
| | √ | | √ | 95 | 88 |
| | | √ | √ | 94 | 89 |
| | √ | √ | √ | 96 | 90 |
| $RUN_{knn}$ | √ | √ | | 94 | 94 |
| | √ | | √ | 94 | 97 |
| | | √ | √ | 93 | 97 |
| | √ | √ | √ | 95 | 97 |

improvement. It showed a significant improvement at the 95% confidence level, and emphasizes the importance of a good feature fusion technique.

Our experiments also show that 3-feature fusion statistically significantly outperforms 2-feature fusion in both $RUN_{linear}$ and $RUN_{knn}$. Therefore we conclude that a larger number of features will increase the overall performance of the system.

## 5   Conclusion

The paper describes WPED, an automatic mining system for bilingual web parallel corpora. This system used several new techniques to extract parallel web pages, and thus has the potential to find more candidate pages than previous systems. We have explored the use of multiple features via a KNN classifier. Experimental results show that the use of the KNN classifier with multiple features achieves substantial improvements over the systems that use any one of these features. WPDE has achieved a precision rate of 95% and a recall rate of 97%, and thus is a significant improvement over earlier work.

## Acknowledgments

This work was done while the first and second authors were visiting Microsoft Research Asia. We thank Professor Jian-Yun Nie for his valuable discussion and advice.

# References

1. Nie, J.Y., Simard, M., Isabelle, P., Durand, R.: Cross-language information retrieval based on parallel texts and automatic mining of parallel texts from the web. In: Proceedings of the 22nd Annual International ACM SIGIR Conference on Research and Development in Information Retrieval, Berkeley, California, United States, ACM Press (1999) 74–81

2. Franz, M., McCarley, J.S., Ward, T., Zhu, W.J.: Quantifying the utility of parallel corpora. In: Proceedings of the 24th Annual International ACM SIGIR Conference on Research and Development in Information Retrieval, New Orleans, Louisiana, United States, ACM Press (2001) 398–399

3. Brown, P.F., Cocke, J., Pietra, S.D., Pietra, V.J.D., Jelinek, F., Lafferty, J.D., Mercer, R.L., Roossin, P.S.: A statistical approach to machine translation. Computational Linguistics **16** (1990) 79–85

4. Ballesteros, L., Croft, W.B.: Resolving ambiguity for cross-language retrieval. In: Proceedings of the 21st Annual International ACM SIGIR Conference on Research and Development in Information Retrieval, Melbourne, Australia, ACM Press (1998) 64–71

5. McEwan, C.J.A., Ounis, I., Ruthven, I.: Building bilingual dictionaries from parallel web documents. In: Proceedings of the 24th BCS-IRSG European Colloquium on IR Research, London, UK, Springer-Verlag (2002) 303–323

6. Chau, R., Yeh, C.H.: Construction of a fuzzy multilingual thesaurus and its application to cross-lingual text retrieval. In: Proceedings of the 1st Asia-Pacific Conference on Web Intelligence: Research and Development, Maebashi City, Japan, Springer-Verlag (2001) 340–345

7. http://www.elda.org/.

8. http://www.ldc.upenn.edu/.

9. http://www.comp.lancs.ac.uk/computing/research/ucrel/.

10. http://www.umiacs.umd.edu/users/resnik/parallel/bible.html.

11. http://people.csail.mit.edu/koehn/publications/europarl/.

12. Kraaij, W., Nie, J.Y., Simard, M.: Embedding web-based statistical translation models in cross-language information retrieval. Computational Linguistics **29** (2003) 381–419

13. Resnik, P., Smith, N.A.: The web as a parallel corpus. Computational Linguistics **29** (2003) 349–380

14. Chen, J., Chau, R., Yeh, C.H.: Discovering parallel text from the world wide web. In: Proceedings of the 2nd Workshop on Australasian Information Security, Data Mining and Web Intelligence, and Software Internationalisation, Dunedin, New Zealand, Australian Computer Society, Inc. (2004) 157–161

15. Lowrance, R., Wagner, R.A.: An extension of the string-to-string correction problem. Journal of the ACM **22** (1975) 177–183

16. Cover, T., Hart, P.: Nearest neighbor pattern classification. IEEE Transactions on Information Theory **13** (1967) 21–27

17. Wilson, D.R., Martinez, T.R.: Instance pruning techniques. In: Proceedings of the 14th International Conference on Machine Learning, San Francisco, CA, USA, Morgan Kaufmann Publishers Inc. (1997) 403–411

# A    A List of Pre-defined Strings

```
english
chinese
simplifiedchinese
chinesesimplified
traditionalchinese
chinesetraditional
englishversion
simplifiedchineseversion
traditionalchineseversion
```

英文     英文首页
简体     中文首页
繁體     中文简体
英文版    中文繁體
中文版    简体中文
简体版    简体中文版
繁體版    繁體中文
英文网站   繁體中文版
中文网站

# Fast Discovery of Similar Sequences in Large Genomic Collections

Yaniv Bernstein and Michael Cameron

School of Computer Science and Information Technology,
RMIT University, Melbourne, Australia
{ybernste, mcam}@cs.rmit.edu.au

**Abstract.** Detection of highly similar sequences within genomic collections has a number of applications, including the assembly of expressed sequence tag data, genome comparison, and clustering sequence collections for improved search speed and accuracy. While several approaches exist for this task, they are becoming infeasible — either in space or in time — as genomic collections continue to grow at a rapid pace. In this paper we present an approach based on document fingerprinting for identifying highly similar sequences. Our approach uses a modest amount of memory and executes in a time roughly proportional to the size of the collection. We demonstrate substantial speed improvements compared to the CD-HIT algorithm, the most successful existing approach for clustering large protein sequence collections.

## 1 Introduction

Similarity between genomic sequences is a strong predictor of functional or phylogenetic relatedness, and thus the identification of sequence similarity is a very important application in bioinformatics. The first step towards identifying a new sequence typically involves searching a large sequence databank for similar sequences using an alignment algorithm such as Smith-Waterman (Smith & Waterman 1981), FASTA (Pearson & Lipman 1988) or BLAST (Altschul et al. 1990, 1997, Cameron et al. 2004, 2005). These algorithms compare a single query sequence against a collection of sequences, and are notable for their accuracy and sensitivity. In many cases, however, it is useful to know not just the similarity between a single sequence and a collection, but between *all* sequences in the collection. The identification of similar sequence pairs is useful for clustering EST (expressed sequence tag) data (Burke et al. 1999, Malde et al. 2003), genome comparison (Kurtz et al. 2004), and reducing redundancy in a collection to improve search speed (Holm & Sander 1998, Li et al. 2001 *b,a*) and accuracy (Park et al. 2000, Li et al. 2002). In such cases, a straightforward application of Smith-Waterman or BLAST is not appropriate: an all-against-all comparison of a 100 Mb collection takes several days with BLAST.

Previous studies have investigated a range of approaches to identifying all pairs of highly similar sequences in a collection. Most of the proposed techniques execute significantly faster than a naïve application of query-based algorithms

M. Lalmas et al. (Eds.): ECIR 2006, LNCS 3936, pp. 432–443, 2006.
© Springer-Verlag Berlin Heidelberg 2006

such as BLAST. However, a majority of these algorithms still have a fundamental $O(n^2)$ complexity in the size of the collection, rendering them increasingly infeasible as genomic databases continue their exponential growth. Malde et al. (2003) have investigated the use of suffix structures such as suffix trees (Gusfield 1997) or suffix arrays (Manber & Myers 1993) to efficiently identify high-scoring pairs in a single pass of the collection. This approach does not suffer from the quadratic complexity problem, however suffix structures have significant memory overheads and long construction times, making them unsuitable for large genomic collections such as GenBank.

In this paper we describe and apply *document fingerprinting* to isolate candidate pairs of highly similar sequences. Our approach is fast, scales linearly with collection size, and has modest memory requirements. We describe our method for applying fingerprinting to genomic sequences and find that it is remarkably accurate and sensitive for this task. We also apply fingerprinting to the creation of representative-sequence databases (Holm & Sander 1998, Park et al. 2000, Li et al. 2001 *b*). We are able to process the GenBank non-redundant database in around 1.5 hours, while the fastest existing approach, CD-HIT (Li et al. 2001 *b*), requires over 9 hours for the same task. Importantly, there is no significant change in accuracy.

## 2    Similarity Detection: Techniques and Applications

Query-based similarity detection in sequence collections is a fundamental task in bioinformatics. It is often the first step in the identification, classification and comparison of new sequence data. A number of well-researched and well-established techniques exist for this task; alignment algorithms such as BLAST compare a single query sequence to every sequence in a collection and are generally considered satisfactory solutions for this task.

For some important applications, however, there is no notion of a query sequence; rather, it is necessary to identify similarity between arbitrary pairs of sequences in a collection. For example, the assembly of EST (expressed sequence tag) data involves arranging a collection of overlapping sequences into a longer consensus sequence. For this application there is no apparent query sequence: rather, we are interested in similarity between any pair of sequences in the collection. Another application where an all-against-all comparison is required is the construction of a representative-sequence database (RSDB), where highly redundant sequences are removed from a collection resulting in faster, more sensitive search for distant homologies using search algorithms such as PSI-BLAST (Altschul et al. 1997).

Several past solutions — including Holm & Sander (1998) and Li et al. (2001 *b*) — use a simple pairwise approach to identify pairs of similar sequences. These schemes use fast BLAST-like heuristics to compare each sequence in the collection to the entire collection. The representative-sequence database tool CD-HIT (Li et al. 2001 *b*) is the fastest approach based on this method. However, despite fast methods for comparing each sequence pair, such approaches require time that is quadratic in the size of the collection and are increasingly infeasible as genomic collections continue to grow. The CD-HIT tool requires over 9 hours to process the current GenBank non-redundant protein database.

An alternative approach to identifying similar sequences involves using a suffix structure such as a suffix tree or suffix array. This approach is taken by Malde et al. (2003), where suffix arrays are used to cluster EST sequences in linear time. While the approach is highly effective for this application — in which collections are typically quite small — suffix structures are known to consume large amounts of main-memory. In our experiments with the freely available XSACT software, this was confirmed: the software required more than 2 Gb of main memory to process a 10 Mb collection of uncompressed nucleotide data. Although more compact suffix structures exist (Grossi & Vitter 2000) they have longer construction and search times.

In the following sections we describe a novel, alternative approach called document fingerprinting with linear time complexity and modest memory requirements.

## 3   Document Fingerprinting and SPEX

Document fingerprinting (Manber 1994, Brin et al. 1995, Heintze 1996), (Broder et al. 1997, Shivakumar & García-Molina 1999) is an effective and scalable technique for identifying pairs of documents within large text collections that share portions of identical text. Document fingerprinting has been used for several applications, including copyright protection (Brin et al. 1995), document management (Manber 1994) and web search optimisation (Broder et al. 1997, Fetterly et al. 2003, Bernstein & Zobel 2005).

The fundamental unit of document fingerprinting techniques is the *chunk*, a fixed-length unit of text such as a series of consecutive words or a sentence. The full set of chunks for a given document is formed by passing a sliding window of appropriate length over the document; this is illustrated below for a chunk length of six words:

|  |  |
|---|---|
|  | `[the quick brown fox jumped over]` |
| the quick brown fox jumped | `[quick brown fox jumped over the]` |
| over the lazy dog | `[brown fox jumped over the lazy]` |
|  | `[fox jumped over the lazy dog]` |

The set of all chunks in a collection can be stored in an inverted index (Witten et al. 1999) and the index can be used to calculate the number of shared chunks between pairs of documents in a collection. Two identical documents will naturally have an identical set of chunks. As the documents begin to diverge, the proportion of chunks they share will decrease. However, any pair of documents sharing a run of text as long as the chunk length will have at least one chunk in common. Thus, the proportion of common chunks is a good estimator of the quantity of common text shared by a pair of documents. The quality of this estimate is optimised by choosing a chunk length that is long enough so that two identical chunks are unlikely to coincidentally occur, but not so long that it becomes too sensitive to minor changes. In the DECO package, for example, the default chunk length is eight words (Bernstein & Zobel 2004).

For practical document fingerprinting, chunks are generally hashed before storage in order to make their representation more compact. Further, some sort of *selection heuristic* is normally applied so that only some chunks from each document are selected for storage. The choice of selection heuristic has a very significant impact on the general effectiveness of the fingerprinting algorithm. Most fingerprinting algorithms have used simple feature-based selection heuristics, such as selecting chunks only if their hash is divisible by a certain number, or selecting chunks that begin with certain letter-combinations. These heuristics are obviously lossy: if two documents share chunks, but none of them happen to satisfy the criteria of the selection heuristic, the fingerprinting algorithm will not identify these documents as sharing text.

Bernstein & Zobel (2004) introduced the SPEX chunk selection algorithm, which allows for *lossless* selection of chunks, based on the observation that singleton chunks (chunks that only occur once and represent a large majority in most collections) do not contribute to identifying text reuse between documents. The SPEX algorithm takes advantage of the fact that, if any subchunk (subsequence) of a chunk is unique, the chunk as a whole is unique. Using a memory-efficient iterative hashing technique, SPEX is able to select only those chunks that occur multiple times in the collection. Using SPEX can yield significant savings over selecting every chunk without any degradation in the quality of results.

Figure 1 provides a pseudocode sketch of how SPEX identifies duplicate chunks of length finalLength within a collection of documents or genomic sequences. The algorithm iterates over chunk lengths from 1 to finalLength, the final chunk length desired. At each iteration, SPEX maintains two hashtables (referred to as lookup in the figure): one recording the number of occurrences of each chunk for the previous iteration, and one for the current iteration. As we are only interested in knowing whether a chunk occurs multiple times or not, each entry in lookup takes one of only three values: zero, one, or more than one ($2^+$). This allows us to fit four hashtable entries per byte; collisions are not resolved. A chunk is only inserted into lookup if its two subchunks of length chunkLength - 1 both

```
for chunkLength = 1 to finalLength
   foreach sequence in the collection
      foreach chunk of length chunkLength in sequence
         if chunkLength = 1
            increment lookup[chunk]
         else
            subchunk1 = chunk prefix of length chunkLength - 1
            subchunk2 = chunk suffix of length chunkLength - 1
            if lookup[subchunk1] = 2+ and lookup[subchunk2] = 2+
               increment lookup[chunk]
```

**Fig. 1.** The SPEX algorithm

appear multiple times in the hashtable from the previous iteration. The iterative process helps prevent the hashtables from being flooded. The SPEX algorithm is able to process quite large collections of text and indicate whether a given chunk occurs multiple times in a reasonable time, and consuming a relatively modest amount of memory. For a full description of how the SPEX algorithm works, we refer the reader to Bernstein & Zobel (2004).

## 4   Fingerprinting for Genomic Sequences

The SPEX algorithm (and, indeed, any fingerprinting algorithm) can be trivially adapted for use with genomic sequences by simply substituting documents with sequences. However, the properties of a genomic sequence are quite different from those of a natural language document. The most significant difference is the lack of any unit in genomic data analogous to natural language words. The protein sequences we consider in this paper are represented as an undifferentiated string of amino-acid characters with no natural delimiters such as whitespace, commas or other punctuation marks.

The lack of words in genomic sequences has a number of immediate impacts on the operation and performance of the SPEX algorithm. First, the granularity of the sliding window must be increased from word-level to character-level. An increased granularity means that there will be far more chunks in a genomic sequence than in a natural-language document of similar size. As a result, the SPEX algorithm is less efficient and scalable for genomic data than for natural language documents.

The distribution of subsequences within genomic data is also less highly skewed than the distribution of words in English text. Given a collection of natural language documents, we expect some words (such as 'and' and 'or') to occur extremely frequently, while other words (such as perhaps 'alphamegamia' and 'nudiustertian') will be *hapax legomena*: words that occur only once. This permits the SPEX algorithm to be effectual from the first iteration by removing word-pairs such as 'nudiustertian news'. In contrast, given a short string of characters using the amino acid alphabet of size 20, it is far less likely that the word will occur only once in any collection of nontrivial size. Thus, the first few iterations of SPEX are likely be entirely ineffectual.

One simple solution to these problems is to introduce 'pseudo-words', effectively segmenting each sequence by moving the sliding window several characters at a time. However, this approach relies on sequences being aligned along segment boundaries. This assumption is not generally valid and makes the algorithm highly sensitive to insertions and deletions. Consider, for example, the following sequences given a chunk length of four and a window increment of four:

|          | Sequence          | Chunks              |
|----------|-------------------|---------------------|
| Sequence 1 | ABCDEFGHIJKLMNOP | ABCD EFGH IJKL MNOP |
| Sequence 2 | AABCDEFGHIJKLMNOP | AABC DEFG HIJK LMNO |
| Sequence 3 | GHAACDEFGHIJKLMQ | GHAA CDEF GHIJ KLMQ |

Despite all three of these sequences containing an identical subsequence of length 11 (in bold above), they do not share a single common chunk. This strong correspondence between the three sequences will thus be overlooked by the algorithm.

We propose a hybrid of regular SPEX and the pseudo-word based approach described above that we call slotted SPEX. Slotted SPEX uses a window increment greater than one but is able to 'synchronise' the windows between sequences so that two highly-similar sequences are not entirely overlooked as a result of a misalignment between them.

```
chunkLength = finalLength - Q × (numIterations - 1)
for iteration = 1 to numIterations
    foreach sequence in the collection
      foreach chunk of length chunkLength in sequence
        if lookup[chunk] ≠ 0
          increment lookup[chunk]
        else
          count number of subchunks of length chunkLength - Q
                where lookup[subchunk] = 2⁺
          if (count ≥ 2 or iteration = 1) and
            (number of chunks processed since increment lookup ≥ Q)
              increment lookup[chunk]
    increment chunkLength by Q
```

**Fig. 2.** The slotted SPEX algorithm

Figure 2 describes the slotted SPEX algorithm. As in standard SPEX, we pass a fixed-size window over each sequence with an increment of one. However, unlike SPEX, slotted SPEX does not consider inserting every chunk into the hashtable. In addition to decomposing the chunk into subchunks and checking that the subchunks are non-unique, slotted SPEX also requires that one of two initial conditions be met. First, that it has been at least $Q$ window increments since the last insertion; or second, that the current chunk already appears in the hashcounter. The parameter $Q$ is the *quantum*, which can be thought of as the window increment used by the algorithm. Slotted SPEX guarantees that at least every $Q^{th}$ overlapping substring from a sequence is inserted into the hashtable. The second precondition — that the chunk already appears in the hashcounter — provides the synchronisation that is required for the algorithm to work reliably.

The operation of slotted SPEX is best illustrated with an example. Using the same set of sequences as above, a quantum $Q = 4$ and a chunk length of four, slotted SPEX produces the following set of chunks:

|  | Sequence | Chunks |
|---|---|---|
| Sequence 1 | ABCDEFGHIJKLMNOP | ABCD **EFGH IJKL** MNOP |
| Sequence 2 | AABCDEFGHIJKLMNOP | AABC ABCD **EFGH IJKL** MNOP |
| Sequence 3 | GHAACDEFGHIJKLMQ | GHAA CDEF **EFGH IJKL** |

For the first sequence, the set of chunks produced does not differ from the naïve pseudo-word technique. Let us now follow the process for the second sequence.

The first chunk — AABC — is inserted as before. When processing the second chunk, ABCD, the number of chunks processed since the last insertion is one, fewer than the quantum Q. However, the condition lookup[chunk] $\neq$ 0 on line 5 of Figure 2 is met: the chunk has been previously inserted. The hashcounter is therefore incremented, effectively synchronising the window of the sequence with that of the earlier, matching sequence. As a result, every $Q^{th}$ identical chunk will be identified across the matching region between the two sequences. In this example, the slotted SPEX algorithm selects two chunks of length four that are common to all sequences. Slotted SPEX also differs from regular SPEX by incrementing the word length by Q rather than 1 between iterations.

In comparison to the ordinary SPEX algorithm, slotted SPEX requires fewer iterations, consumes less memory and builds smaller indexes. This makes it suitable for the higher chunk density of genomic data. While slotted SPEX is a lossy algorithm, it does offer the following guarantee: for a window size finalLength and a quantum Q, any pair of sequences with a matching subsequence of length finalLength + Q - 1 or greater will have at least one identical chunk selected. As the length of the match grows, so will the guaranteed number of common chunks selected. Thus, despite the lossiness of the algorithm, slotted SPEX is still able to offer strong assurance that it will reliably detect highly similar pairs of sequences.

## 5    Fingerprinting for Identity Estimation

In this section, we analyze the performance of slotted SPEX for distinguishing sequence pairs with a high level of identity from those that do not.

Following Holm & Sander (1998) and Li et al. (2001b), we calculate the percentage identity between a pair of sequences by performing a banded Smith-Waterman alignment (Chao et al. 1992) using a band width of 20, match score of 1, and no mismatch or gap penalty. The percentage identity $I$ for the sequence pair $s_i, s_j$ is calculated as $I = S(s_i, s_j)/L(s_i, s_j)$ where $S(s_i, s_j)$ is the alignment score and $L(s_i, s_j)$ is the length of the shorter of the two sequences. This score can be functionally interpreted as being the proportion of characters in the shorter sequence that match identical characters in the longer sequence. We define similar sequence pairs as those with at least 90% identity ($I \geq 0.9$); this is the same threshold used in Holm & Sander (1998) and is the default parameter used by CD-HIT (Li et al. 2001b).

For experiments in this section we use version 1.65 of the ASTRAL Compendium (Chandonia et al. 2004), because it is a relatively small yet complete database that allows us to experiment with a wide range of parameterisations. The ASTRAL database contains 24,519 sequences, equating to 300,578,421 unique sequence-pair combinations. Of these, 139,716 — less than 0.05% — have an identity of 90% or higher by the above measure; this is despite the fact that the database is known to have a high degree of internal redundancy. A vast majority of sequence pairs in any database can be assumed to be highly dissimilar.

Although we do not expect fingerprinting to be as sensitive and accurate as a computationally intensive dynamic-programming approach such as

Smith-Waterman, we hope that the method will effectively distinguish sequence-pairs with a high level of identity from the large number of pairs that have very low identity. Our aim is to use document fingerprinting to massively reduce the search space within which more sensitive analysis must be pursued. For example, even if fingerprinting identifies three times as many false positives (dissimilar sequences) as true positives (similar sequences), less than 0.2% of all sequence pairs in the ASTRAL collection would need to be aligned.

In order to find a good compromise between resource consumption and effectiveness, we have experimented with different parameter combinations. Figure 3 (left) shows the SPEX index size for varying chunk lengths and quanta. The results show that increasing the word length does not result in a large reduction in index size, but increasing the quantum results in a marked and consistent decrease in the size of the index.

Figure 3 (right) plots the average precision (Buckley & Voorhees 2000) as a function of chunk length and quantum. The average precision measure was calculated by sorting pairs in decreasing order of SPEX score — the number of matching chunks divided by the length of the shorter sequence — and using sequence pairs with an identity of 90% or above as the set of positives. We observe that increasing the chunk length results in a small loss in accuracy, however increasing the quantum has almost no effect on average precision. This indicates that slotted SPEX — even with a high quantum — is able to estimate sequence identity nearly as well as the regular SPEX algorithm with reduced costs in memory use, index size and index processing time.

The result in Figure 3 make a strong case for using a shorter word length; however, shorter words place a greater loading on the hashcounter. With larger collections, memory bounds can lead to the hashtable flooding and a consequent blowout in index size. Thus, shorter word lengths are less scalable. Similarly, longer quanta are in general beneficial to performance. However, a larger quantum reduces the number of iterations possible in slotted SPEX. Thus, a very high quantum can result in more collisions in the hashcounter due to fewer iterations, suggesting once again that a compromise is required. Guided by these observations along with the other data, chunk lengths of 25 or 30 with a quantum of 5 to 9 appear to provide a good compromise between the various considerations in all-against-all identity detection for large collections.

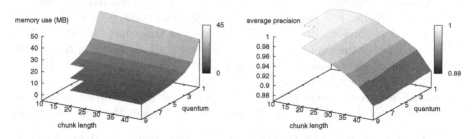

**Fig. 3.** SPEX index size as a function of final chunk length and quantum (left) and average precision as a function of final chunk length and quantum (right)

The high average precision results indicate that slotted SPEX provides an accurate and sensitive prediction of whether sequence pairs have a high level of identity. What is particularly surprising is that the average precision stays high even with reasonably long chunk lengths and high quanta. Earlier efforts by Holm & Sander (1998) and Li et al. (2001b), and Li et al. (2001a) are extremely rigorous and rely upon short matching chunks, typically less than ten characters in length, between sequence-pairs before proceeding with alignment. Our results indicate that longer chunk lengths have only minor impact on result quality.

In our experiments we have focused on identifying sequence-pairs with greater than 90% identity, and we have shown that fingerprinting is effective at this task. However, it is probable that fingerprinting will prove less useful as the identity threshold is lowered.

## 6    Removing Redundant Sequences: An Application

Holm & Sander (1998), Park et al. (2000) and Li et al. (2001b) have all investigated techniques for creating *representative-sequence databases* (RSDBs), culled collections where no two sequences share more than a given level of identity. RSDBs are typically constructed by identifying clusters of similar sequences and retaining only one sequence from each cluster, the cluster representative. Such databases are more compact, resulting in faster search times. More significantly, they have been demonstrated to improve the sensitivity of distant-homology search algorithms such as PSI-BLAST (Li et al. 2002).

The most recent and efficient technique for constructing an RSDB, CD-HIT (Li et al. 2001b), uses a greedy incremental approach based on an all-against-all comparison. The algorithm starts with an empty RSDB. Each sequence is processed in decreasing order of length and compared to every sequence already inserted into the RSDB. If a high-identity match is found, where $I$ exceeds a threshold, the sequence is discarded; otherwise it is added to the RSDB. To reduce the number of sequence pairs that are aligned, CD-HIT first checks for short matching chunks — typically of length four or five — between sequences before aligning them. The approach is still fundamentally quadratic in complexity.

We have replicated the greedy incremental approach of CD-HIT, but use fingerprinting with slotted SPEX as a preprocessing step to dramatically reduce the number of sequence comparisons performed. A list of candidate sequence-pairs, for which the SPEX score exceeds a specified threshold, is constructed. We only perform alignments between sequence pairs in this candidate list. This is significantly faster than comparing each sequence to all sequences in the RSDB.

We measured the performance and scalability of our approach by comparing it to CD-HIT — which is freely available for download — using several releases of the comprehensive Genbank non-redundant (NR) protein database over time[1]. We used the CD-HIT default threshold of $T = 90\%$ and the four releases of

---

[1] Ideally, we would have had more datapoints for this experiment. However, old releases of the NR database are not officially maintained, and thus we could only find four different releases of the database.

**Table 1.** Reduction in collection size for CD-HIT and our approach for various releases of the GenBank NR database

| Release date | Original Size (Mb) | Size reduction | |
|---|---|---|---|
| | | CD-HIT | Our approach |
| 16 July 2000 | 157 | 61.71 Mb (39.56%) | 61.72 Mb (39.57%) |
| 22 May 2003 | 443 | 164.38 Mb (37.33%) | 165.07 Mb (37.48%) |
| 30 June 2004 | 597 | 217.80 Mb (36.71%) | 218.76 Mb (36.87%) |
| 18 August 2005 | 900 | 322.98 Mb (36.08%) | 324.92 Mb (36.30%) |

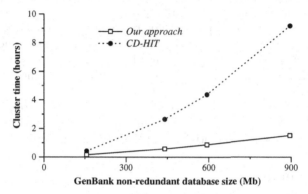

**Fig. 4.** Time required to identify and remove redundant sequences from various releases of the GenBank NR database

GenBank NR database from July 2000 until August 2005 described in Table 1. For tests with CD-HIT we used default parameters except for `max_memory` which we increased to 1.5 Gb. For our approach, we used a final chunk length `finalLength` of 25, a quantum of 9 and 3 iterations. Our threshold for identifying a candidate pair is one matching chunk between the pair. We use this low threshold because we have found that it provides improved accuracy with a negligible increase in execution time. In our experiments with the ASTRAL database described previously and our chosen default parameters, slotted SPEX identifies only 10,143 false positives out of 147,724 sequence pairs identified.

The results in Table 1 show no significant difference in representative collection size between our method and CD-HIT, indicating the two approaches are roughly equivalent in terms of accuracy. Figure 4 shows the runtime for our approach and CD-HIT for the releases of GenBank tested. A visual inspection reveals that our approach scales roughly linearly with the size of the collection while CD-HIT is superlinear. When processing the recent August 2005 collection, our approach is more than 6 times faster than CD-HIT.

## 7   Conclusions

The identification of highly-similar sequence pairs in genomic collections has several important applications in bioinformatics. Previous solutions to this problem involve either an all-against-all comparison with $O(n^2)$ complexity or the use of suffix structures that suffer from large main-memory overheads or long construction times. Therefore, existing approaches are not suitable for processing large collections such as GenBank.

We have applied document fingerprinting techniques to genomic data with the aim of more efficiently identifying pairs of similar sequences in large collections. We have described a new algorithm called slotted SPEX that requires less main-memory and CPU resources when processing genomic collections. We show that slotted SPEX is highly accurate for identifying high-identity sequence pairs, even with long chunk lengths and large quanta. We have also tested the effectiveness of our slotted SPEX approach for removing redundant sequences from large collections. When processing the recent GenBank non-redundant protein database our scheme is more than 6 times faster than the previous fastest approach, CD-HIT, with no significant change in accuracy. Further, our approach scales approximately linearly with collection size.

As future work, we plan to investigate the effectiveness of our approach on nucleotide data. We also plan to apply our slotted SPEX algorithm to English text in applications where the original SPEX algorithm has proved successful.

## Acknowledgements

This work was supported by the Australian Research Council.

## References

Altschul, S., Gish, W., Miller, W., Myers, E. & Lipman, D. (1990), "Basic local alignment search tool", *Journal of Molecular Biology* **215**(3), 403–410.

Altschul, S., Madden, T., Schaffer, A., Zhang, J., Zhang, Z., Miller, W. & Lipman, D. (1997), "Gapped BLAST and PSI–BLAST: A new generation of protein database search programs", *Nucleic Acids Research* **25**(17), 3389–3402.

Bernstein, Y. & Zobel, J. (2004), A scalable system for identifying co-derivative documents, *in* A. Apostolico & M. Melucci, eds, "Proc. String Processing and Information Retrieval Symposium (SPIRE)", Springer, Padova, Italy, pp. 55–67.

Bernstein, Y. & Zobel, J. (2005), Redundant documents and search effectiveness, *in* A. Chowdhury, N. Fuhr, M. Ronthaler, H. Schek & W. Teiken, eds, "Proc. CIKM conference", ACM Press, Bremen, Germany, pp. 736–743.

Brin, S., Davis, J. & García-Molina, H. (1995), Copy detection mechanisms for digital documents, *in* "Proceedings of the ACM SIGMOD Annual Conference", pp. 398–409.

Broder, A. Z., Glassman, S. C., Manasse, M. S. & Zweig, G. (1997), "Syntactic clustering of the web", *Computer Networks and ISDN Systems* **29**(8-13), 1157–1166.

Buckley, C. & Voorhees, E. M. (2000), Evaluating evaluation measure stability, *in* "Proc. ACM SIGIR conference", ACM Press, pp. 33–40.

Burke, J., Davison, D. & Hide, W. (1999), "d2_cluster: A validated method for clustering EST and full-length DNA sequences", *Genome Research* **9**(11), 1135–1142.

Cameron, M., Williams, H. E. & Cannane, A. (2004), "Improved gapped alignment in BLAST", *IEEE Transactions on Computational Biology and Bioinformatics* **1**(3), 116–129.

Cameron, M., Williams, H. E. & Cannane, A. (2005), "A deterministic finite automaton for faster protein hit detection in BLAST", *Journal of Computational Biology* . To appear.

Chandonia, J., Hon, G., Walker, N., Conte, L. L., Koehl, P., Levitt, M. & Brenner, S. (2004), "The ASTRAL compendium in 2004", *Nucleic Acids Research* **32**, D189–D192.

Chao, K., Pearson, W. & Miller, W. (1992), "Aligning two sequences within a specified diagonal band", *Computer Applications in the Biosciences* **8**(5), 481–487.

Fetterly, D., Manasse, M. & Najork, M. (2003), On the evolution of clusters of near-duplicate web pages, *in* R. Baeza-Yates, ed., "Proc. 1st Latin American Web Congress", IEEE, Santiago, Chile, pp. 37–45.

Grossi, R. & Vitter, J. S. (2000), Compressed suffix arrays and suffix trees with applications to text indexing and string matching (extended abstract), *in* "STOC '00: Proceedings of the thirty-second annual ACM symposium on Theory of computing", ACM Press, New York, NY, USA, pp. 397–406.

Gusfield, D. (1997), *Algorithms on Strings, Trees, and Sequences*, Cambridge University Press.

Heintze, N. (1996), Scalable document fingerprinting, *in* "1996 USENIX Workshop on Electronic Commerce".

Holm, L. & Sander, C. (1998), "Removing near-neighbour redundancy from large protein sequence collections", *Bioinformatics* **14**(5), 423–429.

Kurtz, S., Phillippy, A., Delcher, A., Smoot, M., Shumway, M., Antonescu, C. & Salzberg, S. (2004), "Versatile and open software for comparing large genomes", *Genome Biology* **5**(2).

Li, W., Jaroszewski, L. & Godzik, A. (2001a), "Clustering of highly homologous sequences to reduce the size of large protein databases", *Bioinformatics* **17**(3), 282–283.

Li, W., Jaroszewski, L. & Godzik, A. (2001b), "Tolerating some redundancy significantly speeds up clustering of large protein databases", *Bioinformatics* **18**(1), 77–82.

Li, W., Jaroszewski, L. & Godzik, A. (2002), "Sequence clustering strategies improve remote homology recognitions while reducing search times", *Protein Engineering* **15**(8), 643–649.

Malde, K., Coward, E. & Jonassen, I. (2003), "Fast sequence clustering using a suffix array algorithm", *Bioinformatics* **19**(10), 1221–1226.

Manber, U. (1994), Finding similar files in a large file system, *in* "Proceedings of the USENIX Winter 1994 Technical Conference", San Fransisco, CA, USA, pp. 1–10.

Manber, U. & Myers, G. (1993), "Suffix arrays: a new method for on-line string searches", *SIAM Journal on Computing* **22**(5), 935–948.

Park, J., Holm, L., Heger, A. & Chothia, C. (2000), "RSDB: representative sequence databases have high information content", *Bioinformatics* **16**(5), 458–464.

Pearson, W. & Lipman, D. (1988), "Improved tools for biological sequence comparison", *Proceedings of the National Academy of Sciences USA* **85**(8), 2444–2448.

Shivakumar, N. & García-Molina, H. (1999), Finding near-replicas of documents on the web, *in* "WEBDB: International Workshop on the World Wide Web and Databases, WebDB", Springer-Verlag.

Smith, T. & Waterman, M. (1981), "Identification of common molecular subsequences", *Journal of Molecular Biology* **147**(1), 195–197.

Witten, I. H., Moffat, A. & Bell, T. C. (1999), *Managing Gigabytes: Compressing and Indexing Documents and Images*, Morgan Kauffman.

# Using Concept-Based Indexing to Improve Language Modeling Approach to Genomic IR*

Xiaohua Zhou, Xiaodan Zhang, and Xiaohua Hu

College of Information Science & Technology, Drexel University,
3141 Chestnut Street, Philadelphia, PA 19104
xiaohua.zhou@drexel.edu, {xzhang, thu}@cis.drexel.edu

**Abstract.** Genomic IR, characterized by its highly specific information need, severe synonym and polysemy problem, long term name and rapid growing literature size, is challenging IR community. In this paper, we are focused on addressing the synonym and polysemy issue within the language model framework. Unlike the ways translation model and traditional query expansion techniques approach this issue, we incorporate concept-based indexing into a basic language model for genomic IR. In particular, we adopt UMLS concepts as indexing and searching terms. A UMLS concept stands for a unique meaning in the biomedicine domain; a set of synonymous terms will share same concept ID. Therefore, the new approach makes the document ranking effective while maintaining the simplicity of language models. A comparative experiment on the TREC 2004 Genomics Track data shows significant improvements are obtained by incorporating concept-based indexing into a basic language model. The MAP (mean average precision) is significantly raised from 29.17% (the baseline system) to 36.94%. The performance of the new approach is also significantly superior to the mean (21.72%) of official runs participated in TREC 2004 Genomics Track and is comparable to the performance of the best run (40.75%). Most official runs including the best run extensively use various query expansion and pseudo-relevance feedback techniques while our approach does nothing except for the incorporation of concept-based indexing, which evidences the view that semantic smoothing, i.e. the incorporation of synonym and sense information into the language models, is a more standard approach to achieving the effects traditional query expansion and pseudo-relevance feedback techniques target.

## 1 Introduction

Biomedical literature contains a wealth of valuable information. How to help scientists find desired information effectively and efficiently is an important research endeavor. In recent years, genomic information retrieval (GIR) is getting more and more attention from IR community. TREC Genomic Track has attracted lots of talented IR researchers to participate in.

* This research work is supported in part from the NSF Career grant (NSF IIS 0448023). NSF CCF 0514679 and the research grant from PA Dept of Health.

M. Lalmas et al. (Eds.): ECIR 2006, LNCS 3936, pp. 444–455, 2006.
© Springer-Verlag Berlin Heidelberg 2006

However, GIR is challenging IR community most likely due to the following reasons. First, unlike general searching that Google and Yahoo are working on, GIR are working for the scientists who have very specific information need. Second, GIR is dealing with a huge collection of biomedical literature that hinders many existing IR approaches that may be backed by a perfect theoretical model but not scalable to large document collections. Third, in genomic-related literature, a term is often comprised of multiple words; the word-based unigram IR models may lose the semantics of the term. Last, severe synonym and polysemy problem would cause trouble while an IR system tries to match query terms with indexing terms according to their strings instead of meanings.

In this paper, we focus on addressing the synonym and polysemy problem in GIR rather than attempting to solve all the problems. On one hand, synonyms of terms such as genes, proteins, cells and diseases are widely used in biomedical literature. On the other hand, the polysemy of many terms plus the use of partial names and abbreviations have caused the ambiguity of terms. The synonym and polysemy have affected the performance of genomic IR. A fundamental way to solve this problem is to index and search documents through a set of concepts. A concept has a unique meaning in a domain and therefore will not cause any ambiguity. All synonymous terms in the domain will share same concept identities and thus concept-based indexing will easily solve the synonym problem too.

The sense-based information retrieval is a kind of implementation of concept-based indexing and searching. However, word sense disambiguation (WSD) is a challenging task in the area of natural language processing (NLP). The performance (e.g. precision and recall) of WSD in general domain is not satisfying yet, which discourages IR researchers to incorporate word sense into their IR models. Some researchers reported positive outcome of sense-based IR models [15] but most of them failed to show any performance improvement partially due to the low accuracy of WSD in general domain [11]. Furthermore, word senses can not capture well the meaning of many terms in a technical domain such as biomedicine. For example, three individual word senses can not express the meaning of the concept "*high blood pressure*".

Many alternative approaches are then proposed to addressing the synonym and polysemy issue in IR. Latent semantic indexing (LSI) [2] tries to identify the latent semantic structure between terms; thus it can in part solve the synonym problem. However it is not suited to large document collections because the factorization of large matrix is prohibitive. Meanwhile, LSI can not handle the polysemy problem well. Vector space models and other traditional probabilistic models [10, 14] use query expansions to relax the synonym problem. Unlike LSI that is well supported by solid mathematical models, various query expansion techniques are often heuristic. But they achieve great success in IR practice. The translation model [1] extended from the basic unigram language model is a more formal approach for achieving the effects that query expansion techniques target. Berger and Lafferty reported significant improvement of IR performance with translation models [1]. However, there are several difficulties with translation model approach to semantic smoothing under language modeling framework (refer to Section 2 for details) [4].

Recent developments in large domain ontology such as UMLS[1] and statistical language modeling approach to information retrieval lead us to a re-examination of the concept-based indexing and searching. The language modeling approach to IR, initially proposed by Ponte and Croft [9], has been popular with IR community in recent years due to its solid theoretical foundation and promising empirical retrieval performance. We think a well-motivated retrieval framework such as language models might well take the full advantage of concept-based indexing. Meanwhile, the availability of large domain ontology will allow us to extract concepts from documents and queries efficiently and effectively.

To verify our idea, we build a prototyped IR system that indexes and searches documents through both controlled concepts and phrases, and then conduct a comparative experiment on the TREC 2004 Genomic Track data using a basic unigram language model for retrieval. The concept-based approach achieved a 36.94% MAP (mean average precision), significantly higher than the 29.17% MAP of the baseline approach (using phrases for index and search). The result of the concept-based approach is also significantly superior to the average performance (21.72%) of the official runs in TREC 2004 Genomic Track and is comparable to the performance of the best run (40.75%). Considering most official runs including the best run extensively used various query expansion and pseudo-relevance feedback techniques while our approach did nothing except for the incorporation of concept-based indexing, the concept-based approach demonstrated its effectiveness on solving synonym and polysemy issue in IR.

The rest of the paper is organized as follows: Section 2 describes the background of language modeling approach to IR. Section 3 presents a generic ontology-based approach to the concept extraction. Section 4 shows the experiment design and result. A short conclusion finishes the paper.

## 2   Language Modeling Approach to IR

In this section, we shortly review the work on language modeling approach to IR and point out the urgency of the development of semantic smoothing approaches and then propose our concept approach that directly uses concepts to index and search documents with the language modeling framework.

Language modeling approach to information retrieval (IR) was firstly proposed by Ponte and Croft [9]. Basically, the language model uses the generative probability of a query according to the language model of each document in the collection, $p(q \mid d)$, to rank the document for IR. Lafferty and Zhai further made the underlying semantics of the language model clear by linking the notion of relevance to the language model [5]. Under their framework, the relevance of a document to the query is defined as (2.1). Assuming the document is independent of the query conditioned on the event $R = \bar{r}$, the ranking formula is reduced to (2.2). Further ignoring the document prior such as PageRank used by Google in (2.2), the rank formula could be further reduced to be as simple as (2.3).

---

[1] http://www.nlm.nih.gov/research/umls/

$$\log \frac{p(r|Q,D)}{p(\bar{r}|Q,D)} = \log \frac{p(Q|D,r)}{p(Q|D,\bar{r})} + \log \frac{p(rD)}{p(\bar{r}|D)} \qquad (2.1)$$

$$\overset{rank}{=} \log p(Q|D,r) + \log \frac{p(rD)}{p(\bar{r}|D)} \qquad (2.2)$$

$$\overset{rank}{=} \log p(Q|D,r) \qquad (2.3)$$

Let $Q = (A_1, A_2, ..., A_m)$ and assume that the attributes (terms) are independent given $R$ and the document $D$. The ranking formula is then transformed to (2.4) and the term frequency in each document is used to estimate the term $\log p(A_i | D, r)$. For the simplicity of the notation, we will use (2.5) as the basic ranking formula for IR in the present paper.

$$\log p(Q|D,r) = \sum_i \log p(A_i | D, r) \qquad (2.4)$$

$$\log p(Q|D) = \sum_i \log p(A_i | D) \qquad (2.5)$$

However, some query terms may not appear in a given document; thus language models for IR must be smoothed because zero probability can not be assigned to query terms. The *Jelinek-Mercer method* is one of the simplest ways to smooth language models [17]. It involves a linear interpolation of the maximum likelihood model with a background collection model, using a coefficient $\lambda$ to control the influence of the background collection model $C$:

$$\log p_\lambda(a_i | d) = \log\{(1-\lambda)p(a_i | d) + \lambda p(a_i | C)\} \qquad (2.6)$$

Semantic smoothing, which incorporates synonym and sense information into the language model, is regarded as a potentially more effective smoothing approach [4]. With semantic smoothing, a document containing term *high blood pressure* may be retrieved for the query term *hypertension*; a document containing term *ferroportin-1* may not be retrieved for query term *ferroportin-1* because the former refers to a gene in human while the latter refers to a gene in mouse.

Berger and Lafferty present a translation model [1] that maps a document term *t* into a query term $a_i$. With term translations, the estimation of the generative probability for query term $a_i$ becomes (2.7). In the simplest way, a document term can be translated into a query term with high probability if they are synonyms to each other. Thus, the translation model is kind of semantic smoothing. It achieved significant improvement in practice over the baseline system as described in [9].

$$\log p(a_i | d) = \log \sum_j p(a_i | t_j) p(t_j | d) \qquad (2.7)$$

However, there are several difficulties with translation model approach to semantic smoothing in language modeling framework [4]. First, the estimation of translation probability would be a problem due to the lack of sufficient training data. Second, the calculation of the ranking score would be prohibitive for large document collections. Third, it can not incorporate sense information into the language model, i.e. it can not handle polysemy problem well.

We propose in this paper the direct use of controlled concepts for indexing and searching with the framework of language models. Except terms (often words) will be replaced by concepts as indexing and searching unit, no additional modification is required on the basic unigram language model. Thus the concept approach keeps language models as simple as described in (2.5) and (2.6). Furthermore, the calculation of the ranking score will be very efficient in comparison with the translation models. In addition, the concept approach solves both synonym and polysemy problems in IR. The major concern with this approach may be the extraction of concepts. However, with the availability of human-coded domain ontology, we are able to extract multi-word concept names with high accuracy. The further disambiguation of concept name, i.e. mapping a concept name to a unique concept ID in the domain according to the contextual information, is much easier than word sense disambiguation because term polysemy in technical domains such as biomedicine is rarer than generic domains. Therefore, it is reasonable to expect good overall performance of concept extractions.

## 3   Concept Extraction and Indexing Schema

In this section, we will briefly review the past work on biological term extractions and then introduce our generic ontology-based approach. In general, the concept extraction is done in two steps. In the first step, we extract multi-word concept names such as *"high blood pressure"*. We call them *phrases* in this paper. Because a concept name may correspondence to more than one concept ID in UMLS, we need the second step to disambiguate the concept name using the contextual information.

The approaches to biological term extraction roughly fall into two categories, with dictionary [16, 18] or without dictionary [7, 8, 12, 13]. The latter approaches use either hand-coded or machine learned rules to extract terms. It is able to recognize new terms, but it assign semantic class rather than concept IDs to extracted terms. For this reason, we do not use this line of approaches. The dictionary-based approaches use either noun phrase [16] produced by shallow parsers or part of speech patterns [18] to generate term candidates and then check the candidates with the dictionary. Both of them recognize terms based on exact character matching and would yield high precision. However, the extraction recall is often very low because a term name usually has many variants but a dictionary collects very few term variants.

$$I(w) = \max\{S_j(w) \mid j \le n\} = \max\left\{ \frac{1/N(w)}{\sum_i 1/N(w_{ji})} \mid j \le n \right\} \qquad (3.1)$$

To overcome the limitation of exact character matching, we develop an IE system called MaxMatcher that is namely able to recognize concept names by approximate matching. The basic idea of this approach is to capture the important tokens (not all tokens) of a concept name. For example, the token *gyrb* is obviously important to the concept *gyrb protein*; we will treat it as a concept name even if the token *protein* is not present. So the problem is reduced to how to score the importance of each token to a given concept name. Formally, given a concept that has $n$ concept names or variants and let $S_j(w)$ denotes the importance of the token $w$ to the j-th variant name, and let $N(w)$ denotes the number of concepts whose variant names contain token $w$ in the dictionary, and let $w_{ji}$ denotes the $i$-th token in the $j$-th variant name of the concept, the importance of $w$ to the concept is defined as in (3.1).

**Table 1.** Demonstrate the calculation of the importance score of each token to concept C0120543 in UMLS (this concept has three variant names). The number in the parenthesis of the first column is the number of concepts whose variant names contain that token. The final importance score of each token to this concept is listed in the rightmost column.

| Token | gyrb protein | gyrb gene product | DNA gyrase subunit b | Score |
|---|---|---|---|---|
| gyrb (1) | 0.99998 | 0.99990 | | 0.99998 |
| protein (47576) | 0.00002 | | | 0.00002 |
| gene (22186) | | 0.00005 | | 0.00005 |
| product (18724) | | 0.00005 | | 0.00005 |
| b (9548) | | | 0.00083 | 0.00083 |
| DNA (1884) | | | 0.00421 | 0.00421 |
| gyrase (8) | | | 0.98995 | 0.98995 |
| subunit (1580) | | | 0.00501 | 0.00501 |

Using the importance score formula in (3.1), we can easily build a matrix each cell of which stores the importance score of a token (row) to a concept (column) in the dictionary (i.e. UMLS in this paper). Then the concept name extraction is equivalent to tokenize sentences in a document and maximize the match between token sequences and concept names with a few syntactic constraints. The detailed extraction algorithm is presented in Figure 1. We treat a verb, preposition, punctuation and so on as the boundary of a concept name. If two or more concept candidates are found for an extracted concept name, we will further use surrounding tokens (3 to the left and 3 to the right) to narrow down the candidates in the same way as the extraction algorithm shown in Figure 1. The candidate with maximum importance score is chosen in the end unless only one candidate is remained.

*Approximate Matching* is a neat approach to the concept extraction. It completes phrase extraction and phrase meaning disambiguation within one step. More importantly, it achieves high precision as well as high recall. The evaluation of the extraction module on GENIA[2] 3.02 corpus achieved 56.32% *F-score* for exact match and 73.35% for approximate match, which are significantly better than approaches described in [16] and [18] (see table 2). We did not do formal evaluation for meaning disambiguation because no concept is annotated in GENIA corpus.

---

[2] http://www-tsujii.is.s.u-tokyo.ac.jp/GENIA/

Find next starting token $t_s$
$k = 0$
$C = \{c \mid t_s \in T(c)\}$ /*$T(c)$ is the set of tokens appearing in names of concept $c$ */
For each $c \in C$  $S_c = I(t_s,c)$ /*$I(t_s,c)$ is the score of token $t_s$ to concept $c$ */
While  next token $t$ is not bounary token AND $k < skip$
    $N = \{c \mid t \in T(c) \wedge c \in C\}$
    IF $N = \varnothing$ Then  $k = k + 1$
    Else
        $C = N$
        For each $c \in C$  $S_c = S_c + I(t,c)$
    End If
Wend
$C = \{c \mid S_c > threshold \wedge c \in C\}$
If $|C| > 0$ Then
    return concept name and candidate concepts  $c \in C$
End If

**Fig. 1.** The algorithm for extracting one concept name and its candidate concept IDs. The *threshold* is set to 0.95; the maximum number (*skip*) of skipped tokens is set to 1.

**Table 2.** The performance comparison of three different dictionary-based term extraction systems. Please read [16] for the detail of the evaluation method. BioAnnotator actually tested several configurations. But only the configuration with only dictionaries is compared.

| IE Systems | Exact Match | | | Approximate Match | | |
|---|---|---|---|---|---|---|
| | Recall | Precision | F-score | Recall | Precision | F-score |
| MaxMatcher | 57.73 | 54.97 | 56.32 | 75.18 | 71.60 | 73.35 |
| BioAnnotator [16] | 20.27 | 44.58 | 27.87 | 39.75 | 87.67 | 54.70 |
| PatternMatcher [18] | 26.63 | 31.45 | 28.84 | 61.56 | 72.69 | 66.66 |

Given a document, MaxMatcher will extract a set of phrases and concepts. We will use both of them for indexing, called phrase-based indexing and concept-based indexing, respectively. One indexing example is presented below. The advantage of concept-based indexing over phrase-based indexing is twofold. First, it is able to solve synonym problem well because all synonymous terms share same concept IDs. Second, a concept stands for a unique meaning in a domain and thus, it will not cause any ambiguity.

**Example**
*A recent epidemiological study (C0002783) revealed that obesity (C0028754) is an independent risk factor for periodontal disease (C0031090).*
**Phrase Index:** *epidemiological study, obesity, periodontal disease*
**Concept Index:** *C0002783, C0028754, C0031090*

## 4   Experiments

We implement a basic unigram language model as described by formula 2.5 and 2.6. The coefficient $\lambda$ in (2.6) is empirically set to 0.1 in our experiment. The dictionary used for concept extraction is UMLS 2005AA version. With this prototyped IR system, biomedical literature can be indexed and searched either by concepts (*concept approach*) or by phrases (*baseline approach*).

The document collection we used for the experiment is from the TREC 2004 Genomic Track. The collection is a 10-year subset (1994-2003, 4.6 million documents) of the MEDLINE bibliographic database. However, human relevance judgments were merely made to a relative small pool. The pools were built from the top-precedence run from each of the 27 groups. They took the top 75 documents for each topic and eliminated the duplicates to create a single pool for each topic. The average pool size was 976, with a range of 476-1450 [3]. Our prototyped IR system only index and search all human relevance judged documents, i.e. the union of 50 single pools that contains total 42, 255 unique documents.

Following the convention of TREC, we take MAP (Mean Average Precision) as the primary measure for IR performance evaluation. MAP is a comprehensive indicator of IR performance that captures both precision and recall. P@10 (the precision of top 10 documents) and P@100 (the precision of top 100 documents) are treated as secondary measures in our evaluation.

**Table 3.** The comparison of our runs with official runs participated in TREC04 Genomics Track. Runs in TREC are ranked by Mean Average Precision (MAP) [3].

| Run | MAP (%) | P@10 | P@100 |
|---|---|---|---|
| Concept Approach (Our Run) | 36.94 | 59.80 | 44.76 |
| Baseline Approach (Our Run) | 29.17 | 49.53 | 40.82 |
| pllsgen4a2 (the best) | 40.75 | 60.04 | 41.96 |
| uwntDg04tn (the second) | 38.67 | 62.40 | 42.10 |
| pllsgen4a1 (the third) | 36.89 | 57.00 | 39.36 |
| PDTNsmp4 (median) | 20.74 | 40.56 | 23.18 |
| edinauto5 (the worst) | 0.12 | 0.36 | 1.3 |
| Mean@TREC04 (47 runs) | 21.72 | 42.69 | 26.37 |

The concept approach with a basic unigram language model achieves the 36.94% MAP, 59.80% P@10 and 44.76% while the baseline approach (phrase-based indexing and searching) achieves 29.17% MAP, 49.53% P@10 and 40.82% P@100, respectively. The paired-sample T test (M=7.77%, t=3.316, df=49, p=0.002) shows the concept approach is significantly better than the baseline approach in terms of mean average precision. Thus, we can conclude that concept-based indexing and searching in conjunction with language model would significantly improve the performance of IR especially in a very specific domain such as biomedicine. This outcome, however, is slightly different from the result of many previous studies on sense-based IR which failed to show significant performance improvement. A possible explanation is that the concept extraction with an ontology in a very specific domain such as biomedicine would achieve much higher accuracy than word sense disambiguation in generic domains. Furthermore, the language models provide the chance to "smooth" the generative probability (or importance) of terms in a formal manner, which may allow the concept approach to fully take its potential.

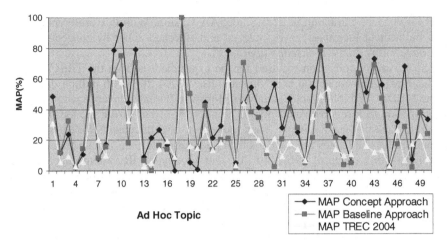

**Fig. 2.** The comparison of the MAP of our runs (Concept Approach and Baseline Approach) with the average MAP of official runs in TREC 2004 Genomic Track on 50 ad hoc topics

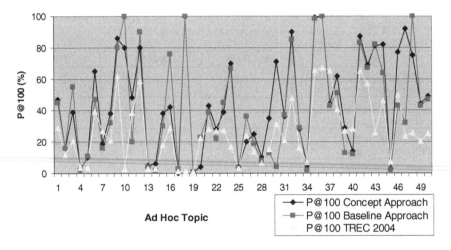

**Fig. 3.** The comparison of the P@100 of our runs (Concept Approach and Baseline Approach) with the average P@100 of official runs in TREC 2004 Genomic Track on 50 ad hoc topics

We further compare the sense approach with the official runs in TREC 2004 Genomic Track. Most runs in the track extensively apply various query expansion and pseudo-relevance feedback techniques to their IR models while our sense approach did nothing except for incorporating concept-based indexing into a basic unigram language model. Surprisingly, the performance of the sense approach is still much better than the average of the runs in the track and is comparable to the best run. The P@100 (44.76%) is even better than that of the best run. This outcome give us more reason to believe that semantic smoothing, i.e. the incorporation of synonym and sense information into the language models, is a more standard approach to achieving the effects the traditional query expansion and pseudo-relevance feedback techniques target.

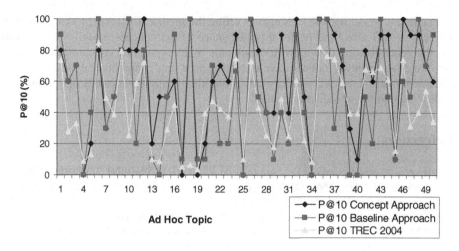

**Fig. 4.** The comparison of the P@10 of our runs (Concept Approach and Baseline Approach) with the average P@10 of official runs in TREC 2004 Genomic Track on 50 ad hoc topics

## 5 Conclusions and Future Work

For biomedical literature, synonyms of terms such as genes, proteins, cells and diseases are widely used while the polysemy of many terms and the use of partial names and abbreviations cause the ambiguity of terms. The synonym and polysemy has affected the performance of genomic IR. Unlike the emerging translation model and the traditional query expansion techniques, we address the issue of synonym and polysemy by incorporating concept-based indexing into a basic language model. In other words, we directly use concepts rather than phrases or individual words to index and search documents under the language modeling framework. It not only maintains the simplicity of language models, but also makes the ranking schema efficient and effective. The comparative experiment on the TREC 2004 Genomic Track data showed that the concept approach achieved significant performance improvement over the baseline approach. This outcome, however, is slightly different from the result of many previous studies on sense-based IR which failed to show significant performance improvement. A possible explanation is that the concept extraction with an ontology in a very specific domain such as biomedicine would achieve much higher accuracy than word sense disambiguation in generic domains. Furthermore, the language models provide the chance to "smooth" the generative probability (or importance) of terms in a formal manner, which may allow the concept approach to fully take its potential.

The performance of the concept model is also significantly superior to the average of official runs in TREC 2004 Genomic Track and is comparable to the performance of the best run. Because most official runs in the track extensively use various query expansion and pseudo-relevance feedback techniques while our approach does nothing except for the incorporation of concept-based indexing, we have more reasons to believe that semantic smoothing, i.e. the incorporation of synonym and sense information into the language models, is a more standard approach to achieving the effects the traditional query expansion and pseudo-relevance feedback techniques target.

For future work, we will continue to refine the method for concept extraction that we believe will affect the retrieval performance of the concept model. We will also test the generalization of our positive outcome by incorporating concept-based indexing into other retrieval models such as vector space model and other traditional probabilistic models. Last, we will take effort on other challenging issues of genomic IR as described in the introduction section.

# References

1.  Berger, A. and Lafferty, J.D., "Information Retrieval as Statistical Translation", *In proceedings of the 1999 ACM SIGIR Conference on Research and Development in Information Retrieval*, 1999, pp. 222-229.
2.  Deerwester, S., Dumais, S. T., Furnas, G. W., Landauer, T. K., and Harshman, R., "Indexing by latent semantic analysis", *Journal of the American Society for Information Science*, 1990, 41(6), pp. 391-407.
3.  Hersh W, et al. "TREC 2004 Genomics Track Overview", The thirteenth Text Retrieval Conference, 2004.
4.  Lafferty, J. and Zhai, C., "Document language models, query models, and risk minimization for information retrieval"**, *2001 ACM SIGIR Conference on Research and Development in Information Retrieval (SIGIR'01)*, 2001
5.  Lafferty, J. and Zhai, C., "Probabilistic relevance models based on document and query generation" , In *Language Modeling and Information Retrieval*, Kluwer International Series on Information Retrieval, Vol. 13, 2003.
6.  Lesk, M., "Automatic Sense Disambiguation: How to Tell a Pine Cone from and Ice Cream Cone", *Proceedings of the SIGDOC'86 Conference, ACM*, 1986.
7.  Mooney, R. J. and Bunescu, R. "Mining Knowledge from Text Using Information Extraction", *SIGKDD Explorations* (special issue on Text Mining and Natural Language Processing), 7, 1 (2005), pp. 3-10.
8.  Palakal, M., Stephens, M.; Mukhopadhyay, S., Raje, R., ,Rhodes, S., "A multi-level text mining method to extract biological relationships" , *Proceedings of the IEEE Computer Society Bioinformatics Conference (CBS2002)*, 14-16 Aug. 2002 Page(s):97 - 108
9.  Ponte, J.M. and Croft, W.B., "A Language Modeling Approach to Information Retrieval", Proceedings of the 21st annual international ACM SIGIR conference on Research and Development in Information Retrieval.
10. Robertson, S. E. and K. Sparck Jones, "Relevance weighting of search terms", *Journal of the American Society for Information Science*, 1976, 27, 129--146.
11. Sanderson, M. 1994, "Word sense disambiguation and information retrieval", *Proceedings of the 17th annual international ACM SIGIR conference on Research and development in information retrieval*, p.142-151, July 03-06, 1994, Dublin, Ireland.
12. Soderland, S., Fisher, D., Aseltine, J., and Lehnert, W., "CRYSTAL: Inducing a Conceptual Dictionary", *Proceedings of the Fourteenth International Joint Conference on Artificial Intelligence*, 1995, pp. 1314-1319.
13. Soderland, S., "Learning Information Extraction rules for Semi-structured and free text", *Machine Learning*, Vol. 34, 1998, pp. 233-272.
14. Sparck Jones, K., Walker, S., and Robertson, S.E., "A probabilistic model of information retrieval: Development and comparative experiments Part I", *Information Processing and Management*, 2000, Vol. 36, pp. 779-808

15. Stokoe, C. and Tait, J. I. 2004. Towards a Sense Based Document Representation for Information Retrieval, in *Proceedings of the Twelfth Text REtrieval Conference (TREC)*, Gaithersburg M.D.
16. Subramaniam, L., Mukherjea, S., Kankar, P., Srivastava, B., Batra, V., Kamesam, P. and Kothari, R., "Information Extraction from Biomedical Literature: Methodology, Evaluation and an Application", *In the Proceedings of the ACM Conference on Information and Knowledge Management*, New Orleans, Louisiana, 2003.
17. Zhai, C. and Lafferty, J., "A study of smoothing methods for language models applied to information retrieval" , *ACM Transactions on Information Systems*, Vol. 2, No. 2, April 2004
18. Zhou, X., Han, H., Chankai, I., Prestrud, A., and Brooks, A., "Converting Semi-structured Clinical Medical Records into Information and Knowledge", *Proceeding of The International Workshop on Biomedical Data Engineering (BMDE) in conjunction with the 21st International Conference on Data Engineering (ICDE)*, Tokyo, Japan, April 5-8, 2005.

# The Effects on Topic Familiarity on Online Search Behaviour and Use of Relevance Criteria

Lei Wen[1], Ian Ruthven[1], and Pia Borlund[2]

[1] Department of Computer and Information Sciences,
University of Strathclyde, Glasgow, G1 1XH, United Kingdom
amanda_wen37@hotmail.com, ir@cis.strath.ac.uk
[2] Department of Information Studies,
Royal School of Library and Information Science,
DK-9000 Aalborg, Denmark
pb@db.dk

**Abstract.** This paper presents an experimental study on the effect of topic familiarity on the assessment behaviour of online searchers. In particular we investigate the effect of topic familiarity on the resources and relevance criteria used by searchers. Our results indicate that searching on an unfamiliar topic leads to use of more generic and fewer specialised resources and that searchers employ different relevance criteria when searching on less familiar topics.

## 1 Introduction

Searchers of online resources make a variety of judgments on the material retrieved by Information Retrieval (IR) systems. In evaluations of IR systems these judgments are often simplified into decisions of relevance: are the documents relevant or not to the searcher? However, studies of how people search for information, and the assessments they make on retrieved material, show that this is overly simplistic and people instead make a range of decisions on material they encounter whilst they are searching. These decisions are generally known as *relevance criteria*, reasons people give for assessing material as relevant. There have been many studies of relevance criteria uncovering either which criteria are used in searching [1], how criteria change over time [7] and how these criteria relate to the search problem being undertaken [8].

Previous work [e.g. 4, 5, 6] also shows that topic familiarity can affect a searcher's search strategy and the type of information they believe they will require. In this paper we present the results of a pilot study to investigate the degree to which a searcher's familiarity with a topic affects their use of resources and their ability to predict which relevance criteria will be important to them in a search.

## 2 Methodology

18 participants took part in this study, all of whom were postgraduate students in Masters' level courses at the University of Strathclyde. Each participant was asked to search on basis of two simulated work task situations [2] both of which had a

M. Lalmas et al. (Eds.): ECIR 2006, LNCS 3936, pp. 456–459, 2006.
© Springer-Verlag Berlin Heidelberg 2006

common structure in which the participant was asked to find 10 or more good resources (books, web pages, or articles) that they would recommend to a colleague interested in that topic. The major difference between the two tasks was the task *topic*.

The first task, given to all participants, asked the participants to find information on the topic of 'multimedia information retrieval'. As all participants took part in a compulsory course in Information Retrieval as part of their degree course, this was a topic with which we expected them to be familiar. For the second task the topic varied between participants. Participants were asked at the start of the study which of three domains (psychology, history, or architecture) was the least familiar to them and they were then given a search task based on that topic. 11 participants chose architecture as the topic of which they had least knowledge, 2 chose history and 5 chose psychology.

Simply asking the participants which topic is least familiar does not guarantee that they are unfamiliar with the topic. However, as part of the study the participants were asked to assess the familiarity of each search topic on a 5-point scale (1 being 'very unfamiliar', 5 being 'very familiar). The average rating given to the familiar task was 4.1, and 2.1 for the unfamiliar task. Using a Wilcoxon Test we found a statistically significant difference between the participants' responses showing that the participants felt more familiar with the topic 'multimedia information retrieval'.

For both search tasks the participants were asked to find a number of resources. As the study was aimed at understanding the effects of topic familiarity on the participants' existing search behaviour we placed no restrictions on the participants search strategies: the participants could search in any way they felt comfortable and could use any search engine, database or visit any website they wished. The only restriction we placed on their searching was that they were not allowed to ask for recommendations from the investigators or to ask for opinions on the resources they found. The participants were restricted to 15 minutes on each search task and the study took place in the departmental laboratory which was the main laboratory for the participants and hence is a familiar place to carry out work tasks.

As well as the effects of topic familiarity on search behaviour we were also interested in how topic familiarity would affect people's relevance criteria: would people with less familiarity use different criteria in assessing relevance? To investigate this we gave the participants a list of 12 relevance criteria drawn from the criteria described in [1]. We selected the relevance criteria that could reasonably be applied to any search task and which were mentioned as being the most frequent in [1]. The relevance criteria we chose were *depth/scope/specificity*, *accuracy/validity*, *clarity*, *currency* (recent information), *tangibility* (material contains specific facts), *quality* of sources, *accessibility* (information is available), *verification* (*verification a.* information is consistent with other information and *verification b.* the participant agrees with the information), *affectiveness* (*affectiveness a.* the participant enjoys reading the material and *affectiveness b.* the document is interesting) and *background experience* (participant is familiar with the topic or source of the document).

The criteria were presented in a list with a simple English description of each criterion as part of the initial study interview rather than before each search task. Each participant was asked to note which criteria they felt would be important to them in assessing material for different types of search task including familiar and unfamiliar tasks. There was a slight, although not significant, difference in the number of criteria chosen per task (average of 6 criteria for familiar task vs. 5.6 criteria for unfamiliar task) and a similar distribution of criteria to both tasks. The main difference was that all participants rated the criterion *background experience* as being important for the familiar task whereas only 4 participants rated this as important for the unfamiliar task. *Currency* and *verification b.* were also more important for the familiar task.

## 3  Findings

The effects of topic familiarity in this study can be seen in two areas of searching: the use and selection of resources and how searchers employed relevance criteria. The participants used more formal resources and search engines when searching on the familiar task than the unfamiliar task (average 2.6 resources in the familiar task vs. average of 3 for the unfamiliar task) with a higher use of domain specific resources on the familiar task, e.g. Google Scholar, or ACM Digital Library, than on the unfamiliar task where more generic resources were used such as Yahoo, or Wikipedia. The participants' reasons for using these generic resources were that they helped either structure their searching, e.g. Yahoo hierarchies, or provided more information on the topic which helped the participant assess the quality of retrieved material, e.g. Wikipedia. This is in line with work by Michel [5] who found that topically experienced searchers are better at assessing the relevancy of retrieved objects.

There was a strong relationship between familiarity and the number of sources recommended: participants recommended significantly more documents on the unfamiliar task than on the familiar task (average 9.9 familiar task vs. 12.6 unfamiliar task). This relates to the work of Byström and Järvelin [3] who found that low task familiarity increases the complexity of a task and that, as task complexity increases, the need for more sources of information increases. The increase in number of sources found could also be due to an increased number of sources available. It is difficult to assess the number of sources available for a given topic on the Internet but we note that 15 of the 18 participants recommended more sources for the unfamiliar task.

In section 2 we explained that the participants were asked to predict which relevance criteria they would use in assessing material. After searching we asked the participants to view the recommended resources and discuss *why* they would recommend them to a colleague. This was to elicit whether the criteria they did use in assessing relevance were the ones that they predicted would be important. For familiar tasks the predicted relevance criteria were generally similar to the ones used in assessing the retrieved material. For unfamiliar tasks, however, they were often not the same and criteria such as depth/scope, or accuracy could not be easily employed. Although the participants were confident before searching that these criteria were important features of the information they sought, these were criteria that could not easily be judged on an unfamiliar topic. Instead, participants compensated for their lack of topic familiarity by using other criteria. For example, *tangibility* was employed as a substitute measure for *accuracy* because the extent to which specific information was provided was seen as a measure of the reliability of information.

The use of a criterion such as *accessibility* was also not straightforward. On unfamiliar tasks participants would recommend resources that were less accessible, e.g. a book from Amazon rather than a freely available book from the University Library, because generic sites such as Amazon gave more information on the resources. As one participant noted "Amazon represented more book details…even a few paragraphs from each chapters, this information is very helpful to evaluate a book which I have never seen before". The University library, on the other hand, only supplies limited bibliographic information. The degree to which information is consistent with other information (relevance criterion *verification a*) was more important for unfamiliar tasks because participants reported that in early search stages they were forced to learn about a topic whilst searching and consistent information helped the process of learning about a topic.

# 4  Conclusions

This paper reports on a pilot test to investigate the effects of topic familiarity on search behaviour. We found that topic familiarity can affect the number and type of resources selected by searchers and the ability of a searcher to use relevance criteria.

## Acknowledgements

We gratefully acknowledge the help of our participants and the comments made by the referees. The research is supported by The Royal Society Research Project *Task-centred evaluation methodologies for interactive information retrieval*.

## References

1. Barry, C. and Schamber, L.: Users' Criteria for Relevance Evaluation: a Cross-situational Comparison. Inf. Proc. & Manag. 34. 2/3. (1998) 219–236.
2. Borlund, P.: The IIR Evaluation Model: a Framework for Evaluation of Interactive Information Retrieval Systems. Inf. Res. 8.3. (2003) *http://informationr.net/ir/8-3/paper152.html*
3. Byström, K. and Järvelin, K.: Task Complexity Affects Information Seeking and Use. Inf. Proc. & Manag. 31. 2. (1985) 191–213.
4. Hsieh-Yee, I.: Effects of Search Experience and Subject Knowledge on the Search Tactics of Novice and Experiences Searchers. J. Am. Soc. Inf.  44. 3. (1993) 161–174.
5. Michel, D.: What is Used During Cognitive Processing in Information Retrieval and Library Searching? Eleven Sources of Search Information. J. Am. Soc. Inf. 45. 7. (1994). 498–514.
6. Serola, S. and Vakkari, P.: The Anticipated and Assessed Contribution of Information Types in References Retrieved for Preparing a Research Proposal. J. Am. Soc. Inf. 56. 4. (2005) 373-381.
7. Vakkari, P. and Hakala, N.: Changes in Relevance Criteria and Problem Stages in Task Performance. J. Doc. 56 .5. (2000) 540–562.
8. Yuan, X-J, Belkin, N. J. and Kim, J-Y.: The Relationship Between ASK and Relevance Criteria. In: Järvelin, K., Beaulieu, M., Baeza-Yates, R., and Myaeng, S. H. (eds): Proceedings of the 25th Annual International ACM SIGIR Conference on Research and Development in Information Retrieval. (2002) 359–360.

# PERC: A Personal Email Classifier

Shih-Wen Ke, Chris Bowerman, and Michael Oakes

School of Computing and Technology,
University of Sunderland,
St. Peter's Campus, Sunderland, SR6 0DD, UK
{george.ke, chris.bowerman, Michael.oakes}@sunderland.ac.uk

**Abstract.** Improving the accuracy of assigning new email messages to small folders can reduce the likelihood of users creating duplicate folders for some topics. In this paper we presented a hybrid classification model, PERC, and use the Enron Email Corpus to investigate the performance of kNN, SVM and PERC in a simulation of a real-time situation. Our results show that PERC is significantly better at assigning messages to small folders. The effects of different parameter settings for the classifiers are discussed.

## 1 Introduction

Automatic categorising emails into user-defined folders is still an under-explored area in automatic text categorisation. In our initial user study we found that a large proportion of users sometimes cannot remember which folders they have created or which folders they should file the email under. In these circumstances, users tend to create new folders, which results in creating duplicate folders for some topics. Bekkerman et al. [1] reported that newly-created folders significantly affect the performance of classifiers for two main reasons: usually these new folders contain a relatively small number of emails, which means fewer positive training examples are available, and classifiers need be re-trained in order to recognise these new folders. Therefore, reducing the likelihood of users creating new folders when they forget which folders they already have can significantly improve the performance of an email classifier. To achieve this, the accuracy of assigning emails to folders that are created in the first place needs to be improved, i.e. improve the accuracy of assignment to small folders.

Klimt and Yang [6] investigated the performance of a Support Vector Machine (SVM) on the Enron email corpus using different fields, such as "From", "Subject" and "To, CC". No field was clearly more useful than the others. Zhang and Yang [9] examined the different behaviour of three selected linear classification methods – linear SVM, linear regression and logistic regression – on rare categories with few positive training examples by randomly extracting small samples of positive examples from the 12 most common categories of Reuters-21578. However, this collection of news stories is not directly comparable with the Enron corpus of email messages used in the experiments described here. Kiritchenko and Matwin [5] applied the co-training technique to iteratively train classifiers starting with a small number of positive examples and a larger number of unlabelled examples. None of the authors cited in this section evaluated the k-Nearest Neighbour (kNN) technique.

M. Lalmas et al. (Eds.): ECIR 2006, LNCS 3936, pp. 460–463, 2006.
© Springer-Verlag Berlin Heidelberg 2006

## 2  The PERC Classifier

We propose a hybrid classification model, PERC (PERsonal email Classifier) here. PERC combines the characteristics of kNN and centroid-based classification [3]. One centroid $c_i$ for each category $C_i$ is obtained by summing the weight values of each attribute in all training examples of the category [4], then the weight value of each attribute is divided by the number of training examples in the category. In the test phase PERC finds the k nearest neighbours in the training data set to each test document in turn. The similarity between a test document $x$ and the training document $d_j$ is added to the similarity between $x$ and $c_i$, the centroid of the category that $d_j$ belongs to. Hence PERC's algorithm can be written as:

$$sim(x, C_i) = \sum_{d_j \in kNN} (sim(x, d_j) y(d_j, C_i) + sim(x, c_i) y(d_j, C_i))$$

where $y(d_j, C_i) \in \{0, 1\}$ is the classification for document $d_j$ with respect to category $C_i$; and $sim(x, d_j)$ is the similarity of $x$ to $d_j$; and $sim(x, c_i)$ is the similarity of $x$ to the centroid $c_i$ of the category that $d_j$ belongs to. The $sim(x, C_i)$ values for each category are then sorted in descending order when k nearest neighbours are calculated. The decision to assign $x$ to $C_i$ can be made using different thresholding strategies [8].

Similar work has been carried out by [7] and [2]. Lam and Ho [7] proposed the generalised instance set (GIS) algorithm which constructs one set of generalised instances (GI) to replace the original training examples of each category. Lam and Ho assigned a test document to the category by determining the product of similarity score of each GI and the test document and the association factor between the GI and the category. One of the disadvantages of GIS is that the performance of GIS depends on the order in which positive instances are selected. The kNN model-based approach proposed by Guo et al. [2] tried to tackle the drawbacks of the GI and Rocchio methods by building several local centroids for each category and the GI as a model to represent the whole training dataset. However, the performance of GIS and kNN model-based approach on rare categories are unknown and their results are not directly comparable.

## 3  Evaluation

We applied SVM [1], kNN [8] and PERC to seven large email directories selected from the Enron Corpus [1]. Unlike [1,6] we divided each user's emails according to the week in which they were received,  regardless of how many emails they received in that week, because it takes different lengths of time for different users to accumulate the same number of messages. For example it took *sanders-r* 26 weeks to collect the first 100 messages. Stemming and stopword removal were applied to all messages, which were then represented as term frequency vectors using a bag-of-words document representation. We assumed mono-classification, i.e. only one folder could be assigned to each message in the experiment. In our simulation, the classifiers were evaluated and updated "weekly" (i.e. after consideration of the all the messages received in the space of one week) over a period of 26 weeks, starting at the second week because the first week's messages were all training data. Test messages belonging to folders that did not exist in the current week's training data were ignored in that week's evaluation, but were used as training data in the following week.

In order to investigate the overall performance of these three classifiers, results were averaged over each user in the dataset. We set $k$ to be 1, 3, 5, 7, 10, 15, 20, and 25 for different kNN and PERC trials and used the RCut thresholding strategy ($t=1$) and the cosine similarity function as the similarity measure. We fixed the SVM parameters $c$ (trade-off between training error and margin) = 0.01 [1] or $c = 1$ (the default value) and kept cost-factor $j = 1$ at all times.

## 4   Results

Figures 1 and 2 summarise the performance of SVM, kNN and PERC. SVM with $c = 1$ is denoted as SVM1 and SVM with $c = 0.01$ is denoted as SVM2. Macro-$F_1$ and micro- $F_1$ averaging are presented. Note that micro-precision, micro-recall and micro-$F_1$ are all equal in mono-classification. In the micro-averaging evaluation SVM1, kNN and PERC performed similarly with SVM2 performing much more poorly. In the macro-averaging evaluation PERC outperformed the other classifiers, except where kNN performed slightly better than PERC when k =15. We performed paired-t tests on the results shown in Figures 1and 2. There were no significant differences between PERC, kNN and SVM1 for the micro-averaging evaluations. However, for the macro-averaging evaluations, PERC significantly outperformed kNN (t=2.786, p=0.032), SVM1 (t=2.533, p=0.044) and SVM2 (t=5.926, p=0.001). This suggests that PERC can reduce the likelihood of users creating new folders as the macro-averaged scores are more influenced by the classifier's performance on small folders.

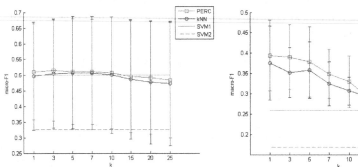

**Fig. 1.** Micro-averaging $F_1$ over all users with standard deviation for kNN, SVM and PERC

**Fig. 2.** Macro-averaging $F_1$ over all users with standard deviation for kNN, SVM and PERC

## 5   Conclusions

In this paper we have presented a hybrid classification model, PERC, and investigated the performance of kNN, SVM and PERC in a simulation of a real-time situation where classifiers were trained weekly. We also investigated the behaviour of kNN and

PERC with different values of $k$ and that of SVM with different settings of trade-off between training error and margin. Bekkerman [1] points out that incoming messages are usually more related to those that are recently received. This may be the reason why kNN and PERC performed better with smaller k, where a small number of the most related messages in the training data are considered. SVM2 performed poorly in our experiments which indicates that the parameters of SVM can be very sensitive to the number of training data available and the way it is trained (such as on a weekly basis), but it is not clear what setting of SVM parameters will achieve the optimal performance in email classification as the training dataset grows over time. PERC takes the advantage of the centroids which summarise the content of each category. This can be very important in email classification because centroids contain information about both the older and the newer messages. In our future work we will investigate the effect of various parameter settings and use of time on email classification. A questionnaire-based study is being conducted in order to indicate the behaviour of real users in email management.

# References

1. Bekkerman, R., McCallum, A. and Huang, G.: Automatic Categorization of Email into Folders: Benchmark Experiments on Enron and SRI Corpora. CIIR Technical Report IR-418. Available at: http://www.cs.umass.edu/~ronb/papers/email.pdf (2004)
2. Guo, G., Wang, H., Bell, D., Bi, Y. and Greer., K.: KNN Model-Based Approach in Classification. In ODBASE (2003)
3. Han, E. & Karypis. G.: Centroid-Based Document Classification: Analysis and Experimental Results. In Proceedings of the 4th European Conference on Principles of Data Mining and Knowledge Discovery (2000) 424-431
4. Ke, S., Bowerman, C., Oakes, M.: Mining Personal Data Collections to Discover Categories and Category Labels. In International Workshop of Text Mining Research, Practice and Opportunities, RANLP (2005) 17-22
5. Kiritchenko, S. & Matwin, S.: Email Classification with Co-Training. In CASCON (2001)
6. Klimt, B. & Yang, Y.: The Enron Corpus: A New Dataset for Email Classification Research. In ECML (2004)
7. Lam, W. & Ho, C.: Using a Generalized Instance Set for Automatic Text Categorization. In SIGIR (1998) 81-89
8. Yang, Y.: A Study on Thresholding Strategies for Text Classification. In SIGIR (2001) 137-145
9. Zhang, J. & Yang, Y.: Robustness of Regularized Linear Classification Methods in Text Classification. In SIGIR (2003) 190-197

# Influence Diagrams for Contextual Information Retrieval

Lynda Tamine-Lechani and Mohand Boughanem

Université de Paul Sabatier, Laboratoire IRIT,
118 Route de Narbonne, 31400 Toulouse CEDEX 06, France

**Abstract.** The purpose of contextual information retrieval is to make some exploration towards designing user specific search engines that are able to adapt the retrieval model to the variety of differences on user's contexts. In this paper we propose an influence diagram based retrieval model which is able to incorporate contexts, viewed as user's long-term interests into the retrieval process.

**Keywords:** personalized information access, influence diagrams, user context.

## 1  Introduction

A key challenge in information retrieval is the use of contextual evidence within the ad-hoc retrieval.Several approaches explored in contextual retrieval area, techniques for building the user's profile [3, 6, 2] and using it in the retrieval process [2, 7, 5, 8]. Most of these approaches employ implicit user feedback to model the related long-term interests as contexts represented by word vectors [2], classes of concepts [3] or a hierarchy of concepts [6]. Since the contexts are modeled, they are exploited in order to refine the query [2, 8], re-rank the documents [7] or model the whole retrieval process [5, 8]. The latest goal is precisely our own one. Our contribution is particularly based on the belief that contextual retrieval is a decision-making problem. For this reason we propose to apply influence diagrams witch are an extension of Bayesian networks to such problems, in order to solve the hard problem of user's relevance estimation.

## 2  The Influence Diagram Based Model

An influence diagram [4] is a graphic model used to represent and resolve a decision-making problem. Our interest in influence diagrams is namely to model the decision problem of document relevancy by taking into account the influence of both user's long-term interests and the query submitted.

### 2.1  Diagram Topology

Figure 1 illustrates the qualitative component of our influence diagram based retrieval model. The set of nodes $V$ is composed of four different types of nodes

M. Lalmas et al. (Eds.): ECIR 2006, LNCS 3936, pp. 464–467, 2006.
© Springer-Verlag Berlin Heidelberg 2006

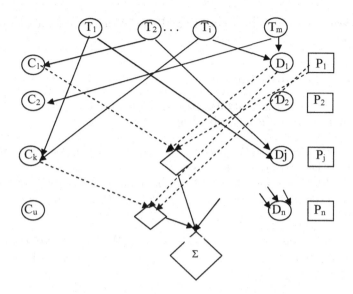

**Fig. 1.** Influence diagram-based retrieval model

$V = D \cup T \cup P \cup C$. The set $D = \{D_1, D_2, , D_n\}$ represent the set of documents in the collection, $T = \{T_1, T_2, , T_m\}$ represent the set of terms used to index these documents, $P = \{P_1, P_2, .., P_n\}$ represent the decisions to state that these documents are relevant and $C = \{C_1, C_2, , C_u\}$ represent the set of a specific user's contexts expressing his long-term interests. These different types of nodes are described below:

- *Chance nodes.* There are three types of chance nodes: documents, terms and contexts. Each document node $D$, represents a binary random variable taking values in the set $\{d, \overline{d}\}$, where $d$ represents 'the document d is relevant for a given query', and $\overline{d}$ represents 'the document d is not relevant for a given query'. Each term node $T$ represents a binary random variable taking values in the set $\{t, \overline{t}\}$, where $t$ represents 'the term t is representative for a given query' and $\overline{t}$ represents 'the term t is not representative for a given query'. Each context node $C$ represents a binary random variable taking values in the set $\{c, \overline{c}\}$, where $c$ represents 'the context c is relevant for a given query' and $\overline{c}$ represents 'the context c is not relevant for a given query'.
- *Utility nodes.* There is an utility node corresponding to each decision node.
- *Decision nodes.* Each decision node $P$ represents a binary random variable $p$, taking values in the set $\{p, \overline{p}\}$ . These values correpsonds to each pair $\{d, \overline{d}\}$ corresponding to a document node.

Influence arcs join each node term $T_i \in \tau(D_j)$ and each document node $(D_j) \in D$. Similarly there are influence arcs joining each node term $T_i \in \tau(C_k)$ and each context node $C_k \in C$. We note $Pa(.)$ the parent sets for each node in the network: $\forall T_i \in T, Pa(T_i) = \varnothing, \forall D_j \in D, Pa(D_j) = \tau(D_j), \forall C_k \in C, Pa(C_k) = \tau(C_k)$.

The informative arcs point to utility nodes for which ordered numerical values are assigned.

## 2.2 Probability Distributions

The estimation of the probability distributions stored in chance and decision nodes is carried out in the following ways:

- *Term node:* $p(t_i/pa(t_i)) = p(t_i)$ as $Pa(T_i) = \varnothing$. We assume that $p(t_i) = \alpha$, $p(\overline{t_i}) = (1-\alpha)$ $\forall t_i \in T$ $(0 \le \alpha \le 1)$.
- *Document node:* $p(d_j/pa(d_j)) = \sum_{t_i \in rel(pa(d_j))} Wtd(i,j)$ where $rel(pa(d_j)) = \{T_i \in Pa(D_j)/t_i \in pa(d_j)\}$, $Wtd(i,j) = \frac{wtd_{ij}}{\sum_{t_l \in \tau(D_j)} w_{lj}}$ $wtd_{ij}$ is the weight of the term $T_i$ in the document $D_j$.
- *Context node:* $p(c_k/pa(c_k)) = \sum_{t_i \in rel(pa(c_k))} Wtc(i,k)$ where $rel(pa(c_k)) = \{T_i \in Pa(C_k)/t_i \in pa(c_k)\}$, $Wtc(i,k) = \frac{wtc_{ik}}{\sum_{t_l \in \tau(C_k)} wtc_{lk}}$ $wtc_{ik}$ is the weight of the term $T_i$ in the context $C_k$.

# 3 Query Evaluation

The query evaluation consists in the propagation of new evidence through the diagram, like in Bayesian networks [1], in order to maximize a re-ranking utility measure. More precisely, given a query $Q$ represented by a set of positive terms $(\tau(Q) = \{T_1, T_2, ..., T_r\})$, the retrieval process starts placing the evidence in the term nodes (marginally independent): $p(t_i/Q) = 1$ if $T_i \in \tau(Q)$ and $p(t_i/Q) = \alpha$ if $T_i \notin \tau(Q)$. Then, the inference process is run by maximizing the re-ranking utility measure $\frac{EU(p/Q)}{EU(\overline{p}/Q)}$ computed as follows: (we assume that documents are independent given the query and context)

$$EU(p/Q) = \sum_{c_k \in \{c,\overline{c}\}, d_j \in \{d,\overline{d}\}} u(p/c_k, d_j) p(c_k/Q) p(d_j/Q) \tag{1}$$

$$EU(\overline{p}/Q) = \sum_{c_k \in \{c,\overline{c}\}, d_j \in \{d,\overline{d}\}} u(\overline{p}/c_k, d_j) p(c_k/Q) p(d_j/Q) \tag{2}$$

When using the probability functions used respectively for document and context nodes, we compute respectively $p(d_j/Q)$ and $p(c_k/Q)$ as follows:

$$p(d_j/Q) = \alpha + (1-\alpha) \sum_{T_i \in (\tau(D_j) \cap \tau(Q))} Wtd(i,j) \tag{3}$$

$$p(c_k/Q) = \alpha + (1-\alpha) \sum_{T_i \in (\tau(C_k) \cap \tau(Q))} Wtc(i,k) \tag{4}$$

# 4    Conclusion

We proposed in this poster, an influence diagram based model for contextual information retrieval. This model allows to make inferences about the user's search intention and to take ideal actions based on probability query term distributions over the document collection and the user' contexts. We are currently experimenting with the graph representation, identification of user' contexts and parameters to be used for query evaluation.

# Acknowledgment

This research was partially supported by the French Ministry of Research and New Technolologies under the ACI program devoted to Data Masses (ACI-MD), project MD-33.

# References

1. S. Acid, L..M. De Campos, J.M, Fernadez-Luna J.F. An information retrieval model based on simple Bayesian networks. International Journal of Intelligent Systems, 18, pages, 251-265, 2003
2. J. Budzik, K.J Hammond, Users interactions with everyday applications as context for just-in-time information access. In Proceedings of the 5th international conference on intelligent user interfaces, pages 44-51, 2000
3. J.P Mc Gowan , A multiple model approach to personalised information access. Master Thesis in computer science, Faculty of science, University College Dublin, February 2003
4. F. Jensen : Bayesian networks and decision graphs. Berlin: Springer Verlag, 2001
5. Lin C., Xue G.R., Zeng H.J., Yu Y., Using probabilistic latent semantic analysis for personalized Web search. In Proceedings of the APWeb Conference, Springer Verlag Eds, pages 707-711, 2005
6. F. Liu, C. Yu, Personalized Web search for improving retrieval effectiveness, IEEE Transactions on knowledge and data engineering, 16(1), pages 28-40, 2004
7. M. Speretta, S. Gauch, Personalizing search based on user search histories, In 30th Conference on information retrieval and management, CIKM, 2004
8. J.R Wen, N. Lao, W.Y. Ma, Probabilistic model for contextual retrieval. In Proceedings of the 27th Annual International ACM SIGIR Conference on Research and development in information retrieval, pages 57-63, Sheffield, 2004

# Morphological Variation of Arabic Queries

Asaad Alberair and Mark Sanderson

Department of Information Studies, University of Sheffield,
Regent Court, 211 Portobello St, Sheffield, S1 4DP, UK
{a.alberair, m.sanderson}@shef.ac.uk

**Abstract.** Although it has been shown that in test collection based studies, stemming improves retrieval effectiveness in an information retrieval system, morphological variations of queries searching on the same topic are less well understood. This work examines the broad morphological variation that searchers of an Arabic retrieval system put into their queries. In this study, 15 native Arabic speakers were asked to generate queries, morphological variants of query words were collated across users. Queries composed of either the commonest or rarest variants of each word were submitted to a retrieval system and the effectiveness of the searches was measured. It was found that queries composed of the more popular morphological variants were more likely to retrieve relevant documents that those composed of less popular.

## 1 Introduction

In a text retrieval system, a query is posted to the retrieval system to satisfy an information need. Retrieval systems apply matching functions; measuring the similarity between the query terms and documents in the collection. Languages are dynamic and humans are capable of expressing similar ideas in both queries and documents with the use of different vocabulary. There is always a chance for a query to be formulated with terms that are different from terms in the document. A query term can retrieve morphologically related terms in the collection by means of stemming, where words are reduced to their root or stem forms with the aim of improving retrieval system effectiveness. A number of test collection-based evaluations have shown that normalizing user queries with stemmers generally improves retrieval effectiveness (Hull, 1996; Krovetz, 1993), however, there is to the best of our knowledge, little research that studies morphological variation of queries analyzed across a user population. As part of a wider study of the expectations Arabic users have of the processing IR systems might perform, a study of the morphological variation that might be found in Arabic language queries was conducted.

## 2 Methodology

Studying morphological variation within a topic is somewhat challenging as there is little existing data on the variability of queries: test collections at best hold different versions of topics that vary in length. Eliciting from a group of users a variety of

M. Lalmas et al. (Eds.): ECIR 2006, LNCS 3936, pp. 468–471, 2006.
© Springer-Verlag Berlin Heidelberg 2006

queries for a particular topic was the task of the TREC Query Track, which ran in 1999 and 2000 (Buckley, 2000). Simply asking users to think of a query after being shown the text of a topic, is likely to result in users generating query words based purely on the topic text, resulting in queries failing to show the broad morphological variations of queries for a particular topic that maybe observed in operational settings. Buckley attempted to address this issue in the TREC query track by using a number of different approaches to inform users of the subject of a topic. The approaches informed users of the topic area by showing them both topic text and relevant documents before asking users to write a query related to the topic. Even with such a variation, however, it is still quite possible that users' choice of terms will be influenced by the texts they are shown. Therefore, in this experiment, we extended Buckley's approach to user topic generation, by recruiting users who were bilingual. Participants were asked to formulate Arabic language queries based on topics and sample relevant documents that were written in English. It was hoped that the process of translating English to Arabic would reduce the influence on users' word choices. The three approaches used were as follows:

- Length-Free Query: Participants were shown a topic, but no supporting material. After reading the topic each participant was asked to formulate a query freely, without any restrictions.
- Natural Language Sentence Query: Each participant was shown two documents relevant to a particular topic. After reading the two, participants were asked to formulate appropriate natural language sentence queries that could retrieve similar documents.
- Short Query: Participants were shown a topic and two examples of relevant documents to that topic. Participants were then asked to formulate a short query. The length of this form of query was not specified to the participants.

The topics used were the 25 topics of the TREC-2001 Arabic collection; each participant formulated 25 queries (one from each topic). Fifteen native Arabic speakers were used. Topics and query generation approaches were arranged in a Latin Square to avoid any bias in topic generation. All participants were male and either students studying at the university or working in an academic institute in the United Kingdom. Participants were volunteers.

In total, 375 queries were created. For each topic, the words of the fifteen user queries were manually arranged into separate classes, where each class contained morphologically related terms (i.e. terms that conflate to one root). (Note, that an Arabic root encompasses a much broader range of word forms than a morphological root in a language like English.) For each root-class, the number of times each term occurred in a class was counted. Out of each topic's classes, three types of queries were generated, namely:

- All Morphological Variants (AMV) - A query of this category includes the union of all terms produced for a topic. Therefore, for each topic, queries of this category were the longest and morphologically the richest. For the purposes of these experiments, AMV can be regarded as a stemming run.
- Most Repeated Terms (MRT) - It was observed that a number of terms from each topic were used more than once by different participants to formulate a query.

A query of this category therefore, was formed by selecting the most repeated term from each class. If more than one term shared the same frequency of being mentioned in a class, then a term was chosen at random to be put in the query.

- Least Repeated Terms (LRT) - A query of this category contained terms that are the least used by participant. Conditions used in formulating queries of the MRT category were also applied when formulating queries of this category. The MRT and LRT query categories were identical in length.

The three queries were posted to an Arabic Information Retrieval System (InQuery). The collection as described in (Voorhees and Harman 2001) consisted of 869 megabytes of news articles taken from Agence France-Presse (AFP) Arabic newswire. It contained 383,872 documents or articles dated from May 1994 through December 2000. InQuery was set to a cut-off level of twenty documents.

There are some variations in the way Arabic text was presented across Arabic speaking countries, beside differences in the individual style of writing. In view of these variations and the fact that participants were from different backgrounds, it was found that the unification of text presentations was a necessity. Therefore, queries were normalized, where punctuations, full stops and diacritics were removed. Also, regardless in which position of a word any of the two alifs (إ and أ) and/or the alif-mamdood (آ) was found, it was replaced with the bare alif ا)). Furthermore, the Hamza when placed under the Ya (ئ) was replaced with the one over the Ya (ئ); and the final Ya if it was written without the below two dots (ى) was replaced with the one that has the two dots (ي). Finally, the final Ta-marboota if it was written with the above two dots (ة) was replaced with the one without the two dots (ه).

# 3   Results and Analysis

The three types of queries for each topic were generated and on the basis of TREC relevance judgments, the number of relevant documents for each query category was counted and precision at rank 20 was calculated. Results for the retrieval effectiveness of the three query types is shown below.

|          | AMV  | LRT  | MRT  |
|----------|------|------|------|
| P@20     | 0.50 | 0.24 | 0.36 |
| % of AMV | 100% | 47%  | 72%  |

Pair wise comparisons between the three types were tested for statistical significance using the t-test; each was found to be significant at a level of $p<0.01$. As expected, AMV, a query composed of all morphological variants, produced the best retrieval effectiveness. This is in agreement with past work showing the benefit of stemming over user queries, (e.g. Hull, 1996; Krovetz, 1993). What the results also show however is that popular terms that native Arabic language speakers use to formulate queries (i.e. those occurring in the MRT column), were capable of retrieving many more relevant documents than the terms users used less frequently (i.e. the LRT column). To the best of our knowledge such a result has not been shown before.

While a preliminary study, the result based on fifteen users and 25 topics is striking as it shows that users can generally be expected to type in a query composed of morphological forms that retrieve a substantial fraction of relevant documents. Although stemming can help, it is only likely to add a minority of relevant documents to that already retrieved. The least commonly entered query terms were the ones that stemming can help the most. Such a result suggests a possible reason for the limited use of stemming in many operational IR systems: namely that the greatest benefit stemming can provide is rarely needed.

## 4   Conclusions and Future Work

This poster presented a new form of a previous method for eliciting a variety of queries from users on a set of topics. The method was used to create a large set of queries, which was used to study the relationship of Arabic morphological variation to retrieval effectiveness. It was found that the morphological form used most often by users was commonly the form that retrieved a substantial number of relevant documents. This is a result that we believe has not been reported before in Arabic nor, we believe in other languages. The work is part of a wider study of both the methodology and results. The methodology of eliciting queries from users needs further study to determine its effectiveness and to better understand any influence on users on which words or morphological variants of words they choose to use. The methodology could also be studied in the context of the results. For example, rather than merge all fifteen query variants of a topic into a single LRT or MRT, each of the query formation approaches could themselves contribute to an individual LRT or MRT query. For the runs themselves, a number of additional processes could be applied, one example would be to stem the three query types (AMV, MRT, LRT) and measure the difference in retrieval effectiveness. Finally the experiment is planned to be re-run with queries formed in other languages to test the consistency of the effects observed and reported here.

## References

Buckley, C. (2000) The TREC-9 Query Track. In E. M. Voorhees and D. K. Harman, eds., *Proceedings of the 9th Text REtrieval Conference (TREC-9)*, pp. 81-85.

Hull, D. (1996) Stemming Algorithms: A Case Study for Detailed Evaluation, *Journal of the American Society of Information Science*, 47(1), 70-84.

Krovetz, R (1993) Viewing morphology as an inference process, in *Proceedings of ACM SIGIR Conference*, 191-202.

Voorhees, E.M, Harman, D. (2001) Overview of TREC 2001 in *Proceedings of the 10th Text REtrieval Conference (TREC 2001)*, 1-15.

# Combining Short and Long Term Audio Features for TV Sports Highlight Detection

Bin Zhang[1,*], Weibei Dou[1], and Liming Chen[2]

[1] Tsinghua University, Beijing 100084, China
bin-zhang@tsinghua.org.cn, douwb@tsinghua.edu.cn
[2] LIRIS CNRS UMR 5205, Ecole Centrale de Lyon, France
Liming.Chen@ec-lyon.fr

**Abstract.** As bearer of high-level semantics, audio signal is being more and more used in content-based multimedia retrieval. In this paper, we investigate TV tennis game highlight detection based on the use of both short and long term audio features and propose two approaches, decision fusion and hierarchical classifier, in order to combine these two kinds of audio features. As more information is included in decision making, the overall performance of the system is enhanced.

## 1 Introduction

As bearer of high-level semantics, audio signal has been recognized as a key component in content-based multimedia information retrieval. In this paper, we investigate a prospective application of multimedia information retrieval, namely TV sports highlight detection based on audio analysis. Many approaches were proposed in the literature [1] [2]. However, short or long term features were employed separately by the highlight detection systems. We can use, for example, only spectrum envelope as short term feature, or the variance of spectrum envelopes as long term feature, to discriminate speech and silence, respectively. Because short and long term features are extracted in completely different ways, different aspects of information are carried by these two kinds of features. More specifically, some instantaneous characteristics of the audio signal are presented by short term features, while some long time and time-dependent characteristics are expressed by long term features. The performance is therefore limited if we use only one of them, and this drawback can be overcome if both features are employed. Yet, these two kinds of features are generated in different time scales, making the combination of the two rather difficult.

Two novel approaches, which combine short and long term features in decision making, are proposed in this paper. By employing both short and long term features, more information about audio signal can be considered in classification, and thus higher accuracy can be attained. The experiment also reveals the enhancement of overall performance.

* This work has been supported by Programme de Recherches Avancées de Coopérations Franco-Chinoises (PRA SI04-02).

M. Lalmas et al. (Eds.): ECIR 2006, LNCS 3936, pp. 472–475, 2006.
© Springer-Verlag Berlin Heidelberg 2006

## 2   Combination of Short and Long Term Audio Features

Audio features used in most papers are two categories: short term features and long term features. Short term features are generated in short, usually overlapping windows (typically 10 to 20 ms) named *analysis windows* [3]. They can present some instantaneous characteristics of the signal, e.g., the short time spectrum envelope. To the contrary, long term features, also referred as *texture* [3], are extracted in relatively long windows (*texture window* [3], usually 1 seconds), by exploiting some time-dependent characteristics of the audio signal. In this paper, Mel Frequency Cepstral Coefficient (MFCC) [4] is used as short term feature, and is extracted in every analysis window with a length of 10ms. The statistics, more specifically, the mean and variance, of MFCC in every texture window (1 second long) are used as texture in this paper. The mean of the first MFCC coefficient, logarithmic energy, is excluded from the texture feature in our experiment, because poor performance is observed with this component used.

Short term features and long term features were used separately in the literature, both yielding good performance [1] [2]. They can represent the behavior of audio signal from different aspects. We believe, consequently, the overall performance of the classifier can be enhanced, by combining together the information provided by these two kinds of features. Because they are generated in different scales, however, it is difficult to combine them in the same feature space, i.e., to concatenate both short term and long term features and form an expanded feature vector. Two approaches, decision fusion and hierarchical classifier, are proposed in this paper as solutions to combination. The structures of the two approaches are shown in Fig. 1. In both approaches, Support Vector Machines (SVM) [5] with the Radial Basis Function (RBF) kernel are employed to classify the data into three audio classes (silence, applause, and speech). To some extent, games can be considered as a composition made up of these three basic audio classes. Although we are only interested in applause detection in the following experiment, it should be noted that the discrimination of these audio classes is crucial to semantical understanding. As the boundary of these classes may be vague sometime, we consider them, however, distinct audio classes in this paper for simplicity. Fuzzy segmentation of audio classes will be applied in future work.

In the decision fusion approach (Fig. 1(a)), two distinct classifiers, which are based on short term and long term features respectively, are built. Each classifier assigns a decision to the same texture window. A Bayesian inference [6] module is employed to fuse the decisions of two classifiers. The a posterior probability $P(d_\mathrm{F}|d_1 d_2)$ is computed as follows according to the Bayes' rule:

$$P(d_\mathrm{F}|d_1 d_2) = \frac{P(d_1 d_2|d_\mathrm{F})P(d_\mathrm{F})}{P(d_1 d_2)} = \frac{P(d_\mathrm{F}|d_1)P(d_\mathrm{F}|d_2)}{P(d_\mathrm{F})} \ , \tag{1}$$

where, $d_i$ is the decision of classifier $i$ ($i = 1, 2$), $d_\mathrm{F}$ the final decision (hypothesis), and $P(d_i|d_\mathrm{F})$ the likelihood function of classifier $i$. The decisions of two classifiers are assumed independent here.

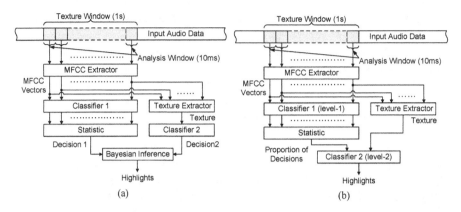

**Fig. 1.** The structures of two approaches: (a) decision fusion, (b) hierarchical classifier

**Table 1.** Fusion matrix

| Fused Output | | Output of Classifier 1 | | |
|---|---|---|---|---|
| | | silence | applause | speech |
| Output of Classifier 2 | silence | silence | applause | silence |
| | applause | silence | applause | applause |
| | speech | silence | applause | speech |

The system needs to be trained in three steps: 1) train classifier 1, 2) train classifier 2, 3) train the Bayesian inference module. Step 1 and 2 can be done in parallel, and step 3, however, has to be done alone after step 1 and 2. By approximating $P(d_F|d_i)$ and $P(d_F)$ in (1) using the statistics of the results from both classifiers, the a posteriori probability function can be obtained. Since the probability space is discrete, we have only $3 \times 3 = 9$ combinations of $d_1 d_2$. It is very easy to calculate the a posteriori probability matrix. Finally, a fusion matrix (Tab. 1) can be attained based on maximization of the a posterior probability (MAP). Alternatively, we can also determine the fusion matrix manually according to our prior knowledge of a specific application. By applying Bayesian inference, decision relying on only one classifier is avoided, and every final decision is made based on the consideration of results from both classifiers. However, the drawback of this approach is that no information other than the decisions of classifiers is included in fusion, making its accuracy lower than Dempster-Shafer algorithm or fuzzy logic [6].

In the hierarchical classifier approach (Fig. 1(b)), two classifiers are built in a style of cascade composed of two levels. The level-1 classifier assigns decision to every analysis window, and the proportion of decisions belonging to each class is calculated in every texture window. These statistics, together with the texture features, are inputted into the level-2 classifier, which makes the final decision, as combined features. Compared with the first approach, decision fusion, more information about short term and long term features is included and fused in the level-2 classifier, and the performance is therefore better.

# 3   Experimental Results and Conclusion

We use one tennis game in our experiment, in which highlights can be basically located by the occurrence of applause. The training for decision fusion is accomplished using two sets of training sequences. The training sequences in the first set, which are 20 seconds in length (for each sound class), are used to train classifier 1 and 2. The training sequences in the second set, which are 1 minute in length (for each sound class), are used to train the Bayesian inference module. Since there is normally no single audio class lasting for 1 minute in real games, fragmentary audio clips are manually segmented from the game and concatenated together for training. For the hierarchical classifier approach, however, the first training set mentioned above is used to train classifier 1 and the second set to train classifier 2, respectively. The testing data set for both approaches is the whole game, which is about 30 minutes long.

**Table 2.** Experimental results

|  | Short term feature only | Long term feature only | Decision fusion | Hierarchical classifier |
|---|---|---|---|---|
| Precision | 98% | 91% | 92% | 98% |
| Recall | 91% | 87% | 96% | 96% |

The performance of highlight detection is listed in Tab. 2. The conventional precision-recall metric [2] is used for evaluation. It can be seen from the results that, by consider precision and recall comprehensively, combination of short term and long term features outperforms either short term or long term features. Especially, the hierarchical classifier approach performs the best. Nevertheless, the improvement is not yet great enough. One possible solution is to explore more information from the decisions of classifiers. From this point of view, conventional classifiers with crisp outputs can not meet the needs. Fuzzy classifiers are therefore to be used in the future, by which some advanced fusion techniques [6] can be involved to make the performance even better.

# References

1. Rui, Y., Gupta, A., Acero, A.: Automatically extracting highlights for TV baseball programs. In: Proc. of the 8th ACM MULTIM. (2000) 105 – 115
2. Harb, H., Chen, L.: Highlights detection in sports videos based on audio analysis. In: Proc. of CBMI03. (2003)
3. Tzanetakis, G., Cook, P.: Musical genre classification of audio signals. IEEE Transactions on Speech and Audio Processing **10**(5) (2002) 293 – 302
4. Rabiner, L., Juang, B.H.: Fundamentals of Speech Recognition. PTR Prentice-Hall, Inc. (1993)
5. Duda, R.O., Hart, P.E., Stork, D.G.: Pattern Classification. 2nd edn. John Wiley & Sons, Inc. (2001)
6. Klein, L.A.: Sensor and Data Fusion. SPIE Press (2004)

# Object-Based Access to TV Rushes Video

Alan F. Smeaton, Gareth J.F. Jones, Hyowon Lee,
Noel E. O'Connor, and Sorin Sav

Centre for Digital Video Processing & Adaptive Information Cluster,
Dublin City University, Glasnevin, Dublin 9, Ireland
`Alan.Smeaton@dcu.ie`

## 1 Introduction

Recent years have seen the development of different modalities for video retrieval. The most common of these are (1) to use text from speech recognition or closed captions, (2) to match keyframes using image retrieval techniques like colour and texture [6] and (3) to use semantic features like "indoor", "outdoor" or "persons". Of these, text-based retrieval is the most mature and useful, while image-based retrieval using low-level image features usually depends on matching keyframes rather than whole-shots. Automatic detection of video concepts is receiving much attention and as progress is made in this area we will see consequent impact on the quality of video retrieval. In practice it is the combination of these techniques which realises the most useful, and effective, video retrieval as shown by us repeatedly in TRECVid [5].

For many types of query we seek video which contains an *object* of interest such as a car, a building or an animal, something where the background is of no importance. Here we introduce a technique we have developed for object-based video retrieval. We outline the processes involved in analysing and indexing video to support this and we present an interactive system to support user searching using objects and/or using matching of whole keyframes.

The data used in our work is 50 hours (c. 4.5M frames) of rushes video provided by BBC as part of the TRECVid evaluation in 2005. Rushes is a term used to refer to raw video footage which is unedited and contains lots of redundancy, overlap and "wasteful" material. Shots tend to be much longer than in post-produced video and it generally contains a lot of re-takes, bloopers and content where nothing much happens. It is very similar to home movies or personal video material since it often contains camera shake and re-focus, and little or no dialogue. The task for participants in this track in TRECVid 2005 was to explore how to develop techniques to automatically analyse such video given that there is no text dialogue to work with and to build systems which allow users who know nothing about the content of the data to navigate through it with some information need in mind.

## 2 Object-Based Video Retrieval

In work reported elsewhere [2] we developed a video retrieval and browsing system which allowed users to search using the text of closed captions, using the

M. Lalmas et al. (Eds.): ECIR 2006, LNCS 3936, pp. 476–479, 2006.
© Springer-Verlag Berlin Heidelberg 2006

keyframe for locating similar keyframes in terms of colour, texture and edges, and using the occurrence (or non-occurrence) of a set of pre-defined video objects. The content used was several seasons of the Simpsons TV series and the video objects corresponded to the faces of the 10 major characters in the series, Homer, Bart, Marge, etc. We evaluated the ways in which different video retrieval modalities (text search, image search, object search) were used [3] and we concluded that certain queries can benefit from using objects as part of their search, but this is not true for all query types.

In moving from object detection and retrieval on synthetic video (e.g. the Simpsons) to object retrieval on natural video as in [4], we are faced with a problem of object segmentation. This is hard because in video objects can deform and turn, cameras can move, objects can become occluded when other objects move in front of them, lighting conditions can change, and so on. Nevertheless we have developed a semi-supervised technique for object segmentation based on an RSST region segmentation which requires the user to indicate some regions both within and outside the contours of the object to be segmented and this can be done easily with two mouse-strokes, one inside and one outside the object [1]. This approach is feasible for the BBC rushes video corpus in comparison with the amount of manual effort currently placed on video annotation, and we've segmented objects from this corpus of video data in order to support object retrieval. Our retrieval system also supports whole keyframe based retrieval where a number of images can be used as the query and in object based retrieval a number of example objects can be used as the query. These two approaches can also be combined into one query for retrieval and our interest is in seeing under what circumstances users find object-based retrieval to be useful.

We used a standard approach to shot boundary determination, comparing adjacent frames over a certain window and using low-level colour features, in order to determine boundaries [5]. We detected 8,717 shots (a rate of 174 keyframes per hour) for the 50 hours and for each of these we automatically extracted a single keyframe by examining the whole shot for levels of visual activity using features extracted directly from the encoded video. The rationale for this is that the approach of choosing the first, last or middle frame as the keyframe would be quite inappropriate given the amount of "dead" time there is in shots within rushes video. Much of the unusable video footage in rushes is there because the camera is left running while the main action of the shot is prepared and then takes place. In rushes footage the camera is left running in order to ensure the action, whatever that may be, is not missed. Thus our approach to automatic keyframe selection based on choosing the frame where the greatest amount of action is happening, seems to make sense, although this is certainly a topic for further investigation.

Each keyframe was manually examined to determine if there was a single dominant object present and if so it was segmented from its background using our semi-automatic tool [1] described in the previous section [1] which yielded 1,210 objects. Once segmentation was completed we extracted features for keyframes using global MPEG-7 colour and texture features for whole keyframes and dominant colour, homogeneous texture and shape compactness MPEG-7 features for objects. We then pre-computed two $8,717 \times 8,717$ matrices of keyframe similarities using the two image features for the whole keyframe, and three $1,210 \times 1,210$ matrices of similarities between objects in those keyframes using object features.

For retrieval we cannot assume that the user knows the archive's content since rushes content is not catalogued in any way. In order to begin a user's retrieval we ask the user to locate one or more external images using some other image searching resource. The aim here is to find one or more images, or even better one or more video objects, which can be used for searching. In our experiments our users use Google Image Search to locate such external images but any image searching facility could be used. Once external images are found they are indexed in the same way as keyframes in terms of colour and texture for the whole image and the user is also allowed to segment one object in the external image if s/he wishes. This is done in real time.

At search time the user indicates which visual characteristics in each query image are important — colour or texture in the case of the whole image, or colour, shape or texture in the case of an object. The set of query images is then used for retrieval and the user is presented with a list of keyframes from the archive. The similarity between these and the user query is a combination of image-image similarity (using colour and texture) and object-object similarity (using colour, shape and texture). For the 1,210 of 8,717 keyframes where there is a segmented object present the object is highlighted when the keyframe is presented. The user browses these keyframes and can either play the video, save the shot, or add the keyframe (and its object, if present) to the query panel and the query-browse iteration continues. The overall architecture and a sample screen taken from the middle of a search is shown as Figure 1 where there are 3 query images (the first is a whole keyframe added from within the collection as relevance feedback; the second and third are external images and the user has segmented objects in these), 5 pages of search results and 4 saved keyframes. Objects appearing in frames with segmented objects, either in the query panel or search result, are outlined in red and the facets of the query images which are to be used for the search (colour, texture, object shape) are shown in the query panel.

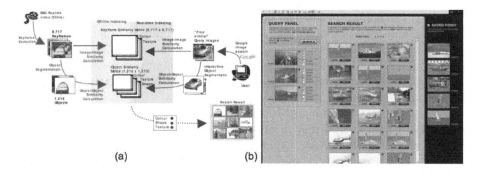

(a)                                              (b)

**Fig. 1.** (a) System architecture and (b) sample screen for video rushes search system

# 3    Experiments and Plans

We now have two versions of our system allowing us to explore how useful video objects are in video browsing and search. One supports image similarity based only on whole keyframes, while the other supports object-object similarity as well as whole keyframe matching. A small user experiment with 12 users is being run to compare the performance of the two systems for a number of searches. We are using a Latin squares design for rotating the order of users for topics, and systems. Since there was no formal evaluation task for BBC rushes at TRECVid 2005 (it was an exploratory task only), we take a "do-it-yourself" approach to formulating search topics and performing relevance assessments. We will share our topics, pool retrieved shots and share relevance judgments with at least one other TRECVid participating group in a a mini-TRECVid for the BBC rushes data. Search topics are taken from a log of actual search topics from a broadcaster's archive to which we have access.

The use of video objects in searching offers interesting potential to expanding the set of possible modalities for video search and browsing but our dependency on using objects from single keyframes is limiting. We index objects in a keyframe rather than in a shot, and as we know during a shot an object can turn or deform, and the camera and/or the object can move, all yielding different object representations. To overcome this we would like to track an object throughout a shot and to index each *instance* of the object throughout the frame. Although this is very ambitious it would reduce dependency on keyframes rather than whole shots and is planned as further work.

# References

1. Adamek, T. and O'Connor, N. (2003). Efficient Contour-based Shape Representation and Matching. MIR 2003 - 5th International ACM SIGMM Workshop on Multimedia Information Retrieval, Berkeley, CA, 7 November 2003.
2. Browne, P. and Smeaton, A.F. (2004). Video Information Retrieval Using Objects and Ostensive Relevance Feedback. In Proceedings of SAC 2004 - ACM Symposium on Applied Computing, Nicosia, Cyprus, 14-17 March 2004.
3. Browne, P. and Smeaton A.F. (2006). A Usage Study of Retrieval Modalities for Video Shot Retrieval. *Information Processing and Management*, (in press),
4. Sivic, J. and Zisserman, Z. (2003) Video Google: A Text Retrieval Approach to Object Matching in Videos. Proceedings of the Ninth IEEE International Conference on Computer Vision (ICCV 2003).
5. Smeaton, A.F., Kraaij, W., and Over, P. (2004). The TREC Video Retrieval Evaluation (TRECVID): A Case Study and Status Report. In: RIAO 2004 - Coupling Approaches, Coupling Media and Coupling Languages for Information Retrieval, Avignon, France, 26-28 April 2004.
6. Smeulders, A.W.M., Worring, M., Santini, S., Gupta, A. and Jain, R. (2000). Content-Based Image Retrieval at the End of the Early Years. IEEE Trans. Pattern Anal. Mach. Intell. **22(12)**, pp. 1349-1380.

# An Efficient Computation of the Multiple-Bernoulli Language Model

Leif Azzopardi[1] and David E. Losada[2],[*]

[1] Dept. of Computer and Information Sciences,
University of Strathclyde, Scotland
Leif.azzopardi@cis.strath.ac.uk
[2] Grupo de Sistemas Inteligentes, Departamento de Electrónica y Computación,
Universidad de Santiago de Compostela, Spain
dlosada@dec.usc.es

**Abstract.** The Multiple Bernoulli (MB) Language Model has been generally considered too computationally expensive for practical purposes and superseded by the more efficient multinomial approach. While, the model has many attractive properties, little is actually known about the retrieval effectiveness of the MB model due to its high cost of execution. In this paper, we show how an efficient implementation of this model can be achieved. The resulting method is comparable in terms of efficiency to other standard term matching algorithms (such as the vector space model, BM25 and the multinomial Language Model).

## 1 Introduction

The Multiple-Bernoulli Language Model was originally proposed for Information Retrieval (IR) in [3] and has been recently extended in the context of Bayesian Learning[2, 1]. The MB language model is an appealing IR model, providing a coherent framework in which queries and documents are treated in a uniform manner. Also, the model provides implicit length normalization, because documents which contain many non-query terms are penalized for being off topic. This feature would suggest that the applicability of the model would favor particular IR tasks where length normalization is critical (such as in element retrieval). Already, some evidence to this tune has been shown in the context of sentence retrieval[1].

Although the computational complexity of the MB model could be thought to be too high for the model to be implemented in a practical setting, we show here that an efficient method can be designed to do retrieval efficiently. If we examine the formulation of the MB model in Eq. 1, we can see that the probability of generating a query $q$ given the document model $\theta_d$ involves a computation across all terms $t_i$ in the vocabulary $T$, (i.e. $t_i \in T$).

[*] The second author is supported by the "Ramón y Cajal" R&D program, which is funded in part by "Ministerio de Educación y Ciencia" and in part by FEDER funds. This work was financially supported by "Ministerio de Educación y Ciencia" through research project ref. TIN2005-08521-C02-01.

M. Lalmas et al. (Eds.): ECIR 2006, LNCS 3936, pp. 480–483, 2006.
© Springer-Verlag Berlin Heidelberg 2006

$$p(q|\theta_d) = \prod_{t_i \in q} p(t_i|\theta_d) \prod_{t_i \notin q} (1 - p(t_i|\theta_d)) \tag{1}$$

In the worse case scenario a direct implementation for a collection of documents would be equal to the number of terms in the vocabulary, $|T|$ multiplied by the number of documents in the collection, $|D|$ (i.e. $|T| \times |D|$).

## 2   Optimization

Instead of directly computing $p(q|\theta_d)$ for every $d$ in the collection of document $D$, an optimization of the model is possible, by decomposing the scoring procedure. First, we require a pre-computation given the set of model parameters which define $\theta_d$, before query time. This estimates the probability of a hypothetical 'empty' query being generated from the document model. Then, at query time, the pre-computed document score is adjusted according to the terms that appear in the query. To facilitate the optimization, we shall require some extra definitions. Let $q_e$ be the empty query, and let $d_e$ be an empty document, where the number of times $t_i$ occurs in the document is zero for any $t_i$ (denoted as $n(t_i, d_e) = 0$). The document model of $d_e$ is denoted as $\theta_{d_e}$.

### 2.1   Pre-computation Before Query Time

The probability of the empty query $q_e$ given each document model $\theta_d$ is computed offline.

$$p(q_e|\theta_d) = \prod_{t_i \notin q_e} (1 - p(t_i|\theta_d)) \tag{2}$$

Since the query is empty, this involves a product across all vocabulary terms. Whilst this value is document dependent, we can design an efficient method for computing the $p(q_e|\theta_d)$. This is accomplished by first scoring a hypothetical 'empty' document and then updating this score given the terms seen in the actual document. Thus, we pre-compute the probability of the empty query given the empty document model, $p(q_e|\theta_{d_e})$ as follows:

$$p(q_e|\theta_{d_e}) = \prod_{t_i \notin q_e} (1 - p(t_i|\theta_{d_e})) \tag{3}$$

Note that any term $t_i$ is unseen in the empty document and, therefore, the value $p(t_i|\theta_{d_e})$ is computed using $n(t_i, d_e) = 0$. Once we see the actual document $d$ we can compute the probability of producing the empty query, $p(q_e|\theta_d)$, starting from $p(q_e|\theta_{d_e})$. The approach can be illustrated as follows. Starting from $p(q_e|\theta_{d_e})$ can be thought as an initial assumption that any document is empty. As we see the actual document terms, we update the probability score, removing $(1 - p(t_i|\theta_{d_e}))$ which was computed assuming $n(t_i, d) = 0$. And then multiplying by $(1 - p(t_i|\theta_d))$, which is computed using the actual term document counts (i.e. $n(t_i, d) > 0$). Formally,

$$p(q_e|\theta_d) = p(q_e|\theta_{d_e}) \cdot \prod_{t_i \in d} \frac{1 - p(t_i|\theta_d)}{1 - p(t_i|\theta_{d_e})} \tag{4}$$

That is, we only need to go on the seen terms whereas the unseen terms take its probability from the pre-computed $p(q_e|\theta_{d_e})$, which needs only to be computed once. This is the first significant saving because the number of unique terms in the documents is usually several orders of magnitude less than the size of the vocabulary, $|T|$. The reader may note that this imposes an implicit constraint on the optimization, because of the assumption that $p(t_i|\theta_d) = p(t_i|\theta_{d_e})$ for all the terms which are unseen in the document $d$. This equality holds in the original Ponte and Croft formulation [3] as the unseen terms' probabilities are assumed to be equal to the probability in a background model. That is, there is no document dependent factor in the unseen term probability. On the other hand, in the context of Bayesian Learning, the case is slightly different. The basic MB formulation of the $p(t_i|\theta_d)$ formula in [2] and [1] also depend only on background probabilities for unseen terms and, therefore, the same efficient approach can be taken. However, in a variation of the MB model to deal with non-binary term-document counts (called Model B in [2]), the above method cannot be immediately applied as $p(t_i|\theta_d)$ is not equal to $p(t_i|\theta_{d_e})$ because the final term estimate is proportional to the length of a document. When this is the case, then a generalization of the process designed here can be employed. Instead of assuming one hypothetical document, which is empty (i.e. $\sum_{t_i} n(t_i, d_e) = 0$), a set of hypothetical documents need to be constructed, where the length of each hypothetical document is $1, \ldots, n$, $n$ being the document length of the largest document[1]. This enables the computation to be performed almost as efficiently, but incurs higher storage/memory costs.

## 2.2 Computation at Query Time

For each query term we adjust the contribution from the query terms in the empty document model (eq. 5). Next, we compute the factor involving the query-document matching terms (eq. 6).

$$p(q|\theta_d) = p(q_e|\theta_d) \cdot \prod_{t_i \in q} \frac{p(t_i|\theta_{d_e})}{1 - p(t_i|\theta_{d_e})} \tag{5}$$

$$\times \prod_{t_i \in q \cap d} \frac{p(t_i|\theta_d)}{p(t_i|\theta_{d_e})} \cdot \frac{1 - p(t_i|\theta_{d_e})}{1 - p(t_i|\theta_d)} \tag{6}$$

Note that the product across query terms in eq. 5 is document independent and, thus, it only needs to be computed once for each query. The product across matching terms in eq. 6 introduces the right score for a matching term, $p(t_i|\theta_d)$, and removes the score introduced in the previous steps[2]. This speed up uses a similar tactic to that suggested in [4] for the multinomial approach. However, in the multinomial model unseen query terms are not considered and, hence, there is no need for an initial query score.

---

[1] Actually, only one hypothetical document is needed for each unique document length.

[2] Note that, for a matching term, after applying eqs 3, 4 and 5, we have a contribution equal to $\frac{p(t_i|\theta_{d_e}) \cdot (1 - p(t_i|\theta_d))}{(1 - p(t_i|\theta_{d_e}))}$. We just multiply by the inverse of this value.

# 3    Complexity Analysis

We described the computation complexity according to the number of term score calculations required. The before query time pre-computation of calculating $p(q_e|\theta_{d_e})$ (eq. 3) takes $|T|$ steps and to compute the value $p(q_e|\theta_d)$ for all the documents (eq. 4) takes $|D| \cdot |T| \cdot s$ steps, where $s$ is the sparsity expressed as the percentage of non-zero entries in the document-term matrix. This is computed offline and so does not directly affect on-line performance. At query time, the online computations in eq. 5 involves $|q|$ steps, and eq. 6 takes $|d| \cdot |q| \cdot s$ iterations, where $|q|$ is the number of query terms. Under this optimization a very significant reduction in the run time of the MB retrieval model can be achieved which makes it comparable to other state of the art retrieval models.

# 4    Conclusion

We have presented an efficient method for computing the MB model, which reduces significantly the expected matching time[3]. From prior research and our own intuitions we believe that the MB model will be more effective in specific retrieval scenarios, such as when the elements to be retrieved are short and need to be focused or when the variation in size of retrievable elements is high. Further work will be directed at identifying retrieval scenarios that can exploit the attractive properties of the MB model.

# References

1. D. E. Losada. Language modeling for sentence retrieval: a comparison between multiple-bernoulli models and multinomial models. In *Information Retrieval and Theory Workshop*, Glasgow, UK, 2005.
2. D. Metlzer, V. Lavrenko, and W. B. Croft. Formal multiple-bernoulli models for language modeling. In *Proc. 27th ACM Conference on Research and Development in Information Retrieval, SIGIR'04*, pages 540–541, Sheffield, UK, 2004. ACM press.
3. J. Ponte and W. B. Croft. A language modeling approach to information retrieval. In *Proc. 21st ACM Conference on Research and Development in Information Retrieval, SIGIR'98*, pages 275–281, Melbourne, Australia, 1998.
4. C. Zhai and J. Lafferty. A study of smoothing methods for language models applied to information retrieval. *ACM Transactions on Information Systems*, 22(2):179–214, 2004.

---

[3] We have implemented the MB proposed in [1] in LEMUR 4.0, and this code will be made freely available.

# Title and Snippet Based Result Re-ranking in Collaborative Web Search*

Oisín Boydell and Barry Smyth

Adaptive Information Cluster, UCD School of Computer Science and Informatics,
University College Dublin, Belfield, Dublin 4, Ireland
{Oisin.Boydell, Barry.Smyth}@ucd.ie

**Abstract.** Collaborative Web search is a form of meta-search that manipulates the results of underlying Web search engines in response to the learned preferences of a given community of users. Results that have previously been selected in response to similar queries by community members are promoted in the returned results. However, promotion is limited to these previously-selected results and in this paper we describe and evaluate how relevant results without a selection history can also be promoted by exploiting snippet-text and title similarities.

## 1 Introduction

Collaborative Web Search (CWS) records the search behaviours of communities of like-minded searchers with a view to capturing their preferences in order to personalize result lists for their needs [1]. CWS accommodates different types of communities—for example the set of searchers who use a search box on a motoring Web site, the employees of a given company or a class of students—and has been shown to be especially effective when it comes to dealing with the type of vague queries that are commonplace in Web search.

The key to CWS is its ability to record and exploit the search behaviour of individual communities of searchers as a matrix of *query-result* selections, $H$ [1]. Thus when a searcher selects a result $p_j$ for query $q_i$, $H_{ij}$ is incremented. In turn, the relevance of a page $p_j$ to some target query $q_T$ is calculated from a weighted sum of the proportion of times that this page has been selected in the past for $q_T$ and similar queries (Equation 1); the contributions of more similar queries to $q_T$ are weighted higher than the contributions of less similar queries. Query similarity is estimated using a simple term overlap metric.

$$\text{WRel}(p_j, q_T, q_1, \ldots, q_n) = \sum_{i=1}^{n} \left( \frac{H_{ij}}{\sum_{\forall j} H_{ij}} \right) \cdot \text{Sim}(q_T, q_i) \tag{1}$$

Thus, for each new search $q_T$, in addition to combining the results from a set of underlying search engines, CWS seeks to identify a set of similar queries, $q_1, \ldots, q_n$, and produces a list of results that have previously been selected for

* This material is based on works supported by Science Foundation Ireland under Grant No. 03/IN.3/I361.

M. Lalmas et al. (Eds.): ECIR 2006, LNCS 3936, pp. 484–487, 2006.
© Springer-Verlag Berlin Heidelberg 2006

these queries, ranking them in descending order of their weighted relevance. These results are then promoted ahead of the normal meta-search results.

One important limitation of this approach is that only previously-selected results can be promoted, which leads to a *cold-start* problem for young communities. In this paper we propose a solution to this problem in which the promoted results in a given search session, i.e. the results selected for similar searches in the past, are used as a basis for selecting additional relevant results from the meta-search results based on title and snippet-text similarity. Accordingly, even in sessions where there is only a single promoted result it is possible to use this method to re-rank the meta-results in line with community preferences so that similar results are effectively promoted.

## 2   Title and Snippet Based Re-ranking

For a given search, the promoted results tell us something about the preferences of the corresponding search community because these are the results that have frequently been selected in the past for the current and similar queries. It seems reasonable to assume then that the terms contained in the titles and snippet-texts of these promoted results will capture, at least in part, the community's preferences; after all, selections from a result-list are often made on the basis of title and snippet-text. By comparing these titles and snippet-texts to the other meta-search results for the current session it may be possible to identify other results that similarly conform to community preferences. This idea has its origins in the work of [2], which looked at snippet-based re-ranking based on the results selected by an individual user in the current session, and [3], which focused on multiple sessions for a given user. However, in our work we are leveraging the multiple-session histories of a community of users.

Thus, we adapt the standard CWS approach to accommodate a two-stage promotion model. First, results that have been selected in the past for similar queries are promoted ahead of the meta-search results in the normal way. Second, we re-rank the remaining meta-results in decreasing order of their similarity to the results promoted during stage one. During stage two we use a standard TFIDF weighted cosine similarity measure [4] as our similarity metric (Equation 2) where $r$ and $p$ are the TFIDF weighted term vectors of the combined title and snippet text of the meta-result, and the combined titles and snippet texts of all the promoted results respectively. The query terms are first removed, as these generally occur in all the snippets returned by the underlying Web search engine(s). We also remove common stop words and stem the terms.

$$\text{Sim}(r, p) = \frac{\sum_{i=1}^{t} r_i p_i}{(\sum_{i=1}^{t} (r_i)^2 \sum_{i=1}^{t} (p_i)^2)^{\frac{1}{2}}}. \tag{2}$$

## 3   Evaluation

To evaluate the effectiveness of this new promotion model we used search logs generated from a recent live-user trial of CWS [5], which cover an eight month period. These logs provide information about the queries used and the results selected during an extended period of time. However, the logs do not contain snippet or title texts for search results and so this data was retrieved from Google and HotBot for the purpose of the current evaluation. In fact this eliminated a portion of the log data when titles and snippets could not be retrieved because the page no longer existed, for example.

The key to our evaluation is the ability to judge the relevance of particular meta-results; ultimately we were interested in measuring the mean average precision (MAP) of the top 10 meta-results returned by the standard CWS approach and by our modified promotion technique. To do this we rely on explicit user selections and thus we were only interested in search sessions that had at least one CWS-promoted result and at least one selected meta-result. This provided 160 separate search sessions. However there is a problem arising from the selection bias that naturally exists in search in which most user selections occur at the top of a result-list [6]. As a consequence, for many of the sessions the selected meta-results tended to occur at the top of the meta-result list and so there is little opportunity for improved MAP as a result of re-ranking.

To account for this we looked at two options for coping with this bias. In the first (which we denote *original CWS trial order*) we focused on sessions where the first selected meta-result was not at the top of the meta-results to see whether our new promotion technique would be able to push this relevant result (and any other selected meta-results) higher in the result-list. This reduced our evaluation set to leave 81 search sessions and the MAP for the top 10 meta-results for these sessions using standard CWS (*original ranking*) and using our new technique (*after re-ranking*) is presented in Figure 1. The results show a 9% relative increase in MAP for the new technique.

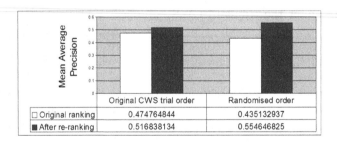

**Fig. 1.** Results of the Evaluation

The second option for coping with this bias is to randomise the order of the meta-results prior to re-ranking. This is not as extreme as it sounds since we are after all only focusing on the top 10 meta-results, results which are likely to be just as relevant to the query as far as the underlying search engines (Google and HotBot in this case) are concerned. This option allowed us to use the full set of 160 search sessions and the MAP shown in Figure 1 indicates a significant 27% relative increase for the new re-ranking method compared to standard CWS.

# 4   Conclusions

Collaborative Web Search personalizes meta-search results for a community of like-minded searchers based on their prior search histories, by promoting results that have previously been judged to be relevant by the community. In this paper we have described and evaluated a method to enhance the effectiveness of CWS by facilitating additional result promotions by exploiting textual similarities between promoted results and results without a selection history. Our preliminary evaluation suggests that our new approach has the potential to significantly improve result precision by leveraging similarities between result titles and snippet-texts, thus avoiding the need for any processing of full-page content.

As already mentioned, the work of [2, 3] has also looked at result personalization by leveraging the snippet-texts of the results selected by a user (within the current session or beyond). The use of snippet text for result page clustering has also been extensively researched [7, 8]. We believe that our approach adds to this growing body of work and helps to clarify the value and importance of snippet-text data as a source of result re-ranking and personalization.

# References

1. Smyth, B., Balfe, E., Freyne, J., Briggs, P., Coyle, M., Boydell, O.: Exploiting query repetition and regularity in an adaptive community-based web search engine. User Modeling and User-Adapted Interaction **14** (2005) 383–423
2. Shen, X., Tan, B., Zhai, C.: Implicit User Modeling for Personalized Search. In: Proceedings of the Fourteenth ACM Conference on Information and Knowledge Management (CIKM 05). (2005)
3. Teevan, J., Dumais, S.T., Horvitz, E.: Personalizing search via automated analysis of interests and activities. In: Proceedings of the 28th annual international ACM SIGIR conference. (2005) 449–456
4. Rijsbergen, C.J.V.: Information Retrieval, 2nd edition. Dept. of Computer Science, University of Glasgow (1979)
5. Smyth, B., Balfe, E., Boydell, O., Bradley, K., Briggs, P., Coyle, M., Freyne, J.: A Live-user Evaluation of Collaborative Web Search. In: Proceedings of the 19th International Joint Conference on Artificial Intelligence. (2005) 1419–1424
6. Joachims, T., Granka, L., Pan, B., Hembrooke, H., Gay, G.: Accurately interpreting clickthrough data as implicit feedback. In: Proceedings of the 28th annual international ACM SIGIR conference. (2005) 154–161
7. Ferragina, P., Gulli, A.: A personalized search engine based on web-snippet hierarchical clustering. In: Special interest tracks and posters of the 14th international conference on World Wide Web. (2005) 801–810
8. Vivísimo Inc.: The Vivísimo Clustering Engine. (http://vivisimo.com)

# A Classification of IR Effectiveness Metrics

Gianluca Demartini and Stefano Mizzaro

Dept. of Mathematics and Computer Science,
University of Udine, Udine, Italy
{demartin, mizzaro}@dimi.uniud.it

**Abstract.** Effectiveness is a primary concern in the information retrieval (IR) field. Various metrics for IR effectiveness have been proposed in the past; we take into account all the 44 metrics we are aware of, classifying them into a two-dimensional grid. The classification is based on the notions of *relevance*, i.e., if (or how much) a document is relevant, and *retrieval*, i.e., if (how much) a document is retrieved. To our knowledge, no similar classification has been proposed so far.

## 1 Introduction

Evaluation is an important issue in Information Retrieval (IR). Evaluation initiatives (Cranfield, TREC, CLEF, NTCIR, INEX) have a strong tradition, and user studies experiments are frequently performed. Whatever the approach (test collection or user study), the effectiveness metrics chosen are crucial. We are aware of 44 metrics proposed so far. We propose a novel classification of all of them, based on the notions of *relevance*, i.e., if (or how much) a document is relevant, and *retrieval*, i.e., if (how much) a document is retrieved. The simple and traditional approach is based on the *binary* relevance and retrieval assumptions: either a document is relevant or not, and either a document is retrieved or not. By relaxing these two assumptions, one can speak of: *ranking* relevance and/or retrieval (a document is more relevant/retrieved than another), and of *continuous* relevance and/or retrieval (the value of relevance/retrieval is a real number on a continuum, measuring the amount of relevance/retrieval). Combinations, like binary relevance and ranking retrieval are possible, and indeed frequent.

## 2 IR Metrics: A Survey and a Classification

Table 1 shows the (approximated) year in which each metric has been made public, the metric name, a bibliographic reference, the category(ies) to which it belongs (•), the category(ies) to which it can belong with straightforward extensions (○), and in which evaluation initiatives it is used (×). We take into account also the metrics used in INEX 05, made public a few weeks ago. For space limitations, being most of the metrics described in well known textbooks [19, 18, 13], we briefly recall only the following, less common, ones:[1]

---

[1] $N$ is the set of documents in the database; $R$ is the set of relevant documents; $r$ is the set of retrieved documents; $\overline{x}$ is the complement of $x$; $|x|$ is the cardinality of $x$.

M. Lalmas et al. (Eds.): ECIR 2006, LNCS 3936, pp. 488–491, 2006.
© Springer-Verlag Berlin Heidelberg 2006

**Table 1.** A classification of IR effectiveness metrics (sorted by year)

| Year | Relevance: / Retrieval: | Binary B | R | C | Rank B | R | C | Cont. B | R | C | TREC | INEX | NTCIR |
|---|---|---|---|---|---|---|---|---|---|---|---|---|---|
| 1960 | Precision [19] | • | | | | | | | | | | | |
| | Recall [19] | • | | | | | | | | | | | |
| | Fallout [19] | • | | | | | | | | | | | |
| | Generality Factor [19] | • | | | | | | | | | | | |
| 1965 | E-Measure F-measure | • | | | | | | | | | | | |
| | R/P curve | | • | | | | | | | | × | × | × |
| | R/fallout curve | | • | | | | | | | | | | |
| | Normalized Recall [13] | | • | | | | | | | | | | |
| | Normalized Precision [13] | | • | | | | | | | | | | |
| | Expected Search Length [5] | | • | | | | | | | | | | |
| | Sliding Ratio [13] | | | | | | | • | | | | | |
| 1970 | Novelty Ratio [13] | • | | | | | | | | | | | |
| | Coverage Ratio [13] | • | | | | | | | | | | | |
| | Relative Recall [13] | • | | | | | | | | | | | |
| | Recall effort [13] | • | | | | | | | | | | | |
| | Utility [18] | • | | | | | | | | | | | |
| 1975 | MAP | | • | | | | | | | | × | × | × |
| | P@N | | • | | | | | | | | × | × | × |
| | R-Precision | | • | | | | | | | | × | | × |
| | Interpolated MAP | | • | | | | | | | | | | |
| 1990 | Satisfaction [13] | | | | | | | • | | | | | |
| | Frustration [13] | | | | | | | • | | | | | |
| | Total [13] | | | | | | | • | | | | | |
| | Usefulness measure [8] | | | | | • | | | | | | | |
| | Average Search Length [14] | | | | • | | | | | | | | |
| 1995 | NDPM [20] | | | | | • | | | | | | | |
| | Ranked Half Life [2] | | | | | | | | • | | | | |
| | Relative Relevance [2] | | | | | • | | | | | | | |
| 2000 | Classification accuracy [1] | • | | | | | | | | | | | |
| | DCG [9] | | • | | | • | | • | | | | | |
| | AWP [10] | | • | | | • | | | | | | | |
| | Weighted R-Precision [10] | | • | | | • | | | | | | | |
| | ADM [7] | • | • | • | • | • | • | • | • | • | | | |
| | XCG [11] | | • | | | • | | • | | | | × | |
| | bpref [4] | | • | | | | | | | | | | |
| | Q-measure [17] | | • | | | • | | | | | | | × |
| | R-measure [17] | | • | | | • | | | | | | | × |
| | Tolerance to Irrelevance [6] | | • | | | | | | | | | | × |
| | Estimated Ratio of Relevant [16] | | • | | | | | | | | | | × |
| | Kendall, Spearman [3] | | | | | • | | | | | | | |
| | Normalized xCG [12] | | • | | | • | | | | | | × | |
| | Mean average nxCG at rank n [12] | | • | | | • | | | | | | × | |
| | Effort-precision/gain-recall @ std. gain-recall p. [12] | | • | | | • | | | | | | × | |
| | Non-interpolated mean average effort-precision [12] | | • | | | • | | | | | | × | |
| | Interpolated mean average effort-precision [12] | | • | | | • | | | | | | × | |

- *R/fallout curve*: a plot of the recall values corresponding to the fallout values.
- *Expected Search Length*: average number of documents which must be examined before the total number of relevant documents is reached.
- *Sliding Ratio*: sum of the relevance judgments of the documents retrieved so far divided by the sum of the relevance judgments of the documents the ideal system would have retrieved so far.
- *Novelty Ratio*: percentage of the relevant retrieved documents which were previously unknown to the user.
- *Coverage Ratio*: percentage of relevant and known documents which are retrieved.

- *Relative Recall* (aka *sought recall*): percentage of the documents the user would have liked to examine which are relevant, retrieved, and examined.
- *Recall effort*: ratio of desired to examined by the user documents.
- *Satisfaction* (and *Frustration*): sliding ratio on documents in $R$ ($\overline{R}$) only.
- *Total*: weighted mean of satisfaction and frustration.
- *Usefulness measure*: which of two IR systems delivers more useful information to the user.
- *Average Search Length*: average number of documents examined moving down in a ranked list before the average position of a relevant document is reached.
- *NDPM*: normalized distance between user and system ranking of documents.
- *Ranked Half Life*: degree to which relevant documents are located on the top of a ranked retrieval result.
- *Relative Relevance*: degree of agreement between the types of relevance applied in a non-binary assessment context.
- *Classification Accuracy*: if the classification is correct $((|r \cap R| + |\overline{r} \cap \overline{R}|)/|N|)$.
- *Average Weighted Precision (AWP)*: based on Cumulative Gain (CG), but more statistically reliable since it performs comparison with an ideal ranked output before averaging across topics.
- *Weighted R-Precision*: an extension of R-Precision.
- *Average Distance Measure (ADM)*: average difference between the relevance amount of documents and their estimates by the IR system.
- *eXtended Cumulative Gain (XCG)*: extends DCG-based metrics via the definition of a set of relevance value functions modeling different user behaviors.
- *bpref*: the average number of nonrelevant documents before a relevant document in the ranking, using the documents in the pool only.
- *Q-measure*: is based on CG, but it is better than AWP because it imposes a penalty for going down the ranked list.
- *R-measure*: is based on CG and it is the counterpart of Q-measure for R-Weighted Precision.
- *Tolerance to Irrelevance (t2i)*: maximum time that the user would keep reading nonrelevant documents before she proceeds to the next result.
- *Estimated Ratio of Relevant*: expectation of the number of relevant documents a user sees in the list of the first $k$ returned documents, divided by the number of documents a user would see in the collection.
- *Kendall, Spearman*: statistical correlation between the ranked retrieval result and the user ranking of the documents.
- *Normalized xCG*: reflects the relative gain the user accumulated up to that rank, compared to the gain she could have attained if the system would have produced the optimum best ranking.
- *Mean average nxCG at rank n*: the average of nxCG[i] values for i=1 to $n$.
- *Effort-precision/gain-recall at standard gain-recall points*: the amount of relative effort (where effort is measured in terms of number of visited ranks) that the user is required to spend when scanning a systems result ranking compared to the effort an ideal ranking would take in order to reach a given level of gain (relative to the total gain that can be obtained).
- *Non-interpolated (Interpolated) mean average effort-precision*: the average of effort-precision values at each natural (standard) gain-recall point.

# 3   Conclusions and Future Work

The evolution over time shows that: (i) INEX initiative has caused a steep increase in the number of metrics; and (ii) the earlier metrics are usually classified under binary relevance and retrieval, and more recent metrics are often rank- or continuous-based, thus reflecting the changes in the underlying notion of relevance [15]. We hope that this classification will be useful for IR researchers, and will enable them to choose more consciously the most appropriate metrics for their purpose.

# References

1. R. Belew. *Finding Out About*. Cambridge Univ. Press, 2000.
2. P. Borlund and P. Ingwersen. Measures of relative relevance and ranked half-life: Performance indicators for interactive IR. In *21st SIGIR*, pages 324–331, 1998.
3. R. Brache. Personal communication, 2005.
4. C. Buckley and E. Voorhees. Retrieval evaluation with incomplete information. In *27th SIGIR*, pages 25–32, 2004.
5. W. S. Cooper. Expected search length: A single measure of retrieval effectiveness based on weak ordering action of retrieval systems. *JASIST*, 19:30–41, 1968.
6. A. de Vries, G. Kazai, and M. Lalmas. Tolerance to irrelevance: A user-effort oriented evaluation of retrieval systems without predefined retrieval unit. In *RIAO 2004 Conference Proceedings*, pages 463–473, 2004.
7. V. Della Mea and S. Mizzaro. Measuring retrieval effectiveness: A new proposal and a first experimental validation. *JASIST*, 55(6):530–543, 2004.
8. H. Frei and P. Schauble. Determining the effectiveness of retrieval algorithms. *IPM*, 27(2):153–164, 1991.
9. K. Järvelin and J. Kekäläinen. Cumulated gain-based evaluation of IR techniques. *TOIS*, 20:422–446, 2002.
10. N. Kando, K. Kuriyama, and M. Yoshioka. Information retrieval system evaluation using multi-grade relevance judgments. In *IPSJ SIGNotes*, 2001.
11. G. Kazai. Report of the INEX 2003 metrics working group. In *Proceedings of the 2nd INEX Workshop*, pages 184–190, 2004.
12. G. Kazai and M. Lalmas. INEX 2005 evaluation metrics. http://inex.is.informatik.uni-duisburg.de/2005/inex-2005-metricsv4.pdf.
13. R. R. Korfhage. *Information Storage and Retrieval*. John Wiley & Sons, 1997.
14. R. M. Losee. Upper bounds for retrieval performance and their use measuring performance and generating optimal boolean queries: Can it get any better than this? *IPM*, 30(2):193–204, 1994.
15. S. Mizzaro. Relevance: The whole history. *JASIS*, 48(9):810–832, 1997.
16. B. Piwowarski and P. Gallinari. Expected ratio of relevant units: A measure for structured information retrieval. In *INEX'03 proceedings*, pages 158–166, 2004.
17. T. Sakai. New performance metrics based on multigrade relevance: Their application to question answering. In *NTCIR 4 Meeting Working Notes*, 2004.
18. G. Salton and M. J. McGill. *Introduction to Modern Information Retrieval*. McGraw-Hill, 1984.
19. C. J. van Rijsbergen. *Information Retrieval*. Butterworths, 2nd edition, 1979.
20. Y. Y. Yao. Measuring retrieval effectiveness based on user preference of documents. *JASIS*, 46(2):133–145, 1995.

# Experiments on Average Distance Measure

Vincenzo Della Mea[1], Gianluca Demartini[1],
Luca Di Gaspero[2], and Stefano Mizzaro[1]

[1] Dept. of Mathematics and Computer Science
[2] Dept. of Electrical, Management and Mechanical Engineering,
University of Udine, Udine, Italy
{dellamea, demartin, mizzaro}@dimi.uniud.it,
l.digaspero@uniud.it

**Abstract.** ADM (Average Distance Measure) is an IR effectiveness
metric based on the assumptions of continuous relevance and retrieval.
This paper presents some novel experimental results on two different
test collections: TREC 8, re-assessed on 4-levels relevance judgments,
and TREC 13 TeraByte collection. The results confirm that ADM correlation with standard measures is high, even when using less data, i.e.,
few documents.

## 1 Introduction

Common effectiveness measures for Information Retrieval Systems (IRSs) are
based on the assumptions of binary relevance (either a document is relevant to
a given query or not) and binary retrieval (either a document is retrieved or
not). Several measures go beyond this and work with category relevance and
ranked retrieval; almost no measures are available for the continuous relevance
and retrieval case. One exception is ADM (*Average Distance Measure*) [1, 2, 3].

ADM measures the average distance between the amount of User Relevance
Estimate (UREs, the actual relevances of documents) and the amount of System
Relevance Estimates (SREs). ADM values lie in the [0, 1] range, with 0 representing the worst performance and 1 the performance of the ideal IRS. As discussed
in detail in previous papers [1, 2, 3], ADM presents some nice theoretical properties; also, ADM has been experimentally validated on TREC and NTCIR data,
with encouraging results, although the experimentation was somewhat limited.
Indeed, an experimental confirmation of ADM effectiveness is both needed and
difficult because very few data are available featuring continuous UREs and
SREs, so that some approximations and assumptions are necessary.

The present work aims at providing further experimental evidence on the
suitability of ADM for measuring the effectiveness of IRSs, especially when only
a limited number of documents is available. In particular, this work aims at
answering to the following two research questions: How many documents are
needed to compute ADM in order to obtain results comparable to those of conventional measures like Average Mean Precision and R-Precision? What is the
difference between computing ADM on the basis of two relevance levels or more?

In the experiments presented here, we used two document collections that
include non-binary relevance scales (which are not continuous, yet provide more

M. Lalmas et al. (Eds.): ECIR 2006, LNCS 3936, pp. 492–495, 2006.
© Springer-Verlag Berlin Heidelberg 2006

information than binary values): TREC 13 TeraByte, assessed on a 3-levels relevance scale, and TREC 8, re-assessed on a 4-levels relevance scale [4]. We compare ADM, by means of the Kendall's correlation, with the traditional effectiveness measures used by TREC, i.e., Mean Average Precision (MAP), R-Precision (R-Prec), and precision at $N$ retrieved documents (P@$N$).

## 2    Experiments on TREC 13 TeraByte

The TREC 13 TeraByte test collection features data from 70 IRSs, 57 of which retrieved at least 1,000 documents for each topic. To study ADM effectiveness when considering only few documents, we compare the correlations among ADM@$N$ (ADM calculated after $N$ documents retrieved) and the reference measures.

For this test collection, Kendall's correlation between the two reference measures MAP and R-Prec is 0.82, whereas, as reported in Figure 1, the correlation

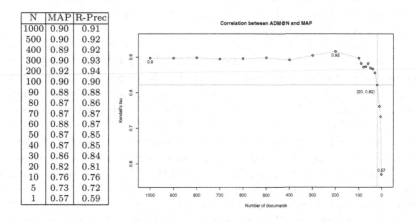

| N | MAP | R-Prec |
|------|------|--------|
| 1000 | 0.90 | 0.91 |
| 500 | 0.90 | 0.92 |
| 400 | 0.89 | 0.92 |
| 300 | 0.90 | 0.93 |
| 200 | 0.92 | 0.94 |
| 100 | 0.90 | 0.90 |
| 90 | 0.88 | 0.88 |
| 80 | 0.87 | 0.86 |
| 70 | 0.87 | 0.87 |
| 60 | 0.88 | 0.87 |
| 50 | 0.87 | 0.85 |
| 40 | 0.87 | 0.85 |
| 30 | 0.86 | 0.84 |
| 20 | 0.82 | 0.81 |
| 10 | 0.76 | 0.76 |
| 5 | 0.73 | 0.72 |
| 1 | 0.57 | 0.59 |

**Fig. 1.** Correlation between ADM@$N$ and the two standard metrics MAP and R-Prec

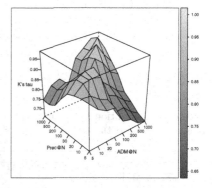

|  |  | ADM | | | | | | | |
|---|------|------|------|------|------|------|------|------|------|
|  | N | 5 | 10 | 20 | 30 | 100 | 200 | 500 | 1000 |
| Precision | 5 | **0.89** | 0.88 | 0.88 | 0.86 | 0.82 | 0.76 | 0.75 | 0.75 |
|  | 10 | 0.84 | 0.88 | **0.91** | 0.91 | 0.88 | 0.83 | 0.80 | 0.80 |
|  | 20 | 0.82 | 0.85 | 0.92 | **0.94** | 0.89 | 0.85 | 0.82 | 0.82 |
|  | 30 | 0.81 | 0.83 | 0.91 | **0.94** | 0.87 | 0.81 | 0.78 | 0.77 |
|  | 100 | 0.72 | 0.74 | 0.81 | 0.85 | **0.94** | 0.93 | 0.90 | 0.90 |
|  | 200 | 0.71 | 0.75 | 0.79 | 0.82 | 0.91 | **0.98** | 0.94 | 0.93 |
|  | 500 | 0.67 | 0.71 | 0.75 | 0.77 | 0.85 | 0.92 | **0.99** | 0.97 |
|  | 1000 | 0.66 | 0.68 | 0.72 | 0.75 | 0.83 | 0.87 | **0.92** | **0.92** |

**Fig. 2.** Correlation between ADM@$N$ and P@$N$

between ADM@$N$ and the reference measures is higher than 0.82 for $N \geq 20$. This suggests that, at least for this test collection, ADM calculated on only the first 20 documents provides the same information value as R-Prec and MAP computed on the whole set of retrieved documents.

Figure 2 shows how the correlation between ADM@$N$ and P@$N$ varies depending on the value of $N$. As expected, the higher correlation values for each $N$ (shown in boldface) lie on the diagonal of the table or in its proximity, so that the two measures correlates most for equal (or very close) $N$ values. This confirms that ADM@$N$ and P@$N$ measure similar phenomena.

# 3    Experiments on 4-Levels Relevance TREC

Sormunen [4] has re-assessed 18 topics from TREC 7 and TREC 8 using 4 levels of relevance (0, 1, 2 and 3). For the sake of applying traditional binary measures, these levels can (and have to) be binarized as either a *Rigid* mapping (levels 0 and 1 become 0, levels 2, and 3 become 1) or a *Relaxed* mapping (level 0 becomes 0, levels 1, 2, and 3 become 1).

We calculated ADM using both the 4 levels of relevance (denoted by ADM[4]) and the rigid and relaxed binary data (ADM[2rig] and ADM[2rel], respectively). These three ADM values were then compared with the reference measures MAP and R-Prec calculated on the Sormunen data (see Table 1). We then compared Sormunen and ADM values with the original MAP and R-Prec measures calculated on the TREC 8 data (see Table 2 and Figure 3).

ADM computed on the binary relaxed mapping has a higher correlation with the reference measures than ADM computed on the 4 levels of relevance. We conjecture that this phenomenon is related to the TREC evaluation rules: the TREC guidelines state that a document is judged relevant if any piece of it is relevant, thus the relaxed mapping matches better with the reference measures calculated by the original TREC assessments. This is a confirmation of the results

**Table 1.** Correlation between ADM and R-Prec and MAP. All measures are computed on the basis of the Sormunen's 4 levels reassessment.

|  | ADM[2rig] | ADM[2rel] | ADM[4] |
|---|---|---|---|
| R-Prec[rig] | 0.75 | 0.70 | 0.77 |
| R-Prec[rel] | 0.80 | 0.83 | 0.90 |
| MAP[rig] | 0.41 | 0.40 | 0.39 |
| MAP[rel] | 0.67 | 0.67 | 0.64 |

**Table 2.** Correlation between ADM computed on the basis of the Sormunen's 4 levels reassessment and the original TREC 8 measures

| | | Sormunen | | | | | | |
|---|---|---|---|---|---|---|---|---|
| | | ADM[2rig] | ADM[2rel] | ADM[4] | R-Prec[rig] | MAP[rig] | R-Prec[rel] | MAP[rel] |
| TREC 8 | ADM | 0.80 | 0.94 | 0.86 | 0.69 | 0.39 | 0.82 | 0.66 |
| | MAP | 0.79 | 0.85 | 0.82 | 0.72 | 0.43 | 0.82 | 0.79 |
| | R-Prec | 0.79 | 0.84 | 0.80 | 0.68 | 0.46 | 0.78 | 0.79 |

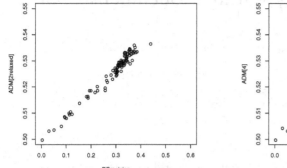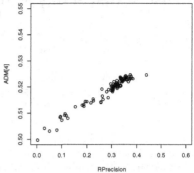

**Fig. 3.** Correlation between ADM[2rel] and R-Prec and between ADM[4] and R-Prec

shown in [4]. However, differences between ADM calculated on rigid and relaxed data are lower than those between either MAP or R-Prec calculated on rigid and relaxed data. This fact may be interpreted as either a greater robustness of ADM or a lower sensitivity to relevance variations, and thus needs further experimentations to be fully understood.

## 4   Conclusions and Future Work

The results on ADM presented in this paper are to be considered still preliminary. However, when considered together those already presented in [1, 2, 3], give insights on the capabilities of ADM as an effectiveness measure for information retrieval systems. In particular, the results show that ADM correlation with standard measures (R-Prec, MAP, P@$N$) is high, and that the correlation is still high also when using just few documents. The latter capability makes ADM easier to use for IRS evaluation than traditional binary measures.

In the future, we plan to further study the phenomena emphasized above; we are experimenting with ADM on INEX 2004 data and we intend to build an IRS capable of estimating the amount of relevance on a continuous scale.

## References

1. V. Della Mea, L. Di Gaspero, and S. Mizzaro. Evaluating ADM on a four-level relevance scale document set from NTCIR. In *Proceedings of NTCIR Workshop 4 Meeting - Supplement Vol. 2*, pages 30–38, 2004.
2. V. Della Mea and S. Mizzaro. Measuring retrieval effectiveness: A new proposal and a first experimental validation. *JASIS&T*, 55(6):530–543, 2004.
3. S. Mizzaro. A new measure of retrieval effectiveness (Or: What's wrong with precision and recall). In T. Ojala, editor, *International Workshop on Information Retrieval (IR'2001)*, pages 43–52, 2001.
4. E. Sormunen. Liberal relevance criteria of TREC - Counting on negligible documents? In K. Jarvelin, M. Beaulieu, R. Baeza-Yates, and S. Myaeng, editors, *Proceedings of the 25th ACM SIGIR Conference*, pages 324–330, August 11–15 2002.

# Phrase Clustering Without Document Context

Eric SanJuan[1] and Fidelia Ibekwe-SanJuan[2]

[1] LITA, University of Metz – URI, INIST-CNRS, France
eric.sanjuan@univ-metz.fr
[2] URSIDOC – University of Lyon 3, France
fidelia.ibekwe@univ-lyon3.fr

**Abstract.** We applied different clustering algorithms to the task of clustering multi-word terms in order to reflect a humanly built ontology. Clustering was done without the usual document co-occurrence information. Our clustering algorithm, CPCL (Classification by Preferential Clustered Link) is based on general lexico-syntactic relations which do not require prior domain knowledge or the existence of a training set. Results show that CPCL performs well in terms of cluster homogeneity and shows good adaptability for handling large and sparse matrices.

## 1 Introduction

We test the ability of clustering methods in an *out-of-context clustering* (OTC) task, i.e., clustering without document co-occurrence information. The methods are evaluated against categories issuing from a humanly built ontology. For this purpose, we chose as test corpus the GENIA dataset which comes with an existing *ideal partition*. Domain terms in this corpus have been manually annotated by specialists, yielding $31,398$ terms. The GENIA ontology consists of 36 categories at the leaf nodes. Each term in the GENIA corpus has been assigned a semantic category at the leaf node of the ontology. The goal of the evaluation is to determine the method whose output requires the least effort to reproduce the categories at the leaf nodes of the ontology.

## 2 Our Clustering Methodology

We developed a fast and efficient clustering algorithm, CPCL that builds clusters of multi-word terms (MWTs) without relying on document context. Details of our clustering methodology can be found in [1]. Here we only sketch out its principle. Terms are clustered depending on the presence and number of shared lexico-syntactic relations. Two types of lexico-syntatic operations are studied: the expansion of an existing term by the addition of one or more modifier words (*information retrieval – efficient retrieval of information*); the substitution a word in a term, either in the modifier position (*coronary heart disease – coronary lung disease*) or in the head position (*mutant motif – mutant strain*). We call $COMP$ the subset of relations that affects modifier words in

M. Lalmas et al. (Eds.): ECIR 2006, LNCS 3936, pp. 496–500, 2006.
© Springer-Verlag Berlin Heidelberg 2006

a term and $CLAS$ the subset that affects the head word in a term. Clustering is based on $COMP$ and $CLAS$ relations and CPCL, a graph-based algorithm called which implements a variant of hierarchical clustering. Let us refer to this principle of clustering as "clustering by lexico-semantic similarity" (LSS). $COMP$ relations are used in an initial phase to form connected components and $CLAS$ relations are used in the 2nd phase to form clusters of such components in a hierarchical process. The particularity of $CPCL$ is to compute at each iteration the local maximal similarity values in the graph of non null similarity relations. Average link clustering is then performed on the resulting subgraph.

## 3   Evaluation Metrics

For the OTC task, we need a measure that focuses on cluster quality (homogeneity) vis-à-vis an existing partition (here the GENIA categories) and that is also adapted to the comparison of methods producing a great number of clusters (hundreds or thousands) and of very differing sizes. Pantel & Lin's editing distance [2] appears as the most suitable for this task. We focus on two of the elementary operations in their measure: "merges" which is the union of disjoint sets and "moves" that applies to singular elements. In this restricted context, Pantel & Lin's measure has a more deterministic behaviour with some inherent bias which we correct hereafter.

Let $\Omega$ be a set of objects for which we know a crisp classification $\mathcal{C} \subseteq 2^{\Omega}$. Consider now a second disjoint family $\mathcal{F}$ of subsets of $\Omega$ representing the output of a clustering algorithm. For each cluster $F \in \mathcal{F}$, we denote by $\mathcal{C}_F$ the class $C \in \mathcal{C}$ such that $|C \cap F|$ is maximal. We thus propose a corrected version of this measure where the weight of each move is no more 1 but $|\Omega|/(|\Omega| - \max\{|C| : C \in \mathcal{C}\})$ and the weight of a merge is $|\Omega|/(|\Omega| - |\mathcal{C}|)$:

$$\mu_{ED}(\mathcal{C}, \mathcal{F}) = 1 - \frac{\max\{0, |\mathcal{F}| - |\mathcal{C}|\}}{|\Omega| - |\mathcal{C}|} - \frac{\sum_{F \in \mathcal{F}}(|F| - |\mathcal{C}_F \cap F|)}{|\Omega| - \max\{|C| : C \in \mathcal{C}\}} \tag{1}$$

The maximal value of $\mu_{ED}$ is 1 in the case where the clustering output corresponds exactly to the target partition. It is equal to 0 in the case that $\mathcal{F}$ is a trivial partition (discrete or complete). Based on the corrected $\mu_{ED}$ index, we propose a complementary index, *cluster homogeneity* ($\mu_H$) defined as:

$$\mu_H(\mathcal{C}, \mathcal{F}) = \frac{\mu_{ED}(\mathcal{C}, \mathcal{F})}{1 + \sum_{F \in \mathcal{F}}(|F| - |\mathcal{C}_F \cap F|)} \times |\Omega| \tag{2}$$

$\mu_H$ takes its maximal value $|\Omega|$ if $\mathcal{F} = \mathcal{C}$ and, like the $\mu_{ED}$ measure, it is null if $\mathcal{F}$ is one of the two trivial partitions. We will use $\mu_H$ to distinguish between algorithms having similar editing distances but not producing clusters of the same quality.

## 4    Experimental Setup

For statistical clustering methods to find sufficient *co-occurrence* information, it was necessary to represent *term-term* similarity. Co-occurrence is defined here as internal word co-occurrence within a term. We then built a *term × word* matrix where the rows were the terms and the columns the unique constituent words. We further adapted this matrix as follows: words are assigned a weight according to their grammatical role in the term and their position with regard to the head word. Since a head word is the noun focus (the subject), it receives a weight of 1. Modifier words are assigned a weight which is the inverse of their position with regard to the head word. Let $M$ be the term×word matrix such that $M_{i,j}$ refers to the weight of word $j$ in term $i$. We derive two other matrices from $M$. A similarity matrix $S = M.M^t$ whose cells give the similarity between two terms as the scalar product of their vectors (for hierarchical algorithms). A core matrix $C$ for partitioning algorithms by removing all rows and columns of $M$ with less than 5% of non null values.

We experimented three types of clustering relations on four clustering methods. The three clustering relations were:

- Coarse Lexical Similarity (CLS). This consists in grouping terms by identical head word and will serve as a "baseline" against which the other algorithms can be aligned.
- Lexico-Syntactic Similarity (LSS). This is based on the linguistic relations identified by our clustering methodology as described in section §2.
- Lexical Cohesion (LC). This is based on the vector representation of terms in the space of words they contain as described in section §4.

The following clustering algorithms were tested:

- **Baseline with CLS:** No particular parameter is necessary. All terms sharing the same head word are grouped in the same cluster.
- **CPCL with LSS:** Custering is based on LSS relations. No threshold was set so as not to exclude terms and relations. The algorithm was stopped at iteration 1. We also tested the performance of the 1st step of CPCL, i.e., the connected components formed at the $COMP$ level.
- **Hierarchical with LC:** Clustering is based on the similarity matrix $S[S \geq th]$ where $th$ is a threshold with the following values: 0.5 and 0.8.
- **Partitioning with LC:** This is based on the computation of k-means centers and medoids on the core matrix $C$. We used the standard functions of k-means and CLARA (Clustering LARge Applications).We ran these two variants for the following values of $k$: 36, 100, 300, 600 and 900.

## 5    Results

The baseline clustering grouped the whole list of terms in 3,220 clusters. CPCL on LSS generated 1,897 non trivial components at the COMP phase and 3,738 clusters at the CLAS phase. Hierarchical clustering on LC, based on similarity

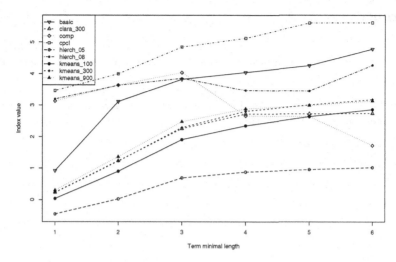

**Fig. 1.** Cluster homogeneity measure $\mu_{ED}$

matrix generated $1,090$ clusters for a threshold of $th = 0.5$ and $1,217$ clusters for $th = 0.8$.

The hierarchical algorithm with $th=0.8$ and CPCL obtain a better $\mu_{ED}$ score ($\geq 0.36$) than the baseline ($\leq 0.24$) and partitioning methods ($\leq 0.14$) when considering all terms (length $\leq 2$). When fewer and longer terms are considered (length $\geq 3$), partitioning methods obtain $\mu_{ED}$ scores between 0.58 and 0.79 and outperform the baseline, CPCL and hierarchical algorithms ($\leq 0.59$). However, the $\mu_{ED}$ measure masks important features of the evaluation: how homogeneous a cluster is with regard a category in the target partition.

Cluster homogeneity is measured by the $\mu_H$ index which computes the ratio between the value of $\mu_{ED}$ and the number of movings. This is plotted on figure 1. Since the majority of the clustering methods showed sensitivity to term length, we plotted the score obtained by each of the measure (y-axis) by term length (x-axis). Note that at each length, only terms of that length and above are considered. Thus, the further we move down the x-axis, the fewer the input terms for clustering. The baseline clustering is noted "basic" on this figure.

It appears clearly that CPCL outperforms the other methods. It forms the most homogeneous clusters that need the least number of moves and merges in order to obtain the target partition. Also, CPCL is the only algorithm that significantly outperforms the baseline, irrespective of term length.

## 6   Conclusion

Overall, this experiment has shown that even without adequate context (document co-occurrence), clustering algorithms can be adapted to partially reflect a human semantic organisation of scientific concepts. Moreover, clustering based on simple linguistic relations outperforms other criteria in terms of cluster quality.

# References

1. SanJuan, E., Dowdall, J., Ibekwe-SanJuan, F., Rinaldi, F.: A symbolic approach to automatic multiword term structuring. Computer Speech and Language **19**(4) (2005) 524 – 542
2. Pantel, P., Lin, D.: Clustering by Committee. In: Annual International conference of ACM on Research and Development in Information retrieval - ACM SIGIR, Tampere, Finland (2002) 199–206

# Rapid Development of Web-Based Monolingual Question Answering Systems

Edward W.D. Whittaker, Julien Hamonic, Dong Yang,
Tor Klingberg, and Sadaoki Furui

Dept. of Computer Science, Tokyo Institute of Technology,
2-12-1, Ookayama, Meguro-ku,
Tokyo 152-8552, Japan
{edw, yuuki, raymond, tor, furui}@furui.cs.titech.ac.jp

**Abstract.** In this paper we describe the application of our statistical pattern classification approach to question answering (QA) to the rapid development of monolingual QA systems. We show how the approach has been applied successfully to QA in English, Japanese, Chinese, Russian and Swedish to form the basis of our publicly accessible web-based multilingual QA system at http://asked.jp.

## 1  Introduction

The approach to question answering (QA) that we adopt has previously been described in [3, 4, 5] where the details of the mathematical model and how it was trained for English and Japanese were given. In this paper we demonstrate how this new statistical pattern classification approach to QA has been successfully applied to monolingual QA for the five distinct languages of English, Japanese, Chinese, Russian and Swedish. Using our approach and given appropriate training data it is found that a proficient developer can build a QA system in a new language in approximately 10 hours. The systems, built using this method, form the basis of our web demo which is publicly available at http://asked.jp.

Our approach to QA is significantly different to that commonly employed in contemporary QA systems. Specifically, our approach was designed to exploit the vast amounts of data available on the web, to require an absolute minimum of linguistic knowledge about the language to be encoded in the system and to be robust to the kinds of input errors that might come from a spoken interface to the system. For example, in our English-language system we only use capitalised word tokens in our system and do not use WordNet, named-entity (NE) extraction, regular expressions or any other linguistic information e.g. from semantic analysis or from question parsing. We do, however, rely heavily on the web and a conventional web search engine as a source of data for answering questions, and also require large collections of example questions and answers (q-and-a). Nonetheless, our approach is still very different to other purely web-based approaches such as askMSR and Aranea. For example, we use entire documents rather than the snippets of text returned by web search engines; we do not use structured document sources or databases and we do not transform the query

M. Lalmas et al. (Eds.): ECIR 2006, LNCS 3936, pp. 501–504, 2006.
© Springer-Verlag Berlin Heidelberg 2006

in any way neither by term re-ordering nor by modifying the tense of verbs. These basic principles apply to each of our language-specific QA systems thus simplifying and accelerating development.

Our approach has been successfully evaluated in the 2005 text retrieval conference (TREC) question answering track evaluations [1] where our group placed eleventh out of thirty participants [3]. Although the TREC QA task is substantially different to web-based QA this evaluation showed that the approach works and provides an objective assessment of its quality. Similarly, for our Japanese language system we have evaluated the performance of our approach on the NTCIR-3 QAC-1 task [5]. Although our Japanese experiments were applied retrospectively, the results would have placed us in the mid-range of participating systems.

We briefly describe our statistical pattern classification approach to QA in Section 2. In Section 3 we describe the basic building blocks of our QA system and how they can typically be trained. We also give a breakdown of the data used to train each language specific QA system and the approximate number of hours required for building each system.

## 2    Statistical Pattern Classification Approach to QA

The answer to a question depends primarily on the question itself but also on many other factors such as the person asking the question, the location of the person, what questions the person has asked before, and so on. For simplicity, we choose to consider only the dependence of an answer $A$ on the question $Q$. In particular, we hypothesize that the answer $A$ depends on two sets of features extracted from $Q$: $W = \mathcal{W}(Q)$ and $X = \mathcal{X}(Q)$ as follows:

$$P(A \mid Q) = P(A \mid W, X), \tag{1}$$

where $W$ can be thought of as a set of $l_W$ features describing the "question-type" part of $Q$ such as *who, when, where, which*, etc. and $X$ is a set of features comprising the "information-bearing" part of $Q$ i.e. what the question is actually about and what it refers to. For example, in the questions, *Where is Mount Everest?* and *How high is Mount Everest?* the information-bearing component is identical in both cases whereas the question-type component is different.

Finding the best answer $\hat{A}$ involves a search over all $A$ for the one which maximizes the probability of the above model:

$$\hat{A} = \arg\max_A P(A \mid W, X). \tag{2}$$

This is guaranteed to give us the optimal answer in a maximum likelihood sense if the probability distribution is the correct one. Making various conditional independence assumptions to simplify modelling we obtain the final optimisation criterion:

$$\arg\max_A \underbrace{P(A \mid X)}_{\substack{retrieval \\ model}} \cdot \underbrace{P(W \mid A)}_{\substack{filter \\ model}}. \tag{3}$$

The $P(A \mid X)$ model is essentially a language model which models the probability of an answer sequence $A$ given a set of information-bearing features $X$. It models the proximity of $A$ to features in $X$. This model is referred to as the *retrieval model*.

The $P(W \mid A)$ model matches an answer $A$ with features in the question-type set $W$. Roughly speaking this model relates ways of asking a question with classes of valid answers. For example, it associates names of people or companies with *who*-type questions. In general, there are many valid and equiprobable $A$ for a given $W$ so this component can only re-rank candidate answers retrieved by the retrieval model. Consequently, we call it the *filter model*.

## 3   System Components

There are four basic ingredients to building a QA system using our approach: (1) a collection of example question-and-answer (*q-and-a*) pairs used for answer-typing (answers need not necessarily be correct but must be of the correct answer type); (2) a classification of words (or word-like units cf. Japanese/Chinese) into classes of similar words (*classes*) e.g. a class of country names, of given names, of numbers etc.; (3) a list of question words (*qlist*) such as *"Who"*, *"Where"*, *"When"* etc.; and (4) a stop list of words that should be ignored by the retrieval model (*stoplist*).

The q-and-a for different languages can often be found on the web or in commercial quiz software that is relatively cheap to acquire. To obtain the classes $C$ for each language a fast automatic clustering algorithm taken from the statistical language modelling literature was applied [2]. To obtain word classes in this manner only a large source of training text $T$ comprising $|T|$ words in the target language is required. Typically, the vocabulary $V$ is taken to be the most frequent $|V|$ word tokens in $T$ which are then clustered into $|C|$ classes. The qlist is generated by taking the most frequently occurring terms in the q-and-a examples and the stoplist is formed from the 50 or so most frequently occurring words in $T$.

At run time Google is used to select web documents related to the question being asked. The question is passed as-is to Google after the removal of stop words. In our web demos the top 100 documents are downloaded in their entirety, HTML markup removed, the text cleaned and upper-cased. We have found that the more documents used the better the performance with no observed performance degradation even up to 10000 documents in Japanese, for example. For consistency, all data in our system in encoded using UTF-8.

The data and relevant system details for each language-specific QA system are given in Table 1 where the estimated number of man-hours to build each of the new systems is also shown. For the Japanese system Chasen[1] is used to segment character sequences into word-like units. For Chinese each sentence is mapped to a sequence of space-separated characters.

---

[1] http://chasen.naist.jp/hiki/ChaSen

**Table 1.** System description and number of hours to build each new language's QA system

| Language | # q-and-a examples | $T$ (corpus name) | $|T|$ | $|V|$ | $|C|$ | # hours |
|----------|--------------------|--------------------|------|------|------|---------|
| English  | 290k               | AQUAINT            | 300M | 300k | 5k   | —       |
| Japanese | 270k               | MAINICHI           | 150M | 215k | 500  | —       |
| Chinese  | 7k                 | TREC Mandarin      | 68M  | 33k  | 1k   | 10      |
| Russian  | 98k                | LUB [2]            | 100M | 500k | 1k   | 10      |
| Swedish  | 5k                 | PAROLE             | 19M  | 367k | 1k   | 10      |

## 4   Conclusion and Further Work

In this paper we have shown how our recently introduced statistical pattern classification approach to QA can be applied successfully to create with minimal effort monolingual web-based QA systems in many languages. In the official TREC2005 QA evaluation our approach was shown to be comparable to the state-of-the-art for English language QA. On the NTCIR-3 QAC-1 Japanese-language QA task comparable performance with the state-of-the-art was also obtained. Although no official results are available for Chinese, Russian and Swedish QA systems our subjective evaluations show that performance is lower but competitive with the English and Japanese systems. In future we aim to develop QA systems in many more languages and evaluate performance objectively for example by participating in the annual CLEF evaluations.

## Acknowledgments

This research was supported by JSPS and the Japanese government 21st century COE programme. The authors also wish to thank Dietrich Klakow for all his contributions.

## References

1. E. Voorhees and H. Trang Dang. Overview of the TREC 2005 Question Answering Track. In *Proceedings of the TREC 2005 Conference*, 2005.
2. E. Whittaker. *Statistical Language Modelling for Automatic Speech Recognition of Russian and English*. PhD thesis, Cambridge University, 2000.
3. E. Whittaker, P. Chatain, S. Furui, and D. Klakow. TREC2005 Question Answering Experiments at Tokyo Institute of Technology. In *Proceedings of the 14th Text Retrieval Conference*, 2005.
4. E. Whittaker, S. Furui, and D. Klakow. A Statistical Pattern Recognition Approach to Question Answering using Web Data. In *Proceedings of Cyberworlds*, 2005.
5. E. Whittaker, J. Hamonic, and S. Furui. A Unified Approach to Japanese and English Question Answering. In *Proceedings of NTCIR-5*, 2005.

# Filtering Obfuscated Email Spam by means of Phonetic String Matching*

Valerio Freschi, Andrea Seraghiti, and Alessandro Bogliolo

STI - University of Urbino, Urbino, IT-61029, Italy
{freschi, seraghit, bogliolo}@sti.uniurb.it

**Abstract.** Rule-based email filters mainly rely on the occurrence of critical words to classify spam messages. However, perceptive obfuscation techniques can be used to elude exact pattern matching. In this paper we propose a new technique for filtering obfuscated email spam that performs approximate pattern matching both on the original message and on its phonetic transcription.

## 1  Introduction

The increasing amount of unsolicited emails (a.k.a. *junk email* or *spam*) that circulate over the Internet has prompted research efforts aiming at building effective *anti-spam filters*. An ideal filter should stop all spamming messages without preventing the delivery of regular emails. In practice, however, any filter is based on an error-prone classification algorithm that can produce both *false-negative* results (FN), delivering spamming messages, and *false-positive* results (FP), blocking regular emails.

Existing approaches can be broadly classified into *rule-based* and *statistical* approaches. Rule-based filters classify an incoming message as spam if it meets user-specified rules that characterize known unsolicited emails. Statistical approaches rely on corpora of unsolicited and regular e-mails to infer distinguishing features to be used for classifying incoming email messages [6, 8]. A message is classified as spam if its statistical properties are closer to those of the unsolicited corpus than to those of the regular one. Both approaches look not only at the content of the message, but also at its header (list of recipients, source IP address, subject, ...). Since none of the approaches clearly outperforms the other, available tools usually integrate both of them. In this paper we focus only on rule-based spam filtering.

Since junk emails are often characterized by recurrent words (*keywords*) that do not appear in regular traffic, rule-based approaches make use of pattern matching to detect such words in the incoming messages. The list of keywords needs to be periodically updated, possibly using pattern-discovery algorithms that automatically find recurrent words in the emails discarded by the user [5].

To elude keyword-detection, spammers apply perceptive obfuscation techniques that change the orthography of the words in order to prevent exact pattern matching without avoiding the user to properly recognize them. For instance, the term 'viagra' is easily identified by a human reader even if it is changed in '\/1@gr@', 'v-i-a-g-r-a' or 'vaigra'.

Generalized rules based on regular expressions have been introduced to contrast deliberate misspellings [7]. However, regular expressions are hard to maintain and they

---

* This work was partially supported by *PIT Consulting SpA* and *Zone-H.org*.

© Springer-Verlag Berlin Heidelberg 2006

are not expressive enough to deal with all possible obfuscations. In alternative, statistical de-obfuscation techniques have been proposed to reduce obfuscated words to the corresponding keywords [4]. Finally, *approximate pattern matching* (APM) [2] can be used in place of exact matching to directly compare obfuscated words and keywords.

The key problem with de-obfuscation techniques is that the generalization of rules (or the relaxation of matching criteria) decreases the number of FNs at the cost of increasing the number of FPs. Moreover, new obfuscation strategies have been recently devised that exploit the complexity of English spelling rules to significantly change the orthography of a word without affecting its pronunciation. Since this kind of obfuscations work at phonological level, the orthographic effects they produce are not easily captured by orthographic de-obfuscation techniques. For instance, 'vyaggrra' has *edit distance* [2] 3 from 'viagra', but it has exactly the same pronunciation in English. This means that an orthographic APM tool should set a threshold 3 in order to detect the keyword despite its obfuscation (thus also recognizing the words 'diagram', 'via', 'vagrant' and 'anagram' as possible obfuscations of viagra). A filter based on English pronunciation could use threshold 0 to detect the keyword without any FP.

In this work we propose a new spam filtering technique that applies APM both to the original messages and to their phonetic transcriptions. Phonetic de-obfuscation is combined with orthographic APM to achieve the best trade off between FPs and FNs.

## 2   Proposed Approach

Figure 1 shows the tool flow of the proposed approach. The incoming message propagates through a message-transformation chain composed of 4 tasks (represented on the first row of the flow): *normalization*, *null-char removal*, *key-specific deambiguation* and *phonetic transcription*. The original message, together with the results of each transformation, are then passed to the APM modules (represented on the second row) that work in parallel providing independent flags that are eventually combined by the *rule-composition module*.

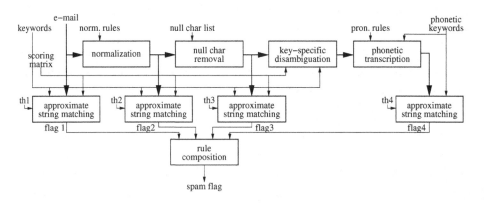

**Fig. 1.** Tool flow of the proposed approach

Orthographic obfuscations are handled in three steps. First, normalization rules are applied to restrict as much as possible the character set by replacing the original characters (or their combinations) with the graphically closest lower-case letters (e.g., â,ä,á, @ and å, are all mapped into 'a', ©into 'c' and \/ into 'v'). Normalization rules are applied only when the transformation is considered to be non-ambiguous (e.g., character '1' can be used to obfuscate either 'I' or 'l', hence it is left unchanged by the normalization step). Second, non-alphabetic characters that do not represent any letter (e.g., '-') are considered as null characters and removed from the string.

Finally, APM modules are used to search for the approximate occurrences of the keywords under a modified version of the *Damerau distance metric* [1], where insertion, deletion and possible swapping of adjacent characters are assigned with a unitary cost, while the costs of character substitutions are specified by a scoring matrix. In particular, the scoring matrix is used to handle ambiguous graphical obfuscations by assigning cost 1 to pairs of strongly dissimilar characters, cost 0 to identical characters (that correspond to diagonal entries) and cost 0 to all possible de-obfuscations of non-alphabetical characters (e.g., character '1' can be replaced at no cost either with 'i' or with 'l'). The choice of the proper de-obfuscation is implicitly made by the APM algorithm by finding the best alignment with the keyword (e.g., the '1' that appears in 'v1agra' is aligned with the 'i' of 'viagra' at no cost).

Phonetic de-obfuscation entails: key-specific disambiguation, phonetic transcription and APM with phonetic keywords. The strings returned by normalization and null-char removal steps still contain non-alphabetic characters that couldn't be normalized because of ambiguity. As previously observed, ambiguities can be conservatively solved when searching for a specific keyword. Key-specific deambiguation exploits the APM algorithm to decide which letter to use in place of all residual non-alphabetic characters. The resulting string is then processed by the phonetic transcription module that returns a sequence of phonetic symbols that represents the most likely English pronunciation. The same pronunciation rules are applied off-line to the keywords to build a list of phonetic keywords. The last step consists of searching for the approximate occurrences of the phonetic keywords in the phonetic transcription of the incoming message.

Phonetic transcription is based on hierarchical pronunciation rules (expressed as *grapheme* to *phoneme* correspondences) inferred from a dictionary [3]. Level-1 rules provide the most likely context-independent pronunciation of each grapheme, while level-$n$ rules provide context-specific exceptions derived by looking at up to $n$ context graphemes.

## 3   Experimental Results

The proposed tool flow was implemented in C and tested on a real-world benchmark composed of 2377 e-mail messages received by the authors during Summer 2005. For the sake of simplicity our analysis was restricted to the email subjects. This allowed us to manually annotate the benchmark finding 162 messages containing obfuscations of 'viagra' in the subject field.

SpamAssassin [7] was used for comparison. In particular, we applied the filter to the benchmark and we checked the logs to single out the messages satisfying the rules

**Table 1.** Experimental results for ortographic matching, phonetic matching (rule depth 1) and phonetic matching (rule depth 5)

| Ortographic (flag 3) | | | | | Rule depth 1 (flag 4) | | | | | Rule depth 5 (flag 4) | | | | |
|---|---|---|---|---|---|---|---|---|---|---|---|---|---|---|
| th3 | FP | FP/Nn | FN | FN/Ns | th4 | FP | FP/Nn | FN | FN/Ns | th4 | FP | FP/Nn | FN | FN/Ns |
| 0.0 | 0 | 0.00 | 104 | 0.64 | 0 | 0 | 0.00 | 68 | 0.42 | 0 | 0 | 0.00 | 72 | 0.44 |
| 1.0 | **0** | 0.00 | **25** | 0.15 | 1 | **0** | 0.00 | **11** | 0.07 | 1 | **0** | 0.00 | **45** | 0.28 |
| 2.0 | 42 | 0.02 | 20 | 0.12 | 2 | 25 | 0.01 | 0 | 0.00 | 2 | 35 | 0.02 | 4 | 0.03 |
| 3.0 | 688 | 0.31 | 0 | 0.00 | 3 | 279 | 0.13 | 0 | 0.00 | 3 | 270 | 0.12 | 0 | 0.00 |
| 4.0 | 1846 | 0.83 | 0 | 0.00 | 4 | 1481 | 0.67 | 0 | 0.00 | 4 | 1342 | 0.61 | 0 | 0.00 |

specifically designed to detect the obfuscations of 'viagra' in the subject. SpamAssassin classified as obfuscations of 'viagra' 48 messages, with 3 FPs and 117 FNs[1].

We applied the proposed approach with a keyword list containing only the word 'viagra'. The results achieved are reported in Table 1, that shows the separate effectiveness of ortographic (flag3) and phonetic (flag4) de-obfuscations. For the sake of conciseness we do not report separate results for the first two flags.

For each instance of the APM algorithm a different threshold can be specified to span the trade off between FPs and FNs: The higher the threshold the lower the number of FNs and the higher the number of FPs. We evaluated the effect of phonetic pattern matching with different sets of pronunciation rules, ranging from context-free rules (rule depth 1) to context-dependent rules (up to rule depth 5). As expected, the best results were achieved with the simplest rule set. In fact, phonetic obfuscations rely on the most intuitive (i.e., most likely) pronunciation of each grapheme. From Table 1 we observe that the best tradeoff between FPs and FNs separately provided by each flag (highlighted in boldface) outperforms the results of SpamAssassin.

Finally, flag composition rules were tested to build a classifier combining the information provided by flag3 and flag4. The best result was provided by $flag3^{(th3=1)} + flag4^{(th4=1)}$, returning 0 (i.e., 0%) FPs and 5 (i.e., 3.08%) FNs. These results demonstrate that ortographic and phonetic pattern matching provide complementary information, allowing us to properly recognize heavily obfuscated words (such as '\/1@grr/A') using only the exact spelling of the undesired word (e.g., 'viagra') as a keyword.

# References

1. F. Damerau: A technique for computer detection and error correction of spelling errors. Comm. of the ACM **7** (3), 171-176. (1964)
2. D. Gusfield: Algorithms on Strings, Trees, and Sequences, Cambridge University Press. (1999)
3. J. Hochberg, S.M. Mniszewski, T. Calleja, G.J. Papcun: A default hierarchy for pronouncing English. IEEE Trans. on Pattern Matching and Machine Intelligence (1991) **13**, 957-964
4. H. Lee, A.Y. Ng: Spam deobfuscation using a Hidden Markov Model. Proceedings of the Second Conference on Email and Anti-Spam. (CEAS05). (2005)

---

[1] We remark that these numbers do not represent the overall performance of SpamAssassin, but just the effectiveness of the rules directly comparable with the algorithms presented in this work.

5. I. Rigoutsos, T. Huynh: Chung-Kwei: a pattern-discovery-based system for the automatic identification of unsolicited E-mail messages (SPAM). Proceedings First Conference on Email and Anti-Spam (CEAS04). (2005)
6. M. Sahami, S. Dumais, D. Heckerman, E. Horvitz: A Bayesian approach to filtering junk E-Mail. Proceedings of AAAI-98 Workshop on Learning for Text Categorization. (1998)
7. http://spamassassin.apache.org/
8. S. Stolfo, S. Hershkop, K. Wang, O. Nimeskern, C.W. Hu: Behavior-Based Approach to Securing Email Systems. Second International Workshop on Mathematical Methods, Models, and Architectures for Computer Network Security, ACNS03 (2003), LNCS 2776, 57-81

# Sprinkling: Supervised Latent Semantic Indexing

Sutanu Chakraborti, Robert Lothian, Nirmalie Wiratunga, and Stuart Watt

School of Computing, The Robert Gordon University,
Aberdeen AB25 1HG, Scotland, UK
{sc, rml, nw, sw}@comp.rgu.ac.uk

**Abstract.** Latent Semantic Indexing (LSI) is an established dimensionality reduction technique for Information Retrieval applications. However, LSI generated dimensions are not optimal in a classification setting, since LSI fails to exploit class labels of training documents. We propose an approach that uses class information to influence LSI dimensions whereby class labels of training documents are endoded as new terms, which are appended to the documents. When LSI is carried out on the augmented term-document matrix, terms pertaining to the same class are pulled closer to each other. Evaluation over experimental data reveals significant improvement in classification accuracy over LSI. The results also compare favourably with naive Support Vector Machines.

## 1 Introduction

Supervised text classification systems are typically based on the Vector Space Model (VSM) or the Probabilistic Model. Latent Semantic Indexing (LSI) [1] uses a two-mode factor analysis on the VSM term-document representation to construct a lower-dimensional space where term co-occurrence patterns are used to infer "latent" associations between terms (words). LSI has been shown to be effective in handling synonymy, and to a lesser extent polysemy [1].

LSI has been successfully used previously for text classification applications [2,3]. One limitation of LSI in classification is that it fails to exploit class labels of training documents. If taken into account, class labels can help LSI promote inferred associations between words representative of the same class and attenuate word associations otherwise.

In this paper, we investigate how additional terms corresponding to class labels of documents can be appended to each training document, so as to promote class specific word associations. We call this process "sprinkling". When LSI is performed on a term-document matrix augmented with sprinkled terms, documents belonging to the same class are moved closer to each other. Furthermore, since LSI maps documents and words to a homogeneous space, words pertaining to concepts associated with the same class are drawn closer to each other.

## 2 Latent Semantic Indexing and Sprinkling

LSI [1] uses singular value decomposition (SVD) to factor a term-document matrix into three matrices $U$, $\Sigma$ and $V$ where $U$ and $V$ contain the left and right singular vectors of $A$ and the matrix $\Sigma$ is a diagonal matrix containing the singular values

M. Lalmas et al. (Eds.): ECIR 2006, LNCS 3936, pp. 510–514, 2006.
© Springer-Verlag Berlin Heidelberg 2006

$$A = U \Sigma V^T$$

Retaining only top $k$ singular values in $\Sigma$, we can construct an approximation $A_k$ to the original matrix that is the best k-rank approximation to A in the least-squares sense. Terms which occur in similar documents will be drawn close to each other in the $k$ dimensional factor space even if they never actually co-occur in the same document.

Two limitations of LSI in a classification setting are: top k singular values correspond neatly to class structure mostly in the absence of overlapping terms between documents from different classes; and infrequent words with high discriminatory power are watered down. To address these issues, we incorporate class knowledge into LSI by generating a set of artificial terms corresponding to the class labels and appending these terms to the training documents. We refer to this process as 'sprinkling'. LSI is then carried out on this augmented matrix, and a lower-rank approximation of this matrix is obtained. The resulting matrix has the same dimensionality as the augmented matrix. Columns corresponding to additional

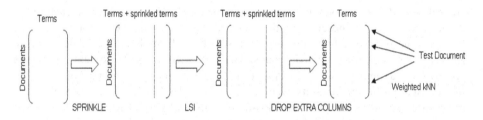

**Fig. 1.** Classification using Sprinkled LSI

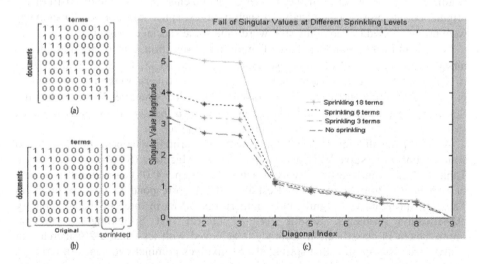

**Fig. 2.** (a) Original Term Doc Matrix (b) Matrix after Sprinkling 3 terms (c) Fall of Singular Values before and after sprinkling

sprinkled terms are dropped from this matrix and test documents are classified using weighted kNN using an Euclidean distance metric. These steps are illustrated in Fig.1.While in principle it is possible to augment the matrix with real valued elements, we retain the binary-valued nature of the matrix in the interest of efficiency.

Sprinkling aims to make explicit any implicit associations between terms indicative of underlying classes. Since sprinkled terms are essentially class labels, the inclusion of them helps to artificially promote co-occurrences between existing terms and classes. Fig. 2(a) shows a trivial term-doc matrix which is sprinkled with additional terms. We assume that documents 1, 2, 3 belong to class 1; documents 4, 5 and 6 to class 2; documents 7, 8 and 9 to class 3. With increased sprinkling the top three singular values get promoted with respect to the remaining ones. This has the desired effect of creating a document space that is separable into class specific clusters.

## 3 Evaluation

We evaluate classification effectiveness of Sprinkled LSI using routing datasets created from the 20 Newsgroups [4] corpus. One thousand messages from each of the 20 newsgroups were chosen at random and partitioned by the newsgroup name [4]. We form the following four sub corpuses: SCIENCE from 4 science related groups; REC from 4 recreation related groups; HARDWARE from 2 problem discussion groups on Mac and PC and RELPOL from 2 groups on religion and politics. Two further Spam filtering datasets were used: USREMAIL [8] which contains 1000 personal emails of which 50% are Spam and LINGSPAM [7] which contains 2893 email messages, of which 83% are legitimate messages related to linguistics and the rest are Spam. Equal sized disjoint training and test sets were created, where each stratified set contains 20% of the dataset of documents randomly selected from the original corpus. For repeated trials, 15 such train test splits were formed. Documents were pre-processed by removing stop words and some special characters.

We use an Information Gain based feature (term) selection. Results are presented at nine different choices of LSI dimensionality: 5, 10, 15, 20, 40, 60, 80, 100 and 120. It is important to note that sprinkling too many terms (over-sprinkling) may fail to preserve interesting variations in the original term-doc structure. When evaluating Sprinkled LSI, we used 16 sprinkled terms over each dataset, as this was found to strike a good tradeoff between under- and over-sprinkling.

Accuracy results for LSI with and without Sprinkling appear in Fig. 3 and comparisons with Naïve VSM and Support Vector Machines (SVM-Light [9]) are in Table 1. Significance testing involved paired t-tests ($p = 0.05$) carried out over each of 6 pairs (of four algorithms). Results in bold correspond to best accuracy in Table 1. Sprinkled LSI significantly outperforms SVM in three of the four binary classification problems. Results further confirm that Sprinkling's significant improvement in classification accuracy is achieved with less than a 2% increase in matrix size. This implies that sprinkled LSI involves nominal overheads in terms of computation time.

**Table 1.** Comparison of optimal performance of algorithms

|  | Routing | | | | Filtering | | | |
|---|---|---|---|---|---|---|---|---|
|  | REC Accuracy | SCIENCE Accuracy | HARD WARE Accuracy | RELPOL Accuracy | USREMAIL | | LINGSPAM | |
|  |  |  |  |  | Acc | Prec | Acc | Prec |
| Naïve VSM | 62.79 | 54.89 | 59.51 | 70.51 | 59.23 | 62.84 | 85.09 | 58.89 |
| LSI | 79.32 | 72.55 | 66.30 | 91.17 | 94.67 | 93.71 | **97.37** | **99.05** |
| Sprinkled LSI | **86.99** | **80.60** | **80.42** | **93.89** | **96.13** | **96.40** | 98.34 | 98.32 |
| SVM | --- | --- | 78.82 | 91.86 | **95.83** | **97.37** | 95.63 | 98.32 |

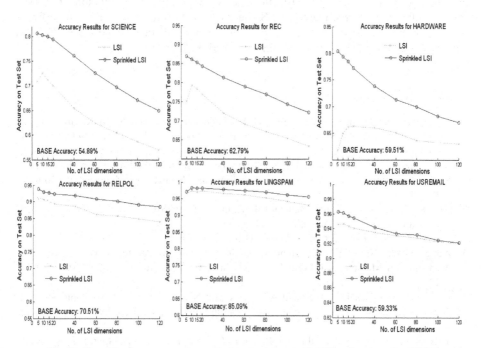

**Fig. 3.** Classification accuracy results for six datasets (BASE refers to naïve VSM)

## 4 Related Work

Zelikovitz et al.[2] use background texts in addition to training data. This is useful when the training data set is small and each document has few words. The significant difference with our approach is that instead of using an extended corpus, we attempt to integrate additional knowledge by way of additional terms that represent the underlying class structure. Wang and Nie [5] have an objective similar to ours; they present a theoretical model to extend LSI to classification domains. The authors do not present any experimental validation for their algorithm, but observe that the algorithm slows down in situations where a document can belong to more than one class. In contrast, sprinkling is, in principle, insensitive to the number of classes, which only affects the encoding of the sprinkled terms. Wiener et al. [6] approach the problem of text classification using LSI by introducing a local LSI in addition to the global LSI. Local LSI representations are created separately for each class and the test document is compared with each local LSI representation separately. The disadvantage is that similarities between test documents across different representations are not easily comparable.

# 5  Conclusion

We have presented Sprinkling, a novel approach to incorporating knowledge of classes into LSI for text classification tasks. Experimental evaluation shows its superior effectiveness compared to LSI on its own. Sprinkled LSI also outperforms SVM on binary classification problems. Future work will investigate the problem of empirically arriving at the optimal number of sprinkled terms.

# References

1. Deerwester, S., Dumais, S.T., Furnas G.W., Landauer T.K., Harshman R.: Indexing by Latent Semantic Analysis, Journal of the American Society of Information Science, 41(6), 1990, pp. 391-407
2. Zelikovitz S., Hirsh, H.: Using LSI for Text Classification in the Presence of Background Text, International Conference on Information and Knowledge Management 2001,pp. 113- 118
3. Gee, Kevin R.: Using Latent Semantic Indexing to Filter Spam, Proc. of the 2003 ACM Symposium on Applied Computing, 2003, pp. 460-464
4. Mitchell, T: Machine Learning. Mc Graw Hill International,1997
5. Wang, M.W., Nie, J.Y.: A Latent Semantic Structure Model for Text Classification, Workshop on Mathematical/Formal methods in Information Retrieval, 26th ACM-SIGIR, 2003
6. Wiener E., Pedersen J.O., Weigend A.S.: A Neural Network Approach To Topic Spotting, Proc. of Symposium on Document Analysis and Information Retrieval-95,  1995, pp. 317-332
7. Sakkis,  G.,  Androutsopoulos,  I.,Paliouras,G.,  Karkaletsis,V.,  Spyropoulos,  C.D., Stamatopoulos,P.: A Memory-based Approach to Anti-Spam Filtering for Mailing Lists. Information Retrieval, 6:49–73, 2003
8. Delany S.J., Cunningham P.: An Analysis of Case-base Editing in a Spam Filtering System in Proc of the 7th European Conference on Case-Based Reasoning, Springer., 2004. pp. 128–141
9. Joachims, T.: Making Large-Scale SVM Learning Practical. Advances in Kernel Methods - Support Vector Learning, Schölkopf B., Burges, C. and Smola, A. (ed.), MIT-Press, 1999

# Web-Based Multiple Choice Question Answering for English and Arabic Questions

Rawia Awadallah and Andreas Rauber

Department of Software Technology and Interactive Systems,
Vienna University of Technology, Vienna, Austria
rradi@mail.iugaza.edu, rauber@ifs.tuwien.ac.at

**Abstract.** Answering multiple-choice questions, where a set of possible answers is provided together with the question, constitutes a simplified but nevertheless challenging area in question answering research. This paper introduces and evaluates two novel techniques for answer selection. It furthermore analyses in how far performance figures obtained using the English language Web as data source can be transferred to less dominant languages on the Web, such as Arabic. Result evaluation is based on questions from both the English and the Arabic versions of the TV show "Who wants to be a Millionaire?" as well as on the TREC-2002 QA data.

## 1 Introduction

A large body of research exists on Question Answering (QA) where user queries are received in a natural language and precise answers are returned, decomposing the problem into three steps: (1) retrieving documents that may contain answers, (2) extracting answer candidates, and (3) selecting the most probably correct answer. Early TREC QA systems were looking for an answer that was known to be included in a given local corpus. Now, many QA systems use the Web as a corpus, either by extracting answers or by learning lexical patterns from the Web which are then used to improve the system itself. Studies suggest that the resulting data redundancy provides more reliable answer extraction [1]. Different approaches to improve system performance exist, such as using probabilistic algorithms to learn the best question paraphrase [2] or training a QA system to find possible sentence-length answers [3]. When several potential answers are retrieved, answer validation techniques rank them, selecting the most probable answer. This basically resembles multiple-choice QA. Approaches to answer validation range from purely statistical methods [7] based on Web search to the use of semantic techniques [4].

In this paper we present and evaluate two new answer selection techniques within a multiple-choice QA settings, comparing them to exciting answer validation techniques. These are evaluated on both English and Arabic language questions to evaluate the impact of the different sizes of the Web in the respective languages. Questions stem from both the TREC-2002 QA task questions as well as the English and the Arabic versions of the TV show "Who wants to be a Millionaire?", a quiz-show that originated in the UK and has been exported around the world, where candidates have to answer 4-choice trivia general-interest questions.

M. Lalmas et al. (Eds.): ECIR 2006, LNCS 3936, pp. 515–518, 2006.
© Springer-Verlag Berlin Heidelberg 2006

The remainder of the paper is organized as follows: Section 2 describes our multiple-choice QA module. Experiments are detailed in Section 3, with conclusions being presented in Section 4.

## 2   The MCQAS Module

The core procedure of our Multiple Choice Question Answering System (MC-QAS) is roughly as follows: A set of representative keywords both from the question and from each individual answer is extracted using simple linguistic techniques. Tokenization is performed to extract individual terms followed by (attached and detached) stop word and punctuation removal. The stem of each of the remaining words is obtained. For Arabic, a normalization process is further applied on the remaining words as described in [8]. The set of these remaining words along with their stems form the keywords set which is transformed into a set of individual queries combining the question keywords and the answer keywords of each individual answer. This is then submitted to, in our case, the Google search engine. A core task now is to assess the relevance of the candidate answers. Using search engines and the Web as a basis for answer selection, several different techniques utilizing different amounts of information can be applied. Those range from simple hit counts, via using the text snippets returned for each document providing context information on the query words found, to full-fledged analysis of the documents retrieved by the search engine. As the latter results in a rather high overhead in terms of document downloads, our work focuses on utilizing the result snippets for answer selection. In MCQAS, six answer selection techniques are used – four were previously used in answer validation task and two new ones. These are either based on the number of documents retrieved from the Web (Hits, CCP, KA), or on the analysis of snippets returned by the search engine (CW, AQC, AQA):

1. **Hits:** simple hit counts returned by a search engine [5].
2. **Corrected Conditional Probability (CCP):** based on the conditional probability of answer keyword based hits, given query keywords [7].
3. **Key Words Association (KA):** based on forward and backward associations of the query using hand crafted rules, calculating probabilities for hits using the set of question and answer keywords.
4. **Co-occurrence Weight (CW):** based on the distance (number of non-stopwords) between question and answer keywords in result snippets [7].
5. **Answer and Question words Count (AQC):** based on the number of question and/or answer keywords ocurring in result snippets.
6. **Answer and Question words Association (AQA):** based on the co-occurrence of both question and answer keywords within the same result snippet's context.

In a nutshell, the two new techniques are calculated as follows: The snippets of the first 10 (or all, if less than 10) search results for each query are weighted, and their average should be the answer score. For AQC, a snippet weight is the number of query words it contains. For AQA, a snippet weight is the sum of its sub-snippets weights where the sub-snippet (context) is defined by the text between the ellipsis symbols "...", and in which at least one question keyword and at least one answer keyword co-occur. A sub-snippet weight is the percentage of the different question keywords added to the percentage of the different answer keywords.

## 3   Experiments

In order to check the validity of the different answer validation techniques experiments have been carried out using questions from the English[1] and the Arabic version of the TV Show "Who Wants to Be a Millionaire?", as well as the TREC-2002 QA track questions. To transform the latter into a multiple choice QA setting four answers returned during the TREC sessions were selected manually for each question, making sure that exactly one correct answer is among the four.

**Table 1.** QA accuracy of different techniques for different questions categories

| Category | Hits | CCP | KA | CW | AQC | AQA |
|---|---|---|---|---|---|---|
| **Arabic** | 38.0% | 43.0% | 45.0% | 50.0% | 44.0% | **55.0%** |
| **English** | 43.0% | 45.0% | 48.0% | 59.0% | **63.0%** | 60.0% |
| **TREC** | 35.0% | 40.0% | 42.0% | 59.0% | **62.0%** | 56.0% |

A random subset of 100 questions was used to run the experiments in each case. An overview of the results is provided in Table 1. The snippet-based techniques outperformed the hits-based ones. For Arabic, AQA outperforms the other techniques, while for English, AQC is dominant. An analysis of the Arabic queries search results has revealed, that the returned number of snippets for most queries was less than 10 and most of these snippets were irrelevant and only few relevant precise phrases were found to exist on the Web. This is because there are many Arabic words with the same spelling but with different meanings. So the use of more restrictive schemas (CW and AQA) is essential. More over, using general search engines such as Google for Arabic queries does not satisfy the redundancy issue required by the hits-based techniques since Arabic specific features to query correction such as word morphology or word root is not implemented, which emphasizes the need for more linguistic efforts. On the other hand, for English queries the redundancy is higher and more restrictive schemas may ignore the cases where the question and the right answer keywords appear frequently but in different contexts (sub-snippets).

A more detailed analysis reveals that the various techniques tend to answer different questions correctly. This opens room for ensemble methods. However,

---

[1] Thanks to Shyong K. Lam for providing us with their test data from [5].

more detailed analysis of question types and answer characteristics will be required to reveal an optimized strategy.

## 4 Conclusions

In this paper we proposed two new techniques for answer selection based on analyzing the text snippets returned by a search engine when confronted with modified question–answer pairs as queries. Evaluations have been performed both on English and Arabic questions from the TV show "Who wants to be a Millionaire?" as well as TREC-2002 data. Experiments reveal an average performance of 55-62%, with the AQA strategy performing better on the Arabic language questions, while AQC is superior for English language tasks. This may be attributed to the morphological complexity of the Arabic language, resulting in only precise phrases returned if they exist on the Web, rather than having split segments returned as well. Analysis reveals that further improvements can be obtained by both more complex linguistic pre-processing, specifically for the Arabic language, and by using ensemble methods for answer selection.

## References

1. Clarke, C. L. A. and Cormack, G. V. and Lynam, T. R., *Exploiting redundancy in question answering*, Proc. of th 24th Annual Int'l ACM SIGIR Conf. on Research and Development in Information Retrieval, 2001.
2. Radev, H.R and Qi, H. and Zheng, Z. and Blair-Goldensohn, Zhang, Z. and Fan, W.and Prager, J., *Web for Answers to Natural Language Questions*, Proc. of the 10th Int'l Conf. on Information and Knowledge Management, 2001.
3. Mann, S., *A Statistical Method for Short Answer Extraction*, Proc. of the 39th Annual Meeting of the Association for Computational Linguistics, 2001.
4. Harabagiu, S. and Maiorano, S., *Finding Answers in Large Collections of Texts: Paragraph Indexing + Abductive Inference*, Proc. of the AAAI Fall Symposium on Question Answering Systems, 1999.
5. Shyong, K. Lam and David, M. Pennock and Dan, Cosley and Steve, Lawrence, *1 Billion Pages = 1 Million Dollars? Mining the Web to Play "Who Wants to be a Millionaire?"*, Proc. of the 19th Conf. on Uncertainty in Artificial Intelligence, 2003.
6. Masatsugu, T. and Takehito, U. and Satoshi, S., *Answer Validation by Keyword Association*, Proc. of the 3rd Workshop on Robust Methods in Analysis of Natural Language Data, 2004.
7. Magnini, B. and Negri, M. and Prevete, R. and Tanev, H., *Mining the Web to Validate Answers to Natural Language Questions*, Proc. of the 3rd Int'l Conf. on Data Mining, 2002.
8. Ballesteros, L. and Connell, E.M., *Improving stemming for Arabic information retrieval: light stemming and co-occurrence analysis*, Proc. of the 25th Annual International ACM SIGIR Conference on Research and Development in Information Retrieval, 2002, 275-282.

# Authoritative Re-ranking of Search Results

Toine Bogers and Antal van den Bosch

ILK / Language and Information Sciences, Tilburg University,
P.O. Box 90153, NL-5000 LE Tilburg, The Netherlands
{A.M.Bogers, Antal.vdnBosch}@uvt.nl

**Abstract.** We examine the use of authorship information in information retrieval for closed communities by extracting expert rankings for queries. We demonstrate that these rankings can be used to re-rank baseline search results and improve performance significantly. We also perform experiments in which we base expertise ratings only on first authors or on all except the final authors, and find that these limitations do not further improve our re-ranking method.

## 1  Introduction

Professionals have several options available to fulfill their information needs. One particularly rich source of useful information is the combined body of publications of the workgroup that the professional is a part of. Colleagues share both interests and vocabulary, and publications of colleagues are also often considered to be more trustworthy compared to random documents found in libraries and on the WWW. Workgroup members are bound by the common research focus of the workgroup, but each member also has separate interests and may be the group's expert on specific topics. By adopting a wider perspective and by disregarding institutional proximity, scientific communities or collectives of people who publish articles in a specific journal can also be considered a workgroup; in the remainder of this paper we use "workgroup" to refer to both meanings.

In this paper we present *authoritative re-ranking*, a novel method of re-ranking search results which utilizes information on topical expertise of workgroup members to improve the information retrieval process within these workgroups. We assume that we can estimate the expertise of each member of the workgroup from the aggregated content of his or her publications. Based on this, we estimate how well a term or phrase points to a certain expert, by calculating the author-term co-occurrence weights. We describe a method to create expertise rankings of the workgroup members for a query, and use these rankings to re-rank the search results produced by a baseline system. We performed experiments to determine which authors contribute the most to this re-ranking.

Constructing rankings of author expertise is a relatively new subfield of information retrieval research. TREC 2005 marked the introduction of the 'Expert Search Task', aimed at solving the problem of identifying employees who are the experts on a certain topic or in a certain situation [6]. Campbell et al. [2] performed similar experiments on a corpus of e-mail messages sent between people in the same company. Neither approach uses these expertise rankings to

M. Lalmas et al. (Eds.): ECIR 2006, LNCS 3936, pp. 519–522, 2006.
© Springer-Verlag Berlin Heidelberg 2006

improve search results. A considerable amount of research has been devoted to improving the search results of information retrieval systems. Among the more successful approaches are query expansion [7] and using cluster analysis [5] or citation analysis for re-ranking purposes [4].

## 2  Authoritative Re-ranking

Our re-ranking approach was designed to be used on top of a basic TF·IDF vector space model of information retrieval. In our experiments, we used the formulas for document weights and query weights as determined by [3]. We incorporated some tried and tested low-level NLP-techniques into our baseline system, such as stop word filtering and stemming. We also experimented with statistical and syntactic phrases and optimized the use of these techniques for every test collection, as recommended by [1].

We partitioned the documents into one-vs-all data sets for each author and then calculated the co-occurrence weights of each author-term pair for each term (words and phrases) that occurred in the collection. The weights were determined using the following feature selection metrics from text categorization: Information Gain, Chi-Square, and Mutual Information [8]. We also tested using the average TF·IDF value as a measure of term informativeness; collection terms that did not occur in the author's documents were assigned a score of zero.

Combining these term weights for each author yielded a matrix of term-author weights for each of these metrics. For each query-author combination an expert score was calculated that signified the expertise of the author on the query topic. Calculating the expert scores is based on the straightforward assumption that if terms characteristic for author $A$ occur in query $Q$, $A$ is likely to be more of an expert on $Q$. For each author separately, the informativeness weights were collected for each of the query terms and combined into an expert score. We experimented with taking an unweighted average of the weights and an average weighted by the TF·IDF values of the query terms.

Re-ranking the baseline results using these expert rankings was the final step in authoritative re-ranking. It is based on the premise that the documents authored by the experts on the current query topic are more likely to be relevant to the query, i.e. more *suitable* to fulfill the query. Since many documents have multiple authors, the expert scores associated with each document had to be combined. Early experimentation showed that weighting the expert scores with the total number of publications of each author gave the best performance. We also investigated abating the influence of high numbers of publications with the square root and the natural logarithm of these counts as weighting factors. After computing this 'suitability' score, which is computed for each query–document combination, it is combined with the original baseline similarity score to form a new score on the basis of which the authoritative re-ranking is performed.

We performed additional experiments to test and fine-tune the ways in which similarity scores and suitability scores can be combined. The most successful combinations involved multiplying the original similarity score with the (normalized) suitability score $S$ and transforming the original similarity score by multiplying it with $1 + S$. Experiments showed that the optimal re-ranking settings were collection-dependent, so the settings were optimized for each collection, similar to the NLP techniques used in the baseline [1].

## 3    Evaluation

Investigating the merits of authoritative re-ranking in workgroups required testing our approach on test collections that (1) contain information about the authors of each document, and (2) are a realistic representation of a workgroup. We used two well-known test collections, **CACM** (3204 documents, 52 queries, and 2963 unique authors) and **CISI** (1460-76-1486), and we created a third collection called **ILK** (147-80-89), because to our knowledge no real workgroup test collections exist. **ILK** contains 147 document titles and abstracts of publications of current and ex-members of the ILK workgroup. The paper topics focus mainly on machine learning for language engineering and linguistics[1]. We also performed some experiments to determine which author rank contributes most to expertise re-ranking. We created special versions of each corpus where only the primary authors were included (**CACM–first**, **CISI–first**, and **ILK–first**), and versions where the last author was removed from the author listings (**CACM–m1**, **CISI–m1** and **ILK–m1**). Our hypothesis was that, on average, first authors contribute the most to a paper and final authors the least.

We evaluated the performance of our approach using R-precision, the precision at the cut-off rank of the number of relevant documents for a query. It emphasizes the importance of returning more relevant documents earlier. The reliability of the comparisons between our baseline system and the re-ranking approach was determined by performing paired t-tests.

**Table 1.** Comparison of the re-ranking approaches in terms of R-precision scores. The underlined scores are statistically significant improvements.

| collection–author selection | re-ranked | baseline | |
|---|---|---|---|
| CACM | 0.313 | 0.233 | (+34.3%) |
| CACM–first | 0.302 | | (+20.2%) |
| CACM–m1 | 0.304 | | (+30.5%) |
| CISI | 0.206 | 0.203 | (+1.5%) |
| CISI–first | 0.206 | | (+1.5%) |
| CISI–m1 | 0.206 | | (+1.5%) |
| ILK | 0.649 | 0.647 | (+0.3%) |
| ILK–first | 0.650 | | (+0.5%) |
| ILK–m1 | 0.656 | | (+1.4%) |

Table 1 shows the results of our experiments. Authoritative re-ranking produced statistically significant performance improvements on the **CACM** and

---

[1] Publicly available at http://ilk.uvt.nl/~tbogers/ilk-collection/.

**CISI** collections, ranging from +1.5% to +34.3%. The improvements seem to be dependent on the corpus, but even the optimal performance on the **ILK** collection yielded very small improvements. A possible reason for the differences in performance might be the topical diversity of the test collections: **CACM** seems to have a more diverse range of topics than **CISI** and **ILK** which might make it easier for different fields of expertise to be recognized.

The experiments with different author selections did not confirm our initial hypothesis. Using the expertise of all authors associated with a document yields the best results and using less authors did not increase performance significantly.

## 4   Conclusions

Under optimized settings, authoritative re-ranking is able to significantly boost R-precision, with the exact performance increase dependent on the document collection. The technique appears to be suited for collections with a fair topical heterogeneity, such as publications in a journal, and perhaps less so for collections of workgroups with more topical coherence among publications. Furthermore, optimal re-ranking performance requires using the expertise of all the authors associated with a document.

**Acknowledgements.** This research was funded by the IOP-MMI-program of SenterNovem / The Dutch Ministry of Economic Affairs, as part of the À Propos project. The authors would like to thank Frank Hofstede (Intelli-Gent B.V.) for the fruitful discussions and useful comments.

## References

1. Brants, T. Natural Language Processing in Information Retrieval. In *Proc. of CLIN 2004*, Antwerp, Belgium, pp. 1–13, 2004
2. Campbell, C.S., Maglio, P.P., Cozzi, A., and Dom B. Expertise Identification using Email Communications. In *Proc. of CIKM2003*, New Orleans, LA, pp. 528–531, 2003
3. Chisholm, E. and Kolga, T.G. *New Term Weighting Formulas for the Vector Space Method in Information Retrieval.* Technical report ORNL/TM-13756, Computer Science and Mathematics Division, Oak Ridge National Laboratory, 1999
4. Giles, C.L., Bollacker, K., and Lawrence, S. CiteSeer: An Automatic Citation Indexing System. In *Proc. of Digital Libraries 98*, Pittsburgh, PA, pp. 89–98, 1998
5. Lee, K.-S., Park, Y.-C., and Choi, K.-S. Re-ranking model based on document clusters. In *Information Processing & Management*, vol. 37, no. 1, pp. 1–14, 2001
6. TREC. *TREC Enterprise Track.* http://www.ins.cwi.nl/projects/trec-ent/, 2005
7. Xu, J. and Croft, W.B. Query Expansion Using Local and Global Document Analysis. In *Proc. of SIGIR'96*, Zurich, Switzerland, pp. 4–11, 1996
8. Zheng, Z. and Srihari, R. Optimally Combining Positive and Negative Features for Text Categorization. In *Workshop for Learning from Imbalanced Datasets II, Proc. of the ICML*, Washington, DC, 2003

# Readability Applied to Information Retrieval*

Lorna Kane, Joe Carthy, and John Dunnion

Intelligent Information Retrieval Group,
School of Computer Science and Informatics,
University College Dublin, Belfield, Dublin 4, Ireland

## 1 Introduction

Readability refers to all characteristics of a document that contribute to its 'ease of understanding or comprehension due to the style of writing' [1]. The readability of a text is dependent on a number of factors, including but not constrained to; its legibility, syntactic difficulty, semantic difficulty and the organization of the text [2]. As many as 228 variables were found to influence the readability of a text in Gray and Leary's seminal study [2]. These variables were classified as relating to document content, style, format or, features of organization.

However, the concept of readability does not simply refer to properties of text but incorporates the engagement or interaction of a particular reader with the text. A number of reader characteristics affect readability alongside the reader's level of literacy. How motivated a reader is will affect how much effort they are willing to expend in order to understand a difficult text [3, 4]. Entin and Klare have shown that a reader's levels of interest, their prior knowledge and the readability of a text influence the reader's comprehension of the text [3].

Traditionally, information retrieval systems have concentrated on improving topical relevance, however relevance has been shown to be a multi-faceted concept [5]. Information seekers have listed various relevance criteria that relate directly to readability, including technicality, depth of treatment of topic, clarity of explanation and presentation, understandability, and the extent to which the information presented is novel to the user [6, 7]. From this we can conclude that information seekers desire documents that are topically relevant to their information need but also relevant in terms of readability in their context.

In particular, it is hypothesized that an information seeker with a high degree of domain knowledge [relating to their information need] will find documents of an introductory style to contain predominantly redundant information. Such documents will thus be irrelevant in their context. In turn, information seekers with a low level of domain knowledge who encounter documents containing domain specific concepts, without sufficient explanation, will be unable to learn from the document. This follows Kintsch's hypothesis concerning 'zones of learnability' [8].

The objective of our research is to match a user with a given level of domain knowledge to documents that they can learn the most from, documents that

---

* Enterprise Ireland Grant No. SC/2003/0255.

M. Lalmas et al. (Eds.): ECIR 2006, LNCS 3936, pp. 523–526, 2006.
© Springer-Verlag Berlin Heidelberg 2006

have the optimum balance of redundant and new information. We propose to achieve this aim by re-ranking a topically relevant set of documents as obtained from a traditional retrieval system. Readability analysis would be used to boost documents of suitable readability according to the user's context. This objective must be carried out without compromising topical relevance.

## 2    Related Work

A number of readability formulae have been developed since research into the area began in the early part of the 20th century. Some of the most widely used of these are the Flesch Reading Ease formula [9], the Dale-Chall formula [10], the Fog-Index [11], and the Fry Readability Graph [12].

Most readability formulae calculate some measure of syntactic complexity and semantic difficulty. These are commonly operationalised using sentence length to determine syntactic complexity and a syllable count or word frequency list to measure semantic difficulty. Other variables that have been found to affect readability include prepositional phrases, personal pronouns and number of indeterminate clauses. See [2] for a review of criteria that have been correlated with reading difficulty in traditional readability research.

Contemporary work relating to readability includes the use of latent semantic analysis [13], textual coherence [14], and statistical language models [15].

## 3    Corpus and Experimental Setup

To the authors' knowledge no corpus annotated with readability data is freely available. Thus, a corpus was assembled for the purpose of this research. The corpus is made up of news articles, expository in nature, that are written for target age groups (either children or adult) from disparate topic areas. A total of 2394 'easy' and 'difficult' documents were collected.

We use a machine learning approach to classify the documents for readability. The C5.0 [16] decision tree learning algorithm was utilised as it has been successfully used for a similar task (classifying text genre) [17]. C5.0 is also suitable as the rule set generated is amenable to intuitive human analysis.

We selected parts of speech (POS) as features for classifying the documents to obtain a measure of the documents' syntactic complexity. A number of studies have found particular parts of speech to correlate with readability, as mentioned in Section 2. The number of words of each part of speech, divided by the total number of words in the passage, produced the set of continuous attributes.

For comparative purposes, a close approximation of the Flesch readability formula was applied to the documents, as implemented by Talburt [18]. This measure is one of the most commonly used of the readability formulae. Classification was carried out using the metrics embedded in the Flesch formula, average words per sentence and average syllables per word, along with the Flesch score.

# 4 Evaluation

Results from classification experiments are shown in Table 1. Error rates were measured using ten-fold cross-validation repeated ten times.

**Table 1.** Comparison of error rates across feature sets

| Fold | POS | Flesch | Combined |
|------|--------|---------|----------|
| 0 | 12.0 % | 9.8 % | 6.9 % |
| 1 | 12.4 % | 9.7 % | 6.4 % |
| 2 | 14.0 % | 9.6 % | 6.5 % |
| 3 | 12.5 % | 9.5 % | 6.8 % |
| 4 | 12.5 % | 9.6 % | 6.9 % |
| 5 | 10.8 % | 9.5 % | 7.0 % |
| 6 | 11.4 % | 9.8 % | 6.2 % |
| 7 | 11.8 % | 9.8 % | 6.2 % |
| 8 | 11.8 % | 10.0 % | 6.9 % |
| 9 | 12.5 % | 9.7 % | 7.2 % |
| Mean | 12.2% | 12.2% | 6.7% |
| SE | 0.3% | 0.3% | 0.1% |

Upon examination of the decision trees generated using the part of speech feature set, C5.0 considered the proportion of personal pronouns, prepositions and subordinating conjunctions, and adjectives to be the most informative when classifying readability. In the combined feature set, C5.0 considered Flesch measures to be most indicative of readability.

# 5 Conclusions and Future Work

Our part of speech features performed well at classifying readability, though not as well as the Flesch measures. When part of speech and Flesch features were combined misclassifications were significantly decreased. We have shown that the performance of traditional readability measures can be boosted in a machine learning environment using part of speech features that are cumbersome to measure via human analysis. We have shown that high accuracy can be achieved using a machine learning approach to classifying readability.

While personal pronouns and prepositions have previously been correlated with readability, adjectives have not commonly appeared in readability literature [2]. However, it is intuitive that writers may often use more adjectives to assist a reader to create a cognitive 'image' of the topic under discussion.

Experiments completed thus far have been exploratory and confined to the task of measuring text characteristics. A fuller feature set that will incorporate measures of sentence construction, textual coherence, idea complexity and density with some rhetorical structure analysis is expected to give a more accurate and natural measure of document readability.

Once the optimal readability analysis technique is found, further work must include finding the most beneficial method of incorporating readability analysis into an existing IR system. This will entail investigating methods of inferring the level of readability that is suitable for a particular user. Integration into an IR system will also necessitate developing a re-ranking formula that does not trivialise the importance of topical relevance.

# References

1. Klare, G.: The Measurement of Readability. Iowa State University Press (1963)
2. Chall, J.: Readability: An Appraisal of Research and Application. Number 34 in Bureau of Educational Research Monographs. The Bureau of Educational Research Ohio State University (1958)
3. Entin, E., Klare, G.: Relationships of measures of interest, prior knowledge, and readabilty to comprehension of expository passages. Advances in reading/language research **3** (1985) 9–38
4. Schiefele, U.: Topic interest and free recall of expository text. Learning and Individual Differences **8**(2) (1996) 141–160
5. Borlund, P.: The concept of relevance in ir. JASIST **54**(10) (2003) 913–925
6. Cool, C., Belkin, N., Frieder, O., Kantor, P.: Characteristics of text affecting relevance judgments. In: Proceedings of the 14th National Online Meeting, Learned Information, Inc (1993) 74–84
7. Barry, C.L., Schamber, L.: Users' criteria for relevance evaluation: a cross-situational comparison. Information Processing Management **34**(2-3) (1998) 219–236
8. Kintsch, W.: Learning from text. American Psychologist **49** (1994) 294–303
9. Flesch, R.: A new readability yardstick. Journal of Applied Psychology **32** (1948) 221–233
10. Dale, E., Chall, J.: A formula for predicting readability. Educational Research Bulletin **27** (1948) 11–20
11. Gunning, R.: The Technique of Clear Writing. 2nd edn. McGraw-Hill (1968)
12. Fry, E.: Fry's readability graph: Clarifications, validity, and extension to level 17. Journal of Reading **21**(3) (1977) 242–252
13. Wolfe, M., Schreiner, M., Rehder, B., Laham, D., Kinstch, W., Landauer, T.: Learning from text: Matching readers and texts by latent semantic analysis. Discourse Processes **25** (1998) 309–336
14. Dufty, D.F., McNamara, D., Louwerse, M., Cai, Z., Graesser, A.C.: Automatic evaluation of aspects of document quality. In: SIGDOC '04: Proceedings of the 22nd annual international conference on Design of communication, ACM Press (2004) 14–16
15. Collins-Thompson, K., Callan, J.: Predicting reading difficulty with statistical language models: Research articles. Journal of the American Society for Information Science and Technology **56**(13) (2005) 1448–1462
16. Quinlan, J.R.: C4.5: programs for machine learning. Morgan Kaufmann Publishers Inc. (1993)
17. Finn, A., Kushmeric, N.: Learning to classify documents according to genre. IJCAI-03 Workshop on Computational Approaches to Style Analysis and Synthesis (2003)
18. Talburt, J.: The flesch index: An easily programmable readability analysis algorithm. In: SIGDOC '85: Proceedings of the 4th annual international conference on Systems documentation, ACM Press (1985) 114–122

# Automatic Determination of Feature Weights for Multi-feature CBIR

Peter Wilkins, Paul Ferguson, Cathal Gurrin, and Alan F. Smeaton

Centre for Digital Video Processing,
Dublin City University, Dublin 9, Ireland
{pwilkins, pferguson, cgurrin, asmeaton}@computing.dcu.ie

## 1 Introduction

Image and video retrieval are both currently dominated by approaches which combine the outputs of several different representations or features. The ways in which the combination can be done is an established research problem in content-based image retrieval (CBIR). These approaches vary from image clustering through to semantic frameworks and mid-level visual features to ultimately determine sets of relative weights for the non-linear combination of features. Simple approaches to determining these weights revolve around executing a standard set of queries with known relevance judgements on some form of training data and is iterative in nature. Whilst successful, this requires both training data and human intervention to derive the optimal weights.

We address the problem of determining the optimal set of relative weights for different features by automatically determining the weights *at query time*. This has advantages in that it does not require any prior training data or query history. Our approach calculates a ratio of the distance between result scores in a top subset of results, versus the distance between results over a larger result set. This provides an indication of how tightly clustered results are in the top subset as opposed to the larger set. For this paper we compute one of these ratios per visual feature for a given query image, and compare these ratios across features to arrive at a set of weights that can be applied to those features.

We also apply this technique to image and video queries where multiple example query images are used. This allows us to determine weights to apply to the results generated from each query image, giving greater weights to those query images which are more likely to aid retrieval performance. Whilst our work is at an early stage, results to date have been positive and demonstrate that this approach warrants further investigation.

## 2 Automatic Determination of Weights

### 2.1 Visual Features

We first extract the visual features that we are going to retrieve against. Our work uses MPEG-7 [1] visual features. We extract an edge histogram descriptor and a local colour descriptor from the images using the aceToolbox, developed

M. Lalmas et al. (Eds.): ECIR 2006, LNCS 3936, pp. 527–530, 2006.
© Springer-Verlag Berlin Heidelberg 2006

as part of our participation in aceMedia [2]. The edge histogram descriptor captures the spatial distribution of edges by dividing the image into 4 × 4 subimages (16 non-overlapping blocks) and categorizing the edges into one of 5 types $0°, 45°, 90°, 135°$ and *non-directional*. The local colour descriptor partitions the colour information of the image in 8 × 8 blocks and for each block the representative colour is determined by using the average colour from each block. To compare one feature representation against another of the same type, we employ an L2/Euclidian distance measure, scores are then normalized.

## 2.2   Feature Weight Determination

The calculation of feature weights is based upon the following assumption. That given a set of normalized similarity scores, if we calculate the average difference between adjacent scores across the result set, and then compare that to the average distance among the very top subset of the ranking, we would expect to find that the mean of the top subset shows a tighter clustering of similarity scores than that of the larger set. But that the closer these values, the more likely that there is similar scores at a greater depth.

We assert that given a result list of 1,000 normalized similarity scores, that the top subset of these results (we have explored a range of 10 - 100) would have a mean average distance ($MAD$) between these results that is less than the mean average distance between the top 1000 results, but the closer these scores the greater the depth of the similar results. The calculation of the $MAD$ measure can be expressed as:

$$mad(UB) = \frac{\sum_{n=1}^{n=UB}[score(n) - score(n+1)]}{UB - 1} \qquad (1)$$

where $UB$ (or Upper Bound) defines the set size. By calculating the $MAD$ value for a given subset, and for that of a larger result set, we can define a ratio that represents the degree of clustering of similar scores that occurs in the results. The higher the value of this ratio, the greater the amount of clustering over the entire set. We can define this similarity cluster (sc) ratio as:

$$sc = \frac{MAD(subset)}{MAD(1000)} \qquad (2)$$

Whilst this equation looks similar to standard deviation, standard deviation informs us of the degree of compactness around a mean, whereas in this formula, it is the comparison of the actual means that we are interested in.

For each feature we calculate a score, *sc*. To arrive at our feature weights, we simply determine the relative percentage of that score, against the sum of the scores. For example, the colour weight is defined as:

$$Colour_{Weight} = \frac{Colour_{SC}}{Colour_{SC} + Edge_{SC}} \qquad (3)$$

The final combination of the features involves normalising each complete result list, applying the weight for that feature, and linearly interpolating the results using CombSUM [3].

## 2.3   Query Image Weight Determination

Another problem for CBIR where each query topic contains multiple example query images, is that all query images are equally weighted. We know that some images will perform better than others. Just as text retrieval has developed techniques to weight query terms differently, our approach can be used to apply weights to query images. Text retrieval achieves this through the use of IDF in ranking formula, where common terms are given lower weights. Our approach assigns weights to images based upon the score distribution of an images' result set.

If we take the result list generated by each query image and normalise it we are left with a result list that is similar to the data that we were previously dealing with, i.e. a list of scores with varying degrees of distribution. We can make a similar assumption as previously, that result lists which have a higher value for $sc$ should provide better retrieval performance and thus give these greater weight.

## 3   Experiment

Our experiment used the TRECVid 2004 and 2005 video collections. These are collections of video materials for which keyframe images are made available by the TRECVid organisers. We acknowledge that this is a video collection, however the matching of query images against video keyframes does form a part of many of the video retrieval systems used in TRECVid. The TRECVid keyframe collection for 2004 consisted of 33,367 keyframes and 45,675 keyframes for 2005. For each collection, 24 search topics with multiple query images were available, with a total of 145 query images for 2004 and 227 for 2005. These query images were either example images supplied by the organisers or as keyframes extracted from the development set of videos.

The search task we performed was fully automatic image-only retrieval with no user intervention in query formulation, and no iteration through the search. For each run we processed all 24 topics. We compared two systems in our experiments. The baseline (referred to as `Oracle Manual Weights`) used the same static feature weights across all topics to fuse the feature data. These weights were selected based upon the best results achieved through manual training (i.e. select the weights, run the experiment, evaluate results, refine weights). The `Auto. Feature & Query Image Weights` system used our automatic weight techniques to fuse feature data and weight the example query images. We used '25' as the value of $UB$ in the calculation of $MAD$ for both feature weights and query image weights. To reiterate, each example query image in each topic had a set of unique feature weights automatically determined for fusion of feature data. Weights were also determined when fusing the results of multiple example query images, as opposed to the equal weight given in the baseline system. The results can be seen in Table 1.

The results demonstrate several things, such as performance on TRECVid 2005 is much better than on TRECVid 2004 which is in line with the results of others, and that the automatic weight assignment is better than the baseline

**Table 1.** Experimental results

|      |                                       | MAP    | P@5    | P@10   | Recall |
|------|---------------------------------------|--------|--------|--------|--------|
| 2004 | Oracle Manual Weights                 | 0.0298 | 0.1391 | 0.1043 | 246    |
|      | Auto. Feature & Query Image Weights   | 0.0324 | 0.1478 | 0.1174 | 251    |
| 2005 | Oracle Manual                         | 0.0668 | 0.2250 | 0.2250 | 870    |
|      | Auto. Feature & Query Image Weights   | 0.0689 | 0.2667 | 0.2375 | 862    |

when assessed against MAP, P@5 and P@10. Yet it is hard to make definitive conclusions about whether we can dynamically determine the best feature combination weights at query time, without performing a thorough analysis of the results at the topic level. We can see that the approaches put forward here do generate results that are comparable with the best static weights that can be obtained through training and this is encouraging.

## 4  Conclusion

We have presented an approach towards automatically generating feature weights for fusion of similarity scores from different image features, and for weighting query images. Our approach makes use of the distribution of result scores to derive weights which aid in retrieval performance, that can be calculated at query time without the need for prior training. The approach achieves better results to manual weights obtained from oracle training for the same sets of queries. These results whilst encouraging highlight the work yet to be done, and there are several future directions that this work needs to undertake. The first will be to increase the number of low-level image features. Increasing the number of features to be fused will increase the complexity of the weight determination and will better test its applicability.

## Acknowledgments

This work was supported by Science Foundation Ireland under grant 03/IN.3/I361. We are grateful to our aceMedia colleagues who provided us with output from the aceToolbox image analysis tooklit.

## References

1. Manjunath, B., Salembier, P., Sikora, T., eds.: Introduction to MPEG-7: Multimedia Content Description Language. Wiley (2002)
2. The AceMedia Project, available at http://www.acemedia.org.
3. Fox, E.A., Shaw, J.A.: Combination of multiple searches. In: Proceedings of the 2nd Text REtrieval Conference. (1994)

# Towards Automatic Retrieval of Album Covers

Markus Schedl[1], Peter Knees[1], Tim Pohle[1], and Gerhard Widmer[1,2]

[1] Dept. of Computational Perception, Johannes Kepler University, Linz, Austria
markus.schedl@jku.at
http://www.cp.jku.at
[2] Austrian Research Institute for Artificial Intelligence, Vienna, Austria
http://www.ofai.at

**Abstract.** We present first steps towards intelligent retrieval of music album covers from the web. The continuous growth of electronic music distribution constantly increases the interest in methods to automatically provide added value like lyrics or album covers. While existing approaches rely on large proprietary databases, we focus on methods that make use of the whole web by using *Google*'s or *A9.com*'s image search. We evaluate the current state of the approach and point out directions for further improvements.

## 1  Introduction and Context

Today's digital music players provide a wide variety of meta-information (e.g. ID3-tags of MP3-files, song lyrics, or album cover images) to the user. Considering the trend towards digital music distribution via online stores and the need of offering additional and valuable meta-data to catch a decisive advantage in competition makes automatic retrieval of e.g. cover images an interesting and important task. Furthermore, cover images can be used to enrich visual interfaces to music collections like [3], or serve as data source for applying collaging techniques [1] to facilitate browsing in digital music libraries. In [2], the authors use color histogram representations of cover images together with lyrics and musical scores to build a basis for clustering pieces of music.

While we could not find previous scientific publications on automatic retrieval of album covers, there exist a number of applications for this task. For example, programs like the "Album Cover Art Downloader"[1] or the "Essential MP3 Player"[2] offer functions to crawl the web for album covers. However, the main drawback of these programs is that they only perform semi-automatic retrieval. This means that the user is presented with some candidate covers and he/she has to select the most appropriate.

An alternative to programs that crawl the web are specialized web pages like "CoverUniverse"[3] that provide access to cover image databases. Also online

---

[1] *http://louhi.kempele.fi/~skyostil/projects/albumart*
[2] *http://www.twistermp3.com/emp3player*
[3] *http://www.coveruniverse.com*

M. Lalmas et al. (Eds.): ECIR 2006, LNCS 3936, pp. 531–534, 2006.
© Springer-Verlag Berlin Heidelberg 2006

stores that sell music like *Amazon* or *Wal-Mart* usually maintain such databases. Although these web pages frequently offer high quality scans of cover images, the number of available covers is obviously quite small compared to the number accessible by crawling the web.

In this paper, we investigate approaches that use image search functions of popular search engines and complement them with simple, robust image content analysis to retrieve covers. We aim at combining the advantages of both semi-automatic cover image retrieval by web crawling and cover image databases, namely, access to an enormous number of images and high certainty to retrieve the correct cover image. For evaluation, we use two international collections of CD covers. We report on occurring problems and point out possible solutions.

## 2    First Explorations

To get a first impression of the performance of image search functions for cover retrieval, we ran a set of experiments on a small private collection of 225 CDs. For retrieval, we query the image search functions provided by *A9.com* and *Google* using two schemes, `"artist name" "album title" cover` (abbreviated as $C$ in the following) and `"artist name" "album title" cover album` ($CA$). The $CA$ scheme was introduced to omit images of scanned discs that were sometimes returned in preliminary experiments when using $C$. Since it is often quite difficult to figure out if an album cover is correct, for example due to different versions for different sales regions, covers that became censored after release, or remastered versions with new covers, we have to inspect every retrieved cover manually and decide whether it is a correct one.

Table 1 shows the results for the query settings $C$ and $CA$ (in the rows labeled *baseline*). It can be seen that the search engine *Google* generally performs better than *A9.com*. Moreover, it is obvious that using $CA$ instead of $C$ not only eliminates images of scanned discs, but unfortunately also decreases the number of found cover images considerably.

From these insights we conclude that improvements are unlikely to be achieved by adding additional query constraints other than `cover`. Thus, in subsequent steps we focus on implementing content-based techniques and filtering with respect to image dimensions to eliminate erroneous covers. To this end, we reject all returned images that have non-quadratic dimensions within a tolerance of 15 percent. With this simple constraint on retrieved images we can improve accuracy for all settings by more than 4 percentage points in average (Table 1, rows labeled *quad. filter*). While this approach remedies problems with misdimensioned images, it cannot distinguish between actual covers and scanned discs. To address this issue, we propose a simple circle detection technique in order to filter out scanned disc images. We found all images of scanned discs to be cropped to the circle-shaped border of the CD which allows us to use a simple algorithm instead of complex circle detection techniques usually used in pattern recognition. For every potential cover image returned by the search engine, we examine small rectangular regions along a circular path that is touched by the

**Table 1.** Evaluation results on the test collection of 225 albums. The upper part of the table shows the results using the scheme $C$, the lower those using $CA$. The column labels indicate the following: *correct* – correct cover image, *dim. err.* – image does not fit to cover dimensions, *other* – other album or single by same artist, *scanned* – scanned disc, *related* – other artist-related material, *wrong* – something completely wrong, *not found* – no images returned. The values indicate the fraction on the total collection.

| | | cover | | | | | | |
|---|---|---|---|---|---|---|---|---|
| | | correct | dim.err. | other | scanned | related | wrong | not found |
| *Google* | *baseline* | 0.78 | 0.01 | 0.06 | 0.02 | 0.02 | 0.03 | 0.07 |
| | *quad. filter* | 0.81 | 0.00 | 0.06 | 0.02 | 0.01 | 0.02 | 0.07 |
| | *quad, circle* | 0.83 | 0.00 | 0.07 | 0.00 | 0.01 | 0.02 | 0.07 |
| *A9.com* | *baseline* | 0.63 | 0.05 | 0.05 | 0.01 | 0.06 | 0.05 | 0.15 |
| | *quad. filter* | 0.68 | 0.00 | 0.07 | 0.03 | 0.01 | 0.03 | 0.18 |
| | | cover album | | | | | | |
| | | correct | dim.err. | other | scanned | related | wrong | not found |
| *Google* | *baseline* | 0.63 | 0.01 | 0.06 | 0.00 | 0.02 | 0.04 | 0.23 |
| | *quad. filter* | 0.68 | 0.00 | 0.05 | 0.00 | 0.00 | 0.04 | 0.23 |
| *A9.com* | *baseline* | 0.56 | 0.02 | 0.07 | 0.00 | 0.02 | 0.04 | 0.28 |
| | *quad. filter* | 0.60 | 0.00 | 0.08 | 0.00 | 0.00 | 0.03 | 0.29 |

image borders tangentially. We then determine the contrast between subareas of these regions using RGB histograms. If there is a strong contrast between subareas that would show the imprint of the CD in case of a scanned CD and subareas that would show the background, the image is classified as scanned CD and removed from the set of potential cover images.

Applying this technique to our test collection further improves results, as it can be seen in Table 1 for the $C$ scheme in conjunction with Google.[4] Using the quadratic dimension constraint together with the circle detection approach improves results from a baseline of 78% to 83%.

## 3   Evaluation on a Large Collection

The approach was also tested on a large commercial collection of 3311 albums. This collection comprises albums by various artists from all around the world. Thus, it should give better insights into the behavior of our approach on a broader spectrum of music. Again, we had to laboriously classify each album manually for the reasons mentioned above. The results of this evaluation can be found in Table 2. It can be seen that only about 60% are correct. The main reason for this is the high amount of covers that could not be found (27%). This suggests that even in the best case we can only expect accuracies around 73%. However, for covers available on the web we can improve results by 3 percentage points.

---

[4] Since this setting performed significantly better than the others in the preliminary experiments, we decided to focus on it in all subsequent investigations.

**Table 2.** Evaluation results on the test collection of 3 311 albums. Labels as in Table 1.

| | | correct | dim.err. | other | scanned | related | wrong | not found |
|---|---|---|---|---|---|---|---|---|
| | | \multicolumn{7}{c}{cover} | | | | | | |
| *Google* | *baseline* | 0.57 | 0.02 | 0.08 | 0.00 | 0.02 | 0.06 | 0.27 |
| | *quad, circle* | 0.60 | 0.00 | 0.08 | 0.00 | 0.01 | 0.05 | 0.27 |

## 4   Conclusions and Future Work

We explored first steps towards fully automatic album cover retrieval from the web. Compared to the simplest approach of taking the first proposed image returned by an image search, we could raise accuracy of correctly found covers from 57% to 60% by incorporating very simple filtering techniques. Moreover, we noticed that it is unlikely to achieve more than 70-75% accuracy on large international collections due to not available images.

As for future work, we plan to improve performance by decreasing the number of covers from the correct artist but from another album by examining the pages from which the presumed covers were taken instead of taking the suggested picture. Comparing the found pictures across multiple sites may help to identify the correct cover, even though first histogram-based attempts to find the most frequent cover among the displayed results yielded disappointing results. We suppose that this was caused by the fact that Google performs similar preprocessing steps to omit duplicate images, which may interfere with our attempts. Finally, we aim at combining different approaches for automatic meta-data retrieval, e.g. for lyrics, into a single media player application.

## Acknowledgments

This research is supported by the Austrian Fonds zur Förderung der Wissenschaftlichen Forschung (FWF) under project number L112-N04 and by the EU 6th FP project SIMAC (project number 507142). The Austrian Research Institute for Artificial Intelligence is supported by the Austrian Federal Ministry for Education, Science, and Culture and by the Austrian Federal Ministry for Transport, Innovation, and Technology.

## References

1. D. Bainbridge, S. J. Cunningham, and J. S. Downie. Visual Collaging of Music in a Digital Library. In *Proc. of the 5th Intl. Symposium on Music Information Retrieval (ISMIR'04)*, Barcelona, Spain, October 2004.
2. E. Brochu, N. de Freitas, and K. Bao. The Sound of an Album Cover: Probabilistic Multimedia and IR. In *Proc. of the 9th Intl. Workshop on AI and Statistics*, Key West, Florida, USA, January 2003.
3. M. Schedl, P. Knees, and G. Widmer. Using CoMIRVA for Visualizing Similarities Between Music Artists. In *Proc. Compendium of the 16th IEEE Visualization 2005 Conference (Vis'05)*, Minneapolis, Minnesota, October 2005.

# Clustering Sentences for Discovering Events in News Articles

Martina Naughton, Nicholas Kushmerick, and Joe Carthy

School of Computer Science and Informatics, University College Dublin, Ireland
{martina.naughton, nick, joe.carthy}@ucd.ie

**Abstract.** We investigate the use of clustering methods for the task of grouping the text spans in a news article that refer to the same event. We provide evidence that the order in which events are described is structured in a way that can be exploited during clustering. We evaluate our approach on a corpus of news articles describing events that have occurred in the Iraqi War.

## 1  Introduction

A news event is defined as a specific thing that happens at a specific time and place [1], which may be reported by one or more news sources. Multiple news articles often contain duplicate information concerning the same event, but differ in choice of language used. Specific details regarding the event may vary from source to source. For example, one article about a given bombing in Iraq may say *"at least 5 people were killed"* while a second may contain the phrase *"6 people were found dead"*.

Our research focuses on merging descriptions of events from multiple sources to provide a concise description that combines the information from each source. We decompose this problem into three sub-problems: (1) Annotation: identifying the spans of text in an article corresponding to the various events that it mentions; (2) Matching: identifying event descriptions from different articles that refer to the same event; and (3) Aggregation: converting the event descriptions into a structured form so that they can be merged into a coherent summary.

In this paper we focus on the first sub-problem. Specifically, we describe and evaluate methods for annotating each sentence in an article with a set of identifiers specifying which event(s) the sentence mentions. This set can be empty (if the sentence does not mention any event) or it can contain multiple identifiers.

Event annotation is challenging for several reasons. Most news articles refer to multiple events. Moreover, sentences that refer to the same event are usually scattered through the article with no simple sequential pattern. Fig. 1 shows a sample article that demonstrates these issues.

The task of clustering similar sentences is a problem that has been investigated particularly in the area of text summarization. In SimFinder [2], a flexible clustering tool for summarisation, the task is defined as grouping small paragraphs of text containing information about a specific subject. However, we examine the use of clustering at sentence level.

M. Lalmas et al. (Eds.): ECIR 2006, LNCS 3936, pp. 535–538, 2006.
© Springer-Verlag Berlin Heidelberg 2006

> **World News**
> **Suicide Bombs Kills 30 in Iraq**
>
> Suicide Bombers killed at least 30 people in attacks in two Iraqi cities Monday, in the worst bloodshed since the country's historic election eight days ago.
> ................
> ................
> In the Northern city of Mosul, 12 people were killed and four wounded when a suicide bomber targeted a crowd of police officers in a hospital compound

**Fig. 1.** Sample news article that describes multiple events

## 2   Event Extraction as Sentence Clustering

This paper investigates the use of clustering to automatically group sentences in terms of the event they describe. We generated sentence clusters using average link, complete link and single link agglomerative clustering. Hierarchical agglomerative clustering (HAC) initially assigns each data point to a singleton cluster, and then repeatedly merges clusters until a specified termination criteria is satisfied [3]. HAC clustering methods require a similarity metric between two sentences. We use the standard cosine metric over a bag-of-words encoding of each sentence. We removed stopwords, but did not employ term weighting.

We evaluated our clustering algorithms using a collection of 219 news stories describing events related to the recent war in Iraq. Excess HTML (image captions etc.) was removed, and sentence boundaries were identified. The corpus was then annotated by two volunteers. Within each article, events were uniquely identified by integers. Starting at the value 1, the annotators were asked to assign labels to each sentence representing the event(s) it describes. If a sentence did not refer to any event, it was assigned the label 0. Sentences may refer to multiple events. For example, consider the sentence *"These two bombings have claimed the lives of 23 Iraqi soldiers"*. This sentence would be annotated with two labels, one for each of the two bombings. Note that sentences from the same document that refer to the same event are assigned the same label.

To evaluate our clustering method, we define precision and recall as follows. We assign each pair of sentences into one of four categories: a, clustered together (and annotated as referring to the same event); b, not clustered together (but annotated as referring to the same event); c, incorrectly clustered together; d, correctly not clustered together. Precision and recall are thus found to be computed as $P = \frac{a}{a+c}$ and $R = \frac{a}{a+b}$, and $F1 = \frac{2PR}{P+R}$.

We also need to consider sentences annotated with multiple event labels. For each pair, where one or both of the sentences were annotated as referring to multiple events, we consider them as belonging in the same event cluster if the intersection between their labels is not empty. For example, we consider that a sentence pair with labels "1,2" and "1,3" respectively as belonging to the same cluster.

A fully-automated approach must use some termination criteria to decide when to stop clustering. In this preliminary work, we simply compare the results

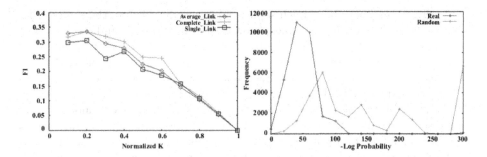

**Fig. 2.** Left: F1 at each value of normalized $k$, for complete link, single link and average link clustering algorithms. Right: Distribution in the probability that actual and random event sequences are generated by the tuned FSA.

emitted by the HAC algorithm for various values of $k$, where $k$ is the number of remaining clusters.

As seen in Fig. 2, F1 increases slightly as $k$ is increased, but then rapidly falls with increasing $k$. We also implemented a semi-supervised approach in which $k$ is manually set to the annotated number of incidents in each article. We found that precision ranges between 0.58 and 0.39 and recall falls between 0.29 and 0.25 for all three algorithms. Interestingly, we observe that the "correct" value for $k$ is not necessarily the value of $k$ that maximizes accuracy.

## 3   Sequential Event Structure

Our clustering approach ignores an important constraint on the event associated with each sentence: the position of the sentence within the document. Intuitively, adjacent sentences are more likely refer to the same event, later sentences are likely to introduce new events, etc.

To confirm the intuition that such latent structure indeed exists, we treat each document as a sequence of event labels (namely, one label per sentence). We trained a finite state automaton (FSA) from the sequences, where states corresponded to event labels, and transitions corresponded to adjacent sentences that mention the pair of events. The automaton is stochastic: we counted the number of each transition across a set of training documents (as well as the fraction of documents whose first and last sentences are labeled with each event). We can calculate the probability that the trained automaton generated a given document as the product of the probability that the first sentence's event is an initial state, the probabilities of each transition in turn, and the probability that the last sentence's label is a final state. (This assumes that each sentence mentions at most one event. We deal with multi-event sentences in various ways, such as making a "copy" of each article for each permutation of its labels; for example, the article sequence "1, {1,2}, 2, {2,3}" is mapped to 4 sequences, "1 1 2 2", "1 2 2 2", "1 1 2 3" and "1 2 2 3".)

Finally, we estimate how much sequential structure exists in the sentence labels as follows. The document collection was split into training and test sets. The automaton parameters were learned from the training data, and the probability that each test sequence was generated by the automaton was calculated. These probabilities were compared with those of a set of random sequences (generated to have the same length distribution as the test data).

The probabilities of event sequences from our dataset and the randomly generated sequences are shown in Fig. 2. The test and random sequences are sorted by probability. The horizontal axis shows the rank in each sequence and the vertical axis shows the negative log probability of the sequence at each rank. The data suggest that the documents are indeed highly structured, as real document sequences tend to be much more likely under the trained FSA than randomly generated sequences.

## 4   Discussion

We have presented exploratory work on the use of clustering for event annotation in news articles. We are currently trying variations of our approach, such as using WordNet [4] to deal synonymy (eg, *"killed"* and *"died"*).

Although the precision of our approach is approximately 50%, we are encouraged since the similarity metric ignored the sequential structure demonstrated in Sec. 3. We have developed a revised distance metric that incorporates the sequential regularities demonstrated in Fig. 2. Preliminary experiments show that this enhancement provides a modest increase in F1.

Finally, our approach did not use term weighting. We have developed a TFIDF-like weighting scheme where we define a "document" to be the set of sentences which discuss a given event and then weight terms according to their frequency in the document compared to the entire corpus. Of course, these "documents" are precisely what the clustering algorithm is trying to discover. We therefore initialize the term weights uniformly, and then iterate the clustering process, re-calculating the term weights based on the previous output, stopping when the event labels converge. Preliminary results show that this approach converges rapidly and also produces a modest increase in F1.

## References

1. Li, Z., Wang, B., Li, M., Ma, W.Y.: A probabilistic model for retrospective news event detection. In: Proceedings of the 28th annual international ACM SIGIR Conference on Research and Development in Information Retrieval, ACM Press (2005) 106–113
2. Hatzivassiloglou, V., Klavans, J., Holcombe, M., Barzilay, R., Kan, M.Y., McKeown, R.: Simfinder; a flexible clustering tool for summarisation. In: NAACL Workshop on Automatic Summarisation. (2001) 41–49
3. Manning, C.D., Schtze, H.: Foundations of Statistical Natural Language Processing. MIT Press (1999)
4. Miller, G. A., E.: Wordnet: An on-line lexical database. International Journal of Lexicography (1990) 235–312

# Specificity Helps Text Classification

Lucas Bouma and Maarten de Rijke

ISLA, University of Amsterdam,
Kruislaan 403, 1098 SJ Amsterdam, The Netherlands
{lbouma, mdr}@science.uva.nl

**Abstract.** We examine the impact on classification effectiveness of semantic differences in categories. Specifically, we measure broadness and
narrowness of categories in terms of their distance to the root of a hierarchically organized thesaurus. Using categories of four different levels
degrees of broadness, we show that classifying documents into narrow
categories gives better scores than classifying them into broad terms,
which we attribute to the fact that more specific categories are associated with terms with a higher discriminatory power.

## 1 Introduction

While text categorization has a long history [7], the increased availability of
large scale semantically rich thesauri and ontologies, raises a number of challenging scientific questions. If we classify text documents into categories that
are organized in such a semantic structure, how can we exploit the structure?
How does the position of a category in such a hierarchy impact a classifier's
performance?

Specifically, in this paper we aim to find out whether classification accuracy is
influenced by the level of "broadness" (or "narrowness") of a category. A priori,
one may entertain one of two clear intuitions here. One is that classification into
broader classes is more effective than into narrow categories due to more training
examples [9]. The competing intuition is that classification into more narrow
categories is more effective because the terms associated with such categories
tend to be more discriminating. Our experiments show that the latter is the
case.

The rest of the paper is organized as follows. In Section 2 we describe our
experimental set-up. We follow with our results and a discussion in Section 3,
and conclude in Section 4.

## 2 Experimental Set-Up

We addressed our research question by working with data provided by TREC
as part of the classification task for the 2004 edition of the Genomics track [8].
Here, Medline documents need to be classified in categories that correspond to
term descriptions in the MeSH thesaurus [6]. Categories are organized in levels,
from broad to narrow, depending on the length of the shortest path to the root
of the thesaurus. A total of eleven levels are found in MeSH.

M. Lalmas et al. (Eds.): ECIR 2006, LNCS 3936, pp. 539–542, 2006.
© Springer-Verlag Berlin Heidelberg 2006

**Table 1.** Categories chosen for our experiments, grouped by level, together with the number of examples per selected category

| Level 1 | Level 3 |
|---|---|
| 6847 Pharmaceutical_Preparations | 8383 Bladder |
| 3937 Eye_Diseases | 8186 Education,_Medical |
| 2472 Parasitic_Diseases | 4203 Malondialdehyde |
| 1421 Archaea | 1990 Philosophy,_Medical |
| 1110 Organic_Chemicals | 1365 Product_Surveillance,_Postmarketing |
| 947 Animal_Diseases | 1118 Work_Schedule_Tolerance |
| 910 Endocrine_System | 844 Disasters |

| Level 8 | Level 10 |
|---|---|
| 8409 Xenopus_laevis | 8360 Macaca_mulatta |
| 7226 Mice,_Mutant_Strains | 7943 Cercopithecus_aethiops |
| 4216 Motor_Cortex | 2396 Trypanosoma_cruzi |
| 2376 Receptors,_Antigen,_T-Cell,_gamma-delta | 1530 Trypanosoma_brucei_brucei |
| 1421 Medroxyprogesterone_17-Acetate | 1183 Entamoeba_histolytica |
| 1162 Goldfish | 4190 Macaca_fascicularis |
| 1024 Receptors,_Kainic_Acid | 981 Leishmania_donovani |

From the eleven levels found in MeSH, we selected four for our experiments—1, 3, 8 and 10—, and from each we selected seven categories, which we hoped would allows us to demonstrate differences in classification effectiveness across levels. Level 10 had the smallest number of categories (32); we selected the seven categories with the most examples. Level 3 had the most categories (2525). For levels 1, 3, and 8 we selected seven categories with roughly the same number of examples as the selected categories at level 10. Table 1 shows the chosen categories and the number of positive examples used in the experiments. To rule out other possible semantic influences we made sure that the selected categories are all unambiguous (that is, they have one, and only one, level in the MeSH thesaurus).

To build the training material for our experiments, we took a sample of documents from the Medline corpus used at TREC. One hundred categories were randomly selected from MeSH. We used around 40 thousands documents that are classified with these categories, these were used as negative instances. We made sure that the term distributions in the different MeSH levels in the sample were statistically the same as in the entire corpus. In the experiments the positive instances of the chosen category were merged with this sample.

For text representation, we employed Weka [10]. Following standard practice, documents were turned into word vectors, each consisting of one thousand most significant words after eliminating stopwords; here, significance was measured by using TF.IDF. Stemming was not used.

Finally, we carried out single-label classification experiments using the SVM-Light [5] and BBR [2] classifiers for each of the 28 categories chosen. Both classifiers have been shown to perform well on the classification task at the TREC Genomics track [4]. The classification effectiveness is measured in Precision, Recall, and F-score, all averaged over all categories per level.

# 3    Results

Classification into narrow categories was found to be significantly more effective than into broad categories: for each level considered, the F-scores for that level were higher (in many cases significantly so) than the F-scores for all broader levels.

**Table 2.** Average scores per level (SVM and BBR)

| | SVM | | | BBR | | |
|---|---|---|---|---|---|---|
| Level | Precision | Recall | F-score | Precision | Recall | F-score |
| 1 | 90.33 | 61.98 | 72.89 | 67.50 | 65.21 | 66.22 |
| 3 | 90.21 | 73.93 | 80.76 | 75.66 | 74.64 | 75.07 |
| 8 | 94.80 | 85.41 | 89.78 | 86.84 | 85.19 | 85.94 |
| 10 | 96.80 | 87.48 | 91.80 | 92.71 | 88.51 | 90.52 |

Specifically, Table 2 shows the averaged Precision, Recall, and F-scores for each of the levels. Observe that the F-scores increase, for both classifiers, as the category level increases. The two classifiers behave quite differently, however. For SVM the precision is high for all levels, even for the broadest categories (level 1); for BBR precision and recall increase almost in sync.

A significant ($\alpha = 0.1$) difference of 10 points in F-score was found between level one and level ten. Level one compared with level three and level three compared with level eight both gave a significant difference of 5 points in F-score, but with weaker evidence ($\alpha = 0.25$). No significant difference was found between levels eight and ten.

For finding a possible explanation for the observed differences in classification effectiveness, we carried out an analysis of the TF.IDF scores in the word vectors used to represent documents. For every category, we ranked the features according to their TF.IDF score, and found no differences between the TF.IDF scores of the most discriminating terms for levels 1 and 3, while the scores for the most discriminating terms at levels 8 and 10 as much as 50% higher—supporting the intuition that more specific categories are associated with terms with a higher discriminatory power.

# 4    Conclusion

Our findings refute claims by Wibowo and Williams [9] that classification into broader categories is more accurate than into narrow categories. We explain the different findings in terms of the fact that 80 of narrow categories used by Wibowo and Williams [9] had only one training example. In our study the number of positive examples for the narrow categories ranged from 981 to 8360. The larger amount of narrow category examples can be seen as a positive influence on the discriminatory power of the features. Also the specific domain of the MeSH thesaurus should help in that matter.

As to future work, in our research so far we ignored the fact that many category labels are ambiguous, in the sense that they may occur at different levels in the thesaurus: we did not investigate whether the ambiguity of a category label impacts categorization accuracy. Additionally, for a broad category like *Animal diseases* the singular and plural form of the words *animal* and *disease* are both scored separately. Scoring according to the same morphological root could increase their influence, and we conjecture that multiple word representations [1] will probably have a positive effect on classification effectiveness here. Finally, Granitzer [3] uses the hierarchy as a path for classification. More attention could be advised for top level decisions, also since they are propagated downwards.

**Acknowledgments.** This research was supported by the Netherlands Organization for Scientific Research (NWO) under project numbers 017.001.190, 220-80-001, 264-70-050, 365-20-005, 612.000.106, 612.000.207, 612.013.001, 612.-066.302, 612.069.006, 640.001.501, and 640.002.501.

# References

[1] S. Bloehdorn and A. Hotho. Boosting for text classification with semantic features. In *Proceedings of the Workshop on Mining for and from the Semantic Web at the 10th ACM SIGKDD Conference on Knowledge Discovery and Data Mining*, pages 70–87, 2004. http://www.aifb.uni-karlsruhe.de/WBS/sbl/publications/2004-08-ws-msw-bloehdorn-hotho_boosting-semantic-features.pdf.

[2] A. Dayanik, D. Fradkin, A. Genkin, P. Kantor, D. Madigan, D. Lewis, and V. Menkov. Dimacs at the TREC 2004 genomics track. In *The Thirteenth Text Retrieval, Conference (TREC 2004)*, 2005.

[3] M. Granitzer. Hierarchical Text Classification using Methods from Machine Learning. Master's thesis, Graz University of Technology, 2003.

[4] W. Hersh, R. Bhuptiraju, L. Ross, P. Johnson, A. Cohen, and D. Kraemer. TREC 2004 genomics track overview. In *The Thirteenth Text Retrieval, Conference (TREC 2004)*, 2005.

[5] T. Joachims. Making large-scale SVM learning practical. In B. Schölkopf, C. Burges, and A. Smola, editors, *Advances in Kernel Methods*. 1999.

[6] MeSH. National library of medicine, medical subject headings (MeSH), 2005. URL: http://www.nlm.nih.gov/mesh/MBrowser.html.

[7] F. Sebastiani. Machine learning in automated text categorization. *ACM Comput. Surv.*, 34(1):1–47, 2002.

[8] TREC Genomics Track. Trec genomics 2004 ad hoc task documents, 2005. URL: http://ir.ohsu.edu/genomics/.

[9] W. Wibowo and H. Williams. On using hierarchies for document classification. In *Proceedings of the Fourth Australasian Document Computing Symposium*, Coffs Harbour, Australia, 1999.

[10] I. H. Witten and E. Frank. *Data mining: practical machine learning tools and techniques with Java implementations*. Morgan Kaufmann Publishers Inc., San Francisco, CA, USA, 2000. ISBN 1-55860-552-5.

# A Declarative DB-Powered Approach to IR

Roberto Cornacchia and Arjen P. de Vries

CWI, INS1, Amsterdam, The Netherlands
{R.Cornacchia, Arjen.de.Vries}@cwi.nl

**Abstract.** We present a prototype system using array comprehensions to bridge the gap between databases and information retrieval. It allows researchers to express their retrieval models in the General Matrix Framework for Information Retrieval [1], and have these executed on relational database systems with negligible effort.

## 1 Introduction

Information Retrieval (IR) researchers develop methods to assess the degree of relevance of data to user queries. While ideally such a retrieval model could be considered 'just' a (somewhat complicated) query for a database system, in practice the researcher attempting to deploy database technology to information retrieval will stumble upon two difficulties. First, database implementations of IR models are still inefficient in runtime and resource utilisation if compared to highly optimised custom-built solutions. The second difficulty, which is the focus of this paper, is that the set-oriented query languages provided by relational database systems provide a fairly poor abstraction in expressing information retrieval models. Specifically, the lack of explicit representation of ordered data has long been acknowledged as a severe bottleneck for developing scientific database applications [2], and we believe the same problem has hindered the integration of databases and information retrieval.

Recently, Roelleke et al. [1] have developed a mathematical framework that maps IR concepts to matrix spaces and matrix operations (Matrix Framework in the remainder). We explain how this theoretical framework to IR can be operationalised in a prototype for array data management in relational database systems (RAM) [3]. RAM defines operations over arrays declaratively in comprehension syntax (see [4]). For example, the expression

$$A = [ f(x,y,z) + 1 \mid x<5, y<3, z<10 ]$$

defines a three-dimensional array, whose axes x, y and z have dimensions 5, 3 and 10, respectively. Each cell $(x, y, z)$ of such an array is filled with the value of the function f(x,y,z) + 1. While comprehension syntax allows to express array operations on an element by element basis, the RAM system translates such element-at-a-time operations to collection-oriented database queries, suited for (potentially more efficient) bulk processing.

The remainder of the paper demonstrates how the Matrix Framework combines nicely with the RAM system, using the Language Modelling (LM) retrieval

M. Lalmas et al. (Eds.): ECIR 2006, LNCS 3936, pp. 543–547, 2006.
© Springer-Verlag Berlin Heidelberg 2006

model (see [5]) as an example. The results apply likewise to the other retrieval models discussed by [1].

## 2   Language Modelling in the Matrix Framework

First define matrices $L$ (locations), $LT$ (location-term), $LD$ (location-document) and $QT$ (query-term) to represent documents $d \in D$ and queries $q \in Q$:

$$L = [l_i]_{L \times 1}, \quad LT = [lt_{ij}]_{L \times T}, \quad LD = [ld_{ij}]_{L \times D}, \quad QT = [qt_{ij}]_{Q \times T}$$

$$l_i = 1, \quad lt_{ij} = \begin{cases} 0, & \text{if } t_j \notin l_i \\ 1, & \text{if } t_j \in l_i \end{cases}, \quad ld_{ij} = \begin{cases} 0, & \text{if } l_i \notin d_j \\ 1, & \text{if } l_i \in d_j \end{cases}, \quad qt_{ij} = \begin{cases} 0, & \text{if } t_j \notin q_i \\ 1, & \text{if } t_j \in q_i \end{cases} \quad (1)$$

Following the language modelling approach to IR, result matrix RSV containing retrieval status values for documents $d$ and queries $q$ is defined as

$$RSV = [rsv_{dq}]_{D \times Q} = \begin{bmatrix} \log P(t_1|d_1, r) & \cdots & \log P(t_{N_t}|d_1, r) \\ \vdots & \ddots & \vdots \\ \log P(t_1|d_{N_d}, r) & \cdots & \log P(t_{N_t}|d_{N_d}, r) \end{bmatrix}_{D \times T} \cdot QT^T, \quad (2)$$

where the probability $P(t|d,r)$ is a linear combination of foreground and background probabilities $P(t|d)$ and $P(t)$, defined in terms of within-document term frequency and collection term frequency:

$$P(t|d, r) = \lambda \cdot P(t|d) + (1 - \lambda) \cdot P(t), \quad (3)$$

using their maximum likelihood estimators

$$P(t|d) = tf(d, t) = \frac{NL(d, t)}{NL_D(d)}, \quad P(t) = tf(t) = \frac{NL_T(t)}{|L|}, \quad (4)$$

where

$$NL = LD^T \cdot LT, \quad NL_D = L^T \cdot LD, \quad NL_T = L^T \cdot LT \quad (5)$$

Here, $NL(d, t)$ denotes the number of locations at which $t$ occurs in $d$, $NL_D(d)$ the number of locations belonging to document $d$, and $NL_T(t)$ the number of locations at which $t$ occurs in the collection.

## 3   Language Modelling in RAM

We now present the corresponding array expressions in RAM. First, introduce two macros for matrix transposition and matrix multiplication (the pre-processor expands macro-definitions symbolically):

```
mxT(A)      = [ A(j,i) | i,j ]
mxMult(A,B) = [ sum([ A(n,m) * B(m,p) | m ] ) | n,p ]
```

```
        | 1  | LD = ([$Nlocs,$Ndocs],      bool)  sparse("0",0.01)   "LD_table"
F. (1)  | 2  | LT = ([$Nlocs,$Nterms],     bool)  sparse("0",0.01)   "LT_table"
        | 3  | QT = ([$Nqueries,$Nterms],bool)    sparse("0",0.001)  "QT_table"

F. (2)  | 4  | RSV = mxMult( [log(p_rel(d,t)) | d<$Ndocs, t<$Nterms] , mxT(QT) )
F. (3)  | 5  | p_rel(d,t)   = ($Lambda * p_dt(d,t)) + ((1.0 - $Lambda) * p_t(t))
F. (4)  | 6  | p_dt(d,t) = NL(d,t) / NL_d(d)
F. (4)  | 7  | p_t(t)    = NL_t(t) / $Nlocs
F. (5)  | 8  | NL        = mxMult( mxT(LD), LT )
F. (5)  | 9  | NL_d      = mxMult( mxT(L), LD )
F. (5)  | 10 | NL_t      = mxMult( mxT(L), LT )
F. (1)  | 11 | L         = [ 1 | l<$NLocs, x<1 ]
```

**Fig. 1.** Matrix Framework-compliant RAM query for Language Modelling retrieval

The LM retrieval model is then expressed as shown in Fig. 1. Each piece of code is a straightforward rewrite of the formulas in Section 2, as indicated by the leftmost column.

The upper part of the query (lines 1-3) declares the input matrices (in the next prototype, a data dictionary will replace explicit declaration of properties such as axis length, element type, sparsity, and name of the physical table).

The actual retrieval algorithm is implemented by the lower part of Fig. 1 (lines 4-11). The one-to-one relation between such expressions and the formulas in Section 2 clearly shows that RAM syntax is simple and fully declarative. This example gives a further evidence of the importance of the declarative nature of the RAM approach. The array NL_t (line 10) is computed as in (5), by the matrix multiplication $L^T \cdot LT$. However, it is easily verified that such a matrix multiplication is equivalent to a summation over the $L$ axis, which is natively supported in RAM: NL_t = [ sum([LT(1,t) | l<$Nlocs]) | t<$Nterms ].

Because the RAM query optimiser detects and removes unneeded arithmetic operations, the matrix multiplication $L^T \cdot LT$ (potentially more expensive) and the equivalent summation over the $L$ axis would result in the same physical query plan (the same considerations hold for the computation of NL_d). This allows us to make the RAM query fully compliant with the Matrix Framework without compromising the performance.

## 4  Query Processing

**Multi-layer approach.** The front-end translates the high level array comprehensions into an intermediate array-algebra before final transformation to the relational domain. This algebraic expression is then rewritten by a traditional rule-based optimiser. A second step translates the array-algebra plan into the native query language of the database system. Currently, translations are available for SQL and (binary) relational algebra. For testing purposes, RAM supports direct translation into stand-alone programmes (Matlab and C++). A $k$-dimensional array is represented as relation $R(I_1, \ldots, I_k, V)$, where columns $I_1, \ldots, I_k$ identify the coordinates of each cell and $V$ contains their values.

**Sparse arrays.** While the Matrix Framework is an elegant formalism, representation of its matrix spaces is only feasible if the materialisation of the absence of
a term can be avoided. Matrices like $LT$, for instance, are extremely sparse (the
density of the non-0 values is lower than 0.0001%). Therefore, we extended the
RAM prototype with specific query processing techniques to handle sparse arrays.

The relational representation of sparse arrays is relatively easy: tuples
$(i_1, \ldots, i_k, v)$ are only stored if $v \neq 0$ (more precisely, we allow arrays to be
sparse on *any* value, not only 0). The evaluation of query plans involving sparse
arrays is however more complicated, to ensure correct results when the input values are not physically stored. We have found experimentally that the increased
complexity starts to pay off when input array density drops below 20%, while
performance improves dramatically with smaller densities.

The RAM extension for the evaluation of expressions involving sparse arrays
has made it possible for the user to deal with well-defined array structures,
regardless of their theoretical sizes; the low-level, physical details are handled by
the system. Remarkably, the resulting set-based and bulk-oriented query plans
are not dissimilar to what an expert database developer would devise.

## 5    Summary and Future Work

The Matrix Framework for information retrieval captures a wide spectrum of
IR in a consistent way, including indexing, retrieval, relevance feedback, and
evaluation measures. Also, it establishes a consistent notation for frequencies in
event spaces (see (4)), readily available as building blocks in common libraries
for matrix operations.

Thanks to its array-based data model, the RAM query language remedies
many of the interfacing hurdles encountered when implementing computation
oriented algorithms in database systems. It provides for arrays a level of abstraction which is similar to that provided by SQL for sets: queries can be expressed
in a declarative manner, such that application logic and physical implementation
are clearly separated, and can be improved independently.

The research presented in this paper demonstrates how RAM provides an elegant implementation platform for information retrieval research. It justifies the
development of optimisations, under investigation at present, that are specific
for a matrix-based computational model. Future work topics include the implementation of sparse arrays evaluation for all backends (currently available only
for relational algebra), and the usage of lightweight data compression provided
by MonetDB/X100 [6], which is expected to be highly effective in the presented
scenario.

## References

1. T. Roelleke, T. Tsikrika, and G. Kazai. A general matrix framework for modelling
   information retrieval. *IP&M*, 42(1):4–30, 2005.
2. D. Maier and B. Vance. A call to order. In *SIGMOD*, pages 1–16. ACM Press, 1993.

3. A. R. van Ballegooij, A. P. de Vries, and M. L. Kersten. RAM: Array processing over a relational DBMS. Technical Report INS-R0301, CWI, Amsterdam, The
   Netherlands, March 2003.
4. P. Buneman, L. Libkin, D. Suciu, V. Tannen, and L. Wong. Comprehension syntax.
   *SIGMOD Record*, 23(1):87–96, 1994.
5. D. Hiemstra. A linguistically motivated probabilistic model of information retrieval.
   In *ECDL*, pages 569–584, 1998.
6. M. Zukowski, S. Hman, N. Nes, and P. A. Boncz. Super-Scalar RAM-CPU Cache
   Compression. In *Proceedings of the IEEE International Conference on Data Engineering (ICDE)*, Atlanta, GA, USA, April 2006. Accepted for publication.

# Judging the Spatial Relevance of Documents for GIR[*]

Paul D. Clough[1], Hideo Joho[2], and Ross Purves[3]

[1] Department of Information Studies, University of Sheffield, UK
p.d.clough@sheffield.ac.uk
[2] Department of Computer Science, University of Glasgow, UK
hideo@dcs.gla.ac.uk
[3] Department of Geography, University of Zurich, Switzerland
rsp@geo.unizh.ch

**Abstract.** Geographic Information Retrieval (GIR) is concerned with the retrieval of documents based on both thematic and geographic content. An important issue in GIR, as for all IR, is relevance. In this paper we argue that spatial relevance should be considered independently from thematic relevance, and propose an initial scheme. A pilot study to assess this relevance scheme is presented, with initial results suggesting that users can distinguish between these two relevance dimensions, and that furthermore they have different properties. We suggest that spatial relevance requires greater assessor effort and more localised geographic knowledge than judging thematic relevance.

## 1 Introduction

Geographic Information Retrieval (GIR) is a relatively new research area, concerned with the retrieval and ranking of documents from collections based on queries that specify both thematic and geographic scopes [1,2]. As with any new form of retrieval appropriate methodologies and resources are required to evaluate GIR systems [3][4]. In IR, test collections are often used to benchmark system performance (e.g. TREC, CLEF and INEX), however existing resources do not necessarily distinguish spatial aspects of information, an important point to consider when evaluating GIR [5].

Assessing the relevance of documents across multiple dimensions is not a new problem in IR. For example, INEX has implemented such a scheme to assess both structural and conceptual relevance of XML documents. Cai [2] suggests two subspaces for GIR which represent two different cognitive aspects of relevance: geographic and thematic. In the former, relevance is judged based upon spatial relationships (e.g. overlap and adjacency) between the query location and spatial footprints identified within a document. It is therefore necessary to assess whether different relevance schemes are required to evaluate GIR systems based upon the specifically geographic aspects of documents.

This paper investigates the usability of an assessment scheme which takes into account both thematic and spatial relevance for the evaluation of GIR systems. The following sections present our proposed relevance scheme and a pilot test evaluating the usability of such a scheme, before briefly discussing some aspects of our results and considering the implications.

---

[*] Research part-funded by EU-IST Projects IST-2001-35047 (SPIRIT) and IST-2002-2.3.1.12 (BRICKS).

M. Lalmas et al. (Eds.): ECIR 2006, LNCS 3936, pp. 548–552, 2006.
© Springer-Verlag Berlin Heidelberg 2006

## 2  Relevance Scheme

Our initial proposed scheme (shown in Table 1) was based on assessing the relevance of Web documents and used a three-point scale to indicate the degree of relevance (we intentionally did not label the scales as highly relevant, partially relevant, or relevant to avoid the influence of preconceived ideas about relevance).

**Table 1.** Relevance scheme

| Thematic relevance | |
| --- | --- |
| Score 1 | A document which contains relevant information about the concept queried AND on its own allows you to form a judgment about the document (i.e. requires no external knowledge). |
| Score 2 | A document is relevant, since it points to a resource MENTIONING the concept, but you must consult further pages referenced by the document to perform a judgment. |
| Score 3 | A document does not provide information about the concept provided. |
| **Spatial relevance** | |
| Score 1 | A document refers to a location that is/near the query location AND you think that the location in the document has sufficient detail for you to find it on a local map of the area. |
| Score 2 | A document refers to a location that is in/near the query location BUT you think that there is insufficient information for you to find that location on a local map of the area. |
| Score 3 | A document does not fall within the query location. |

## 3  Experiment and Results

A pilot user study was carried out to investigate the effectiveness of the proposed scheme. Subjects were asked to make relevance judgments regarding the thematic and spatial relevance of 10 documents per topic using the proposed schemes. Each subject was given five topics to judge. The judged scores were analysed in relation to their distribution across the topics, inter-assessor agreement, ease of assessment, confidence in judgments and any difficulties they faced in assessing topics through the use of pre-topic, post-topic and post-session questionnaires.

Documents were retrieved using SPIRIT, a prototype spatially-aware search engine [6], based on a set of approximately 20,000 web pages. A set of 10 documents were retrieved based for each of the following five topics: 1) Caving in Derbyshire (UK), 2) Castles in Wales (UK), 3) Skiing near Glencoe (UK), 4) Art festivals in Edinburgh (UK), and 5) Music in Montreux (Switzerland).

In addition, a paragraph-length description of each topic was provided to subjects in order to help them make their judgments. Subjects were also allowed to use the Internet as a source of geographical knowledge and could also select "Not sure" when unable to make an appropriate decision for a particular document. A total of 11 subjects participated in the experiment giving a total of 1,100 judgments (550 judgments for each type of relevance). The results of our experiment are as follows.

### 3.1  Perception of Subject Assessments

Subjects were asked three questions: (Q1) Was the three-point scale suitable, (Q2) Were the schemes easy to understand, and (Q3) Did you make a judgment confidently? And

**Table 2.** Participants' perception of the assessment scheme (T: Thematic S: Spatial)

|        | Strongly disagree | Disagree | Neutral | Agree | Strongly agree |
|--------|-------------------|----------|---------|-------|----------------|
| Q1 (T) | 0 | 2 | 0 | 7 | 2 |
| Q1 (S) | 0 | 1 | 0 | 7 | 3 |
| Q2 (T) | 0 | 0 | 1 | 5 | 5 |
| Q2 (S) | 1 | 1 | 0 | 6 | 2 |
| Q3 (T) | 0 | 0 | 4 | 6 | 1 |
| Q3 (S) | 1 | 2 | 3 | 3 | 2 |

results are shown in Table 2. Assessors agreed that a ternary scheme was suitable for judging and most found the scheme easy to understand, especially for thematic relevance. Assessors appeared to be more confident in judging thematic than spatial relevance.

### 3.2 Relevance Assessments

Although our subjects appeared to have been somewhat confident about making relevance judgements in both the thematic and spatial cases, on initial investigation of our data we found that inter-annotator agreement was in many cases relatively poor (a multi-rater Kappa test gave k=0.1886, p<.05 for thematic relevance and k=0.1388, p<.05 for spatial relevance). We decided to investigate this contradiction in more detail and, to ease analysis, reduced both the thematic and spatial relevance judgements to a binary scale.

Figure 1 shows a histogram illustrating summed relevance judgements for each document, where a single judgement of not relevant scored -1, and a judgement of relevant scored 1. Thus, 10 documents were judged to be thematically relevant by all 11 of our subjects. The histogram is biased towards relevant documents since the judgements were made on documents retrieved by a GIR system which we expect to retrieve at least some relevant documents. However, it is clear that there is considerably more inter-annotator agreement for thematic judgements than spatial judgements. Furthermore, thematic relevance judgments are only moderately correlated with spatial relevance (r= 0.63).

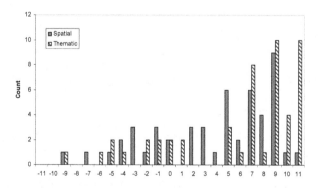

**Fig. 1.** Sum of relevant and non-relevant judgments per document

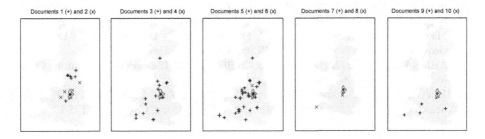

**Fig. 2.** Distribution of spatial references in documents for topic 1 (mapped as pairs)

Since it appeared that, although our subjects were happy with the scheme for making spatial judgements, in many cases they disagreed about the spatial relevance of indidvidual documents, we decided to investigate such judgements in more detail. We parsed location names from documents, and where possible geocoded them for each of the 10 documents from each topic. Figure 2 shows the results for the 10 documents retrieved for Topic 1 (caving in Derbyshire). The spatial relevance judgement for each of these documents was as follows: (doc:score): 1:2, 2:9, 3:-5, 4:7, 5:-1, 6:0, 7:5, 8:0, 9:-1 and 10:-7. Therefore, documents 2, 4 and 7 were judged to be spatially relevant by more than 2/3 of our subjects, and documents 3 and 10 was judged to be spatially irrelevant by more than 2/3 of our subjects. Documents 1, 5, 6, 8 and 9 are all more or less ambiguous in terms of judgements of spatial relevance.

## 4   Discussion

The spatially relevant documents (2,4,7) all appear to have a small set of locations tightly focussed around Derbyshire (indicated in the centre of Figure 2). However, much less of a pattern is evident in the case of both the ambiguous or irrelevant documents. We suggest that this is because documents which have a well-defined geographic focus and are centred on the query location are probably much easier to assess, in particular for subjects with less geographic knowledge of the query region. Documents referring to many locations appear difficult to assess according to the subject's background knowledge of the area resulting in poor inter-annotator agreement.

These initial qualitative results show that, in general, spatial relevance appears more difficult than thematic relevance to judge. However, they also suggest that use of a "spatially-aware" relevance scheme is appropriate. Further work is required with larger subject and topic groups to refine the scheme and to propose guidelines for making appropriate judgements of spatial relevance.

## References

[1] McCurley, S.K. 2001. Geospatial mapping and navigation of the web. In Proceedings of the Tenth International WWW Conference, Hong Kong, 221-229.
[2] Cai. G. (2002) GeoVSM: An Integrated Retrieval Model for Geographic Information. LNCS 2489, 70-85.

[3] Bucher, B., Clough, P., Joho, H., Purves, R., and Syed, A. K. (2005) Geographic IR Systems: Requirements and Evaluation. In Proceedings of the 22nd ICC, A Coruña, Spain.

[4] Martins, B. Silva, M.J. and Chaves, M. (2005) Challenges and Resources for Evaluating Geographical IR, In Proceedings of GIR'05, Bremen, Germany.

[5] András Kornai (2005) MetaCarta at GeoCLEF 2005, In "The working notes of the CLEF workshop", Vienna, Austria, 21-23 September 2005.

[6] Jones, C.B, A.I. Abdelmoty, D. Finch, G. Fu and S. Vaid, 2004. The SPIRIT Spatial Search Engine :Architecture, Ontologies and Spatial Indexing. LNCS 3234, 125-39.

# Probabilistic Score Normalization for Rank Aggregation

Miriam Fernández, David Vallet, and Pablo Castells

Universidad Autónoma de Madrid, Escuela Politécnica Superior,
Ciudad Universitaria de Cantoblanco,
28049 Madrid, Spain
{miriam.fernandez, david.vallet, pablo.castells}@uam.es

**Abstract.** Rank aggregation is a pervading operation in IR technology. We hypothesize that the performance of score-based aggregation may be affected by artificial, usually meaningless deviations consistently occurring in the input score distributions, which distort the combined result when the individual biases differ from each other. We propose a score-based rank aggregation model where the source scores are normalized to a common distribution before being combined. Early experiments on available data from several TREC collections are shown to support our proposal.

## 1 Introduction

Rank aggregation is a pervading operation in IR technology [6]. To name a few examples, rank aggregation takes place in the combination of multiple criteria for document/query similarity assessment in most search engines; in merging the outputs of different engines for meta-search; in the combination of query-based and preference-based relevance for personalized search [1]; or even in the combination of preferences from multiple users for collaborative retrieval [5]. Both rank-based and score-based aggregation techniques have been explored in prior research on this topic [7]. We hypothesize that that the performance of score-based aggregation may be affected by artificial, usually meaningless deviations consistently occurring in the input score distributions, which do not affect the performance of each ranking technique separately, but distort the combined result when the individual biases differ from each other, and therefore it should be possible to improve the results by undoing these deviations.

In order to devise a general method to merge the output of several ranking techniques, no a-priori assumption on the interpretation of the scores values should be made. The values may correspond to a degree of relevance, probability of relevance, odds of relevance, user preference, or other interpretations in a variety of retrieval models, often undergoing further mathematical transformations (scaling, dampening, logs, etc.) for practical purposes. However, in order to combine the scores, the values should be first made comparable across input systems [2], which usually involves a normalization step [6]. In this poster we propose an aggregation model where the source scores are normalized to a common *ideal* score distribution, and then merged by a linear combination. Early experiments on available data from several TREC collections are shown to support our proposal.

M. Lalmas et al. (Eds.): ECIR 2006, LNCS 3936, pp. 553–556, 2006.
© Springer-Verlag Berlin Heidelberg 2006

## 2  Score Normalization

In prior work, normalization typically consists of linear transformations [3], and other relatively straightforward, yet effective methods, such as normalizing the sum of scores (rather than the max) of each input system to 1, or shifting the mean of values to 0 and scaling the variance to 1 [6]. But none of these strategies takes into account the detailed distribution of the scorings, and is thus sensitive to "noise" score biases.

A work where the score distribution is taken into account is that of Manmatha et al [4], who analyze the probabilistic behavior of search engines, in order to derive a better combination of their outputs. They observe that the scoring values have an exponential distribution for the set of non-relevant documents, and a Gaussian distribution for the set of relevant ones. According to this, a score $s$ output by a given engine for a document $d$ is normalized to P ($d$ is relevant | $score(d) = s$), which is computed by applying Bayes' rule, and approximating the probabilities by a mixture of an exponential and a Gaussian distribution, using the Expectation Maximization method.

Starting from Manmatha's analysis of typical score distributions, we propose an alternative approach, where input scores are mapped to an *optimal score distribution* (OSD), which we define as the distribution of an ideal scoring function that matches the ranking by actual relevance. Of course this is a difficult concept to define, let alone to obtain, but we claim that an acceptable approximation can provide good results.

Our method works as follows. Let $\Omega$ be the universe of information objects to be ranked, and $\mathcal{R}$ the set of rank lists to be combined. Each rank source $\tau \in \mathcal{R}$ can be represented as a bijection $\tau : \Omega_\tau \to \mathbb{N}^+_{|\Omega_\tau|}$ for some $\Omega_\tau \subset \Omega$, where for each $x \in \Omega_\tau$, $\tau(x)$ is the position of $x$ in the ranking returned by $\tau$. For each $\tau \in \mathcal{R}$, we shall denote by $s_\tau : \Omega \to \mathbb{R}$ the scoring function associated to $\tau$, where we take $s_\tau(x) = 0$ if $x \notin \Omega_\tau$. Our approach consists of two phases. The first one is performed offline, as follows:

1. For each ranked list $\tau \in \mathcal{R}$, compute the cumulative score distribution $F_\tau$ of the values $s_\tau$ returned by the ranking system that outputs $\tau$. This can be approximated by running a significant number of calls to each system with different random inputs (e.g. queries and documents).

2. Build a strictly increasing OSD $\overline{F} : [0,1] \to [0,1]$. This step is discussed below.

In the second phase, which takes place at query-time, the outputs of the rank sources are normalized and merged:

3. Normalization: For each $x \in \Omega$ and $\tau \in \mathcal{R}$, map the score of each rank source to the OSD: $s_\tau(x) \to \overline{s}_\tau(x) = \overline{F}^{-1} \circ F_\tau \circ s_\tau(x)$.

4. Combination: merge the normalized scores, e.g. by a linear combination or some other score-based technique.

The idea of step 3 is illustrated in figure 1. The normalization respects the order of each rank list (except in intervals where $F_\tau$ is constant, i.e. where by definition it is unlikely that any score value should fall), since $\overline{F}^{-1} \circ F_\tau$ is monotonically

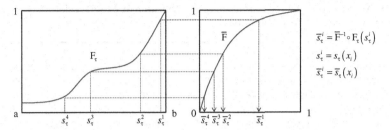

**Fig. 1.** Mapping scores to a common distribution

non-decreasing. The resulting scores $\bar{s}_\tau = \bar{F}^{-1} \circ F_\tau \circ s_\tau$ range in [0,1], and their distribution is $\bar{F}$ for all $\tau \in \mathcal{R}$, thus undoing potential distributional biases, as intended.

The choice of $\bar{F}$ as an appropriate OSD, in step 2 above, is critical to our method. Our proposed approach consists of computing the average distribution of several good scoring systems, as a rough approximation to an actual relevance distribution. This can be obtained empirically on a statistically significant sample of scoring systems (the ones to be merged, or different ones) and input values. In this estimation, the scores of each system are first linearly normalized to [0,1] by a variation of the standard normalization technique [3], where rather than taking the min and max scores of a single ranked list, all the scores collected from the system over several runs are included.

## 3 Evaluation and Results

We have tested our techniques in four different test collections from the TREC Web Results, namely TREC8, TREC9, TREC9L, and TREC2001. For the comparative evaluation we have tried our technique with two reference combination functions after the normalization step, to which we will refer as: a) DCombSUM, where the fused score is computed as $s_\mathcal{R}(x) = \sum_{\tau \in \mathcal{R}} \bar{s}_\tau(x)$, i.e. our score normalization step is followed by the so-called CombSUM method [6]; and b) DCombMNZ, where $s_\mathcal{R}(x) = h(x,\mathcal{R}) \sum_{\tau \in \mathcal{R}} \bar{s}_\tau(x)$, and $h(x,\mathcal{R}) = \left| \left\{ \tau \in \mathcal{R} \mid s_\tau(x) > 0 \right\} \right|$ is the number of engines that return $x$, a technique named as CombMNZ in prior work [6].

We have compared these functions with other ones where the same combination step is used, but a different normalization method is applied. As a benchmark for comparison, we have taken the results published in [7], which we label as SComb-SUM (CombSUM with standard score normalization), RCombSUM (CombSUM with Rank-sim normalization), and SCombMNZ (CombMNZ with standard score normalization). Table 1 shows the average results over the four collections. It can be seen that both DCombSUM and DCombMNZ are globally better that the other techniques. Although we only show the averaged results, this behavior is consistent over the four collections. DCombMNZ is only surpassed on average by SCombMNZ in TREC 2001, while the performance of DCombSUM, which could be thought of as a non-tuned version of our algorithm, performs slightly below DCombMNZ, but still globally better than any other of the benchmarks taken from [7].

**Table 1.** Average precision for 10 trials of the combination of 2 to 12 rank lists. The results are averaged over the four TREC collections.

|  | 2 | 4 | 6 | 8 | 10 | 12 | Avg |
|---|---|---|---|---|---|---|---|
| **SCombSUM** | 0.2598 | 0.2886 | 0.3084 | 0.3172 | 0.3204 | 0.3241 | 0.3031 |
| **RCombSUM** | 0.2567 | 0.2884 | 0.2847 | 0.2877 | 0.2971 | 0.2994 | 0.2857 |
| **SCombMNZ** | 0.2599 | 0.2884 | 0.3058 | 0.3176 | 0.3156 | 0.3231 | 0.3017 |
| **DCombSUM** | 0.2614 | 0.2942 | 0.3096 | 0.3184 | 0.3237 | 0.3268 | 0.3057 |
| **DCombMNZ** | 0.2637 | 0.2979 | 0.3090 | 0.3194 | 0.3228 | 0.3268 | 0.3066 |

## 4 Further Work

The possibilities for the continuation of this work are manifold. Studying score distributions is a research topic by itself. For instance, we foresee that a finer, more specialized analysis of score distributions could be achieved by identifying and separating certain conditions on which the distribution may depend, such as properties of the queries (e.g. query length), the search space, the result set, or other domain-specific factors. Also, we are currently exploring techniques where the coefficients in the linear combination are a function of application-specific variables of the ranking system, such as the uncertainty in the rankings [1].

## Acknowledgements

This research was supported by the EC (FP6-001765 – aceMedia), and the Spanish Ministry of Science and Education (TIN2005-06885). The content expressed is the view of the authors but not necessarily the view of the aceMedia project as a whole.

## References

1. Castells, P., Fernández, M., Vallet, D., Mylonas, P., Avrithis, Y. Self-Tuning Personalised Information Retrieval in an Ontology-Based Framework. 1st IFIP Intl. Workshop on Web Semantics (SWWS 2005). LNCS Vol. 3532. Agia Napa, Cyprus, 2005, pp. 455-470.
2. Croft, W. B. Combining approaches to information retrieval. In: Advances in Information Retrieval: Recent Research from the Center for Intelligent Information Retrieval. Kluwer Academic Publishers, 2000, pp. 1-36.
3. Lee, J. H. Analysis of multiple evidence combination. 20th ACM SIGIR Conf. on Research and Development in Information Retrieval (SIGIR 97). New York, 1997, pp. 267-276.
4. Manmatha. R., Rath, R., Feng, F. Modelling score distributions for combining the outputs of search engines. 24th Annual International ACM SIGIR Conference on Research and Development in Information Retrieval (SIGIR 2001). New Orleans, LA, pp. 267-275.
5. Masthoff, J. Group Modeling: Selecting a Sequence of Television Items to Suit a Group of Viewers. User Modeling and User-Adapted Interaction 14 (1), 2004, pp. 37-85.
6. Montague, M., Aslam, J.A. Relevance score normalization for metasearch. 10th Conf. on Information and Knowledge Management (CIKM 2001). Atlanta, GA, 2001, pp. 427-433.
7. Renda, M. E., Straccia, U. Web metasearch: rank vs. score based rank aggregation methods. ACM symposium on Applied Computing. Melbourne, Florida, 2003, pp. 841-846.

# Learning Links Between a User's Calendar and Information Needs

Elena Vildjiounaite and Vesa Kyllönen

Technical Research Centre of Finland,
Kaitovayla 1, 90571 Oulu, Finland
{firstname.lastname}@vtt.fi

**Abstract.** Personal information needs depend on long-term interests and on current and future situations (contexts): people are mainly interested in weather forecasts for future destinations, and in toy advertisements when a child's birthday approaches. As computer capabilities for being aware of users' contexts grow, the users' willingness to set manually rules for context-based information retrieval will decrease. Thus computers must learn to associate user contexts with information needs in order to collect and present information proactively. This work presents experiments with training a SVM (Support Vector Machines) classifier to learn user information needs from calendar information.

## 1 Introduction

If asked, people can usually explain why they were looking for certain pieces of information. Computer systems also need to take into account these cause-and-effect relations as they become increasingly capable of context recognition. However, recommender and IR systems do not detect the user context via wired networks, while mobile devices are aware of user contexts, but not aware of user information needs because, with the exception of mobile context-based reminding and location-based guiding systems, it is mainly a desktop that is used for information search purposes.

We suggest that user context data should be connected to information retrieval, so that dependences between them can be learned and used in recommender systems and for proactively collecting and uploading to an appropriate mobile device multimedia and information which the user might be interested in while on the move. This approach poses the following research problems: first, which context types (among the many contexts which it is possible to detect) affect user interests most of all; second, what are the advantages and disadvantages of different machine learning methods that could be applied to the task; and third, which threats or benefits to privacy are involved in such data linkages. Using context data for personalisation purposes is not yet an active area of research, but its importance has recently been acknowledged. Work [1] suggests using social context by merging the profiles of users whose individual interests are known beforehand; works [2] and [3] present benefits of learning the dependence of TV programme selection on day and time. The work [4] proposes that user interests can be modelled in context as multidimensional spaces.

M. Lalmas et al. (Eds.): ECIR 2006, LNCS 3936, pp. 557–560, 2006.
© Springer-Verlag Berlin Heidelberg 2006

## 2  Summary of User Interviews

We found during user interviews that users are interested in having a proactive information/multimedia retrieval system provided that it will not require much prior configuration and will be unobtrusive (that is, it will collect and store information and multimedia until the user needs it or until it becomes outdated). Such offline delivery can be useful e.g. in cases when a user needs guiding or wants to watch videos and to read news while on the move. A network connection can be too costly or imperfect, e.g. problems are common underground and in the wild. Moreover, wireless connections are not allowed in aeroplanes or in some hospitals. Proactive context-based Multimedia and Information Retrieval and corresponding application goals could include the following:

1. Learning of complex dependences within a set of metadata on a set of contexts. This can include regular routines (e.g. checking the weather forecast in the morning of every workday to decide how to dress the children, or looking for news on interesting topics during breakfast), or not so regular (such as the selection of videos for several family members to watch together, or the selection of home videos to show to guests, or looking at news during free time at work). The application goal is to learn desired topics for different sets of people and other factors, such as when information is needed, the time available (e.g. a 10-minute digest on a workday morning vs. more detailed information at weekends) and event dependence (e.g. Christmas videos in Christmas time).

2. Learning of the dependence of a set of metadata on a particular context, usually an event, either in the user's life (weather forecast for a destination), or a global event (people often watch news about a major terrorist attack even if they rarely watch news generally). The application goal is to learn person-dependent links between events and desired information, and also when the user needs this information: some people check the weather and collect things at the last moment, while others do so in advance.

3. Privacy concerns (e.g. to hide completely the existence of erotic or cruel videos from children or girlfriends). The goal here is not to suggest anything if it was not retrieved previously in a similar social context.

## 3  Learning of Links Between Contexts and IR

User context is a complex notion described by many parameters. We have chosen to represent context as a vector in a multidimensional space which points at certain topics of user interests. The choice of dimensions was made on the basis of user interviews:

- time (time of day; day of week; time available)
- event (personal event; close person event ("wife's birthday"); world-wide event ("crash of twin towers").
- social context (people located together or involved in the same activity);
- location (e.g. at home, at work, on the move)
- activity (e.g. gymnastics needs to be accompanied by rhythmic music)
- device (desktop; PDA; phone)

Each of these contexts can refer to a user's current situation or future situation, or even past situation for some applications (e.g. a reminder to take the latest holiday photos when going to visit friends). We have selected only context types which are fairly easy to detect, e.g. social context recognition is described in [5]. Each case of information retrieval is associated with a long list of contexts, for example:

*Time of Day: morning; Day of week: Monday; Location: work; Device: desktop; Social Context: alone; Near Future Event: work trip to Brussels; its Social Context: alone; Near Future Event: child's birthday; its Social Context: family, relatives...* Similar, corresponding list of retrieved information might contain many descriptors, e.g.: *Shopping Pages: books; Source: Amazon; News: Sports: skiing; Source: local newspaper; News: weather Brussels; Source: CNN....*

The initial data were collected by means of user interviews: users reported information/multimedia retrieval cases and corresponding contexts over a period of one week. To these cases we added 30% noise (retrieval of similar and arbitrary information in arbitrary contexts), taking into account that some cases were not described correctly or were simply forgotten. This resulted in 210 IR cases on 45 topics, among which were ten favourite (almost everyday) topics and one event-related topic.

For learning associations between contexts and information/multimedia retrieval we used SVM (Support Vector Machines) and its implementation in the TORCH library of machine learning methods [6], because of the following advantages:

- SVM has good generalization capabilities and should thus be able to provide valuable recommendations even after training on only a small amount of data
- SVM allows utilizing user feedback and treating most recent examples as more important by assigning different penalties for misclassification of different examples
- SVM training is very fast and allows retraining of the model as often as additional information comes in, at least during the initial phases of learning (less than several thousand examples), when this is especially important.

We trained SVM to provide recommendations on each topic separately (distinct models for news, documents, videos, etc). Since each topic has its own model, each new IR case means that either a few corresponding models need to be updated or new models created, but not the whole system. During training several "good" sets of contexts (sets which perform sufficiently well on a randomly selected subset of training data) are selected for each topic. During testing four test examples per topic of interest were generated, as follows: two contained all the contexts described by a user as important predicates for an IR case, while contexts described as irrelevant were different, whereas in the other examples all the contexts were different.

We tested the ability of the method to learn the links between the list of relevant contexts and the list of relevant topics for these contexts; to learn one relevant context (e.g. *Near Future Event: work trip to Brussels*) from among many irrelevant ones in order to provide specific information (*News: weather Brussels*); and to learn when the system should not present certain information. We have found that SVM learns regular user activities fast (the five favourite topics for mornings and three for evenings were always among the top twelve suggestions for the corresponding context, while two other favourite topics retrieved in random contexts were not learned as favourites based on one week data). At the moment, however, the method lacks the ability to learn when it should not present information, which is not a desirable situation as far as privacy protection is concerned, and treats all context types as equally important. We therefore added the rule that the method should not recommend a given topic (i.e. it can only reject it) if there are no positive examples in same social context.

As for the need to find one relevant context for a certain IR case, such as (*weather Brussels*) for a trip, the method has learned to associate "*trip to Brussels soon*" with interest in *weather Brussels* after meeting with only three examples (this was among top five suggestions for a similar context). One good feature of SVM is that it does not forget training examples easily (it is mainly engaged in detecting differences between examples). In contexts where there were a few training examples on different topics, however, the suggestions were unpredictable and unusable.

## 4   Conclusions

This work has suggested trained classifier-based approach to learning the dependence of user information needs on user context, and presented the choice of most important context dimensions. The first experiments made with one week history of IR cases, calendar data and social context, collected via user interviews, suggest that the classifier can learn topics which are generally interesting to a user in different contexts, and can select the context dimensions which are most important for current topic. However, the classifier currently can not learn fast which topics should not be presented in certain contexts, and thus additional rule for user privacy protection was added on top of the learned models. Another drawback is that the method generates as many models as there are users' topics of interests, which allows for system flexibility but requires disk space. The scalability of the method; its ability to adapt to concept drift and its applicability to real-time recommender systems need to be tested further.

The work has been carried out in EU project Amigo, contract number IST 004182.

## References

1. Masthoff, J., Group Modeling: Selecting a Sequence of Television Items to Suit a Group of Viewers, User Modeling and User-Adapted Interaction 14: 37-85, 2004
2. Goren-Bar, D., Glinansky, O., FIT-recommending TV programs to family members, Computers & Graphics 28 (2004) 149-156
3. Ardissono, L., Gena, C., Torasso, P., Bellifemine, F., Chiarotto, A., Difino, A., Negro, B., User Modeling and Recommendation Techniques for Personalized electronic Program Guides, Personalized Digital Television, Vol. 6, 2004
4. Adomavicius, G., Sankaranarayanan, R., Sen, Sh., Tughilin, A., Incorporating Contextual Information in Recommender Systems Using a Multidimensional Approach, ACM Trans. Inf. Syst., Vol. 23, No. 1. (January 2005), pp. 103-145
5. Mäntyjärvi, J., Gfeller, B., Social Cliques: Group Awareness for Mobile Terminals, EI 2005
6. http://www.torch.ch/

# Supporting Relevance Feedback in Video Search

Cathal Gurrin[1,2], Dag Johansen[1], and Alan F. Smeaton[2]

[1] Dept. of Comp. Sci, Universitetet i Tromsø, 9037 Tromsø, Norway
dag@cs.uit.no
[2] Centre for Digital Video Processing, Dublin City University,
Glasnevin, Dublin 9, Ireland
{cgurrin, alan.smeaton}@computing.dcu.ie

**Abstract.** WWW Video Search Engines have become increasingly common-place within the last few years and at the same time video retrieval research has been receiving more attention with the annual TRECVid series of workshops. In this paper we evaluate methods of relevance feedback for video search engines operating over TV news data. We show for both video shots and TV news stories, that an optimal number of terms can be identified to compose a new query for feedback and that in most cases; the number of documents employed for feedback does not have a great effect on these optimal numbers of terms.

## 1 Introduction

Within the last few years we have seen the major search engines provide video searching and we are now able to search through large collections of video as if searching for web pages. At the same time, video retrieval research has continued apace, fostered to a great extent, by the TRECVid series of workshops. One aspect of interactive video retrieval systems, both research systems and WWW video search engines, has been the facility for a user to engage in relevance feedback. The research we present in this paper evaluates the effect of query size on relevance feedback performance for video archives of TV news shots and TV news stories where, like WWW video search engines, retrieval uses text surrogates of the video data. We examine scenarios where a user may choose to feedback one video document, or more than one video document in a relevance feedback process. Typically single document feedback is employed in WWW video search, whereas multi-document feedback has been employed primarily in research systems. For recommendation of video content based on user histories, the ability to automatically generate meaningful (and optimal) queries based on multiple user history documents is an important consideration and motivates this research.

Major search engines (such as Google and Yahoo!) have recently begun to provide video retrieval services. In addition there are a number of dedicated video search engines such as Truveo.com and Blinkx.com. WWW video search engines normally operate using a text surrogate of a video and process textual user queries. One possible option for generating text surrogates is the ASR (Automatic Speech Recognition) text from the audio track of the video; however the most widely used technique uses the surrounding text from a web page, in a similar manner to the WWW image search engines. Search and relevance feedback is then supported using these text surrogates.

M. Lalmas et al. (Eds.): ECIR 2006, LNCS 3936, pp. 561–564, 2006.
© Springer-Verlag Berlin Heidelberg 2006

Research into video retrieval has been ongoing since the early 90s and two of the best known projects are Informedia [1] from CMU the Físchlár [2] Digital Video suite from DCU. Since 2001, the annual TRECVid Workshop [3] has fostered and encouraged such research by providing video test collections and a comparison and evaluation framework for participants. Many research video retrieval systems (e.g. [2]) support single video document feedback, but also 'more like these' relevance feedback where more than one document can be selected for feedback. Conventional relevance feedback techniques, when presented with a video document (a text surrogate), or many video documents, can then select terms to append to a query or compose a new query. We are interested in identifying the optimal number of terms (for both video shots and video news stories) used to compose a new query from text surrogates of video documents and how the number of feedback video documents influences this.

## 2   Relevance Feedback Experiment from Digital Video Libraries

The data used for this experiment was the TRECVid 2004 test collection, (33,367 video shots from TV news video and 24 topics). We represented each video shot by a document (textual surrogate) generated from the ASR transcript. In addition, we constructed a similar test collection of 1,757 news stories (with relevance judgments) from the TRECVid 2004 video shots, using predefined manually generated story boundaries (which excluded story transition shots). The basic text retrieval engine employed for this work implemented BM25 [4] with parameters trained on the TRECVid 2003 collection, which was similar in nature and size to TRECVid 2004. A custom stopword list was employed, based on the SMART list, but employing thirteen additional terms and the Porter stemmer was applied.

To evaluate relevance feedback, we automatically modeled a user selecting from one to nine video documents for feedback and examined system performance when between one and thirty terms were selected from these surrogates (270 evaluations). This feedback process generated a new query, not an expanded version of the original query. We assumed that the user would only feedback relevant video documents and that the user's information need, as expressed in the TRECVid topic did not change during the feedback process. Therefore, we only selected relevant (judged) video documents for feedback from the top ranked videos returned by the BM25 retrieval engine for each of the 24 topics and evaluated performance using the relevance judgments (which excluded the video documents already chosen for feedback). For feedback of 1 to 3 video documents we evaluated 5 different random combinations of documents from the top 5 relevant documents and averaged the results[1]. Feedback of 4 to 9 video documents was performed similarly, though we evaluated 10 different random combinations from the top 10 relevant documents.

Two feedback techniques were examined for this study, TF-IDF and a variation on Robertson's Relevance Weight formula [4]. These algorithms are used to select the $N$ most useful terms from the feedback documents to compose a new query. The TF-IDF algorithm employed *log* normalised TFs. The second algorithm incorporates a

---

[1] E.g. two document feedback: 5 random pairs of unique documents from the top 5 relevant documents were chosen and evaluated for all 1-30 terms with the results averaged across the five pairs of documents producing 30 results (1-30 terms) for two document feedback.

*log* nomalised TF weight into Robertson's RW formula and will be called TFRW. Having $(r=R=0)$ where $N$ is the size of the collection and $n$ is the number of segments that term $i$ occurs in, the formula is:

$$TFRW_i = \log(TF_i) \times \log((0.5/(N-n+0.5))/((n+0.5) \times 0.5)). \tag{1}$$

Our findings suggest that there is no significant difference between the performances of these techniques in the experiments we present, and therefore we focus on TFRW in our results, which performed marginally better than TFIDF.

## 2.1 Shot-Level and Story-Level Feedback

The shot-level search engine achieved a MAP of 0.0465 over the 24 TRECVid 2004 topics (optimal parameter MAP is 0.0511). While low in absolute terms this is comparable to the expected performance of an automatic system on the TRECVid 2004 data.

Examining the results in detail (Fig. 1), it is clear that performance increases significantly for relevance feedback of shots as terms are added up to a maximum of 7-8 terms, after which performance decreases or remains relatively static, regardless of the number of video documents chosen for feedback. The addition of any additional terms will not only affect query response time but also effectiveness.

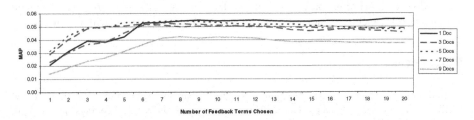

**Fig. 1.** Plot of 1,3,5,7 & 9 video shots chosen for feedback. The average MAP is shown as the number of feedback terms increased up to twenty (2,4,6 &8 removed for clarity).

The 2004 story-level search engine achieved a MAP of 0.2310 when using the 2003 parameters (optimal parameter MAP is 0.2318). With TV news story video, the optimal performance occurs between 10 and 13 terms in the feedback query (see Fig. 2).

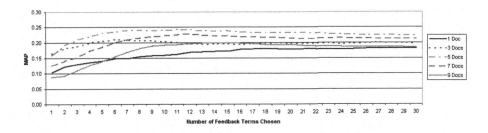

**Fig. 2.** Plot of 1,3,5,7 & 9 TV news story videos chosen for feedback. The average MAP is shown as the number of feedback terms increased up to twenty (2,4,6 & 8 removed for clarity).

The notable exception is when a single video document is chosen for feedback, when the optimal number of terms was found to be 30, though only a minor improvement in performance (6%) was noted over queries comprised of the top 13 terms. Adding additional terms above the top 30 has a negative effect on MAP. This negative effect increases with the number of video documents chosen for feedback.

## 3   Conclusions and Future Work

The purpose of this experiment was to evaluate the influence of query size on relevance feedback for video retrieval systems that index video shots or news stories. We have shown that for shots a system will perform at or near its peak when 7-8 terms are used to generate a new feedback query and for TV news stories that the peak can be found in most cases when 10-13 terms comprise the query. The number of video documents chosen for feedback does not affect these optimal numbers of terms noticeably (except for a single news story). The addition of more terms (beyond the optimal) from feedback video documents will be expected to hamper performance, while also having a negative effect on processing time. This is an important consideration for commercial WWW video search engines for whom processing time for each query is an important consideration. Future work planned includes optimising the feedback algorithms for general video data and we also plan to evaluate video search and relevance feedback on real-world WWW video content, with real users.

## References

1. Hauptmann, A., Thornton, S., Houghton, R., Qi, Y., Ng, T.D., Papernick, N., Jin, R. Video Retrieval with the Informedia Digital Video Library System. In: Proceedings of the Tenth Text Retrieval Conference (TREC'01), Gaithersburg, Maryland, November 13-16, (2001).
2. Gurrin, C., Lee, H., Smeaton, A.F. Físchlár @ TRECVID2003: System Description. In 12th ACM International Conference on Multimedia 2004, New York, NY, 15-16 October (2004) 938-939.
3. TRECVid Workshop. WebLink: http://www-nlpir.nist.gov/projects/trecvid/. Last Visited 21st Nov. 2005.
4. Robertson, S. E., Sparck Jones, K. Simple, proven approaches to text retrieval. Tech. Rep. TR246, University of Cambridge, (1997).

# Intrinsic Plagiarism Detection

Sven Meyer zu Eissen and Benno Stein

Faculty of Media: Media Systems,
Bauhaus University Weimar, 99421 Weimar, Germany

**Abstract.** Current research in the field of automatic plagiarism detection for text documents focuses on algorithms that compare plagiarized documents against potential original documents. Though these approaches perform well in identifying copied or even modified passages, they assume a closed world: a reference collection must be given against which a plagiarized document can be compared.

This raises the question whether plagiarized passages within a document can be detected automatically if no reference is given, e. g. if the plagiarized passages stem from a book that is not available in digital form. We call this problem class *intrinsic plagiarism detection*. The paper is devoted to this problem class; it shows that it is possible to identify potentially plagiarized passages by analyzing a single document with respect to variations in writing style.

Our contributions are fourfold: (*i*) a taxonomy of plagiarism delicts along with detection methods, (*ii*) new features for the quantification of style aspects, (*iii*) a publicly available plagiarism corpus for benchmark comparisons, and (*iv*) promising results in non-trivial plagiarism detection settings: in our experiments we achieved recall values of 85% with a precision of 75% and better.

**Keywords:** plagiarism detection, style analysis, classifier, plagiarism corpus.

## 1  Introduction

Plagiarism refers to the use of another's information, language, or writing, when done without proper acknowledgment of the original source [10]. A recent large-scale study on 18,000 students by McCabe shows that about 50% of the students admit to plagiarize from extraneous documents [5]. Plagiarism in text documents happens in several forms: plagiarized text may be copied one-to-one, passages may be modified to a greater or lesser extent, or they may even be translated. Figure 1 shows a taxonomy of plagiarism delicts, which organizes delicts and possible detection methods.

**State of the Art in Plagiarism Detection.** The success of current approaches in plagiarism detection varies according to the underlying plagiarism delict. The approaches stated in [1; 3] employ cryptographic hash functions to generate digital fingerprints of so-called text chunks, which are then compared against a database of original text passage fingerprints. Since cryptographic fingerprints identify a text chunk exactly, the quality of these approaches depends on offsets and sizes of chunks within both plagiarized and original texts. An approach given in [8] overcomes these limitations: unlike cryptographic fingerprints, the proposed method generates fingerprints that are robust against modifications to some extent.

M. Lalmas et al. (Eds.): ECIR 2006, LNCS 3936, pp. 565–569, 2006.
© Springer-Verlag Berlin Heidelberg 2006

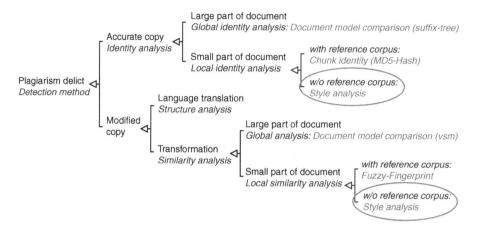

**Fig. 1.** A taxonomy of plagiarism delicts and analysis methods [7]. The encircled parts indicate our contributions: the detection of plagiarism delicts without having a reference corpus at hand.

**Intrinsic Plagiarism Detection.** The mentioned approaches have one constraint in common: they require a reference collection of potential original documents. Observe that human readers may identify suspicious passages within a document without having a library of reference documents in mind: changes between brilliant and baffling passages, or the change of person narrative give hints to plagiarism. Situations where such an intrinsic plagiarism detection can be applied are shown encircled in Figure 1.

Basically, the power of a plagiarism approach depends on the quality of the quantified linguistic features. We introduce features which measure—simply put—the customariness of word usage, and which are able to capture a significant part of style information. To analyze the phenomenon of intrinsic plagiarism detection we have constructed a base corpus from which various application corpora can be compiled, each of which modeling plagiarism delicts of different severity. Section 3 reports on experiments that we have conducted with this corpus.

## 2   Quantification of Writing Style

Intrinsic plagiarism detection can be operationalized by dividing a document into "natural" parts, which may be sentences, paragraphs, or sections, and analyzing the variance of certain style features. Within the experiments presented below the size of a part is chosen rather small (40-200 words), which is ambitious from the analysis standpoint—but which corresponds to realistic situations.

**Stylometric Features.** Stylometric features quantify aspects of writing style, and some of them have been used successfully in the past to discriminate between books with respect to authorship [4]. Most stylometric features fall in one of the following five categories: (*i*) text statistics, which operate at the character level, (*ii*) syntactic features, which measure writing style at the sentence-level, (*iii*) part-of-speech features to quantify the use of word classes, (*iv*) closed-class word sets to count special words, and (*v*) structural features, which reflect text organization.

In addition to these features we now introduce a new statistic, the averaged word frequency class, which turned out to be the most powerful concept with respect to intrinsic plagiarism detection that we have encountered so far.

**Averaged Word Frequency Class.** The frequency class of a word is directly connected to Zipf's law and can be used as an indicator of a word's customariness. Let $C$ be a text corpus, and let $|C|$ be the number of words in $C$. Moreover, let $f(w)$ denote the frequency of a word $w \in C$, and let $r(w)$ denote the rank of $w$ in a word list of $C$, which is sorted by decreasing frequency.

In accordance with [9] we define the word frequency class $c(w)$ of a word $w \in C$ as $\lfloor \log_2(f(w^*)/f(w)) \rfloor$, where $w^*$ denotes the most frequently used word in $C$. In the Sydney Morning Herald Corpus, $w^*$ denotes the word "the", which corresponds to the word frequency class 0; the most uncommonly used words within this corpus have a word frequency class of 19. A document's averaged word frequency class tells us something about style complexity and the size of an author's vocabulary—both of which are highly individual characteristics [6].

Note that, based on a lookup-table, the averaged word frequency class of a text passage can be computed in linear time in the number of words. Another salient property is its small variance with respect to text length, which renders it ideal for our purposes.

# 3 Experimental Analysis

Since no reference collection is available for our concern, we constructed a new corpus, oriented at the following corpus-linguistic criteria [2]: (*i*) authenticity and homogeneity, (*ii*) possibility to include many types of plagiarism, (*iii*) easy processable for both human and machine, (*iv*) clear separation of text and annotations.

We chose genuine computer science articles from the ACM digital library that we "plagiarized" with both copied as well as reformulated passages from other ACM computer science articles, contributing to criterion 1. With respect to criteria 2-4, all documents in the base corpus are represented in XML and validate against an XML schema. The schema declares a mixed content model and provides element types for plagiarism delict, plagiarism source, and other meta information.

An XML document with $k$ plagiarized passages defines a template from which $2^k$ instance documents can be generated, depending on which of the $k$ plagiarized parts are actually included. Instance documents contain no XML tags, in order to ensure that they can be processed by standard algorithms. Instead, a meta information file is generated for each, containing information about the exact locations of plagiarized passages.

**Experiments.** For the experiments presented here more than 450 instance documents were generated each of which containing between 3 and 6 plagiarized passages of different lengths. During the plagiarism analysis these instance documents were decomposed into 50 - 100 passages from which the feature vectors were computed; the feature set included average sentence length, 18 part-of-speech features, average stopword number,

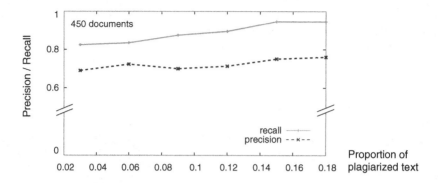

**Fig. 2.** Analysis performance versus severity of plagiarism delicts: The plot shows the averaged values for precision and recall of a series of experiments, where the sizes of the plagiarized passages are successively increased

**Table 1.** The table shows significance scores for the three best-discriminating features. Lower Lambda-values and higher F-ratios indicate better performance.

| Ranking | Feature | Wilks Lambda | F-Ratio | significant |
|---------|---------|--------------|---------|-------------|
| 1 | av. word frequency class | 0.723 | 152.6 | yes |
| 2 | av. preposition number | 0.866 | 61.4 | yes |
| 3 | av. sentence length | 0.880 | 54.0 | yes |

and the averaged word frequency class. Figure 2 illustrates good detection rates for plagiarism delicts in terms of precision and recall with respect to the plagiarism severity. These results were achieved using a classical discriminant analysis; however, an SVM classification showed similar results. Table 1 quantifies the discrimination power of the best features.

# References

[1] S. Brin, J. Davis, and H. Garcia-Molina. Copy detection mechanisms for digital documents. In *Proc. SIGMOD '95*, pages 398–409, 1995.

[2] R. Garside, G. Leech, and A. McEnery. *Corpus Annotation: Linguistic Information from Computer Text Corpora*. Longman, 1997.

[3] T. C. Hoad and J. Zobel. Methods for Identifying Versioned and Plagiarised Documents. *JASIST*, 54(3):203–215, 2003.

[4] M. Koppel and J. Schler. Authorship verification as a one-class classification problem. In *Proc. of ICML'04*, 2004.

[5] D. McCabe. Research Report of the Center for Academic Integrity. http://www.academicintegrity.org, 2005.

[6] S. Meyer zu Eißen and B. Stein. Genre Classification of Web Pages: User Study and Feasibility Analysis. In *Proc. of KI'04: Advances in AI*, volume 3228 LNAI. Springer, 2005.

[7] B. Stein. Fuzzy-Fingerprints for Text-based Information Retrieval. In *Proc. of 5th Int. Conf. on Knowledge Management, Graz, Austria.* JUCS, 2005.

[8] B. Stein and S. Meyer zu Eissen. Near similarity search and plagiarism analysis. In *Proc. of GfKl '05.* Springer, 2005.

[9] University of Leipzig. Wortschatz. `http://wortschatz.uni-leipzig.de`, 1995.

[10] Wikipedia. Plagiarism. `http://en.wikipedia.org/wiki/Plagiarism`, 2005.

# Investigating Biometric Response for Information Retrieval Applications

Colum Mooney, Micheál Scully, Gareth J.F. Jones, and Alan F. Smeaton

Centre for Digital Video Processing & School of Computing,
Dublin City University, Dublin 9, Ireland
{gareth.jones, alan.smeaton}@computing.dcu.ie

**Abstract.** Current information retrieval systems make no measurement of the user's response to the searching process or the information itself. Existing psychological studies show that subjects exhibit measurable physiological responses when carrying out certain tasks, e.g. when viewing images, which generally result in heightened emotional states. We find that users exhibit measurable biometric behaviour in the form of galvanic skin response when watching movies, and engaging in interactive tasks. We examine how this data might be exploited in the indexing of data for search and within the search process itself.

## 1 Introduction

There is currently significant interest in the topic of *context* in information retrieval (IR). It is widely held that taking account of the context in which IR takes place might be used to increase search effectiveness. There are a great range of context features which could potentially be incorporated into the search, although these in general all seek to better express and exploit the user's information need within the IR system. Such features include information details such as the ongoing interests and previous searches of a specific user, but of interest in this paper are features associated with measurable biometric responses to information presentation and the search process.

Recent neuro-scientific research has demonstrated relations between measurable physiological attributes and psychological states (often related to emotional or affective states) [1] [2]. A number of measurements can be made which are shown to be related to these states, including galvanic skin conductivity (GSR), skin temperature and heart rate. These features can be used to measure variations in user arousal (activity levels) and valence (positive vs negative response) which have been shown to be correlated with affective state [3]. Using these measurements studies have demonstrated a number of results of potential relevance in IR. For example, using machine learning, models can be built that enable a predefined group of emotional states to be recognized with good reliability [4], a user's frustration response to interacting with a poorly performing computer application can be recognised [5], and variations in physiological responses to different images presentation to a user can be captured [6].

In this paper we describe two of our current experiments to capture biometric information which can be exploited in IR applications. The first of these relates to the indexing of data and the second explores biometric response in search.

M. Lalmas et al. (Eds.): ECIR 2006, LNCS 3936, pp. 570–574, 2006.
© Springer-Verlag Berlin Heidelberg 2006

## 2   Measuring Biometric Response

The biometric responses most easily captured and associated with emotional stimuli are GSR, skin temperature and heart rate. In our work we are currently using a SenseWear PRO2 armband produced by BodyMedia Inc. [7]. This monitors GSR, skin temperature, heat flux (loss), and acceleration. The SenseWear PRO2 armband is a small lightweight device which straps unobtrusively to the back of the upper arm. Sensors on the back of the device monitor user response. GSR is measured using electrical skin conductance (in $\mu$Siemens) between two electrodes placed on the skin - associated with sweat gland activity. Changes in the levels of sweat in the eccrine sweat glands have been shown to be linked to measures of emotion, arousal, and attention. The rate of sampling can be varied, and we informally optimised this to capture short variations in signals. The captured data is uploaded to a PC for analysis and further processing. We find that GSR is more significant than skin temperature, and for reasons of space only include GSR results here. We are also exploring the use of separate heart rate monitors, but we do not describe results of this work here.

## 3   Measuring Affective Response to Movies

Documents in IR are conventionally indexed in terms of objective features appearing in the documents; words or phrases in text documents, or objects and named individuals and places in images and video. Indexing features can potentially be augmented by describing more subjective features such as their emotional content or user response. In related work our group are currently exploring the affective labelling of movies [8] based on their audio-visual content. Indexing using features of this type enables searching, for example, for exciting or sad sections of a movie. In this paper we introduce our study of movies based on user biometric response.

Based on the observation in previous work that users respond in measurable ways to visual stimuli [6], we have recently recorded the responses of small groups of viewers watching a wide range of movies using the BodyMedia device and heart rate monitors. As an example of the initial output of this work, Figures 1 and 2 show the GSR response of two viewers of the first 10 minutes of the film *Finding Nemo*. We can see considerable

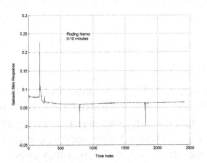   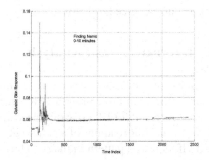

**Fig. 1.** *Finding Nemo*: Viewer 1                    **Fig. 2.** *Finding Newo*: Viewer 2

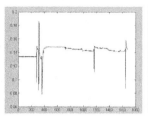 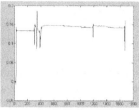 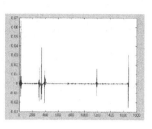

**Fig. 3.** Raw GSR signal        **Fig. 4.** Low-pass filtered GSR        **Fig. 5.** FFD of filtered GSR

variation in these two graphs. This difference between individuals is to be expected, and means that it is not possible to directly compare GSR measurements across individuals (there are no "normal" baselines). However, there is a significant consistent response after around one minute which we know to correspond to a very significant event in the film. While we can clearly see this event and discriminate from it personal variations in GSR caused by less significant events in the movie or from the user's environment, a key challenge is to do this automatically.

In order to better understand variations and detect significant events, we conducted an investigation of 10 individuals watching one movie. For the collected data we measured average GSR range, mean GSR, and the size and rate of peaks. An example result is shown in Figures 3, 4 and 5. Figure 3 is the raw signal for one subject, Figure 4 shows the results of using a low-pass filter to remove high frequency noise, finally Figure 5 shows the absolute value of the first forward difference (FFD) showing the size of changes between consecutive points. The FFD values can be thresholded to include only large changes. We explored variations in absolute and relative threshold values. Analysis across our test subjects revealed similar levels of GSR activity, although there were significant variations in mean level and variation, indicating that the GSR must be personalised to individuals.

Variations in affective state will generally be gradual, and thus it is tempting to consider applying a smoothing function to the GSR output to take account of this, as is applied in [8]. However, while affective state may vary gradually, the results indicate that GSR responses are rapid pulses. We are continuing to explore methods to identify the significant events in a GSR output. A further consideration is that in order to be able to relate biometric response to specific classes of affective state, we need to relate it to arousal and valence levels [3].

## 4   Interactive Task Analysis

Previous work has shown that users exhibit anticipatory GSR responses to risky decisions, before they are consciously aware that the decision is a risky one [2]. This is an interesting result for IR. For example, can we exploit this information so that a computer is aware via GSR readings of a pattern in a users search results before they are conscious of it? If there is a pattern in the search results that the user is not consciously aware of and the biometric measurements can pick up, can we use this usefully in retrieval?

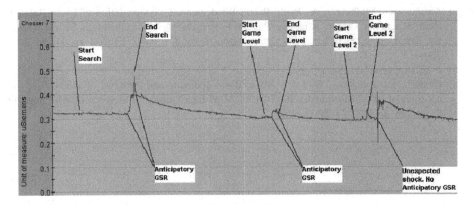

**Fig. 6.** GSR response for tasks with negative reward

In order to explore anticipatory response measurements, we set out an investigation with individuals performing a timed puzzle where a "negative reward" was administered for failure. Participants perform a Google image search to find 5 images within 3 minutes, and a strategy game to reach level 2 in 60 seconds. The result of the experiment for one subject is shown in Figure 6, in this graph there are visible peaks in GSR before anticipated negative rewards, but not before unexpected ones. Having demonstrated that we can capture anticipatory response in a highly stressed task, we plan to investigate its potential appearance and exploitation in interactive search.

## 5    Conclusions and Current Work

Our investigation of biometric response has so far demonstrated that we can observe measurable features in response to events in movies, and within engaging computer mediated tasks. We are currently examining the results of our collection of biometric data for a large number of movie viewers, and exploring further methods for identifying significant features in the signals. We are also planning to record biometric signals within an image search task requiring high levels of cognitive engagement.

## References

[1]  A. Damasio, A.: *Descartes' Error* New York: Grosset-Putman, 1994.
[2]  Bechara, A., Damasio, H., Tranel, D., Damasio, A.: Deciding Advantageously Before Knowing the Strategy. *Science*, 275:1293-5, 1997.
[3]  Bradley, M. M.: Emotional Memory: A Dimensional Analysis. In (S. van Groot, N. E. van de Poll and J. Sargent eds) The Emotions: Essays on Emotion Theory, Erlbaum, pp.97-134, 1994.
[4]  Kim, K. H., Bang, S. W., and Kim, S. R.: Emotion Recognition System using Short-Term Monitoring of Physiological Signals. *Medical & Biological Engineering & Computing*, 42:419-427, 2004.
[5]  Scheirer, J., Fernandez, R., Klien, J., and Picard, R. W.: Frustrating the User on Purpose: A Step Toward Building an Affective Computer. *Interacting with Computers*, 14(2):93-118, 2002.

[6] Amrhein, C., Mhlberger, A., Pauli, P. and Wiedemann, G.: Modulation of Event-Related Brain Potentials During Affective Picture Processing: A Complement to Startle Reflex and Skin Conductance Response? *International Journal of Psychophysiology*, 54:231-240, 2004.

[7] www.bodymedia.com

[8] Chan, C. H., and Jones, G. J. F.: Affect-Based Indexing and Retrieval of Films, In Proceedings of ACM Multimedia 2005 - 13th ACM International Conference on Multimedia, Singapore, pp.427-430, 2005.

# Relevance Feedback Using Weight Propagation

Fadi Yamout, Michael Oakes, and John Tait

School of Computing and Technology,
University of Sunderland, U.K.
{Fadi.Yamout, Michael.Oakes, John.Tait}@sunderland.ac.uk

**Abstract.** A new Relevance Feedback (RF) technique is developed to improve upon the efficiency and performance of existing techniques. This is based on propagating positive and negative weights from documents judged relevant and not relevant respectively, to other documents, which are deemed similar according to one of a number of criteria. The performance and efficiency improve since the documents are treated as independent vectors rather than being merged into a single vector as is the case with traditional approaches, and only the documents considered in a given neighbourhood are inspected. This is especially important when using large test collections.

## 1 Introduction

In Information Retrieval (IR), documents are usually retrieved using lexical matching (LM), where terms in a user's query are matched with those in a set of documents. Using a standard interface for Relevance Feedback (RF), the user will mark the retrieved documents as either relevant or non-relevant [1]. In a positive RF, index terms are taken from documents deemed relevant, and added to the initial query. The search process is then repeated using this new query. It is also possible to make use of documents declared not relevant, by removing index terms in those documents from the query. It has been found that standard RF algorithms usually do not perform any better given the evidence of negative judgments [2]. This poster describes a new RF technique that outperforms existing RF techniques in term of computational time and quality of the retrieval results.

## 2 The Weight Propagation Technique

The technique described here uses weight propagation (WP). A relevant document will propagate positive weights to neighbouring documents, and negative weights if chosen to be non-relevant. Similar techniques have been used in statistical telecommunications fraud detection to identify 'communities of interest' [3] and in web retrieval where similarities between web pages affect similarity of queries and vice versa [4]. Similarity matching and propagating weights have also been used in data mining to obtain the subset of the most relevant and authoritative Web pages [5]. However, the Weight Propagation technique has never been used before for query reformulation. To illustrate the technique we have adopted, in Figure 1, "doc1" is a

M. Lalmas et al. (Eds.): ECIR 2006, LNCS 3936, pp. 575–578, 2006.
© Springer-Verlag Berlin Heidelberg 2006

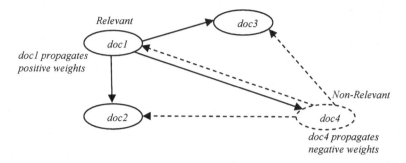

**Fig. 1.** Documents propagating positive and negative weights

relevant document; therefore, it will propagate positive weights to "doc2", "doc3", and "doc4" while "doc4", which is not relevant, will propagate negative weights to "doc1", "doc2", and "doc3". This process is repeated for all the relevant and non-relevant documents and the documents with highest weights are then retrieved as the result of the RF process. The weights propagated from a document to other documents in the neighbourhood are influenced by how far away those documents are from the given document in vector similarity space.

The weight propagated, $w_{ij}$, from a document $i$ to a document $j$, is based on the distance between the two documents as defined by the equation:

$$w_{ij} = 1 / \text{distance (document i, document j).} \tag{1}$$

where

- $w_{ij}$ is the weight propagated from a document i to a document j
- distance (document i, document j) is the conceptual distance between document i and document j estimated by the numeric cosine similarity measure.

To reduce the time complexity, it would be enough for the document to propagate weights only to nearby documents. The time complexity for performing RF is $O(n)$ [6] where $n$ is the number of documents in the collection. The time complexity for the WP technique is $O(q\ n')$, where $q$ is the number of documents most highly ranked in the original hit list and marked relevant or non-relevant by the user, and $n'$ is the number of documents found in close proximity to each of the retrieved documents and consequently affected by the propagation. The user chooses the value of $q$, and in our experiments $n'$ is set to a maximum of 12. Therefore, WP is sufficiently efficient to work in a search engine, taking into account the size of the WWW and the speed users expect.

## 3   Experimental Design

The weight propagation technique is inspired by both the Rocchio and the Ide techniques, as shown in Figure 2. WP inspired by Rocchio (WPR) takes the following format:

$$w_t = w_{i+} (1/r)\ \Sigma\ w_r - (1/n)\ \Sigma\ w_n. \tag{2}$$

where

- $w_t$ is the total weights propagated from neighbourhood documents
- $w_i$ is the weight derived from the initial query
- r  is the number of relevant documents
- $w_r$ is the weight propagated from relevant documents
- n is the number of non-relevant documents
- $w_n$ is the weight propagated from non-relevant documents

In a second variant of WP, inspired by Ide (WPI), weight propagation is taken to be

$$w_t = w_{i+} \Sigma\, w_r - \Sigma\, w_n. \tag{3}$$

A third variant of WP, WPY, the primary focus of this poster (Figure 2), counts only the maximum weight propagated to the document. The system, as a result, produces better results than summing all the weights or computing their averages.

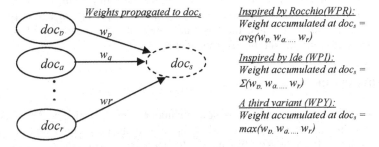

**Fig. 2.** WP expressed in 3 variant ways

## 4  Results and Analysis

The experiment was conducted on the TREC WT18G test collection. Both the standard Rocchio and Ide techniques were compared against the WPY method and tested with different values of $n'$ (the number of documents affected by the propagation). In this experiment only positive feedback was employed. The assessments were done as follows: For each query, an initial document ranking was obtained. The relevant documents, as determined by the list of relevance judgments that comes with the test collection, are taken from the top $N$ retrieved documents ($N$ is set equal to 20) and used for one iteration of query reformulation.

WPY gave better precision than the baselines when tested on the TREC WT18G collection. Precision was better at low recall levels, meaning that the user will find more relevant documents on the first pages of search hits as is preferable in a search engine. WPY shows improvement in recall when propagating between 2 and 6 documents. When propagating to 2 documents, for instance, WPY and the baselines cross at 15% recall. The baselines, however, performed better at low recall levels. When the number of propagated documents increases, the recall level increases as well. WPY shows that when propagating to 6 documents, WPY and the baselines

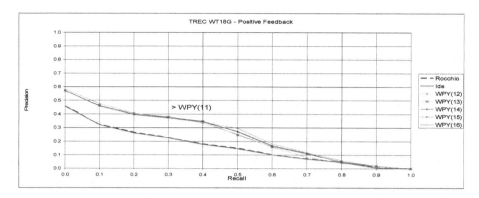

**Fig. 3.** Propagating over 11 documents

cross at 40% recall. The performance of the system kept improving as the number of propagated documents was increased to 11 (Figure 3), but no further improvement was noted after that. WPY and the baselines cross at 70% recall for 11 propagated documents, which means WPY performs better.

## 5   Conclusions

In this poster, we have developed a new technique for RF, called WPY, which uses Weight Propagation where positive and negative weights are propagated to documents in given vicinity. Both the Rocchio and the Ide technique inspire the technique.

This new technique improves precision since the documents are treated as independent vectors rather than having them merged into a single vector, as is the case with Ide and Rocchio. In addition, the WPY approach consumes less computation time since it inspects only nearby documents.

## References

1.   Baeza-Yates R. and Ribeiro-Neto B.: Modern Information Retrieval. New York: Addison-Wesley. P 118 (1999)
2.   Dunlop, M.D.: The effect of accessing non-matching documents on relevance feedback. ACM Transactions on Information Systems, 15(2):137-153, (1997)
3.   Cortes. C., Pregibon D., and Volinsky C.: Communities of Interest. Proceedings of IDA 2001 - Intelligent Data Analysis. (2001)
4.   Xue Z., Zeng H.J., Chen Z., Yu Y., Ma W.Y., Xi W., Fan W.: Optimizing Web Search Using Web Click-through Data. Proceedings of the thirteenth ACM conference on Information and knowledge management CIKM (2004) :http://portal.acm.org/citation. cfm?id=1031192
5.   Kantardzic M.: Data Mining.: Concepts, Models, Methods, and Algorithms. Wiley-Interscience. P 179 (2003)
6.   Yamout F., Moghrabi I., Oakes M.: Query and Relevance Feedback in Latent Semantic Index with Reduced Time Complexity. IASTED International Conference on Database Applications - DBA (2004)

# Context-Specific Frequencies and Discriminativeness for the Retrieval of Structured Documents

Jun Wang and Thomas Roelleke

Computer Science Department,
Queen Mary, University of London
{wangjun, thor}@dcs.qmul.ac.uk

**Abstract.** Structured document retrieval requires the ranking of document elements. Previous approaches either aggregate term weights or retrieval status values, or propose alternatives to *idf*, for example, *ief* (inverse element frequency). We propose and investigate in this paper a new approach: Context-specific *idf*, which is, in contrast to aggregation-based ranking functions, parameter-free.

## 1  Introduction

The structure of XML documents makes XML retrieval different from traditional information retrieval, since the retrieval result contains document elements rather than just whole documents.

One of the main issues of element retrieval is to assign a retrieval status value ($RSV$) to each element. Previous approaches are based on:(1) the aggregation of term weights from that of the sub-elements', then computing the RSV's ([8], [4], [7]), or (2) the aggregation of RSV's directly from that of their sub-elements ([1], [2]), or (3) alternative the inverse element frequency (*ief*,[5],[9], [6]).

Approaches (1) and (2) need to assign each element an aggregation parameter, which decides the sub-elements' contribution to its parent's $RSV$ or term weight. The estimation of aggregation parameters is not easy; (3) provides a different *idf* calculation method according to the retrieval requirements, but it didn't prove superior to *idf*.

## 2  Context-Specific Frequencies, Discriminativeness and RSV's

Structured documents can be viewed as a document tree. Document collections can also be organized in a tree structure. Then documents and collections are in the same framework. In definition 1, we generalize the frequencies for each node. Then, $RSV$ computation depends on the root, which is defined in definition 2.

M. Lalmas et al. (Eds.): ECIR 2006, LNCS 3936, pp. 579–582, 2006.
© Springer-Verlag Berlin Heidelberg 2006

**Definition 1.** *Tree-based frequencies. Let $c_1, \ldots, c_n$ be the children of node $c$.*

$$n_D(t,c) := \sum_i n_D(t,c_i), \ N_D(c) := \sum_i N_D(c_i)$$

$$n_E(t,c) := \sum_i n_E(t,c_i), \ N_E(c) := \sum_i N_E(c_i)$$

$$n_L(t,c) := \sum_i n_L(t,c_i), \ N_L(c) := \sum_i N_L(c_i)$$

**Definition 2.** *Retrieval Function with Context-Specific Discriminativeness*

$$\mathrm{RSV}_{ief}(d,q) := \sum_t \mathrm{tf}(t,q) \cdot \mathrm{tf}(t,d) \cdot \mathrm{ief}(t, root(d))$$

$$\mathrm{RSV}_{idf}(d,q) := \sum_t \mathrm{tf}(t,q) \cdot \mathrm{tf}(t,d) \cdot \mathrm{idf}(t, root(d))$$

$$\mathrm{RSV}(d,q) := \begin{cases} \mathrm{RSV}_{ief}(d,q) & \textit{if } d \textit{ is an element} \\ \mathrm{RSV}_{idf}(d,q) & \textit{if } d \textit{ is a document} \end{cases}$$

## 3   Experimental Results and Their Analysis

The implementation of our model requires to maintain element and location frequencies for each element in the collection tree. This sounds like a lot of overhead, but actually, the implementation is very modular since local frequency-spaces are created, and the local frequency-spaces form the frequency-space of their parent, and so on (see definition 1).

Experiment is running on INEX2003. Currently we only maintain frequencies for sub-collections, including $df$, $ef$ and $lf$.

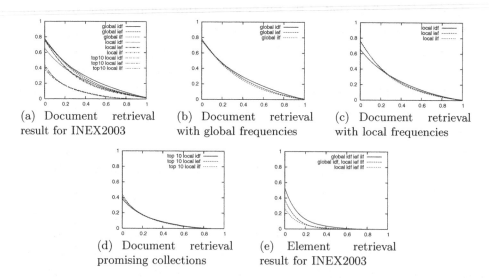

(a) Document retrieval result for INEX2003

(b) Document retrieval with global frequencies

(c) Document retrieval with local frequencies

(d) Document retrieval promising collections

(e) Element retrieval result for INEX2003

**Fig. 1.** Retrieval result for INEX2003

For investigating our approach to structured document retrieval, we choose the following retrieval functions:

- *tf* with Global *idf* vs *ief* vs *ilf*
- *tf* with Local *idf* vs *ief* vs *ilf*: to see whether the relevant documents come from several promising sub-collections, we select 10 highest *idf* summarization collections to retrieve.
- Context-specific discriminativeness: Ranking of documents based on the *idf* of the collection to which the document belongs to, and, analogously, ranking of elements based on the *ief* in the document to which the element belongs to (see definition 2).

Figure 1 shows the performance of global *idf*, *ief* and *ilf*, and local *idf*, *ief*, and *ilf*.

The overall conclusion is that the performance increases with the abstraction of the discriminativeness measure: *ilf* as the least abstract measure shows the worst performance; this confirms the result of [3], and the argument on the burstiness/clinginess of good terms. The positioning of *ief* between *ilf* and *idf* perfectly fits the picture, as *ief* is more abstract than *ilf* and less abstract than *idf*.

## 4   Normalization of Context-Specific *idf*

Considering the subject of a collection may impact on the discriminativeness of local *idf*, we also did another interesting experiment. We mixed all the documents from INEX sub-collections and regrouped them into 20 new sub-collections. After sub-collection regrouping, statistic result shows, all the query terms occur in the each sub-collection almost the same times. The local retrieval strategy was run again. This time the result improves a little more than previous local strategy run on INEX original sub-collection. The result is shown in figure 2.a. To be conveniently observed, only *idf* runs are shown on the figure.

We also take into account Zipf's law (Luhn's analysis, a very rare term is not necessarily a good term), and divergence from randomness (the more a term's distribution diverge from randomness, the more discriminative is the term). Currently rare terms are given very high weights and frequent terms are given

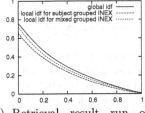

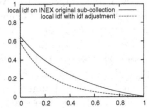

(a) Retrieval result run on INEX original sub-collection and mixed sub-collection

(b) Retrieval result with df adjustment

**Fig. 2.** Normalization with context-specific idf

pretty low weights. Therefore, we decreased the term weight of rare terms, and increased the term weight of frequent terms. Then we investigated whether this improves the retrieval result. The adjustment of term weights is based on the term distribution among the different sub-collections. The idea is that $df$ is up-level frequency of $tf$. Figure 2.b shows that this approach did not improve the retrieval quality, and we will reconsider the adjustment of the term weights.

## 5   Summary and Conclusion

We have presented and investigated a new retrieval model for structured document retrieval: The basic idea of the model is the context-specific discriminativeness. By context-specific we mean that the retrieval function selects the discriminativeness measure based on the properties of a context. This is different to classical retrieval, and in contrast to aggregation-based approaches, parameter-free.

Our investigation indicates (confirms) that global $idf$ yields the best retrieval quality, despite the intuition that $ief$ or context-specific discriminativeness cover better the specialties of element retrieval.

In the future study, we would like to maintain a discriminativeness space for each node in a structured document collection. We intend to look closer at the divergence of randomness as an alternative to $idf$-based discriminativeness spaces, since our initial observations show a surprisingly strong correlation between randomness-based and idf-based discriminativeness.

## References

1. J. P. Callan. Passage-level evidence in document retrieval. *Proceedings of the Seventeenth Annual International ACM SIGIR* , pages 302–310, 1994.
2. J.P. Callan, Z. Lu, and W.B. Croft. Searching distributed collections with inference networks. *Proceedings of the 18thAnnualInternationalACM SIGIR*, pages 21–29, 1995.
3. K. Church and W Gale. Inverse document frequency (idf): A measure of deviation from poisson. In *Proceedings of the Third Workshop on Very Large Corpora*, pages 121–130, 1995.
4. Norbert Fuhr and Kai Grossjohann. XIRQL: A query language for information retrieval in XML documents. *Proceedings of the 24th Annual International ACM SIGIR* , New York, August 2001. ACM.
5. T. Grabs and H.-J. Schek. Generating vector spaces on-the-fly for flexible xml retrieval. In *Proceedings of the ACM SIGIR Workshop on XML and Information Retrieval*, pages 4–13, Tampere, Finland, 2002.
6. Y. Mass and M Mandelbrod. Retrieving the most relevant xml component. In *Proceedings of the Second Workshop of INEX*, pages 53–58, Germanny, 2003.
7. P. Ogilvie and J. Callan. Language models and structured document retrieval, 2003.
8. T. Roelleke, M. Lalmas, and etal. The accessibility dimension for structured document retrieval. In *Proceedings of the BCS-IRSG European ECIR*, March 2002.
9. Torsten Schlieder and Holger Meuss. Querying and ranking xml documents. *J. Am. Soc. Inf. Sci. Technol.*, 53(6):489–503, 2002.

# Author Index

# Author Index